About the Author

A major leader in the international critical thinking movement, Richard Paul is a passionate reformer who sees educational problems at the heart of our social and economic ones. He sees ineffectual educational systems mirroring obsolete economic and social institutions and structures, economic and social malaise exacerbating educational bankruptcy. He sees that, although the 12st Century is upon us, we are still trapped in 19th Century thinking and 20th Century arrogance and narrow-mindedness.

We are not educating our children, Paul argues, and we are not planning, as rational people would, for the economic and social well-being of our country. These two needs are deeply interconnected. In a world of shallow values, instant gratification, and quick fixes, critical thinking is a tool necessary for survival. We need its sharp cutting edge to slice through propaganda generated daily not only by self-serving educational bureaucrats but also by a rainbow of vested interest groups all too ready to sacrifice the well-being of the country to their short-term gain.

Through Paul's efforts, and those of thousands of like-minded persons, critical thinking is finally becoming a national educational goal (so say the National Goals Panel, the U.S. Departments of Commerce and Labor, and the U.S. Department of Education). Yet just as the concept of critical thinking is finally gaining currency — and a window of opportunity is opening up — individuals and groups are ripping it from its substantial intellectual foundations and reducing it to easy-to-learn tricks, gimmicks, and quick fixes. Paul is leading the counter-attack on the pseudo critical thinking that is springing up everywhere in the educational marketplace — from textbooks to state assessment instruments designed to bolster the falling images of state departments of education.

Director of the Center for Critical Thinking, and Chair of the National Council for Excellence in Critical Thinking, author of over 50 articles and five books on critical thinking at every grade level (K–3, 4–6, 6–9, high school, and university), a committed teacher, Paul has given hundreds of workshops at the K–12 level and made a series of eight critical thinking video programs for PBS.

His views on critical thinking have been canvassed in *The New York Times, Education Week, The Chronicle of Higher Education, American Teacher, Educational Leadership, Newsweek, U.S. News and World Report,* and *Reader's Digest.*

Besides publishing extensively in the field, he has organized two national and eleven international conferences on critical thinking. He has given invited lectures at many universities and colleges, including Harvard, University of Chicago, University of Illinois, University of Amsterdam, and the universities of Puerto Rico and Costa Rica, as well as workshops and lectures on critical thinking in every region of the United States. Paul worked with the late Edward M. Glaser on revising the Watson-Glaser Critical Thinking Appraisal. Working with Gerald Nosich, he has developed a model for the national assessment of critical thinking at the post-secondary level for the U.S. Department of Education. He is actively sought as a keynote speaker and staff development leader.

About the Center for Critical Thinking and Moral Critique

The Center conducts advanced research and disseminates information on critical thinking and moral critique. It works closely with the Foundation for Critical Thinking, the National Council for Excellence in Critical Thinking, the College Board, numerous school districts, the Association for Supervision and Curriculum Development, the National Education Association, and the U. S. Department of Education to facilitate implementation of high standards of critical thinking instruction from kindergarten through the university.

Its major work includes:

* International Conferences on Critical Thinking
  Each summer, in early August, the Center hosts the oldest and largest critical thinking conference with registrants from virtually every state of the union and numerous foreign countries. Over 300 distinguished experts in the field present 350 sessions on critical thinking and critical thinking instruction over four days. These sessions are designed to meet the needs of the widest variety of educational levels and concerns from kindergarten through graduate school. A variety of subject matters and subject fields are used as examples of critical thinking infusion. The two days preceding the conference are used for intensive sessions that lay a foundation for the conference and for critical thinking instruction.

* Staff Development Services
  The Center provides staff development services at every level of education from kindergarten through graduate school. Staff development programs emphasize an exploration of the rich, underlying concepts of critical thinking and how to excite students to the power and potential of developing a mind that reasons well. There is a focus on the critique and redesign of instruction to infuse critical thinking principles into subject matter instruction.

About the Foundation for Critical Thinking

The Foundation for Critical Thinking is an independent, non-profit, institution not associated with Sonoma State University. It publishes a variety of critical thinking resources.

Resources for Instruction
* PBS Videotapes
* Ground-Breaking Books
* Four Grade-Level Critical Thinking Handbooks
* The Leaders of the Critical Thinking Movement on Audio and Videotape
* Audio and Videotapes for Critical Thinking Staff Development

About the National Council for Excellence in Critical Thinking

Information regarding the National Council for Excellence in Critical Thinking may be secured by calling the National Office. *(707) 546-0629.*

The Center for Critical Thinking
& Moral Critique
Sonoma State University
Rohnert Park, CA 94928
(707) 664-2940

The Foundation for Critical Thinking
4655 Sonoma Mountain Road
Santa Rosa, CA 95404
(800) 833-3645

Richard W. Paul

CRITICAL THINKING

How to Prepare Students for a Rapidly
Changing World

Edited by
Jane Willsen & A.J.A. Binker
Foundation for Critical Thinking
1993

Acknowledgments

"The Critical Thinking Movement in Historical Perspective", originally appeared as, "The Critical Thinking Movement: A Historical Perspective", in *National Forum*, Winter 1985.

"Dialogical and Dialectical Thinking", will be forthcoming in *Developing Minds*, ASCD, second edition, 1990.

"Teaching Critical Thinking in the Strong Sense: A Focus on Self-Deception, World Views, and a Dialectical Mode of Analysis", and "Background Logic, Critical Thinking, and Irrational Language Games", appeared in Informal Logic, May 1982 and Winter 1985.

"Critical Thinking Staff Development: The Lesson Plan Remodelling Approach", originally appeared as, "Staff Development for Critical Thinking: Lesson Plan Remodelling as the Strategy", in *Journal of Staff Development*, Fall 1987.

"Critical Thinking and Learning Centers", originally appeared as "Critical Thinking and Learning: A Maximalist Versus Minimalist Approach", in *Journal of College Reading and Learning*, 1988, vol. 21.

"Bloom's Taxonomy and Critical Thinking Instruction: Recall is Not Knowledge", originally appeared as, "Bloom's Taxonomy and Critical Thinking Instruction", in *Educational Leadership*, May, 1985.

"Philosophy and Cognitive Psychology: Contrasting Assumptions" and "The Contributions of Philosophy to Thinking", are forthcoming as one paper, "Critical and Reflective Thinking: A Philosophical Perspective", in *Dimensions of Thinking and Cognitive Instruction: Implications for Educational Reform*, Lawrence Erlbaum, 1990.

ISBN number: 0–944583–09–1

Library of Congress number: 93–72691

To the memory of the late Edward Glaser, friend and scholar,
whose foundational book,
An Experiment in the Development of Critical Thinking (1941),
laid the cornerstone for the critical thinking movement.

Table of Contents

Part A: What Is Critical Thinking?

I Overview: What Critical Thinking Is and Why It Is Essential

II Intellectual Standards and Assessment: The Foundation for Critical Thought

III Contrasting Approaches to Thinking

IV The Affective and Ethical Dimension

Part B: How to Teach for Critical Thinking

I Instruction

II Staff Development

III Critical Thinking and Academic Subjects

Appendices

Acknowledgments

I wish to acknowledge the enthusiastic and tireless support and good
will I received from my many colleagues at the Center for Critical
Thinking and Moral Critique and the Foundation for Critical
Thinking, including that of J. J. Jones, David Grady, Jessie Foster,
Annalise O'Brien, Wes Hiler, Kelly Ann Grogan, Stuart Grose, Mike
Lanham, Lincy Castro, Emiko Lewis, Jeanette Martinez, Rena Ferrick,
Joyce Miller-Carpini, and Charles Evans. Their team-spirit and
practical problem-solving are a continual source of strength and joy
to me. Special thanks go to Jill Binker for her editing abilities and
long-standing dedication to the cause of critical thinking.

I owe a special debt of gratitude to John Pruess, Renee Denise, and
Trish Taylor for their exemplary trouble-shooting abilities and
patience in many hours of overload. They demonstrate daily how
critical thinking can be brought into the heart and soul of an
organization and continually breathe new life and energy into it.

And finally, I want to express my appreciation for the dedicated
support, deep insight, and committed vision of my newest friend
and colleague, Jane Willsen. Her incisive questions and practical
sensitivity, her unflinching sense of "Can do!" and of how always to
find new and better ways, have contributed mightily to my work, its
fruitfulness, and its personal satisfaction.

Foreword

Although the papers included in this volume have been written at different times and for a variety of occasions, they have a unity that explains their collection into a single book. All have been written with the express purpose of persuading educators and others concerned with education of the need to place critical thinking at the heart of educational reform. They represent a point of view too often at the periphery of the discussion of what is wrong with education. Their scope reflects something of the breadth with which critical thinking ought to be conceived.

No one in education today has accepted the responsibility to conceptualize education as a whole, or to assess, at any given time, whether it is succeeding or rather, degenerating into mere training, socialization, or indoctrination. No one is keeping education focused on essential questions and concerns and, consequently, attention is typically diffused to any of an endless number of "immediate," day-to-day, and specific lower-order "imperatives." Basic facts and questions — like whether or not students are learning to reason well — are lost in the shuffle. No one is held accountable for the integrity of the core issues.

Indeed, as a result, global failures such as the failure of schooling to improve students' ability to reason are not even recognized as such, except episodically, and then almost always by a scattered few. To the extent that the study of critical thinking develops into a recognized and respected field within education, it can serve as a voice responsible for conceptualizing the whole. It can keep attention focused on the central educational pillars such as, "What is an *educated* person?" For can we not say that if students learn to think critically as a result of their schooling, then, *ipso facto*, they have become educated persons? And if, on the other hand, they merely commit to memory any number of specific facts about this or that domain of study, if they pass any number of courses or gain any number of academic credits or degrees but remain undisciplined in their thinking, then, whatever else can be said of them, they have not yet become educated persons. Whether they recognize it or not — and almost inevitably, by virtue of the defective nature of their thinking they do not — they are still walking in circles in the vestibule of education; they have not yet entered its hallowed chambers.

What is worthwhile in education and in life is never easy: no one ever legitimately claimed that critical thinking would be. Critical thinking is complex because it involves overcoming not only intellectual barriers to progress, but psychological barriers as well. We are comfortable, as a rule, with our ideas, our belief structures, our view of the world. Certainly, if we thought our ideas were flawed, irrational, shallow, or biased in an unfair way, we would have *already* changed them. When questioned about the validity of our ideas or beliefs, particularly the foundational ones, we typically interpret the question to be a challenge to our integrity, often even to our identity.

That we hold tenaciously to our beliefs, however ill-founded, is testimony to the struggle that a commitment to critical thinking will trigger. Yet a commitment to critical thinking is as exhilarating as it is exhausting. Imagine the satisfaction of looking through the inventory of one's beliefs and finding that many of them were consciously, deliberately, and painstakingly chosen for their accuracy, their depth, their clarity, their consistency — in other words, their legitimate merit!

Intellectually, critical thinking is challenging because we must prepare the way for new ideas by rooting out old ones, by breaking down remnants from popular, if incoherent, illogical and insupportable ideologies and prejudices of the day. Until we have thought deeply and critically we are apt to be persuaded by deeply flawed ideas, such as

• the view that every person's opinion, regardless of how poorly it is supported, deserves equal respect;
• the view that all language users hold bona fide, unique definitions for every word they use;
• the view that language itself is vague, rather than our use of it;
• the view that there are no general intellectual standards; and
• the view that appropriate intellectual standards are a reflection of gender, race, culture, or period in history.

However tempting these views can be at any point in time or from any given point of view, or how intuitive they might seem, each is readily refuted under closer scrutiny.

Awash as our culture is with these and many other ideologies and prejudices, we cannot help but have unconsciously absorbed some of them. And, unfortunately because we did not think our way into what we have unconsciously absorbed, we must now laboriously and painfully think our way out. These are bothersome presuppositions, not explicit constructions and conclusions. We want only products of our rational and deliberate thought, for that is the goal of critical thinking.

How will we reach our goal? Where is the path? The fact is there are many paths and they crisscross and double back. Given the complexity of the challenge, our inherent tendencies toward self-deception, and our tenacious grip on unconsciously absorbed beliefs, an effective introduction to critical thinking requires that we come at it from many different angles and prepare ourselves for a lifetime of diligent and rigorous intellectual work. We must hear the story many times, and appreciate many different versions and variations. We must retell the story to ourselves and to others to hear how it sounds, to tighten up our understanding, sharpen our insights, and uncover new and important implications.

If there is one phrase that encapsulates this challenge, it is intellectual discipline. Yet, we live in an age in which intellectual discipline is rare and in which schooling and the media are as rich in trivial information as they are devoid, or virtually devoid, of reasoned discourse. We are the targets of an unprecedented campaign of misinformation about what is important, and why. We are simultaneously put upon by a multiplicity of cultural voices — not to mention an army of academic and professional specialists — besieged with information yet left in ignorance, devoid of the tools that could make sense of the chaos that surrounds us.

We are given no glimpse into the inner sanctum. W*e fail to see the sense in which critical thinking provides a common denominator for all fields of knowledge.* We are given no common standards upon the basis of which we might form our judgment and build our design. We are perplexed and unsure as to how to construct a comprehensive view that would enable us to gain perspective on diversity in culture, language, and knowledge. Often, we blindly accept hollow models we have picked up from the platitudes, truisms, and arrogance of everyday chatter as substitutes for a well-reasoned, disciplined, comprehensive view.

One major obstacle to the successful construction of such a comprehensive view is a lack of understanding of the basis for intellectual criteria and standards. We don't know where the target is, so how can we aim for it? Where do we get appropriate criteria and the standards? What intellectual criteria should we use and how can we justify them?

In this volume, these issues are treated in a way that will certainly not satisfy everyone, for there is no attempt made to couch the analysis in the jargon of a particular discipline nor in the light of some traditional or specialized mode of argumentation. I am, almost always, more concerned to address those who think across multiple disciplinary lines than I am to address those who bury themselves within the boundaries, the jargon, and the presuppositions of any given one. Critical thinking in its legitimate, comprehensive sense applies to every academic discipline as readily as it applies to life beyond the ivory tower.

Of course, this book in no way contains the last word on critical thinking. Indeed, it is merely one of many opening salvos in a field just now beginning to emerge. In the future the field will draw, as it is just now

beginning to do, illuminating contributions from sociologists, anthropol-
ogists, historians, economists, scientists, and mathematicians. At present
the field is still dominated by philosophers and cognitive psychologists.

Critical thinking will come to be the first field in intellectual history, I
believe, that crosses fields at the same time that it draws its contributing
scholars from the very fields it crosses. As such it will, I hope, provide for
the intellectual perspective and synthesis so typically and significantly
absent today from both education and educational research.

Before I close I should provide some explanation of the history of this
third edition. The first two editions were massive (673 pages of fine print).
At the recommendation of many, I have divided the original edition into
two overlapping books: this one which maintains the original title and is
intended for a general audience, and a second which is targeted principally to educators, *Critical Thinking: How to Prepare Students for a Rapidly
Changing World*. Both volumes contain some of the same articles, those
which seemed fundamental to both, since the volumes will not be mar-
keted as a set. Each book becomes a more manageable read. I hope that
this decision helps bring the basic concept of critical thinking to a yet
wider audience. The intellectual quality of the original, for better or
worse, was nowhere compromised.

One final point. Perceptive readers may discern in these papers many
influences including but not limited to Plato, Aristotle, Aquinas, Bacon,
Descartes, Tom Paine, Jefferson, John Stuart Mill, John Henry Newman,
Freud, Marx, Thoreau, Max Weber, William Graham Sumner, Piaget, John
Dewey, C. Wright Mills, Erving Goffman, Bertrand Russell, Ludwig
Wittgenstein, John Wisdom, Gilbert Ryle, and J. L. Austin. Certainly there
is no idea in it that does not have many historical predecessors. Nevertheless, it seems to me that a rich appreciation of what it would take to cultivate fairminded critical persons in fairminded critical societies is just now
beginning to form. I hope this book contributes to this raw beginning.

Preface

Educational Virtue:
Becoming a Critical Thinker

by Gerald Nosich

*W*hat Richard Paul presents us with in this book is a massive, and massively different, vision of what education should always have been (but wasn't), and of what education must certainly become (in a world of accelerating change). It is a vision fundamentally different, not just from contemporary practice in our schools, but from our present-day educational ideal. The breadth of this vision, and the specific details of working it out, are what distinguishes Paul's book from other books either on education or on critical thinking. It does not just present us with a program for how our educational goals can be better achieved through critical thinking. It is not really a treatise on present educational practices and their inadequacy, nor is its aim primarily to get students and teachers to think better, more critically. To construe the book in any (or all) of these ways would be natural, but it would fail to get at the revolutionary nature of what Paul is proposing.

Even if our school system, from kindergarten up, were to turn out students who by *its* standards were ideal, by Paul's standards those students would not, except by accident, be well-educated. That is, they would not be critical thinkers. They would have acquired a great deal of information (at least as measured by standardized achievement tests), a few skills, and even, if they happened to sign up for a reasoning course, an ability to do a slash-and-burn, demolishing critique of positions they disagreed with. This is not the ideal product of the education Paul has in mind.

Many of us would be willing to settle for informed and skilled students, of course, but it is not really our choice. Our school system in fact turns out precious few of them, and not very many near facsimiles either. And the reason is partly that we have had the wrong goal in mind from the beginning; those students who have succeeded in becoming critical thinkers have done so in the teeth of the educational system — both practice *and* theory. And very few are prepared for a world of accelerating change and complexity.

What then is a critical thinker for Paul? It is someone who is able to think well and fairmindedly not just about her own beliefs and viewpoints, but about beliefs and viewpoints that are diametrically opposed to her own. And not just to think about them, but to explore and appreciate their adequacy, their cohesion, their very reasonableness vis-a-vis her own. Moreover, a person who thinks critically is not just willing and able to explore alien, potentially threatening viewpoints, but she also *desires* to do so. She questions her own deeply-held beliefs, and if there are no opposing viewpoints ready at hand, she seeks them out or constructs them herself.

Exploring opposing points of view is just one example — though an important one — of thinking critically, but notice that it involves far more than skills. It involves attitudes and passions as well. It is not just something you do in school and then go home and get on with your life. To the extent that a person acquires the skills, attitudes, and passions of a critical thinker, it will permeate her life. It is not the kind of complex that lends itself to compartmentalization.

What is more, such skills, attitudes, and passions make for an ideal instrumentality of deep change and far-reaching adaptability. For when a thinker can comfortably question her own deeply-held beliefs, and restructure them when they are found wanting, she can certainly comfortably adapt to the rush of everyday social and technological changes, changes which don't usually threaten our image or ego.

Paul sums up this interlocking complex of skills, attitudes, passions (and more besides) in the phrase *critical thinking*. But it is important to see that *critical thinking*, in Paul's hands, is not exactly a species of thinking; rather it is a species of living. It is living, in Socrates' phrase, an examined life, a *deeply* examined life. To become a critical thinker is not, in the end, to be the same person you are now, only with better abilities; it is, in an important sense, to become a different person.

Take another attribute of being a critical thinker: the willingness to suspend judgement. Suppose someone asks you a question, and you don't know the answer. What should you reply? The obviously reasonable response is "I don't know." And that's probably the reasonable response even if the question is a deep one, or one that you have guesses about, or one that everyone has opinions on, or one that's in the news everyday. "Why is there so much more violent crime in the U.S. than in other countries?" Chances are, unless you've really investigated the issue, the only reasonable response is "I don't know" (or maybe, tenuously, "I don't know, but it could possibly be...."). And that is not only the reasonable *external* response, but the internal one as well. You should *feel* ignorant.

Suspending judgment, in this case as well as in innumerable similar cases, is an awkward, uncomfortable, almost unnatural response. It is far more immediately satisfying to plump down for *some* answer, however unexamined. It is more gratifying to be unreasonable.

A critical thinker suspends judgment. How are we to clarify this? The willingness and ability to suspend judgment is not a skill or a passion exactly, though both of those are involved. It is closer to an attitude, but that doesn't really capture it either because it is the kind of attitude that exists only in concert with a host of other attitudes: humility enough to recognize that you don't know, self-confidence enough to assert it, morality enough to feel that there is something wrong in acting as if you know when you don't. It is part of a way of living your life, how you respond, think, feel about the issue, other people, you yourself. This is the kind of person that Paul wants education to try to produce.

For all the breadth of its educational ideal, this is not in the least a head-in-the-air book. It is far more a practical, down-to-earth exploration of the countless avenues involved in implementing the vision: how to set up a staff development program, the necessity of administrative participation, how to get students to discover "answers" themselves, how to promote socialization and dialogue among students, how to get students to relate subject matter to their own lives and to other courses, what kinds of questions to ask, even down to how to teach maps and charts in social studies. The book is far more a practical guide, though of an unusual kind, than it is an abstract or visionary treatise. Teachers can find concrete suggestions and techniques in practically every chapter.

The problem with practical guides generally is that you can become so involved with the details, so involved with, say, asking the right question, that you lose sight of the goal in mind, and your performance slides into a mechanical, uncritical one. That is especially easy to do with critical thinking, where the techniques or applications are often so intrinsically interesting that we can forget they are *merely* techniques and applications, never the end itself. What Paul does is to infuse the goals into every technique, every discussion, so that in the end, to the extent that the book has been useful to you, you will no longer need it. You will be actively engaged in critical thinking and so will be able to (and have the skills, passions, and attitudes to want to) come up with your own techniques and applications, which may well fit your situation better than Paul's do. That, I think, is very close to the guiding principle of the book: to get other people to do it better than he does.

The papers that constitute this volume have expanded the field into areas of inquiry where, just ten years ago, few people in critical thinking had ventured. And in broadening the field, Paul — more I think than any single individual — has helped to transform it, from an almost exclusive concentration on argument to the multifaceted enterprise it is today. Consider his list of the basic *elements* of thought and the manner in which they can be used, along with critical thinking *standards*, to generate critical thinking *abilities*. Here are two examples: "the ability to analyze accurately the problem or question at issue" and "the ability to gather relevant information." It is easy to see not only the importance of these, but also how to formulate other important abilities on one's own. Most of the abilities and intellectual traits he isolates are flexible enough and basic enough to provide guidelines for teaching math, composition, literature, history, and other courses whose subject matter often has little to do with argumentation. He makes clear, for example, the centrality of intellectual perseverance, intellectual humility, intellectual integrity, and intellectual courage.Elsewhere in the book, Paul talks about topics as far-ranging as the structure of questioning, the "logic" of learning, critical approaches to viewing and sometimes changing one's life, personality, and culture.

Or, again, consider his elucidations of basic concepts (weak sense/strong sense, monological/multilogical, for example) or the straightforward introduction of moral categories into critical thinking. Moral concepts, of course, have *always* been implicit in critical thinking (even before there was a field so called), just as they have always lurked in the background of academic fields generally: there is *value* (and it is more than adventitious value) in being reasonable. But what Paul has done in these papers is to bring them out into the open, both as explicit goals to be striven for, and as objects of critical discussion. What *are* the values inherent in this "standard" history of the Renaissance? In our account of Jacobean drama? In this handbook of managerial techniques? Following Paul's guidelines, such questions would be nearly obligatory in any subject-matter course that is taught in a critical manner. And Paul emphasizes that all instruction should be focused on reasoning: historical reasoning in history classes, scientific reasoning in science classes, mathematical reasoning in math classes, and so forth, and so on.

A couple of Paul's points, it should be noted, are controversial among philosophers. It remains to be seen, for instance, whether the concept of *multilogical* can be worked out epistemologically, or how much weight should be given to the weak sense/strong sense distinction.

Take the multilogical issue. The essence of the monological/multilogical distinction is that the logic of some questions, monological questions, allows only one correct answer, with a single or convergent logic of justification for it. (Think of the word problems at the end of the chapter in a physics text.) Multilogical questions, on the other hand, allow more than one rationally defensible answer, and the justifications for answers are frequently divergent. (Think of social or cultural problems, for example.) The controversy centers around whether there is ultimately a single, convergent, complete answer to the latter questions as well. The key word is "ultimately," for both sides in the controversy agree that we certainly do not, at present, have such answers, that there is little prospect for discovering them in the near future, and that we, humans, may in fact never actually discover them.

What is the controversy, then? It is whether there *is* such an answer, a *knowable* answer, regardless of whether it will ever in fact be known to us. Could there be, say, an ideal sociology which would answer all questions about human social behavior, and to which every reasonable person would assent? To this, Paul gives a qualified "No," while others give (on metaphysical or epistemological grounds) a "Yes."

The controversy is too complex and ambiguous to discuss further here, but what is clear is that even if Paul is mistaken on this epistemological question — and I for one grow less and less convinced that he *is* wrong — the perspectival view he is committed to is not a crude one. To maintain that there is not a single, convergent, complete answer to multilogical questions is not at all to say that one answer is as good as another; it is not to say that "it all depends on your point of view."

As Paul repeatedly insists, *rational* discussion — reasons, arguments, explorations of consequences and motives, crucial tests where possible — is the deciding factor. Critical thinking is never mere discussion: it is always reason-backed discussion. It is subjecting one's point of view to critical scrutiny (and perhaps refutation).

My own way of putting the point is that there is an asymmetry between true and false, or, if you like, between establishing *as* true and establishing *as* false. With multilogical questions, the total amount of evidence, plus interpretations, may leave us rationally unable to establish one of two viewpoints as true; but whether the question is monological *or* multilogical, considerations of evidence can and often do give us conclusively good reasons to reject some points of view as false, even points of view that are sincerely and deeply held. In such cases, intellectual integrity should compel the critical thinker to admit that her point of view was mistaken, false. The dodge to saying "Well, it's still my point of view" is just that: an intellectual dodge — and one that is certainly not sanctioned by Paul's concept of the multilogical.

A resolution of the epistemological controversy (were it not question-begging, I would be tempted to say that issue too is multilogical) thus does not bear on the educational point at hand: our ignorance of the ultimate truth (perhaps invincible ignorance), together with considerations about the logic of discovery, dictates that we *teach* (and learn) multilogically, perspectivally. In that sense, the difference between math and physics on the one hand, and social studies on the other, may not be so much that the former are monological while the latter are multilogical; rather, the apparent differences may be the result of the amount of expertise and knowledge required before one reaches the multilogical threshold in a field. It takes a certain amount of knowledge and familiarity to discuss questions intelligently and critically, to entertain contrasting theories and follow out their consequences. We begin to collect information (or misinformation) about the human-related matters that are the topics of social studies by the time we start using language. A ten-year-old can

rationally argue some (though not all) points of view about personal
identity or the causes of crime: she has reached the multilogical threshold
on the basis of "common knowledge" and reasoning skills. But even an
upper-level undergraduate cannot typically engage in a similar level of
informed rational discussion about the big-bang theory. Physics and
math majors themselves are just beginning to acquire the familiarity —
with quarks or singularities, or the rudiments of super-computer-generat-
ed mathematical proofs — that will allow them, several years down the
line, to get to the multilogical thresholds of those fields.

If this speculation is right, it meshes nicely with the techniques Paul
details of teaching multilogical vs. monological subject matter in courses.
The differing teaching techniques are grounded not in an inherent difference in the fields as such, but in the level at which students are operating.
So though Paul *may* be wrong in some of what *may* be his epistemological
assumptions (I emphasize *"may"*), in an educational sense I think he is
right, even profoundly right.

Whether he is talking about such distinctions, or about educational theory or practice, or, for that matter, about how to teach parts of speech to a
fourth-grader, one major impression Paul leaves is that the results often
seem disconcertingly obvious. In that respect the conclusions in the book
are like the conclusions of most good, careful, original thinking: the obvi-
ousness of them is patent — but only by hindsight. I find myself responding to a chapter I read yesterday: "But *obviously* those are the strategies I
should use. Of *course* that's the goal I should have in mind when I teach"
— when the truth is that as recently as the day before yesterday the question had not even occurred to me. (By tomorrow, it will have become so
natural that I may no longer think of it as having originated in Paul's
book.) This reaction occurs because of what Paul has done throughout the
book: guided us to think the questions out ourselves — so the results seem
just as much a product of our own critical thinking as his.

Thus, more than anything, the book demonstrates the great versatility
and fecundity of critical thinking itself. It is a guidebook, of both theory
and practice, in two different senses. In the conventional sense, it guides
us by providing techniques and applications that are the product of Paul's
expertise as a critical thinker. But it is also a guidebook in a very different
sense (the one, I think, that Paul primarily intends): it guides us along
through the argumentation and the thought processes to arrive at conclusions ourselves. We then see with our own eyes, with clarity and insight,
why critical thinking — of the kind Paul envisions, defends, and elaborates — is indispensible for the world of the future.

University of New Orleans, New Orleans
December 10, 1989

Introduction

Critical thinking is the essential foundation for education because it is the essential foundation for adaptation to the everyday personal, social, and professional demands of the 21st Century and thereafter. The most inescapable imperative of the future is continuous change, change that involves complex adjustments to the increasingly complex systems that dominate our lives. Therefore, the distinguishing characteristics of those who will not only survive but thrive in the future, will be abilities and traits, both intellectual and emotional, that entail excellence in evaluating and responding to the conditions of change.

Yet the mind is not by nature adaptable to changes of the breadth and depth that we are facing. Rather the mind is instinctively designed for habit, associating "peace of mind" with routine. The mind's natural inclination is to reduce the new to the old, the complex to the simple, and everything as much as possible, to familiar, well-grooved patterns and habits. It is not natural for the human mind to continuously re-think its systems, its routines, its habits — in fact, it is downright threatening.

If we juxtapose the nature of the future with the nature of the human mind, confusion is the inevitable result. We cannot arrest the accelerating changes of our future, nor can we simplify the challenges to come. Therefore, we must adapt our minds. We must ready them for complexity and change. What will the particulars of this adaptation be?

We need to construct, through socialization and education, a new "second nature" for the mind. We must work within the human propensity toward habit by learning how to shape our minds to a qualitatively different kind of habit: the habit of not only continually changing but of continually expecting to change. We must cultivate the habit of continually raising our systems of routine to a conscious level with the express purpose of reshaping them in an unending series of acts of intellectual self-improvement. No domains of our lives — as teachers, parents, citizens, workers — will be spared if legitimate "peace of mind" is to be restored.

It will never again do to think exclusively within one fixed belief system. The cruel illusion of security in permanence will continue to tantalize us, but we must prepare ourselves to live within flux rather than constancy, to be comfortable with the unexpected and problematic, to expect the unexpected, even, in fact, to create the unexpected and problematic as a "natural" part of day-to-day living and thinking. Ceaseless, incessant, perpetual adjustments to novel, unfamiliar intricacy now becomes the only permanent rule. Skill in turning systems inside out, frequently restructuring and recasting them, will be the basis for high-paid labor and the challenge of sound leadership.

For our adaptations to succeed, we must enhance our abilities to evaluate ideas, changing conditions, and events. We will thrive to the extent that we cultivate minds that habitually probe the logic of the systems of the status quo as well as the logic of the possible variations and alternative systems, approaching each with questions that enable us to assess both strengths and weaknesses.

Our educational institutions, unfortunately, are totally unprepared for this kind of revolutionary change. When one lays 21st Century global imperatives against the routines of modern education, the misfit is obvious. Not only are school administrators and teachers insulated from these imperatives, but even if they recognized them, they are not by preparation, practice, or inclination ready to respond. If for no other reason, their own education was severely lacking in stress on intellectual abilities, intellectual traits, and intellectual standards. They have not learned the art of disciplined reasoning. They are often poor problem solvers; they tend to approach all problems from the point of view of expediency and the protection of their images. In any case, they show no sign of recognizing the profound difference between students memorizing the conclusions of others and students reasoning to those conclusions on the basis of their own disciplined thought.

Indeed, it is clear after twenty odd years of "Educational Reform" that the systems by which schools presently operate strongly resist foundational change. They see no value in the continuous critical assessment of ideas and thinking. They are fixated on self-protection. Historically, schools have lagged behind social, professional, and commercial developments; the problem is compounded because schools are heavily insulated bureaucratically from those developments.

Those who run schools have become unwitting masters of the art of surface change, of seeming to change while not changing, of leap-frogging from fad to fad, of living in a permanent state of delusion, of continually shifting labels for what are, at root, essentially unchanging practices. Intellectual standards are without question largely absent from the day-to-day life of scholastic thinking. Shoddy ideas and shallow thinking — polished up with glitz, rhetoric, and platitudes — rule the day. Wide-ranging critical thinking, as opposed to narrow-focused political thinking, is conspicuous by its absence.

New jargon replaces old jargon in the scholastic world, but the old reality remains: *administrators* not focused on facilitating education but on preventing or minimizing disquiet and unrest; bobbing and weaving, dodging and evading, eluding and equivocating, quibbling and side-stepping; *teachers* in their turn learning to make periodic surface changes in what remains predominantly static: the unending dominance of unimaginative didactic teaching; *students* in their turn, episodically memorizing, reiterating, parroting, ignoring, avoiding, hiding, and opining; in their hearts and minds, heedless, defiant, subservient, impetuous, inconsistent, muted, sluggish, passive, apathetic, undisciplined, clamorous, hazy, confused, dogmatic, indifferent, dulled, blunted, numbed, unsettled, inert, intemperate, irritable, hushed, and moody, the by-products of an ungrounded, poorly led, anti-intellectual culture.

Today this art of counterfeit is being used to create the appearance of a shift to "higher order" thinking. A new lingo is abroad, that of "restructuring," "meaning-centered" instruction, of "effective schools," of "outcome-based" education, of "site-based management," of "cooperative learning" and "whole language," of "total quality management," of "creativity," of "learning styles" and "multiple intelligences," of "multi-culturalism," of "group problem solving" and "shared decision making," etc., but, as usual, the old practices have not changed, the old ground has not shifted.

Without a substantial groundwork of quality in thinking, without the necessary intellectual standards, "restructuring" will be ill-designed, the "meanings" students construct will be ill-formed, the "effectiveness" of schools will be at the expense of quality of thought, the "outcomes" will be lower order, "site-based management" will be "site-based mis-management," the "cooperative learning" will be "cooperative mis-learning," the "whole language" learned will be that of an undisciplined speaker of the language, at best fluent and slick but superficial, the "total quality management" will be a mockery of Deming, all procedure and no substance, the "creativity" will be nothing but "flashy novelty," the "learning styles" will sacrifice well-rounded intellectual development, the "multiple intelligences" will produce one-sided development; all at the expense of the development of universal intellectual traits and standards. The "multi-culturalism" will move society in the direction of cultural anarchy, all diversity and no unity, and the "group problem solving" and "decision making" will confuse group agreement with group rationality, and conformity with depth and quality of reason. These patterns are everywhere illustrated today in the low quality of student performance, despite a large public investment.

It is of little use for educators to talk about a "rich thinking, meaning-centered curriculum for all students," about "authentic performance tasks," about teachers providing "the kind of instruction that enables students to formulate questions and work in groups to solve problems," about "students learning content through processes similar to those which they encounter in their everyday life outside of school." It is not enough to ask that students "construct personal meanings" or be "motivated to learn" or to be "fluent" or "articulate" or even "persuasive" in what they say or write.

None of this is worthwhile if neither the teacher's nor the students' thinking is grounded in intellectual standards and they cannot assess thinking objectively or with discipline.

Ironically, the emphasis is often on distinguishing between fact and opinion, as if those were the only two choices. The category of well-reasoned judgment is entirely absent, both conceptually and in practice. Yet, all of the crucial problems and questions of our day require well-reasoned judgment, neither mere collections of facts nor mindlessly formed opinion.

Virtually all of the programs, all of the staff development, all of the textbooks proceed as if intellectual standards and knowledge of the art of critical thinking are automatically produced in the minds of teachers and students merely by virtue of their using some program or textbook. Nothing could be further from the truth. The textbooks merely reinforce the students' and teacher's perception that they really have grasped the crucial issues, when in fact, they have simply touched upon the surface of them, often in a misleading way.

Neither teachers nor students have a workable idea of what critical thinking is. Neither have a clear idea of what reasoning is, of what an assumption, an inference, an implication is, of what it means to adapt or change one's point of view or frame of reference. Neither has a clear idea of what is required when one sets out to analyze a concept or question. And neither understands what it is to have, to articulate, or to use intellectual standards as a guide in one's thinking.

At every level of education, teachers and students are, for the most part, thinking in lower order ways, quite uncritically. What further complicates the problem is that they are, for the most part again, oblivious of the limited nature and depth of their thinking.

Though students undoubtedly do think, and often think in functional ways, in tune with the lower-order system in place, they do not think in ways that lead to self-assessment and self-improvement of any kind, much less within a model of continuous self-improvement. Students and teachers lack the basic rudiments of what good thinking requires and how the criteria and standards of good thinking cut across every subject area, guiding the well-grounded student to use the logic common to all systems to reconstruct the logic specific to each. Instead, students use their thinking in the only way that seems rational to them: to get the grades they want, often more tuned into the psychology of their instructor than into the logic of the subject.

Perhaps it is the focus of the field of education on the discipline of psychology for its grounding, which has led 20th Century education to progressively move from a focus on "objectivity" to a focus on "subjectivity," "idiosyncrasy," and the art of "doing your own thing." The focus of education has shifted in the 20th Century from the integrity and logic of the various subjects to an emphasis on a myriad of overlapping processes devoid of logic. Most of the psychology that has influenced education has been imbued with latent or overt relativism, leading to an uncritical validation of the primacy of "mere opinion" over "reasoned judgment." There has seemed to be no room, in this atmosphere of the psychologized mind, for an emphasis on intellectual standards, logic, reasoning, intellectual traits, and the imperative for inner discipline of thought.

Of course, there have been many contributions by some important psychologists, yet vulgarized educational psychology has had the impact of indoctrination for both students and teachers, with each group uncritically accepting what is "normal" for what is "rational and worthwhile." We must rediscover the fact that psychology cannot tell "how we *should* think, but only how we *do* think." We need the bigger brush, the sharper tools of reason, and logic, and basic values to guide us to what should be.

Can we sustain an educational model that lacks standards by which to cultivate and assess improvement? Can we support the kind of social indoctrination that prepares students to be compliant, follow orders, habituate themselves to perform routine tasks while they deny responsibility for their conduct and their lives? Can we support intellectual conditioning in the classroom that leaves virtually no room for significant intellectual growth? A cult of subjectivity cannot help us confront the objective fact of the accelerating change and complexity of our world.

The long and the short of the story is this: Schools today do not focus on how to introduce children to the logic of the subjects they study. They do not focus on what it is to reason historically, what it is to reason mathematically or scientifically, what it is to reason sociologically, anthropologically, or geographically, what it is to reason philosophically or morally. Hence, disciplined reasoning — which is at the heart of the logic of every academic subject and profession — is largely absent from the classroom of today.

In this book, I set out the nature of what is missing in education today, the central linchpin of quality thinking and quality evaluation of thinking. Until this substructure is in place, the superstructure is bound to be nothing more than a facade that looks forever new, but remains forever old, a facade merely replicating the past again and again and again in a new set of surface words. Until this substructure is in place, our educational institutions will continue to fail dramatically to support this nation's adaptability to the global imperatives of the 21st Century.

Part A

What Is Critical Thinking?

Section I

Overview: What Critical Thinking Is and Why It Is Essential

Accelerating Change, the Complexity of
Problems, and the Quality of Our Thinking

Critical Thinking: Identifying the Targets

The Critical Thinking Movement in
Historical Perspective

Pseudo Critical Thinking in the Educational
Establishment

Critical Thinking: Basic Questions and
Answers

Chapter 1

Accelerating Change, the Complexity of Problems, and the Quality of Our Thinking

with Jane Willsen

Abstract

The goal of this chapter is to trace the general implications of what are iden-tified as the two central characteristics of the future: accelerating change and intensifying complexity. If change continues to move faster and faster, and if the changes that do occur become more and more complex, how are we to deal with the world? More specifically, how are we to understand how this change and complexity will play itself out? How are we to prepare for it? Paul and Willsen focus on the economic and educational dimensions of these questions. They lead us into and through the vision of four of our most penetrating thinkers: Robert Reich, Lester Thurow, W. Edward Deming, and Robert Heilbroner. The general thesis is that the visions of these thinkers are complementary and that collectively they provide us with a rich and pointed picture of what we must do, not because they are "visionaries," but because they have done the profound analytic work which enables them to shed a clear light on very general patterns, all of which add up to accelerating change, intensifying complexity, and critical thinking. The chapter ends with an analysis of the implications for parenting, work, and educa-tion of the foundational fact that "the work of the future is the work of the mind, intellectual work, work that involves reasoning and intellectual self-discipline."

✦✦ The Nature of the Post-Industrial World Order

*T*he world is swiftly changing and with each day the pace quickens. The pressure to respond intensifies. New global realities are rapidly working their way into the deepest structures of our lives: economic, social, environmental realities — realities with profound implications for teaching and learning, for business and politics, for human rights and human conflicts. These realities are becoming increasingly complex; and they all turn on the powerful dynamic of accelerating change. This chap-ter explores the general character of these changes and the quality of thinking necessary for effectively adapting to them.

1

Can we deal with incessant and accelerating change and complexity without revolutionizing our thinking? Traditionally our thinking has been designed for routine, for habit, for automation and fixed procedure. We learned how to do something once, and then we did it over and over. Learning meant becoming habituated. But what is it to learn to continually re-learn? To be comfortable with perpetual re-learning? This is a new world for us to explore, one in which the power of critical thinking to turn back on itself in continual cycles and re-cycles of self-critique is crucial.

Consider, for a moment, even a simple feature of daily life: drinking water from the tap. With the increase of pollution, the poisoning of ground water, the indirect and long-term negative consequences of even small amounts of a growing number of chemicals, how are we to judge whether or not public drinking water is safe? Increasingly governments are making decisions about how many lives to risk against the so many dollars of cost to save them. How are we to know whether the risk the government is willing to take with our lives is equivalent to our willingness to risk? This is just one of hundreds of decisions that require extraordinary thinking.

Consider also the quiet revolution that is taking place in communications. From fax machines to E-Mail, from bulletin board systems to computer delivery systems to home shopping, we are providing opportunities for people to not only be more efficient with their time, but to build invisible networks where goods, services, and ideas are exchanged with individuals the world over. But how is one to interface with this revolution? How much is one to learn and how fast? How much money should one spend on this or that new system? When is the new system cost effective? When should one wait for a newer development?

These communication innovations have re-introduced a way of life lost in the industrial revolution of the late 1800s. Farmers used to work at home, doctors' offices were routinely downstairs from where they lived. All that is coming back, not for farmers or doctors, but for millions of service and technical professionals for whom, "I work at home," is now a common refrain. But how are we to take these realities into account in planning our lives and careers?

Yes, technological growth brings new opportunities, new safety devices, more convenience, new lifestyles. But we must also juggle and judge work and child care, efficiency and clogged transportation systems, expensive cars and inconvenient office space, increased specialization and increasing obsolescence. We are caught up in an increasing swirl of challenges and decisions.

These changes ask and offer much at the same time, if only we can make sense of them and put them into perspective. For example, what are we to make of altered forms of community, for community in a world of automatic tellers, home shopping, self-service, delivery services, malls, video rentals, and television? How shall we evaluate these social changes and their implications for our lives?

Or consider another facet of the accelerating change: that young people today can expect to make from four to seven career changes in their lifetimes. The question, "What do you want to be when you grow up?" is a poignant reminder of a vision from the past. Our children and students can no longer anticipate the knowledge or data that they will need on the job, because they can no longer predict the kinds of jobs that will be available or what they will entail.

What is more, even if the young could predict the general fields in which they will work, about half of the information which is current in each field will be obsolete in six years. Will people recognize which half? Will they know how to access and use it?

Accelerating change is intermeshed with another powerful force, the increasing complexity of the problems we face. Consider, for a moment, solid waste management. This problem involves every level of government, every department: from energy to water quality, to planning, to revenues, to public health. Without a cooperative venture, without bridging the territorial domains, without overcoming the implicit adversarial process within which we currently operate, the responsible parties at each tier of government cannot even *begin* to solve these problems. When they do communicate, they often do not speak honestly about the issues given the human propensity to mask the limitations of one's position and promote one's narrow but deeply vested interests.

Consider the issues of depletion of the ozone layer, world hunger, overpopulation, and AIDS. Without a grasp of the elements, and internal relationships of the elements, in each of dozens of interrelating systems from specific product emissions to social incentives, from effective utilization of the media to human learning, we are adrift in a stormy sea of information. Without a grasp of the of political realities, economic pressures, scientific data on the physical environment and its changes — all of which are simultaneously changing the as well — we stand no chance of making any significant positive impact on the deterioration of the quality of life for all who share the planet.

These two characteristics, then, accelerating change and increasing complexity — with their incessant demand for a new capacity to adapt, for the now rare ability to think effectively through new problems and situations in new ways — sound the death knell for traditional methods of learning how to survive in the world in which we live. How can we adapt to reality when reality won't give us time to master it before it changes itself, again and again, in ways we cannot anticipate? As we struggle to gain insight, let's look more closely at the operating forces.

Robert Heilbroner, the distinguished American economist, in *Twenty-First Century Capitalism*, identifies capitalism as a global force that brings us "kaleidoscopic changefulness," a "torrent of market-driven change." As he illustrates in example after example, "If capitalism is anything, it is a social order in constant change — and beyond that, change that seems to have a direction, an underlying principle of motion, a logic." The logic, however, is the logic of "creative destruction, the unpredictable displacement of one process or product by another at the hands of giant enterprise" (p. 20).

Furthermore, along with kaleidoscopic change, along with the continual social transformations that follow from those changes, come "both wealth and misery," development and damage, a "two-edged sword" that makes instability permanent in unpredicted and unpredictable forms. Basic change continually destabilizes the system at the micro-level, making for multiple imbalances and upheavals. The complexity and speed of change means that we shall always have to make unpredictable adjustments to both the upsides and downsides that result from this upheaval, for we cannot hope to predict the myriad of micro-level system changes that are continually emerging and putting pressure on the system at the macro level.

We can no longer rely on the past to be the guide for the future. Technology will continually race ahead, creating links that make the world smaller and smaller. New opportunities will continually emerge but within them are embedded new problems, hence the need for acute readiness and disciplined ingenuity. At every step along the way, however, polished, satiny voices will tempt us astray with slick, simplistic messages that appear to guide us back to the "tried and true." Often, these voices in fact coax us into policies and practices that continually sacrifice our long-term interests to someone's short-term gain. In business, education, and politics, the same sirens echo.

Many American business and labor leaders have yet to come to terms with these realities. They yearn for a world of stability in which they can play a predictable game in a predictable way. As Laura Tyson, Chairwoman of the President's Council of Economic Advisors has put it,

> ... the vast majority of American companies ... [continue] to opt for traditional hierarchical work organizations that ... [make] few demands on the skills of their workers. In fact, most American companies interviewed by the Commission on the Skills of the American Workforce continue to prefer this approach, which dooms most American workers to a low-wage future. If American workers are to look forward to anything more than low-wage employment, changes in work organization are required to upgrade their skills and productivity so that American companies can afford to pay higher wages and still compete in world markets. ("Failing Our Youth: America's K–12 Education," p. 52)

What our businesses are failing to change is what European and Japanese companies are changing: namely, "making their high-wage labor more productive not simply by investing in more equipment but by organizing their workers in ways that ... [upgrade] their skills." World-class, internationally-competitive companies recognize the need to play a new game and have re-organized themselves accordingly. As Tyson explains,

High productivity work-place organizations depend on workers who can do more than read, write, and do simple arithmetic, and who bring more to their jobs than reliability and a good attitude. In such organizations, workers are asked *to use judgment and make decisions* rather than to merely follow directions. Management layers disappear as workers take over many of the tasks that others used to do — from quality control to production scheduling. Tasks formerly performed by dozens of unskilled individuals are turned over to a much smaller number of skilled individuals. Often, teams of workers are required to monitor complicated computer-controlled production equipment, to interpret computer output, to perform statistical quality control techniques, and to repair complex and sensitive equipment. (p. 53) [our emphasis]

These new kinds of workers, of course, are not asked merely to "use judgment and make decisions," rather they are asked to use *good* judgment and make *well-thought-out* decisions. How will workers acquire these fundamental abilities to think deeply and well? Are educators able to "make meaning" out of these exhortations of our leaders?

Bold changes in business organization and practices require parallel changes in education. Yet the U.S. public school systems, like most U.S. businesses, remain mired in the past, focused on lower order skills, and unresponsive to the need for higher order abilities. Again, as Laura Tyson puts it, "[Higher-order tasks] ... require higher-order language, math, scientific, and reasoning skills that America's K–12 education system is not providing."

Our students deserve at least a fighting chance to compete, to rise to the challenges of the day. Reconstructing and adapting our business and educational systems to teach our managers as well as our teachers and administrators how to create these higher order workplaces and classrooms, and then to expect them to do so in the ordinary course of their professional obligations, is our first major challenge. Today, at every level, we are failing this test, failing our students and workers, jeopardizing our future. What is missing is a genuine sense of what accelerating change entails and a shared public vision of the need for fundamental changes. Many of our leading economic analysts are struggling to create just such a new frame of reference within which we can come to terms with the new imperatives.

✦ The Vision of Robert Reich: The Thinking of Workers as the New Capital

Robert Reich, Secretary of Labor, in his seminal book, *The Work of Nations*, offers a shocking perspective. No longer will economies be tied to the fate of national corporations. No longer will we be sheltered by the power of our enormous industrial complex, our major corporations. No longer can we say, "What is good for General Motors is good for the United States!" The new form of "wealth" will no longer principally reside in the number of dollars in American pockets. Rather it will reside in the quality of the minds of our workers. As Reich puts it,

> We are living through a transformation that will rearrange the politics and economics of the coming century. There will be no national products or technologies, no national corporations, no national industries. There will no longer be national economies, or at least not as we have come to understand that concept. All that will remain rooted within national borders are the people who comprise a nation. Each nation's primary assets will be its citizens' skills and insights. (p. 3)

The changes triggered and fueled by new opportunities will bring an economy

> ... replete with unidentified problems, unknown solutions, and unknown means of putting them together — mastery of old domains of knowledge isn't nearly enough to guarantee a good income. Nor, importantly, is it even necessary.... What is more valuable is the capacity to effectively and creatively use the knowledge. (p. 182)

Routinely, jobs and production, the income that those jobs generate, and its multiplying effects in commerce, are leaping national boundaries, seeking optimum conditions for competition. We are facing competition for the production work that Americans have habitually taken as their birthright. The competitors are everywhere, as growing pressures of over-population and environmental problems make more people willing to work for lower wages and more governments willing to offer incentives to incoming business.

Certainly, many industries are still located here in the United States; however, there is a hemorrhage of routine production work that is moving to Mexico, to Asia, to Central and South America where workers are able to produce the same product for international markets at a significant savings to the organization. U.S. workers are bewildered and afraid, watching their standard of living decline with every year.

> In the emerging global economy, even the most impressive of positions in the most prestigious of organizations is vulnerable to worldwide competition if it entails easily replicated routines. The only true competitive advantage lies in skill in solving, identifying, and brokering new problems. (p. 184)

Reich claims that the distinguishing characteristic of workers who will retain their jobs will be the ability to "add value" to the production process. This translates into being able to identify and solve problems at every level relative to the job function. It means taking initiative and responsibility for the continuous improvement of production and efficiency, from the shop floor to the executive suite. To the extent that our labor force can shift into a cooperative venture with management, sharing responsibility for enhanced performance and production, jobs are more likely to be retained within our national boundaries.

The possession of capital will not in itself be a sure source of national wealth because American capital, as all other "national" capital, will be drawn to and invested in the nations where the work forces produce the highest level of return. Profit will stem from successful problem solving and brokering. Reich identifies a spiral wherein increasing opportunities for problem solving will provide the fodder for increasing our workers' capacity to solve more and more complex problems. Mastery of each new task requires new learning, thus enhancing each worker's capacity to contribute to the next new task.

Enhancing our capacity to solve problems will also produce more job opportunities, and up the spiral we will march as our workers continue to become better at solving the problems we face and continue to expand our inventories of skills and experience. The effectiveness and quality of our workers' thinking will drive us up the spiral, and will provide the basis for the wealth of the nation.

But do our workers and managers see this spiral? Do we see that it is the effectiveness and quality of our thinking which enables us to climb it? What is patently clear is that the spiral flows both up and down. What is unclear is whether we have the vision and determination to reverse our current course. Assuming we do have the will, we still need to know how to proceed.

Reich identifies four components of the kind of critical thinking that the highly-paid workers of today and the future will increasingly need to master: *1)* abstraction, *2)* system thinking, *3)* experimentation and testing, and *4)* collaboration. He calls the critical thinkers in possession of these basic abilities "symbolic analysts." Let us look briefly at how Reich characterizes each of these four *generic* abilities.

COMMAND OF ABSTRACTIONS

> The capacity for abstraction — for discovering patterns and meanings — is, of course, the very essence of symbolic analysis, in which reality must be simplified so that it can be understood and manipulated in new ways.... Every innovative scientist, lawyer, engineer, designer, management consultant, screenwriter, or advertiser is continuously searching for new ways to represent reality which will be more compelling or revealing than the old.... [But] for most children in the United States and around the world, formal education entails just the opposite kind of learning. Rather than construct meanings for themselves, meanings are imposed upon them. (pp. 229–230)

THINKING WITHIN SYSTEMS

The education of the symbolic analyst emphasizes system thinking. Rather than teach students how to solve a problem that is presented to them, they are taught to examine why the problem arises and how it is connected to other problems. Learning how to travel from one place to another by following a prescribed route is one thing; learning the entire terrain so that you can find shortcuts to wherever you may want to go is quite another. (p. 231)

TESTING IDEAS

Instead of emphasizing the transmission of information, the focus is on judgment and interpretation. The student is taught to get *behind* the data — to ask why certain facts have been selected, why they are assumed to be important, how they were deduced, and how they might be contradicted. The student learns to examine reality from many angles, in different lights, and thus to visualize new possibilities and choices. The symbolic-analytic mind is trained to be skeptical, curious, and creative. (p. 230)

LEARNING TO COLLABORATE AND COMMUNICATE

... in America's best classrooms ... the emphasis has shifted. Instead of individual achievement and competition, the focus is on group learning. Students learn to articulate, clarify, and then restate for one another how they identify and find answers. They learn how to seek and accept criticism from peers, solicit help, and give credit to others. They also learn to negotiate — to explain their own needs, to discern what others need and view things from others' perspectives. (p. 233)

How many critical thinkers (symbolic analysts) will we have the foresight to develop? For each student we fail to reach, we create an economic dependent; for each student we help to possess the requisite abilities and traits, we create a producer who can carry not only himself or herself, but those dependents inevitable in any society. How urgent do we perceive the problem to be? How clearly do we understand the problem and its dimensions?

✦ The Vision of Lester Thurow: Two Forms of Capitalism at War in a World of Economic Revolutions

The world that Lester Thurow looks out upon is a world of multiple revolutions: a green revolution, a materials-science revolution, a telecommunications-computer-transportation-logistics revolution. These revolutions require fundamental changes in all economies around the world. We live in a multi-polar world: the global economy is no longer pivoting solely around the United States as it did in the fifties and sixties. As Thurow sees it, "Nowhere are the necessary changes going to be harder to make than in the United States, for in the past century it has been the most successful economy in the world." (*Head to Head,* p. 16) Our tendency, Thurow believes, will be to continue the strategies that brought us success in the past, even though those strategies no longer fit a "multi-polar" world.

For example, military power is now a distinct disadvantage rather than an advantage, a drain on the national treasury and a limitation on investments necessary for competition. Here are the new questions that in Thurow's view can be used to measure world economic strength.

> Who can make the best products? What expands their standards of living most rapidly? Who has the best-educated and best-skilled work force in the world? Who is the world's leader in investment — plant and equipment, research and development, infrastructure? Who organizes best? Whose institutions — government, education, business — are world leaders in efficiency? (pp. 23–24)

Much of Thurow's argument is based on a distinction between the two forms of capitalism currently in competition for world leadership: communitarian and individualistic capitalism. In every way, Thurow argues, it is clear that communitarian capitalism (such as in Germany and Japan) wins out over individualistic capitalism (such as in U.S. and Great Britain). This is reflected in many statistics including those of the World Economic Forum relating to American, German, and Japanese management (p. 162).

RANKING OF QUALITY OF MANAGEMENT IN 23 INDUSTRIAL NATIONS
World Economic Forum, Swiss-run publisher of *World Competitiveness Report*

	GERMANY	JAPAN	USA
PRODUCT QUALITY	3	1	12
ON-TIME DELIVERY	2	1	10
AFTER-SALES SERVICE	2	1	10
QUANTITY AND QUALITY OF ON-THE-JOB TRAINING	2	1	11
FUTURE ORIENTATION	3	1	22

Thurow sums up the problem as follows:

> Japan and Germany, the countries that are outperforming America in international trade, do not have less government or more motivated individuals. They are countries noted for their careful organization of teams — teams that involve workers and managers, teams that involve suppliers and customers, teams that involve government and business.... But American mythology extols only the individual — the Lone Ranger or Rambo.... History is littered with the wrecks of countries whose mythologies were more important than reality. (p. 298)

In essence, Thurow's analysis calls for a transformed American global view in which we recognize the obsolescence of some of our most fundamental traditional assumptions and the need to shift our world view — to make no less than a fundamental intellectual paradigm shift.

But isn't this asking a lot of a nation that has never put a premium on the ability to think critically? Isn't this asking a lot of a nation that historically has been able to solve its problems with sheer hard work and physical courage? Isn't this asking a lot of a nation that believes deeply in the tried and true, that has been conditioned to think of itself as leading not following and as being the most progressive, as being always *number one?*

Thurow nowhere discusses how this shift is to occur, how the electorate is to be persuaded into such a radical re-orientation. We tend to seek security in the familiar, in the established, in the traditional: if we don't find it immediately, we look harder, but in the same places! Since most Americans have not been prepared by their education to do the requisite critical thinking that would support a paradigm shift such as Thurow suggests, how are they to do it?

If Thurow is right in his analysis of world economic conditions, then it will not be sufficient for a small minority of highly paid workers to learn to think critically as "symbolic analysts." It will not be enough for a few to be comfortable with abstractions, to be able to think in terms of alternative systems, to test ideas for their strengths, and to recognize the value of collaboration. But here, again, is the most pressing problem of the day: How are we to persuade educators, how are we to persuade citizens, how are we to persuade parents, that a new economic era is dawning? How are we to persuade the general public, which itself has not learned to think critically, that it is now in our collective national interest to set as our first priority the development of critical thinking abilities and traits in all of our children?

✦ The Vision of W. Edwards Deming: Everyone a Critical Thinker Contributing to Continuous Improvement

W. Edwards Deming, the American marvel who, after WWII, designed the highly successful Japanese style of management and production, built his whole approach on the assumption that the most important asset of any company is the capacity of the individuals in it to use their ability to think critically to improve their collective performance. Success can be found, in his view, in the ability to devise structures that systematically encourage and reward the critique and improvement of process. He therefore established a system of interrelated networks of "workers and managers" (quality control circles, so called) who use "critical reflection in a formal but unthreatening setting so as to establish what it is good to do." (Holt, p. 383)

When procedures are designed to bring the maximum degree of constructive critical thinking to bear on the problems of production, virtually everyone has a potential contribution to make. The quality of the contribution will not be a function of the worker's position in the hierarchy, but the quality of the critical thinking he or she brings to bear on the problem. This, again, requires the paradigm shift that American businesses seem reluctant to make.

Unfortunately, though Deming is now popular and much has been written about the Deming way and "total quality management," most writings emphasize the "techniques" and "procedures" of Deming while leaving out the critical thinking they require to succeed. They have tried to "formalize" Deming, to reduce Deming to a series of procedures and charts. The inevitable result is a caricature of Deming: Total Quality Control without the "quality." Only excellence in thinking can produce genuine, continuous improvement in quality, and excellence in thinking cannot be produced with simplistic procedures and slogans.

But we are still captive of a traditional American assumption that might be expressed as follows: "Every idea of importance can be expressed simply and learned easily. The true challenges of life are to be found in everyday hard work and extraordinary courage and neither of those require deep or 'intellectual' thinking."

The necessary paradigm shifts, however, do entail the cultivation of critical thinking across the work force, up and down the lines of labor and management, across industries, across educational levels, and into the everyday discussions of national and international issues. This shift is painfully against the American grain, contrary to our traditional folk wisdom, and incompatible with much current thinking of both business and labor leaders.

✦ The Vision of Robert Heilbroner: The Challenge of Large-Scale Disorder

Robert Heilbroner argues, as do Reich and Thurow, that though capitalism will be dominant in the 21st Century, there will be serious conflicts between opposing forms of capitalism. As a result of these conflicts, a new and perplexing dimension to the picture will emerge: the challenge of "macro-disorder," of economy-wide and world-wide problems arising from the market mechanism following its own logic without making critical adjustments. This problem calls for solutions we have yet to think through. He calls this problem that of negative "externalities," of market failures that have large-scale, and to date uncontrolled, negative consequences.

Addressing these large-scale problems requires a new brand of both leadership and followership. We need leaders who become comfortable talking about and thinking through complexities. We need "followers" with the thoughtful ability and patience to grasp the very complexities being explained. Here are some of the large-scale problems that Heilbroner has in mind:

> The overcutting of forests, the overfishing of the seas, the overconsumption of gasoline, ... the indeterminacy of the outlook for investment and for technology; the unequal distribution of incomes; the volatility of credit; the tendency towards monopoly; over-regulation; the technological displacement of labor and the technological impetus towards cartelization; the inflationary tendencies of a successful economy and the depressive tendencies of an unsuccessful one; the vacillation between optimism and pessimism, ... the approach of ecological barriers, ... the internationalizing tendency of capital that continues to outpace the defensive powers of individual governments. (p. 104)

He summarizes our situation as follows:

> ... the problems of capitalist disorder — too many to recite, too complex in their origins to take up one at a time ... arise from the workings of the system.... The problems must be addressed by the assertion of political will ... the undesired dynamics of the economic sphere must be contained, redressed, or redirected by the only agency capable of asserting a counter-force to that of the economic sphere. It is the government. (pp. 108–109)

The unanswered questions are, "Who or what is going to direct governments to make rational decisions in the long-term public interest? Where are we to turn to find this new kind of leader? How are we to cultivate the new kind of electorate?"

If the electorates in the various countries do not learn to think critically about large and vexing questions in the environment, in the economy, in health care and overpopulation, it is likely that government policies will be directed by small groups whose short-range interests *easily* triumph over long-range public good. We are facing basic problems in our capacity to govern ourselves. But all government is finally government made up of people, and people can rise only to the height of their own ability. The crucial issue is, "Will we develop the thinking abilities and intellectual traits of our citizens to a level that will be sufficient for survival?"

✦ The Challenge of the Future

The world of the 21ˢᵗ Century — virtually all commentators agree — will see intensifying economic competition between forms of capitalism. Governmental, economic, social, and environmental problems will become increasingly complex and interdependent. Basic causes will be both global and national. The forces to be understood and controlled will be corporate, national, trans-national, cultural, religious, economic, and environmental, all intricately intertwined. Critical thinking will become a survival need, an external imperative for every nation and for every individual who must survive on his or her own talents, abilities, and traits.

A battle for economic vitality is being fought. Yet consider how unprepared we have been, and continue to be, for that battle. Consider the size of our national debt, the decay of our infrastructure. Consider the intensification of social divisions and divisiveness, the obsolescence of our systems of public education. Consider our traditional but increasingly dangerous assumption that the solutions to our problems lie in a dependence on traditional wisdom. Consider our traditional anti-intellectualism, our traditional parochialism. Can we free ourselves from our own narrow modes of thinking?

Can we accept the fact of accelerating change and complexity? Can we develop intellectual humility and flexibility? Can we develop faith in reason as a tool of discovery? Can we learn to think within points of view other than our own? Can we accept that we are no longer the dominant economic force in the world? Can we learn to think in the long-term and not simply in terms of short-term advantages? Can we begin to make decisions that are in the long-range interest of our children and their well-being? Can we become habitual thinkers rather than reactors and learn to continually inform our action with deep thought? These are the challenges we face. How we respond to them will determine our national fate.

✦✦ *Implications*

What, then, do we need to do?

As a society, our challenge is to recognize that the work of the future is the work of the mind, intellectual work, work that involves reasoning and intellectual self-discipline. Our challenge is to demonstrate intellectual courage in facing our traditional indifference to the development of our minds, our traditional arrogance in assuming that our common sense will always provide the answers, and that our example will always lead the world. We are unaccustomed to this kind of challenge. We are uncomfortable with things *intellectual*. The very word smacks of subversive, egghead, ivory tower, out of touch, impractical, unrealistic. Our collective mindset is now working against us and we must own that fact. We need to "discover," and then genuinely explore in depth this whole notion of substantive critical thinking, of thinking based on intellectual discipline and standards. We need to transform our schools, our businesses, and our lives accordingly. Are we willing to evaluate our own thinking? Are we willing to set ideology aside? Are we willing to re-think our most basic thinking?

To date, we are still under the sway of the misconception that thinking more or less "takes care of itself," that simply by studying "hard" subjects or "concentrating" we can think well. In general, we still treat knowledge as something that can be given to us and inserted into our minds by memory alone. We must begin now to set ourselves a course that will take many, many years to reach.

1) We must parent differently. We must respond differently to our children's "Why?" questions. We must not give them short didactic answers, but must encourage them to conjecture as to the answers. We must call more attention to the extent of our own ignorance and not try to convince our children that adults have good answers for most of their questions.

We must dialogue more with our children about complexities in their lives and in ours. We must help them to discover their own capacity to figure things out, to reason through situations. We must hold them responsible to think and not simply to rotely respond. We must step more into their points of view and help them to step more into the points of view of others. We must help them to identify their own assumptions, clarify their emerging concepts, question their habitual inferences. We must raise our children so that critical thinking becomes an integral part of their everyday lives. They must learn to accept its responsibility and come to discover its power and challenge.

2) We must work differently. We must bring the reality of cooperative critical thinking into the workplace in a thorough way. This means that we must abandon quick-fix strategies and recognize the counterfeits of substantial change. We must become aware of the difference, for example, between the jargon of "Total Quality Management" (which we now have in abundance) and the reality (which we almost entirely lack).

Both managers and workers need to learn how to begin to think in a new way: we must learn how to discipline our thinking to a new level of clarity, precision, relevance, depth, and coherence. CEO's need to learn how to think within alternative models of how to organize and run businesses. Leaders in industry need to learn to broaden their perspectives and think about the long-range interests of the economy and not simply about short-range, vested interests of their businesses. Labor leaders need to concentrate more on support for programs that cultivate broad-based job skills and abilities, that emphasize the basic thinking skills of workers, and less on immediate bread and butter issues.

We must each take it upon ourselves to become lifelong learners, searching for ways to continuously upgrade our reasoning skills, our critical reading skills, our ability and propensity to enter into the points of view of others. Complex problems have many facets, and intellectual humility requires that we become used to exploring multiple perspectives before we make a decision. No more "Ready!... Fire!... Aim!"

3) We must educate differently. We can no longer afford the high cost of educators who have few or no critical thinking skills, and little or no motivation to develop them. Teachers and administrators who do not themselves think critically, cannot design changes in curriculum and instruction that foster critical thinking. We must come to terms with the most fundamental problem in education today and that is "the blind leading the blind." Many educators do not realize that they are functionally blind to the demands of our post-industrial world.

As CEO and Chairman of Apple Computer, John Sculley, has put it,

> In the new economy, strategic resources no longer just come out of the ground. The strategic resources are ideas and information that come out of our minds.
> The result: as a nation, we have gone from being resource-rich in the old economy to resource-poor in the new economy almost overnight! Our public education has not successfully made the shift from teaching the memorization of facts to achieving the learning of critical thinking skills. We are still trapped in a K–12 public education system which is preparing our youth for jobs that no longer exist.

✦ Is There Room for Any Optimism?

Yet there is room for optimism, but only under certain conditions. We have the theoretical foundation and expertise to bring critical thinking to our children, but do we have the vision and the will? If we do, we have an ace in the hole. What Deming did not anticipate was the opportunity of systematically enhancing the critical thinking of the workers as well as the students in our schools, and the competitive advantage that this would provide.

Those countries with the foresight to systematically cultivate the critical thinking of their citizens of all ages, through the educational systems in schools and the workplace, will enjoy a significant competitive advantage over countries that do not make this effort. This is particularly true when this foresight extends to emphasizing high-quality, Deming-style production models. At present, no country in the world systematically fosters critical thinking. Opportunities await those nations who can see the potential to invest intensely in this specific effort.

What we can be sure of is that the persuasiveness of the argument for critical thinking will only grow year by year, day by day — for the logic of the argument is simply the only prudent response to the accelerating change, to the increasing complexity of our world. No gimmick, no crafty substitute, can be found for the cultivation of quality thinking. The quality of our lives can only become more and more obviously the product of the quality of the thinking we use to create them.

Critical thinking is ancient, but until now its practice was for the elite minority, for the few. But the few, in possession of superior power of disciplined thought, used it as one might only expect, to advance the interests of the few. We can never expect the few to become the long-term benevolent caretakers of the many.

The many must become privy to the superior intellectual abilities, discipline, and traits of the traditional privileged few. Progressively, the power and accessibility of critical thinking will become more and more apparent to more and more people, particularly to those who have had limited access to the educational opportunities available to the fortunate few.

The only question is how long and how painful the process will be and what we shall sacrifice of the public good in the meanwhile. How many of our citizens will live lives unemployed and unemployable in the post-industrial age?

We must sooner or later abandon the traditional attempt to teach our fellow citizens *what* to think. Such efforts cannot prepare us for the real world we must, in fact, face. We must concentrate instead on teaching ourselves *how* to think, thus freeing us to think for ourselves, critically, fairmindedly, and deeply. We have no choice, not in the long haul, not in the face of the irrepressible logic of accelerating change and increasing complexity.

✦ References

Holt, R. "The Educational Consequences of W. Edwards Deming." *Phi Delta Kappan.* Jan. 1993.

Heilbroner, Robert. *Twenty-First Century Capitalism.* House of Anansi Press, Limited, Concord, Ontario. 1992.

Reich, Robert. *The Work of Nations.* Vintage Books, New York, NY. 1992.

Sculley, John. Remarks to then President-Elect Clinton, December, 1992.

Thurow, Lester. *Head to Head.* William Morrow and Company, Inc., New York, NY. 1992.

Tyson, Laura D'Andrea. "Failing Our Youth: America's K–12 Education." *New Perspectives Quarterly.* edited by Nathan Gordels. Winter, 1993.

Chapter 2

Critical Thinking:
Identifying the Targets

with Jane Willsen

Abstract

The goal of this chapter is to set out clearly what critical thinking is in general and how it plays itself out in a variety of domains: in reading, in writing, in studying academic subjects, and on the job. Richard Paul and Jane Willsen provide down-to-earth examples that enable the reader to appreciate both the most general characteristics of critical thinking and their specific manifestations on the concrete level. It is essential, of course, that the reader become clear about the concept, including its translation into cases, for otherwise she is apt to mis-translate the concept or fail to see its relevance in a wide variety of circumstances. The danger of misunderstanding and mis-application is touched upon in this chapter at the end, but is developed at great length in another chapter, "Pseudo Critical Thinking in the Educational Establishment" (p. 47).

✔ Is this a good idea or a bad idea?

✔ Is this belief defensible or indefensible?

✔ Is my position on this issue reasonable and rational or not?

✔ Am I willing to deal with complexity or do I retreat into simple stereotypes to avoid it?

✔ If I can't tell if my idea or belief is reasonable or defensible, how can I have confidence in my thinking, or in myself?

✔ Is it appropriate and wise to assume that my ideas and beliefs are accurate, clear, and reasonable, when I haven't really tested them?

✔ Do I think deeply or only on the surface of things?

✔ Do I ever enter sympathetically into points of view that are very different from my own, or do I just assume that I am right?

✔ Do I know how to question my own ideas and to test them?

✔ Do I know what I am aiming for? Should I?

17

Effectively evaluating our own thinking and the thinking of others is a habit few of us practice. We evaluate which washing machine to buy after reading *Consumer Reports*, we evaluate which movie to go see after studying the reviews, we evaluate new job opportunities after talking with friends and colleagues, but rarely do we explicitly evaluate the quality of our thinking (or the thinking of our students).

But, you may ask, how can we know if our thinking is sound? Are we relegated to "trial and error" to discover the consequences of our thinking? Do the consequences always accurately tell the tale? Isn't thinking all a matter of opinion anyway? Isn't my opinion as good as anyone else's? If what I believe is true for me, isn't that all that matters?

In our education and upbringing, have we developed the ability to evaluate, objectively and fairly, the quality of our beliefs? What did we learn about thinking during our schooling?

How did we come to believe what we do believe, and why one belief and not another? How many of our beliefs have we come to through rigorous, independent thinking, and how many have been down-loaded from the media, parents, our culture, our spouses or friends? As we focus on it, do we value the continuing improvement of our thinking abilities? Do we value the continuing improvement of our students' thinking abilities? Important research findings indicate that we need to look closely at this issue. Mary Kennedy reports the findings on the opposite page in the *Phi Delta Kappan*, May, 1991, in an article entitled, "Policy Issues in Teaching Education."

How can we improve our thinking without effective evaluation practices? Can we learn how to evaluate our thinking and reasoning objectively? Let's look at one concrete example for clues into the elements of effective evaluation in a familiar field. In platform diving, there are criteria to be met to receive a score of "10" and standards that judges and competitors alike use to evaluate the dive. These standards guide the divers in each practice session, in each effort off the board. Without these criteria and standards, how would the diver and the judges know what was excellent and what was marginal? Awareness of the criteria and standards are alive in the divers' and coaches' minds. Do we have parallel criteria and standards as we strive to improve our abilities, our performances in thinking?

There is nothing more common than evaluation in the everyday world but for sound evaluation to take place, one must establish relevant standards, gather appropriate evidence, and judge the evidence in keeping with the standards.

There are appropriate standards for the assessment of thinking and there are specific ways to cultivate the learning of them. The research into critical thinking establishes tools that can help us evaluate our own thinking and the thinking of others, if we see their potential benefit and are willing to discipline our minds in ways that may seem awkward at first. This chapter briefly lays out those tools in general terms and acts as a map, so to speak, of their dimensions. We present examples of student

Important Research Findings

First Finding: ...national assessments in virtually every subject indicate that, although our students can perform basic skills pretty well, they are not doing well on thinking and reasoning. American students can compute, but they cannot reason.... They can write complete and correct sentences, but they cannot prepare arguments.... Moreover, in international comparisons, American students are falling behind...particularly in those areas that require higher-order thinking.... Our students are not doing well at thinking, reasoning, analyzing, predicting, estimating, or problem solving.

Second Finding: ...textbooks in this country typically pay scant attention to big ideas, offer no analysis, and pose no challenging questions. Instead, they provide a tremendous array of information or 'factlets', while they ask questions requiring only that students be able to recite back the same empty list.

Third Finding: Teachers teach most content only for exposure, not for understanding.

Fourth Finding: Teachers tend to avoid thought-provoking work and activities and stick to predictable routines.
Conclusion: "If we were to describe our current K–12 education system on the basis of these four findings, we would have to say that it provides very little intellectually stimulating work for students, and that it tends to produce students who are not capable of intellectual work.

Fifth Finding: ... our fifth finding from research compounds all the others and makes it harder to change practice: teachers are highly likely to teach in the way they themselves were taught. If your elementary teacher presented mathematics to you as a set of procedural rules with no substantive rationale, then you are likely to think that this is what mathematics is and that this is how mathematics should be studied. And you are likely to teach it in this way. If you studied writing as a set of grammatical rules rather than as a way to organize your thoughts and to communicate ideas to others, then this is what you will think writing is, and you will probably teach it so.... By the time we complete our undergraduate education, we have observed teachers for up to 3,060 days.

Implication: "We are caught in a vicious circle of mediocre practice modeled after mediocre practice, of trivialized knowledge begetting more trivialized knowledge. Unless we find a way out of this circle, we will continue re-creating generations of teachers who re-create generations of students who are not prepared for the technological society we are becoming."

(Figure 1 condensed from "Policy Issues in Teaching Education" by Mary Kennedy in the *Phi Delta Kappan*, May, 91, pp 661–66.)

thinking that demonstrate critical and uncritical thinking as we define those terms. In other chapters, we identify approaches to teaching critical thinking that are flawed, and explain why they undermine the success of those who attempt to use them.

✦ Critical Thinking: A Picture of the Genuine Article

Critical Thinking is a systematic way to form and shape one's thinking. It functions purposefully and exactingly. It is thought that is disciplined, comprehensive, based on intellectual standards, and, as a result, well-reasoned.

Critical Thinking is distinguishable from other thinking because the thinker is thinking with the awareness of the systematic nature of high quality thought, and is continuously checking up on himself or herself, striving to improve the quality of thinking. As with any system, critical thinking is not just a random series of characteristics or components. All of its components - its elements, principles, standards and values - form an integrated, working network that can be applied effectively not only to academic learning, but to learning in every dimension of living.

Critical thinking's most fundamental concern is excellence of thought. Critical thinking is based on two assumptions: first, that the quality of our thinking affects the quality of our lives, and second, that everyone can learn how to continually improve the quality of his or her thinking.

Critical Thinking implies a fundamental, overriding goal for education in school and in the workplace: always to teach so as to help students improve their own thinking. As students learn to take command of their thinking and continually to improve its quality, they learn to take command of their lives, continually improving the quality of their lives.

COMPREHENSIVE CRITICAL THINKING HAS THE FOLLOWING CHARACTERISTICS

• It is thinking which is responsive to and guided by INTELLECTUAL STANDARDS, such as relevance, accuracy, precision, clarity, depth, and breadth. Without intellectual standards to guide it, thinking cannot achieve excellence. [Note: most so-called "thinking skill" educational programs and approaches have no intellectual standards.]

The chart on the right gives an overview of the concept of critical thinking supported by thirteen years of research from the Center of Critical Thinking and Moral Critique, Sonoma State University, California.

What is Critical Thinking?

A Unique Kind of Purposeful Thinking ——— IN ANY SUBJECT AREA OR TOPIC, WHETHER ACADEMIC OR PRACTICAL, REQUIRING **INTELLECTUAL FITNESS TRAINING FOR THE MIND** AKIN TO PHYSICAL FITNESS TRAINING FOR THE BODY

In Which the Thinker Systematically and Habitually ——— **ACTIVELY DEVELOPS TRAITS** SUCH AS INTELLECTUAL INTEGRITY, INTELLECTUAL HUMILITY, FAIRMINDEDNESS, INTELLECTUAL EMPATHY, AND INTELLECTUAL COURAGE

Imposes Criteria and Intellectual Standards Upon the Thinking ——— **IDENTIFIES THE CRITERIA OF SOLID REASONING**, SUCH AS PRECISION, RELEVANCE, DEPTH, ACCURACY, SUFFICIENCY, AND **ESTABLISHES A CLEAR STANDARD** BY WHICH THE EFFECTIVENESS OF THE THINKING WILL BE FINALLY ASSESSED

Taking Charge of the Construction of Thinking ——— **AWARENESS OF THE ELEMENTS OF THOUGHT** SUCH AS ASSUMPTIONS AND POINT OF VIEW, THAT ARE PRESENT IN ALL WELL-REASONED THINKING; **A CONSCIOUS, ACTIVE AND DISCIPLINED EFFORT** TO ADDRESS EACH ELEMENT IS DISPLAYED

Guiding the Construction of the Thinking According to the Standards ——— **CONTINUALLY ASSESSING** THE COUSE OF CONSTRUCTION DURING THE PROCESS, **ADJUSTING, ADAPTING, IMPROVING,** USING THE CANDLES OF CRITERIA AND STANDARDS TO LIGHT THE WAY

Assessing the Effectiveness of the Thinking According to the Purpose, the Criteria, and the Standards. ——— **DELIBERATELY ASSESSING THE THINKING TO DETERMINE ITS STRENGTHS AND LIMITATIONS,** ACCORDING TO THE DEFINING PURPOSE, CRITERIA AND STANDARDS, **STUDYING THE IMPLICATIONS** FOR FURTHER THINKING AND IMPROVEMENT

• It is thinking that deliberately supports the development of INTELL-ECTUAL TRAITS in the thinker, such as intellectual humility, intellectual integrity, intellectual perseverance, intellectual empathy, and intellectual self-discipline, among others. [Note: most "thinking skill" programs ignore fundamental intellectual traits.]

• It is thinking in which the thinker can identify the ELEMENTS OF THOUGHT that are present in all thinking about any problem, such that the thinker makes the logical connection between the elements and the problem at hand. For example, the critical thinker will routinely ask himself or herself questions such as these about the subject of the thinking task at hand:

What is the *purpose* of my thinking?

What precise *question* am I trying to answer?

Within what *point of view* am I thinking?

What *information* am I using?

How am I *interpreting* that information?

What *concepts* or ideas are central to my thinking?

What *conclusions* am I coming to?

What am I taking for granted, what *assumptions* am I making?

If I accept the conclusions, what are the *implications*?

What would the *consequences* be, if I put my thought into action?

For each element, the thinker must be able to reflect on the standards that will shed light on the effectiveness of her thinking. [Note: Most "thinking skill" programs ignore most or all of the basic elements of thought and the need to apply standards to their evaluation.]

• It is thinking that is ROUTINELY SELF-ASSESSING, SELF-EXAMIN-ING, and SELF-IMPROVING. The thinker takes steps to assess the various dimensions of her thinking, using appropriate intellectual standards. [Note: Most "thinking skill" programs do not emphasize student self-assessment.] *But what is essential to recognize is that if students are not assessing their own thinking, they are not thinking critically.*

• It is thinking in which THERE IS AN INTEGRITY TO THE WHOLE SYSTEM. The thinker is able not only to critically examine her thought as a whole, but also to take it apart, to consider its various parts, as well. Furthermore, the thinker is committed to thinking within a system of inter-related traits of mind; for example, to be intellectually humble, to be intellectually perseverant, to be intellectually courageous, to be intellectually fair and just. Ideally, the critical thinker is aware of the full variety of ways in which thinking can become distorted, misleading, prejudiced, superficial, unfair, or otherwise defective. The thinker strives for wholeness and integrity as fundamental values. [Note: Most "thinking skills" programs are not well integrated and lack a broad vision of the range of thinking abilities, standards, and traits that the successful critical thinking student will develop. Many tend to instruct students with a technique such as mapping of ideas in diagrams or comparing two ideas, yet these ask little of the student and can readily mislead student and teacher to believe that such techniques will be sufficient.]

• It is thinking that YIELDS A PREDICTABLE, WELL-REASONED ANSWER because of the comprehensive and demanding process that the thinker pursues. If we know quite explicitly how to check our thinking as we go, and we are committed to doing so, and we get extensive practice, then we can depend on the results of our thinking being productive. Good thinking produces good results. [Note: Because most "thinking skills" programs lack intellectual standards and do not require a comprehensive process of thinking, the quality of student response is unpredictable, both for the students and for the teacher.]

• It is thinking that is responsive to the social and moral imperative to not only enthusiastically argue from alternate and opposing points of view, but also to SEEK AND IDENTIFY WEAKNESSES AND LIMITATIONS IN ONE'S OWN POSITION. When one becomes aware that there are many legitimate points of view, each of which—when deeply thought through—yields some level of insight, then one becomes keenly aware that one's own thinking, however rich and insightful it may be, however carefully constructed, will not capture everything worth knowing and seeing. [Because most "thinking skills" programs lack intellectual standards, the students are unable to identify weaknesses in their own reasoning nor are they taught to see this as a value to be pursued.]

WHAT DOES COMPREHENSIVE CRITICAL THINKING LOOK LIKE?

The following section highlights examples of legitimate, substantial, comprehensive critical thinking in a variety of contexts. These examples will provide the reader with concrete samples of the criteria, the standards and characteristics integral to genuine critical thinking.

✦ *Identifying the Target:*
Critical Thinking at School

Critical thinking has an appropriate role in virtually every dimension of school learning, very little that we learn that is of value can be learned by automatic, unreflective processes. Textbooks, subject matter, classroom discussion, even relationships with classmates are things to be "figured out" and "assessed." Let's look at two students who are each "reading" a passage from a story and see if we can identify the consequences of critical and uncritical reading habits and abilities.

ARE WE HITTING THE TARGET?
ASSESSING STUDENT THINKING IN READING

Consider the following example of two students engaging in reading the same story. This example is being taken from an important article by Stephen Norris and Linda Phillips, "Explanations of Reading Comprehension: Schema Theory and Critical Thinking Theory," in *Teachers College Record*, Volume 89, Number 2, Winter 1987. We are privy to conversations between each of the two students, Colleen and Stephen and an experimenter. We are thus invited to reconstruct, from the students' responses, our own appraisal of the quality of their thinking. The utility of intellectual standards such as clarity, relevance, accuracy, consistency, and depth of thinking come into sharp focus once one begins to assess specific thinking for "quality."

In what follows we will present episode-by-episode Stephen and Colleen's thinking aloud as they work through the passage. The experimenter's questions are given in brackets. We have chosen to make our example detailed, because we see this as the best route for providing specificity to otherwise vague generalizations about the relationship between reading and thinking. To simulate the task for you we present the passage without a title and one episode at a time as was done with the children.

Episode 1

The stillness of the morning air was broken. The men headed down the bay.

Stephen

The men were heading down the bay, I'm not sure why yet. It was a very peaceful morning. [Any questions?] No, not really. [Where do you think they're going?] I think they might be going sailing, water skiing, or something like that.

Colleen

The men are going shopping. [Why do you think that?] They're going to buy clothes at The Bay. [What is The Bay?] It's a shopping center. [Any questions?] No. [Where do you think they're going?] They're going shopping because it seems like they broke something.

Commentary

Stephen recognizes that there is insufficient information for explaining what the men are doing. On questioning, he tentatively suggests a couple of alternatives consistent with the information given, but indicates there are other possibilities. Colleen presents one explanation of the story, and seems fairly definitive that the men are going to buy clothes at The Bay, a chain of department stores in Canada. On being queried she maintains her idea that the men are going shopping but offers an explanation inconsistent with her first one that they are going to buy clothes. To do this she assumes that something concrete was broken, which could be replaced at The Bay.

Episode 2

The net was hard to pull. The heavy sea and strong tide made it even difficult for the girdie. The meshed catch encouraged us to try harder.

Stephen

It was not a very good day as there were waves which made it difficult for the girdie. That must be some kind of machine for doing something. The net could be for pulling something out of the water like an old wreck. No, wait! It said "meshed catch." I don't know why but that makes me think of fish and, sure, if you caught fish you'd really want to get them. [Any questions?] No questions, just that I think maybe the girdie is a machine for helping the men pull in the fish or whatever it was. Maybe a type of pulley.

Colleen

I guess The Bay must have a big water fountain. [Why was the net hard to pull?] There a lot of force on the water. [Why was it important for them to pull the net?] It was something they had to do. [What do you mean?] They had to pull the net and it was hard to do. [Any questions?] No. [Where do you think they're going?] Shopping.

Commentary

For both children the interpretations of Episode 2 built on those of Episode 1. Stephen continues to question what the men were doing. He raises a number of alternative interpretation dealing with the context of the sea. He refines his interpretations through testing hypothetical interpretations against specific details, and hypotheses of specific word meanings against his emerging interpretation of the story. At the outset he makes an inference that a girdie is a machine, but leaves details about its nature and function unspecified. He tentatively offers one specific use for the net, but immediately questions this use when he realizes that it will not account for the meshed catch, and substitutes an alternative function. He then confirms this interpretation with the fact from the story that the men were encouraged to try harder and his belief that if you catch fish you would really want to bring them aboard. Finally, he sees that he is in a position to offer a more definitive but tentative interpretation of the word girdie.

Colleen maintains her interpretation of going shopping at The Bay. When questioned about her interpretation, Colleen responds in vague or tautological terms. She seems not to integrate information relating to the terms net, catch, and sea, and it seemed satisfied to remain uniformed about the nature of the girdie and the reason for pulling the net. In the end, she concludes definitively that the men are going shopping.

Episode 3

With four quintels aboard, we were now ready to leave. The skipper saw mares' tails in the north.

Stephen

I wonder what quintels are? I think maybe it's a sea term, a word that means perhaps the weight aboard. Yes maybe it's how much fish they had aboard. [So you think it was fish?] I think fish or maybe something they had found in the water but I think fish more because of the word "catch." [Why were they worried about the mares' tails?] I'm not sure. Mares' tails, let me see, mares are horses but horses are not going to be in the water. The mares' tails are in the north. Here farmers watch the north for bad weather, so maybe the fishermen do the same thing. Yeah, I think that's it, it's a cloud

Colleen

They were finished their shopping and were ready to go home. [What did they have aboard?] Quintels. [What are quintels?] I don't know. [Why were they worried about the mares' tails?] There were a group of horses on the street and they were afraid they would attack the car. [Any questions?] No.

formation which could mean strong winds and hail or something which I think could be dangerous if you were in a boat and a lot of weight aboard. [Any questions?] No.

Commentary
Stephen is successful in his efforts to incorporate the new information into an evolving interpretation. From the outset Stephen acknowledges that he does not know the meaning of quintel and seeks a resolution of this unknown. He derives a meaning consistent with his evolving interpretations and with the textual evidence. In his attempt to understand the expression mares' tails he first acknowledges that he does not know the meaning of the expression. Thence, he establishes what he does know from the background knowledge (mares are horses, horses are not going to be in the water, there is nothing around except sky and water, farmers watch the north for bad weather) and textual information (the men are on the bay, they have things aboard, the mares' tails are in the north) and inferences he has previously made (the men are in a boat, they are fishing). He integrates this knowledge into a comparison between the concerns of Alberta farmers with which he is familiar, and what he takes to be analogous concerns of fishermen. On seeing the pertinence of this analogy he draws the conclusion that the mares' tails must be a cloud formation foreboding inclement weather. He claims support for his conclusion in the fact that it would explain the skipper's concern for the mares' tails, indicating that he did not lose sight of the overall task of understanding the story.

Colleen maintains her original interpretation but does not incorporate all the new textual information into it. She works with the information on the men's leaving and the mares' tails, but appears to ignore or remain vague about other information. For example, she says the cargo was comprised of quintels but indicates no effort to determine what these things are. She cites the fact that the men were ready to leave and suggests that they have finished their shopping, but does not attempt to explain the use of such words as skipper, cargo, and aboard in the context for shopping for clothes. She interprets mares' tails as a group of horses the possibly would attack the men, but gives no account of what the horses might be doing on the street. Basically, she appears to grow tolerant of ambiguity and incompleteness in her interpretation.

Interestingly, each student believes that he or she has read the passage. The question becomes, what does it mean "to read" something? Comprehensive, legitimate critical thinking enables us to explore the meaning of the concept "to read" and to come to understand that there is a spectrum of quality of readings, some superficial and mechanical, some deep and thorough.

Specifically, Colleen has scrambled to piece together meanings that have little relationship to the writer's ideas. Colleen has "read" the passage but we can quickly see that the quality of her thinking lacks characteristics that we equate with sound reasoning, with critical thinking. She has been ineffective in thinking within the system of meanings inherent in what was said in the passage she tried to read. That her responses were inconsistent did not seem to disturb her, almost as if she had no sense of how to figure out what she was reading. The consequences for Colleen in this episode of thinking are minimal. However, consider how vulnerable she will be outside school, when much more than grades or teacher approval is riding on her ability to think effectively in other systems, such as health care, parenting, upgrading job skills or becoming a proficient consumer.

On the other hand, Stephen has "read" the passage by means of critical reasoning, effectively decoding not only the words but the writer's thoughts. He has taken the initiative to reconstruct in his mind as much as he can of the logic of the images and concepts that the writer conveyed through the system of language. Stephen also explored the implications of his ideas and was clear about what he understood and failed to understand. He demonstrated intellectual perseverance in striving to make sense when struggling with difficult passages. He expected to make sense of the passage, to grasp the author's ideas, and finally he did. These habits, traits and abilities are among those we find in individuals for whom critical thinking is a comprehensive, substantial system of thought embedded, ideally, in every aspect of their lives.

Although Colleen and Stephen have each "read" the passage, a useful distinction can be drawn between "critical reading" and "uncritical reading."

Most reading is performed at the lower end of the spectrum in school today. Very little instruction is given in the thinking skills that critical readers use. Colleen will only be able to improve with professional assistance, that is, with instruction that helps her assess her thinking using intellectual standards and a sense of the elements of thought. She needs help in learning how to think through the elements of a problem. Of course, instruction alone is insufficient. She will also need to apply her will and acquire self-discipline. She will need extensive practice and expectations placed on her effort.

As we stretch ourselves to develop our bodies we naturally feel some physical stress. So, too, do we feel intellectual stress as we stretch our minds to develop our thinking. Students must learn intellectual perseverance, intellectual responsibility, intellectual integrity to develop true intellectual "fitness." This is a lifetime process that merely begins in school.

Most students are not well informed about the consequences of their uncritical thinking habits. It is likely that no one has presented these ideas to them so that they realistically grasp the possibility of intellectual development. Let's now look at two student written responses and examine the quality of the thinking displayed, keeping in mind the implications for the students' future effectiveness.

ARE WE HITTING THE TARGET?
ASSESSING STUDENT THINKING IN WRITING

The Assignment: The students in Ms. Tamari's 8th grade class were asked to write a paragraph in which they were to explain what the most important characteristics of a "friend" are and why they are most important. Here are the written responses of two students, Susan and Carl.

Susan

A friend is someone who cares a lot about you, who likes to be with you, and who helps you out when you get in trouble. The most important characteristics of a friend are loyalty, helpfulness, and honesty. First, it's important for a friend to be loyal because you want to depend on your friend. If someone is not loyal that person may turn against you, especially if she meets someone he or she likes better than you. Second, it's important for a friend to be helpful, because often a person needs help and if you have no friends it can be real hard to feel so alone. And finally, it's important for a friend to be honest because very few people will tell you something about yourself that you don't want to hear. An honest friend will try to help you improve, even though she knows it may hurt your feelings. It's okay to hear some things from a friend because you know that she isn't trying to hurt you.

Observations

Susan is basically doing a good job critically analyzing which characteristics are desirable in a friend. First of all, it is clear that she understands the issue. First she clarifies the concept of a friend. Then she asserts three characteristics of a good friend. Then she takes each one in order and gives good reasons in support of each of them. Her writing is clear, relevant to the issue, systematic, well-reasoned, and reflects deep thinking for her age.

Now let's look at the writing of Carl.

Carl

The most important thing is to have a lot of friends who like to do the things you like to do. Then you can go places and have fun. I mostly like other boys for my friends because they like sports like me. Girls sometimes play sports too but not as good as boys. I like to play baseball, football, and basketball. Sometimes I like to play Hockey. There are no good places to play in my neighborhood and sometimes my mother makes me come in too early. She sometimes makes me very mad because she screws up my life. All she ever wants me to do is work around the house. I don't think she knows anything about having friends. Maybe if she had played sports when she was little she'd let me play more and not just think about work, work, and more work.

Observations

Almost all of Carl's writing is irrelevant to the issue of what are the most desirable characteristics of a friend. He seems simply to be writing thoughts down as they occur to him in a stream of consciousness, in an associational way. Carl begins by confusing the question "What are the most important characteristics in a friend?" with "Is it important to know a lot of people who share pleasures with you?" He then moves to the question "Who do I like?" Then he moves to the question"What do I like to do?" and then on to "What's wrong with my neighborhood?" The final question, "Why doesn't my mother let me do what I want to do?" indicates that he has ended up far off course, yet it is unlikely that he realizes it. Until Carl learns to discipline his mind to stick to the question at hand, he will have trouble doing any quality thinking.

Learning to write out our thinking is one of the best ways to improve it. It goes without saying that excellence in writing requires excellence in thinking. Writing requires that one systematize one's thinking, arranging thought in a progression that makes the system of one's thought accessible to others. When the writer's thinking lacks a clear purpose, lacks focus, lacks documentation and logic, and standards by which to judge the merit of the ideas, these flaws are revealed in the written work.

Writing, then, which is excellent is excellently thought through, is produced by someone with definite standards for both thinking and writing. (See the chapters: "Why Students and Teachers Don't Reason Well" and "Pseudo Critical Thinking in the Educational Establishment.") It is obvious as we read the responses of Carl and Susan that each has a very different understanding of what is well-thought-out thinking and writing, critical and uncritical thinking and writing. The consequences for Carl's uncritical thinking are minimal in 8th grade, but how will he be affected when he demonstrates the same confusions on the job?

School instruction is focused on "subject matter." We usually, but wrongfully, think of school subjects as little more than masses of facts and definitions to be memorized. We don't often recognize that what is really important about school subjects is that they—when properly learned—provide us raw materials upon which to practice thinking in a more proficient and insightful manner. They introduce us to new "systems" in which to think. As you read the next section, see if you can think of school subjects in this more illuminating and penetrating way.

ARE WE HITTING THE TARGET?
ASSESSING STUDENT THINKING IN ACADEMIC SUBJECTS.

Subject Matter, Especially in High School and College Courses
Though we often do not think of it this way, all subject matter — history, literature, geography, biology, chemistry, physics, mathematics — is part of a system of logically ordered parts. A historian studies a period and creates a "story" that puts events into meaningful patterns. In literature we study periods with their distinctive visions, their distinctive values, their distinctive modes of expression. One period is "romantic," one is "classic," one is "realist," and so forth. Or we study the outlook of an author, the way he or she sees the world: Dickens, Austen, Hemingway, Faulkner. In geography we develop systems for dividing up the surface of the earth: into continents, countries, climates. We develop organized, logical ways to look at the surface, especially the physical surface, of the earth. In geology, we use a system to arrange time into geological time periods, and correlate principal physical and biological features with those periods. In biology, we develop systems for making sense of multiple forms of living and pre-living things. In math, we develop systems—arithmetic, geometry, algebra, calculus—for dealing with the quantitative dimensions of the world.

Everywhere there are systems inherent in subject matter, networks of logically ordered parts functioning in relation to each other for a definite human purpose. Critical thinking, with its *system-unlocking orientation*, is the perfect set of tools to take command of the systems inherent in subject matter. It is perfect, that is, only if we understand what it is and how to use it. Most students, unfortunately, have never been introduced to critical thinking, so cannot systematically use it to guide and empower their learning. Most students try to learn what is in fact systematized, by randomly memorizing fragments of the system as if they had no relation to each other. Compare the two following students talking about studying history.

Anna: "I don't really like history too much. There is too much to try to remember. And it's all about olden times, with a lot of dates and different wars and people doing things we don't do anymore. You learn about presidents and kings and what they did and about when things happened. History is all about the past. It's boring and I never use it. How could you? Things are really different now. "

Carra: "We do it differently in Mrs Brown's class. Do you know that we're all part of history? For example, in my mind I remember all of my past as a kind of story I tell myself. That's how I remember things and that's also how I figure things out. Think about it. Whenever you talk about yourself, you're like a historian trying to help people figure things out about you. Everyone is really interested in their own history and in the history of the people they know. That's what gossip is all about. Also the news. It's like the history of yesterday. In her class we talk about how the history writer puts together the story he writes. We also look at how the story might be told differently, I mean 'cause what we read is only a tiny part of what the writer knows, and what the writer knows is only a tiny part of what actually happened. You have to look at it from different points of view or else you don't have a chance of figuring out what most likely really happened. We are learning how to tell the difference between "facts" and how different people filter and interpret the facts depending on their own interests. We also try to notice what is left out of the history stories we read. Mrs Brown says we are learning to think like history writers do and face the problems that they face. I think its fun to try to figure out history . . . how to tell a story in the most honest way, and how to see when people twist a story to make themselves look good."

Observations

Anna and Carra, in their reactions to history, model the distinction between the way subjects have traditionally been taught (as a lot of stuff to remember for a test) and the way they should be taught (as a way to figure things out). The traditional student never gets the real point of the subject and hence does not transfer what she learns to the "real" world. By teaching history in a critical manner students can readily transfer what they learn to "life-centered" situations. They can improve their own everyday historical thinking.

Critical thinking is valuable, of course, not only in school but in the world beyond school as well. If we are teaching properly, our students not only learn how to apply critical thinking effectively to their reading, writing, and subject-matter learning, they also begin to apply it to their everyday lives. The wonderful result is they not only reason historically about what is in their history textbook, for example, they also begin to reason much better about the "historical" issues in their daily life, as Carra is doing above. They not only reason scientifically about what is in their science textbook, they also begin to reason scientifically about the 'scientific" questions in their daily life. They not only hear about ethical principles when talking about characters in stories in their literature class, they also begin to use ethical reasoning when dealing with the ethical issues embedded in their lives.

Indeed, if we do our job correctly, students begin to discover that all the kinds of reasoning that they learn to do at school have application in the "real" world. They not only start to talk about and value reasoning in school, they also begin to discover how actually to do it, how to realistically and effectively to apply intellectual standards to their own thought in virtually every context of their lives. The result is that students, for the first time in their lives, begin to evaluate their own thinking and do so in a way which is increasingly disciplined and objective. Let's look at three examples of college students beginning to discover the value of applying intellectual standards to their own work and thinking.

Mandy: "I am often inconsistent. The most difficult aspect of my weakness is my attempt at achieving consistency between that of word and deed. That is, I use a double standard. I often say one thing and do another."

Kristin: "This semester I have learned how to organize my thinking through critical thinking. In organizing my thinking logically I have learned to break down my thought processes down into specific parts. By breaking my thought process down into specific parts I can see some of my strengths and weaknesses. When I do not organize my thought logically, my writing often becomes trivial, irrelevant and vague."

Laurie: "It is important to recognize key concepts when one thinks. If I need to figure out a problem and do not understand the key concepts, I will not be able to come to a logical conclusion. I am more and more aware of the need to pay attention to key concepts. One particular example occurred this winter when I went snowboarding for the first time. The relevant concepts of snowboarding are: one needs to torque the body, the back leg is your anchor, and the edges of the board are used to slow down and in turn control the speed of the board. My friend explained to me that it usually takes a whole day to learn to snowboard, but because I paid close attention to the concepts and kept them carefully in mind, I was able to learn quickly. Most students do not realize that concepts are important in learning. In fact, I think that most students don't know what concepts are. I certainly didn't."

These examples demonstrate that some students are prepared to take advantage of critical thinking instruction, though others are less ready. The teacher's challenge, however, is to meet the students needs and respond effectively with appropriate instruction.

✦ Identifying the Target: Critical Thinking in the Workplace

With accelerating change and the increasing complexity of problems facing us at the dawn of the 21st Century, we are striving to compete within the new global economic realities. John Sculley, CEO of Apple Computer, Inc. reported to President-elect Clinton in December of 1992:

Most Americans see our largest corporations going through massive restructurings, layoffs, and downsizing. People know something has changed and they are scared because they don't fully understand it and they see people they know losing their jobs.

They also see their neighbors buying high-quality, lower-priced products from abroad, and they ask why can't we build these same products or better ones here at home?

The answer is, we can. But only if we have a public education system which will turn out a world-class product. We need an education system which will educate all our students, not just the top 15–20 percent.

A highly-skilled work force must begin with a world class public education system. Eventually, the New Economy will touch every industry in our nation. There will be no place to hide!

In the New Economy, low-skilled manual work will be paid less. The United States cannot afford to have the high-skilled work being done somewhere else in the world and end up with the low-wage work.

This is not an issue about protectionism. It is an issue about an educational system aligned with the New Economy and a broad educational opportunity for everyone. maximum flexibility.

In the old economy, America had a real advantage because we were rich with natural resources and our large domestic market formed the basis for economies of scale.

In the New Economy, strategic resources no longer just come out of the ground (such as oil, coal, iron, and wheat). The strategic resources are ideas and information that come out of our minds.

The result is, as a nation, we have gone from being resource-rich in the old economy to resource-poor in the New Economy almost overnight! Our public education system has not successfully made the shift from teaching the memorization of facts to achieving the learning of critical thinking skills. We are still trapped in a K–12 public education system which is preparing our youth for jobs that no longer exist.

Critical thinking is valuable not only in school but in the world beyond school as well. Increasingly, our ever-changing economy demands abilities and traits characteristic of comprehensive critical thinking. They enable us not only to survive but to thrive. They are essential to the new management structures to which successful businesses will routinely and increasingly turn. Consider the news item opposite, from a small town in Wisconsin. It illustrates well a trend which is going to grow enormously, and that is toward high productivity work-place organizations that "depend on workers who can do more than read, write, and do simple arithmetic, and who bring more to their jobs than reliability and a good attitude. In such organizations, workers are asked to use judgment and make decisions rather than to merely follow directions. Management layers disappear as workers take over many of the tasks that others used to do...." [Laura D'Andrea Tyson, Chairwoman of the President's Council of Economic Advisors]. Ladysmith, Wisconsin gives us an opportunity to see this trend displayed.

Mill Interviews 83 for Jobs

Between June 10 and 17, City Forest Corporation completed assessments of 83 candidates for jobs at the soon-to-be-opened paper mill in Ladysmith. The mill, formerly operated by Pope & Talbot, has been idle since last Aug 14.

Candidates for positions at the mill went through a half day "assessment center" to determine their potential for the new work concept to be implemented at the mill. The assessment center included several group problem-solving sessions as well as an oral presentation, written presentation and traditional interview.

When the mill reopens, it will operate under a "self-directed team" method. With that approach there are no first line supervisors. Instead, workers are organized into teams which are responsible for much of the decision making and problem solving previously handled by the supervisor.

Each of the four production shifts will have a team leader. The production teams will be supported by a maintenance team...and a staff team made up of management and other staff support. The beauty of this new system is that it place more of the control of the day-to-day operation in the hands of the individuals who are doing the hands-on work.

—*Ladysmith News*, Ladysmith, Wisconsin Thursday, June 24, 1993.

How important, then, is our role as teachers? Can we rely on parents to understand and to provide these essential abilities and traits for their children? Will the children master them on the streets or with their friends? It seems unlikely. How important, then, is it that we, ourselves, devote our professional energies to examining and assessing our own thinking? Can we do a proficient job of helping our students if we are not equally committed to improving our own abilities, traits and habits as well?

Our professional responsibility extends to recognizing that we may very well find that we need to assert our will, our initiative, our discipline and curiosity to secure the best materials and resources available to meet this obligation. How much care, then, should we use in selecting materials that will take us where we want to go, to a deep and comprehensive understanding and working knowledge of legitimate critical thinking?

✦ Off the Target
Pseudo-Critical Thinking Approaches and Materials

Critical thinking cannot be seen, touched, tasted or heard directly, and thus it is readily subject to counterfeit, readily confused with thinking that sounds like, but is not critical thinking, with thinking that will not lead students to success in school and beyond. Critical thinking is readily falsified in the commercial world by those who seek to capitalize on its growing legitimacy. We increasingly need a regular *Consumer Report* that enables the reader to effectively recognize the counterfeits of good thinking which are multiplying daily, to help us recognize the latest gimmick *du jour*. The characteristics of comprehensive critical thinking outlined in this chapter make available just a beginning set of criteria by which professionals and parents can evaluate educational resources in this field.

Educators, business and governmental leaders must begin to distinguish the genuine from the counterfeit, the legitimate from the specious, the incomplete from the comprehensive. Smooth, slick, and shallow thinking are everywhere around us, filled with promises of simple, quick, instant solutions, or misdirecting us into schemes that misspend our own or public monies. Other chapters of this book will provide many examples, principally from the field of education. The reader will doubtless be able to add other examples from his or her own experience.

That we need sound critical thinking to protect ourselves and the public good is intuitively obvious, once we are clear about what critical thinking is and what it can do. Identifying the target precisely, however, is the first step in facing the challenges ahead.

Chapter 3

The Critical Thinking Movement in Historical Perspective

Abstract

In this paper, originally published in National Forum *(1985) and revised for this edition, Richard Paul discusses the history of critical thinking and intellectual discipline in education. He argues that, from the earliest days, education in the U.S. has emphasized passive learning, lower-order training, and indoctrination. He begins with a cameo of the critical thinking movement today, briefly reflects back to Socrates, then explores the history of intellectualism and anti-intellectualism in U.S. schooling and the teaching profession. He concludes with a discussion of the series of reform efforts and their predictable failure.*

✦ Critical Thinking Emerges as a Movement

T he critical thinking movement is beginning to have a palpable effect on the day-to-day life of some American schooling, though it is becoming increasingly obvious that it will be many years before we routinely graduate students who can think critically about the problems they face and the tasks they must do. The transition from theory to practice is as vexing as one might have realistically expected. At present, though the public awareness of the importance of critical thinking grows with every increase in public awareness of the accelerating pace of change and complexity, there is still no one area of the country that has emerged as leading the way. It appeared in the mid-1980's that California would be the needed bellwether. In 1981, the massive 19-campus California State University system instituted a graduation requirement in critical thinking intended to achieve:

> ... an understanding of the relationship of language to logic, leading to the ability to analyze, criticize, and advocate ideas, to reason inductively and deductively, and to reach factual or judgmental conclusions based on sound inferences drawn from unambiguous statements of knowledge or belief.

Within two years, the even larger community college system established a parallel requirement. The California Department of Education launched into what was billed as an assessment program heavily emphasizing critical thinking skills. Guiding policy statements from the Department — from the *California State Frameworks*, to *It's Elementary*, *Caught in the Middle*, and *Second to None* — all claim that critical thinking is at the core of mandatory reforms. However, things are not as quickly achieved as conceived. In California, for example, the serious efforts that many expected to help prepare teachers to teach for critical thinking have not been made. This raises at least three issues: Do California's educational leaders, and those in other states, mean what they say? Do those people charged with the duty to redesign classroom instruction understand what critical thinking requires? And finally, is the educational establishment so insulated that meaningful change requires, at best, a twenty-year plan?

While public education continues to thrash about, still seeking to establish the educational miracle of foundational change through various combinations of painless quick-fixes, the critical thinking movement continues to grow. In every academic discipline and at every level of education there is increased interest in infusing critical thinking into instruction. There is a growing consensus in the assessment community that critical thinking, problem-solving, and higher order communication must be given a new primacy in educational evaluation. In the 1992 Goals Report of the National Education Goals Panel, reasoning and critical thinking are given special prominence in two key objectives:

• The percentage of students who demonstrate the ability to reason, solve problems, apply knowledge, and write and communicate effectively will increase substantially.

• The proportion of college graduates who demonstrate an advanced ability to think critically, communicate effectively, and solve problems will increase substantially.

Special prominence has also been given to the importance of critical thinking in a long series of reports on medical education, nursing, and allied health. More and more articles and books are being written about critical thinking, many of them focused on particular subject domains. The number of conferences and workshops on critical thinking continues to grow. The number of centers for critical thinking has also increased dramatically. A National Council for Excellence in Critical Thinking has emerged. More and more prominent leaders are calling attention to the importance of critical thinking for the economic future of the nation. All this is progress that will continue to increase the pressure for fundamental change. This powerful emergence of critical thinking did not occur overnight.

Until the mid-1980's, the movement was no more than a small, scattered group of educators calling for a shift from a didactic paradigm of knowledge and learning to a Socratic, critically reflective one. The early stirrings of the modern critical thinking movement can be traced back to Edward Glaser's *An Experiment in the Development of Critical Thinking* (1941) and his development with Watson of the Watson-Glaser Critical Thinking Appraisal (1940). But let's briefly survey the history of the core ideas and the thinkers who generated them.

The deepest intellectual roots are ancient, traceable to the teaching practice and vision of Socrates 2,400 ago who discovered by a method of probing questioning that people could not rationally justify their confident claims to knowledge. Confused meanings, inadequate evidence, or self-contradictory beliefs often lurked beneath smooth but largely empty rhetoric. Since his time, Socrates' insight has been variously articulated by a scattering of intellectuals, certainly by the 18th, and increasingly in the 19th and 20th centuries: Voltaire, John Henry Newman, John Stuart Mill, and William Graham Sumner are a few that come readily to mind. Consider Mill:

> ... since the general or prevailing opinion on any object is rarely or never the whole truth, it is only by the collision of adverse opinions that the remainder of the truth has any chance of being supplied. (*On Liberty,* 1859)

Or Newman:

> ... knowledge is not a mere extrinsic or accidental advantage, ... which may be got up from a book, and easily forgotten again, ... which we can borrow for the occasion, and carry about in our hand ... [it is] something intellectual ... which reasons upon what it sees ... the action of a formative power ... making the objects of our knowledge subjectively our own. (*Idea of A University,* 1852)

Or Sumner:

> The critical habit of thought, if usual in a society, will pervade all its mores, because it is a way of taking up the problems of life. People educated in it cannot be stampeded by stump orators and are never deceived by dithyrambic oratory. They are slow to believe. They can hold things as possible or probable in all degrees, without certainty and without pain. They can wait for evidence and weigh evidence, uninfluenced by the emphasis and confidence with which assertions are made on one side or the other. They can resist appeals to their dearest prejudices and all kinds of cajolery. Education in the critical faculty is the only education of which it can be truly said that it makes good citizens. (*Folkways,* 1906)

This view of knowledge and learning holds that beliefs, without reason and the judgment of the learner behind them, are for that learner mere prejudices; that critical reflection on the part of each learner is an essential precondition of knowledge and of rational action. Until now this view has made little headway against a deeply if unconsciously held contrary mind-set. The everyday world — especially in the U.S. where the agenda has been filled with one pragmatic imperative after another, a nation with a "mission" to perform and a "destiny" to fulfill — provides little time for self-formed, self-reasoned beliefs called for by Socrates and his successors.

✦ Historical Roots of Anti-Intellectualism In United States' Schools

Let us not forget that schools in the U.S. were established precisely to transmit by inculcation self-evident, true beliefs conducive to right conduct and successful "industry". The best seller of 17th Century North America was Michael Wigglesworth's *Day of Doom,* a detailed description of the terrifying fate of condemned sinners. To question this fate was heresy. In 1671, governor Sir William Berkeley of Virginia could say with pride:

> ... there are no free schools, nor printing in Virginia, for learning has brought disobedience, and heresy ... into the world, and printing has divulged them.... God keep us from both!

"Free schools" were set up, as in Massachusetts (1647), "to teach all children to read and write ... [to combat] that old deluder Satan," or, to ensure that "children and servants" are "catechized" (1675). In Plymouth Colony (1671) "Education of Children" was mandated because "Children and Servants [were]... in danger [of] growing Barbarous, Rude, or Stubborn" and hence were becoming "pests". This was hardly the climate in which analytic thinking and critical questioning could thrive. All questioning began and ended with a *"Nil desperandum, Christo duce."* (Don't despair, Christ leads us.) This sense of having a mission or mandate from God has discouraged self-reflective questioning. At times it has generated arrogant self-delusion.

As late as 1840, U.S. schools taught ordinary students nothing but the three R's, some basic catechism, and a smattering of patriotic history. The school term was short and attendance irregular. In 1800, for example, average Americans attended school only 82 days out of their entire lives. By 1840 it had increased to only 208 days.

When the time in school increased, it was not because of a demand for critical thinking, but for better reading and writing, skills increasingly necessary in the commercial and industrial activities of the day. To get a sense of the quality of reading instruction, one need only hear the assessment of Horace Mann:

> I have devoted especial pains to learn, with some degree of numerical accuracy, how far the reading, in our schools, is an exercise of the mind in thinking and feeling and how far it is a barren action of the organs of speech upon the atmosphere. My informa-

tion is derived principally from the written statements of the school committees of the respective towns — gentlemen who are certainly exempt from all temptation to disparage the schools they superintend. The result is that more than $^{11}/_{12}$ths of all the children in the reading classes do not understand the meanings of the words they read; and that the ideas and feelings intended by the author to be conveyed to, and excited in, the reader's mind, still rest in the author's intention, never having yet reached the place of their destination. *(Second Report to the Massachusetts Board of Education,* 1838)

There was an expansion in schooling, triggered not by a change in the basic U.S. mind-set, but by the increasing use of machinery, the rapid expansion of transportation, and the new waves of non-Anglo-Saxon immigrants. For a long time the *McGuffy Readers*, with their parables about the terrible fate of those who gave in to sloth, drunkenness, or wastefulness were as close as the average student got to reflective thinking. Americans were learning to be "doers," not "thinkers". The basic truths necessary for successful living seemed eminently available, for all who cared to sit up and take notice:

Remember, that time is money, ... that credit is money, ... that money is of the prolific, generating nature, that six pounds a year is but a groat a day ... that the good paymaster is lord of another man's purse. (Ben Franklin, 1770)

In 1860 the average American spent little more than a year in school, and by 1900 spent little more than two years. In 1880, 17% of the population still could not read or write. With their homespun views and simplistic picture of the world in hand, the American public was confident it could judge quite well, not only the matters immediately before it, but also what was best for the well being of other peoples far away. Increasingly in this time, the question of empire was before the public, and the electorate was expected to decide, for example, whether or not it was justifiable to "rule a people without their consent." Those, like Senator Beveridge, who favored imperialism, as did the majority of voters, easily formulated a logic whose fallaciousness was not penetrated by the voting majority:

The opposition tells us that we ought not to govern a people without their consent. I answer: The rule of liberty, that all just government derives its authority from the consent of the governed, applies only to those who are capable of self-government. I answer: We govern the Indians without their consent, we govern our territories without their consent, we govern our children without their consent.... Shall we save them ... to give them a self-rule of tragedy? It would be like giving a razor to a babe and telling it to shave itself. It would be like giving a typewriter to an Eskimo and telling him to publish one of the great dailies of the world. (U.S. Senator Albert Beveridge, 1899)

Senator Beveridge could link, without fear of significant dissent from an electorate of thinking people, the voice of liberty, our guns, Christ's gospel, and our profit:

> Ah! as our commerce spreads, the flag of liberty will circle the globe, and the highways of the ocean — carrying trade to all mankind — will be guarded by the guns of the republic. And, as their thunders salute the flag, benighted peoples will know that the voice of liberty is speaking, at last, for them; that civilization is dawning, at last, for them — liberty and civilization, those children of Christ's gospel, who follow and never precede the preparing march of commerce. It is the tide of God's great purposes made manifest in the instincts of our race, whose present phase is our personal profit, but whose far-off end is the redemption of the world and the Christianization of mankind.

It should be no surprise therefore that William Graham Sumner, one of the founding fathers of anthropology, was appalled by the manner in which history was taught and the level of uncritical thinking that followed it:

> The examination papers show the pet ideas of the examiners.... An orthodoxy is produced in regard to all the great doctrines of life. It consists in the most worn and commonplace opinions.... It is intensely provincial and philistine ... [containing] broad fallacies, half-truths, and glib generalizations. [We are given] ... orthodox history ... [so] ... that children shall be taught just that one thing which is "right" in the view and interest of those in control and nothing else.... "Patriotic" history ... never can train children to criticism. (*Folkways*, 1906)

Higher education was little better. It began in the 17th and 18th centuries in primarily upper class "seminaries," providing a classical education though not, of course, in the Socratic sense. Students were drilled in Latin and Greek and theology. Inculcation, memorization, repetition, and forensic display were the order of the day. Not until the latter half of the 19th Century was higher education possible for someone not in the upper class, and then only at the new Land Grant Colleges (150 new colleges opened between 1880 and 1900). These colleges were established to promote "education of the industrial classes in the several pursuits and professions in life." Their emphasis was "agriculture and the mechanic arts." Students graduated with an agricultural, commercial, technical, industrial, scientific, professional, or theological focus. Higher education turned out graduates fit to enter farms, businesses, professions, or the clergy. Their "civic" education was not fundamentally liberal but nationalistic, not fundamentally emancipatory but provincial.

THE TEACHING PROFESSION FALLS IN LINE

The history of teaching fits into this picture like a perfectly carved puzzle piece. In the early days, teachers were selected from those who had no other job and could read, write, and cipher. From the start, teaching was a low prestige, low paying job. Normal schools did not begin springing up until after 1830, and then their curriculum mainly consisted of a review of the subjects taught in elementary school, such as reading, writing, arithmetic, and spelling. Eventually, and in the spirit of industrialism, science, and technology, education — still conceived fully within the traditional U.S. world view — came to be considered, and is still largely considered, a "science" of methods of "delivery."

At no point along the way, even to this day, have prospective teachers been expected to demonstrate their ability to lead a discussion Socratically, so that students explore the evidence that can be advanced for or against their beliefs, note the assumptions upon which their beliefs are based, their implications for, or consistency with, other espoused beliefs. Nor have they been expected to demonstrate ability to think analytically or critically about the issues of the day. The state of affairs (*circa.* 1920–35) is satirically suggested by journalist and social critic H. L. Mencken:

> The art of pedagogics becomes a sort of puerile magic, a thing of preposterous secrets, a grotesque compound of false premises and illogical conclusions. Every year sees a craze for some new solution of the teaching enigma, an endless series of flamboyant arcana.... Mathematical formulae are marked out for every emergency; there is no sure-cure so idiotic that some superintendent of schools will not swallow it. The aim seems to be to reduce the whole teaching process to a sort of automatic reaction, to discover some master formula that will not only take the place of competence and resourcefulness in the teacher but that will also create an artificial receptivity in the child. Teaching becomes a thing in itself, separable from and superior to the thing taught. Its mastery is a special business, a sort of transcendental high jumping. A teacher well grounded in it can teach anything to any child, just as a sound dentist can pull any tooth out of any jaw. (*Baltimore Sun,* 1923)

✦ 1930's to Today: An Endless Series of Pseudo-Reforms

From 1930 to now, education has undergone a series, indeed an endless series, of reform movements, all of which have come aground for one fundamental reason: none provided a means for transforming the thinking of teachers. Critical thinking was not brought into the classroom in a large-scale way. Teachers still taught as they had been taught, that is, *didactically.* Educators still tacitly maintained the view that knowledge was something one memorizes. Students still got the grades they wanted by simply feeding back to teachers what had been fed to them. No intellectual standards were introduced into the classroom. Indeed, to this day, most teachers and educators still have no real conception of the nature of intellectual standards and what it is to hold students to them. Most grading of student performances is still largely a mixture of reward for lower order recall and verbal agreement with the views of the teacher.

In place of substantial reform, professional educators learned to become masters of lip service, adroit at the art of taking on the language of reform without its substance. This 63-year process of pseudo-reform following pseudo-reform began with the bastardization of the views of John Dewey, the movement of so-called "progressive" education. A deep and well-thought-out conception of education was transformed into a series of slogans and catch-phrases. Progressive classrooms became caricatures of what Dewey advocated.

Today, the educational marketplace is deluged with reformist ideas, each being swiftly transformed, one after another, into caricatures of their more insightful originators. And so it will continue unless we recognize that the quality of any reform can be no better than the quality of the thinking of those who put that reform into action. So it will continue unless we recognize that there is no mindless or robotic way to reform education, that every reform, to be substantial, must be implemented by those whose thinking is substantial, that *critical thinking* must be an intrinsic part of every dimension of every reform.

What good is "outcome-based" education, for example, if the "outcomes" are not well-thought-out, if they are no more than jargon or platitude, or lower-order learning masked under higher order terms? What good is education for "self-esteem" if it is based on the false assumption that we can "give" students self-esteem by continually giving them positive feedback — while we ignore the skills and abilities the possession of which gives them a real sense of empowerment? What good is an emphasis on "cooperative learning" that ignores the intellectual standards whose possession prevents the process from descending into "cooperative mis-learning?" What good is an emphasis on "writing across the curriculum" when students are not learning how to intellectually assess their writing, resulting in smooth, articulate fluff being routinely mistaken for deep, substantial thought? What good is an emphasis on "diversity", when teachers are unable to critically assess which forms of "diversity" and "unity" are appropriate and which forms are not? What good is "restructuring" when those engaged in it do not know how to critically assess alternative suggestions or how to distinguish vague platitude from substantial principle or how to assess whether students are learning at a lower or higher order? What good is "total quality management" when the quality of thinking that goes into the "management" of "quality" is intellectually undisciplined?

The system in place in education has displayed a remarkable ability to take on the appearance of any number of reforms without changing in any substantial way. We have not yet learned the fundamental lesson: No substantial change can occur in education without a substantial change in the thinking of educators.

To formulate substantial "outcomes" in such a way that we can truly assess whether they are being achieved requires critical thinking in the design and application of the teaching and assessment process. To achieve genuine self-esteem, students need to develop the skills and abilities which give them a sense of real empowerment. To engage in successful cooperative learning, students need to bring to the process the intellectual standards by which they can assess and improve the quality of their learning. To effectively emphasize "writing across the curriculum", students need intellectual standards to assess their writing and that of their peers. An appropriate emphasis on "diversity" requires students to critically assess which forms of "diversity" and "unity" are justified and which are not. Productive "restructuring" requires that those engaged in it know how to critically assess proposals effectively. "Total Quality Management" that deserves the name must be based on *thinking of quality*, thinking that is tested again and again by appropriate intellectual standards.

Consider this sobering thought: When, between 1917 and 1934, inductees into the armed forces were systematically tested using the *Army Alpha Test* (an I.Q. test based on the Stanford Benet) it was estimated that the average U.S. citizen was probably somewhere around 13 or 14 years old intellectually — about the intellectual level to which, I understand, most present day T.V. programming today is geared. Can we conclude then that most Americans are intellectually incapable of rising above childish reasoning, or should we rather hypothesize that as a nation both socially and scholastically we have not yet challenged most people to think for themselves beyond the most primitive levels? Are we, and if so will we remain, what William J. Lederer characterized us as in his best selling book of the 1960's, *A Nation of Sheep?*

If Boyer, Sizer, Adler, Bloom and others are right, if the Rockefeller Commission on the Humanities, the International Educational Achievement Studies, the College Board, the Education Commission of the States, the National Assessment of Educational Progress, and the Association of American Medical Colleges are right, then our overemphasis on "rote memorization and recall of facts" does not serve us well. We must exchange our traditional picture of knowledge and learning for one that generates and rewards "active, independent, self-directed learning" so that students can "gather and assess data rigorously and critically." We need to abandon "methods that make students passive recipients of information" and adopt those that transform them into "active participants in their own intellectual growth."

It is time to bite the bullet. It is time to focus on the prime condition for all reform: quality thinking. Educators who have not learned to think critically cannot transform education for the better; as a nation, we can no longer afford to subsidize their efforts, however well-intentioned. Finally, we need to resolutely, we need to adamantly press for a long-term, thorough emphasis on critical thinking for both teachers and administrators.

To achieve this we need a new kind of educational leadership, not one which mirrors the status quo, not one which mouths platitudes and high-sounding words. Rather we need leaders with the intellectual courage to admit forthrightly that education is filled with shallow thinking and the shallow practices that inevitably follow from it. We need leaders willing to look seriously at the prospect of long-term evolution that puts quality of thinking first, at every level of reform.

Such leadership can only come from that minority of administrators, teachers, and parents who are willing to put the well-being of students above the propaganda, the defensiveness, the self-flattery of the status quo. That leadership is only now beginning to emerge. The reality of everyday schooling is still to be transformed. Those committed to fundamental change must be patient, persistent, firm, steadfast, insistent, and tenacious. They must continually use their own capacity for critical thinking to out-think those who would defend the status quo, who invent specious reasons why basic change is impossible, or who present superficial change as though it were basic. It will be many years before the back of the present paradigm is truly broken, and the paradigm of critical thinking for all students everywhere finally replaces it in the trenches of everyday schooling.

Chapter 4

Pseudo Critical Thinking
in the Educational Establishment

Abstract

Unfortunately, there is not simply good and bad thinking in the world, both easily recognized as such. There is also bad thinking that appears to be good and therefore wrongfully, sometimes disastrously, is used as the basis of very important decisions. Very often this "bad thinking" is defended and "rationalized" in a highly sophisticated fashion. However flawed, it successfully counterfeits good thinking and otherwise intelligent people are taken in. Such thinking is found in every dimension of human life and in every dimension it does harm; in every dimension it works against human well-being. Very often it is generated in a structural way, as a likely or probable by-product of how we have arranged and ordered things. This is illustrated in the American educational establishment. The manner in which it is structured and operates makes likely the continuous generation of more bad, albeit highly sophisticated, thinking: pseudo-critical thinking, in short. However, because the educational bureaucracy is a powerful shaping force in education, bad thinking at the bureaucratic level leads directly to bad teaching at the classroom level. In this chapter, Paul illustrates this destructive pattern using the California Department of Education (as his model of educational bureaucracy at work) and the new California State Reading and Writing Assessment instrument (as the resultant bad practice). He argues that this poorly designed assessment tool leads directly to bad teaching practices and the exacerbation of a profound problem in instruction: the failure to teach students to reason well in every subject they study. If the educational bureaucracy doesn't understand what reasoning is and how to assess it in reading and writing, argues Paul, is it likely that higher order reading and writing will be taught? No, he claims. And thus the educational bureaucracy creates a deep and serious problem in education.

A Guide to the Reader

✦ *Introduction*

Sometimes when people think poorly, they do so out of simple ignorance. They are making mistakes, they don't know they are making mistakes, but they would willingly correct their mistakes if they were pointed out to them. Often mistakes in thinking are quite humble. No one is apt to take them for models of how to think.

Such thinking may be quite uncritical, but is not pseudo critical thinking. Pseudo critical thinking is a form of intellectual arrogance masked in self-delusion or deception, in which thinking which is deeply flawed is not only presented as a model of excellence of thought, but is also, at the same time, sophisticated enough to take many people in. No one takes a rock to be a counterfeit diamond. It is simply other than diamond. But a zircon mimics a diamond and is easily taken for one and hence can be said to be a pseudo diamond.

There is much "sophisticated" but deeply flawed thinking which is presented as a model for thought. This is nothing new in the history of thought and knowledge. Medieval philosophy and theology, for example, was used as a sophisticated tool to resist, quite unknowingly of course, the advance of science. When deeply flawed thinking is embedded in teaching, then the development of thought and knowledge in the student is retarded or arrested. Teachers at every level of education, for example, tell students how to think. They point out thinking which they in effect encourage students to emulate. When what they point out as a model is deeply flawed, and yet sophisticated enough to take many in, it is a form of destructive pseudo critical thinking.

When deeply flawed thinking is embedded in teaching, then the development of thought and knowledge in the student is retarded or arrested.

Pseudo critical thinking is everywhere in the world, for everywhere there are people who take themselves to be models of good thinking and who are engaged in influencing others by their model. Sometimes they foster an approach to thinking quite explicitly — by, for example, designing a program that purports to foster critical thinking. But more often they simply implicitly propagandize for a form of flawed thinking, not aware of the thinking that they are modeling. In any case, it is a rare person, one who really does think critically, who recognizes fundamental flaws in his or her own thinking. Most people are victims of their bad thinking. They do not know how to analyze and assess thinking. Consequently, most believe that their thinking is instinctively and naturally of good quality. Most believe, in other words, that his or her own thinking is that of a fairminded person who judges persons and events in an impartial and accurate way. Often people, then, inadvertently buy into one or more kinds of pseudo critical thinking: in business, in politics, and, of course, in personal, emotional, and family life. The pseudo critical thinking that I propose to concentrate on in this chapter is pseudo critical thinking in the educational establishment.

I will use as my major illustration, the California State Department of Education's new assessment tool for reading and writing. Its development and nature provide an illuminating example of how deeply-flawed thinking is generated and worked into the system, from the statewide to the classroom level. Of course, we must remember that there is local and statewide bureaucracy and that they exist in symbiosis, each feeding the other. And teachers themselves have learned to think the way they do in bureaucratic settings, so very often they are in effect asking for, from the system, what the system by its nature is ready to give them. It is therefore somewhat misleading to say that the flawed thinking at the statewide bureaucratic level is *the* cause — it is rather *a* cause — of flawed thinking in the classroom.

Before we proceed to our "exemplar," I would like to set the stage for what we shall do by providing the reader in advance with one — hopefully intuitive — example of why it might be that flawed thinking is regularly generated in the educational establishment. It is important that the reader comes to see why the blunders and mistakes of the California reading and writing assessment, which I shall presently document, are not exceptions in a generally good record, but rather representative examples of a typically bad product in a system that, like many others, typically generates bad products.

Consider one way in which the educational environment invites flawed thinking. It is an environment in which many whose education may in fact have been quite narrow and flawed, (see "Research Findings," p. 19) take themselves to be experts in one form of knowledge or another,

---

. . . most people recognize that there is something incoherent about saying that one is well educated but thinks poorly.

---

and of course, not only in a form of knowledge *per se* but in the kind of thinking that has created or discovered the knowledge. These experts — called teachers and administrators — are presumed to be qualified to tell the young not only what to think but how to think about mathematical, scientific, social, and literary questions, for example. It would be odd for someone to say, "I'm a qualified teacher but my thinking is deeply flawed." That is to say, most people recognize that there is something incoherent about saying that one is well educated but thinks poorly. Imagine someone saying, "Jack is very well educated, but with just one minor exception; his thinking is unclear, imprecise, inaccurate, irrelevant, narrow, insignificant, and shallow. Other than that, he is well educated." Clearly this would be absurd. Hence to believe oneself an educator is pretty much tantamount to believing oneself a critical thinker, at least in *some* academic domain. Chemistry teachers take themselves to be experts in sound chemical thinking. Math teachers take themselves to be experts in sound mathematical thinking, and so on.

Yet many educators have been miseducated. Many are poor reasoners. Many confuse issues and questions, are easily diverted from the relevant to the irrelevant. Many lack a comprehensive educational philosophy. Many do virtually no serious reading. Many cannot speak knowledgeably

> *... many educators have been miseducated. Many are poor reasoners. Many confuse issues and questions, are easily diverted from the relevant to the irrelevant.*

outside a narrow field. And many are not even up-to-date in their own field. Furthermore, the educational environment dominant in the schools is not traditionally conducive to critical thinking or to the development of further learning on the part of teachers and administrators. Much of the inservice is episodic, intellectually unchallenging, and fragmented. At most schools there is very little discussion on or about serious educational issues, and when there is such discussion it is often simplistic. And that is not all. The kind of instruction that is prevalent at all levels is didactic instruction. The kind of testing that is prevalent is multiple-choice focused on recall. Most students pass their courses by relying on rote memorization. Most teachers, even college professors, passed most of their courses in the same way. (see "Research Findings," p. 19) It is the thesis of this chapter that the models for thinking and the assessment of thinking presented in the schools are generally deeply flawed, and that the reason why this is so is systemic. I will also make recommendations at the end of this chapter as to the kind of action that is called for.

✦ The Bureaucracy
Ignores Reasoning & Intellectual Standards

Much of the pseudo critical thinking derives from the lack of a coherent understanding of the role of reasoning and intellectual standards in disciplined thought. What do I mean by this? Consider that as soon as we set our minds to the task of figuring anything out — a poem, a book, our bank account, a problem in our personal relationships, whatever — we are engaged in the task of reasoning, and reasoning can be done well or poorly. It can be assessed. And to assess it, we need intellectual standards. The California Department of Education English Language Arts Assessment (ELAA) committees are not clear about the role of reasoning in reading and writing, and therefore they are not clear about the role of intellectual standards in the assessment of reasoning in reading and writing. Unfortunately, when one is confused on a basic point such as this, the confusion inevitably spreads to other matters as well. And so we should not be surprised to find a variety of confusions in their work.

I will enumerate for your convenience some of the major ones just below. In the next section, I list flaws characteristic of the educational establishment in general. Each item in this second list I analyze in detail, to provide a background set of understanding in preparation for an in-

---

The general point, running through-out, is that the ill-constructed California reading and writing assessment is not an anomaly.

---

depth analysis of the California reading and writing assessment. The reason for this is simple. If one understands the general pattern of misunderstanding, then specific instances of the pattern are much easier to see. A third list of flaws follows the analysis of the test. This final list makes clear the significance and instructional implications of the flawed character of the test. The general point, running throughout, is that the ill-constructed California reading and writing assessment is not an anomaly. The mistakes it makes are painfully predictable, mistakes being made all over the country in any number of ill-designed tests, in any number of ill-conceived curricula, in any number of ill-thought-through assignments.

You shall read, then, three lists of flaws. Remember that each has a somewhat different, but related, purpose. Now, the first list.

The California Department of Education English Language Arts Assessment materials, as we shall show below, contain all of the following flaws:

- Its treatment of intellectual standards is confused and erroneous.
- It confuses recall with knowledge.
- It confuses subjective preference with reasoned judgment.
- It confuses irrational with rational persuasion.
- Its key terms are often vague.
- Some key terms are dangerously ambiguous.
- It inadvertently encourages "subjectivism."
- Its scoring is arbitrary.
- It is both invalid and unreliable.

But before we look at the detail of these manifestations of pseudo critical thinking in the California Department of Education's assessment materials, let's make clearer what some of the common confusions of pseudo critical thinking amount to in the domain of educational assessment and why they occur. With these understandings in hand, it will be easier to explain what precisely is wrong with California's reading and writing assessment.

✦ What Does Pseudo Critical Thinking Look Like in Educational Assessment?

The advance of knowledge has been achieved not because the mind is capable of memorizing what teachers say but because it can be disciplined to ask probing questions and pursue them in a reasoned, self-critical way. Scholars pursuing knowledge submit their thinking to rigorous discipline, just as the discipline within which they think must itself submit to the broader discipline of more encompassing intellectual standards. Each academic discipline, in other words, develops special standards in virtue of its specialized concepts, procedures, and assumptions, but each also must submit to general standards which enable it to share its knowledge with

> *Pseudo critical thinking is revealed in educational assessment when the assessment theory or practice — or the approaches to teaching, thinking, or knowledge that follow from it — fails to take into account fundamental conditions for the pursuit or justification of knowledge.*

all disciplines and enable all genuine knowledge to be integrated comprehensively and tested for coherence. All research must be put, therefore, into a form of reasoning taken seriously in a field and the reasoning must then submit to the reasoned critique of others, both within and ultimately without the field, who share not only its standards but the standards of good thinking generally. Every field must be intellectually accountable to every other field by demonstrating its commitment to clarity, precision, accuracy, relevance, consistency, depth, and coherence.

Pseudo critical thinking is revealed in educational assessment when the assessment theory or practice — or the approaches to teaching, thinking, or knowledge that follow from it — fails to take into account fundamental conditions for the pursuit or justification of knowledge. The result is the unwitting or unknowing encouragement of flawed thinking. What are some of the common ways, then, that the assessment of thinking or, indeed, any approach to the teaching of thinking might be flawed? Here are three. These are not by any means the only ones, but they are very common, very basic, and very important.

FIRST BASIC FLAW —
THE LACK OR MISUSE OF INTELLECTUAL STANDARDS

This is one of the most common flaws. It derives from the fact that though all of us think, and think continually, we have not been educated to analyze our thinking and assess it. We don't have explicit standards already in mind to assess our thinking. We may then fall back on "mental process words" to talk about good thinking, words such as analyzing,

---

. . . though all of us think, and think continually, we have not been educated to analyze our thinking and assess it.

---

identifying, classifying, and evaluating. These are words that name *some* of what thinking does. We use our thinking to identify things, to classify them, to analyze them, to apply them, and to evaluate them. It is tempting, then, to think of critical thinking as *merely* thinking engaged in identification, classification, analysis, application, evaluation, and the like. But it is important to remember that responsible critical thinking requires intellectual standards. Hence, it is not enough to classify, one must do it well, that is, in accord with the appropriate standards and criteria. *Misclassification*, though a form of classification, is not an ability. The same goes for analysis, application, and evaluation.

> It might be helpful to remember that all critical thinking abilities have three parts: a process, an object, and a standard. Here are various critical thinking abilities which can serve as examples. As you read them see if you can identify the intellectual standard in each.
>
> - the ability to evaluate information for its relevance
> - the ability to accurately identify assumptions
> - the ability to construct plausible inferences
> - the ability to identify relevant points of view
> - the ability to distinguish significant from insignificant information

The standards used in these examples are "relevance," "accuracy," "plausibility," and "significance." Each of these standards would, needless to say, have to be contextualized. Nevertheless — and this is the key point — there can be no critical thinking without the use of intellectual standards.

Hence, if an approach to teaching or thinking focuses on the use of mental processes without a critical application of standards to that use,

> *There can be no critical thinking without the use of intellectual standards.*

and persuades many to do the same, then, it is an example of pseudo critical thinking. There are in fact many such approaches in use in education today.

Second Basic Flaw — Misconceptions Built Into the System

Flaws occur when thinking or an approach to thinking embodies a misconception about the nature of thinking or about what makes for excellence in it. I will explain just two of the most common misconceptions. The first involves confusing *reasoned judgment* (which is one of the most important modes of thinking leading to the possibility of knowledge) with *subjective preference* (which is not a basis for attaining knowledge). The second misconception involves confusing *recall* (which is a lower order use of the mind) with *knowledge* (which requires higher order thinking). Here are the explanations in brief. See if you can follow the examples and relate them to your experience.

Reasoned Judgment Confused with Subjective Preference

Many pseudo critical thinking approaches present all judgments as falling into two exclusive and exhaustive categories: fact and opinion. Actually, the kind of judgment most important to educated people and the kind we most want to foster falls into a third, very important, and now almost totally ignored category, that of reasoned judgment. A judge in a court of law is expected to engage in reasoned judgment; that is, the judge is expected not only to render a judgment, but also to base that judgment on sound, relevant evidence and valid legal reasoning. A judge is not expected to base his judgments on his subjective preferences, on his personal opinions, as such. You might put it this way, judgment based on sound reasoning goes beyond, and is never to be equated with, fact alone or mere opinion alone. Facts are typically used in reasoning, but good reasoning does more than state facts. Furthermore, a position that is well-reasoned is not to be described as simply "opinion." Of course, we sometimes call the judge's verdict an "opinion," but we not only expect, we demand that it be based on relevant and sound reasoning.

Here's a somewhat different way to put this same point. It is essential when thinking critically to clearly distinguish three different kinds of questions: *1)* those with one right answer (factual questions fall into this category), *2)* those with better or worse answers (well-reasoned or poorly reasoned answers), and *3)* those with as many answers as there are differ-

---

When questions that require better or worse answers are treated as matters of opinion, pseudo-critical thinking occurs.

---

ent human preferences (a category in which mere opinion does rule). Here are examples of the three types: *1)* What is the boiling point of lead? *2)* How can we best address the most basic and significant economic problems of the nation today? and *3)* Which would you prefer, a vacation in the mountains or one at the seashore? Only the third kind of question is a matter of sheer opinion. The second kind is a matter of reasoned judgment — we can rationally evaluate answers to the question (using universal intellectual standards such as clarity, depth, consistency and so forth).

When questions that require better or worse answers are treated as matters of opinion, pseudo critical thinking occurs. Students come, then, to uncritically assume that everyone's "opinion" is of equal value. Their capacity to appreciate the importance of intellectual standards diminishes, and we can expect to hear questions such as these: What if I don't like these standards? Why shouldn't I use my own standards? Don't I have a right to my own opinion? What if I'm just an emotional person? What if I like to follow my intuition? What if I don't believe in being "rational?" They then fail to see the difference between offering legitimate reasons and evidence in support of a view and simply asserting the view as true. The failure to teach students to recognize, value, and respect good reasoning is one of the most significant failings of education today.

Recall Confused With Knowledge

A second common confusion which leads directly to pseudo critical thinking is recall confused with knowledge. As I suggested above this confusion is deeply embedded in the minds of many "educators." It results from the fact that most instruction involves didactic lectures and most testing relies fundamentally on recall. Educators confuse students recalling what was said in the lecture with knowing the *how* and the *why* behind what was said. For example, a teacher might give you information, some of which is true and some of which is not, and you may not know which is which. Another way to see this point is to figure out why we don't think of parrots as gaining any knowledge when they learn to repeat words. Tape recorders get no credit for knowledge either. Do you see the point?

We tend to assume, to carry the point a bit further, that all information in a textbook is correct. Some, of course, is not. We attain genuine knowledge only when the information we possess is not only correct but, additionally, we know that it is and why it is. So, strictly speaking, I don't know that something is true or correct if I have merely found it asserted to be so in a book. I need to have a greater understanding — for example, I need to know what supports it, what makes it true — to properly be said to know it.

So if someone tells me Jack has flown to Paris for the weekend, I don't know if he actually did. I might believe that he had (because I trust the person who told me) and my belief might even be correct (through happen stance), but still I don't yet know for sure that he did. I am operating

---

We attain genuine knowledge only when the information we possess is not only correct but, additionally, we know that it is and why it is.

---

on the basis of "hearsay." The failure to appreciate the significance of this distinction causes a lot of problems in schooling because many who teach do not really know their own subjects well enough to explain clearly why this or that *is* so, and why this or that *is not* so. They know what the textbook says, certainly, but not why the textbook says what it says, or whether what it says is so or not. Having knowledge (for such confused persons) is nothing other than remembering what the textbook said.

THIRD BASIC FLAW — THE MISUSE OF INTELLECT

"Skilled" thinking can easily be used to obfuscate rather than to clarify, to maintain a prejudice rather than to break it down, to aid in the defense of a narrow interest rather than to take into account the public good. If we teach students to think narrowly, without an adequate emphasis on the essential intellectual traits of mind (intellectual humility, intellectual honesty, fairmindedness, etc.) the result can then be the inadvertent cultivation of the manipulator, the propagandist, and the con artist. We unknowingly end up, then, undermining the basic values of education and public service, properly conceived.

It is extremely important to see that intelligence and intellect can be used for ends other than those of gaining "truth" or "insight" or "knowledge." One can learn to be cunning rather than clever, smooth rather than clear, convincing rather than rationally persuasive, articulate rather than accurate. One can become judgmental rather than gain in judgment. One can confuse confidence with knowledge at the same time that one mistakes arrogance for self-confidence. In each of these cases a counterfeit of a highly desirable trait is developed in place of that trait. There

> *One can learn to be cunning rather than clever, smooth rather than clear, convincing rather than rationally persuasive, articulate rather than accurate.*

are many people who have learned to be skilled in merely appearing to be rational and knowledgeable when, in fact, they are not. Some of these have learned to be smooth, articulate, confident, cunning, and arrogant. They lack rational judgment, but this does not dissuade them from issuing dogmatic judgments and directives. They impress and learn to control others, quite selfishly. Unless we carefully design schooling to serve the "higher" ends of education, it can easily, as it now often does, degenerate into merely serving "lower" ends. When this happens, schooling often does more harm than good. It spreads the influence and resultant harm of pseudo critical thinking.

With the above understandings in mind, we are prepared to examine the new California Assessment Program and its evaluation of reading and writing.

✦ *The California Assessment Program: English Language Arts Assessment*

California
Assessment
Program

INTRODUCTION

California has developed the reputation of being a leader in educational reform. It was the first state to mandate critical thinking instruction at all educational levels. However, it is now becoming apparent that at the K–12 level at least, the mandate is not on solid ground, for pseudo critical thinking approaches, and the misunderstandings that underlie them, are becoming rampant in the state. The jargon of reform is everywhere, but substance is virtually nowhere. Unfortunately, the California Department of Education is oblivious of the danger, in fact, is very much part of the problem. Not only is it failing to provide sound leadership in integrating critical thinking into instruction, it is developing an assessment program which is shot-through with pseudo critical thinking confusions.

It is now deeply involved in developing what it calls "authentic" assessment that focuses on student "performances" found in the student "construction of meaning" in language arts and social studies. Now all of these terms — "authentic" and "performance" and "construction of meaning"

— are part of the buzz words of the day in educational circles. Of course, the theoretical insights that led to emphasis on these words are important, so let's briefly review them.

Testing and assessment in this country has come under increasing fire, and for good reason. Much of what has traditionally been tested in the popular, machine scorable, multiple choice tests has contributed to little more than trivial pursuit, more and more emphasis in instruction on the lowest order of thinking: rote memorization. Growing numbers of critics have pointed out that the items on which we have been testing students do not involve reasoning and have little relationship to the kinds of tasks that students will later be called upon to "perform." The tests fail, in other words, to "authentically" test higher order "performances." The reform of assessment has increasingly looked to an increased emphasis on "authentic" items that involve "performances" of a "higher order."

Furthermore, research by cognitive psychologists and others have clearly established the fact that when humans deeply learn something — in contrast to, say, storing it temporarily in short-term memory — that learning involves the "construction of meaning." Here's how you might

---

The reform of assessment has increasingly looked to an increased emphasis on "authentic" items that involve "performances" of a "higher order."

---

look at it. In order to get about successfully in the world in which we live we have to continually "make sense" of things, to give a meaning to what is surrounding us. As we do this we develop networks, systems of meanings that enable us quickly to size up what's in front of us. The result is we don't see "meaningless" colors and shapes and sounds. We see trees, and people, and dogs, and speeding cars, and smog. We immediately construct "meaning" out of our experience. Our experience is made by our minds to "fit into" meanings we have already constructed, or, if we cannot do this, we set about constructing a new meaning out of the old ones.

Now, what puzzled educational researchers was what has come to be called the problem of "transfer." Why don't students take what they are studying at school and use it in their daily acts of "constructing meanings?" Why don't they use scientific concepts when they make everyday predictions or form everyday theories about people and events? Why don't they use concepts from their social studies textbooks when they go about interpreting social situations and trying to figure out solutions to their social problems? Their conclusion was that the students don't use what they study in school in their everyday life because they are not engaged in the construction of meaning in class. In class, they are merely, or at least mainly, memorizing, not constructing meaning, not integrating school learning with everyday life.

Now we are ready to bring the three theoretical concepts together — "authentic," "performance," and the "construction of meaning." In authentic performances students construct meaning. They do not simply memorize. So why not focus school instruction on just such matters? Why not give them tasks that are "authentic?" Why not help them, in "performing" those tasks, to actually "construct meaning," in other words, to integrate what they are learning into the network of meanings they are already using to make sense of the world. This is the basic theoretical idea behind the ELAA materials, and, as far as it goes, there can be no objection. But as one wise person once said, "The important truths are in the details." And the details of the ELAA materials are horrendous.

A close examination of the details of the California Language Arts Assessment reveal that it is flawed in all of the following ways:

• The overall conception is not theoretically coherent. It is filled with vagueness and confusion. This is probably the result of the committee adopting the key buzz words without clearly understanding the theory underlying them. The buzz words are then used vaguely and the details are filled out with terms from the agendas of the various stake-holders.

• It does not provide a realistic model of reasoning, of critical reading and writing. Indeed, it is clear that the developers of the assessment do not realize that both reading and writing intrinsically involve the use of reasoning and that reasoning can be done well or poorly.

• The overall conception does not call attention to definite and clear intellectual standards. The criteria given are typically vague and applied inconsistently. Important intellectual standards are missing.

The test, in fact, leads the teachers in the direction of malpractice, that is, into the systematic misassessment of reading and writing, leading the students in turn to become inaccurate, imprecise, and undisciplined readers and writers.

• There is no way that a teacher might grasp an organized and systematic approach to the role of reasoning in reading and writing by studying the materials being disseminated. The test, in fact, leads the teachers in the direction of malpractice, that is, into the systematic misassessment of reading and writing, leading the students in turn to become inaccurate, imprecise, and undisciplined readers and writers.

A TANGLE OF CONFUSIONS

Let's now look at the details and shed light on some of the theoretical confusions that undermine the approach.

First of all, the ELAA commentators open by confusing knowledge with recall and "constructing meaning" with "reasonably constructing meaning." Since these confusions are basic and lead to indiscriminate scoring, let's look at how this occurs.

California's *New English-Language Arts Assessment: An Integrated Look,* begins by announcing a paradigm shift. As the English Language Arts Assessment (ELAA) document explains, "At the heart of the framework is a paradigm shift in which 'constructing meaning' replaced 'gaining knowledge' as the primary goal." Or, as it says later, "Since the construction of meaning is the essence of both reading and writing, the new assessment allows students to shape the outcome rather than to identify correct meanings that test makers have posited."

It is clear that the writers of the assessment are either not clear about the difference between recall and knowledge, or they are wrongly assuming that the attainment of knowledge is not intrinsically connected to the construction of meaning, or both. Briefly, let's make these relationships clear.

RATIONAL AND IRRATIONAL CONSTRUCTIONS

"Constructing meaning" is a process that is common to all learning which becomes deep-seated in the mind of the learner. It applies, however, just as much to the formation of flawed, irrational meanings as it does to the formulation of defensible, rational meanings. Deep-seated irrational fears, for example, result as much from the personal construction of meaning as do insights and understandings. Knowledge, on the other hand, though also the result of the construction of meaning, requires a clear-cut exercise of the rational faculties of the mind. For example, to appropriately judge a person accused of murder to be guilty or innocent, one's thinking must be guided by a careful and rational use of evidence, legal criteria (the criteria for "murder"), and the canons of sound reasoning. When a jury appropriately attains the knowledge of guilt or innocence, that knowledge, expressed in their verdict, is a product of a rational, a reasoned, construction of meaning. Of course, a jury may not function as it ought. It may be irrational and prejudiced, and the judge may overturn its verdict precisely because it did not properly discharge its responsibility to be "rational."

There is nothing wrong, therefore, with focusing attention on the need of students to "construct meaning" but it must be underscored that the *mere* construction of meaning, as such, is not a significant achievement, since it is done as much by Archie Bunker as by Einstein.

But the authors of The California Student Assessment System are confused on this point, for they talk as if the construction of meaning is an end in itself. They forget that "prejudice," "stereotypes," "misconceptions," "illusions," "delusion," "self-deceptions," "false beliefs," and all manner of other intellectually flawed creations of the mind, are just as much "constructions" and as "meaningful" constructions as ones more insightful and discerning.

We should rather be interested in fostering in children adherence to those intellectual standards that maximize their construction of genuine

> *. . . it must be underscored that the* mere *construction of meaning, as such, is not a significant achievement, since it is done as much by Archie Bunker as by Einstein.*

"knowledge," for otherwise they are likely to engage in a great deal of "irrational" construction and they will not know they are doing so. Education must discriminate between the quality of students' constructions of meaning, both in their reading and in their writing. But this can only defensibly be done by judging them by means of those intellectual standards common to educated thought. A construct that is unclear is not to be confused with one that is clear. One that is inaccurate is not to be confused with one that is accurate. One that is relevant to an assigned task is not to be confused with one that is irrelevant. One that is superficial is not to be confused with one that is deep.

Hence we do not need to decide between emphasizing the construction of meaning and the goal of attaining knowledge. If we properly understand the "dual" character of "meaning construction," we will immediately recognize the need to focus on the "reasoned" and "reasonable" construction of meaning, and not indiscriminately credit *any* construction of meaning.

To underscore the point, the human mind naturally and inevitably constructs meaning. The mere fact that students construct meanings tells us nothing about the quality of those constructs. For example, in the extended example on reading as a form of thinking which we cited (pp. 24–27), both readers, Stephen and Colleen, constructed meanings. But you will remember that the meanings constructed by Colleen were absurd. Both students reasoned about the text's meaning, but there was a stark contrast in the quality of reasoning in the two cases.

The point should now be clear. We want to work with our students' capacity to construct meaning from a text, but we want to do this while teaching them to discipline their reading, to learn how to fit their interpretations to the logic of the words of the text. We want them to develop definite intellectual standards for their reading and not feel free to treat a text as if it were "silly putty," to be shaped into any "meaning" they choose.

In passing, in the workplace, there is no economic value in constructing irrational, fanciful, lively, and entertaining meaning if it is irrational and reflects a flawed understanding of the text. Employers are not looking for a flashy, individualized response to a piece of writing, but rather a solid grasp of the meaning intended by the author. This is a fundamental premise of written communication! We should therefore continually

> *Employers are not looking for a flashy, individualized response to a piece of writing, but rather a solid grasp of the meaning intended by the author. This is a fundamental premise of written communication!*

underscore the pivotal role of intellectual standards, not only in assessment but in any form of intellectual work whatsoever, including of course, reading and writing.

Intellectual Standards *That Apply to Thinking in Every Subject*	
Thinking that is:	*Thinking that is:*
Clear	vs Unclear
Precise	vs Imprecise
Specific	vs Vague
Accurate	vs Inaccurate
Relevant	vs Irrelevant
Plausible	vs Implausible
Consistent	vs Inconsistent
Logical	vs Illogical
Deep	vs Superficial
Broad	vs Narrow
Complete	vs Incomplete
Significant	vs Trivial
Adequate *(for purpose)*	vs Inadequate
Fair	vs Biased or One-Sided

A Pseudo Commitment to Intellectual Standards

Intellectual standards are essential to the appropriate assessment of reading and writing. At some level, the assessment authors are aware of this necessity. Their description of their own criteria imply both impartiality and commitment to intellectual standards. For example, the authors of the English-Language Arts Assessment often speak of their commitment to "encourage students to read widely and in depth." (Depth implies criteria for distinguishing "deep" from "shallow" readings.) Secondly, they imply impartial assessment when they state the three-fold purpose of the new English-Language Arts Assessment (p. I-2):

1) To establish standards for evaluating students' performance when they read diverse kinds of materials for different purposes.

2) To measure how well students are able to construct meaning.

3) To improve the instructional program by providing an assessment that reflects the Framework.

They use language that implies a concern with rational judgment: for example, the ELAA report says when speaking of "meaning-making," that,

We want students to think critically as they explore interests, clarify values, solve problems, resolve conflicts, generate new ideas, synthesize/apply learnings, set goals, and make decisions in response to the literature they read. (p. I - 2)

Now, the processes of thinking critically, clarifying values, solving problems, setting goals, and making decisions all presuppose the importance of rationality, of engaging in sound reasoning. To clarify values, for

---

It becomes clear, from here on, that the California testing experts' glossy, global statements about critical thinking and meaning-making and standards are losing their luster.

---

example, requires that we rationally analyze them. Solving problems is not the product of an arbitrary construction of meaning, but requires, amongst other things, an objective and accurate analysis of the nature of the problems, of the information relevant to the problems, and such like. Effective goal setting requires that we accurately identify possible competing goals and reasonably assess which make most sense. And certainly, decisions can reasonably or unreasonably be arrived at. It becomes clear, from here on, that the California testing experts' glossy, global statements about critical thinking and meaning-making and standards are losing their luster. Empty platitudes and vacuous ideals are a specialty of virtually all bureaucracies. So common are they now that they are hardly noticed anymore.

THE PROBLEM OF SCORING

As you might expect, all of the confusions above come home to roost in the design for scoring student "performances" in reading and writing. For example, in explaining the design with respect to assessing elementary reading, the authors introduce us to a 15-point list under the head of the reading performances of effective readers.

Effective readers *connect* with, *reflect* on, and *challenge* the text. Readers do not need to show evidence of all the performances listed here. The discerning and insightful reader may display a broad spectrum of reading behaviors or may investigate a few selected behaviors in great depth. The exemplary reader may show variety, complexity, breadth, and/or depth. Through their writing and graphics, these readers show convincing evidence of their ability to construct meaning. They may:

1. Experiment with ideas; think divergently; take risks; express opinions (e.g., speculate, hypothesize, explore alternative scenarios; raise questions; make predictions; think metaphorically).

2. Explore multiple possibilities of meaning; see cultural and/or psychological nuances and complexities in the text.

3. Fill in gaps; use clues and evidence in the passage to draw conclusions; make plausible interpretations of ideas, facts, concepts, and/or arguments.

4. Recognize and deal with ambiguities in the text.

5. Revise, reshape and/or deepen early interpretations.

6. Evaluate; examine the degree of fit between the author's ideas or information and the reader's prior knowledge or experience.

7. Challenge the text(s) by agreeing or disagreeing, arguing, endorsing, questioning, and or wondering.

8. Demonstrate understanding of the work as a whole.

9. Show sensitivity to the structure of the text(s): how the parts work together; how characters and/or other elements of the work(s) change.

10. Show aesthetic appreciation of the text(s); see linguistic and structural complexities.

11. Allude to and/or retell specific passages(s) to validate and/or expand ideas.

12. Make connections between the text(s) and their own ideas, experiences, and knowledge.

13. Demonstrate emotional engagement with the text(s).

14. Retell, summarize, and/or paraphrase with purpose.

15. Reflect on the meaning(s) of the text(s), including larger or more universal significance; express a major understanding about or insight into a subject, an aspect of self, or of life in general.

The Escape Hatch

First off, it is clear that since each scorer can pick and chose from such a wide variety of criteria (a number of which as we shall see are extremely vague), the impartiality of application of the criteria is suspect. Also note that any and all of these activities can be done either defensibly or indefensibly. Hence, if these are to be assessed in order to be credited or discredited, criteria must be provided for each of the individual "performances" cited (over 50 are buried in the list). We need some explanation of how they expect someone assessing student reading to apply them. Consider each of the following. The assessor is left to her own intuitions in determining whether or not a student's reading:

- is insightful; discerning; perceptive;

- is sensitive to linguistic, structural, cultural and psychological nuances and complexities;

- entertains challenging ideas; grounds meaning in acute perceptions of textual and cultural complexities.

Do the assessors really know how to *impartially* assess whether or not a student reader is being "sensitive to a psychological nuance" or to a "structural nuance" or a "cultural nuance?" Or can they impartially determine whether or not the student reader is entertaining a "challenging" idea? Or whether a student perception is "acute" or not? Isn't it highly probable that different assessors are going to have somewhat different conceptions of each of these matters, for example, one thinking a given idea is "quite challenging" and another thinking it is not? Surely this much is clear! No criteria, however, are provided, and this invalidates any attempt to use the results to assess one student's performances year after year, as well as to assess all California students collectively, year after year. Instead, having given us an array of vague descriptors, the authors now largely set them aside and focus instead on a six-point "Scoring Guide" that is to be used in distinguishing student reading into the following categories:

- *Exemplary* Reading Performance ....(Six Points)

- *Discerning* Reading Performance ....(Five Points)

- *Thoughtful* Reading Performance ....(Four Points)

- *Literal* Reading Performance ....(Three Points)

- *Limited* Reading Performance ....(Two Points)

- *Minimal* Reading Performance ....(One Point)

These general descriptors are of very little use. For example, consider the words "discerning" and "thoughtful." It is not obvious that one is better off being "discerning" than being "thoughtful." It is also not obvious why "literal" is above "limited." It is certainly not clear why the lowest score is "minimal" reading. What ever happened to just plain "poor" reading? Has it disappeared or is it one of many forms of "minimal" reading. (See Colleen's reading on pp. 24–27.) Is it "minimal" or just plain "poor?")

But that is not all. Each of the terms listed in each of the six point scoring guide create further problems for the conscientious scorer. Consider the terms in the first category alone, that of "exemplary reading performance." A person who takes seriously the characterizations of this first category should be prepared to notice and assess whether or not the student is:

filling in gaps	drawing on evidence
drawing meaning	objecting to text features
entertaining ideas	considering the authority of the author
raising questions	considering the quality of the author's sources
taking exception	suggesting ways of rewriting the text
agreeing; disagreeing	embracing the ideological position of a text
exploring possibilities	resisting the ideological position of a text
developing connections	revising their understanding as they read
making connections	carrying on an internal dialogue

The State Department Criteria for an Exemplary Reading Performance

1) An exemplary reading performance is insightful, discerning and perceptive as the reader constructs and reflects on meaning in a text. Readers at this level are sensitive to linguistic, structural, cultural, and psychological nuances and complexities. They fill in gaps in a text, making plausible assumptions about unstated causes or motivations, or drawing meaning from subtle cues. They differentiate between literal and figurative meanings. They recognize real or seeming contradictions, exploring possibilities for their resolution or tolerating ambiguities. They demonstrate their understanding of the whole work as well as an awareness of how the parts work together to create the whole.

Readers achieving score point six develop connections with and among texts. They connect their understanding of the text not only to their own ideas, experience, and knowledge, but to their history as participants in a culture or larger community, often making connections to other texts or other works of art. Exceptional readers draw on evidence from the text to generate, validate, expand, and reflect on their own ideas.

These readers take risks. They entertain challenging ideas and explore multiple possibilities of meaning as they read, grounding these meanings in their acute perceptions of textual and cultural complexities. They often revise their understanding of a text as they re-read and as additional information or insight becomes available to them. They sometimes articulate a newly developed level of understanding.

Readers demonstrating a score point six performance challenge the text. They carry on an internal dialogue with the writer, raising questions, taking exception, agreeing, disagreeing, appreciating or objecting to text features. They may test the validity of the author's ideas, information, and/or logic by considering the authority of the author and the nature and quality of the author's source(s). They frequently suggest ways of rewriting the text, speculating about the ideology or cultural or historical biases that seem to inform a text, sometimes recognizing and embracing and sometimes resisting the ideological position that a text seems to construct for its reader.

MUST THE STUDENT JUST DO IT OR DO IT WELL?

Even more problematic than the likely disagreement among assessors as to the application of the vague standards provided is, as I suggested above, the problem of the assessors being given many criteria that name processes that can, in principle, be done well or poorly. The directions do not explain whether, to be credited, the student is obliged to use the cited processes well or simply use them in any way whatsoever. That is, there is

---

Unfortunately, once we examine the actual student writing examples along with the commentary provided, it becomes painfully clear that the assessors were simply looking to see if the student in any sense used the process and did not have, or did not use, criteria to assess how well *the students used the processes credited.*

---

no indication as to whether the assessor is to evaluate the "quality" of the way the student is doing these things or simply certify the fact of doing these things — however poorly. Remember, a student who is drawing an *absurd* meaning is still drawing a meaning. A student who is making a *trivial* connection is still making a connection. A student who is drawing on *irrelevant* evidence is still drawing on evidence. A student who is raising a *silly* or *superficial* question is still raising a question. And so forth, and so on.

Unfortunately, once we examine the actual student writing examples along with the commentary provided, it becomes *painfully clear* that the assessors were simply looking to see if the student in any sense used the process and did not have, or did not use, criteria to assess how *well* the students used the processes credited. The California State Department of Education falls directly into the trap of failing to discriminate between these crucial differences. The assessors are left to their own devices. They can draw these distinctions or fail to draw them. It is clear that most failed to draw them. This is a fatal flaw in the assessment. It renders the results of the assessment virtually useless.

THE MISASSESSMENT OF ELEMENTARY READING

The only elementary reading passage which is given with scored examples is from a story by John Gardiner called *Stone Fox*. It is an emotionally explosive story, one chosen perhaps to ensure an emotional response. The children are simply asked to give some of their "thoughts, feelings, and questions" about what they are reading. No other kind of writing is given as an example.

Insufficient Directions Are Given

Now the first remarkable feature of the *Stone Fox* reading prompt is that the student readers are given no indication whatsoever of the purpose for which they are reading the story. This is ironic in the light of the fact that the CAP materials emphasize the fact that one can read and write "for different purposes" (p. I-3). And yet, here, the students are asked to read for no particular purpose. Are they to read in a casual fashion, simply for amusement? Or are they to do a "close reading" for detail? Are they to be analytical and reflective, or not? The students are given no indication of how they will be assessed. Hence, they are asked to engage, at best, in an ill-defined "performance." Nothing is given in the way of directions to the students except "Read to see what happens" and a place to the right in which the student *may* write notes under a column head titled, "My thoughts, feelings, and questions about what I am reading." The students were apparently not even told that they should try to write out as much of their thoughts, feelings, and questions as they could. Some readers might presumably have thoughts, feelings, and questions they would not bother to express.

Consider that you are a student reading the story. You see a column at the right which says, "My thoughts, feelings, and questions about what I am reading." How should you understand it? Wouldn't you wonder which thoughts ... which feelings ... based on what? What am I to think about? Why am I to think about it?

In any case, since the student reader is not told that she is going to be evaluated on what she writes and is told none of the criteria, why should she be motivated to fully express her thoughts and feelings? Consider, on the other hand, what the directions might have said.

Possible Directions

When we read a story we have to try to understand and follow its meaning. We try to figure out what it is saying and we try to connect it with our own life in some way. We want you to read this story and see what it means to you. Why do you think it was written? Do you think that it was written well? Do you think it is true to life? Does it illustrate anything that you believe is important? Please write in as many of your thoughts on these questions as possible as you read. Help us to understand what is going on in your mind as you are reading and trying to relate this story to your life.

Can One Evaluate Purely Subjective Responses to Stories?

When the student reads that she is directed to express her "feelings," with no explanation given why she is so directed, then how can we legitimately go on to judge those feelings and "score" them one through six?

Suppose the student quite sincerely said, "In my view this is a sentimental story that insults my intelligence. I feel disgusted when I read it and bored silly." How should the assessor evaluate that "feeling" response? Is there any way to discredit it according to the directions? Certainly not. It is as good a response to a request for "feelings" as any other. To put the point succinctly, *either we help students understand the difference between a request for a purely subjective response,* (How do you feel when you read this?) *and a request for a more reasoned response* (What feeling do you judge the author wants you to feel and why? In your judgment is the author successful? Tell us the reasons why you think so.) *or we must not indulge in any assessment of the students "feelings."* We have no legitimate grounds for doing so. The student can legitimately take the request to be one that asks for a subjective response and a purely subjective response cannot be impartially assessed or scored.

THE MISASSESSMENT OF WRITING AT THE ELEMENTARY LEVEL

Different kinds of writing will be assessed at different levels: Elementary: persuasive writing ... Middle School: *problem solution, evaluation* and *speculation about cause and effect* ... High School: *evaluation, speculation about cause and effect, interpretation* and *controversial issues* plus a *reflective essay.* (p. I–4)

The grade four writing assessment is designed to reflect a variety of purposes for which children write:

1) **Expressive** writing
    ("This is what I see, think, and feel ...")

2) **Persuasive** writing
    ("This is what I believe and why I think you should believe it ...");

3) **Narrative** writing
    ("This is what happened ..."); and

4) **Informational** writing
    ("This is what I know and how I know it ...").

Criteria For Persuasive Writing

Persuasive writing is explained in the following terms (p. III–12):

Persuasive writing requires students to choose positions, to make judgments, to offer proposals, and to argue convincingly for their beliefs and ideas. However, some students may choose to explore both sides of an issue and then offer a compromise, ... Effective writers use evidence such as examples or anecdotes to support their arguments. Convincing arguments may appeal to logic, emotions, and/or philosophical beliefs.

Persuasive writers establish themselves as informed, knowledgeable individuals. They orient readers... More than any other kind of writing, argument requires writers to consider their audience.... The best persuasive writers systematically develop arguments with a strong sense of coherence and movement throughout the piece.

California's Standards for Exceptional Writing (Six Points)

An exceptional score (6 points) must meet the following standards:

Focus/coherence

Position. Writers of six-point papers usually assert and maintain a clear position throughout the piece; they present evidence and explanations in a purposeful way. Occasionally these writers will effectively evaluate both sides of an issue and offer a reasonable compromise; or they may conclude that neither position is preferable, or they may suggest a third position.

Organization. Writers arrange reasons, examples, information and/or personal anecdotes in a discernible and effective pattern resulting in an overall persuasive effect.

Coherence. Writers provide overall links or transitions; they present arguments, evidence, and reasons logically so that the overall effect is one of coherence.

Elaboration

Depth/Density of Arguments. Writers thoroughly develop and elaborate their reasons, examples, information and/or anecdotes. Some writers may develop only one reason or example, but they do so in depth; others may choose to develop several appropriate reasons, examples, and so forth.

Relevance of Arguments. Writers choose and present appropriate reasons, examples, information, and so forth to support their argument(s). They show their arguments are valid based on prior knowledge, personal experience and reflection.

Audience Awareness. Writers choose and present arguments with a clear awareness of reader needs. They often show credibility and a sense of authority by revealing source(s) of information. They may anticipate possible reader response by including some counter-arguments.

Style

Word Choice. These writers use lively, interesting concrete language that carries precise meanings and emotions. Word choice is appropriate to the writer's purpose.

Sentence Variety. Writers vary sentence length and type, making the writing interesting and readable.

Voice. Writers evidence confidence, conviction, belief and sometimes enthusiasm.

Problems With the Criteria In Assessing Writing

Once again there are a host of problems with the criteria, the most serious being that, just as in the criteria for reading, there is no indication of whether the students are expected to do any of the above well, or simply do them in any form whatsoever. For example, consider the claim that "convincing arguments may appeal to logic, emotions, and/or philosophical beliefs." Suppose a student uses "convincing" but "fallacious" logic — is the student to be credited? Or suppose the student appeals to the emotions of the reader by engaging in *name-calling* ("This stupid communist idea...!") — is the student to be credited? The formulators of the criteria are seemingly oblivious of the problem.

A GRADE FOUR ESSAY JUDGED TO ILLUSTRATE HIGH-RANGE ACHIEVEMENT

"Good-evening ladies and gentelmen. I come to you tonight with a few simple facts. The pack you are ready to face downs this very min it filled with children. It is the favorit place to play of many children, as well as myself. Do you anistly think that children at the age of two and three are going to enjoy a mall more than a park?! I would also like to bring to your atichun that we already have over five stores in one plazza. You can get there very esley. I admit that it's about a half hour away, but

wouldn it be 'hole lot of trouble to spend a little more cash & as long as you know that children are happy and safe. You, and only

you can make that chois to make that difreace!! How would you feel if you were a child playing in your favorit place to play, beutiful shady trees, and fresh green grass. A perfict place to play, take your dog for a walk, play with another pet, or even just sit around and look at the beutiful sky. And then after knoing it had been there for over 100 years, and their going to tare it down! Oh! The feeling

thoes poor children must have! Please! Please! Just stop and think about this matter! This is very sereous. I didnt come here to wach thoes C.A.T.s tare up that park! Pleas consiter my slotion. I bid you good night."

The CAP Commentary

From the opening ... this writer exudes confidence, focuses on an audience and takes a firm stand on the issue. These attributes of persuasive writing are maintained throughout the piece.

Support for the writer's credible arguments in favor of a park versus a mall are drawn from personal experiences. She uses examples: "We already have over five stores in our plaza," and notes that the park is a "perfect place to play, take your dog for a walk." She includes reflection,

"Do you honestly think that children at the age of two or three are going to enjoy a mall ...?" Her arguments are appropriate and appeal to reason (safety) and emotions ("I didn't come here to watch those C.A.T.s tare up that park!")

This writer is consistently aware of and appeals to her audience with appropriate tone and lively language.

The Problem of Subjectivity, Once Again

The problem of subjectivity that was so apparent in the elementary reading assessment reappears again in the writing assessment. It is clear in this, and in other examples, that the commentators are using the criteria for good persuasive writing literally and not making any real judgments of reasonability. Hence, if the student says anything which can be construed as falling under one of the criteria then that is credited. For example, if she uses an emotional appeal then credit the emotion criterion (however irrelevant or inappropriate it might be); if she says something which can be described as "reflection," then credit the reflection criterion (however irrelevant or inappropriate the "reflection" might be). Any kind of a move that would work with an audience, in the view of the commentator, is credited as good (regardless of how irrational it might be). But the

To suggest that this is good persuasive writing is to teach children exactly the wrong lesson. It fails to show them the vital distinction between reason and its counterfeit.

significant question for anyone concerned with the traditional values of education is whether a *reasonable* audience should be persuaded or "moved." The important distinction for students to grasp is that between what might be called "low level rhetorical appeals" and those appeals which would convince or "move" a reasonable audience. No such distinction is recognized by ELAA. The criteria are used crudely, without any important intellectual distinctions in evidence.

The implication of this is that if a student wrote a very rational appeal, which recognized the weaknesses in her position and the need to qualify her claims, she would be downgraded because she would not be "exuding confidence," "taking a firm stand on the issue," etc. Indeed, though her presentation might appeal to a "jury of reasonable persons," the graders of the ELAA would not be impressed.

In this particular essay, for example, though it is good for children to display confidence, etc., the issue of park versus mall should be decided on rational grounds. Yes, it is important that the park is a favorite place for children and that they are safe there, but this is really a decision about options, and alternatives, and relative costs and benefits. This issue should be decided by looking at these factors and weighing them as rationally as possible, not on the basis of emotional appeals, like that of the child. To suggest that this is good persuasive writing is to teach children exactly the wrong lesson. It fails to show them the vital distinction between reason and its counterfeit.

Suppose the child has to present a case before an audience she knows to be racist; if one reads and applies the criteria presented for good persuasive writing in ELAA, the student who plays on those racist sentiments

---

What apparently matters in the mind of the ELAA assessors is that one successfully persuades, not that one argues reasonably. But it is harder to imagine a distinction which it is more vital for the educated person to grasp.

---

will score higher than one who opposes them. What apparently matters in the mind of the ELAA assessors is that one successfully persuades, not that one argues reasonably. But it is harder to imagine a distinction which it is more vital for the educated person to grasp. Indeed, one might almost regard it as a criterion of being educated that one sees the difference between fairminded, reasonable argument, and self-seeking, low-level, persuasive rhetoric. The demagogues may often win the day, but do we want to use public monies to generate armies of demagogues, all having mastered the art of demagogery at the public expense?

In another example, which contains some very good reasoning about why another child should feel good about himself, the commentators say, "She arranges her reasons and evidence in a sophisticated pattern." There is no mention of whether the reasons and evidence are relevant or

---

It is not that the reasons are arranged in a sophisticated pattern, but that they are good reasons!

---

irrelevant, true or false, good or bad. Yet, again, isn't this what really matters? It is not that the reasons are arranged in a sophisticated pattern, but that they are *good* reasons!

In another, mid-range, example, about how to solve problems between children and parents, the commentators say (among other things), "Audience awareness is evident throughout, although appeals lack the vigor and exactness of higher score point papers. The use of bullets to summarize the writer's arguments is an effective tool and adds to her sense of conviction." Why is the writer criticized for a lack of vigor and praised for conveying a sense of conviction? Neither is a virtue in itself. What matters is that one exhibits the *appropriate* degree of vigor and conviction, depending on the strength of one's case. Vigorously arguing a weak case and displaying conviction despite poor supporting reasons ought to be marked down, not praised.

The Young Hitler Scores High on the CAP Test

We can now make our point dramatically by considering how the following piece of persuasive, but highly irrational, writing should be graded according to the ELAA criteria.

... the greatest revolution Germany has undergone was that of the purification of the Volk [people] and thus of the races, which was launched systematically in this country for the first time ever. *[From the opening the writer exudes confidence, focuses on an audience and takes a firm stand on the issue.]*

The consequences of this German racial policy will be more significant for the future of our Volk than the effects of all the other laws put together. For they are what is creating the new man. They will preserve our Volk from doing as so many historically tragic past prototypes of other races have done: lose their earthly existence forever because of their ignorance as regards a single question. *[The writer arranges reasons, examples and information in a discernible and effective pattern resulting in overall persuasive effect.]*

For what is the sense of all our work and all our efforts if they do not serve the purpose of preserving the German being? And what good is any effort on behalf of this being if we omit the most important thing to preserve it pure and unadulterated in its blood? *[The writer asserts and maintains a clear position throughout. He also chooses and presents arguments with a clear awareness of reader needs.]*

Any other mistake can be rectified, any other error can be corrected, but what one fails to do in this area can often never be amended. Whether our work in this area of purifying our race and thus our Volk has been fruitful is something you can best judge for yourselves here during these few days. For what you are encountering in this city is the German being. Come and see for yourselves whether he has become worse under National Socialist leadership or whether he has not indeed become better. Do not gauge only the increasing number of children being born — gauge above all the appearance of our youth. *[The writer presents evidence and explanations in a purposeful way.]*

How lovely are our girls and our boys, how bright is their gaze, how healthy and fresh their posture, how splendid are the bodies of the hundreds of thousands and millions who have been trained and cared for by our organizations! *[The writer shows his arguments are valid based on personal knowledge and reflection.]*

Where are better men to be found today than those who can be seen here? It is truly the rebirth of a nation, brought about by the deliberate breeding of a new being *[The overall effect is one of coherence.]*

—*(Hitler Speech 1937)*

This piece asserts and maintains a clear position throughout and presents evidence and explanations in a purposeful way; the writer arranges reasons, examples, information and/or personal anecdotes in a discernible and effective pattern resulting in overall persuasive effect; the overall effect is one of coherence; the writer shows his arguments are valid based on prior knowledge, personal experience and reflection; the writer chooses and presents arguments with a clear awareness of reader needs; the writer evidences confidence, conviction, belief, and sometimes enthusiasm.

Clearly, for all these reasons we have to give this piece of Hitler's writing a Point 6 score! It meets the CLAS criteria, as does much of his writing. Hitler's writing was widely recognized to meet the needs of his audience, to exude confidence, etc. Is that really what we want to praise? Is that the model of persuasive writing that we want to hold up to our children? If so, shame on the California Learning Assessment System!

THE MISASSESSMENT OF WRITING AT THE HIGH SCHOOL LEVEL

Introduction — Same Problem: Next Level

At the high school level the Writing Assessment assesses four types of writing, Autobiographical Incident, Interpretation, Reflective Essay, and Speculation About Causes and Effects, some of which are successors to the elementary level Persuasive writing.

The same general faults that were mentioned earlier in connection with the elementary level are to be found at this level too. For example, the scoring guide for *interpretation* makes it clear that only subjective reactions to and subjective interpretation of fiction are really being considered. But *interpretation* is important in many other contexts, e.g. history, and in history it is crucial to distinguish between subjective response and objective interpretation, between reasons that persuade irrational audiences and reasons which persuade rational and fairminded persons, between something which is rhetorically convincing and something which is true. None of these distinctions is recognized in the CLAS.

To be specific in our criticisms, consider the scoring guide for **Speculation About Causes and Effects**; once again writing of this kind is judged almost entirely by *subjective* standards, by standards appropriate to one's response to fiction.

Here is what is said about writing of this kind which should score Point 6, for Exceptional Achievement:

A six point essay **engages the reader immediately**. It seems **purposeful**. The writer **seems aware of reader's questions and needs throughout** the essay. The essay seems to be not just written but **written to particular readers**. The writer **convinces the readers of the plausibility** of the speculation.

A six-point essay demonstrates qualities all readers admire: conviction, enthusiasm, freshness. These essays may use an unconventional rhetorical approach. A six-point essay may **take chances and succeed.**

Presenting the Situation. The six-point essay writer clearly defines, identifies, or describes the situation to be speculated about. Though it does not dominate the essay at the expense of speculation, the situation is nevertheless presented fully and precisely. The writer limits the occasion appropriately, focusing reader attention on just those aspects of the situation that the writer will speculate about.

Writers of six-point essays may describe or detail the situation that is established in the prompt, or they might create the situation by using narrative or anecdotal techniques. In either case, they will **use concrete language, rich in sensory detail.**

The writer of the six-point essay acknowledges readers' concerns. For real world situations, the writer of the six-point essay acknowledges the reader's experience or familiarity with a situation and, using narrative or descriptive strategies, builds on this awareness to focus reader attention on a comparable situation. ...

Whether the essay arises from a factual assessment of a real situation or from a fanciful guess about a fanciful situation, the writer **consistently demonstrates broad knowledge and clear understanding of the situation. In this way the writer establishes authority.**

Logic and Relevance of Causes and Effects. In the six-point essay, the proposed causes and effects are clearly related to the particular situation that the writer has defined. Writers use imaginative, inventive argument to convince the reader of the logic of their speculation. The best writers are clearly considering possibilities and are seeing multiple perspectives.... Because speculation is essentially a persuasive type of writing, the best writers will be continually aware of readers' needs. They might refer to the readers directly, trying to enlist their support ...

Elaboration of Argument. The six-point essay **provides substantial elaboration,** convincing the reader that the writer's conjectures are valid for the situation. These writers elaborate their speculated causes and effects **with carefully chosen evidence that is logically and fully developed.** Such **evidence is chosen because it is relevant and convincing.** It is developed fully with precise, explicit detail to convince the reader both of the logic and the authenticity of the proposed cause and effect.

Some strategies writers may use to develop their arguments are the following:

* Cite facts, opinions, projections, and personal experiences or observations (anecdotes) to explain or validate a cause or an effect.

* Elaborate on possibilities arising from proposed causes and effects, showing possible "domino effects" that might determine the direction of the developing situation.

* Give specific examples of comparable causes and effects that have arisen in analogous situations. (p. III–64)

How may we best make the point that these criteria again fail to recognize the crucial distinctions of which we have been speaking — between subjective responses and good reasons, etc? Perhaps the simplest way is to look at another example of persuasive writing, this time **Speculating About Causes and Effects,** and consider how we should grade it according to the CLAS criteria.

Just as every people, as a basic tendency of all its earthly actions possesses a mania for self-preservation as its driving force, likewise is it exactly so with Jewry too. Only here, in accord with their basically different dispositions, the struggle for existence of Aryan peoples and Jewry is also different in its forms. The foundation of the Aryan struggle for existence is the soil, which he cultivates and which provides the general basis for an economy satisfying primarily its own needs within its own orbit through the productive forces of its own people.

Because of the lack of productive capacities of its own the Jewish people cannot carry out the construction of a state, viewed in a territorial sense, but as a support of its own existence it needs the work and creative activities of other nations. Thus the existence of the Jew himself becomes a parasitical one within the lives of other people. Hence the ultimate goal of the Jewish struggle for existence is the enslavement of productively active peoples. In order to achieve this goal, which in reality has represented Jewry's struggle for existence at all times, the Jew makes use of all weapons that are in keeping with the whole complex of his character.

Therefore in domestic politics within the individual nations he fights first for equal rights and later for super-rights. The characteristics of cunning, intelligence, astuteness, knavery, dissimulation, etc, rooted in the character of his folkdom, serve him as weapons thereto.

They are as much stratagems in his war of survival as those of other peoples in combat.

In foreign policy he tries to bring nations into a state of unrest, to divert them from their true interests, and to plunge them into reciprocal wars and in this way gradually rise to mastery over them with the help of the power of money and propaganda.

His ultimate goal is the denationalization, the promiscuous bastardization of other peoples, the lowering of the racial level of the highest peoples as well as the domination of this racial mish-mash through the extirpation of the folkish intelligentsia and its replacement by the members of his own people.

The end of the Jewish world struggle therefore will always be a bloody Bolshevization. In truth this means the destruction of all the intellectual upper classes linked to their peoples so that he can rise to become the master of a mankind become leaderless. *Hitler's Secret Book*, pp. 212-213.

Hitler's Assessment Based on CAP Criteria

• This piece of writing certainly engages the reader immediately;

• it seems purposeful;

• the writer seems aware of reader's questions and needs throughout;

• the piece seems not just to be written but written to particular readers;

• the writer convinced those readers of the plausibility of the speculation;

• the writing shows conviction and enthusiasm;

• the writer clearly defines the situation to be speculated about, acknowledges the reader's experience or familiarity with the situation, and consistently demonstrates broad knowledge and clear understanding of the situation;

• the writer uses imaginative, inventive argument to convince the reader of the logic of his speculation;

• the writer elaborates on possibilities arising from the proposed causes and effects, showing possible "domino effects" that might determine the direction of the developing situation; etc., etc.

Can there be any doubt that Hitler's writing in the category merits a Point 6 grade?! If that is so then once again, shame on the California Learning Assessment System, which has again failed to see the difference between a *proper* and *improper* use of rhetoric and reason.

Summary Judgment
on the California Assessment of Reading & Writing

An assessment of reading and writing should not only underscore the role of reasoning in both, but also firmly establish defensible intellectual standards, appropriately and specifically explained and consistently and

---

No assessment of intellectual work, nor foundation for teaching, should be based on an approach in which intellectual standards are confused and erroneous, confusing recall with knowledge, subjective preference with reasoned judgment, irrational with rational persuasion.

---

appropriately applied. No assessment of intellectual work, nor foundation for teaching, should be based on an approach in which intellectual standards are confused and erroneous, confusing recall with knowledge, subjective preference with reasoned judgment, irrational with rational persuasion. No assessment of intellectual work should use its key terms vaguely or oscillate between two significant uses of a term or score in an arbitrary manner. And, most important of all, no intellectual assessment should encourage irrational subjectivism.

For example, it is striking that in the context of reading and listening, there is little discussion of the need to create an accurate interpretation: there are many contexts in which it is not appropriate for the readers to "create their own meaning" and where accuracy is what is required. This may be equally true if the author is addressing a particular question or problem, or using particular basic concepts; very often the good response to what is said or written is good precisely because it is based on an accurate construal of the text. Nothing in this assessment mentions the virtue of accuracy.

Most importantly however, this approach is flawed again and again because what gets credited is anything that could be construed as fulfilling one of the criteria and the criteria are the wrong ones for the purpose. If the writer is using any emotion (however discreditable) then it is marked positively; if she is giving anything that could be called evidence,

---

Underneath all of this is a question of values. We are obliged to educate our students, not simply to shape them.

---

even if it is bad evidence, it is credited; any kind of a move that would work with an audience, in the view of the reader is credited as good (regardless of how irrational it might be). The end result is that if a student wrote a very rational appeal, one that would persuade a rational audience, it is going to be graded down because it wouldn't appeal to an irrational judge (because it won't be maintaining a strong line, it won't necessarily be persuasive; it will be putting in qualifications; it will be speaking in terms of greys and greys don't persuade; it will not be engaging in hyperbole and hyperbole is effective; it won't be trying to negate everything about the other side, it will be recognizing reasonable objections; it will express the degree of confidence that is appropriate but no more). Given a list of what a rational person would do, you will be able to see that the criteria for success under CLAS are negating these rational qualities and therefore encouraging irrational beliefs about how you communicate to people, indeed encouraging people to become manipulators!

Underneath all of this is a question of values. We are obliged *to educate* our students, *not simply to shape them.*

The educated person is reasonable; the educated person isn't simply concerned with winning. The educated person wants to win when winning is the appropriate thing. However, when the other side is more reasonable, then the educated person, who is more interested in getting at the truth than in winning, will want to make concessions.

If the goal of education is simply to enable people to get what they want, then we should teach them tools of manipulation, ways to win battles, ways to undermine positions whether those positions are rational or not, ways to just get what they want, irrespective of fairness, and of the evidence. Inadvertently and unknowingly, this is what CLAS is supporting. CLAS does not have in mind a clear difference between the educated, fairminded, and rational person, on the one hand, and the person who is simply good at manipulating, winning, and defeating others, on the other.

In effect what CLAS has said is that the name of the game is to persuade the audience by whatever methods work and we'll credit anything that works. Shouldn't they instead have said, "Since we are obliged and committed to educating children, and since this requires they learn to reason well as readers, writers, and thinkers, we will not credit flawed reasoning. We will only credit well-reasoned responses."

TO SUMMARIZE SOME OF OUR CRITICISMS OF THE CLAS APPROACH:

1) The overall conception fails to capture the practices of critical readers, writers, and thinkers the world over.

2) The overall conception does not call attention to definite and clear intellectual standards, and without them, it becomes impossible for both teacher and student to engage in "objective" assessment.

3) The overall conception does not provide an organized and systematic approach to posing, analyzing, and reasoning through problems embedded in everyday personal and professional reading and writing.

4) The teacher who takes this approach seriously will misteach reading and writing.

5) The student who learns through this approach will mislearn the art of reading and writing.

Given these failings, it is clear that the California Learning Assessment System falls into the category of pseudo critical thinking, and will not help students and teachers to develop their critical thinking abilities, but will hinder this process. Indeed, when classroom teachers receive copies, as they surely will, of test items, sample answers, commentary, and scores, they will use them as a guide for instruction. Thousands of school children will lose an opportunity to begin to become critical readers and writers. Thousands of school children will themselves learn to confuse recall with knowledge, subjective preference with reasoned judgment, irrational with rational persuasion. They will learn to use language vaguely and to think that their subjective pronouncements are not to be criticized. Their reasoning skills will remain abysmally low.

✦ Is The California Assessment Fiasco a Fluke?
The Educational Bureaucracy and Self-Deception

One of the most significant facts about the California language arts test fiasco is that *it is not a fluke*. But of course, *neither is it a plot* to undermine education. *The situation is worse than either.* As a fluke it could be corrected. As a plot the perpetrators could be severely dealt with when exposed. No, the pathetic side of the case is that there are systemic reasons why educational bureaucracies, framed as they are, will continue to generate just such fiascos regularly and predictably. And predictably, many will be taken in. Furthermore, because classroom teachers have emerged from a long-term training that reflects a similar background to that of the test designers, they also will fall easily into line with the flawed thinking passed down to them.

To deal with the problem at its roots, we must own the fact that there are significant problems in education due to its wide-spread and large-

> *One of the most significant facts about the California language arts test fiasco is that it is not a fluke. But of course, neither is it a plot to undermine education. The situation is worse than either.*

scale bureaucratization. Large-scale bureaucratization entails, or at least makes highly probable, a high degree of narrow specialization — and specialization tends to bring fragmentation, narrowness of vision, politicization, and self-deception in its wake. The fragmentation and narrowness of vision makes it difficult to effect fundamental changes because the parts do not work together in a rational way and no one sees clearly that this is so, since each element in the structure becomes an end in itself, to itself.

It is almost impossible for the most pressing problems of education to become "issues" in educational bureaucracies because the focus is inevitably on the political, the narrow, the fragmented part or parts. With each part serving itself as an ultimate end — including those on the top — the whole is left to take care of itself. No one is left responsible for it. The executive wing is also focused on itself and typically is satisfied with or driven to manufacture an illusion of serving the announced or official goals and ends. Meanwhile, the politicization and self-deception helps hide those realities most unpleasant to think about, and to have to face, and consequently those realities most in need of change.

This includes, of course, the most significant one today: the fact that modern American bureaucratic schooling is a system that preserves at its heart a mode of instruction that is a hold-over from the 19th Century and whose consistent effect is a superficial one. Most students in most classes most of the time are not actively engaged in learning what is worth learning. Most students are, on their side, not taking their education seriously. On the teaching side, they are not given challenging instruction. They are not engaged in genuine intellectual work. They are not developing intellectual standards or discipline. And, most assuredly, they are not learning to reason scientifically, mathematically, geographically, economically, sociologically, or morally. (See "Research Findings," p. 19.)

On the shoddy foundation of didactic instruction and passive, lower order learning, the rhetoric of high goals and ideals, the propaganda of the schools, is overlaid. Modern educational bureaucracy has developed

---

On the shoddy foundation of didactic instruction and passive, lower order learning, the rhetoric of high goals and ideals, the propaganda of the schools, is overlaid.

---

multiple ways to appear to be, and to appear to be doing, what it is not. In the K–12 domain especially, the history of education in the 20th Century is a triumph of propaganda and self-deception. This is documented in story after story of wave after wave of pseudo reform following pseudo reform, of new buzz words and new jargon replacing old buzz words and old jargon — each set of new words serving as a new mask to obscure the one-and-the-same consistent lower order face. (Cf "Critical Thinking in Historical Perspective chapter.) Unfortunately, virtually everyone in the game has a stake in making their playing of it look more honorable, more lofty, more noble and effective than it really is.

You may remember that it is only some three years now since every state in the union, through the massaging and manipulation of statistics by its own state department of education, proudly announced that its students had scored above the national average!!! This is the kind of self-serving propaganda and trickery that is the daily fare of educational reality.

State departments of education, as I have suggested, are a particularly interesting manifestation of the workings of the educational establishment. Each consists of huge bureaucracies, interlaced with committees that are in turn tied into networks of teachers and administrators spread across their states. The microcosm we analyzed in this chapter (the California State Department of Education's new English-Language Arts Assessment materials) is still officially in draft stage, but already is being highly touted as a refined, future-oriented, testing instrument. We've seen what the ELAA has done. Let's see what CLAS and the Department of Education says it has done. The test is being represented to the public and to teachers within the state and the nation as having,

The goal ... to evaluate students' capacities for insightful, productive thinking with tests that support the finest curriculum and instructional programs in the language arts ... [*California's Learning Assessment System*, CDE Publication]

The most important single component of the new assessment system will be the **statewide performance standards**, and the most important outcome of the assessment process will be the internalization of those standards in the thinking and work of teachers, students, and parents. The **performance standards will undergird all aspects of the educational enterprise; serving as the center of the seamless web of teaching, learning and assessment.** [*Some Principles and Beliefs about the Role of Assessment in California's School Reform Plan*, February 15, 1993, CDE]

Let's see what the legislature mandated, Senate Bill 662 (Hart):

Develop a system for producing **valid, reliable** individual scores and to develop and implement common statewide performance standards of student achievement as a basis for reporting all test results and setting targets for improvement.

It sounded simple enough but it provided us with a classic model of pseudo critical thinking in the educational establishment. The manner in which it is structured provides a textbook case. By mirrors, illusion, and

---

The result is that the most fundamental problem in education today — that students are not learning to reason well — is not only ignored, it is intensified.

---

standard self-deception, it creates the appearance of substantial change and reform. In fact, nothing is really being changed. The result is that the most fundamental problem in education today — that students are not learning to reason well — is not only ignored, it is intensified.

FRAGMENTATION AND VESTED INTERESTS

There are a number of reasons why it is unlikely that fundamental reforms will be effected by state departments of education or that this critique, by itself, will bring about fundamental change. In the first place, most of the positions within the state departments of education are for specialists, for example, positions for those specializing in nutrition, for those specializing in transportation, for those specializing in the laws regarding education, for those specializing in learning disorders, for those specializing in a and b and c and d and e and f and g. Virtually no one, however, has a responsibility directly connected to the fundamental goals of education (except possibly the director of instruction). Each specialist has his or her own special interest to focus on and a special group of stake-holders to represent.

When there is a need to develop an assessment instrument, like the one we examined of the California Department of Education, a large group of teachers and administrators from around the state are appointed. For example, there are 33 members of the CAP English-Language Arts committee. In addition to the main committee there is a supporting committee ("Reserve Team") consisting of 46 additional members. According to the California State Department: "These development team teachers have been responsible for shaping the test format, developing prompts for the assessment, and constructing scoring rubrics." (p. I-2)

Many political considerations go into the selection of the members of the development teams; most of the members, for example, are not scholars with publications that could be used as the basis of selection. There is an effort made to balance the committee by region, gender, race, and ethnicity. In addition, many members will have personal agendas to advance. There are usually three "Consultants/Advisors" selected from

The test becomes, then, both invalid and unreliable. In fact, it becomes a hot-bed of pseudo critical thinking, with a variety of misconceptions and flaws emerging. But while its intellectual value is low, its political value is high.

universities to bring in the over-arching theoretical framework. These consultants are usually the pipeline to the latest buzz words and to the theory behind them. The consultants concede to each other the right to get their favored terms into the language of the test materials.

The result of this process, as we have seen, is that the official "standards" embodied in the test become extraordinarily numerous. Many of them remain vague and ill-defined. Others take on a dangerous ambiguity. The diverse criteria and the open-ended nature of the directions combined with the ill-defined nature of the terms, opens the way to arbitrary and inconsistent grading of student responses. The test becomes, then, both invalid and unreliable. In fact, it becomes a hot-bed of pseudo critical thinking, with a variety of misconceptions and flaws emerging. But while its intellectual value is low, its political value is high. The various political interests around the state are served. The media has a simplistic event to cover. Parents can delight in the fact that the scores will go up. (How can they go down when anything can count as a good answer?) The politicians will gain because they can speak of their state as in the vanguard. And so it goes. A new pseudo reform is put in place and the educational bureaucracy grinds on until the next wave of public criticism requires it to generate a new and fresh illusion of change, a new catalogue of counterfeit, bogus, and superficial "reforms."

✦ So What Can We Do? Recommendations

There is a pressing need to develop networks of educators, parents, politicians, and business people who see the need for truly fundamental reform. That reform must be advanced simultaneously on many levels, for it is not going to result from action on one level alone. Because it must go to the roots of things, because it must be substantial, because it involves deep understandings, it must be incremental, evolutionary, and long-term. Everyone with the insight to see the problem comprehensively should act within the sphere of his or her greatest influence. There is a role for everyone concerned to exercise influence for the better: for parents, for public citizens, for business people, for civic leaders, for superintendents, for teachers, for college professors, and ... yes, even for those in state educational bureaucracies. Let us consider each briefly in turn.

WHAT CAN PARENTS DO?

Insightful parents can make the case for an emphasis on intellectual discipline and reasoning in the school curriculum. They can ask whether there is any long-term inservice in critical thinking and reasoning. They can ask what intellectual standards the students are being taught and how they are being taught them. They can make the case to other parents. They can write letters to the local papers. They can organize groups of parents who petition the school board. And most important they can develop a home environment in which the reasonability and intellectual discipline of their children is fostered, in which both they and their children routinely ask and give good reasons in support of their decisions and reason together about issues of importance not only to the family but to the broader society as well.

WHAT CAN CITIZENS DO?

Insightful public citizens can make the case for an emphasis on intellectual discipline and reasoning in the school curriculum in virtue of the need to develop voters who will help the country maintain a democratic form of government. They, too, can go to the local school board and ask whether there is any long-term inservice in critical thinking and reasoning. They, too, can make the case to parents and other citizens. They can contact civic groups. They can write letters to the local papers. They can organize groups of interested citizens to petition the school board.

WHAT CAN BUSINESS PEOPLE DO?

Insightful business people can use the respect that their success commands to exercise influence, alone or in concert with others, over educational decisions about what to teach and how to teach it. Since their success will be increasingly dependent upon their bringing critical thinking into the inner workings of their own businesses, on workers learning how to continually relearn and improve in their performances and in the systems they use, they will have ready access to models and paradigms that can be used to illuminate what should be happening in the classroom. Increasingly, cutting-edge businesses are moving away from an emphasis on hierarchy to an emphasis on group problem solving. Since critical thinking is essential to effective group problem solving, progressive business people will be able to talk intelligibly with educators and other citizens about how problem solving structures function in business and how parallel classroom problem solving groups might be set up. And, certainly, there are any number of civic groups that business people with insight might address on the problem of educational reform, putting emphasis, of course, on the missing foundation: the failure of teachers to learn how to think critically themselves and to teach for that thinking in their instruction, the failure to focus education, in other words, on "carefully-reasoned" problem solving. Finally, insightful business people can form alliances with insightful educators, to create symbiotic, reflective, mutually useful dialogues on what each group can learn from the other and how each can profit by working together.

WHAT CAN CIVIC LEADERS DO?

Insightful civic leaders can draw public attention to the need for intellectual discipline and reasoning in instruction. They can articulate publicly the key links to developing responsible citizens, moral persons, and workers on the cutting edge of development. They can use their access to a more public forum by focusing the discussion of educational reform on the historical problem of the educational bureaucracy and its tendency to generate pseudo reform. They can create a public awareness of the importance of reasoning, critical thinking, and problem solving. They can help organize civic groups. They can use their superior access to other persons of leadership and influence to facilitate significant pressure on the educational bureaucracies. They can make contact with insightful and responsible politicians who are in a position to facilitate appropriate legislation.

WHAT CAN SUPERINTENDENTS DO?

Insightful superintendents can make the case for an emphasis on intellectual discipline and reasoning in the school curriculum to the school board, administration members, teachers, and parents. They can ensure that there is long-term inservice in critical thinking and reasoning. They can ensure that students are being taught intellectual standards in depth. They can create incentives to teachers motivated to move in this direction. They can make the case to civic groups. Most importantly they can model reasonability and help create an atmosphere conducive to making the school a network of communities of inquiry.

WHAT CAN TEACHERS DO?

Insightful teachers can make the case for an emphasis on intellectual discipline and reasoning in the school curriculum. They can request and help design long-term inservice in critical thinking and reasoning. They can bring intellectual standards into the classroom. They can make the case to parents. They can work with other teachers to foster a school environment in which reasonability and intellectual discipline are accepted school norms. Most importantly, they can routinely ask for and give good reasons in the classroom. They can foster student reasoning in history, science, math, and so forth. They can ensure that students must regularly assess their own work using intellectual standards.

WHAT CAN COLLEGE PROFESSORS DO?

Insightful college professors can make the case for an emphasis on intellectual discipline and reasoning in the college curriculum. They can request and help design long-term faculty development in critical thinking and reasoning. They can bring intellectual standards into the classroom. They can do research on the significance of critical thinking and reasoning in their discipline. They can work with schools and departments of education to ensure that those studying to become teachers take classes that require reasoning and disciplined thought. They can articulate the need for prospective teachers to learn how to design assignments that require reasoning and critical thinking. Most importantly, they can routinely foster reasoning in their own classrooms and ensure that their students must regularly assess their own work using intellectual standards.

WHAT CAN THOSE IN STATE-WIDE BUREAUCRACIES DO?

Insightful members of state-wide bureaucracies (who recognize the systemic ways that educational bureaucracies have fostered pseudo reforms and constructed ill-designed assessments) can play a number of significant roles. They can inform themselves and others they work with of the fundamental changes that are being made in businesses adopting structures contrary to those of traditional bureaucratic organization. They can foster movement toward problem-solving teams. They can raise broader and deeper issues. They can recommend hiring people with broader vision and more developed reasoning abilities. They can help to work against narrow specialization. At the same time, they can argue for more appropriate use of experts, so that those who lack expertise in a subject will not become, for example, principal designers in tests or assessment instruments in that subject. They can argue for the construction of assessment instruments that assess reasoning in every subject area and so help to integrate emphases across subject areas.

CAVEAT

Doubtless you noticed my emphasis on "insightful" in characterizing those who can make important contributions to reform. It is important to underscore the problem of pseudo reform, which emerges when well-meaning persons use their intelligence inadvertently to re-duplicate an old problem in new form, creating the illusion of change. Many persons today are unwilling to think through the implications of accelerating change and intensifying complexity. Many are subconsciously wedded to rigid ideas and a static way of thinking. Many are taken in by their own platitudes and high-sounding words. These facts guarantee that a long struggle will be required to work through the superficial and work into the substantial.

✦ Final Conclusion

Pseudo critical thinking is more or less inevitable in the educational bureaucracies, given the way we have traditionally arranged and ordered things. This is illustrated, as we have seen, in the way the American educational establishment goes about designing assessment. Unfortunately, faulty assessment leads to faulty teaching, which leads to more faulty thinking in society, in business, in politics, and in everyday social life. The California Department of Education is a model case of American educational bureaucracy at work and the new California reading and writing assessment instrument is the typical resultant bad practice. Good thinking is now a fundamental human need. And though it will take generations to fully evolve from a society in which pseudo critical thinking is dominant to one in which sound, fairminded, ethically-informed reasoning is dominant, every step in that direction will reduce the amount of suffering and injustice that exists and increase, by degrees, human well being and quality of life. It is our intellectual and moral responsibility to make some contribution to this evolution. Though we are only at the beginnings of this evolution, the irresistible dynamic of accelerating change and intensifying complexity will eventually force it upon us. I hope we learn our lessons sooner rather than later, that the price of waste and unnecessary human misery may be as little as possible.

✦ References

All of the references in this chapter (unless otherwise noted) are from the *Samplers for English Language Arts Assessment,* for Elementary and High School, disseminated statewide in the Spring, 1993, by the California Department of Education.

Chapter 5

Critical Thinking:
Basic Questions and Answers

Abstract

In this interview for Think *magazine (April '92), Richard Paul provides a quick overview of critical thinking and the issues surrounding it: defining it, common mistakes in assessing it, its relation to communication skills, self-esteem, collaborative learning, motivation, curiosity, job skills for the future, national standards, and assessment strategies.*

Question: Critical thinking is essential to effective learning and productive living. Would you share your definition of critical thinking?

Paul: First, since critical thinking can be defined in a number of different ways consistent with each other, we should not put a lot of weight on any one definition. Definitions are at best scaffolding for the mind. With this qualification in mind, here is a bit of scaffolding: critical thinking is thinking about your thinking while you're thinking in order to make your thinking better. Two things are crucial: *1)* critical thinking is not just thinking, but thinking which entails self-improvement and *2)* this improvement comes from skill in using standards by which one appropriately assesses thinking. To put it briefly, it is self-improvement (in thinking) through standards (that assess thinking).

To think well is to impose discipline and restraint on our thinking — by means of intellectual standards — in order to raise our thinking to a level of "perfection" or quality that is not natural or likely in undisciplined, spontaneous thought. The dimension of critical thinking least understood is that of intellectual standards. Most teachers were not taught how to assess thinking through standards; indeed, often the thinking of teachers themselves is very "undisciplined" and reflects a lack of internalized intellectual standards.

Question: Could you give me an example?

Paul: Certainly, one of the most important distinctions that teachers need to routinely make, and which takes disciplined thinking to

make, is that between reasoning and subjective reaction. If we are trying to foster quality thinking, we don't want students simply to assert
things; we want them to try to reason things out on the basis of evidence and good reasons. Often, teachers are unclear about this basic
difference. Many teachers are apt to take student writing or speech
which is fluent and witty or glib and amusing as good thinking. They
are often unclear about the constituents of good reasoning. Hence,
even though a student may just be asserting things, not reasoning
things out at all, if she is doing so with vivacity and flamboyance,
teachers are apt to take this to be equivalent to good reasoning. This
was made clear in a recent California state-wide writing assessment in
which teachers and testers applauded a student essay, which they said
illustrated "exceptional achievement" in reasoned evaluation, an
essay that contained no reasoning at all, that was nothing more than
one subjective reaction after another.

The assessing teachers and testers did not notice that the student failed
to respond to the directions, did not support his judgment with reasons and evidence, did not consider possible criteria on which to base
his judgment, did not analyze the subject in the light of the criteria,
and did not select evidence that clearly supported his judgment.
Instead the student 1) described an emotional exchange, 2) asserted —
without evidence — some questionable claims, and 3) expressed a variety of subjective preferences. The assessing teachers were apparently
not clear enough about the nature of evaluative reasoning or the basic
notions of criteria, evidence, reasons, and well-supported judgment to
notice the discrepancy. The result was, by the way, that a flagrantly
mis-graded student essay was showcased nationally (in ASCD's *Developing Minds*), systematically misleading the 150,000 or so teachers who
read the publication.

Question: Could this possibly be a rare mistake, not representative of
teacher knowledge?

Paul: I don't think so. Let me suggest a way in which you could begin to
test my contention. If you are familiar with any thinking skills
programs, ask someone knowledgeable about it the "Where's the beef?"
question, namely, "What intellectual standards does the program articulate and teach?" I think you will first find that the person is puzzled
about what you mean. And then when you explain what you mean, I
think you will find that the person is not able to articulate any such
standards. Thinking skills programs without intellectual standards are
tailor-made for mis-instruction. For example, one of the major programs asks teachers to encourage students to make inferences and use
analogies, but is silent about how to teach students to assess the inferences they make and the strengths and weaknesses of the analogies

they use. This misses the point. The idea is not to help students to make *more* inferences but to make *sound* ones, not to help students to come up with *more* analogies but with more *useful* and *insightful* ones.

Question: What is the solution to this problem? How, as a practical matter, can we solve it?

Paul: Well, not with more gimmicks or quick-fixes. Not with more fluff for teachers. Only with quality long-term staff development that helps the teachers, over an extended period of time, over years not months, to work on their own thinking and come to terms with what intellectual standards are, why they are essential, and how to teach for them. The city of Greensboro, North Carolina has just such a long-term, quality, critical thinking program. [See, "The Greensboro Plan: A Sample Staff Development Plan", p. 409.] So that's one model your readers might look at. In addition, there is a new national organization, the National Council for Excellence in Critical Thinking Instruction, that is focused precisely on the articulation of standards for thinking, not just in general, but for every academic subject area. It is now setting up research-based committees and regional offices to disseminate its recommendations. I am hopeful that eventually, through efforts such as these, we can move from the superficial to the substantial in fostering quality student thinking. The present level of instruction for thinking is very low indeed.

Question: But there are many areas of concern in instruction, not just one, not just critical thinking, but communication skills, problem solving, creative thinking, collaborative learning, self-esteem, and so forth. How are districts to deal with the full array of needs? How are they to do all of these rather than simply one, no matter how important that one may be?

Paul: This is the key. Everything essential to education supports everything else essential to education. It is only when good things in education are viewed superficially and wrongly that they seem disconnected, a bunch of separate goals, a conglomeration of separate problems, like so many bee-bees in a bag. In fact, any well-conceived program in critical thinking requires the integration of all of the skills and abilities you mentioned above. Hence, critical thinking is not a set of skills separable from excellence in communication, problem solving, creative thinking, or collaborative learning, nor is it indifferent to one's sense of self-worth.

Question: Could you explain briefly why this is so?

Paul: Consider critical thinking first. We think critically when we have at least one problem to solve. One is not doing good critical thinking, therefore, if one is not solving any problems. If there is no problem there is no point in thinking critically. The "opposite" is also true. Uncritical problem solving is unintelligible. There is no way to effectively solve problems unless one thinks critically about the nature of the problems and of how to go about solving them. Thinking our way through a problem to a solution, then, is critical thinking, not something else. Furthermore, critical thinking, because it involves our working out afresh our own thinking on a subject, and because our own thinking is always a unique product of our self-structured experience, ideas, and reasoning, is intrinsically a new "creation", a new "making", a new set of cognitive and affective structures of some kind. All thinking, in short, is a creation of the mind's work, and when it is disciplined so as to be well-integrated into our experience, it is a new creation precisely because of the inevitable novelty of that integration. And when it helps us to solve problems that we could not solve before, it is surely properly called "creative".

The "making" and the "testing of that making" are intimately interconnected. In critical thinking we make and shape ideas and experiences so that they may be used to structure and solve problems, frame decisions, and, as the case may be, effectively communicate with others. The making, shaping, testing, structuring, solving, and communicating are not different activities of a fragmented mind but the same seamless whole viewed from different perspectives.

Question: How do communication skills fit in?

Paul: Some communication is surface communication, trivial communication — surface and trivial communication don't really require education. All of us can engage in small talk, can share gossip. And we don't require any intricate skills to do that fairly well. Where communication becomes part of our educational goal is in reading, writing, speaking and listening. These are the four modalities of communication which are essential to education and each of them is a mode of reasoning. Each of them involves problems. Each of them is shot through with critical thinking needs. Take the apparently simple matter of reading a book worth reading. The author has developed her thinking in the book, has taken some ideas and in some way represented those ideas in extended form. Our job as a reader is to translate the meaning of the author into meanings that we can understand. This is a complicated process requiring critical thinking every step along the way. What is the purpose for the book? What is the author trying to accomplish? What issues or problems are raised? What data, what experiences, what evidence are given? What concepts are used to organize this data, these experiences? How is the author thinking about the world? Is her thinking justified as far as we can see from our perspective? And how does she justify it from her perspective? How can we enter her perspective to appreciate what she has to say? All of these are the kinds of questions that a critical reader raises. And a critical reader in this sense is simply someone trying to come to terms with the text.

So if one is an uncritical reader, writer, speaker, or listener, one is not a good reader, writer, speaker, or listener at all. To do any of these well is to think critically while doing so and, at one and the same time, to solve specific problems of communication, hence to effectively communicate. Communication, in short, is always a transaction between at least two logics. In reading, as I have said, there is the logic of the thinking of the author and the logic of the thinking of the reader. The critical reader reconstructs (and so translates) the logic of the writer into the logic of the reader's thinking and experience. This entails disciplined intellectual work. The end result is a new creation; the writer's thinking for the first time now exists within the reader's mind. No mean feat!

Question: And self esteem? How does it fit in?

Paul: Healthy self-esteem emerges from a justified sense of self-worth, just as self-worth emerges from competence, ability, and genuine success. If one simply feels good about oneself for no good reason, then one is either arrogant (which is surely not desirable), or, alternatively, has a dangerous sense of misplaced confidence. Teenagers, for example, sometimes think so well of themselves that they operate under the illusion that they can safely drive while drunk or safely take drugs. They often feel much too highly of their own competence and powers and are much too unaware of their limitations. To accurately sort out genuine self-worth from a false sense of self-esteem requires, yes you guessed it, critical thinking.

Question: And finally, what about collaborative learning? How does it fit in?

Paul: Collaborative learning is desirable only if grounded in disciplined critical thinking. Without critical thinking, collaborative learning is likely to become collaborative mis-learning. It is collective bad thinking in which the bad thinking being shared becomes validated. Remember, gossip is a form of collaborative learning; peer group indoctrination is a form of collaborative learning; mass hysteria is a form of speed collaborative learning (mass learning of a most undesirable kind). We learn prejudices collaboratively, social hates and fears collaboratively, stereotypes and narrowness of mind, collaboratively. If we don't put disciplined critical thinking into the heart and soul of the collaboration, we get the mode of collaboration which is antithetical to education, knowledge, and insight.

So there are a lot of important educational goals deeply tied into critical thinking just as critical thinking is deeply tied into them. Basically the problem in the schools is that we separate things, treat them in isolation and mistreat them as a result. We end up with a superficial representation, then, of each of the individual things that is essential to education, rather than seeing how each important good thing helps inform all the others.

Question: One important aim of schooling should be to create a climate that evokes children's sense of wonder and inspires their imagination to soar. What can teachers do to "kindle" this spark and keep it alive in education?

Paul: First of all, we kill the child's curiosity, her desire to question deeply, by superficial didactic instruction. Young children continually ask why. Why this and why that? And why this other thing? But we soon shut that curiosity down with glib answers, answers to fend off rather than respond to the logic of the question. In every field of knowledge, every answer generates more questions, so that the more we know the more we recognize we don't know. It is only people who have little knowledge who take their knowledge to be complete and entire. If we thought deeply about almost any of the answers which we glibly give to children, we would recognize that we don't really have a satisfactory answer to most of their questions. Many of our answers are no more than a repetition of what we as children heard from adults. We pass on the misconceptions of our parents and those of their parents. We say what we heard, not what we know. We rarely join the quest with our children. We rarely admit our ignorance, even to ourselves. Why does rain fall from the sky? Why is snow cold? What is electricity and how does it go through the wire? Why are people bad? Why does evil exist? Why is there war? Why did my dog have to die? Why do flowers bloom? Do we really have good answers to these questions?

Question: How does curiosity fit in with critical thinking?

Paul: To flourish, curiosity must evolve into disciplined inquiry and reflection. Left to itself it will soar like a kite without a tail, that is, right into the ground! Intellectual curiosity is an important trait of mind, but it requires a family of other traits to fulfill it. It requires intellectual humility, intellectual courage, intellectual integrity, intellectual perseverance, and faith in reason. After all, intellectual curiosity is not a thing in itself — valuable in itself and for itself. It is valuable because it can lead to knowledge, understanding, and insight, because it can help broaden, deepen, sharpen our minds, making us better, more humane, more richly endowed persons. To reach these ends, the mind must be more than curious, it must be willing to work, willing to suffer through confusion and frustration, willing to face limitations and overcome obstacles, open to the views of others, and willing to entertain ideas that many people find threatening. That is, there is no point in our trying to model and encourage curiosity, if we are not willing to foster an environment in which the minds of our students can learn the value and pain of hard intellectual work. We do our students a disservice if we imply that all we need is unbridled curiosity, that with it alone knowledge comes to us with blissful ease in an atmosphere of fun, fun, fun. What good is curiosity if we don't know what to do next, how to satisfy it? We can create the environment necessary to the discipline, power, joy, and work of critical thinking only by modeling it before and with our students. They must see our minds at work. Our minds must stimulate theirs' with questions and yet further question, questions that probe information and experience, questions that call for reasons and evidence, questions that lead students to examine interpretations and conclusions, pursuing their basis in fact and experience, questions that help students to discover their assumptions, questions that stimulate students to follow out the implications of their thought, to test their ideas, to take their ideas apart, to challenge their ideas, to take their ideas seriously. It is in the totality of this intellectually rigorous atmosphere that natural curiosity thrives.

Question: It is important for our students to be productive members of the work-force. How can schools better prepare students to meet these challenges?

Paul: The fundamental characteristic of the world students now enter is ever-accelerating change, a world in which information is multiplying even as it is swiftly becoming obsolete and out of date, a world in which ideas are continually restructured, retested, and rethought, where one cannot survive with simply one way of thinking, where one must continually adapt one's thinking to the thinking of others, where one must respect the need for accuracy and precision and meticulousness, a world in which job skills must continually be upgraded and perfected — even transformed. We have never had to face such a world before. Education has never before had to prepare students for such dynamic flux, unpredictability, and complexity, for such ferment, tumult, and disarray. We as educators are now on the firing line. Are we willing to fundamentally rethink our methods of teaching? Are we ready for the 21st Century? Are we willing to learn new concepts and ideas? Are we willing to learn a new sense of discipline as we teach it to our students? Are we willing to bring new rigor to our own thinking in order to help our students bring that same rigor to theirs? Are we willing, in short, to become critical thinkers so that we might be an example of what our students must internalize and become?

These are profound challenges to the profession. They call upon us to do what no previous generation of teachers was ever called upon to do. Those of us willing to pay the price will yet have to teach side by side with teachers unwilling to pay the price. This will make our job even more difficult, but not less exciting, not less important, not less rewarding. Critical thinking is the heart of well-conceived educational reform and restructuring because it is at the heart of the changes of the 21st Century. Let us hope that enough of us will have the fortitude and vision to grasp this reality and transform our lives and our schools accordingly.

Question: National Standards will result in national accountability. What is your vision for the future?

Paul: Most of the national assessment we have done thus far is based on lower-order learning and thinking. It has focused on what might be called surface knowledge. It has rewarded the kind of thinking that lends itself to multiple choice machine-graded assessment. We now recognize that the assessment of the future must focus on higher – not lower – order thinking, that it must assess more reasoning than recall, that it must assess authentic performances, students engaged in bona fide intellectual work.

Our problem is in designing and implementing such assessment. In November of this last year, Gerald Nosich and I developed and presented, at the request of the U.S. Department of Education, a model for the national assessment of higher order thinking. [Included as Chapter 6, p. 103.] At a follow-up meeting of critical thinking, problem-solving, communication, and testing scholars and practitioners, it was almost unanimously agreed that it is possible to assess higher-order thinking on a national scale. It was clear from the commitments of the Departments of Education, Labor, and Commerce that such an assessment is in the cards. [See figure 1, "Today's and Tomorrow's Schools".]

Today's and Tomorrow's Schools

Schools of Today	Schools of Tomorrow
• Focus on development of basic skills	• Focus on development of thinking skills
• Testing separate from teaching	• Assessment integral to teaching
• Students work as individuals	• Cooperative problem solving
• Hierarchically sequenced — basics before higher order	• Skills learned in context of real problems
• Supervision by administration	• Learner-centered, teacher-directed
• Elite students learn to think	• All students learn to think

figure 1   From "What Work Requires of Schools" *A Scans Report for America 2000,* The Secretary's Commission on Achieving Necessary Skills, U.S. Department of Labor, June 1991

The fact is we must have standards and assessment strategies for high-er-order thinking for a number of reasons. First, assessment and accountability are here to stay. The public will not accept less. Second, what is not assessed is not, on the whole, taught. Third, what is mis-assessed is mis-taught. Fourth, higher-order thinking, critical thinking abilities, are increasingly crucial to success in every domain of personal and professional life. Fifth, critical thinking research is making the cul-tivation and assessment of higher-order thinking do-able.

The road will not be easy, but if we take the knowledge, understanding, and insights we have gained about critical thinking over the last twelve years, there is much that we could do in assessment that we haven't yet done — at the level of the individual classroom teacher, at the level of the school system, at the level of the state, and at the national level. Of course we want to do this in such a way as not to commit the "Harvard Fallacy", the mistaken notion that because graduates from Harvard are very successful, that the teaching at Harvard necessarily had something to do with it. It may be that the best prepared and well-connected stu-dents coming out of high school are going to end up as the best who graduate from college, no matter what college they attend. We need to focus our assessment, in other words, on how much value has been added by an institution. We need to know where students stood at the beginning, to assess the instruction they received on their way from the beginning to the end. We need pre- and post-testing and assess-ment in order to see which schools, which institutions, which districts are really adding value, and *significant* value, to the quality of thinking and learning of their students.

Finally, we have to realize that we already have instruments available for assessing what might be called the fine-textured micro-skills of crit-ical thinking. We already know how to design prompts that test stu-dents' ability to: identify a plausible statement of a writer's purpose; distinguish clearly between purposes, inferences, assumptions, and consequences; discuss reasonably the merits of different versions of a problem or question; decide the most reasonable statement of an author's point of view; recognize bias, narrowness, and contradictions in the point of view of an excerpt; distinguish evidence from conclu-sions based on that evidence; give evidence to back up their positions in an essay; recognize conclusions that go beyond the evidence; distin-guish central from peripheral concepts; identify crucial implications of a passage; evaluate an author's inferences; draw reasonable inferences from positions stated; and so on.

With respect to intellectual standards, we are quite able to design prompts that require students to: recognize clarity in contrast to unclar-ity; distinguish accurate from inaccurate accounts; decide when a state-ment is relevant or irrelevant to a given point; identify inconsistent positions as well as consistent ones; discriminate deep, complete, and significant accounts from those that are superficial, fragmentary, and trivial; evaluate responses with respect to their fairness; distinguish well-evidenced accounts from those unsupported by reasons and evidence; tell good reasons from bad.

With respect to large scale essay assessment we know enough now about random sampling to be able to require extended reasoning and writing without having to pay for the individual assessment of millions of essays.

What remains is to put what we know into action: at the school and district level to facilitate long-term teacher development around higher-order thinking, at the state and national level to provide for long-term assessment of district, state, and national performance. The project will take generations and perhaps in some sense will never end. After all, when will we have developed our thinking far enough, when will we have enough intellectual integrity, enough intellectual courage, enough intellectual perseverance, enough intellectual skill and ability, enough fairmindedness, enough reasonability? One thing is painfully clear. We already have more than enough rote memorization and uninspired didactic teaching, more than enough passivity and indifference, cynicism and defeatism, complacency and ineptness. The ball is in our court. Let's take up the challenge together and make, with our students, a new and better world.

Section II

Intellectual Standards and Assessment:
The Foundation for Critical Thought

*A Model for the National Assessment of
Higher Order Thinking*

*Using Intellectual Standards to Assess
Student Reasoning*

*Why Students — and Teachers — Don't
Reason Well*

Chapter 6

A Model for the
National Assessment of
Higher Order Thinking

with Gerald M. Nosich

Abstract
This paper, co-authored by Richard Paul and Gerald Nosich, was commissioned by the United States Department of Education, Office of Educational Research and Improvement of the National Center for Education Statistics. It provides exactly what its title implies: a model for the national assessment of higher order thinking. The paper consists of a preface and five main sections.

The preface delineates the problem of lower order learning, summarizes the state of research into critical thinking and educational reform, and explains the five-part structure of the paper. The first main section of the paper states and explicates 21 criteria for higher order thinking assessment. The second section makes the case for how a "rich, substantive concept of critical thinking" meets those criteria. In making this case, Paul and Nosich spell out the dangers of a non-substantive concept of critical thinking. The third section of the paper spells out four domains of critical thinking: elements of thought, abilities, affective dimensions, and intellectual standards. The fourth section of the paper makes substantive recommendations regarding how to assess the various domains of critical thinking, the test strategies that may be used, the value of the proposed strategy for the reform of education, and the suggested implementation of the proposal.

✦✦ Preface: The Problem of Lower Order Learning

*V*irtually all informed commentators agree that schooling today does not foster the "higher order thinking skills and abilities" which represent the "basics" of the future. America 2000, President Bush's education initiative, seeks to bring schooling in line with changing global and economic conditions, to engender sweeping educational reform in what are now admittedly largely static institutions, systems highly resistant to substantial change. America 2000 raises the following vital question: "How can we reverse the pervasive emphasis in education on lower rather than on higher order learning, on recall rather than on reasoning, on students merely 'reproducing' rather than 'producing' knowledge?"

The state of research regarding this problem was summarized recently by Mary Kennedy in an article for the Kappan:

> ...national assessments in virtually every subject indicate that, although our students can perform basic skills pretty well, they are not doing well on thinking and reasoning. American students can compute, but they cannot reason.... They can write complete and correct sentences, but they cannot prepare arguments.... Moreover, in international comparisons, American students are falling behind ... particularly in those areas that require higher order thinking.... Our students are not doing well at thinking, reasoning, analyzing, predicting, estimating, or problem solving.

In this summary, Dr. Kennedy linked the problem to the established mode of instruction:

> ...teachers are highly likely to teach in the way they themselves were taught. If your elementary teacher presented mathematics to you as a set of procedural rules with no substantive rationale, then you are likely to think that this is what mathematics is and that this is how mathematics should be studied. And you are likely to teach it in this way. If you studied writing as a set of grammatical rules rather than as a way to organize your thoughts and to communicate ideas to others, then this is what you will think writing is, and you will probably teach it so.... By the time we complete our undergraduate education, we have observed teachers for up to 3,060 days.

Though not as commonly realized, this problem of the dominance of lower order learning is as serious in post-secondary as it is in primary and secondary education. In both undergraduate and graduate programs students are typically enrolled in content heavy courses taught by professors who feel a greater obligation to cover subject matter through lecture than to generate thought-provoking activities or assignments that may seriously reduce what they can cover or significantly add to their work load, or both.

Alan Schoenfeld has explored this problem with respect to both pre-secondary and post-secondary mathematics instruction. To illustrate the detailed nature of what Schoenfeld's research is disclosing, here is a summary from one of his studies:

> At the University of Rochester 85% of the freshman class takes calculus, and many go on ... [but] most of these students will never apply calculus in any meaningful way (if at all) in their studies, or in their lives. They complete their studies with the impression that they know some very sophisticated and high-powered mathemat-

ics. They can find the maxima of complicated functions, determine exponential decay, compute the volumes of surfaces of revolution, and so on. But the fact is that these students know barely anything at all. The only reason they can perform with any degree of competency on their final exams is that the problems on the exams are nearly carbon copies of problems they have seen before; the students are not being asked to think, but merely to apply well-rehearsed schemata for specific kinds of tasks. Tim Keiter and I studied students' abilities to deal with pre-calculus versions of elementary word problems.... We were not surprised to discover that only 19 of 120 attempts at such problems ... yielded correct answers, or that only 65 attempts produced answers of any kind.

Schoenfeld summarizes the results, in general, of research into mathematics instruction as follows:

In sum: all too often we focus on a narrow collection of well-defined tasks and train students to execute those tasks in a routine, if not algorithmic fashion. Then we test the students on tasks that are very close to the ones they have been taught. If they succeed on those problems, we and they congratulate each other on the fact that they have learned some powerful mathematical techniques. In fact, they may be able to use such techniques mechanically while lacking some rudimentary thinking skills. To allow them, and ourselves, to believe that they 'understand' the mathematics is deceptive and fraudulent.

There is good reason, in our view, to link instructional reform with the need for a special emphasis on critical thinking, problem solving, and communication skills, for it is precisely these higher order thinking skills that are routinely sacrificed when coverage and lower order recall dominate the classroom at either the pre- or post-secondary level, as they now do.

✦ The State of Research into Critical Thinking and Instructional Reform

One major value of the last ten years of research into critical thinking is the focus on the need for reform of instruction at all levels: on the need for students to reason mathematically in mathematics courses, to reason historically in history courses, to reason scientifically in science courses, to reason sociologically in sociology courses. Indeed, critical thinking research has emphasized three basic needs for all learning: for all students to reason out all basic concepts and understandings, to reason to all basic conclusions and solutions, and to reason through and across the curriculum.

This emphasis has been embedded in the structure of the 11 major international conferences on research into critical thinking and educational reform (1980–1991) held at Sonoma State University. The 1991

Conference attracted 1400 registrants from 20 countries and featured over 300 sessions representative of education from kindergarten through graduate school. This same emphasis is reflected in the 25 or so other conferences focused on critical thinking in the last ten years (at Harvard, the University of Chicago, Montclair State, Oakton College, and elsewhere) and in most of the articles published concerning critical thinking.

What is more, the research into critical thinking has focused not only on the cultivation of reasoning in all subjects and at all educational levels, but also on generalizable standards for the assessment of reasoning as well. The concepts and distinctions embedded in critical thinking research are, as a result, well-suited for the design of a process to assess higher order thinking. In this paper, we shall set out both the conceptual foundations for such a process as well as a viable model for carrying out that process.

Before we spell out the detailed structure of this paper, however, it is important to note that the concept of critical thinking has not played a central role in the design of educational assessment instruments to date, principally because the concept has been developed extensively only over the last ten years, and therefore has not had time to permeate already developed assessment tools. Now that we possess a rich, substantive concept, however, we have an unprecedented opportunity to assess central rather than peripheral aspects of critical thinking, and to do so in an authentic and representative way. If anything less than this concept and its central aspects is assessed, the ultimate goal of fostering higher order thinking as an academic, social, and vocational need will be ill served.

✦ The Structure of the Paper

The substance of this paper is divided into four sections, each focused on a major question, as follows:

Section One: What should be the main objectives of a process to assess higher order thinking?

Section Two: How does a rich, substantive concept of critical thinking meet these criteria?

    a) What is included in a rich, substantive concept of critical thinking?

    b) How, specifically, does this concept meet the criteria?

    c) What, specifically, are the dangers of a non-substantive concept of critical thinking?

Section Three: What are the four component domains of critical thinking and the implications of each of these domains for the assessment of higher order thinking?

Section Four: What is the most workable solution to the design of a process to assess higher order thinking, given the findings in the three sections above?

The first section of the paper formulates 21 objectives that should be met by any process adequate to the task. The second outlines the basic concept of critical thinking which informs the paper and explains how a rich, substantive concept of critical thinking, grounded in the research on critical thinking, provides a plausible foundation for accomplishing these objectives. The third section of the paper explicates the four domains essential to critical thinking:

A) The *Elements of Thought* (eight essential dimensions of all reasoning crucial for understanding and assessing reasoning),

B) *Abilities* (basic modes of reasoning — including reading, writing, speaking, and listening — that represent modal "orchestrations" of the elements of thought),

C) *Traits of Mind* (the affective dimensions without which critical thinking skills are merely episodically used, and often in a limiting rather than an expansive manner), and

D) *Universal Intellectual Standards* (presupposed by critical thinking).

As we give a brief explication of the elements of thought, the abilities, essential traits of mind, and intellectual standards, we briefly comment on the implications for assessment purposes of each conception.

In the fourth and final section of the paper, we lay out our recommendations for a process and a time-table for assessing higher order thinking.

✦✦ *Section One: Objectives*

What should be the main objectives of a process to assess higher order thinking?

1) It should assess students' skills and abilities in analyzing, synthesizing, applying, and evaluating information.

2) It should concentrate on thinking skills that can be employed with maximum flexibility, in a wide variety of subjects, situations, contexts, and educational levels.

3) It should account for both the important differences among subjects and the skills, processes, and affective dispositions that are crucial to all the subjects.

4) It should focus on fundamental, enduring forms of intellectual ability that are both fitted to the accelerating pace of change and deeply embedded in the history of the advancement of the disciplines.

5) It should readily lead to the improvement of instruction.

6) It should make clear the inter-connectedness of our knowledge and abilities, and why expertise in one area cannot be divorced either from findings in other areas or from a sensitivity to the need for interdisciplinary integration.

7) It should assess those versatile and fundamental skills that are essential to being a responsible, decision-making member of the work-place.

8) It should be based on clear concepts and have well-thought-out, rationally articulated goals, criteria, and standards.

9) It should account for the integration of communication skills, problem-solving, and critical thinking, and it should assess all of them without compromising essential features of any of them.

10) It should respect cultural diversity by focusing on the common-core skills, abilities, and traits useful in all cultures.

11) It should test for thinking that is empowering and that, when incorporated into instruction, promotes (to quote the September, 1991 Kappan) "the active engagement of students in constructing their own knowledge and understanding."

12) It should concentrate on assessing the fundamental cognitive structures of communication, for example:

with reading and listening, the ability to

- create an accurate interpretation,
- assess the author's or speaker's purpose,
- accurately identify the question-at-issue or problem being discussed,
- accurately identify basic concepts at the heart of what is said or written,
- see significant implications of the advocated position,
- identify, understand, and evaluate the assumptions underlying someone's position,
- recognize evidence, argument, inference (or their lack) in oral and written presentations,
- reasonably assess the credibility of an author or speaker,
- accurately grasp the point of view of the author or speaker,
- empathetically reason within the point of view of the author or speaker.

with writing and speaking, the ability to

- identify and explicate one's own point of view and its implications,

- be clear about and communicate clearly, in either spoken or written form, the problem one is addressing,

- be clear about what one is assuming, presupposing, or taking for granted,

- present one's position precisely, accurately, completely, and give relevant, logical, and fair arguments for it,

- cite relevant evidence and experiences to support one's position,

- see, formulate, and take account of alternative positions and opposing points of view, recognizing and evaluating evidence and key assumptions on both sides,

- illustrate one's central concepts with significant examples and show how they apply in real situations,

- empathetically entertain strong objections from points of view other than one's own.

13) It should assess the skills, abilities, and attitudes that are central to making sound decisions and acting on them in the context of learning to understand our rights and responsibilities as citizens, as well-informed and thinking consumers, and as participants in a symbiotic world economy.

14) It should avoid any reductionism that allows a multi-faceted, theoretically complex, and authentically usable body of abilities and dispositions to be assessed by means of oversimplified parts that do not adequately reflect the whole.

15) It should enable educators to see what kinds of skills are basic for the future.

16) It should be of a kind that will assess valuable skills applied to genuine problems as seen by a large body of the populace, both inside and outside of the educational community.

17) It should include items that assess both the skills of thoughtfully choosing the most reasonable answer to a problem from among a pre-selected set and the skills of formulating the problem itself and of making the initial selection of relevant alternatives.

18) It should contain items that, as much as possible, are examples of the real-life problems and issues that people will have to think out and act upon.

19) It should be affordable.

20) It should enable school districts and educators to assess the gains they are making in teaching higher order thinking.

21) It should provide for a measure of achievement against national standards.

✦✦ Section Two: Critical Thinking and Criteria for Assessment

✦ What Is Included in a Rich, Substantive Concept of Critical Thinking?

Most of the language we shall use is drawn from draft statements of the *National Council for Excellence in Critical Thinking Instruction*. The National Council has been established precisely to articulate standards in critical thinking by 50 key leaders in critical thinking research and 105 leading educators. It is in the process of establishing regional offices and setting up 75 research-based committees to articulate the state of research in the field.

NATIONAL COUNCIL DEFINITION

Critical thinking is the intellectually disciplined process of actively and skillfully conceptualizing, applying, analyzing, synthesizing, or evaluating information gathered from, or generated by, observation, experience, reflection, reasoning, or communication, as a guide to belief and action.

This is the working definition of the National Council for Excellence in Critical Thinking Instruction. Though the definition as well as the other draft statements of the Council are subject to modification and refinement, the basic idea is one that is common to practitioners and researchers in critical thinking.

GLOSS ON THE DEFINITION

"In its exemplary form, [critical thinking] is based on universal intellectual values that transcend subject-matter divisions: clarity, accuracy, precision, consistency, relevance, sound evidence, good reasons, depth, breadth, and fairness." (National Council Draft Statement)

a) "It entails the examination of those structures or elements of thought implicit in all reasoning: purpose; problem, or question-at-issue; assumptions; concepts; empirical grounding; inferences; implications and consequences; objections from alternative viewpoints, and frame of reference." (National Council Draft Statement)

b) It entails larger-scale abilities of integrating elementary skills in such a way as to be able to apply, synthesize, analyze, and evaluate complicated and multidimensional issues. These include such abilities as clarifying issues, transferring insights into new contexts, analyzing arguments, questioning deeply, developing criteria for evaluation, assessing solutions, refining generalizations, and evaluating the credibility of sources of information. Among the abilities are included also the central forms of communication: critical reading, writing, speaking, and listening. Each of them is a large-scaled mode of thinking which is successful to the extent that it is informed, disciplined, and guided by critical thought and reflection. (Paraphrased from National Council Draft Statement.)

c) Critical thinking entails the possession and active use of a set of traits of mind and affective dimensions: independence of thought, fairmindedness, intellectual humility, intellectual courage, intellectual perseverance, intellectual integrity, curiosity, confidence in reason, and the willingness to see objections, to enter sympathetically into another's point of view, and to recognize one's own egocentricity or ethnocentricity. (Paraphrased from National Council Draft Statement.)

Critical thinking — in being responsive to variable subject areas, issues, and purposes — is incorporated in a family of interrelated modes of thinking, among them: scientific thinking, mathematical thinking, historical thinking, anthropological thinking, economic thinking, moral thinking, and philosophical thinking (National Council Draft Statement).

✦ How Does a Rich, Substantive Concept of Critical Thinking Meet the 21 Criteria?

In our view, a rich, substantive concept of critical thinking, and it alone, provides an intelligible and workable means of meeting all 21 criteria. In this section we will briefly consider each objective in turn, not as a definitive response to the criteria, but merely to suggest the fuller response in Section Three below.

CRITERION # 1

Can it be used to test information processing skills? Critical thinking includes at its core "a set of information and belief generating and processing skills and abilities."

CRITERION # 2

Can it be used to test flexible skills and abilities that can be used in a wide variety of subjects, situations, contexts, and educational levels? Since the art of critical thinking "entails proficiency in the examination of those structures or elements of thought implicit in all reasoning — purpose, problem or question-at-issue, assumptions, concepts, empirical grounding, reasoning leading to conclusions, implications and consequences, objections from alternative viewpoints and frames of reference" — it provides for maximum flexibility of use. It can be used in any subject, with respect to any situation to be figured out, in any context in which reasoning is germane, and, if adapted to the proficiency of students, at any educational level.

CRITERION # 3

Can it account for important differences among the subject areas? Subjects differ not because some make assumptions and others do not, not because some pose questions or problems and others do not, not because some have purposes and others do not, but rather because each has somewhat different purposes, and hence asks somewhat different questions, poses somewhat different problems, gathers somewhat different evidence, uses somewhat different concepts, etc. Critical thinking highlights these differences while underlining common structural features.

CRITERION # 4

Can it be used to focus on fundamental abilities fitted to the accelerating pace of change and embedded in intellectual history? Basic critical thinking skills and abilities are readily shown to be implicit in the rational development and critique of ideas at the core of intellectual history. They explain, for example, how new disciplines emerge from established ones: that is, by asking new questions, pursuing new purposes, framing new concepts, gathering new data, making new assumptions, reasoning in new directions, etc. They also explain how it is that a new field of study can ground itself, even at the outset, on definite intellectual standards that transcend any particular academic field: clarity, precision, accuracy, relevance, consistency, evidentiary force, valid reasoning, consistency . . . (standards implicit in the history of critical thinking and rational discourse in every domain).

CRITERION # 5

Can it be used to improve instruction? Critical thinking is not an isolated good, unrelated to other important goals in education. Rather it is a seminal goal which, done well, simultaneously facilitates a rainbow of other ends. It is best conceived, therefore, as the hub around which all other educational ends cluster. For example, as students learn to think more critically, they become more effective readers, writers, speakers, and listeners because each ability requires well-reasoned thought. They increase their mastery of content because all content is embedded in a system of understandings which, to be grasped, must be reasoned through. They become more proficient in — because they must be practiced within — a variety of modes of thinking: for example, historical, scientific, and mathematical thinking. Self-confidence increases with the intellectual empowerment critical thinking engenders. Finally, they develop skills, abilities, and traits of mind (intellectual discipline, intellectual perseverance, intellectual humility, intellectual empathy, intellectual integrity, ...) crucial to success in the educational, professional, and everyday world.

CRITERION # 6

Can it make clear the inter-connectedness of our knowledge and abilities, and why expertise in one area cannot be divorced either from findings in other areas or from a sensitivity to the need for interdisciplinary integration? In learning to think critically, one learns to transfer what one has learned about the logic of questions in one field to logically similar questions in other fields. Typically this begins with a recognition of the need to ask questions based on logical parallels between all fields of study, for example, skilled practice in questioning concepts and theories, in questioning data, in questioning the source or interpretation of data, in questioning the nature or organization of data, in questioning inferences, in questioning assumptions, in questioning implications and consequences, in questioning points of view and frames of reference, etc.

CRITERION # 7

Can it be used to assess those versatile and fundamental skills essential to being a responsible, decision-making member of the work-place? Critical thinking skills and abilities are highly transferable to the work-place. Since in learning to think critically we learn to take increasing charge of our minds as an instrument of learning — for example, reading, writing, speaking, and listening with greater discipline and skill — we are well situated to engage in collective problem solving and goal attainment, wherever they occur. The kind of "work" increasingly required in industry and business is "intellectual", that is, it requires workers to define goals and purposes clearly, seek out and organize relevant data, conceptualize those data, consider alternative perspectives, adjust thinking to context, question assumptions, modify thinking in the light of the continual flood of new information, and reason to legitimate conclusions. Furthermore, the intellectual work required must increasingly be coordinated with, and must profit from the critique of, fellow workers. There is no avoiding the need, therefore, to express ideas well, accurately represent and consider fairly the ideas of others, write clear and precise memos and documents, and coordinate and sequence all of these so that well-reasoned policies and decisions can be accurately understood and effectively implemented.

CRITERION # 8

Can it generate clear concepts and well-thought-out, rationally articulated goals, criteria, and standards? Since critical thinking is based on the art of monitoring one's thinking with standards implicit in the universal structure of thought, and since the use of these standards is implicit in intellectual history from Socrates through Einstein, there is no problem using critical thinking to generate clear concepts for testing, as well as rationally articulated goals, criteria, and standards.

CRITERION # 9

Can it account for the integration of adult-level communication skills, problem-solving, and critical thinking, and legitimately assess all of them without compromising essential features of any of them? Shallow concepts of critical thinking often distinguish critical thinking from problem solving and decision making as well as from reading, writing, and speaking skills. Once one considers a rich, substantive concept of critical thinking, however, it is clear that each of the basic skills of critical thinking are presupposed by each of the other skills, just as each of them is deeply interrelated to critical thinking as a whole. Consider, does it make sense to analyze potential solutions to problems or the implications of choosing an alternative in making a decision without using critical thinking? Clearly not. Every problem to be solved (or question to be settled) requires a *critical* analysis of the conditions under which it can be solved or settled. We, as problem-solvers, need to look critically at the purpose for solving the problem, we need to critically examine contextual factors, our assumptions, our concepts, what we are using as data, our organization of the data, the source of the data, our reasoning, the implications of our reasoning, our point of view, objections from other points of view. All of these are essential to higher order problem solving and decision making.

Furthermore, all of these intellectual abilities are crucial to higher order reading, writing, speaking, and listening. To read must we analyze the text and re-create its logic in our own minds. To write we must construct a logic our readers can translate into the logic of their thought. To speak we must articulate our thoughts in such a way that our audience can translate our thoughts into their experiences. To listen we must analyze the logic of the thinking of the speaker. Intellectually disciplined reading, writing, speaking, and listening require, in other words, that we work explicitly with the logic we are constructing or re-constructing, using our grasp of the standards of critical thinking to communicate accurately and precisely, effectively solve problems, and rationally make decisions.

CRITERION # 10

Does it respect cultural diversity by focusing on the common-core skills, abilities and traits useful in all cultures? As the criterion presupposes, we can respect cultural diversity best by constructing tests in higher order thinking that focus on skills and abilities necessary in all modern cultures. In this way we can legitimately justify assessing it in all cultural groups. Basic critical thinking skills and abilities — because they are based on fundamental elements implicit in the structure of all reasoned thought *per se*, and because their mastery is essential to higher order thinking in all academic, professional, personal, and public life — are an appropriate foundation for assessment.

CRITERION # 11

Does it test for thinking that promotes (to quote the September, 1991 Kappan) "the active engagement of students in constructing their own knowledge and understanding?" Narrow concepts of critical thinking sometimes characterize it in negative terms, as a set of tools for detecting mistakes in thinking. A rich, substantive concept of critical thinking, however, highlights its central role in all rationally defensible thinking, whether that thinking is focused on assessing thought or products already produced, or actively engaged in the construction of new knowledge or understandings. Well-reasoned thinking, whatever its end, is a form of creation and construction. It devises and articulates purposes and goals, translates them into problems or questions, seeks data that bear upon problems or questions, interprets those data on the basis of concepts and assumptions, and reasons to conclusions within some point of view. All of these are necessary acts of the reasoning mind and must be done "critically" to be done well. Hence all require critical thinking.

CRITERION # 12

Does it concentrate on assessing the fundamental cognitive structures of communication? Each of the dimensions identified in the objective is either straightforwardly a critical thinking ability or depends on a critical thinking ability. The writer's or speaker's *purpose, implications, assumptions, point of view,* etc., are all elements of thought, and the ability to identify and assess those as one reads or listens — the ability to construct in one's mind an accurate and fertile interpretation — is simply thinking *by* listening, thinking *by* reading.

A similar reliance on elements of thought is central to writing or speaking effectively at any educational level. The knowledge of how to gather and present evidence, to make clear one's own assumptions, to see the implications of a position: these are critical thinking abilities.

All forms of communication, moreover, rely on critical thinking standards. Essays and interpretations of essays, utterances and interpretations of utterances, need to be *relevant, logical, consistently* worked out; evidence needs to be recorded and reported *accurately;* points need to be made *clearly* and with as much *precision* as the subject permits; topics need to be covered in *depth* and presented *fairly.*

CRITERION # 13

Can it be used to assess the central features of making rational decisions as a citizen, a consumer, and a part of a world economy? Both public and private life increasingly require mastery of the basic skills and abilities of critical thinking. When this mastery is absent the public degenerates into a mass society susceptible to manipulation by public relations specialists who can engineer political victories by an adroit use of mud slinging, scare tactics, shallow nationalism, fear, envy, stereotypes, greed, false idealism, and maudlin sentimentality. Modern citizenship requires basic critical thinking skills and abilities throughout. The modern citizen should be able to assess the arguments presented for his or her assent, must rationally adjudicate between conflicting points of view, must attempt to understand a culturally complex world, must assess the credibility of diverse sources of information, must translate between conflicting points of view and diverse appeals, must rationally decide priorities, must seek to understand complex issues that involve multiple domains (for example, the environmental, moral, economic, political, scientific, social, and historical domains). Without a solid gr0ounding in critical thinking, citizens are intellectually disarmed, incapable of discharging their civic responsibilities or rationally exercising their rights.

CRITERION # 14

Can it avoid reducing a complex whole to oversimplified parts? Testing for a rich, substantive concept of critical thinking is testing for skills of reasoning in terms of elements of thought, for the ability to orchestrate those elementary skills, for the affective dimensions that make critical thinking actualizable in practice, and for universal intellectual standards, in short for a rich and complex whole rather than for fragmented parts.

CRITERION #15

Can it articulate what is central to basic skills for the future? Basic skills are constituted by the structures explicated in a rich, substantive concept of critical thinking. To teach reading is to teach the ability not merely to repeat content, but to reconceptualize that content, to see applications of the main ideas, to generalize from them, critique them, see them in context, to enter with empathy into another's point of view. To teach writing as a basic skill is to teach not merely grammar and punctuation, but the ability to arrange one's ideas logically and consistently, to anticipate reasonable objections, to transfer ideas to the page in a way that makes them decipherable in all their complexity by a reader. To teach math as a basic skill is not primarily to teach how to solve pre-selected, individual, isolated problems out of context, but to teach the ability to begin to make sense of the world mathematically, to think quantitatively, to be able to see mathematical patterns, to set up the construction of problems and then creatively go about solving them. Critical thinking abilities like these do not exist somehow *in addition to* the basic skills of life; they *constitute* the basic skills of life.

CRITERION #16

Can it provide the kind of skills that are seen as valuable outside the school as well as inside it? Critical thinking provides skills that are seen as valuable by practitioners of the academic disciplines, by responsible leaders of government, of the professions, of business, by citizens interested in their environmental, physical, and economic welfare. In all such areas what is needed are ways to adapt to rapidly changing knowledge, to recognize problems and see their implications before they become acute, to formulate approaches to their solution that recognize legitimately different points of view, to draw reasonable conclusions about what to do. Increasingly, one is hearing statements such as the one made by David Kennedy, the president of Stanford University, to 3,000 college and university presidents:

> It simply will not do for our schools to produce a small elite to power our scientific establishment and a larger cadre of workers with basic skills to do routine work. Millions of people around the world now have these same basic skills and are willing to work twice as long for as little as one-tenth our basic wages. To maintain and enhance our quality of life, we must develop a leading-edge economy based on workers who can think for a living. If skills are equal, in the long run wages will be too. This means we have to educate a vast mass of people capable of thinking critically, creatively, and imaginatively.

CRITERIA #17 AND #18

Can critical thinking be assessed in a way that requires evaluation of authentic problems in realistic contexts, where the abilities assessed include those of formulating the problem and initial screening of plausible solutions? Yes. Testing of authentic skills, abilities and dispositions in authentic contexts can be accomplished by using a combination of *a)* standard multiple-choice items, *b)* machine-gradable multiple-rating items and *c)* short essay items.

a) The standard multiple-choice part of the assessment would be an expanded version of established critical thinking tests, such as the Watson-Glaser or Cornell tests. It is suitable for assessing micro-dimensional critical thinking skills, like identifying the most plausible assumption, recognizing an author's purpose, selecting the most defensible inferences, and such like.

b) The multiple-rating part of the assessment would test more open-ended and larger-domained abilities, like thinking within opposing points of view, the willingness to suspend judgment, the ability to synthesize disparate data into a logical scheme, to take established findings and generalize them into new contexts, etc.

The multiple-rating portion of the assessment, to be reliable, must:

    i) embody a rich and substantive idea of critical thinking,

    ii) be constructed and monitored by critical thinking experts who have such a concept, *iii)* be changed often (5% annually) to assess critical thinking with respect to authentic contemporary issues.

c) The essay part of the assessment would be designed to address critical thinking abilities and traits that involve creating a logic to capture a situation rather than selecting from among possibilities suggested by the test. Examples include the ability to construct an interpretation, to make a logical outline of a text, to figure out ways to gather information, to take an unclear and complex real issue and reformulate it so as to make it more amenable to solution.

Validity on the essay part of the assessment requires that the test be:

i) constructed by experts in critical thinking,

ii) assembled from a large and rotating bank of short essay questions to allow for items that show no significant differences,

iii) centrally graded by teams well-trained in a full concept of critical thinking in order to assure quality control.

CRITERION #19

Can critical thinking be assessed nationally in a way that is financially affordable? To make it affordable, the constructed response segment of the assessment should be administered not to the population of students as a whole, but rather to a representative sample of the student population of a school system. The assessment should be *a)* paid for by school systems that contract to have their students tested, and *b)* constructed, monitored, administered, and graded by a private agency with critical thinking credentials, or at least under the direction of scholars with a solid grounding in the research into critical thinking.

CRITERIA #20 AND #21

Can critical thinking be assessed so as to gauge the improvement of students over the course of their education and to measure the achievement of students against national standards? To evaluate students in both these dimensions requires:

a) an assessment administered as a pre-test at the 6th grade and then as a follow up at the 9th and 12th grades (to provide for value-added judgments).

b) a criterion-referenced assessment that is built on clear, consistently applied quality-norms that are derived from a rich and substantive concept of critical thinking (to provide for the measuring of national progress).

✦ What, Specifically, Are the Dangers of a Non-Substantive Concept of Critical Thinking?

It is important to be alert to the dangers posed by a non-substantive concept of critical thinking. Such a concept exists when, separate from a consideration of the research in the field, a person or institution presupposes *a)* that the meaning or terminology of critical thinking is intuitively obvious (hence not in need of scholarly analysis), or *b)* that each concept underlying critical thinking (such as assumption, inference, implication, reasoning, ...) can be analyzed separately from a theory that accounts for the interrelation of these concepts, or *c)* that the skills of critical thinking can be adequately cultivated without reference to the values, traits of mind, and dispositions that underlie those skills.

There are at least three serious problems that may result from the use of a theoretically superficial concept of critical thinking:

a) important critical thinking concepts, which must be clearly defined to be used effectively in assessment, may be used vaguely, inconsistently, incorrectly, or misleadingly,

b) a false, misleading, or simplistic over-arching concept of critical thinking may be fostered, or

c) an unrealistic strategy for the assessment and cultivation of critical thinking may be incorporated into testing and teaching.

Many examples of the unwitting use of a non-substantive concept of critical thinking could be cited — such as "thinking skills" programs devoid of intellectual standards (which, for example, systematically confuse "inferences" with "valid inferences" and "analogies" with "sound analogies"), or testing personnel who lack adequate grounding in critical thinking theory (and so, for example, frequently confuse assumptions with inferences or inferences with implications). The most far-reaching danger occurs when influential educational systems or institutions, like state departments of education, inadvertently incorporate a non-substantive concept of critical thinking into statewide curriculum standards or into statewide testing programs. This can result in significant, unintended negative consequences, for example: thousands of teachers encouraged to follow a misconceived model for the assessment of reasoning, leading to mis-instruction on a grand scale.

Illustration: The California Direct Writing Assessment

We shall look at one important case. Unfortunately, given the brevity of this paper, one case must stand for all. The case we have chosen concerns the *Integrated Language Arts Assessment of the California Assessment Program,* a massive statewide program that has impact not only on every student in the public schools of California, but also, because of the leadership role of California in assessment, on national teaching and testing practices as well. It appears that three fundamental mistakes occurred in the design of the direct writing assessment:

a) Though one of the goals of the program was to place an emphasis on the quality of reasoning and critical thinking in writing, it appears that no one with a research background in critical thinking reviewed the articulation or implementation of the assessment prompts. (We infer this from the fact that fundamental conceptual errors occur both in the prompts themselves and in the application of criteria to student constructed responses.)

b) It was assumed, inappropriately, that classroom teachers without extended training in critical thinking are able to effectively assess student essays that call for evaluative reasoning. We infer this from statements descriptive of the assessment design like:

> Teachers on the CAP writing Development Team develop all the testing and instructional materials for assessment. For every type of writing assessed, the team develops a special set of prompts ... and a scoring guide that identifies the thinking and writing requirements for that type of writing....
>
> Essays are scored in four to six days by several hundred teachers at four regional scoring centers. A special handbook for each grade level provides teachers with practical instructional materials for each type of writing, including sample prompts, illustrative essays, and related readings.

c) The resulting assessment was not monitored by anyone with a research background in critical thinking. (We infer this from the fact that model "strong" answers purporting to illustrate critical reasoning are showcased that are in fact patently very weak answers, containing virtually no reasoning at all.)

Consider Figure 1 and Figure 2 used as illustrations of the nature and quality of the writing assessment program in an article authorized and developed by the staff of the California Assessment Program. It is entitled "California: The State of Assessment" and was written for an important national anthology, *Developing Minds* (more than 150,000 copies disseminated by ASCD). The show-piece article, in which these figures occur, argues that the examples illustrate a "state-of-the-art teacher-developed writing assessment" that is sophisticated in "its testing, scoring, and reporting systems" and designed to "include only those tasks that will stimulate high-quality instruction."

There are a number of problems illustrated in these figures that a substantive understanding of critical thinking would have avoided:

1) A description of subjective reactions was systematically confused with sound evaluative reasoning. It is important to distinguish questions like, "Is rock music good music?" or "Does rock music excel as a form of

Evaluative Essay Sample

EVALUATION. Students were asked to write an evaluative essay, make judgments about the worth of a book, television program, or type of music and then support their judgments with reasons and evidence. Students must consider possible criteria on which to base an evaluation, analyze their subject in light of the criteria, and select evidence that clearly supports their judgments. Each student was assigned one of the following evaluative tasks:

- To write a letter to a favorite author telling why they especially liked one of the author's books.
- To explain why they enjoyed one television program more than any others.
- To justify their preference for a particular type of music.

The tasks made clear that students must argue convincingly for their preferences and not just offer unsupported opinions.

This is a sample essay from a student who demonstrated exceptional achievement.

Rock Around the Clock

"Well, you're getting to the age when you have to learn to be responsible!" my mother yelled out.

"Yes, but I can't be available all the time to do my appointed chores! I'm only thirteen! I want to be with my friends, to have fun! I don't think that it is fair for me to baby-sit while you go run your little errands!" I snapped back. I sprinted upstairs to my room before my mother could start another sentence. I turned on my radio and "Shout" was playing. I noted how true the song was and I threw some punches at my pillow. The song ended and "Control" by Janet Jackson came on. I stopped beating my pillow. I suddenly felt at peace with myself. The song had slowed me down. I pondered briefly over all the songs that had helped me to control my feelings. The list was endless. So is my devotion to rock music and pop rock. These songs help me to express my feelings, they make me wind down, and above all they make me feel good. Without this music, I might have turned out to be a violent and grumpy person.

Some of my favorite songs are by Howard Jones, Pet Shop Boys, and Madonna. I especially like songs that have a message in them, such as "Stand by Me", by Ben E. King. This song tells me to stand by the people I love and to not question them in times of need. Basically this song is telling me to believe in my friends, because they are my friends.

My favorite type of music is rock and pop rock. Without them, there is no way that I could survive mentally. They are with me in times of trouble, and best of all, they are only a step away.

California classroom teachers wrote comments like these after reading and scoring students' evaluative essays:

- "Evidence of clear thinking was heavily rewarded in our scoring."
- "I am struck by how much some students can accomplish in 45 minutes; how well they can sometimes marshal the ideas; and with how much flair and sparkle they can express themselves."
- "More emphasis should be placed on critical thinking skills, supporting judgments, and tying thoughts and ideas together. Far too many papers digress, summarize, underdevelop, or state totally irrelevant facts."
- "Students generally need to develop skills in giving evidence to support their judgments. I plan to spend more time on these thinking skills next year."

Source: California State Department of Education, 1988.

figure 1   Figures 1 and 2 come from "California: The State of Assessment", Anderson, Robert L. in *Developing Minds,* edited by Art Costa, pp. 314–25.

CAP Grade 8 Direct Writing Assessment
Achievement in Evaluation

Score Point	Percentage of California Grade 8 Students*	Cumulative Percentage	Description of Achievement
6 Exceptional Achievement	0.5		The student produces convincingly argued evaluation; identifies a subject, describes it appropriately, and asserts a judgment of it; gives reasons and specific evidence to support the argument; engages the reader immediately, moves along logically and coherently, and provides closure; reflects awareness of reader's questions or alternative evaluations.
5 Commendable Achievement	8.1	8.6	The student produces well-argued evaluation; identifies, describes, and judges its subject; gives reasons and evidence to support the argument; is engaging, logical, attentive to reader's concern; is more conventional or predictable than the writer of a 6.
4 Adequate Achievement	25.5	34.1	The student produces adequately argued evaluation; identifies and judges its subject; gives at least one moderately developed reason to support the argument; lacks the authority and polish of the writer of a 5 or 6; produces writing that, although focused and coherent, may be uneven; usually describes the subject more than necessary and argues a judgment less than necessary.
3 Some Evidence of Achievement	42.4	76.5	The student states a judgment and gives one or more reasons to support it; either lists reasons without providing evidence or fails to argue even one reason logically or coherently.
2 Limited Evidence of Achievement	19.2	95.7	The student states a judgment but may describe the subject without evaluating it or may list irrelevant reasons or develop a reason in a rambling, illogical way.
1 Minimal Evidence of Achievement	3.6	99.3	The student usually states a judgment but may describe the subject without stating a judgment; either gives no reasons or lists only one or two reasons without providing evidence; usually relies on weak and general personal evaluation.
No response	0.3		
Off Topic	0.5		

*This column does not total to 100% because of rounding.

figure 2

music?" (which call for objective evaluation) from questions like, "Do you enjoy rock music?" or "Does rock music stir powerful emotions in you?" (which call, not for reasoning, but for the description of subjective reactions). Apparently the test developers were unclear about this distinction.

2) *The assessing teachers did not notice that the student failed to respond to the directions.* The student did not develop evaluative reasoning, did not support his judgment with reasons and evidence, did not consider possible criteria on which to base his judgment, did not analyze the subject in the light of the criteria, and did not select evidence that clearly supported his judgment. Instead the student described an emotional exchange, asserted — without evidence — some questionable claims, and expressed a variety of subjective preferences (a fuller critique of the student essay is available on page 170 of, "Why Students — and Teachers — Don't Reason Well"). The assessing teachers were apparently too confused about the nature of evaluative reasoning or the basic notions of criteria, evidence, reasons, and well-supported judgment to notice the discrepancy.

3) *The California State Department of Education assessment staff did not notice these errors once they were made.* Instead of catching the errors once made, the California Department of Education chose to use the mis-graded student essay *as a showcase model* to disseminate nationally as illustrating "exceptional achievement" in reasoned evaluation, and as a *model* of their assessment of reasoned writing. We conclude that the California Assessment Program does not use scholars with a background in critical thinking research, any of whom would surely have recognized the problem.

Fundamental misconceptions of the nature of critical thinking and reasoned discourse, such as those documented above, must not be replicated in a national assessment program. Steps should be taken to insure that a substantive concept of critical thinking and a well-supervised implementation of that concept form the basis of the finished assessment program.

✦✦ Section Three: The Four Domains of Critical Thinking

What are the four component domains of critical thinking and their implications for the assessment of higher order thinking?

✦ Elements of Thought

As soon as we move from thought which is purely associational and undisciplined, to thinking which is conceptual and inferential, thinking which attempts in some intelligible way to figure something out, to use the power of reason, then it is helpful to think about what can be called "the elements of thought." The elements of thought are the basic building blocks of thinking, essential dimensions of reasoning whenever and wherever it occurs. Working together, they shape reasoning and provide a general logic to reason. We can articulate these elements by paying close attention to what is implicit in the attempt on the part of the mind to figure anything out whatsoever. Once we make them clear, it will be obvious that each of them can serve as an important touchstone or point of assessment in critical analysis and in the assessment of thinking.

For each of the elements of thought there is a cluster of attendant basic thinking skills. Because they involve fundamental structures of thought, these skills can be characterized as micro-skills, those skills out of which larger-domained critical thinking abilities are built. Being able to think critically about a particular issue, then, will include the ability to identify, clarify, and argue for and against alternative formulations of the elements of thought.

The basic conditions implicit whenever we gather, conceptualize, apply, analyze, synthesize, or evaluate information — the elements of thought — are as follows:

1) *Purpose, Goal, or End in View.* Whenever we reason, we reason to some end, to achieve some objective, to satisfy some desire or fulfill some need. One source of problems in reasoning is traceable to defects at the level of goal, purpose, or end. If the goal is unrealistic, for example, or contradictory to other goals we have, confused or muddled in some way, then the reasoning used to achieve it is problematic.

An assessment of critical thinking, then, would test, at the appropriate educational level, skills of being able to state an author's purpose, to identify a plausible statement of an author's goals from a list provided, to rank formulations of an author's objectives according to which are more or less reasonable in light of a particular passage, to distinguish clearly between purposes, consequences, assumptions, and other elements of thought.

2) *Question at Issue, or Problem to be Solved.* Whenever we attempt to reason something out, there is at least one question at issue, at least one problem to be solved. One area of concern for reasoners, therefore, will be the formulation of the question to be answered or problem to be solved, whether with respect to their own reasoning or to that of others.

Assessing skills of mastery of this element of thought would test students' ability to formulate a problem in a clear and relevant way, to choose from among alternative formulations, to discuss the merits of different versions of the question at issue, to recognize key common elements in statements of different problems, to structure the articulation of problems so as to make possible lines of solution more apparent.

3) Point of View, or Frame of Reference. Whenever we reason, we must reason within some point of view or frame of reference. Any "defect" in that point of view or frame of reference is a possible source of problems in the reasoning. A point of view may be too narrow, too parochial, may be based on false or misleading analogies or metaphors, may contain contradictions, and so forth.

Levels of skill here would be tested with reference to being able to enunciate an author's point of view in a passage, to adjudicate between different statements of that point of view, to recognize bias, narrowness, and contradictions when they occur in the point of view, to recognize relations between the frame of reference being used and its implications, assumptions, and main concepts.

4) The Empirical Dimension of Reasoning. Whenever we reason, there is some "stuff", some phenomena about which we are reasoning. Any "defect", then, in the experiences, data, evidence, or raw material upon which a person's reasoning is based is a possible source of problems.

Students would be tested, again, based on their level, on their ability to distinguish evidence from conclusions based on that evidence, to give evidence themselves, to identify from a pre-selected list data that would support an author's positions, data that would oppose it, data that would be neutral, to notice the presence or lack of relevant evidence, to recognize, to be intellectually courageous in recognizing (and labeling as such) mere speculation that goes beyond the evidence.

5) The Conceptual Dimension of Reasoning. All reasoning uses some ideas or concepts and not others. These concepts can include the theories, principles, axioms and rules implicit in our reasoning. Any "defect" in the concepts or ideas of the reasoning is a possible source of problems.

The assessment of the relevant higher order thinking would test the ability to identify main concepts of a passage, to choose among different versions of those concepts (some perhaps equally good), to see relations among concepts, to reason about the similarity of points of view on the basis of similarity of fundamental concepts, to distinguish central from peripheral concepts, derived concepts from basic concepts, to see the implications of using one concept rather than another.

6) Assumptions. All reasoning must begin somewhere, must take some things for granted. Any "defect" in the assumptions or presuppositions with which the reasoning begins is a possible source of problems.

Assessing skills of reasoning about assumptions would test the ability to identify assumptions underlying given inferences, points of view, and goals, to evaluate the accuracy of different formulations of the assumptions, to distinguish between assumptions and inferences, to rank assumptions with respect to their plausibility, to be intellectually fairminded by choosing the most plausible version of assumptions underlying points of view with which they disagree.

7) *Implications and Consequences.* No matter where we stop our reasoning, it will always have further implications and consequences. As reasoning develops, statements will logically be entailed by it. Any "defect" in the implications or consequences of our reasoning is a possible source of problems.

Skills to be assessed would include the ability to identify important implications, to do so by selecting from a list of possible implications, to make fine discriminations among necessary, probable, and improbable consequences, to distinguish between implications and assumptions, to recognize the weakness of an author's position as shown by the implausibility of its implications, to exercise intellectual fairmindedness in discriminating between the likelihood of dire and mild consequences of an action to which one is opposed.

8) *Inferences.* Reasoning proceeds by steps in which we reason as follows: "Because this is so, that also is so (or probably so)," or "Since *this*, therefore *that*." Any "defect" in such inferences is a possible problem in our reasoning.

Assessment would test, in a way geared to their educational level, students' ability to recognize faulty and justified inferences in a passage, to rank inferences with respect to both their plausibility and their relevance, to make good inferences in their own reasoning, to discriminate among various formulations of an author's inferences with respect to which is most accurate, to take something they do not believe but to entertain it for the sake of argument and draw reasonable inferences from it.

ASSESSMENT OF ELEMENTS OF THOUGHT

Any program for the assessment of critical thinking skills must itself be assessed in terms of its validity and reliability in testing for the ability to think about, and in terms of, the elements of thought. These abilities can be successfully assessed in three related ways: by a restricted use of standard multiple-choice items, by multiple-rating items, and by short essay items. Both multiple-choice and multiple-rating items are machine-gradable, while essay items are not.

Although our recommendations about the content of the assessment will be spelled out in detail in Section Four, some of these can be anticipated here with respect to the assessment of reasoning abilities centering around the elements of thought.

Multiple-choice testing (as in the existing *Watson-Glaser Critical Thinking Appraisal* or the *Cornell Critical Thinking Tests*) is an important part of an assessment of critical thinking, but its legitimate use is restricted to testing only the most basic skills of identifying and recognizing elements of thought, and then only as they occur in relatively short and unambiguous excerpts.

Within this domain, multiple-choice questions will require students:

- to identify an author's purpose in a passage;
- to rate selected inferences as justified, probably true, insufficiently evidenced, probably false, unjustified;
- to select among formulations of the problem at issue in a passage those that are clearly reasonable, probably reasonable, probably unreasonable, clearly unreasonable;
- to recognize unstated assumptions;
- to distinguish evidence from hypotheses and conclusions;
- to rate described evidence as reliable, probably reliable, probably not reliable, unreliable.

✦ Abilities

The elements of thought do not exist in isolation from one another, nor — more importantly for the concept of an assessment procedure — do they exist outside a particular context of application. In the practice of good critical thinking, skills more closely associated with elements of thought are orchestrated into larger-domained abilities which are applied to thinking about complex and sometimes ambiguous issues, problems, decisions, theories, states of affairs, social institutions, and human artifacts.

These critical thinking abilities include being skillful at:

1) refining generalizations and avoiding over-simplifications,
2) comparing analogous situations: transferring insights into new contexts,
3) developing one's perspective: creating or exploring the implications of beliefs, arguments, or theories,
4) clarifying issues, conclusions, or beliefs,
5) clarifying and analyzing the meanings of words and phrases,
6) developing criteria for evaluation: clarifying values and standards,
7) evaluating the credibility of sources of information,
8) questioning deeply: raising and pursuing root or significant questions,
9) analyzing or evaluating arguments, interpretations, beliefs, or theories,
10) generating or assessing solutions,
11) analyzing or evaluating actions or policies,

12) reasoning dialogically: comparing perspectives, interpretations, or theories,

13) reasoning dialectically: evaluating perspectives, interpretations, or theories,

14) reading critically: constructing an accurate interpretation of, understanding the elements of thought in, and evaluating, the reasoning of a text,

15) listening critically: constructing an accurate interpretation of, understanding the elements of thought in, and evaluating, the reasoning of an oral communication,

16) writing critically: creating, developing, clarifying, and conveying, in written form, the logic of one's thinking,

17) speaking critically: creating, developing, clarifying, and conveying, in spoken form, the logic of one's thinking.

Abilities like these play a central role in a rich and substantive concept of critical thinking. They are essential to approaching actual issues, problems, and situations rationally. Understanding the rights and duties of citizenship, for example, requires that one at least have the ability to compare perspectives and interpretations, to read and listen critically, to analyze and evaluate policies. In fact, there is no macro-ability on the list that would not be relevant or even crucial to thinking deeply about the rights and duties of citizenship. Similarly, the capacity to make sound decisions, to participate knowledgeably in the work-place, to function as part of a global economy, to master the content in anything as complex as the academic disciplines, to apply those subject area insights to real-life situations, to make insightful cross-disciplinary connections, to communicate effectively — each of these relies in a fundamental way on having a significant number of the abilities listed. Take, for example, the capacity to make sound decisions: such decision-making is hardly possible without an attendant ability to (going down the list of abilities in order) refine generalizations, compare analogous situations, develop one's perspective, clarify issues, and so forth.

The last four abilities listed — the ability to read, write, listen, and speak, each in a critical, informed, constructive way — are best considered not as in the usual model, not as manifestations of thinking already accomplished, but as being themselves actual modes of constructive thinking. As such, they are structured amalgams of elementary skills together with any number of other abilities.

ASSESSMENT OF ABILITIES

The assessment of abilities, too often neglected, is essential to assessment of critical thinking. Since these *are* the abilities implicit in the realistic use of thinking, no assessment tool that fails to assess a significant number of these abilities could justifiably be called an assessment of higher order thinking. The assessment, moreover, needs to address such abilities *directly* (rather than through secondary indicators), *systematically* (rather than haphazardly as a result of an attempt to assess other variables like academic achievement), and in settings as *authentic* as possible given the requirement of *uniform, relevant grading*.

Assessment of abilities that meets these four criteria cannot be accomplished within the confines of a standard multiple-choice-type test. It can be accomplished, however, for all of the abilities (except those having to do with oral communication), by means of a combination of machine-gradable multiple-rating items and essay items.

For any macro-ability, there will be dimensions of the ability that are *generative* and other dimensions of it that are selective. In trying to solve a real problem, for example, much of one's thinking is devoted to *generating* a formulation of the problem that will make it more susceptible to solution. Another, and quite different, aspect of problem solving, is the ability to *select*, from among a large variety of possibilities, that avenue of thought which will most likely result in a solution. Students who are trained using a rich, substantive concept of critical thinking tend to improve in both dimensions of this ability, and both are genuine dimensions of real problem-solving.

The selective dimensions of an ability can be assessed accurately, even in complex, ambiguous, and subtle cases, using multiple-rating items. The generative dimension, on the other hand, cannot. Since it requires students to come up with their own critical thinking approaches within that macro-ability, this dimension can be assessed adequately only by carefully constructed and carefully graded essay tests. Details of the assessment and samples of assessment items will be presented in Section Four.

✦ *Affective Dimensions*

Higher order thinking requires more than higher order thinking *skills*. Critical thinking, in any substantive sense, includes more than abilities. The concept also includes, in a crucial way, certain attitudes, dispositions, passions, traits of mind. These affective dimensions are not merely important to critical thinking, they are essential to the effective use of higher order thinking in real settings.

These affective dimensions include:

1) thinking independently,

2) exercising fairmindedness,

3) developing insight into egocentricity and sociocentricity,

4) developing intellectual humility and suspending judgment,

5) developing intellectual courage,

6) developing intellectual good faith and integrity,

7) developing intellectual perseverance,

8) developing confidence in reason,

9) exploring thoughts underlying feelings and feelings underlying thoughts,

10) developing intellectual curiosity.

Without *intellectual perseverance*, one could not solve the complicated, multi-faceted problems one confronts in industry. Without *intellectual courage*, one could not maintain a defense of citizenship rights in the face of scare tactics. Without *fairmindedness*, one could not enter into another's point of view and thus would lack that empathetic understanding necessary for a reasonable approach to living in a pluralistic society. Without *developing insight into egocentricity and sociocentricity* one could employ one's reasoning skills in a merely self-serving and prejudiced way. Without *confidence in reason* one could not adequately address those complex and frequently ambiguous real-life problems that require reasonable decisions in the face of crucial uncertainties.

ASSESSMENT OF AFFECTIVE DIMENSIONS

The assessment of affective dimensions of critical thinking is an important part of an assessment of higher order thinking. An initial problem is that from the fact that all these dimensions are essential, it does not follow that all are directly testable, nor does it follow that *any* of them is *easily* testable. For some of these affective dimensions (intellectual perseverance, for example), any testing would have to take place over an appropriately long period of time and thus could not be legitimately assessed at all during a time-frame suitable for a national test.

Nevertheless, a number of affective dimensions can be assessed in a relatively straightforward way using essay items and, especially, machine-gradable multiple-rating items.

"Reasoning Within Conflicting Points of View," a central aspect of the disposition of fairmindedness, is already being assessed on the revised version of the *Watson-Glaser Critical Thinking Appraisal*. This section of the *Appraisal* asks students to select the strongest (that is, the most defensible) argument in favor of each side of a pair of conflicting and sometimes emotionally charged points of view. Proficiency on these items indicates a fairminded willingness to distinguish the concept of *reasonable defensibility* from that of *personal belief*.

Multiple-rating items are currently being prepared that address aspects of intellectual courage, other aspects of fairmindedness, aspects of intellectual humility, and aspects of the development of insight into one's own egocentricity and sociocentricity.

✦ *Intellectual Standards*

In any domain where assessment is taking place, there are standards implicit in that assessment. Higher order thinking is thinking that meets universal intellectual standards. Thus, when assessing a student's ability to compare and evaluate perspectives (a macro-ability) and to do so with fairmindedness (a trait of mind), we would judge whether she had made such evaluations in a *relevant* and *consistent* way, with attention to *accuracy, fairness,* and *completeness* in describing each perspective, and with a sensitivity to the degree of *precision* appropriate to the topic. We would assess critical thinking about and in terms of the elements of thought in very much the same way: to judge a person's skill at recognizing the frame of reference underlying a position, we would want to judge whether she could see *relevant* alternatives, whether the frame of reference she identified fits the available *evidence,* whether her answer was *deep* or merely mechanical, *clear* or vague, *fair* or biased. Intellectual standards apply to thinking in every subject.

Intellectual Standards
That Apply to Thinking in Every Subject

Thinking that is:		*Thinking that is:*
Clear	vs	Unclear
Precise	vs	Imprecise
Specific	vs	Vague
Accurate	vs	Inaccurate
Relevant	vs	Irrelevant
Plausible	vs	Implausible
Consistent	vs	Inconsistent
Logical	vs	Illogical
Deep	vs	Superficial
Broad	vs	Narrow
Complete	vs	Incomplete
Significant	vs	Trivial
Adequate *(for purpose)*	vs	Inadequate
Fair	vs	Biased or One-Sided

The process of learning to teach so as to foster critical thinking is the very process by means of which one establishes intellectual standards for assessing thinking, and, by extension, for assessing instruction itself.

Such standards are more useful if they are made explicit — to the students who are taking the test, to those doing the assessing, and to classroom teachers. Making standards explicit benefits student test-takers because they can then see that there are standards, that the standards are not arbitrary, and that understanding the standards gives them insight into what good critical thinking is. It benefits those doing the assessing because, in addition to the reasons already mentioned, it fosters both a uniformity in grading and a strong correlation between the grade and the skills being graded. Judging a response by how *clearly* and *completely* it states a position, for example, is using a critical thinking standard and dictates a certain level of assessment; judging a response by how *concisely* or how *elegantly* it states a position, on the other hand, is using a standard that is inappropriate to critical thinking assessment. Explicit standards — part of a rich and substantive concept of critical thinking — might have avoided at least some of the mistaken assessment on the *California Assessment Program*, cited earlier. Thus, making standards explicit promotes both the reliability and the validity of the assessment. Finally, it benefits classroom teachers because such standards can readily be built into classroom instruction. The standards, after all, are those implicit in teaching for higher order thinking; they are therefore invaluable both for teachers to use explicitly with their classes and — an essential feature of critical thinking-internalized — for students to learn to use as part of assessing themselves.

✦✦ Section Four: Recommendations of the Center for Critical Thinking and Moral Critique

What is the most workable solution to the design of a process to assess higher order thinking?

In this section we will 1) briefly survey existing assessment tools; 2) make recommendations regarding the substance and format of a national assessment tool — the critical thinking domains to be assessed, the varieties of assessment strategies to be used (including sample test items), and the dual inter disciplinary and intra disciplinary scope of the assessment — 3) appraise the value of the proposed assessment strategy for the reform of instruction, and 4) make recommendations regarding the implementation of the assessment.

✦ Existing Assessment Tools

There are limitations in all twelve of the commercially available critical thinking tests as instruments for assessing higher order thinking:

Cornell Class Reasoning Test, Form X (1964)

Cornell Conditional Reasoning Test, Form X (1964)

Cornell Critical Thinking Test, Level X (1985)

Cornell Critical Thinking Test, Level Z (1985)

The Ennis–Weir Critical Thinking Essay Test (1985)

Judgement: Deductive Logic and Assumption Recognition (1971)

Logical Reasoning (1955)

New Jersey Test of Reasoning Skills (1983)

Ross Test of Higher Cognitive Processes (1976)

Test on Appraising Observations (1983)

Test of Enquiry Skills (1979)

Watson–Glaser Critical Thinking Appraisal (1980)

In addition there are limitations in all of the other available "higher studies" tests which might be taken as a possible model for the assessing of higher order thinking: the SAT, LSAT, the Test of Academic Aptitude (British), ACT, the Graduate Record Exam, the Commonwealth Secondary Scholarships Exam (Australia). We do not have the space here to review each of these tests one-by-one. Instead we will summarize the general situation as we see it.

Though aspects and dimensions of critical thinking are tested, some more and some less, in all of the above tests, none has been designed with the 21 criteria in Sections one and two in mind. Most importantly, none was designed to serve as a national assessment tool which establishes national standards in higher order thinking and as a motivation for and guide to instruction.

Behind none of these tests was there a comprehensive model for the elements of thought, the abilities of critical thinking, or the affective dispositions (as we have here provided). The relative recentness of the bulk of scholarship in critical thinking makes it unlikely that long-established tests will fill the bill.

Of course any new test for assessing higher order thinking should be based on a thorough review of established test strategies to incorporate those with significant application.

Given the need for assessment on the basis of a rich and substantive concept of critical thinking, there are two areas where competing values and objectives come into play. The first concerns the *substance and format* of the test itself: Which domains exactly are to be covered, and with what emphases? What kinds of question will be asked? Will it include both interdisciplinary and intradisciplinary items? What kind of assessment questions best test for skills of citizenship and the challenges of the workplace? The second area concerns the *implementation* of the test and how it is conceived: Should it be value-added or simply criterion-referenced? Who will do the assessing and who will be assessed? How much will the assessment cost and who will pay for it? How often will the test be given?

Some of these are difficult questions, with genuine values and goals on different sides, where reasonable cases can be made for more than one position. Others of these questions are clearer, especially once the objectives of the test as a whole are brought into focus.

✦ Substance and Format

The overall recommendations of the Center for Critical Thinking are set forward below.

1) DOMAINS TO BE ASSESSED

The national assessment of higher order thinking must test for a rich and substantive concept of critical thinking, and this testing must be geared to assessment within all four domains of critical thinking.

a) Elements of Thought

Skills of identifying, explicating, and using the elements of thought need to be assessed. They are necessary for any of the abilities to be employed with precision, depth, or accuracy. They are required if essential affective traits are to be rooted in solid, locatable, intellectual skills and the concepts they presuppose.

Lack of a solid grounding in these skills, and the concepts behind them, results in thinking which, good intentions notwithstanding, is far removed from the close, careful reasoning demanded by the rigors of higher order thinking. Among testing personnel, lack of the informed use of these concepts is part of what results in such poor assessment tools and grading as we found in the *California Direct Writing Assessment.*

Critical thinking in students requires them to be able to perform well, with an expertise appropriate to their grade level, on items testing a list of skills that center around the elements of thought:

- identify a plausible statement of a writer's purpose;
- rank formulations of an author's objectives;
- distinguish clearly between purposes, consequences, assumptions, and inferences;
- choose the most reasonable statement of the problem an author is addressing;
- discuss reasonably the merits of different versions of the question at issue;

- recognize key common elements in formulations of different problems;
- give a clear articulation of an author's point of view;
- identify the most reasonable statement of an author's point of view;
- recognize bias, narrowness, and contradictions in the point of view behind an excerpt;
- identify assumptions and implications of a writer's point of view;
- distinguish evidence from conclusions based on that evidence;
- give evidence to back up their position in an essay;
- recognize data that would support, data that would oppose, and data that would be neutral with respect to, an author's position;
- recognize conclusions that go beyond the evidence;
- note, in an evaluative essay, the presence, or the absence, of evidence in an excerpt;
- identify the main concepts in a passage;
- distinguish central from peripheral concepts;
- identify the assumption underlying a given inference;
- evaluate the aptness of different versions of an assumption;
- choose the most reasonable statement of a background theory involved in a passage;
- distinguish between inferences and assumptions;
- rank different formulations of assumptions with respect to which is the most reasonable;
- identify crucial implications of a passage;
- discriminate between consequences that are necessary, probable, and improbable;
- evaluate an author's inferences;
- make, in an evaluative essay, justified inferences;
- choose the most accurate version of an author's inferences;
- draw reasonable inferences from positions they disagree with.

b) Abilities

Abilities, grounded in a thorough familiarity with the elements of thought, are the activities we actually use to perform our higher order thinking. Abilities like clarifying values and standards, comparing analogous situations, generating and assessing solutions, analyzing and evaluating actions or policies are the stuff of reasoning. They are the means whereby decisions are to be made, problems are to be solved, thinking in the work-place is to be strengthened, and understanding of rights and responsibilities deepened.

The abilities of critical reading and critical writing are keystones of any process to assess higher order thinking in that each of them, when considered at any level, is permeated by other critical thinking abilities. It is not as if we read *and* clarify values, read *and* compare analogous situations, write *and* generate solutions. To read critically *is* to clarify values, compare analogous situations, and to exercise the other abilities as well; to write *is* to generate solutions and much more besides.

Assessment of proficiency in the abilities can be keyed to student performance on test items that are geared to as many of the abilities listed on p. 127 as is feasible given the time constraints of the test.

c) Affective Traits

Without assessing affective traits, only a diminished idea of critical thinking will be addressed. What allows us to confront our prejudices and analytically break them down is not just abilities but a *commitment* to use them for this purpose. What allows us to solve our problems in a sufficiently diligent way as to address complicated and intricate real-life problems, is again not just cognitive abilities. It is intellectual perseverance — a drive, a disposition, an affective trait. A similar point can be made for each of the intellectual traits which are the driving force behind sound and penetrating reasoning.

Assessment of the affective dimensions will concentrate on those aspects it is plausible to test for within the constraints imposed by a national assessment. These will include aspects of fairmindedness, of the willingness to suspend judgment, of intellectual courage and intellectual integrity.

d) Intellectual Standards

Assessment has to involve explicit universal standards. If we are not testing students' abilities to be relevant, precise, logical, consistent, and the rest, then we are not assessing students' abilities to engage in higher order thinking. And if testing personnel do not employ these same explicit standards, then they are grading for something other than higher order thinking.

Relative mastery of these intellectual standards requires students to be able to

- recognize *clarity* vs. unclarity;
- distinguish *accurate* from inaccurate accounts;
- decide when a statement is *relevant* or irrelevant to a given point;
- identify inconsistent positions as well as (relatively) *consistent* ones;
- discriminate *deep, complete, and significant* accounts from those that are superficial, fragmentary, and trivial;
- evaluate responses with respect to their *fairness;*

- prefer *well-evidenced* accounts to accounts that are unsupported by evidence;
- tell *good reasons* from bad.

2) VARIETIES OF ASSESSMENT STRATEGIES

The assessment should contain three kinds of items: *a)* machine-gradable multiple-choice items; *b)* machine-gradable multiple-rating items; *c)* essay items.

a) Multiple-Choice Items

Legitimate use of multiple-choice items on the assessment is limited. This type of item is geared toward relatively straightforward skills of reasoning, particularly with respect to recognizing elements of thought, distinguishing one element of thought from another, and recognizing clear examples of faulty reasoning.

Two detailed samples of assessment items follow (the first, Figure 3, is on Inferences, the second, Figure 4, on Recognition of Assumptions).

Other abbreviated samples of appropriate multiple-choice items are as follows:

1) In the following excerpt, mark E for each item that is a piece of empirical *evidence;* mark C for each item that is a *conclusion* based on evidence; mark N for each item that is neither....

2) In this test, each exercise consists of several statements (premises) followed by several suggested conclusions.... If you think the conclusion *necessarily* follows from the statements given, make a heavy black mark under *"Conclusion Follows"*; if you think it is not a necessary conclusion, put a mark under *"Conclusion Does Not Follow."*

3) The following is a list of possible findings in relation to the experiment quoted above. For each, say whether it would *support* the author's hypothesis, *oppose* the author's hypothesis, or be neutral with respect to the author's hypothesis....

4) Below is a series of questions. Each question is followed by several reasons. For the purpose of this test, you are to regard each reason as true. The problem then is to decide whether it is a *strong reason* or a *weak reason....*

5) Which of the following conclusions is C completely supported by the stated evidence, *P* partially supported by the stated evidence, or *U* unsupported by the stated evidence?

6) Which of the following is an *implication* of the author's position in the passage cited?

Inferences

DIRECTIONS: An inference is a conclusion a person can draw from certain observed or supposed facts. For example, if the lights are on in a house and music can be heard coming from the house, a person might infer that someone is at home. But this inference may or may not be correct. Possibly the people in the house did not turn off the lights and the radio when they left the house.

In this test, each exercise begins with a statement of facts that you are to regard as true. After each statement of facts you will find several possible inferences — that is, conclusions that some persons might draw from the stated facts. Examine each inference separately and make a decision as to its degree of truth or falsity.

For each inference you will find spaces on the answer sheet labeled J, PJ, ID, PU, and U. For each inference make a mark on the answer sheet under the appropriate heading as follows:

> J if you think the inference is definitely JUSTIFIED; that it properly follows beyond a reasonable doubt from the statement of facts given.

> PJ if you think the inference is PROBABLY JUSTIFIED; that it is more likely to be true than false in the light of the facts given.

> ID if you decide that there are INSUFFICIENT DATA; that you cannot tell from the facts given whether the inference is justified or not; if the facts provide no basis for judging one way or the other.

> PU if you think the inference is PROBABLY UNJUSTIFIED; that it is more likely to be false than true in the light of the facts given.

> U if you think the inference is definitely UNJUSTIFIED; that it does not follow, either because it misinterprets the facts given, or because it contradicts the facts or necessary inferences from those facts.

Example

The first newspaper in America, edited by Ben Harris, appeared in Boston on September 25, 1690, and was banned the same day by Governor Simon Bradstreet. The editor's subsequent long fight to continue to publish his paper and print what he wished marks an important episode in the continuing struggle to maintain a free press.

1) The editor of the first American newspaper died within a few days after his paper was banned on September 25,1690.

2) Information about the first issue of Ben Harris's newspaper promptly came to Governor Bradstreet's attention.

3) The editor of this paper wrote articles criticizing Governor Bradstreet.

4) Ben Harris persisted in holding to some of his aims.

5) Governor Bradstreet objected to some of the items published in Ben Harris's paper.

In the above example:

> Inference 1 is (U) unjustified because in the facts given it mentions "the editor's long fight to continue to publish his paper..."

> Inference 2 is (J) justified because the facts state that the first newspaper appeared on September 25, 1690, and was banned the same day by the Governor.

> Regarding inference 3, there is no information given about the precise nature of the articles appearing in the paper; thus (ID) Insufficient data.

> Regarding inference 4, the item mentions "the editor's subsequent long fight to continue to publish his newspaper and print what he wished..."; thus (J) justified.

> Inference 5 is deemed (PJ) probably justified because the Governor banned the paper the day it appeared. However this is PJ rather that J because there may have been reasons for the ban other than objections to some of the items that appeared in the paper.

figure 3

b) Multiple-Rating Items

Though the use of multiple-choice questions is justified in assessing some micro-skills, the bulk of the machine-gradable items will be *multiple-rating* rather than multiple-choice. Multiple-rating items allow one to ask questions where any number of answers from a provided list may be correct, or incorrect. It further allows students to *rank*, from a number of

---

Recognition of Assumptions

DIRECTIONS: Careful reasoners often find it necessary to complete partially stated arguments in order to evaluate those arguments. For example, someone might say, "John is selfish; we are good friends, but he never lends me money." The conclusion that "John is selfish" is supported by two explicit claims:

    1) John never lends me money.
    2) John and I are good friends.

But an important part of the argument was left out:

    3) People who never lend money to their good friends are selfish.

This third assertion is an *unstated assumption* of the argument.

In this test each exercise begins with a brief argument. Each argument is followed by three numbered statements. Examine each of the numbered statements individually and make a decision about its logical relationship to the argument. For each numbered statement there are spaces on your answer sheet labeled: EC, UA, and N. Select just one of the following alternatives for each numbered statement, and make a mark on your answer sheet under the appropriate heading:

  EC if you think the idea expressed in the numbered statement is an *explicit claim* made in the argument (even if the wording is not the same).

  UA if you think the idea expressed in the numbered statement is a probable *unstated assumption* of the argument.

  N if you think the idea expressed in the numbered statement is *neither* an explicit claim nor an unstated assumption of the argument.

Example
Argument: "We need to save time in getting there, so we'd better go by plane."

1) Going by plane will take less time than going by some other means of transportation.

[Saving time is given as a reason for going by plane; this only makes sense if the person giving the argument believes that going by plane would take less time than other available means of transportation. So the idea expressed here is an *unstated assumption* of the quoted argument.] (UA)

2) We should try to cut down how long we spend travelling to our destination.

[The idea expressed here is directly asserted, though in different words, in the argument, so it is not an unstated assumptions of the argument; rather, it is an *explicit claim* made in the argument.] (EC)

3) Travel by plane is more convenient than travel by train.

[No mention is made in the argument of either trains or convenience. The idea expressed here is *neither* an explicit claim nor an unstated assumption of the argument.] (N)

---

figure 4

possibilities provided, those that are more correct. Thus students can be tested on their ability to arrange items on a continuum of reasonability. This allows much more subtle testing and grading.

The same list of possible answers can pertain to any number of independent test items. Thus, a list of twenty possibilities can be provided, and students can be asked to choose the appropriate response from that list to six different questions. There is no restriction on the number of times a given answer may be correct. Nor is there any guarantee that there will be a reasonable answer on the list to every question. Guessing, using the process of elimination, and scoring well because of test-taking skills are all but impossible.

By including clearly unreasonable choices among the multiple-rating possibilities, a grade can be much more sensitive to the *degree* of a macro-ability or to the *intensity* of an affective dimension. Thus, if there are five possible answers to a given question, they need not be graded 5, 4, 3, 2, 1. Rather, they may be graded, say, 5, 4, 1, 1, -3.

We have provided two detailed samples of multiple-rating items: Figure 5 is on Reasoning Within Conflicting Points of View (and thus is an assessment of an aspect of the affective trait of fairmindedness) and Figure 6 is on Comparing Analogous Situations (and is thus an assessment of a macro-ability). Each sample is limited here by having only four possible answers, a limitation that would not obtain on an actual test.

The following is a list of abbreviated samples of multiple-rating items, having to do with elements of thought, with abilities, with affective dimensions, and with intellectual standards.

Multiple-Rating Items, Elements of Thought

- Here is a list of formulations of the writer's objectives in this excerpt. Rank them from 1 to 5 with respect to which is the most reasonable in the light of the quoted passage....

- For each of the underlined passages in the excerpts below, mark P on the answer sheet if it is a statement of the writer's *Purpose*, C if it is a statement of the *Consequences*, A if it is a statement of the writer's *Assumptions*, and I if it is an *Inference* the writer is making.

- Which of the following would the author most likely give as the statement of the problem she is attempting to solve?

- Read the excerpt; then, from the following list, identify the most plausible statement of the writer's purpose.

- Of the following statements of the author's *point of view* in this passage, select the one from the following list that is both most reasonable and most relevant to the passage....

- List A below is a list of various possible statements of the writer's point of view in the quoted passage; List B is a list that includes possible assumptions and implications of those points of view. Match the items on list A with the items on list B...

- Which of the following are main *concepts* in the passage cited; which are *peripheral concepts?*
- For each inference below, decide whether the accompanying statement is *U* an unstated assumption, *A* an assertion, or *N* neither...
- Rank the following items on a scale of 1 to 5 according to how reasonable it is as a statement of the author's *assumptions...*
- Look at each of the statements below as a possible consequence of the writer's position in the excerpt cited. Rank each statement on a scale of 1 to 7, where 7 means that you consider the statement a *necessary* consequence of the passage, and 1 means that you consider the statement a *highly unlikely* consequence of the passage.

Reasoning Within Conflicting Points of View

DIRECTIONS: In the following questions, rank the answers in order of reasonability. In each case you are being asked to rank answers as to which is the strongest argument in favor of a position. By the strongest we mean the one that is most defensible, not necessarily the one which claims the most. To rank a defense for a position high does not mean that you actually hold that position but only that if you had to defend it before an audience of unbiased and openminded people, the options you rank higher would be easier to defend on rational grounds than the ones you rank lower.

1) Children under the age of twelve should have all of their important decisions made for them by their parents and other appropriate adults because:
   1) allowing them to make all important decisions for themselves will encourage false pride and stubbornness.
   2) allowing them to make all important decisions for themselves will undermine parental respect and authority.
   3) children are not mature enough to make all important decisions for themselves.
   4) children should not be expected to take life's problems so seriously until they grow up.
   5) children can be expected to make grave mistakes, some of which could harm them for life.

2) Children under the age of twelve should make some important decisions for themselves because:
   1) children are less prejudiced than adults and more open to the truth.
   2) children spend a lot of time watching T.V. so they know a lot about what is going on in the world.
   3) children are likely to make many reasonable decisions affecting themselves.
   4) children will become depressed if they are not allowed to make some important decisions.
   5) children will be more apt to become responsible adults if they are allowed to make some important decisions for themselves as they are growing up.

figure 5

Comparing Analogous Situations

"Having a population to study instead of an individual fossil is enormously important. No two people today are exactly alike; no two Australopithecines were either.
It is for that reason that drawing conclusions from a single fossil is risky. Measurements taken of it, and theories spun off as a result of those measurements, may be
misleading because the part being measured may not be typical. It is only when a
large number of specimens is available that all their variations can be taken into
account, and a norm derived from them. If a visitor from outer space were to
describe and name *Homo sapiens sapiens* by examining one skeleton, that of a
short, squat, heavy-boned New Guinea tribesman, he would certainly be excused
if he set up another species on the basis of a second skeleton discovered later a few
thousand miles away — that of a seven-foot, slender-boned Watutsi tribesman
from central Africa." (Edey, *The Emergence of Man*, pp. 47–48)

The author of the above passage makes an analogy between an anthropologist
studying fossils and a visitor from outer space studying one or two single skele-
tons. Rank each of the following comments 1 to 3, according to whether it would
be crucial in judging the strength of the analogy for the point the author is making. Give a comment a 3 if it is CRUCIAL in judging the worth of the analogy; give
it a 1 if it is IRRELEVANT to judging the worth of the analogy; give it a 2 if it lies in
between.

a) The analogy illustrates the point well because in both cases we are called
upon to draw general conclusions based on a limited sample. The more
items you have in your sample, the more justified your generalization will
be.

b) It is a bad analogy because the visitors from outer space would draw the
same erroneous conclusion even if they had a whole population of New
Guinea tribesmen to study.

c) It is a good analogy but it shows that we need, not simply *more* fossils of
Australopithecus, but fossils of it from other geographical areas.

d) It is a bad analogy because we have no idea what visitors from outer space
would conclude from seeing a skeleton of a New Guinea tribesman. The
visitors might refrain from making the generalization for the same reason
that makes the author say it is "risky."

figure 6

- Each of the following is an *inference* one might draw from the passage.
  Rank each one on a scale from 1 to 5, according to whether it is
  completely justified (5) or completely unjustified (1)...
- Which of the following is the most accurate formulation of the
  author's *inference* in the cited passage?

Multiple-Rating Items, Abilities

- Which of the following would be relevant to deciding whether A is a
  credible source of information on the topic...?
- Here is a list of observations about the behavior of X's, made by a
  responsible investigator. Which of the items from the following list
  would be a *justified generalization* about X's?

- A has the following beliefs about astrology. Which of the questions below would be *root* or *significant questions* that A would have to answer to claim his beliefs about astrology were rational?

- A refuses to refund a customer's money and, when asked, defends her action by stating that it is "dictated by store policy". Which of the following would be *relevant* to deciding whether her action was indeed "dictated by store policy"? Which of the questions would be relevant to deciding if the store policy was rational?

- Judge A makes the following ruling in a case... Which of the following is the clearest statement of the standards Judge A is using?

- A compares the relation between managers and employees to the relation between teachers and students. Which of the following would A have to answer in order to continue using the analogy rationally?

- A gives the following argument for.... Which of the listed comments would be the *strongest objection* to her argument?

- Listen to the accompanying excerpt from an audiotape of a lecture by A. Which of the following questions would be of most help in clarifying A's views?

Multiple-Rating Items, Affective Traits

- Here are position-statements from both sides, A and B, of a controversial and inflammatory debate. From list X below, choose those items which are the most reasonable *inferences* to draw from position A; then choose those items which are the most reasonable *inferences* to draw from position B.

- Here are position-statements from both sides, A and B, of a controversial and inflammatory debate. From list X below, choose those items which state the most reasonable *assumptions* underlying position A; then choose those items which state the most reasonable *assumptions* underlying position B.

- For each of the items below, tell which is the most reasonable action to take under the circumstances described. If, in your view, there is not enough information to make a reasonable decision, you may choose the action of *suspending judgment* as the most reasonable response.

- A disposition to take a measured response rather than an exaggerated, disproportionate response will be measured by requiring students to discriminate between the likelihood of dire versus mild consequences of positions they dislike.

Multiple-Rating Items, Intellectual Standards

- The following are four definitions from *Webster's New World Dictionary*. Which of them gives the clearest definition of...?

- Rank the following definitions for their *precision* on a scale of 1 to 7. 1 means "not precise at all"; 7 means "too precise for the subject matter"; and 4 means "exactly as precise as it should be".

- Here is a list of data and a series of accounts summarizing the data. Which of the accounts is the *most accurate* summary of the data?
- For each statement below, tell whether it is *relevant* or *irrelevant* to the hypothesis in the passage cited.
- Which of the following is the *fairest* restatement of the author's position [where the author is stating a highly controversial position]?
- Rank the following statements according to which are the *best-evidenced* and which are the *least-evidenced*.
- Which of the following is a good reason for believing the statement in question? Which is a bad reason? Which is somewhere in the middle?

c) Essay Items

The full range of the use of critical thinking cannot be assessed without requiring writing on the part of the student. To confront real issues, balance competing interests, weigh objections and alternatives, and make a reasonable decision about a matter of some consequence — this is a major part of what it is to think critically.

The ability and the disposition to engage in full-fledged critical thinking is measured only in part by a person's ability to choose from among a pre-selected list. A true measure of critical thinking, and thus of a program's capacity to improve critical thinking, can be obtained only by including in the assessment *generative* as well as *selective* dimensions. Neither multiple-rating nor, obviously, multiple-choice items are adequate for testing this dimension.

Essay items will require proficiency in handling the elements of thought, in using appropriate abilities, in applying intellectual standards, and, what is more, it will require integrating these and bringing them to bear on a substantive issue.

Three detailed samples of essay items follow on the next page. Each has the same set of general directions.

In addition to full-blown essay tests, a series of short-justification items are currently being prepared. These would not ask students to write an essay on a topic, but would rather have them choose an answer from a pre-selected multiple-rating list and then justify their answer in a sentence of their own writing.

This type of test, if it were sufficiently developed, would have several advantages: it could be administered, because of the brevity and straightforwardness of students' written answers, to the student population as a whole rather than merely to a representative sample (see #1, under "Implementation", below); it would assess some, though not all, generative dimensions of critical thinking; it would allow flexibility in grading the machine-gradable keyed answers (thus, one could adjust the rating of

Critical Thinking, Problem Solving, & Communication Skills Essay Exam

Directions

This test is designed to assess your critical thinking, problem solving, and communication skills. Your answer will be judged for its clarity, relevance, consistency, logic, depth, coherence, and fairness. More specifically, the reader will be asking the following questions:

1) Is the question at issue well stated? Is it clear and unbiased? Does the expression of the question do justice to the complexity of the matter at issue?

2) Does the writer cite relevant evidence, experiences, and/or relevant information essential to the issue?

3) Does the writer clarify key concepts when necessary?

4) Does the writer show a sensitivity to what he or she is assuming or taking for granted (insofar as those assumptions might reasonably be questioned)?

5) Does the writer develop a definite line of reasoning, explaining well how he or she is arriving at his or her conclusions?

6) Is the writer's reasoning well-supported?

7) Does the writer show a sensitivity to alternative points of view or lines of reasoning? Does he or she consider and respond to objections framed from other points of view?

8) Does the writer show a sensitivity to the implications and consequences of the position he or she has taken?

Issue #1: Ecology

The nation is facing a variety of ecological problems that have the following general form: an established practice, whether on the part of business and industry or on the part of the public, is contributing to serious health problems for a large number of people. At the same time it would be costly to modify the practice so as to reduce the health problem. People often say that the answer is one of achieving a "balance" between the amount of money we spend to correct the problem and the number of lives we would save by that expenditure. Develop a point of view and some plausible criteria for telling how one would determine this "balance." Make sure you address any dilemmas inherent in your strategy for solving such problems.

Issue #2: Politics

There is a growing number of Americans who do not vote in national and local elections. Many of them explain their non-participation by saying that their vote would not make a difference. Some go on to argue that this is true because "money plays such a large role in elections that the candidate with the highest paid, and the highest quality, media campaign wins." Most people agree that money sometimes plays an inappropriate role in determining the outcome of elections. Develop a proposed solution to this problem that takes into account the view that people and organizations with money have a right to use their money to advance political causes they believe in. If you like, you may decide to develop a position to the effect that there is no solution to the problem and that we have no choice but to accept the status quo.

Issue #3: Morality

Sociologist Erving Goffman has pointed out that all social groups, including professions, develop a protective attitude toward members of their group, even when what some of the members do is seen as morally wrong. A sense of loyalty to the group often overrides what they would otherwise deem immoral. Consider the arguments for and against exposing people with whom you are personally close or with whom you have close professional ties. Develop a position on this issue that could serve as a guide for anyone in such a position.

an item up or down depending on the justification); it would be no more difficult to grade by trained personnel than the math work on currently administered standardized calculus tests.

✦ Interdisciplinary and Subject-Specific

SCOPE OF THE ASSESSMENT

An assessment of the results of critical thinking instruction ought to focus both on thinking within the framework of particular academic subjects, and on thinking in the interdisciplinary contexts that are so important to functioning as an autonomous, well-informed, productive member of a democracy.

A basic principle of critical thinking instruction, as applied to teaching subject matter in an area, is that (to quote the National Council for Excellence in Critical Thinking Instruction) "to achieve knowledge in any domain, it is essential to think critically". A related principle is that in any domain where one is thinking well, one is thinking critically. Any example of good scientific thinking, or good historical thinking, or good anthropological thinking, or thinking in any other subject, will necessarily be an example of critical thinking: It will involve basic skills dealing with elements of thought; it will involve at least some, and probably many, of the abilities; it will involve affective traits like independent thinking and intellectual perseverance. And as far as instruction is concerned, there is a real sense in which learning biology is learning to think within and about the logic of biology.

Including critical thinking items taken from individual subject areas would also properly test those thinking skills that are more subject-specific, and it would do so in the context of presupposing a good deal of specialized knowledge. A critical thinking test in nursing or in history of art or in geology might well (in their different ways) test for skills of critical observation, while a test in sociology might assess thinking skills involved in constructing an unbiased questionnaire; a critical thinking test in English literature might well presuppose a knowledge of who Milton was, while a thinking test in physics might justifiably ask about a problem for which a knowledge of the second law of thermodynamics was taken for granted.

Even if we already had a series of critical thinking items within the various subject areas, however, we would not be testing for many of the interdisciplinary abilities we most want critical thinking for. Many of these have already been mentioned: the ability to make sound decisions in the context of understanding our rights and responsibilities as citizens, in the context of the work-place, as well-informed and thinking consumers, as members of our families, as participants in what is becoming a symbiotic and fragile world economy — the ability to reason about the gaps between subject areas, the bridges between them, and the generalizability of subjects to other areas.

To test critical thinking abilities, as they apply to these areas, what is needed are interdisciplinary questions. These are questions of broad interest, ones that shed light on the quality of and improvement in student thinking about realistic and fundamental issues; they ought to be the kind of questions which can be at least partially illuminated by well-integrated knowledge in any number of academic areas.

The national assessment we are proposing would offer a range of subject-specific items, from which students would choose those relevant to their subject-matter knowledge. The interdisciplinary items, on the other hand, would not provide choices because of the desirability of avoiding the loss of equivalency that is almost always involved. (That loss would have to be minimized in the case of subject-specific items by field testing and rewriting.)

The interdisciplinary part is constructable by experts well versed in a rich and substantive concept of critical thinking. Subject-specific critical thinking assessment items will be constructed by members of the discipline working in consultation with experts in critical thinking, perhaps the standing committees on the various disciplines of the National Council for Excellence in Critical Thinking Instruction. Both groups would work in conjunction with grade-level experts to construct appropriate levels of items, from the 6th-grade test through the college-graduate test.

✦ *The Value of the Proposed Assessment Strategy for the Reform of Instruction*

Since higher order thinking has always been considered an important object of education, and since this assessment would furnish a measure of that concept, and since performance on this assessment would have a significant impact on the standing of the school not only in the eyes of the intellectual community but in the eyes of the public as well, administrators and teachers would have a strong motivation to become familiar with the concepts and program behind the assessment. Most importantly, teachers and others in charge of instruction and the formulation of educational goals would find in it a clear model for the articulation and integration of higher order thinking across the curriculum. Note the following:

1) The concept of the elements of thought not only provides a realistic analysis of the common dimensions of reasoning in every domain, it also encourages the explicit use in instruction of those critical/analytic terms which are the common possession of the intellectual community (question-at-issue, problem, evidence, data, concept, inference, assumption, implication, conclusion, point of

view, frame of reference, etc.) and makes explicit the intellectual standards implicit in every subject as well as in the closely reasoned professional work in business and industry (clarity, precision, accuracy, logic, consistency, ...)

2) By highlighting reading, writing, speaking, and listening as modes of critical reasoning, the necessity of having instruction go beyond mere didactic coverage of content would become more intelligible. As long as reading, writing, speaking, and listening skills appear the sole province of specialized subjects and at specialized levels rather than modes of reasoning intrinsic to the construction and mastery of knowledge in any subject at any level, there will continue to be a significant lack of fit between modes of instruction and modes of necessary learning.

3) By highlighting the other abilities of critical thinking, each analyzed into the same elements of thought, there would be significant transfer of emphasis to important modes of higher order thinking within a larger number of student assignments. At present, many teachers fail to notice the extent to which they either presuppose that students already grasp the nature of fundamental intellectual processes, or they make assignments which, though they appear to call for such processes, can be successfully completed by simply repeating to the teacher what was said in lecture or written in the text.

4) By highlighting a common critical/analytic language across the curriculum, students are encouraged to seek to transfer learning and intellectual discipline emphasized in one domain of learning to other domains of learning and application. The fragmentation of the subject areas, in the minds of the students if not in fact, is now a serious problem in education. This problem is mirrored, of course, in business, industry, and government in the tendency to engage in fragmented, over-specialized problem-solving which fails to address the multi-dimensional nature of many complex problems.

5) By highlighting the importance of intellectual discipline and grounding it in specific skills and abilities, teachers and other educational leaders will be given a reasonable impetus to help students make connections of a broader, more interdisciplinary nature. This will also be strongly re-enforced by the inclusion of everyday, multi-logical, interdisciplinary essay questions.

✦ Implementation of the Proposed Assessment

Our recommendations about implementation can be summarized as follows:

1) The essay assessment should be administered to a representative sample of the student population at each educational institution, the machine-gradable items to the total student population;

2) it should be administered at the 6th, 9th, and 12th grades, and three times during a student's college career — at entrance, at the start of the junior year, and just prior to graduation — and thus yield value-added information to schools;

3) the test should be constructed to be roughly three-hours long;

4) test items should be constructed from item shells, rather than from a simple pool of actual items;

5) it should be administered by a private agency with critical thinking credentials;

6) it should be paid for by school districts, colleges, and universities that contract to have their students tested;

7) it should provide educational institutions with detailed information about central aspects of their students' higher order thinking;

8) it should be developed according to the costs and timetables listed below.

Details of our recommendations center around the answers to five practical questions about the administration of the test:

WHO WILL BE ASSESSED?

Our *minimal* recommendation is that all portions of the assessment be given to, at the very least, a representative sample of the student population at each educational institution. Since the problems implicit in testing a random sample can be easily worked out, this recommendation avoids the expense of administering an essay test to the student population as a whole.

The assessment strategies we have proposed include two broad areas of testing: a *machine-gradable portion* that includes multiple-choice items and multiple-rating items and an *essay portion*. Both portions will assess, in their different ways and with their different emphases, micro-skills, abilities, affective traits, and intellectual standards.

There are, therefore, really two options with respect to who is assessed using the strategies we propose. First, the machine gradable portion of the assessment can be administered to the student population as a whole, while the essay portion can be administered to a representative sample of students at each institution. Second, both portions could be given only to a representative sample of the population at each institution. Both options will hold down costs, though the latter will clearly be less expensive than the former. Which option is ultimately chosen will depend on the amount of detail desired, the precise role the assessment is to play, and the funds available.

HOW OFTEN WILL THE ASSESSMENT TAKE PLACE?

The maximum benefit to educational institutions will be provided to the extent that they are enabled to measure the progress of their students' higher order thinking during the course of their educational career. This will enable school systems not only to gauge their contribution to their students' progress, but also to measure the success of attempts to re-design their instruction so as to increase critical thinking capabilities.

These objectives can be accomplished by having students assessed often enough to reflect such progress, optimally: at the 6th, 9th, and 12th grades, and at the time of their college entrance, at the beginning of their junior year, and just before graduation from college.

How Long Will the Test Take?

The test should last about three hours in order to cover multiple-choice, multiple-rating, and essay items without becoming a speeded test to an inappropriate degree. To span all difficulty levels, it would be best to have a total of at least 30 items. While two of these could be short essay items requiring 20 minutes each to answer, the machine-gradable items would be faster to answer, and hence could be handled in 3–8 minutes.

How Will a Sufficiently Large Pool of Items Be Constructed?

While it might be possible to release a pool of items which would pro-vide the equivalent of 6 tests at each level, hence 6 x 6 x 30, it would be better to increase flexibility by using item shells, which would be items that include identified variables, each of which could be replaced from a list of acceptable values. This would greatly increase the number of items that could be generated, but without "surprises". A pool of shells would generate over a thousand items at each level, possibly several thousand.

Who Will Do the Assessing?

In order to avoid problems in the reliability of the assessment (like those we have seen occur in the *California Direct Writing Assessment*), the assessment needs to be monitored, administered, and graded by a private agency whose personnel have critical thinking credentials or are at least under the direction of scholars with a solid grounding in research in crit-ical thinking.

Who Will Bear the Costs of the Assessment?

The assessment should be paid for by the school systems, colleges, and universities that contract to have their students tested. This not only puts least burden on the public but represents an established precedent in dis-tributing costs of testing.

What Will Institutions Be Able to Learn from the Results of the Assessment?

We anticipate that educational institutions will receive an analytic report that will document all of the following:

- where their students are strongest and weakest with respect to particular micro-skills;
- where their students are strongest and weakest with respect to important abilities;
- how students stand in each of the school's subject-matter areas;
- how their students stand in relation to students at other institutions;
- how their students at one educational level stand in relation to their students at other educational levels;
- how their students stand with respect to established performance criteria.

This information would enable institutions to target instruction to remediate weaknesses and build on strengths, as well as to measure what students are gaining as a result of attending their classes.*

---

* The authors wish to acknowledge the invaluable advice provided us by Michael Scriven on evaluation theory in general, and, more particularly, on the logistics of test construction, it is he who originally developed the concept of multiple-rating items.

Chapter 7

Using Intellectual Standards to Assess Student Reasoning

with Gerald M. Nosich

Abstract

In this paper, co-authored by Richard Paul and Gerald Nosich, the emphasis is on providing the reader with specific examples of what is involved in applying intellectual criteria and standards to students' reasoning, especially with reference to the "elements of reasoning" which, they explain, are the logical components of all reasoning. Paul and Nosich first explain the significance of reasoning having "elements", then the need for "standards" in assessing reasoning. They then take us through each of the elements of reasoning, giving us a general sense of the interface between elements and standards, and then, finally, provide a series of three columned charts, one for each of the elements of reasoning. Each chart briefly characterizes the differences between how good and bad reasoners handle the components of their reasoning, as well as articulating samples of the sort of feedback which we as teachers might give to students with regard to each of the components of their performance as reasoners. Their goal is clearly both theoretical and practical.

*T*o assess student reasoning requires that we focus our attention as teachers on two inter-related dimensions of reasoning. The first dimension consists of the elements *of reasoning;* the second dimension consists of the *universal intellectual standards* by which we measure student ability to use, in a skillful way, each of those elements of reasoning.

Elements of reasoning. Once we progress from thought which is purely associational and undisciplined, to thinking which is conceptual and inferential, thinking which attempts in some intelligible way to figure something out, in short, to reasoning, then it is helpful to concentrate on what can be called "the elements of reasoning". The elements of reasoning are those essential dimensions of reasoning whenever and wherever it occurs. Working together, they shape reasoning and provide a general logic to the use of reason. We can articulate these elements by paying close attention to what is implicit in the the act of figuring anything out by the the use of reason. These elements, then — purpose, question at issue, assumptions, inferences, implications, point of view, concepts and evidence — constitute a central focus in the assessment of student thinking.

Standards of Reasoning. When we assess student reasoning, we want to evaluate, in a reasonable, defensible, objective way, not just *that* students are reasoning, but *how well* they are reasoning. We will be assessing not just that they are using the elements of reasoning, but the degree to which they are using them well, critically, in accord with appropriate intellectual standards.

To assess a student response, whether written or oral, in structured discussion of content or in critical response to reading assignments, by how *clearly* or *completely* it states a position, is to assess it on the basis of a standard of reasoning. Similarly, assessing student work by how *logically* and *consistently* it defends its position, by how *flexible* and *fair* the student is in articulating other points of view, by how *significant* and *realistic* the student's purpose is, by how *precisely* and *deeply* the student articulates the question at issue — each of these is an evaluation based on standards of reasoning.

Distinct from such reasoning standards are other standards that teachers sometimes use to assess student work. To evaluate a student response on the basis of how concisely or elegantly it states a position is to use standards that are inappropriate to assessing student reasoning. Similarly unrelated to the assessment of reasoning is evaluating student work by how humorous, glib, personal or sincere it is, by how much it agrees with the teacher's views, by how "well-written" it is, by how exactly it repeats the teacher's words, by the mere quantity of information it contains. The danger is that such standards are often conflated with reasoning standards, often unconsciously, and students are assessed on grounds other than the degree to which they are reasoning well.

The basic conditions implicit whenever we gather, conceptualize, apply, analyze, synthesize, or evaluate information — the elements of reasoning — are as follows:

1) Purpose, Goal, or End in View. Whenever we reason, we reason to some end, to achieve some objective, to satisfy some desire or fulfill some need. One source of problems in student reasoning is traceable to defects at the level of goal, purpose, or end. If the goal is unrealistic, for example, or contradictory to other goals the student has, if it is confused or muddled in some way, then the reasoning used to achieve it is problematic.

A teacher's assessment of student reasoning, then, necessarily involves an assessment of the student's ability to handle the dimension of purpose in accord with relevant intellectual *standards*. It also involves giving *feedback* to students about the degree to which their reasoning meets those standards.

Is the student's purpose — in an essay, a research project, an oral report, a discussion — *clear*? Is the purpose *significant* or trivial or somewhere in between? Is the student's purpose, according to the most judicious evaluation on the teacher's part, *realistic*? Is it an *achievable* purpose? Does the student's overall goal dissolve in the course of the project, does it change, or is it *consistent* throughout? Does the student have contradictory purposes?

2) Question at Issue, or Problem to be Solved. Whenever we attempt to reason something out, there is at least one question at issue, at least one problem to be solved. One area of concern for assessing student reasoning, therefore, will be the formulation of the question to be answered or problem to be solved, whether with respect to the student's own reasoning or to that of others.

Assessing skills of mastery of this element of reasoning requires assessing — and giving feedback on — students' ability to formulate a problem in a *clear* and *relevant* way. It requires giving students direct commentary on whether the question they are addressing is an important one, whether it is *answerable*, on whether they understand the requirements for settling the question, for solving the problem.

3) Point of View, or Frame of Reference. Whenever we reason, we must reason within some point of view or frame of reference. Any "defect" in that point of view or frame of reference is a possible source of problems in the reasoning.

A point of view may be too narrow, too parochial, may be based on false or misleading analogies or metaphors, may contain contradictions, and so forth. It may be restricted or unfair. Alternatively, student reasoning involving articulation of their point of view may meet the relevant standards to a significant degree: their point of view may be *broad, flexible, fair*; it may be *clearly* stated and *consistently* adhered to.

Feedback to students would involve commentary noting both when students meet the standards and when they fail to meet them. Evaluation of students' ability to handle the dimension of point of view would also appropriately direct students to lines of reasoning that would promote a richer facility in reasoning about and in terms of points of view.

4) The Empirical Dimension of Reasoning. Whenever we reason, there is some "stuff," some phenomena about which we are reasoning. Any "defect," then, in the experiences, data, evidence, or raw material upon which a person's reasoning is based is a possible source of problems.

Students would be assessed and receive feedback on their ability to give evidence that is gathered and reported *clearly, fairly,* and *accurately*. Does the student furnish data at all? Is the data *relevant*? Is the information *adequate* for achieving the student's purpose? Is it applied *consistently*, or does the student distort it to fit her own point of view?

5) The Conceptual Dimension of Reasoning. All reasoning uses some ideas or concepts and not others. These concepts can include the theories, principles, axioms and rules implicit in our reasoning. Any "defect" in the concepts or ideas of the reasoning is a possible source of problems in student reasoning.

Feedback to students would note whether their understanding of theories and rules was *deep* or merely superficial. Are the concepts they use in their reasoning *clear* ones? Are their ideas *relevant* to the issue at hand, are their principles slanted by their point of view?

6) Assumptions. All reasoning must begin somewhere, must take some things for granted. Any "defect" in the assumptions or presuppositions with which the reasoning begins is a possible source of problems for students.

Assessing skills of reasoning involves assessing their ability to recognize and articulate their assumptions, again according to the relevant standards. The student's assumptions may be stated *clearly* or unclearly; the assumptions may be *justifiable* or unjustifiable, *crucial* or extraneous, *consistent* or contradictory. The feedback students receive from teachers on their ability to meet the relevant standards will be a large factor in the improvement of student reasoning.

7) Implications and Consequences. No matter where we stop our reasoning, it will always have further implications and consequences. As reasoning develops, statements will logically be entailed by it. Any "defect" in the implications or consequences of our reasoning is a possible source of problems.

The ability to reason well is measured in part by an ability to understand and enunciate the implications and consequences of the reasoning. Students therefore need help in coming to understand both the relevant standards of reasoning out implications and the degree to which their own reasoning meets those standards.

When they spell out the implications of their reasoning, have they succeeded in identifying *significant* and *realistic* implications, or have they *confined themselves to unimportant and* unrealistic ones? Have they enunciated the implications of their views clearly and precisely enough to permit their thinking to be evaluated by the validity of those implications?

8) Inferences. Reasoning proceeds by steps in which we reason as follows: "Because this is so, that also is so (or probably so)," or "Since this, therefore that." Any "defect" in such inferences is a possible problem in our reasoning.

Assessment would evaluate students' ability to make sound inferences in their reasoning. When is an inference *sound?* When it meets reasonable and relevant standards of inferring. Are the inferences the student draws *clear?* Are they *justifiable?* Do they draw *deep* conclusions or do they stick to the trivial and superficial? Are the conclusions they draw *consistent?*

Purpose
(All reasoning has a purpose.)

Fundamental Standards: 1) Clarity of Purpose, 2) Significance of Purpose, 3) Achievability of Purpose, 4) Consistency of Purposes

Failures of Purpose: 1) Unclear Purpose, 2) Trivial Purpose, 3) Unrealistic Purpose, 4) Contradictory Purposes

Good Reasoners:	Bad Reasoners:	Feedback to Students:
take the time to state their purpose clearly	are often unclear about their central purpose	(-) You have not made the purpose of your reasoning clear. What are you trying to achieve? Whom are you trying to persuade? (+) Your paper reflects an excellent sense of unity of purpose. It all fits together like pieces of a puzzle.
distinguish it from related purposes	oscillate between different, sometimes contradictory, purposes	(+) You do a good job of distinguishing different but related goals. (-) You seem to have a number of different purposes in mind. I am not sure how you see them as related. You seem to be going off in somewhat different directions.
periodically remind themselves of their purpose to determine whether they are straying from it	lose track of their fundamental end or goal	(-) After the second paragraph you seem to wander from your purpose. How do your 3rd and 4th paragraphs relate to your central goal? (+) I like the way you periodically show the reader how the points you are making all add up to a central conclusion.
adopt realistic purposes and goals	adopt unrealistic purposes, set unrealistic goals	(+) You make a wise decision not to try to accomplish too much. Accomplishing a little, well, is almost always better than failing in a grand and sweeping design. (-) You try to accomplish too much in so short a paper.
choose significant purposes and goals	adopt trivial purposes and goals as if they were significant	(-) Your paper would have been stronger if you had chosen a more important goal. (+) The goal of your paper is worthwhile and well-chosen.

Purpose continued

Good Reasoners:	Bad Reasoners:	Feedback to Students:
choose goals and purposes that are consistent with other goals and purposes they have chosen	inadvertently negate their own purposes do not monitor their thinking for inconsistent goals	(-) One part of your paper seems to undermine what you are trying to accomplish in another part. You first try to persuade the reader how realistic Dickens' characters are, but after that you seem to be showing that they are caricatures.
adjust their thinking regularly to their purpose	do not adjust their thinking regularly to their purpose	(+) Your unity of purpose is reflected in every section of your paper.

Question at Issue or Central Problem
(All reasoning is an attempt to figure something out, to settle some question, solve some problem.)

Fundamental Standards: *1)* Clarity of Question, *2)* Significance of Question, *3)* Answerability, *4)* Relevance

Flawed Questions: *1)* Unclear, *2)* Insignificant, *3)* Not Answerable, *4)* Irrelevant

Principle: To settle a question you must understand what it requires.

Good Reasoners:	Bad Reasoners:	Feedback to Students:
are clear about the question they are trying to settle	are often unclear about the kind of question they are asking	(-) The main question at issue is never made clear. (+) You do a good job of clarifying the question at issue.
can re-express a question in a variety of ways	express questions vaguely and find them difficult to reformulate	(-) You need to reformulate your question in a couple of ways to recognize the complexity of it. (+) I like the way you reformulate your question in different ways. It helps the reader see it from different points of view.
can break a question into sub-questions	are unable to break down the questions they are asking	(+) You do a good job of analyzing the main question into sub-questions. (-) It would be easier to solve your main problem if you would break it down somewhat.

Good Reasoners:	Bad Reasoners:	Feedback to Students:
have sensitivity to the kind of question they are asking routinely distinguish questions of different types	have little sensitivity to the kind of question they are asking confuse questions of different types often respond inappropriately to the questions they ask	(-) You are confusing a legal question with a moral one. (+) You do a good job of keeping the economic issues separate from the social ones.
distinguish significant from trivial questions	confuse trivial questions with significant ones	(-) You begin with a significant question but seem to wander off into some insignificant ones. (+) The problem you raise is a very significant one.
distinguish relevant questions from irrelevant ones	confuse irrelevant questions with relevant ones	(-) The questions you raise in the second part of your paper do not seem to be relevant to the main question at issue.
are sensitive to the assumptions built into the questions they ask	often ask loaded questions	(-) The way you put the question is loaded. You are taking for granted from the outset the correctness of your own position. (+) You put your question in a neutral and unbiased form.
distinguish questions they can answer from questions they can't		

Point of View

(All reasoning is done from some point of view.)

Fundamental Standards: *1)* Flexibility in Point of View, *2)* Fairness of Point of View, *3)* Clarity of Point of View, *4)* Breadth of Point of View

Defects in point of view: *1)* Restricted, *2)* Biased, *3)* Unclear, *4)* Narrow

Principle: Reasoning is better when multiple, relevant points of view are sought out, articulated clearly, empathized with fairly and logically, applied consistently and dispassionately.

Good Reasoners:	Bad Reasoners:	Feedback to Students:
keep in mind that people have different points of view, especially on controversial issues	don't realize that people approach the question at issue from different points of view	(-) You haven't articulated the point of view from which you are approaching this issue. (+) You have reasoned out this controversial issue clearly from multiple relevant points of view.

Point of View *continued*

Good Reasoners:	Bad Reasoners:	Feedback to Students:
consistently articulate other points of view and reason from within those points of view seek other viewpoints especially when the issue is one they believe in passionately	cannot see issues from points of view that are significantly different from their own; cannot reason with empathy from alien points of view can sometimes give other points of view when the issue is not emotionally charged, but cannot do so for issues they are deeply committed to	(-) You have characterized your own point of view, but what are the most significant aspects of the problem from X's point of view? (+)You have done an excellent job of spelling out the other side of this issue. This is especially difficult when a person is as deeply committed to one side as you are. (-) This is an unfair way of presenting X's point of view.
confine their monological reasoning to problems that are clearly monological	confuse multilogical with monological issues, insist that there is only one frame of reference within which a given multilogical question must be decided	(-) Is the question here monological or multilogical? How can you tell? (-) You are reasoning as if only one point of view is relevant to this issue.
recognize when they are most likely to be prejudiced	are unaware of their own prejudices	(+/-) Is this prejudice or reasoned judgment?
approach problems and issues with a richness of vision and an appropriately broad point of view	reason from within inappropriately narrow or superficial points of view	(-) Your approach to this question is too narrow. (+) You have considered this problem with the depth it requires.

Empirical Dimension
(All reasoning is based on data, information, evidence.)

Fundamental Standards: *1)* Clear Evidence, *2)* Relevant Information, *3)* Fairly Gathered and Reported Evidence, *4)* Accurate Data, *5)* Adequate Evidence, *6)* Consistently Applied Data

Flawed Empirical Dimension: *1)* Unclear, *2)* Unfairly or Self-Servingly Gathered, *3)* Inaccurate, *4)* Insufficient

Principle: Reasoning can only be as sound as the evidence it is based on.

Good Reasoners:	Bad Reasoners:	Feedback to Students:
assert a claim only when they have sufficient evidence to back it up	assert claims without considering any evidence	(+) This is a clear statement of the relevant data. (-) This claim can't merely be asserted but must be supported by evidence.

Good Reasoners:	Bad Reasoners:	Feedback to Students:
can articulate and therefore evaluate the evidence behind their claims	don't articulate their evidence even when they have it, and so do not subject it to rational scrutiny	(-) I think you probably *have* evidence to support your claim here; you just haven't articulated it.
actively search for information *against* (not just *for*) their own position	gather evidence only when it supports their own point of view	(+) You have gathered and reported evidence fairly on both sides of this issue. (-) Where is a good place to look for evidence on the opposite side? Have you looked there?
focus on relevant information and disregard what is irrelevant to the question at issue	do not carefully distinguish between relevant data and irrelevant data	(+) The information you cite is relevant and to the point. (-) The data you supply is irrelevant. (-) How is this relevant to the claim you are making?
draw conclusions only to the extent that they are supported by the data	make inferences that go beyond what the data support	(-) Though you give some evidence to back up your claim, the claim goes beyond the evidence you've cited. (+) Your claims are well-supported by the evidence you cite.
state their evidence clearly and fairly	distort the data, or state it inaccurately	(+) This is a clear and coherent presentation of the pertinent information.

Concepts and Ideas

(All reasoning is expressed through, and shaped by, concepts and ideas.)

Fundamental Standards: *1)* Clarity of Concepts, *2)* Relevance of Concepts, *3)* Depth of Concepts, *4)* Neutrality of Concepts

Failure of Concepts: *1)* Unclear, *2)* Irrelevant, *3)* Superficial, *4)* Biased

Principle: Reasoning can only be as clear, relevant, and deep as the concepts which shape it.

Good Reasoners:	Bad Reasoners:	Feedback to Students:
are aware of the key concepts and ideas they use	are unaware of the key concepts and ideas they use	(-) The concept of democracy, central to your essay, is not analyzed in your paper. You assume that if people are in any sense allowed to vote, they are living in a democracy. You need to consider the idea of democracy more deeply.

Concepts & Ideas continued

Good Reasoners:	Bad Reasoners:	Feedback to Students:
are able to explain the basic implications of the key words and phrases they use	do not accurately explain basic implications of their key words and phrases	(+) You do well in distinguishing training, socialization, indoctrination, and education. (+) Yes, the word 'cunning' has negative implications that the word 'clever' does not.
are able to distinguish special, non-standard uses of words from standard uses	are not able to recognize when their use of a word or phrase departs from educated usage	(-) Where did you get your definition of this central concept? (-) You assume that abortion is murder, but you won't find a dictionary that defines it as "the murder of a very young person". Don't put your conclusion into the definition.
are aware of irrelevant concepts and ideas use concepts and ideas in ways relevant to their functions	use concepts in ways inappropriate to the subject or issue	(-) Do you think that the notion of "dog-eat-dog" applies to moral situations? Isn't the question one of moral responsibility?
can distinguish superficial from deep concepts	confuse superficial with deep concepts	

Assumptions

(All reasoning is based on assumptions.)

Fundamental Standards: 1) Clarity of Assumptions, 2) Justifiability of Assumptions, 3) Consistency of Assumptions

Failure of Assumptions: 1) Unclear, 2) Unjustified, 3) Contradictory

Principle: Reasoning can only be as sound as the assumptions it makes.

Good Reasoners:	Bad Reasoners:	Feedback to Students:
make assumptions that are clear	often make assumptions that are unclear	(-) It is not clear what you are assuming. (-) It is not clear what you base your main assumption on. (+) Your assumptions seem clear and reasonable.
make assumptions that are reasonable	often make unjustified or unreasonable assumptions	(-) It seems unreasonable to make assumptions about the future based on just one experience from the past.

Good Reasoners:	Bad Reasoners:	Feedback to Students:
make assumptions that are consistent with each other	often make assumptions that are contradictory	(-) The assumptions you make in the first part of your paper seem to contradict the assumptions you make in the last section of your paper.

Implications and Consequences
(All reasoning leads somewhere, has implications and consequences.)

Fundamental Standards: 1) Significance of Implications, 2) Realistic Nature of Implications, 3) Clarity of Articulated Implications, 4) Precision of Articulated Implications, 5) Completeness of Articulated Implications

Flawed Implications and Consequences: 1) Unimportant, 2) Unrealistic, 3) Unclear, 4) Imprecise, 5) Incomplete

Principle: To reason through an issue or decision, you must understand the implications and consequences that follow from it.

Good Reasoners:	Bad Reasoners:	Feedback to Students:
trace out a number of significant implications and consequences of their reasoning	trace out few or none of the implications and consequences of holding a position or making a decision	(-) You don't spell out the consequences of the action you are advocating. (-) If you took this course of action, what other consequences would follow?
articulate the implications and consequences clearly and precisely	are unclear and imprecise in the consequences they articulate	(+) You have spelled out the implications of your reasoning in as clear and precise a way as the subject permits. (-) You will be much clearer about whether the action is reasonable if you are more precise when you delineate the consequences likely to follow from it.
search for negative as well as for positive consequences	trace out only the consequences they had in mind at the beginning, either positive or negative, but usually not both	(-) You've done a good job of spelling out some positive consequences of the decision at issue, but what are some of the negative consequences?

Implications & Consequences *continued*

| anticipate the likelihood of unexpected negative and positive implications | are surprised when their decisions have unexpected consequences | (-) In addition to the ones you've traced out, there are several important consequences you've missed. (-) Would other factors in the decision lead to significant consequences you left out? |

Inference & Conclusion

(All reasoning contains inferences by which we draw conclusions and give meaning to data.)

Fundamental Standards: 1) Clarity of Inferences, 2) Justifiability of Inferences, 3) Profundity of Conclusions, 4) Reasonability of Conclusions, 5) Consistency of Conclusions

Failure of Inferences and Conclusions: 1) Unclear, 2) Unjustified, 3) Superficial, 4) Unreasonable, 5) Contradictory

Principle: Reasoning can only be as sound as the inferences it makes and conclusions it comes to.

Good Reasoners:	Bad Reasoners:	Feedback to Students:
make inferences that are clear and precise	often make inferences that are unclear	(-) It is not clear what your main conclusion is. (-) It is not clear what you base your main conclusion on. (+) Your reasoning is very clear and easy to follow.
usually make inferences that follow from the evidence or reasons presented	often make inferences that do not follow from the evidence or reasons presented	(-) The conclusion you come to does not follow from the reasons presented. (+) You justify your conclusion well with supporting evidence and good reasons.
often make inferences that are deep rather than superficial	often make inferences that are superficial	(+) Your central conclusion is well-thought-out and goes right to the heart of the issue. (-) Your conclusion is justified, but it seems superficial, given the problem.
often make inferences or come to conclusions that are reasonable	often make inferences or come to conclusions that are unreasonable	(-) It is unreasonable to infer a person's personality from one action.
make inferences or come to conclusions that are consistent with each other	often make inferences or come to conclusions that are contradictory	(-) The conclusions you come to in the first part of your paper seem to contradict the conclusions that you come to at the end.

Chapter 8

Why Students — and Teachers — Don't Reason Well

Abstract

Paul begins this essay by developing the notion that all human action presupposes the use of humanly created logical systems that model, abridge, and summarize the features of the world about us, and that abstract inferential systems, and the reasoning they make possible, are as natural to us as a species as swimming is to a dolphin or flying is to a bird. As Paul puts it, we are continually "making inferences within a system we have created — about what is going on in our lives." Unfortunately, according to Paul, to reason well we must do more than simply engage in it. We must become aware of that engagement and use our knowledge of the nature of that engagement to improve it. Paul compares the good reasoner to the good ballet dancer, the good chess and tennis players. All three must explicitly study the principles and practice the moves involved (with explicit standards of performance in mind).

Having suggested what good reasoning requires, Paul presents evidence to show that most students are not good at it. What is more, he presents evidence to suggest that most teachers are not good at it either — at least not at assessing it when students are called upon to use it in their work. One of the major reasons, combining with ignorance of what reasoning requires, is a systematic confusion between intelligent subjectivity (wit, articulateness, cleverness without substance), and reasoned objectivity (careful, disciplined, reasoning about an issue), between subjective opinion (however "bright"), and reasoned judgment (however mundane).

Paul documents this problem with an analysis of a major mistake in a California Department of Education statewide assessment of reasoned evaluation in writing. He follows up this documentation of a mistake on the part of testing experts with the same mistake made by teachers. He then briefly explicates a model for the analysis and assessment of reasoning (based on the logic of the question at issue) complete with a series of samples of student reasoning, all duly analyzed for the reader.

Paul concludes the paper with a brief argument to the effect that "the logical structures implicit in an educated person's mind are highly systematized." In contrast he argues:

"When the logical structures by which a mind figures out the world are confused, a jumble, a hodgepodge, a mere conglomeration, then that figuring out is radically defective.... Then the mind begins it knows not where, takes things for granted without analysis or questioning, leaps to conclusions without sufficient evidence..., meanders without a consciousness of its point of view.... Then the

mind wanders into its own prejudices and biases, its own egocentricity and socio-centricity. Then the mind is not able to discipline itself by a close analysis of the question at issue and ignores the demands that the logic of that question puts on it and us as rational, logic-creating, logic-using animals."

✦ The Ability to Reason: A Defining Feature of Humans

Our capacity to reason is at the heart of all disciplined thinking. It explains how we alone of all the creatures of the earth have been able to develop full-fledged academic disciplines: biology, physics, botany, zoology, chemistry, geography, history, psychology, sociology, etc. We can go beyond immediate, instinctive reactions to reflective, reasoned responses precisely because we are able to develop small-scale and large-scale systems in which to intellectually operate and act. These systems enable us to mentally manipulate our possible responses to situations — to formulate them explicitly, to hold them at intellectual arm's length, to analyze and critique them, and to decide what their implications are for us. Let me explain.

We understand the various particulars of everyday life by constructing abstract models or systems that abridge and summarize their features. In simplest form, we call these models or systems *ideas*. For example, our abstract concept of a bird is a model or system for thinking about actual birds in order to make sense of their behavior — in contrast to the behavior, say, of cats, dogs, turtles, beetles, and people. As we construct these abstract systems or models, we are enabled to use the reasoning power of our minds to go beyond a bare unconceptualized noticing of things to the making of inward interpretations of them, and hence derivations from them. In short, our concepts provide our minds with systems in which to experience and think; our minds operate (reason) within them to invest the world we experience with meanings rich in implications and consequences. Much of this is done, of course, quite automatically and subconsciously.

I can reason to any number of conclusions as the result of my having one simple model for a thing. For example, if I recognize a creature to be a dog, I can quickly infer it will:

1) bark rather than meow or chirp
2) wag its tail when pleased
3) growl when irritated
4) be unable to fly
5) have no feathers
6) be unable to live under water
7) be carnivorous

    8) need oxygen
    9) have teeth
    10) have paws rather than feet, etc.

This word ('dog') is part of a much larger logical map upon which our minds can move in virtue of our capacity to reason. As we act bodily in the world, we act intellectually in our minds. These intellectual moves guide our actions in the world. Without these maps and the capacity to locate particulars on them, we would either thrash about aimlessly or be paralyzed by the bewildering mystery of things and events before us. In every situation in our lives we "construct" a response that results from how we are modeling the situation in our minds.

Hence, put us in any situation and we start to give it meaning, to figure it out with the logical structures we have at our disposal. So quickly and automatically do we make inferences — as the result of the way we are modeling the situation in our minds — that we do not typically notice those inferences.

For example, we see dark clouds and infer rain. We hear the door slam and infer someone has arrived. We see a frowning face and infer the person is angry. Our friend is late and we infer she is being inconsiderate. We meet a tall boy and infer he is good at basketball, an Asian and infer he will be good at math. We read a book, and infer what the various sentences and paragraphs, indeed what the whole book, is saying. We listen to what people say, and make a continual series of inferences as to what they mean. As we write we make inferences as to what others will make of what we are writing. We make inferences as to the clarity of what we are saying, as to what needs further explanation, as to what needs exemplification or illustration. We could not do this without "logical structures" by means of which to draw our inferences.

Many of our inferences are justified and reasonable. But, of course, many are not. One of the most important critical thinking skills is the skill of noticing and reconstructing the inferences we make, so that the various ways in which we inferentially shape our experiences become more and more apparent to us. This skill, this sensitivity or ability, enables us to separate our experiences into analyzed parts. We learn to distinguish the raw data of our experience from our interpretations of those data (in other words, from the inferences we are making about them). Eventually we realize that the inferences we make are heavily influenced by our point of view and the assumptions we have made. This puts us in the position of being able to broaden the scope of our outlook, to see situations from more than one point of view, to become more openminded. This requires that we recognize our point of view as a "logical system" that guides our inferences, a system that we can exchange for another (an alternative point of view), depending on our assumptions.

Often, then, different people make different inferences because they bring to situations a different point of view. They see the data differently. Or, to put it another way, they have different assumptions about what they see. For example, if two people see a man lying in a gutter, one might infer, "There's a drunken bum." The other might infer, "There's a man in need of help." These inferences are based on different assumptions about the conditions under which people end up in gutters and these assumptions are connected to the point of view about people that each has formed. The first person assumes: "Only drunks are to be found in gutters." The second person assumes: "People lying in the gutter are in need of help." The first person may have developed the point of view that people are fundamentally responsible for what happens to them and ought to be able to take care of themselves. The second may have developed the point of view that the problems people have are often caused by forces and events beyond their control. The two are modeling the situation differently. They are using a different system for experiencing it.

In any case, if we want our students to become good reasoners, we must become concerned to help them begin to notice the inferences they are making, the assumptions they are basing those inferences on, and the point of view about the world they are taking — hence the systems in which they are thinking. To help our students do this, we need to give them clear examples of simple cases, and lots and lots of practice analyzing and reconstructing them. For example, we could display the above inferences in the following way:

Person One:
Situation: "A man is lying in the gutter."
Assumption: "Only bums lie in gutters."
Inference: "That man's a bum."

Person Two:
Situation: "A man is lying in the gutter."
Assumption: "Anyone lying in the gutter is in need of help."
Inference: "That man is in need of help."

Our goal of sensitizing students to the inferences they make and to the assumptions that underlie their thinking enables them to begin to gain command over their thinking (the way they are using logical structures to model the world). Of course, it may seem odd to put any effort into making explicit such obvious examples. In the harder instances, however, the value of the explication becomes more evident. In any case, because all human thinking is inferential in nature, and all inferences are embedded in a system, we cannot gain command of our thinking unless we can recognize, one way or another, the inferences embedded in it and the assumptions that underlie it.

Consider the way in which we plan and think our way through everyday events. We think of ourselves as washing up, eating our breakfast, getting ready for work, arriving on time, sitting down at our desks, making plans for lunch, paying bills, engaging in small talk, etc. Another way to put this is to say that we are continually interpreting our actions, giving them meanings — making inferences within a system we have created — about what is going on in our lives.

And this is to say that we must choose among a variety of possible systems for thinking about things. Again, consider some simple cases. As I am sitting in my easy chair, am I "relaxing" or "wasting time"? Am I being "determined" or "stubborn", or worse, "pig-headed"? Did I "join" the conversation or "butt in"? Is Jack "laughing with me" or "laughing at me"? Am I "helping him" or "being taken advantage of"? Every time I interpret my actions within one of these systems that each word in the language represents, every time I give them a meaning, I make one or more inferences on the basis of one or more assumptions within some point of view.

As humans we continually make assumptions about ourselves, our jobs, our mates, our children, about the world in general. We take some things for granted, simply because we can't always be questioning everything. Sometimes we take the wrong things for granted. For example, I run off to the store (assuming that I have enough money with me) and arrive to find that I have left my money at home. I assume that I have enough gas in the car only to find that I have run out. I assume that an item marked down in price is a good buy only to find that it was "marked up" before it was "marked down". I assume that it will not, or that it will, rain. I assume that my car will start when I turn the key and press the starter. I assume that I mean well in my dealings with others. We make hundreds of assumptions, use hundreds of concepts, make hundreds of inferences, without noticing that we are doing so. Most of them are quite sound and justifiable. Some however are not.

The question then becomes: "How can we teach our students to begin to recognize the inferences they are making, the assumptions they are basing those inferences on, and the point of view, the perspective on the world that they are beginning to form?" That is, "How can we help students to recognize how they are reasoning about the world?"

✦ Our Students Are Not Learning to Reason Well

Though we are "logic-creating" and "logic-using" animals, we typically operate with little awareness of this fact. We create and apply logical systems without knowing that we are doing so. Our intellectual modeling of the world is done *sub rosa*, without mindfulness. It is small wonder, then, that we often reason poorly.

Imagine a ballet dancer improving her ballet without knowing that she is a dancer or how and when she is dancing. Imagine a chess player who does not know she is playing chess. Or a tennis player who does not know she is playing tennis. We can hardly imagine people developing these physical and intellectual abilities without high consciousness of how and what they are doing in the doing of it. Yet we expect students to develop the ability to reason well without any mindfulness of the nature of reasoning, the elements of reasoning, or the criteria for assessing reasoning. We expect students to become good reasoners, in other words, without any knowledge of the logic of reasoning. Not surprisingly our approach doesn't work. Most students are very poor reasoners.

WHAT DOES RESEARCH ON LEARNING AND TEACHING TELL US?

By any measure whatsoever, most students are not learning to reason well. A recent summary of research by Mary Kennedy regarding student learning and instruction at the K–12 level documents serious reasoning deficiencies on the part of students. (See figure next page.)

✦ California State-Wide Test Fiasco: Teachers and Testers Who Don't Understand Reasoning

Before teachers will be able to help students to reason well, it is essential that they learn what reasoning is and how to assess it. A recent statewide test in California demonstrated that many teachers, and even some educational testing experts, have serious misunderstandings about the nature of reasoning and how to assess it.

The student essay below (figure 2) should have been graded at the lower rather than the higher end of the continuum of eight levels: "minimal evidence of achievement" or, at best, "limited evidence of achievement" rather than the highest grade of "exceptional achievement". For though the essay may have "flair and sparkle" (as one teacher expressed it), it is a poor example of evaluative reasoning, since it systematically confuses the objective goal of reasoned evaluation with the very different goal of explaining subjective preference, an important distinction in critical thinking which the teacher-evaluators apparently missed entirely.

First of all, the instructions themselves are confused. They begin with a clear requirement of "objective" evaluation:

"Students were asked to write an evaluative essay, make judgments about the worth of a book, television program, or type of music and then support their judgments with reasons and evidence. Students must consider possible criteria on which to base an evaluation, analyze their subject in the light of the criteria, and select evidence that clearly supports their judgments."

Important Research Findings

First Finding: "...national assessments in virtually every subject indicate that, although our students can perform basic skills pretty well, they are not doing well on thinking and reasoning. American students can compute, but they cannot reason.... They can write complete and correct sentences, but they cannot prepare arguments.... Moreover, in international comparisons, American students are falling behind...particularly in those areas that require higher-order thinking.... Our students are not doing well at thinking, reasoning, analyzing, predicting, estimating, or problem solving."

Second Finding: "...textbooks in this country typically pay scant attention to big ideas, offer no analysis, and pose no challenging questions. Instead, they provide a tremendous array of information or 'factlets', while they ask questions requiring only that students be able to recite back the same empty list."

Third Finding: "Teachers teach most content only for exposure, not for understanding."

Fourth Finding: "Teachers tend to avoid thought-provoking work and activities and stick to predictable routines."

Conclusion: "If we were to describe our current K–12 education system on the basis of these four findings, we would have to say that it provides very little intellectually stimulating work for students, and that it tends to produce students who are not capable of intellectual work."

Fifth Finding: "... our fifth finding from research compounds all the others and makes it harder to change practice: teachers are highly likely to teach in the way they themselves were taught. If your elementary teacher presented mathematics to you as a set of procedural rules with no substantive rationale, then you are likely to think that this is what mathematics is and that this is how mathematics should be studied. And you are likely to teach it in this way. If you studied writing as a set of grammatical rules rather than as a way to organize your thoughts and to communicate ideas to others, then this is what you will think writing is, and you will probably teach it so.... By the time we complete our undergraduate education, we have observed teachers for up to 3,060 days."

Implication: "We are caught in a vicious circle of mediocre practice modeled after mediocre practice, of trivialized knowledge begetting more trivialized knowledge. Unless we find a way out of this circle, we will continue re-creating generations of teachers who re-create generations of students who are not prepared for the technological society we are becoming."

(Figure 1 condensed from "Policy Issues in Teaching Education" by Mary Kennedy in the *Phi Delta Kappan*, May, 91, pp 661–66.)

Evaluative Essay Sample

EVALUATION. Students were asked to write an evaluative essay, make judgments about the worth of a book, television program, or type of music and then support their judgments with reasons and evidence. Students must consider possible criteria on which to base an evaluation, analyze their subject in light of the criteria, and select evidence that clearly supports their judgments. Each student was assigned one of the following evaluative tasks:

* To write a letter to a favorite author telling why they especially liked one of the author's books.
* To explain why they enjoyed one television program more than any others.
* To justify their preference for a particular type of music.

The tasks made clear that students must argue convincingly for their preferences and not just offer unsupported opinions.

This is a sample essay from a student who demonstrated exceptional achievement.

Rock Around the Clock

"Well, you're getting to the age when you have to learn to be responsible!" my mother yelled out.

"Yes, but I can't be available all the time to do my appointed chores! I'm only thirteen! I want to be with my friends, to have fun! I don't think that it is fair for me to baby-sit while you go run your little errands!" I snapped back. I sprinted upstairs to my room before my mother could start another sentence. I turned on my radio and "Shout" was playing. I noted how true the song was and I threw some punches at my pillow. The song ended and "Control" by Janet Jackson came on. I stopped beating my pillow. I suddenly felt at peace with myself. The song had slowed me down. I pondered briefly over all the songs that had helped me to control my feelings. The list was endless. So is my devotion to rock music and pop rock. These songs help me to express my feelings, they make me wind down, and above all they make me feel good. Without this music, I might have turned out to be a violent and grumpy person.

Some of my favorite songs are by Howard Jones, Pet Shop Boys, and Madonna. I especially like songs that have a message in them, such as "Stand by Me", by Ben E. King. This song tells me to stand by the people I love and to not question them in times of need. Basically this song is telling me to believe in my friends, because they are my friends.

My favorite type of music is rock and pop rock. Without them, there is no way that I could survive mentally. They are with me in times of trouble, and best of all, they are only a step away.

California classroom teachers wrote comments like these after reading and scoring students' evaluative essays:

* "Evidence of clear thinking was heavily rewarded in our scoring."
* "I am struck by how much some students can accomplish in 45 minutes; how well they can sometimes marshal the ideas; and with how much flair and sparkle they can express themselves."
* "More emphasis should be placed on critical thinking skills, supporting judgments, and tying thoughts and ideas together. Far too many papers digress, summarize, underdevelop, or state totally irrelevant facts."
* "Students generally need to develop skills in giving evidence to support their judgments. I plan to spend more time on these thinking skills next year."

Figure 2, Source: California State Department of Education, 1988. Reprinted in, "California: The State of Assessment", Anderson, Robert L. *Developing Minds*, edited by Art Costa, pp. 314–25.

Unfortunately, this request for reasoned evaluation is blended in the second half of the instruction with what might possibly be taken, with a little stretching and selective reading, as a request for the expression of a "subjective" preference:

> Each student was assigned one of the following evaluative tasks: to write a letter to a favorite author telling why they especially liked one of the author's books, to explain why they enjoyed one television program more than any others, or to justify their preference for a particular type of music. The tasks made clear that students must argue convincingly for their preferences and not just offer unsupported opinions.

Let's look closely at this confusion. In the first place, there is still an emphasis on objective evaluation ("The tasks made clear that students must argue convincingly for their preferences and not just offer unsupported opinions") while the task itself is defined as the justification of a "preference".

Now most people prefer books, television programs, and types of music for fundamentally subjective, not objective, reasons. They like a particular book, television program, or song for no reason other than that they like it, that is, because they enjoy it or find pleasure in it or are interested or absorbed or excited or amused by it. Their reasons for liking what they like are not the result of an objective evaluation. They have no relation to the objective quality of what is judged. They are about the personal responses of the experiencer, not about the objective qualities of that which is experienced.

Most people, to take the point a step further, do not have "evidence" — other than the stuff of their subjective reactions — to justify their preferences. They prefer because of the way they feel not because of the way they reason. To choose because of these subjective states of feeling is precisely to lack criteria of evaluation or evidence that bears upon objective assessment. When challenged to support subjective preferences, people usually can do little more than repeat their subjective reactions ("I find it boring, amusing, exciting, dull, interesting, etc.") or rationalize them ("I find it exciting because it has a lot of action in it.")

A *reasoned evaluation* of a book, a program, or a type of music requires more than this; it requires some knowledge of the qualities of what we are evaluating and of the criteria appropriate to the evaluation of those qualities. One needs to be well-informed about books, about programs, about music if one is to claim to be in a position to objectively evaluate them. If one is not well-informed, one is unable to render a justified evaluative judgment, though one can always subjectively react and freely express one's subjective reactions as (mere) personal preferences. This is what the student (graded as having written an objective evaluation of "exceptional achievement") actually does. But his evaluators, not having this distinction clear in their own minds, completely miss the difference.

The sample student essay can, for analytic purposes, be divided into three parts. We shall comment briefly on each in turn. The first segment of the essay is an account of a highly emotional exchange between the student and his mother:

> "Well, you're getting to the age when you have to learn to be responsible!" my mother yelled out. "Yes, but I can't be available all the time to do my appointed chores! I'm only thirteen! I want to be with my friends, to have fun! I don't think that it is fair for me to baby-sit while you run your little errands!" I snapped back. I sprinted upstairs to my room before my mother could start another sentence.

It is clear that in this segment there is no analysis, no setting out of alternative criteria, no clarification of the question at issue, no hint at reasoning or reasoned evaluation.

In the second part, the student makes a sweeping claim about a purported causal relationship between listening to rock music and his asserted, but unsupported, ability to control his emotions. He does not consider "possible criteria on which to base an evaluation". He does not present any evidence, though he does cite two examples, one where a song prompts him to punch his pillow and one where another song prompts him to stop. This gives little credence to the notion that rock music leads to his "controlling" his emotions. If anything, his examples seem to imply that, rather than learning control from, he is learning to be controlled by, the music he listens to. His major claim that "Without this music, I might have turned out to be a violent and grumpy person" is without reasoned or evidentiary support. He merely brashly asserts that it is true:

> I turned on my radio and "Shout" was playing. I noted how true the song was and I threw some punches at my pillow. The song ended and "Control", by Janet Jackson came on. I stopped beating my pillow. I suddenly felt at peace with myself. The song had slowed me down. I pondered briefly over all the songs that had helped me to control my feelings. The list was endless. So is my devotion to rock music and pop rock. These songs help me to express my feelings, they make me wind down, and above all they make me feel good. Without this music, I might have turned out to be a violent and grumpy person.

In the third, and final, section of the essay the student closes his remarks with a series of subjective, unsupported, even irrelevant statements:

> Some of my favorite songs are by Howard Jones, Pet Shop Boys, and Madonna. I especially like songs that have a message in them, such as "Stand by Me", by Ben E. King. This song tells me to stand by the people I love and to not question them in time of need. Basically this song is telling me to believe in my friends, because they are my friends.

My favorite type of music is rock and pop rock. Without them, there is no way that I could survive mentally. They are with me in times of trouble, and best of all, they are only a step away.

If this is reasoning, it is very bad reasoning: "Believe in your friends because they are your friends", "If you feel you cannot survive without rock music, then it follows that you can't." Of course, a more appropriate interpretation of what is going on is that the student is not reasoning at all but merely asserting his subjective opinions. Consider, the student doesn't examine alternative criteria on which to base an evaluation of music. He doesn't analyze rock music in the light of evaluative criteria. He doesn't provide evidence that clearly supports his judgment. His writing is vague where it needs to be precise, logically rambling where it needs to be critically reasoned. We don't really know what he means by songs "controlling" his feelings. We are not provided with any evidence on the basis of which we could assess whether there is any truth in his sweeping claims about himself, for example, that he could not survive mentally without rock music. Indeed, common sense experience strongly suggests, we believe, that the student is simply deluding himself on this point, or, alternatively, engaging in unbridled hyperbole.

When a blatantly weak essay such as this is disseminated nationally as an example of "exceptional achievement" in the writing of a *reasoned* evaluative essay, then it is clear that there are large numbers of educators who are not clear about the assessment of reasoning. Remember, the California Assessment Program of the California State Department of Education is the second largest assessment unit in the country. (I should add that Dale Carlson, the head of CAP, is now putting a major effort into rectifying this problem.)

The Many Ways Teachers Mis-Assess Reasoning

If many teachers take bad reasoning to be good, do they also take good reasoning to be bad? Unfortunately the answer appears to be, "Yes." This became apparent in a Center for Critical Thinking research project in which teachers were provided with a well-reasoned response to the California prompt, in addition to the poorly reasoned one. The participants were teachers enrolled in critical thinking workshops. They were given the two essays to assess after receiving a morning's instruction on critical thinking. What is significant is the myriad of confusions and misunderstandings about the assessment of reasoning that emerged and the inconsistencies in both grading and in justifying grades.

Here is the "well-reasoned response" they were asked to assess alongside the poorly-reasoned "Rock Around the Clock".

This second essay (next page) was written by one of the research staff members of the Center who made sure that it was responsive to the directions and displayed all of the critical thinking abilities called for:

1) it distinguished mere subjective preference from well-reasoned assessment,

2) it was responsive to the logic of the question at issue,

3) it formulated and discussed alternative relevant criteria,

4) it distinguished having evidence relevant to a question from lacking such evidence,

5) it displayed intellectual humility,

6) it displayed intellectual integrity,

7) it drew only those conclusions the evidence warranted.

The results highlighted the problem. On one occasion 81 teachers and administrators assessed the two essays. The poorly-reasoned essay was given an average score of 5.4 (out of 8) while the well-reasoned essay was given an average score of 3.9. Forty-nine of the teachers gave the poorly-reasoned essay a 6, 7, or 8, while only 18 teachers gave the well-reasoned essay a 6, 7, or 8.

Can I Prove Rock Music is Better?

It's certainly hard to objectively judge music based on justifiable criteria because most people don't have any real standards for the music they listen to other than they like it. My friends and I are probably no different from other people. We listen to music we like because we like it. But this assignment asks me to give good reasons why we like what we like. I'm not sure I can, but I'll try.

I first wonder what would be a really good reason for liking any kind of music (other than it sounds good to you). Well, I suppose that one possible good reason for preferring one kind of music to another is that it expresses better the problems we face and what we can do to solve those problems.

Does this give me a good reason for preferring rock music to other kinds? Perhaps so. Certainly, rock music is often about problems that we have: problems of love and sex, school and parents, drugs and drink. I'm not sure, however, whether the "answers" in the songs actually are really good answers or just answers that appeal to us. They might even increase our prejudices about parents, teachers, school, and love. I'm not sure.

Another possible good reason for preferring one kind of music to another is that it is written better or more skillfully performed. Can I truthfully say that rock music is more skillfully written or performed than other kinds of music? In all honesty I cannot.

So what is my conclusion? It is this. I am unable to give any objective reason for liking rock music. My friends and I are like most people. We like the music we listen to just because we like it. For better or for worse, that's all the reason we have. What do you think? Can 15 million teenagers be wrong?

Even more illuminating than the raw scores were the reasons given by the teachers and administrators. Multiple confusions surfaced, as I suggested above, about the nature of reasoning and the appropriate way to assess it. Let's look at some of the responses. Try to imagine students actually receiving these grades along with the often mistaken, confused, or unintelligible commentary.

I have divided teacher assessments for convenience into two groups. The first consists of those teachers who grade the poorly reasoned essay higher than the well-reasoned essay. The second consists of those teachers who grade the poorly reasoned essay lower than the well-reasoned essay. Reading the teachers' justifications for their grades reveals a great deal of misunderstanding of the nature of reasoning. [First Essay: "Rock Around the Clock" (the poorly reasoned essay) Second Essay: "Can I Prove Rock Music is Better?" (the well-reasoned essay)]

FIRST GROUP OF TEACHERS

The following teachers give a high grade to the poorly reasoned essay and a low grade to the well-reasoned essay. In virtually every case, the teachers reveal no awareness of the importance of intellectual humility, wherein one does not claim to justify a conclusion when one lacks the evidence to do so, instead, one gives good reasons for suspending judgment.

1) *A Physical Education Teacher:* *[#1]* "The first essay better fulfills the criteria for the assignment because the writer justifies (his or her) preference for a particular type of music. I think I would give it a 7 though because it was kind of confusing how the writer got on the subject.

   [#2] "The second essay did not justify a preference for any particular type of music. So the writer did not meet the criteria for the assignment. Strangely enough it was easier to read but possibly because the way the writer feels is how I feel about music in general. I think the essay deserves a '0'."

2) *An English Teacher:* *[#1]* "I would give this essay a 7 because he/she gave experience from his/her life to support their opinion — gave reasons and evidence by example.

   [#2] "I would give this essay a grade of 2 because he/she did not prove a point — merely rambled from one thing to another searching for a reason."

3) *A Math Teacher:* *[#1]* "I would give the first essay a 5 because it did not support the judgment well but did make many references.

   [#2] "I would give the second essay a 3 because it is not very evaluative! It did analyze the subject but provided no real support of any judgment."

4) A Math Teacher: *[#1]* "I would give this paper a grade of 7 because criteria were evident, analysis was good and it had lots of supporting evidence.

[#2] "I would give this paper a 3 because criteria are given but nothing was analyzed and no supporting evidence."

5) Freshman Studies Teacher: *[#1]* "I would give 'Rock Around the Clock' a grade of 6 because: *a)* a more flowing style of writing than a series of loosely related points, *b)* a personal approach, *c)* specific information as to records and effects of the songs, *d)* valid and accurate comparisons, *e)* personalization, *f)* availability, *g)* a well-supported point of view, and *h)* R&R as an avoidance tool.

[#2] "I would give 'Can I Prove Rock Music is Better?' a 3 because *a)* statement of problem OK, *b)* no exploration about 'Why we like it', *c)* discusses what it is about, not why we listen. Do we listen to the words or music?, *d)* the idea of 'better performances' not followed through on, and *e)* How do they know they are like 'most people'?"

6) A Math Teacher: *[#1]* "The first essay: grade 6. The writer has set up some criteria for his choice, the music gives him a calming influence.... Since the writer is given the opportunity to set his own criteria, this will suffice. He gives examples to justify his conclusions.

[#2] "The second essay: grade 3. An attempt is made to give reasons for supporting the music but no conclusions are made. The writer cannot make an argument for his case in any area. It is difficult, as the writer has said, to justify choice or preference, but since one can choose one's own criteria it would seem any position well-argued and justified would fulfill the assignment. The author did not succeed in doing that."

7) Subject Taught Not Identified: *[#1]* "'Rock Around the Clock' Score: 6. This student does not give any clear criteria to start off as to possible criteria to base their evaluation on. This student based their evaluation on how it made them feel or respond. It was based on reactions — not facts to choose music by, but at least this student used something to justify their preference.

[#2] "'Can I Prove Rock Music Is Better?' Score: 2 Too vague — never really makes a decision about their preference of music. This student talks about possible criteria but never really says anything about it. Shows no support to justify the preference."

8) Former English Teacher: *[#1]* "I would give this essay a grade of 8 because: *a)* essay cites specific examples, *b)* catchy opening, *c)* the criteria used was based on student's personal experience, *d)* student was asked to justify their preference. I think she did.

[#2] "I would give this essay a grade of 2 because: *a)* very generalized, *b)* few, if any, concrete examples, *c)* essay is not personalized to any extent, *d)* no specific conclusions drawn."

9) *Special Ed. Teacher:* *[#1]* "Point total: 7. This essay listed three criteria on which to base a judgment. It gave examples of each — maybe better examples could be found. The writer attempted to analyze a basically subjective issue in concrete terms — what the songs do for them: not objective, but a fairly concrete assessment of music's subjectivity.

[#2] "Point total: 0. This essay did not seriously attempt to answer the issue at hand. Instead it concluded, quite lamely, that no objective statement of worth could be made. While this may be accurate in the broadest sense, no effort was made to justify that position."

10) *English Teacher:* *[#1]* "I would give this essay a 7 because the author is not afraid to take a stand. Although the 'proof' is emotionally based, that was the direction of his/her argument.

[#2] "I would give this essay a 3 because the writer was not able to take a position. He/she beats around the bush and asks the reader to make the decision when that was the assignment to the writer. The insecurity and negative attitude runs through the entire paper."

SECOND GROUP OF TEACHERS

The following teachers give a low grade to the poorly reasoned essay and a high or higher grade to the well-reasoned essay. In some cases the teachers revealed some awareness of the importance of intellectual humility. Some are, however, confused or mistaken in part about reasoning and its assessment. For most, thankfully, this confusion is conjoined with some insight into reasoning. For some few others, the fact that they graded the poorly-reasoned essay lower is not based on insight but chance. This is apparent from some of the reasons they give.

1) *A Library-Media Teacher:* *[#1]* "Grade: 3 or 4. Reasons: My first thought that it wasn't a typical essay but rather starts out with a rather clever, attention-getting device. In that sense, the student did catch my attention — and also confused me somewhat. That is, it doesn't start out as a typical essay. The student is a good writer in that their word choices make sense and there are supporting reasons for why they chose rock music and pop music.... Now that I read this again, I can see that really the writer has only supplied one reason for their selection: the control/expression of feelings. Well, it's the same old problem in grading a paper, i.e., the student writes well but hasn't followed the criteria strictly.

[#2] "Grade: 7. Reasons: Just a first critical response before I re-read it. It strikes me as thoughtful and honest (which always impresses me). Now I'll see how it fits the criteria. The writer states he needs good reasons for his judgment. I don't think that 'good' is the word he wants.... Why do we like what we like? That's a provocative question!... A quickie, yes, I think they've fulfilled most of the criteria, just not in the usual fashion. Also, it's an essay (as I define one)."

2) *A Special Ed. Teacher: [#1]* "The student in this essay never really makes a statement that involves an evaluation of a judgment made concerning a type of music, except to say 'My favorite type of music is rock and pop rock. Without them there is no way I could survive mentally.' He does try to show what he means by this statement when he offers examples of music that affect his mood. He lacks a clear evaluation or supportive evidence toward the topic. I think his statement about surviving mentally is a bit much. I give it a 4.

[#2] "This student doesn't know what he thinks and he lets you know it continually. His closing paragraph summarizes what he is trying to put down in the essay and it is the most straightforward part of the essay. His title doesn't quite jibe with the rest of the essay. He was supposed to prove rock music is better, but what he really talked about was whether there was any justification for why people like rock music. I give it a 5."

3) *A Social Studies Teacher: [#1]* "I would give essay one a grade of 6. Essay number one lists reasons for liking rock music, but it is very superficial in analyzing them in the light of the criteria. It really does not approach the subject in a way that logically lists possible criteria as a basis for analysis and then applies the criteria to the music. The essay is generally Bull Shit with only a general connection to the instructions.

[#2] "I would give essay #2 an 8 because the possible criteria for analyzing the issue are covered...."

4) *An English Teacher: [#1]* "Score: 3. The writer in essay one has discussed how he/she feels about rock and pop music, but generalities are given and his/her statements aren't supported with evidence. The assignment is to 'justify' preference, not discuss that it makes him/her 'feel good' period. No criteria have been established, so the essay just rambles on about 'feelings' and not much else. Reasons and evidence are lacking.

[#2] "Score: 5. This essay does a little bit better in attempting an argument. The essay establishes two 'criteria' on which to base his/her essay.... Examples of 'answers' in paragraph 3 are needed as

evidence.... Paragraph 4 isn't developed. Needs reasons and evidence/ examples. Weak Conclusion."

5) *A Physical Education Teacher: [#1]* "I would grade the essay 0. The essay does not show their judgment about worth with reason and evidence as asked in the directions. There are no criteria for evaluation, analysis with criteria or evidence that clearly supports the judgments.

[#2] "I would grade the essay 5. The essay attempts to set up criteria for evaluation, yet not as completely as it could have been done. There was an attempt to analyze the subject with the criteria, but not complete. There was no evidence to clearly support the judgment."

6) *A Second Grade Teacher: [#1]* "The first essay should have a 3 because the stated criterion is subjective. The conclusion comes down to, 'I like it because I like it.'

[#2] "The second essay would have a 6 because there was a search for good criteria and no evidence was found to support the good criteria."

7) *A Counselor: [#1]* "I would give this essay a 1 because the student did select a topic to evaluate which fit the directions. However, she reported her subjective taste (how some songs have affected her, which songs she likes) rather than evaluating 'rock music'.

[#2] "I would give this essay a 7 because: a) she selects an appropriate topic, 2) she considered what criteria would be appropriate to evaluate rock music, c) she made judgments based on the criteria she listed, 4) her conclusion was based on her criteria/judgment. However, she might have considered/used other criteria."

8) *A Sixth Grade Language Arts Teacher: [#1]* "A grade of 1. There was no evaluation, went strictly by senses.

[#2] "A grade of 8. The writer did a good job on a subject that is a matter of preference no matter how you look at it! He tried to objectively judge rock music, but in the end... 'We like it just because we like it.'"

9) *A First Grade Teacher: [#1]* "I would give 'Rock Around the Clock' a 4 because the writer did give some facts for liking rock music but wrote mostly from emotion without questioning if her facts were sound. For example, 'believe in my friends because they are my friends'.

[#2] "I would give 'Can I Prove Rock Music is Better?' a 7. The writer stated the purpose, criteria, facts, and gave a conclusion. The writer considered more than just feeling. More facts for liking rock music are needed."

✦ Introduction to the Analysis and Evaluation of Reasoning

There are two obstacles that stand in the way of fostering sound reasoning K–12: 1) teachers must learn how to devise assignments that require reasoning, and 2) teachers must learn how to analyze and evaluate reasoning objectively. This process will not happen overnight, but the sooner it begins, the sooner it can be achieved.

We will shortly take a look at three assignments that call for reasoning as well as at three examples of student work for each of those assignments: student work with no reasoning in it, student work with poor reasoning in it, and student work with good reasoning in it. In each case, we will provide a brief commentary to help make clear what one should look for in the reasoning. But first we will provide a brief overview of what is involved, in general, in the analysis and evaluation of reasoning.

WHAT IS INVOLVED IN ANALYZING AND EVALUATING REASONING?

The fundamental criteria to use in analyzing and evaluating reasoning comes from an analysis of the purpose of the reasoner and the logic of the question or questions raised. For example, if a person raises the question, say, as to whether democracy is failing in the USA (in the light of the dwindling number of people who vote and the growing power of vested interest groups with significant money to expend on campaign contributions), we can establish general criteria for assessing the reasoning by spelling out what in general one would have to do to settle the question. Those criteria would include such matters as the following:

1) *An Analysis of the Concept of the Ends of Democracy.* What would it be for democracy to succeed? What would it be for it to fail? What do we take the fundamental objective of democracy to be? For democracy to succeed is it enough that it simply ensure the right of the people at large to vote or must it also serve the well being of the people as well?

2) *Collection of the Facts About the Numbers of People Not Voting.* What is the actual number of people not voting? Is it growing? By what percentage?

3) *An Interpretation of the Significance of the Facts Collected in #2.* What are the reasons why growing numbers of people are not voting? What are the implications of those facts?

4) *Collection of Facts About the Number of Vested Interest Groups Influencing Elections.* How many vested interested groups are influencing elections today in comparison to the past? What is the nature and extent of their influence in money spent?

5) *An Interpretation of the Significance of the Facts Collected in #4.* What is the significance of the growing influence of vested interest groups on election outcomes? What is gained and lost by means of that influence?

6) Synthesis of Numbers 1 through 5. What is the overall significance of what we have found out in 1 through 5? What does it all add up to? What exactly are we gaining and losing as a result of the growing influence of vested interest groups and diminished numbers of voters? In attempting to put everything together we would want to see reflection on this issue from more than one point of view. We would want to assess how the reasoner responds to reasonable objections from other points of view.

These are some of the considerations relevant to reasoning well about the issue. A rational analysis of someone's response to this issue would involve, then, checking to see if the above considerations were reasonably addressed, to see if the reasoner had done a plausible job in analyzing the functions of democracy, collecting relevant facts and information, interpreting those facts, and putting everything together, with a sensitivity to more than one point of view, into one coherent line of reasoning.

Many of the teachers assessing the reasoning of the essays on rock music above failed to analyze or review the logic of the question at issue. Instead they read the essays impressionistically, allowing the grade they gave to be determined more by whether their impressions were positive or negative than by any close analysis of the degree to which the student responded adequately to the demands inherent in the precise question at issue.

It is the logic of the question at issue which is the "system for thinking" that should guide our reasoning. If we do not develop skill in explicating that logic, our reasoning is apt to become impressionistic, guided by our prejudices and biases, by our egocentrism and ethnocentrism, rather than disciplined by rational considerations.

✦ Three Examples of Student Reasoning

What follows below are three assignments designed to call for reasoning on the part of the students, along with three examples of student "reasoning" in response to those assignments. Two of the assignments are in history and the other in literature. The three issues the students are asked to develop their reasoning on involve: reasoning about the character of the American people, reasoning about the meaning of a poem, and reasoning about the comparative importance of inventions. It would be useful if you thought a little about your own assessment of the students' reasoning before you looked at ours'. You could then compare the two.

AMERICAN HISTORY: REASONING ABOUT THE AMERICAN CHARACTER

Question at Issue: "Are the Americans you know capable of the kind of mass hysteria which occurred in 1919 and is described in a textbook as the 'Red Scare'?"

Directions: One of the most important reasons to write our history is to discover who we are and who we are not, how we can develop ourselves, what faults we have to watch out for, and what strengths we can build upon. Read the passage in your textbook on the "Red Scare". Then write a couple of paragraphs in which you try to figure out whether the Americans you know are "capable" or "not capable" of reacting as many Americans did in 1919. (See textbook, p. 731.) Be sure you show us your reasoning. Support and explain why you think as you do.

Reading Excerpt: The "Red Scare"
(from *America: Past and Present*, by Divine, Breen, Fredrickson, and Williams; Scott, Foreman and Company, 1984, p. 731.)

The first and most intense outbreak of national alarm came in 1919. The heightened nationalism of World War I, aimed at achieving unity at the expense of ethnic diversity, found a new target in bolshevism. The Russian Revolution and the triumph of Marxism frightened many Americans. A growing turn into communism among American radicals (especially the foreign-born) accelerated the fears, although the numbers involved were tiny — at most there were sixty thousand Communists in the United States in 1919. But they were located in the cities, and their influence appeared to be magnified with the outbreak of widespread labor unrest.

A general strike in Seattle, a police strike in Boston, and a violent strike in the iron and steel industry thoroughly alarmed the American people in the spring and summer of 1919. A series of bombings led to panic. First the mayor of strike-bound Seattle received a small brown package containing a homemade bomb; then an alert New York postal employee detected sixteen bombs addressed to a variety of famous citizens (including John D. Rockefeller); and finally, on June 2, a bomb shattered the front of Attorney General A. Mitchell Palmer's home. Although the man who delivered it was blown to pieces, authorities quickly identified him as an Italian anarchist from Philadelphia.

In the ensuing public outcry, Attorney General Palmer led the attack on the alien threat. A Quaker and progressive, Palmer abandoned his earlier liberalism to launch a massive roundup of foreign-born radicals. In a series of raids that began on November 7, federal agents seized suspected anarchists and Communists and held them for deportation with no regard for due process of law. In December, 249 aliens — including such well-known radical leaders as Emma Goldman and Alexander Berkman — were sent to Russia aboard the *Buford,* dubbed the "Soviet Ark" by the press. Nearly all were innocent of the charges against them. A month later, Palmer rounded up nearly four thousand suspected Communists in a single evening. Federal agents broke into homes, meeting halls, and union offices without search warrants. Many native-born Americans were caught in the dragnet and spent several days in jail before being released; aliens rounded up were deported without hearings or trials.

For a time, it seemed that this Red Scare reflected the prevailing views of the American people. Instead of condemning their government's actions, citizens voiced their approval and even urged more drastic steps. One patriot said his solution to the alien problem was simple: "S.O.S. — ship or shoot." General Leonard Wood, the army chief of staff, favored placing Bolsheviks on "ships of stone with sails of lead," while evangelist Billy Sunday preferred to take "these ornery, wild-eyed Socialists" and "stand them up before a firing squad and save space on our ships." Inflamed by public statements like these, a group of legionnaires in Centralia, Washington, dragged a radical from the town jail, castrated him, and hanged him from a railway bridge. The coroner's report blandly stated that the victim "jumped off with a rope around his neck and then shot himself full of holes."

The very extremism of the Red Scare led to its rapid demise. Courageous government officials in the Department of Labor insisted on due process and full hearing before anyone else was deported. Prominent public leaders began to speak out against the acts of terror. Charles Evans Hughes, the defeated GOP candidate in 1916, offered to defend six Socialists expelled from the New York legislature; Ohio Senator Warren G. Harding, the embodiment of middle-class values, expressed his opinion that "too much has been said about bolshevism in America." Finally, Palmer himself, with evident presidential ambition, went too far. In April 1920, he warned of a vast revolution to occur on May 1; the entire New York City police force, some eleven thousand strong, was placed on duty. When no bombings or violence took place on May Day, the public began to react against Palmer's hysteria. Despite a violent explosion on Wall Street in September that killed thirty-three people, the Red Scare died out by the end of 1920. Palmer passed into obscurity, the tiny Communist party became torn with factionalism, and the American people tried hard to forget their momentary loss of balance.

Student #1

The people I know are not like the people who lived in 1919. They obey the law and, though they might make some mistakes or do some things they ought not to, they would never hurt someone who was innocent. Most of the people I know go to church and believe in God. They are good Christians. They read the Bible. They try to raise their children to be good and avoid evil. They are kind people. So I don't believe that what happened in 1919 could ever happen again. It won't happen in my neighborhood.

Commentary on the Student's Reasoning

There is very little reasoning in this student's work and, on the whole, what there is seems uncritical and self-serving: in essence, "My friends are good. Therefore they wouldn't do anything bad." There are obvious objections to this reasoning. Presumably, most of the people in 1919 also went to church and believed in God. Presumably, they too would have thought themselves to be good Christians. Presumably, their friends thought of them as kind and as trying to raise their children to be good and to avoid evil. As a result, the student has not really responded to the logic of the question which implicitly requires that we think about mass hysteria, how it occurs, and how it influences otherwise morally sensitive people to behave in a morally insensitive way.

Student #2

Certainly there are always people who go overboard. That is human nature. And it is unreasonable to think that we will ever abandon human nature. The American people rightly recognized the threat that communism posed to our way of life and fought against it. After all, if we had defeated it then we would not have to have fought the Cold War and spent so much money and resources to defeat the communists after WW II. So what is the lesson. Watch out for human nature. Don't go overboard. But on the other hand, don't forget who your enemies are and don't give up the fight against them just because some people punish them too severely or go to an extreme.

Commentary on the Student's Reasoning

There is more reasoning in this student's work, but still not very good reasoning: in essence, "It is human nature for some people to lose control. So (by implication) some of us might do so, but whether or not some of us might act as some people in 1919 did, the people in 1919 were right to fight against communists". This reasoning is weak because it largely ignores the issue raised. The question at issue is not whether it was right for the people in 1919 to oppose communism, such as it was, in the USA at the time. The question is rather how it came to pass that, as we expressed above, otherwise morally sensitive people came to behave in a morally insensitive way. The student didn't take this question seriously.

Student #3

It is hard to answer the question as to what anyone is capable of. Perhaps what we are capable of is largely a result of the circumstances we are under. If we assume that all humans share human nature and that because of human nature we are capable of acting out of intense fear or insecurity or hate, then a lot depends upon whether something or someone is able to stir those things up in us. Perhaps, of course, there is a way to raise people so that they have so much good character that even when someone tries to stir up the "worst" in them, they do not give in, they resist the temptation to let their worst side take control of them. The question could then be asked whether I and my friends and neighbors are in the first or the second group. Since we have never been "tested" in a crisis situation, since we have never felt deeply threatened, I don't think I can honesty say we would pass the test. I don't know whether we would act like a "Charles Evans Hughes" or a "Billy Sunday". It's a scary thought.

Commentary on the Student's Reasoning

This is better reasoning than in either of the two passages above: in essence, "Everyone has a worse and a better side. Everyone's worse side can be appealed to. Whether you have the "character" to withstand an appeal to your worse cannot be known until you are "tested". My friends and I have not been tested. Therefore, we cannot know whether we have the character to withstand such an appeal. Therefore, we don't know whether we would or would not act as many did in 1919."

ENGLISH: INTERPRETING POEMS

Question At Issue: What is John Donne saying in his poem "Death Be Not Proud"?

Directions: Carefully read the poem below, trying to figure out what the poet is saying. Be careful to explain what your interpretation is and what exactly it is based on. Show us your reasoning. Make sure your interpretation is consistent with (all of) what the poem says.

Death Be Not Proud
(John Donne 1572–1631)

Death be not proud, though some have called thee
Mighty and dreadful, for, thou art not soe,
For, those, whom thou think'st, thou dost overthrow,
Die not, poore death, nor yet canst thou kill mee.
Much pleasure, then from thee, much more must flow,
And soonest our best men with thee doe goe,
Rest of their bones, and soules deliverie.
Thou art slave to Fate, Chance, kings, and desperate men,
And dost with poyson, warre, and sicknesse dwell,
And poppie, or charmes can make us sleepe as well,
And better then thy stroake; why swell'st thou then?
One short sleepe past, wee wake eternally,
And death shall be no more; death, thou shalt die.

Student #1

I don't like this poem. It is boring and confusing. The guy does not spell correctly. He talks a lot about death but he does not say anything. I don't see why he thinks death is mighty or why he thinks it can't kill him. He says a lot of confusing things. At one time he says it gives pleasure and then talks about bones resting, which makes no sense. Then he talks about flowers and sleeping.

Finally he says that death shall be no more and that it shall die. I don't get it. Why doesn't he just say what he wants to say? This is a terrible poem. Why do we have to read such stupid stuff?

Commentary on the Student's Reasoning

This student provides us with virtually no reasoning at all. Rather than attempt to figure out what the poet is saying by closely reading what is said, the student rejects the poem, dismisses it emotionally. The result is that the student flagrantly mis-reads the poem and blames his mis-reading on the poem itself and the poet. The student needs to be introduced to the concept of critical reading in which the reader uses the text as evidence to use in interpreting the meaning.

Student #2

Mr. Donne says that death should not be proud. It is not mighty or dreadful. He says this because death is like sleep and when you go to sleep you rest. Therefore, because it is restful even the best people sleep, even slaves. And sleeping is better than being poisoned or being sick. Finally, he says that we only sleep a while and then we awake. And then death is gone. In fact, it is dead. He thinks this is good.

Commentary on the Student's Reasoning

There is more reasoning in this student's work but most of it ignores the evidence of what the poem says. The poem does not say or imply, for example, that "because it [death] is restful even the best people sleep, even slaves". The poem does not say or imply that "sleeping is better than being poisoned or being sick". Finally, it is clear that the student is not getting the major point of the poem, namely, that because of the promised resurrection, last judgment, and eternal life in heaven or hell, there is a sense in which "death" is not real and lasting, but only something that will "die". Like the first student, this student also needs to be introduced to the concept of critical reading in which the reader uses the text as evidence in interpreting meaning.

Student #3

It is clear that Donne believes in God or at least in an afterlife. This is implied in the first four lines which I interpret as saying something like this: "Don't think you're so powerful because no one really dies but only appears to die" (People who "die" are really just awaiting their resurrection). This interpretation is supported in the next line which implies that what we call death is really a kind of "sleepe" and is not, therefore, very bad. In fact, as he says sleep often gives us "pleasure". The next lines make a different kind of point but still are a criticism of the view that death is "mighty" and "dreadful". Death, he says, is not able to control "Fate, Chance, kings, and desperate men". Furthermore, not only is it not able to control these other forces, it can't even get away from such unpleasant associates as "poyson, warre, and sicknesse". Finally, he reasons, narcotics makes us sleep as well as death does and when everyone is resurrected for final judgment (which I infer is what he means) then death itself will be gone forever, and therefore "shalt die".

Commentary on the Student's Reasoning

Finally, we have a student who illustrates the process of critical reading, carefully reasoning her way through the poem, using the words of the poem to carefully back up her interpretation.

HISTORY: REASONING ABOUT THE SIGNIFICANCE OF INVENTIONS

Question at Issue: "Of two inventions discussed in your textbook, which was the most important and why?"

Directions: The textbook for the course describes a number of important inventions, including those of Gutenberg, Edison, and George Washington Carver. Take two inventions, either from those mentioned in the book or some other inventions you know of, and compare their importance. Defend your answer by giving reasons in favor of your judgment.

Student #1

An invention that is very important is the printing press. It was invented by Johann Gutenberg, who was a man that lived in Germany. He invented the printing press in the Fifteenth Century. The first book ever printed by Gutenberg was the Bible. But he soon printed many other books as well. The first printing press worked by using movable type.

Another important invention mentioned in the textbook was the dehydration of foods. This was invented by George Washington Carver. When you dehydrate foods you take the water out of them. George Washington Carver wanted many people to use his inventions, so he did not take out any patents on them. He made many other inventions besides dehydration. He even thought of more than 300 uses for the peanut, including facial cream, shoe polish, and ice cream.

Both inventions are very important. Many people read books that are printed on a printing press. Many people eat food that has been dehydrated. But to me the printing press was more important than dehydration.

Commentary on the Student's Reasoning

The student does not provide any reasoning to support his conclusion. He discusses no criteria for assessing inventions for their importance, nor any evidence to support one or the other with respect to those criteria. Most of the factual detail is irrelevant to the issue.

Student #2

R-r-r-r-ring.

The first sound I hear in the morning is my alarm clock going off. It's an invention I truly hate.

R-r-r-r-ring.

It is not a pretty sound, and as soon as I hear it I feel myself getting angry. If only I didn't have to get up so early! All my muscles cry out that I want to sleep! Most mornings when I hear that sound, I even cover my ears with my pillow in the hope that I won't hear it going off.

It is an old-fashioned wind-up alarm clock that loses ten minutes a day. It is not a digital alarm clock because all the digital alarm clocks I've ever tried have alarms that are too soft to awaken a really sound sleeper. And believe me I am a *very* sound sleeper.

R-r-r-r-ring. But no matter what I do, or how I feel, I end up wide awake and out of bed and getting dressed for school.

Once I am awake I look at my other clock, the one that is hanging on the wall over my dresser. It is a great invention too. It's a digital clock that keeps perfect time. It has a red LED display and it glows in the dark. It has an emergency battery backup, so that even if the electricity cuts out in the night, my wall clock never loses a second.

Which of the two inventions is more important? That's the question I ask myself as I head off for school. And then the answer comes to me. No matter how perfectly the digital wall clock keeps time, without the alarm clock I wouldn't be awake to see it. So without doubt the alarm clock wins the prize as most important.

Commentary on the Student's Reasoning

The student provides some reasoning but when considered closely it is apparent that the reasoning is absurd. The notion that without the alarm clock people would never wake up is ridiculous. What does this student think happened before the alarm clock was invented? Furthermore, does she really think that loud alarms cannot be built into digital clocks? Once again, the student has not learned to think about the logic of the question at issue. Therefore, the student gives no time to reflecting on the general criteria by means of which we might assess the social worth of inventions by relating that worth to the most basic human values, like the preservation of life, the minimization of pain and suffering, the development of a more just society, and so forth. It is only in terms of the concepts of basic human values that criteria can be generated that give a solid logic to the question and hence a means to assess the reasoning which purports to settle the question.

Student #3

Two inventions mentioned in the book are television and the dehydration of food. Each is important in different ways. The television set, for example, affects many people's lives. I watch television almost every night and so do all of my friends. But it's not just me and my friends. The same is true for people all across the country, and in most foreign countries as well. Television allows more people to be entertained than was ever possible before. We witness world news, nature programs, comedies and many other programs. Television lets us see much of what is going on in the world.

Dehydration of foods is important in a very different way. The main effects of dehydration are that it allows food to be kept for a long time without spoiling, and to be shipped for a lower cost. I don't know how many people in the world today use dehydrated foods, but I'm pretty sure that it's far smaller than the number of people who enjoy TV. So that seems to show that TV is more important.

And yet I don't feel right saying that one invention is more important than another simply because it has affected more people. If dehydration is used more than it is now, it could help cut down on the number of people who are starving in the world. Saving just a few people from dying of starvation is more important than taking a lot of people and entertaining them.

Commentary on the Student's Reasoning

The student provides some reasoning which might at first appear absurd, but on reflection makes good sense. This student is thinking about the logic of the question at issue and hence is reflecting on the general criteria by means of which we might assess the social worth of inventions by relating that worth to the most basic human values: like the quality or preservation of life, the minimization of pain and suffering, the development of a more just society, and so forth. To say that this student's reasoning is better than the first two students — because she does respond to the logic of the question at issue — does not mean that her reasoning is perfect, for perhaps there are yet further considerations that might be mentioned about the effects of television which might persuade us that television itself is making so large a contribution to the quality or preservation of human life that it is indeed more important than food dehydration. We may know the basic logic of a question without knowing whether we yet have the best answer to that question, the answer that best fulfills its logic.

✦ Conclusion

The whole of this book is concerned with the process of developing students who reason through what they are learning so as to grasp the logic of it, students who know clearly the difference between coming to terms with the logic of something and merely rotely memorizing it. But reasoning is not a matter to be learned once and for all. It is a matter of life-long learning, a matter of bringing insightful mindfulness into the fabric of our thinking and our action. For the teacher, it is a matter of learning how to design instruction so that students take command of the logic of their own thinking while they are thinking and through that insightful grasp, improve it.

We figure things out better if we can monitor what we are doing, intellectually, in trying to figure them out, so that we go beyond simply using logical structures, so that we go beyond simply making logical moves, so that we start to intentionally, deliberately, and willfully examine and take apart the logical structures we are using, so that we designedly, purposively, and alertly assess our use of the structures in everyday situations, and, of course, so that we do these things well: clearly, accurately, precisely, etc.

To understand logical structures is to integrate them, to establish logical connections between them, to make it possible for the mind to make an extended series of nuanced inferences, deductions, and derivations. "This is so, therefore that also is so, and that, and that." The logical structures implicit in an educated person's mind are highly systematized. The well-educated person is able to reason quite directly and deliberately, to begin somewhere, know where one is beginning, and then reason with awareness from that point to other points, all with a given question in mind, with specific evidence in mind, with specific reasons to advance, with specific conclusions to support, with consciousness of one's point of view and of contrasting points of view. The good reasoner is always reasoning within a system that disciplines and restrains that reasoning.

When the logical structures by which a mind figures out the world are confused, a jumble, a hodgepodge, a mere conglomeration, then that figuring out is radically defective, typically in any of a variety of ways: incomplete, inaccurate, distorted, muddled, inexact, superficial, rigid, inconsistent, and unproductive. Then the mind begins it knows not where, takes things for granted without analysis or questioning, leaps to conclusions without sufficient evidence to back them up, meanders without a consciousness of its point of view or of alternative points of view. Then the mind wanders into its own prejudices and biases, its own egocentricity and sociocentricity. Then the mind is not able to discipline itself by a close analysis of the question at issue and ignores the demands that the logic of that question puts on it and us as rational, logic-creating, logic-using animals.

Section III

Contrasting Approaches to Thinking

The Logic of Creative and Critical Thinking

*Bloom's Taxonomy and Critical Thinking
Instruction: Recall Is Not Knowledge*

*Philosophy and Cognitive Psychology:
Contrasting Assumptions*

Chapter 9

The Logic of
Creative and Critical Thinking

Abstract

In this paper Richard Paul develops an extended explication of the relationship between creative and critical thinking. He does so by first setting out the
relationship in general, arguing that both are perfections of thought which are, in
fact, inseparable in everyday reasoning. "Creativity", according to Paul, masters
a process of "making" or "producing", "criticality" a process of "assessing" or
"judging". He then argues that insofar as the mind — in thinking — is thinking
well, it must, virtually simultaneously, both produce and assess, make and judge
that making.

Having set out this relationship in general, Paul works out the details with
respect to a series of theoretically basic structures and processes: 1) thinking
through the logic of things, 2) taking command of reasoning and logic, 3) making
fundamental assumptions about learning and knowing, 4) understanding the
logic of concepts, 5) understanding the logic of academic disciplines, 6) the logic
of language, 7) the logic of questions, 8) the logic of student thinking, 9) the logic
of teaching, 10) the logic of reading, writing, speaking, and listening, and 11) the
logic of logic. Throughout, the underlying theme of the paper is sustained: that
intellectual discipline and rigor are not only quite at home with originality and
productivity but that both so-called "poles" of thinking are really inseparable
aspects of excellence of thought.

Beyond exploring the relation of creativity and criticality, this paper is one of
the best in the collection for giving the reader a unified sense of the importance to
critical thinking of the concept, "the logic of..." On Paul's analysis, this concept
is indispensable and, if one reads with a sensitivity to it, one will find that it plays
a role in virtually everything he writes.

✦ Introduction

C reative and critical thinking often seem to the untutored to be
polar opposite forms of thought, the first based on irrational or
unconscious forces, the second on rational and conscious processes, the
first undirectable and unteachable, the second directable and teachable.
There is some, but very little, truth in this view. The truth in it is that
there is no way to generate creative geniuses, nor to get students to gen-

erate highly novel ground-breaking ideas, by some known process of systematic instruction. The dimension of "creativity", in other words, contains unknowns, even mysteries. So does "criticality" of course. Yet there are ways to teach simultaneously for both creative and critical thinking in a down-to-earth sense of those terms. To do so, however, requires that we focus on these terms in practical everyday contexts, that we keep their central meanings in mind, and that we seek insight into the respect in which they overlap and feed into each other, the respect in which they are inseparable, integrated, and unitary. This paper will develop these insights.

OVERVIEW

Good thinking is thinking that does the job we set for it. It is thinking that accomplishes the purposes of thinking. If thinking lacks a purpose, that is, is aimless, it may chance upon something of value to the thinker, but more often it will simply wander into an endless stream of unanalyzed associations from one's unanalyzed past: "hotdogs remind me of ball games, ball games remind me of Chicago, Chicago of my old neighborhood, my old neighborhood of my grandmother, of her pies, of having to eat what I didn't like, which reminds me ... which reminds me ... which reminds me...." Few people need training in aimless thinking such as this, or in daydreaming or fantasizing. For the most part we are "naturals" at aimless thinking.

Where we have trouble is in purposeful thinking, especially purposeful thinking that involves figuring things out, thinking, in other words, that poses problems to be solved and intricacies to reason through. "Criticality" and "creativity" have an intimate relationship to the ability to figure things out. There is a natural marriage between them. Indeed, all thinking that is properly called "excellent" combines these two dimensions in an intimate way. Whenever our thinking excels, it excels because we succeed in designing or engendering, fashioning or originating, creating or producing results and outcomes appropriate to our ends in thinking. It has, in a word, a *creative* dimension.

But to achieve any challenging end, we must also have *criteria:* gauges, measures, models, principles, standards, or tests to use in judging whether we are approaching that end. What is more, we must apply our criteria (models, gauges, measures, models, principles) in a way that is discerning, discriminating, exact, fastidious, judicious, and acute. We must continually monitor and assess how our thinking is going, whether it is plausibly on the right track, whether it is sufficiently clear, accurate, precise, consistent, relevant, deep, or broad for our purposes.

We don't achieve excellence in thinking with no end in view. We don't design for no reason, fashion and create without knowing what we are trying to fashion and create. We don't originate and produce with no sense of why we are doing so. Thinking that is random, thinking that roams aimlessly through half-formed images, that meanders without an organizing goal is not a candidate for either "creativity" or "criticality". It is not a candidate for excellence.

Why? When the mind thinks aimlessly, its energy and drive are typically low, its tendency is commonly toward inertness, its results usually barren. What is aimless is also normally pointless and moves in familiar alliance with indolence and dormancy. But when thinking takes on a challenging task, the mind must then come alive, ready itself for intellectual labor, engage the intellect in some form of work upon some intellectual object — until such time as it succeeds in originating, formulating, designing, engendering, creating, or producing what is necessary for the achievement of its goal. Intellectual work is essential to *create* intellectual products, and that work, that production, involves intellectual standards *judiciously* applied, ... in other words, creativity and criticality interwoven into one seamless fabric.

Like the body, the mind has its own form of fitness or excellence. Like the body, that fitness is caused by and reflected in activities done in accordance with standards (criticality). A fit mind can successfully engage in the designing, fashioning, formulating, originating, or producing of intellectual products worthy of its challenging ends. To achieve this fitness, the mind must learn to take charge of itself, to energize itself, press forward when difficulties emerge, proceed slowly and methodically when meticulousness is necessary, immerse itself in a task, become attentive, reflective, and engrossed, circle back on a train of thought, recheck to ensure that it has been thorough, accurate, exact, and deep enough.

Its generativeness and its judiciousness can only be artificially separated. In the process of actual thought they are one. Such thought is systematic when being systematic serves its end. It can also cast system aside and ransack its intuitions for a lead — when no clear maneuver, plan, strategy, or tactic comes to mind. Nor is the generative, the productive, the creative mind without standards for what it generates and produces. It is not a mind lacking judiciousness, discernment, and judgment. It is not a mind incapable of acuteness and exactness. It is not a mind whose standards are unclarity, imprecision, inaccuracy, irrelevance, triviality, inconsistency, superficiality, and narrowness. The fit mind generates and produces precisely because it has high standards for itself, because it cares about how and what it creates.

Serious thinking originates in a commitment to grasp some truth, to get to the bottom of something, to make accurate sense of that about which it is thinking. This "figuring out" cannot simply be a matter of arbitrary creation or production. There must be specific restraints and requirements to be met, something outside the will to which the will must be bent, some unyielding objectivity we must painstakingly take into account and neither ignore nor thrust aside. It is exactly the severe, inflexible, stern fact of reality that forces intellectual criticality and productivity into one seamless whole. If there were no "objectivity" outside our process of "figuring out", then we would have literally nothing to figure out. If what we figure out can be anything we want it to be, anything we fantasize it as being, then there is no logic to the expression "figure out".

In a sense, of course, all minds create and produce in a manner reflective of their fitness or lack thereof. Minds indifferent to standards and disciplined judgment tend to judge inexactly, inaccurately, inappropriately, prejudicially. Prejudices, hate, irrational jealousies and fears, stereotypes and misconceptions — these too are "created", "produced", "originated" by minds. Without minds to produce them, they would not exist. Yet they are not the products of "creative" minds. They reflect an undisciplined, an uncritical mode of thinking and therefore are not properly thought of as products of "creativity". In short, except in rare circumstances, creativity presupposes criticality and criticality creativity. This is the essential insight behind this paper.

In what follows, therefore, we shall explore the intimate connection between a well-grounded sense of creativity in thinking, the sense of thinking as a *making,* as a process of *creating* thought, as a process that *brings thoughts into being* to organize, shape, interpret, and make sense of our world — thinking that, once developed, enables us to achieve goals, accomplish purposes, solve problems, and settle important issues we face as humans in a world in which rapid change is becoming the only constant. This sense of *thought as a creative making* is the most important sense of creativity, pedagogically speaking, and cannot be understood, as I have briefly argued, separate from understanding the development of "critical judgment" and a critical mind. When a mind does not systematically and effectively embody intellectual criteria and standards, is not disciplined in reasoning things through, in figuring out the logic of things, in reflectively devising a rational approach to the solution of problems or in the accomplishment of intellectual or practical tasks, that mind is not "creative". In this sense, there is a reciprocal logic to both intellectual creation and critical judgment, to the intellectual "making" of things and to the on-going "critique" of that making. Let us examine that reciprocal logic more closely.

✦ Thinking That Grasps the Logic of Things

All intellectual products, in order to be intellectually assessed and validated, require some logic, some order or coherence, some intellectual structure that makes sense and is rationally defensible. This is true whether one is talking of poems or essays, paintings or choreographed dances, histories or anthropological reports, experiments or scientific theories, philosophies or psychologies, accounts of particular events or those of general phenomena or laws. A product of intellectual work that makes no sense, that cannot be rationally analyzed and assessed, that cannot be incorporated into other intellectual work, or used — and hence that cannot play a role in any academic tradition or discipline — is unintelligible. Whether we are designing a new screw driver, figuring out how to deal with our children's misbehavior, or working out a perspective on religion, we must order our meanings into a system of meanings that make sense to us, and so, in that respect, have a logic.

This is to say that there is an important role for reason and reasoning, for constructing and working within a logic, for creative producing and critical assessing of what is produced, in every intellectual enterprise. Let us now explore that role in brief.

WHAT IS REASONING? WHAT IS LOGIC?

The words 'reasoning' and 'logic' each have both a narrow and a broad use. In the narrow sense, 'reasoning' is drawing conclusions on the basis of reasons, and, in the narrow sense, 'logic' refers simply to the principles that apply to the assessment of that process. But in the broad sense, 'reason' and 'reasoning' refer to the total process of figuring things out, and hence to every intellectual standard relevant to doing that. And parallel to this sense is a broad sense of 'logic' which refers to the basic structure that one is, in fact, figuring out (when engaged in reasoning something through).

One can draw conclusions about poems, microbes, numbers, historical events, languages, social settings, psychological fears, everyday situations, character traits — indeed, about anything whatsoever. And this drawing of conclusions is part of a broader process of reasoning things through. The particular inferences made have a specific logic that can be assessed and the total process of reasoning things through has a general logic that also can be assessed. In this broad sense of 'logic', one focuses on the logic of the poem or the logic of a microbe or the logic of numbers or the logic of a historical event or the logic of a language, and so forth. In the narrow sense, one focuses on the logic of this or that inference within a given poem or about a given microbe or within some train of mathematical thought. Hence, Sherlock Holmes tries to figure out the logic of the murder by making a number of specific inferences from the available evidence. The broader logic contains the narrower logic.

IN THE BROAD SENSE, WHAT MAKES GOOD REASONING GOOD REASONING?

Becoming adept at drawing justifiable conclusions on the basis of good reasons is more complex than it appears. This is because drawing a conclusion is always the tip of an intellectual iceberg. It is not just a matter of avoiding a fallacy in logic (in the narrow sense). There is much more that is implicit in reasoning than is explicit, there are more components, more "logical structures" that we do not express than those we do. To become skilled in reasoning things through we must become practiced in making what is implicit explicit so that we can "check out" what is going on "beneath the surface" of our thought.

Thus, when we draw a conclusion, we do so in some circumstances, making inferences (that have implications and consequences) based on some reasons or information (and assumptions), using some concepts, in trying to settle some question (or solve some problem) for some purpose within some point of view.

Good reasoners can consider and plausibly assess any of these elements as they function in their thought in any act of reasoning something out. Good reasoners therefore use good logic in both the narrow and the broad sense. Furthermore, in most circumstances in which we are *using* logic we are *creating* it simultaneously. This needs explanation.

✦ Whenever We Are Reasoning Something Through We Are Ipso Facto Engaged in Creative Thinking

In the broad sense, all reasoned thinking is thinking within a logic, and when we have not yet learned a given logic — e.g., not yet learned the logic of the internal combustion engine, the logic of right triangles, or the logic of dolphin behavior — our minds must bring that logic into being, create it in the fabric, within the structure, of our established ways of thinking. Hence, when we are thinking something through for the first time, to some extent, we create the logic we are using. We bring into being new articulations of our purposes and of our reasons. We make new assumptions. We form new concepts. We ask new questions. We make new inferences. Our point of view is worked out in a new direction, one in which it has never been worked out before.

Indeed, there is a sense in which all reasoned thinking, all genuine acts of figuring out anything whatsoever, even something previously figured out, is a new "making", a new series of creative acts, for we rarely recall our previous thought whole cloth. Instead we generally remember only some part of what we figured out and figure out the rest anew, based on the logic of that part and other logical structures more immediately available to us. We continually create new understandings and re-create old understandings by a similar process of figuring.

In what follows, I will articulate a frame of reference that highlights the intimate interplay between creative and critical thinking, between the thinking that creates a set of logically interrelated meanings and the thinking that assesses the logic being created. I will begin with a basic assumption that underlies the model being developed. The theme that shall run throughout is as follows:

In all contexts that demand the reasoned figuring out of something, there are, as it were, *three logics* involved: *1)* the logic to be figured out (the logic it is our aim to create), *2)* the logic we use to do the figuring (chosen by us from the logics we have already learned), and *3)* the logic that results, in the end, from our reasoning (and which needs to be assessed for its "fit", for the degree to which it has captured the logic to be figured out). For example, I may use my understanding of the logic of one D.H. Lawrence novel (say, *Sons and Lovers*) as an initial framework for understanding the logic of another (say, *Lady Chatterley's Lover*). The understanding I end up with may or may not fully make sense of the actual story. The logic I make of it may be inadequate. Or again, in studying history, I may use my understanding of the logic of one economic crisis (say that of the thirties in the USA) to understand another one (say that of the nineties in the USA). The reconstruction I come up with may or may not make sense of the logic of what was actually going on economically in the nineties. In all our learning we must seek out provisional models (mini logical systems) for figuring out what we are trying to learn (the system we are trying to grasp). We then end up with a product of thought, a system we create. That system may or may not be adequate to the task.

A BASIC ASSUMPTION

In all of our behavior we assume there is order, regularity, and potential intelligibility in everything; that every portion of "reality" can sooner or later be figured out, explained, and related to other portions; that our innate capacity to form conceptions of, and make inferences about, ourselves and the things around us is adequate for our purposes. This basic assumption implies that in some sense there is a discoverable logic to each dimension of reality. Of course, in making this assumption, we need not also assume that what we discover about the logic of things, from our various concepts and inferences, is some form of "Absolute Truth", nor that our knowledge of things exhausts, completely spells out, or totally captures the ultimate nature of things, or even that things have an "ultimate" nature. For one thing, our knowledge is always limited by the perspectives that are inherent in our various ways of forming concepts and making inferences. We are limited, not infinite, creatures; humans, not gods.

✦ The Logic of ...

To say that something has a logic, then, is to say that it can be understood by use of our reason, that we can form concepts that accurately — though not necessarily thoroughly — characterize the nature of that thing. Only when we have conceptualized a thing in some way, and only then, can we reason through it. Since nature does not tell us how to conceptualize it, we must create that conceptualization, individually or socially. Once conceptualized, a thing is integrated by us into a network of ideas (since no concept ever stands alone) and, as such, becomes the subject of many possible inferences.

Furthermore, once we begin to make inferences about something, we can do so either well or poorly, justifiably or unjustifiably, in keeping with the meaning of the concept and the nature of what we know of the thing conceptualized, or not so in keeping. If we are not careful, for example, we may (and very often do) infer more than is implied. If I hear a sound at the door and conceptualize it as "scratching at the door", I may then infer that it is my dog wanting to come in. I have used my reason (my capacity to conceptualize and infer) to interpret the noise as a "scratch" and I have assumed, in the process, that the only creature in the vicinity who could be making that scratch at my door is my dog... my reasoning may be off. I may have mis-conceptualized the noise as a "scratch" (I may even have misheard where the noise is coming from) or I may have wrongly assumed that there are no other creatures around who might make it. Notice that in these acts, I create the conceptualizations that are at the root of my thinking.

We approach virtually everything in our experience as something that can be thus "decoded" by the power of our minds to create a conceptualization and to make inferences on the basis of it (hence to create further conceptualizations). We do this so routinely and automatically that we don't typically recognize ourselves as engaged in processes of reasoned creation. In our everyday life we don't first experience the world in "concept-less" form and then deliberately place what we experience into categories in order to make sense of things.

Rather, it is as if things are given to us with their "names" inherent in them. So we see "trees", "clouds", "grass", "roads", "people", "men", "women", and so on. We apply these concepts intuitively, as if no rational, creative act were involved. Yet, if we think about it, we will realize that there was a time when we had to learn names for things and hence, before we knew those names, we couldn't possibly have seen these phenomena through the mediation of these concepts. In learning these concepts we had to create them in our own minds out of the concepts we already had learned.

I want to highlight the importance of this power of creative conceptualization and inference in human life, for it is precisely this power of mind that we must take charge of in forming disciplined habits of thought, thought which we summarize with the expression 'thinking critically'. In thinking critically we take command of our conceptual creations, assessing them more explicitly than is normally done. Concepts, like all human creations, can be well or poorly designed. Critical judgment is always relevant to the process of design and construction, whether that construction be conceptual or material.

For example, we study living organisms to construct "bio-logic", that is, to establish ways to conceptualize and make valid inferences about life forms. We study social arrangements to construct "socio-logic", that is, to establish ways to conceptualize and make valid inferences about life in society. We study the historical past to construct "the logic of history", ways to conceptualize and make valid inferences about the past. Since no one is born with these logical structures at his or her command, everyone must "create" them.

THE LOGIC OF CONCEPTS

In this paper, we are using the word 'concept' to mean simply "a generalized idea of a class of things". We understand "conceptualization" to be a process by which the mind infers a thing to be of a certain kind, to belong properly to some given class of things. Hence, if I call something, or interpret something to be, an apple, I have placed it into a generalized class of things (the class of all apples). Our minds understand any particular aspect of things in relation to generalized ideas that highlight perceived similarities and differences in our experience. For example, the word 'dog' represents one concept, the word 'cat' another, the word 'cloud' a third, the word 'laughter' a fourth. We reason about, and so interpret the world, by putting the objects of our experience into "categories" or "concepts" each one of which highlights some set of similarities or differences for us, links the thing up with other concepts, and validates a certain set of inferences. For example, if I see a creature before me and take it to be a dog — that is, if I place it mentally into the category of 'dog' — I can reasonably infer that it will bark rather than meow or purr. Of course, I cannot reasonably infer that it will not bite me if I attempt to chase it away. Furthermore, by placing something into the concept of 'dog' I locate the thing in relation to other concepts, such as 'animal', 'furry', 'muzzle', 'paw', 'tail', and so forth.

In learning to speak our native language, we learn thousands of concepts which, when properly used, enable us to make countless legitimate inferences about the objects of our experience. Unfortunately, there is nothing in the way we ordinarily learn to speak a language that forces us to use concepts carefully or that prevents us from making unjustifiable inferences while engaged in their use. Indeed, a fundamental need for critical thinking is given by the fact that as long as the mind remains undisciplined in its use of concepts, it is susceptible to any number of illegitimate inferences.

The process of learning the concepts implicit in a natural language like English, is a process of creating facsimiles of the concepts implicit in the language usage, to which we are exposed. However, we cannot give anyone the meaning of a word or phrase; that meaning must be individually created by every person who learns it. When we mis-learn the meaning of a word, we create in our own minds a meaning that it doesn't have.

THE LOGIC OF ACADEMIC DISCIPLINES

We can now understand each academic discipline to represent a domain in which humans are creating specialized concepts (and inferences that follow from those concepts) that enable them to approach that domain through an ordered set of logical relationships structured by human reason. Critical judgment is essential to all of the acts of construction; all acts of construction are open to critical assessment. We not only assess *what* we create; we assess as we create.

Each student who would learn the logic of a discipline has to create that logic in his or her own mind. Each moment of that creation requires the presence of critical thought and judgment. There is no way to create the logic for the student or simply to "give", transfer, or inject the logic in pre-fabricated form. By the same token, the logic of a text within a discipline enters the student's thinking only through the mediation of the logic of the student's thinking. But the logic of the student's thinking must be continually re-shaped and modified. The logic the student fashions in learning represents, if done well, an analytically modified logic, the result of a process of measured accommodation, not simply one of uncritical assimilation.

Hence, if a student reads a text within a discipline well, that is, critically, the logic he or she creates through reading matches the logic of the text well. Reading proficiently is both a creative task (a making, a creating) and a critical task (an assessing, a judging). The making and the assessing, the creating and the judging are integral to one seamless process of good reasoning. We create the logic of the text in our minds as we critically dialogue with it. We raise and answer probing questions as we read, generating and fashioning ideas and meanings in and through our responses.

This picture is complicated by those domains in which competing logics develop, each rationally defended by different, apparently equally expert, apparently equally rational, proponents. To some extent, of course, questions which call for the adjudication of competing logics emerge in all disciplines. On the other hand, some disciplines, namely those which attempt to conceptualize and make sense of human realities, seem to be inescapably "multi-logical": history, psychology, sociology, philosophy, anthropology, economics, literature, fine arts, and so forth. In these domains, seminal thinkers continue to emerge with alternative and conflicting ideas for reasoning about basic questions in the field. In this case, students have to create and reason within conflicting logics. Problems of confusion abound in this circumstance.

The creativity in reasoning one's way into disciplines which are multi-logical demands exacting and discriminating restraint and self-regulation. In reading, for example, the writings of Freud, Adler, and Jung, I must create in my mind three overlapping systems of thought, systems which complexely agree and disagree. If I come to understand what I have read, I have come to develop the ability to think within three different systems of thought. Only I, through a process of disciplined intellectual work, can generate, fabricate, engender in my mind Freudian, Adlerian, and Jungian thoughts. Only I can create the inner understandings which enable me to draw fine distinctions among their views, fine distinctions which honor the multiple logics they collectively developed. Instruction should provide incentives for students to actively create the logics of these conflicting perspectives and to critically assess that creation at one and the same time.

THE LOGIC OF LOGIC

Critical thinking can now be understood as a deep interest in *the logic of logic,* the art of taking charge of the large variety of ways in which we create concepts and make inferences by means of them, the various ways, in other words, in which we use human reason well or poorly in attempting to make sense of things and our created interpretations of them. Critical thinkers, on this view, attempt to heighten their awareness of the conditions under which their self-created conceptualizations — and inferences from them — are rationally justified. They not only use their innate capacity to reason, they also study how to improve the use of their reason, to discipline and "perfect" it (to make it more clear, precise, accurate, relevant, logical, consistent, respectful of evidence, responsive to good reasons, open to new ideas, and so forth). They habitually, therefore, reason about their reasoning. They routinely scrutinize their thinking as an act of on-going creation which must be continually monitored and checked for its "match".

In this way, critical thinkers maintain an acute and abiding interest in their own intellectual self-improvement. They carefully attend to their personal concept-creating and concept-using practices. They exercise special discipline in taking charge of their thinking by taking charge of the ideas that direct that thinking, by close examination of the ideas which they are generating and using to create an ordered set of meanings.

THE LOGIC OF LANGUAGE

Many of our ideas or concepts come from the languages we have learned to speak (and in which as a matter of course we do our thinking). Embedded in the educated use of words are criteria or standards that we must respect in order to think clearly and precisely by means of those words. We are free, of course, to use a particular word in a special way in special circumstances, but only if we have good reason for modifying its meaning. Such special stipulations should proceed from a clear understanding of established educated use. We are not free, for example, to use the word 'education' as if it were synonymous with the word 'indoctrination' or 'socialization'. We are not free to equate pride with cunning, truth with belief, knowledge with information, arrogance with self-confidence, desire with love, and so on. Each word has its own established logic, a logic that cannot, without confusion or error, be ignored.

Though each word has an established logic, we still have to recreate that logic in our thinking, and we must base that creation on meanings we have previously created. Learning the meaning of a word is therefore not a simple task because in each case we must create a new concept in our minds out of modified old understandings. This requires that our creation be ordered, restrained, regulated, and controlled. The undisciplined creation of meaning in the context of learning the logic of language is nothing more nor less than the mis-learning of that logic.

THE LOGIC OF STUDENT THINKING

Unfortunately many students do not understand the significant relationship between care and precision in language usage and care and precision in thought. Students often say, when talking about the nature of language, that people have their own meanings for all the words they use, not noticing that, were this true, we would not be able to understand each other. Students often speak and write in vague sentences because they have no criteria for choosing words other than that one word rather than another occurred to them. They do not seek to put their sentences into clear logical relationships to one another because they do not recognize any responsibility to do so nor any clear idea of what that would entail. They do not read, write, speak, or listen well because they have never had to think clearly about the logic of reading, writing, speaking, or listening.

All of the rational processes of mind are assumed by them to take care of themselves, automatically and effortlessly. Or better, they are unaware that there are any rational processes of mind to be tended to, in the first place. It goes without saying that students do not generally have any grasp of the creative dimension of all learning. They do not see themselves designing, fashioning, or shaping meanings. They think of themselves as simply absorbing meanings, as simply receiving what is being given to them by the teacher, the textbook, or experience itself.

The result of this common mind-set is that students find it very difficult, if not impossible, to master any well-developed or refined set of conceptual relationships. The logic of their own thinking is vague, fragmented, often contradictory, highly egocentric, typically sociocentric, pervasively undisciplined, and lacking in foundational insights. Since one begins to develop critical thinking significantly only insofar as one begins to discipline one's own thinking with respect to at least one framework of concepts, and since one learns a new set of concepts only by means of a set of previously learned concepts, the development of student thinking must take place over an extended period of time and must be heavily dialogical. Only by moving back and forth between their own undisciplined thought and some set of disciplined concepts, can they work their minds into disciplined thought.

Furthermore, there is the very real danger that, once developed, their emerging discipline in one domain will remain isolated and segregated from the rest of their thinking. Even expert thinkers in one domain are often atrocious in another. The human mind does not necessarily develop as an integrated whole. This is one of the reasons why it is important to emphasize critical thinking as critical thinking, in its most generalizable form. Hence, when learning to think with discipline in one domain of concepts, it is highly useful to be exposed to logically illuminating parallel examples from other domains.

Finally, lacking the discipline of critical thinking and judgment, the creative dimension of student thinking is commonly quite undistinguished. What they "create" is typically poorly designed and constructed. For example, since their own thinking is vague and fragmented, they routinely generate vague and fragmented meanings in the process of learning; their minds bring into being disjointed meanings which often have no single, definite logic whatsoever. It is important to recognize that in a literal sense there is no necessary virtue in "creating" meaning. Prejudices, self-delusions, distortions, misconceptions, and caricatures are all products of the mind as maker and creator.

THE LOGIC OF QUESTIONS

Every question, when well put, imposes specific demands upon us, demands implicit in the logic of the words of the question and in the contexts in which those words are intelligibly used by educated speakers of the language. If I ask, "What is the sum of 434 and 987?", the question requires an answer consonant with the established logic of the word 'addition'. If I ask, "Is Jack your friend or merely an acquaintance?", the question requires an answer in keeping with the logic of the established distinction between the words 'friend' and 'acquaintance'. If I ask you "To what extent are your students learning to think critically?", the question requires that you 1) understand precisely what is implied by the expression 'thinks critically' and 2) assess your students' thinking by some means appropriate to determining the relative standing of your students either with respect to a fixed ideal of critical thinking or some standardized norm to which your students' performances (of thinking) can appropriately be compared. An appropriate answer is one that is constructed in accordance with the logical demands of the question.

Very often, people are cavalier in their putting and answering of questions. They rarely put their own questions precisely, and, when answering the questions of others, they often respond impressionistically or otherwise inappropriately, without care, discipline, or sensitivity to what is implied by the established logic of the question (or by the context in which the question is asked). When called upon to sharpen their questions or to respond more carefully and precisely, many respond with irritation or annoyance, exasperated that they are expected to be clear or precise or accurate or relevant or consistent in their question-asking or - answering behaviors.

This general insensitivity to the logic of questions is part of the broader phenomenon of insensitivity to the logic of language, which is itself part of the even broader phenomenon of insensitivity to the need for care and discipline in our use of reason — our use of concept and inference — in figuring out the logic of the world within and around us. All of these, in turn, are part of the general insensitivity to the need to discipline our mind's creative productions, to shape them in accord with restraining conditions. Sometimes these restraining conditions are given by the logic of language, sometimes by the logic of the material world.

✦ The Elements of Thought

As soon as we move from thought which is purely associational and undisciplined, to thought which is conceptual and inferential, which attempts in some intelligible way to figure something out, to use the power of creative reason, then it is possible, and helpful, to think about what might be called "the elements of thought", the basic building-blocks of thinking, the essential dimensions of all reasoning whenever and wherever it creates meaning. There is, in other words, a general logic to the use of reason. We can deduce these elements, these essential dimensions of reasoning, by paying close attention to what is implicit in the attempt on the part of the mind to figure anything out whatsoever. Once we make these elements of thought clear, it will be obvious that each of them can serve as an important touchstone or point of assessment in our critical analysis and assessment of the constructed process and products of our thinking. As meaning makers we must be exacting, discriminating, and fastidious. Without a guiding logic, thinking is aimless and random. Productive thinking needs some structure, some basic logic to follow.

We have already noticed that the attempt to render something intelligible requires the construction of concepts, the creation of interpretations and understandings based on them, and inferences drawn from them. We can now set out the basic set of conditions implicit in these creative, critical acts of the mind, whenever they occur. They are as follows:

1) *Purpose, Goal, or End in View:* Whenever we reason, we reason to some end, to achieve some purpose, to satisfy some desire or fulfill some need. One source of problems in reasoning is traceable to "defects" at the level of goal, purpose, or end. If our goal itself is unrealistic, contra-

dictory to other goals we have, confused or muddled in some way, then the reasoning we use to achieve it is problematic. The goal, purpose, or end of our thinking is something our mind must actively create.

2) *Question at Issue (or Problem to Be Solved):* Whenever we attempt to reason something out, there is at least one question at issue, at least one problem to be solved. One area of concern for the reasoner should therefore be the very formulation of the question to be answered or problem to be solved. If we are not clear about the question we are asking, or how the question relates to our basic purpose or goal, then it is unlikely that we will be able to find a reasonable answer to it, or one that will serve our purpose. The question at issue in our thinking is something our mind must actively create.

3) *Point of View or Frame of Reference:* Whenever we reason, we must reason within some point of view or frame of reference. Any defect in our point of view or frame of reference is a possible source of problems in our reasoning. Our point of view may be too narrow or too parochial, may be based on false or misleading analogies or metaphors, may not be precise enough, may contain contradictions, and so forth. The point of view which shapes and organizes our thinking is something our mind must actively create.

4) *The Empirical Dimension of Our Reasoning:* Whenever we reason, there is some "stuff", some phenomena about which we are reasoning. Any defect, then, in the experiences, data, evidence, or raw material upon which our reasoning is based is a possible source of problems. We must actively decide which of a myriad of possible experiences, data, evidence, etc. we will use.

5) *The Conceptual Dimension of Our Reasoning:* All reasoning uses some ideas or concepts and not others. Any defect in the concepts or ideas (including the theories, principles, axioms, or rules) with which we reason, is a possible source of problems. The concepts and ideas which shape and organize our thinking must be actively created by us.

6) *Assumptions* — The Starting Points of Reasoning: All reasoning must begin somewhere, must take some things for granted. Any defect in the starting points of our reasoning, any problem in what we are taking for granted, is a possible source of problems. Only we can create the assumptions on the basis of which we will reason.

7) *Inferences:* Reasoning proceeds by steps called inferences. To make an inference is to think as follows: "Because this is so, that also is so (or probably so)". Any defect in the inferences we make while we reason is a possible problem in our reasoning. Information, data, and situations do not determine what we shall deduce from them; we create inferences through the concepts and assumptions which we bring to situations.

8) Implications and Consequences — Where Our Reasoning Takes Us: All
reasoning begins somewhere and proceeds somewhere else. No reasoning is static. Reasoning is a sequence of inferences that begin somewhere and take us somewhere else. Thus all reasoning comes to an end,
yet could have been taken further. All reasoning has implications or
consequences beyond those the reasoner has considered. Any problem
with these (implications that are false, undesirable consequences),
implies a problem in the reasoning. The implications of our reasoning
are an implicit creation of our reasoning.

If we taught each school subject in such a way that students had to reason their way into the subject, and if we routinely questioned students so
they came to habitually look into each basic dimension of their thinking
— purpose, question at issue, point of view, data, concepts, assumptions,
inferences, implications and consequences — they would progressively
become more disciplined in their reasoning, more self-critical and self-
directed in the process and products of their thinking.

THE LOGIC OF READING, WRITING, SPEAKING, AND LISTENING

Reading, writing, speaking, and listening are all "dialogical" in nature.
That is, in each case there are at least two logics involved, and there is an
attempt being made by someone to translate one logic into the terms of
another. Consider reading and listening. In both of these cases we are
attempting to make sense of the logic or reasoning of another person.
Whatever is written must, if it is reasoned, contain all of the elements of
thought, and as a critical reader one can question the text as one goes
seeking to determine: What is the central purpose of the writer of the
text, what problems or issues does she raise? Within what point of view is
she reasoning? What is she assuming or taking for granted? What evidence, information, or data is presented to us? How is that evidence interpreted or conceptualized? What are the key concepts or ideas in the text?
What lines of reasoning are formulated? What key inferences are made?
Where is the reasoning taking us? What is implied by it? If this reasoning
were taken seriously and made the basis for action or policy, what consequences would follow? Furthermore, each of these dimensions of reasoning could be looked at from the point of view of the "perfections" of
thought, those intellectual standards which individually or collectively
apply to all reasoning. (Is it clear, precise, accurate, relevant, consistent,
logical, broad enough, based on sound evidence, utilizing appropriate
reasons, adequate to our purposes, and fair, given other possible ways of
conceiving things?)

To read well, to read critically, one needs to actively construct an interpretation, imagine alternative meanings, imagine possible objections —
one must think creatively. But "creative reading" (as the phrase is often
understood) is not good reading — accurate, clear, plausible — unless it is

also critical, disciplined reading. Consider the following example of two students engaged in reading a text. (This example is taken from an article by Stephen Norris and Linda Phillips "Explanations of Reading Comprehension: Schema Theory and Critical Thinking Theory" in *Teachers' College Record,* Volume 89, Number 2, Winter 1987). We can see in these two readers a striking difference between good and bad reasoning embedded in the act of reading (the questions and commentaries within the text below are those of Norris and Phillips).

In what follows we will present, episode-by-episode, Steven's and Colleen's thinking aloud as they work through the passage. The experimenter's questions are given in brackets. We have chosen to make our example detailed, because we see this as the best route for providing specificity to otherwise vague generalizations about the relationship between reading and thinking. To simulate the task for you we present the passage without a title and one episode at a time, as was done with the children.

Episode 1

The stillness of the morning air was broken. The men headed down the bay.

Steven

The men were heading down the bay, I'm not sure why yet. It was a very peaceful morning. [Any questions?] No, not really. [Where do you think they're going?] I think they might be going sailing, water skiing, or something like that.

Colleen

The men are going shopping. [Why do you say that?] They're going to buy clothes at The Bay. [What is The Bay?] It's a shopping center. [Any questions?] No. [Where do you think they're going?] They're going shopping because it seems like they broke something.

Steven recognizes that there is insufficient information for explaining what the men are doing. On questioning, he tentatively suggests a couple of alternatives consistent with the information given, but indicates there are other possibilities. Colleen presents one explanation of the story, and seems fairly definite that the men are going to buy clothes at The Bay, a chain of department stores in Canada. On being queried she maintains her idea that the men are going shopping, but offers an explanation inconsistent with her first one that they are going to buy clothes. To do this she assumes that something concrete was broken, which could be replaced at The Bay.

Episode 2

The net was hard to pull. The heavy sea and strong tide made it even difficult for the girdie. The meshed catch encouraged us to try harder.

Steven

It was not a very good day as there were waves which made it difficult for the girdie. That must be some kind of machine for doing something. The net could be for pulling something out of the water like an old wreck. No, wait! It said "meshed catch." I don't know why but that makes me think of fish and, sure, if you caught fish you'd really want to get them. [Any questions?] No questions, just that I think maybe the girdie is a machine for helping the men pull in the fish or whatever it was. Maybe a type of pulley.

Colleen

I guess The Bay must have a big water fountain. [Why was the net hard to pull?] There's a lot of force on the water. [Why was it important for them to pull the net?] It was something they had to do. [What do you mean?] They had to pull the net and it was hard to do. [Any questions?] No. [Where do you think they're going?] Shopping.

For both children the interpretations of Episode 2 built on those of Episode 1. Steven continues to question what the men were doing. He raises a number of alternative interpretations dealing with the context of the sea. He refines his interpretations through testing hypothetical interpretations against specific details, and hypotheses of specific word meanings against his emerging interpretation of the story. At the outset he makes an inference that a girdie is a machine, but leaves details about its nature and function unspecified. He tentatively offers one specific use for the net, but immediately questions this use when he realizes that it will not account for the meshed catch, and substitutes an alternative function. He then confirms this interpretation with the fact from the story that the men were encouraged to try harder and his belief that if you catch fish you would really want to bring them aboard. Finally, he sees that he is in a position to offer a more definitive but tentative interpretation of the word girdie.

Colleen maintains her interpretation of going shopping at The Bay. When questioned about her interpretation, Colleen responds in vague or tautological terms. She seems not to integrate information relating to the terms net, catch, and sea, and she seemed satisfied to remain uninformed about the nature of the girdie and the reason for pulling the net. In the end, she concludes definitively that the men are going shopping.

Episode 3

With four quintels aboard, we were now ready to leave. The skipper saw mares' tails in the north.

Steven

I wonder what quintels are? I think maybe it's a sea term, a word that means perhaps the weight aboard. Yes maybe it's how much fish they had aboard. [So you think it was fish?] I think fish or maybe something they had found in the water but I think fish more because of the word *"catch."* [*Why were they worried about the mares' tails?*] *I'm not sure. Mares' tails, let me see, mares are horses but horses are not going to be in the water. The mares' tails are in the north. Here farmers watch the north for bad weather, so maybe the fishermen do the same thing. Yeah, I think that's it, it's a cloud formation which could mean strong winds and hail or something which I think could be dangerous if you were in a boat and had a lot of weight aboard.* [*Any questions?*] *No.*

Colleen
  They were finished with their shopping and were ready to go home. [*What did they have aboard?*] *Quintels.* [*What are quintels?*] *I don't know.* [*Why were they worried about the mares' tails?*] *There were a group of horses on the street and they were afraid they would attack the car.* [*Any questions?*] *No.*

Steven is successful in his efforts to incorporate the new information into an evolving interpretation. From the outset Steven acknowledges that he does not know the meaning of quintel and seeks a resolution of this unknown. He derives a meaning consistent with his evolving interpretation and with the textual evidence. In his attempt to understand the expression *mares' tails* he first acknowledges that he does not know the meaning of the expression. Thence, he establishes what he does know from the background knowledge (mares are horses, horses are not going to be in the water, there is nothing around except sky and water, farmers watch the north for bad weather) and textual information (the men are on the bay, they have things aboard, the mares' tails are in the north) and inferences he has previously made (the men are in a boat, they are fishing). He integrates this knowledge into a comparison between the concerns of Alberta farmers with which he is familiar, and what he takes to be analogous concerns of fishermen. On seeing the pertinence of this analogy he draws the conclusion that the mares' tails must be a cloud formation foreboding inclement weather. He claims support for his conclusion in the fact that it would explain the skipper's concern for the mares' tails, indicating that he did not lose sight of the overall task of understanding the story.

Colleen maintains her original interpretation but does not incorporate all the new textual information into it. She works with the information on the men's leaving and the mares' tails, but appears to ignore or remain vague about other information. For example, she says the cargo was comprised of quintels but indicates no effort to determine what these things are. She cites the fact that the men were ready to leave and suggests that they have finished their shopping, but does not attempt to explain the use of such words as skipper, cargo, and aboard in the context of shopping for clothes. She interprets mares' tails as a group of horses that possibly would attack the men, but gives no account of what the horses might be doing on the street. Basically, she appears to grow tolerant of ambiguity and incompleteness in her interpretation.

Notice how both readers illustrate the relationship between creative and critical thinking. Steve is creating an interpretation, actively constructing — building it, if you will — and in so doing, he makes creative and constructive use of previous knowledge and of his imagination, critically assessing his interpretation as he goes. Colleen, on the other hand, is certainly "creative" in one sense: wildly building a bizarre interpretation, un-restrained by mere reality or plausibility. (Later, after reading that the men cut up the fish they have caught, she, believing the fish to be guppies, says that after the men cut them up, they probably put them in an aquarium.) This "creativity run amok" is not the kind of creative thinking we want to foster in our students, does not enable them to make sense of, and sensibly evaluate, what they read. Only a disciplined process of critical analysis enables one to create in one's mind the logic of the text, to construct a system of meanings that mirror, to the best of one's ability, the system of meanings inherent in the text.

✦ Intellectual Standards

All intellectual standards are derived from some humanly created logic or are implied in the very nature of things themselves, including *universal criteria* implicit in intellectual history and educated discourse within that history, *the logic of concepts and words* implicit in educated usage, *the logic of questions* implicit in academic practice and educated usage, and *the logic of subject matter* implicit in the nature of things themselves. For example, it would be unintelligible to say, "I want to reason well but I am indifferent as to whether or not my reasoning is clear, precise, accurate, relevant, logical, consistent, based on appropriate evidence and reasons, ..." By the same token, it would be unintelligible — unless very special circumstances prevailed — to say "I am trying to determine whether or not I am a 'selfish' person, but I am not concerned with what the word 'selfish' implies." The logic of the question, "Is Jack a selfish person?" is basically revealed by understanding the established uses of the word 'selfish' in educated discourse.

✦ The Logic of Teaching

(Assuming that the most basic goal of education is to foster the general, reasoned, intellectual development of students.) To teach a student critically is to devise activities and an environment conducive to the general, reasoned, intellectual development of students. By the model we present, the goal will be seen to entail cultivating students' ability to reason "creatively and critically" (viewed as inseparable dimensions of good thinking) with respect to the logic of any subject matter they study, in such a way as to maximize the development, over an extended period of time, of general intellectual standards and disciplined minds, minds strongly motivated to reason rigorously and analytically with respect to any problem, issue, or intellectual task to which they afterward set themselves. The ability to read, write, speak, and listen as forms of disciplined reasoning, as forms of disciplined questioning, become central goals on the model because each is a basic modality of reason through which we learn much of what we learn. As teachers committed to the intellectual development of our students, we introduce our students not only to the logic of what they are studying but also to the very logic of logic, i.e., critical thinking, so that they begin as soon as possible to discipline their minds in a general and not simply in a subject-specific way. Through that discipline, the created products of their thinking become useful products, products fashioned, to the degree that they develop critical judgment, with acute discrimination and fastidious discernment. That minds will create meanings is not in doubt; that they will create meanings that are sound, insightful, or profound is.

✦ Conclusion

Creativity, as a term of praise, involves more than a mere haphazard or uncritical making, more than the raw process of bringing something into being. It requires that what is brought into being meet criteria intrinsic to what it is we are trying to make. Novelty alone will not do, for it is easy to produce worthless novelty. Intellectual standards and discipline do not stand in the way of creativity. Rather, they provide a way to begin to generate it, as it must be generated: slowly and painfully, one student at a time, one problem at a time, one insight at a time. If we can engage each of our students passionately in genuine intellectual work on genuine intellectual problems worthy of reasoned thought and analysis, and continually help each student to become a more judicious critic of the nature and quality of his or her thought, we have done all we can do to make likely both the critical and the creative development of each student. It is stimulating intellectual work that develops the intellect simultaneously as both a creator and evaluator: as a creator that evaluates and as an evaluator that creates. Fitness of mind, intellectual excellence, is the result.

Chapter 10

Bloom's Taxonomy and Critical Thinking Instruction:
Recall Is Not Knowledge

Abstract

In this brief article, Richard Paul analyses and critiques Bloom's Taxonomy from the perspective of the critical thinking movement. He points out Bloom's achievements in Cognitive Domains and Affective Domains: the analysis of cognitive processes of thought and their interrelationships; the emphasis on the need for these processes (including critical thinking skills and abilities) to be explicitly and mindfully taught and used; the emphasis on critical thinking values, such as openmindedness and faith in reason.

Dr. Paul then argues that Bloom's approach suffers from the following two flaws: 1) the attempt to be "value neutral" is impossible and incompatible with the values presupposed in critical thinking education and 2) Bloom confuses recall with knowledge.

As a result of the way the taxonomy is explained, many teachers identify learning to think critically with merely learning how to ask and answer questions in all of Bloom's categories: knowledge, comprehension, application, analysis, synthesis, and evaluation. Teachers typically take the categories to express objectives which they should teach to in strict order: first give the students "knowledge", then show them how to comprehend it, then how to apply it, etc. Paul, while recognizing that Bloom's distinctions themselves are important, argues that the common understanding of their link to critical thinking is largely misconceived. Teaching critical thinking is not a simple matter of asking questions from each of Bloom's categories; moreover, the categories themselves are not independent but interdependent. Paul shows, for example, how knowledge is not something that can be given to a student before he or she comprehends it. He explains how the critical thinking movement has properly emphasized that getting knowledge is in fact a complex achievement involving thought, and so should be understood as the product of rational thought processes, rather than as recall. This insight needs to be brought into the heart of instruction.

*I*t would be difficult to find a more influential work in education today than *The Taxonomy of Educational Objectives* (Bloom, et al. 1979). Developed by a committee of college and university examiners from 1949 to 1954 and published as two handbooks — *Cognitive Domain* and *Affective Domain* — its objectives were manifold. Handbook I, *Cognitive Domain*, for instance, lists four encompassing objectives.

1. To "provide for classification of the goals of our educational system ... to be of general help to all teachers, administrators, professional specialists, and research workers who deal with curricular and evaluation problems ... to help them discuss these problems with greater precision ...".

2. To "be a source of constructive help ... in building a curriculum ...".

3. To "help one gain a perspective on the emphasis given to certain behaviors ...".

4. To "specify objectives so that it becomes easier to plan learning experience and prepare evaluation devices ...". (pp. 1–2)

The authors also note that the categories of the Taxonomy below can be used "as a framework for viewing the educational process and analyzing its workings" and even for "analyzing teachers' success in classroom teaching." (p. 3)

A generation of teachers have now come of age not only familiar with and acceptant of the general categories of the Taxonomy, but also persuaded that the Taxonomy's identified higher-order skills of analysis, synthesis, and evaluation are essential to education at all levels. For these teachers, critical thinking is essential because higher-order skills are essential. To learn how to think critically, in this view, is to learn how to ask and answer questions of analysis, synthesis, and evaluation. To help teachers incorporate critical thinking in the classroom is to help them ask questions that call for analysis, synthesis, and evaluation. In this view, then, learning to teach critical thinking is quite straightforward. The teacher's thinking does not need to be significantly altered, and no fundamental shifts in educational philosophy are required. The Taxonomy and the ability to generate a full variety of question types are all that an intelligent teacher really needs to teach critical thinking skills.

This view is seriously misleading. According to most advocates of critical thinking, no neat set of recipes can foster critical thinking in students. The single most useful thing a teacher can do is to take at least one well-designed college course in critical thinking, in which the *teacher's own* thinking skills are analyzed and nurtured in numerous ways. In other words, teachers need a solid foundation in critical thinking skills before they can teach them.

What follows is a succinct analysis and critique of Bloom's Taxonomy, from the perspective of the values and epistemological presuppositions of the critical thinking movement. I hope it will contribute to a deeper understanding of the nature and demands of critical thinking instruction.

✦ A One-Way Hierarchy

Though not designed to further critical thinking instruction as such, *Cognitive Domain* contains a wealth of information of use in such instruction. Reading it in its entirety is most rewarding, particularly the sections on analysis, synthesis, and evaluation. These sections disclose that most of the cognitive processes characterized as essential to higher-order questions in fact presuppose use of basic critical thinking concepts: assumption, fact,

Bloom's Taxonomy

The Taxonomy of Educational Objectives: Cognitive Domain
1.00 *Knowledge*
  1.10 Knowledge of Specifics
  1.11 Knowledge of Terminology
  1.12 Knowledge of Specific Facts
  1.20 Knowledge of Ways and Means of Dealing with Specifics
  1.21 Knowledge of Conventions
  1.22 Knowledge of Trends and Sequences
  1.23 Knowledge of Classifications and Categories
  1.24 Knowledge of Criteria
  1.25 Knowledge of Methodology
  1.30 Knowledge of the Universals and Abstractions in a Field
  1.31 Knowledge of Principles and Generalizations
  1.32 Knowledge of Theories and Structures

2.00 *Comprehension*
  2.10 Translation
  2.20 Interpretation
  2.30 Extrapolation

3.00 *Application*
  The use of abstractions in particular and concrete situations. The abstractions may be in the form of general ideas, rules of procedures, or generalized methods. The abstractions may also be technological principles, ideas, and theories which must be remembered and applied.

4.00 *Analysis*
  4.10 Analysis of Elements
  4.20 Analysis of Relationships
  4.30 Analysis of Organizational Principles

5.00 *Synthesis*
  5.10 Production of a Unique Communication
  5.20 Production of a Plan, or Proposed Set of Operations
  5.30 Derivation of a Set of Abstract Relations

6.00 *Evaluation*
  6.10 Judgments in Terms of Internal Evidence
  6.20 Judgments in Terms of External Criteria

(From the *Taxonomy of Educational Objectives,* Bloom et al. 1974 p. 201)

concept, value, conclusion, premise, evidence, relevant, irrelevant, consistent, inconsistent, implication, fallacy, argument, inference, point of view, bias, prejudice, authority, hypothesis, and so forth. This is clear, for example, in the explanation of analysis:

> Skill in analysis may be found as an objective of any field of study. It is frequently expressed as one of their important objectives by teachers of science, social studies, philosophy, and the arts. They wish, for example, to develop in students the ability to distinguish fact from hypothesis in a communication, to identify conclusions and supporting statements, to distinguish relevant from extraneous material, to note how one idea relates to another, to see what unstated assumptions are involved in what is said, to distinguish dominant from subordinate ideas or themes in poetry or music, to find evidence of the author's techniques and purposes. (*Cognitive Domain*, p. 144)

In other words, if the ability to analyze usually requires students to do such things as distinguish facts from hypotheses, conclusions from evidence, relevant from irrelevant material, note relationships between concepts, and probe and detect unstated assumptions, then it seems essential that students become not only familiar with these words (by teachers introducing them frequently into classroom discussion) but also comfortable with using them as they think their way through analytic problems. This need becomes more evident if we recognize that by analysis, synthesis, and evaluation, the authors of the Taxonomy have in mind only their *explicit* (not subconscious) uses. They rightly emphasize what has become a virtual platitude in cognitive psychology — that students (and experts) who do the best analyses, syntheses, and evaluations tend to do them mindfully with a clear sense of their component elements. So, if the concepts of critical thinking are presupposed in mindful analysis, synthesis, and evaluation, we can best heighten that mindfulness by raising those component concepts to a conscious level.

Although *Affective Domain* implies that it is *value neutral,* many of the examples of higher-order valuing illustrate values intrinsic to education conceived on a critical thinking paradigm, wherein a student:

Deliberately examines a variety of viewpoints on controversial issues with a view to forming opinions about them.

[Develops] faith in the power of reason in methods of experimental discussion.

Weighs alternative social policies and practices against the standards of the public welfare rather than the advantage of specialized and narrow interest groups.

[Achieves] readiness to revise judgments and to change behavior in the light of evidence.

Judges problems and issues in terms of situations, issues, purposes, and consequences involved rather than in terms of fixed, dogmatic precepts or emotionally wishful thinking.

Develops a consistent philosophy of life. (pp. 181–185)

Along with the usefulness of Bloom's Cognitive and Affective Taxonomies, we must bear in mind their limitations for critical thinking curriculum construction. To some extent, the Taxonomies represent an attempt to achieve the impossible: a perfectly neutral classification of cognitive and affective processes that makes no educational value judgments and favors no educational philosophy over any other — one that could be used by any culture, nation, or system whatsoever, independent of its specific values or world view:

> ... to avoid partiality to one view of education as opposed to another, we have attempted to make the taxonomy neutral by avoiding terms which implicitly convey value judgments and by making the taxonomy as conclusive as possible. This means that the kinds of behavioral changes emphasized by *any* institution, educational unit, or educational philosophy can be represented in the classification. Another way of saying this is that any objective which describes an intended behavior should be classifiable in this system. (*Cognitive Domain*, p. 14)

This approach to knowledge, cognition, and education is partly irreconcilable with a commitment to critical thinking skills, abilities, and dispositions:

> To a large extent, knowledge as taught in American schools depends upon some external authority: some expert or group of experts is the arbitrator of knowledge. (*Cognitive Domain*, p. 31)
> ... the scheme does provide levels for the extreme inculcation of a prescribed set of values if this is the philosophy of the culture. (*Affective Domain*, p. 43)
> It is possible to imagine a society or culture which is relatively fixed. Such a society represents a closed system in which it is possible to predict in advance both the kinds of problems individuals will encounter and the solutions which are appropriate to those problems. Where such predictions can be made in advance, it is possible to organize the educational experience so as to give each individual the particular knowledge and specific methods needed for solving the problems he will encounter. (*Cognitive Domain*, p. 39–40)

But precisely because of this attempt at neutrality the category of "knowledge" is analyzed in such a restricted way and the relationship of the categories is assumed to be hierarchical in only one direction. For instance, according to Bloom's Taxonomy, "comprehension" presupposes "knowledge", but "knowledge" does not presuppose "comprehension". The second of these conceptual decisions would be questioned by those who hold that the basic skills and dispositions of critical thinking must be brought into schooling from the start, and that for any learning to occur, they must be intrinsic to every element of it.

✦ Knowledge as Achievement

The critical thinking movement has its roots in the practice and vision of Socrates, who discovered by a probing method of questioning that few people could rationally justify their confident claims to knowledge. Confused meanings, inadequate evidence, or self-contradictory beliefs often lurked beneath smooth but largely empty rhetoric. This led to a basic insight into the problem of human irrationality and to a view of knowledge and learning which holds that to believe or assent without reason, judgment, or understanding is to be prejudiced. This belief is central to the critical thinking movement. This view also holds the corollary principle that critical reflection by each learner is an essential precondition of knowledge. Put another way, those who advocate critical thinking instruction hold that knowledge is not something that can be *given* by one person to another. It cannot simply be memorized out of a book or taken whole cloth from the mind of another. Knowledge, rightly understood, is a distinctive construction by the learner, something that issues out of a *rational* use of mental processes.

To expect students to assent before they have developed the capacity to do so rationally is to indoctrinate rather than to educate them and to foster habits of thought antithetical to the educative process. Peter Kneedler (1985) observed "an unfortunate tendency to teach facts in isolation from the thinking skills" — to *give* students knowledge and some time later expect them to *think* about it. Knowledge, in any defensible sense, is an *achievement* requiring a mind slow rather than quick to believe — which waits for, expects, and weighs evidence before agreeing. The sooner a mind begins to develop rational scruples, in this view, the better.

As Quine and Ullian (1970) put it:

> ... knowledge is in some ways like a good golf score: each is substantially the fruit of something else, and there are no magic shortcuts to either one. To improve your golf score you work at perfecting the various strokes; for knowledge you work at garnering and sifting evidence and sharpening your reasoning skills ... knowledge is no more guaranteed than is a lowered golf score, but there is no better way. (p. 12)

We don't actually know whether students have achieved some knowledge until we have determined whether their beliefs represent something they actually know (have rationally assented to) or merely something they have memorized to repeat on a test. Dewey, as the authors of the Taxonomy recognize, illustrated this point with the following story in which he asked a class:

> "What would you find if you dug a hole in the earth?" Getting no response, he repeated the question: again he obtained nothing but silence. The teacher chided Dr. Dewey, "You're asking the wrong question." Turning to the class, she asked, "What is the state of the center of the earth?" The class replied in unison, "Igneous fusion."

The writers of the Taxonomy attempt to side-step this problem by defining "knowledge" as "what is currently known or accepted by the experts or specialists in a field, whether or not such knowledge, in a philosophical sense, corresponds to 'reality'". (*Cognitive Domain*, p. 32)

The writers of the Taxonomy erroneously assume that the only issue here is the relative *value* of the knowledge, not whether statements merely memorized should be called knowledge at all:

> In these latter conceptions [those which link knowledge to understanding and rational assent] it is implicitly assumed that knowledge is of little value if it cannot be utilized in new situations or in a form very different from that in which it was originally encountered. The denotations of these latter concepts would usually be close to what have been defined as "abilities and skills" in the Taxonomy. (*Cognitive Domain*, p. 29)

This inadvertently begs the question whether blindly memorized true belief can properly be called knowledge at all — and hence whether inculcation and indoctrination into true belief can properly be called education. If knowledge of any kind is to some extent a skilled, rational achievement, then we should not confuse knowledge and education with belief inculcation and indoctrination, just as we should not confuse learning more with acquiring knowledge (we *learn*, are not born with bias, prejudices, and misconceptions, for example). This point, crucial for the critical thinking movement, was well formulated by John Henry Newman (1852):

> ... knowledge is not a mere extrinsic or accidental advantage ... which may be got up from a book, and easily forgotten again, ... which we can borrow for the occasion, and carry about in our hand ... [it is] something intellectual ... which reasons upon what it sees ... the action of a formative power ... making the objects of our knowledge subjectively our own.

The reductio ad absurdum of the view that knowledge can be distinguished from comprehension and rational assent is suggested by William Graham Sumner (1906), one of the founding fathers of anthropology, commenting on the failure of the schools of his day:

> The examination papers show the pet ideas of the examiners ....
> An orthodoxy is produced in regard to all the great doctrines. It
> consists in the most worn and commonplace opinions .... It is
> intensely provincial and philistine ... [containing] broad fallacies,
> half-truths, and glib generalizations ... children [are] taught just
> that one thing which is "right" in the view and interest of those in
> control and nothing else.

Clearly, Sumner maintained that provincial, fallacious, or misleading beliefs should not be viewed as knowledge at all, however widely they are treated as such, and that inculcating them is not education, however widely described as such.

✦ Rational Learning

To sum up, the authors of the Taxonomy organized cognitive processes into a one-way hierarchy, leading readers to conclude that knowledge is always a simpler behavior than comprehension, comprehension a simpler behavior than application, application a simpler behavior than analysis, and so forth through synthesis and evaluation. However, this view is misleading in at least one important sense: achieving knowledge *always* presupposes at least minimal comprehension, application, analysis, synthesis, and evaluation. This counter-insight is essential for well-planned and realistic curriculum designed to foster critical thinking skills, abilities, and dispositions, and it cannot be achieved without the development of the teacher's critical thinking.

From the very start, for any learning, we should expect and encourage those rational scruples realistically within the range of student grasp, a strategy that requires critical insight into the evidentiary foundation of everything we teach. We should scrutinize our instructional strategies lest we inadvertently nurture student *irrationality,* as we do when we encourage students to believe what, from the perspective of their own thought, they have no good reason to believe. If we want rational learning (and again, *not all learning is rational*), then the process leading to belief is more important than belief itself. Everything we believe we have in some sense *judged* to be credible. If students believe something just because we or the text assert it, they learn to accept blindly.

Right-answer inculcation is not a preliminary step to critical thought. It nurtures irrational belief and unnecessarily generates a mind-set that must be broken down for rational learning and knowledge acquisition to begin. The structure of our lifelong learning generally arises from our early cognitive habits. If they are irrational, then they are likely to remain so. There are twin obstacles to the development of rational learning: *1)* being told and expecting to be told what to believe (belief inculcation);

and *2)* being told and expecting to be told precisely what to do (the over-proceduralization of thought). Together they fatally undermine independence of thought and comprehension.

Bloom's Taxonomy, all of the above notwithstanding, is a remarkable tour de force, a ground-breaking work filled with seminal insights into cognitive processes and their interrelations. Nevertheless, the attempt to remain neutral with respect to all educational values and philosophical issues is a one-sided hierarchical analysis of cognitive processes that limits our insight into the nature of critical thinking. (To minimize misunderstanding, let me express in another way one basic sense in which I consider it misleading to call Bloom's Taxonomy "neutral". By labeling the first category "knowledge" rather than "rote recall", the Taxonomy legitimates calling the product of rote recall "knowledge". Such labeling is educationally tendentious and therefore not neutral.) Successful critical thinking instruction requires that:

- teachers have a full range of insights into cognitive processes and their complex interrelationships.
- Bloom's hierarchy become two-sided.
- teachers see that rational learning is *process-* rather than *product-*oriented — a process that brings comprehension, analysis, synthesis, and evaluation into every act of the mind that involves the acceptance, however provisional, of beliefs or claims to truth, and that thereby fosters *rational* habits of thought and *rational* learning:

> ... the teacher's primary job is that of making clear the bases upon which he weighs the facts, the methods by which he separates facts from fancies, and the way in which he discovers and selects his ultimate norms .... This concept of teaching ... requires that the purported facts be accompanied by the reasons why they are considered the facts. Thereby the teacher exposes his methods of reasoning to test and change. If the facts are in dispute ... then the reasons why others do not consider them to be facts must also be presented, thus bringing alternative ways of thinking and believing into dialogue with each other.
>
> — Emerson Shideler

✦ References

Bloom, Benjamin S., and others. *The Taxonomy of Educational Objectives: Affective and Cognitive Domains.* New York: David McKay Company, Inc., 1974.

Kneedler, Peter. "Critical Thinking in History and Social Science" (pamphlet). Sacramento: California State Department of Education, 1985.

Newman, John Henry. *Idea of a University.* New York: Longmans, Green and Company, 1912.

Sumner, William Graham. *Folkways.* New York: Dover Publications, 1906.

Chapter 11

Philosophy and Cognitive Psychology:
Contrasting Assumptions

Abstract

This paper was originally written for the Association for Supervision and Curriculum Development (ASCD) meeting, held at Wingspread in 1987 to discuss the ASCD publication, Dimensions of Thinking. *In it, Paul critiques the book for its pedagogical and theoretical bias toward a cognitive-psychological approach to thinking, a bias that largely ignores the contributions of philosophy, as well as those of affective and social psychology. Paul contrasts the very different assumptions that philosophers and cognitive psychologists make when analyzing the nature of thinking.*

One of the major objectives of the authors of *Dimensions of Thinking* was to produce a comprehensive, theoretically balanced, and pedagogically useful thinking skills framework. Unfortunately, the value of the present framework is limited by its bias in every important respect toward the approach of cognitive psychology. Virtually all of the research cited, the concepts and terminology used, and the recommendations made for implementation are taken from the writings of scholars working principally in cognitive psychology. The work and perspective of many of the philosophers concerned with thinking is minimally reported. Those whose work is not significantly used include these:

> Michael Scriven, Harvey Siegel, Mortimer Adler, John Passmore, Israel Scheffler, Mark Weinstein, R. S. Peters, Ralph Johnson, J. Anthony Blair, Stephen Norris, John Dewey, Vincent Ruggiero, Edward D'Angelo, Perry Weddle, Sharon Bailin, Lenore Langsdorf, T. Edward Damer, Howard Kahane, Nicholas Rescher, Paulo Freire, Robert Swartz, Max Black, James Freeman, John Hoaglund, Gerald Nosich, Jon Adler, Eugene Garver, (to name some who come readily to mind).

Nor does *Dimensions of Thinking* incorporate significant philosophical contributions to our understanding of thinking from the great philosophers of the last three hundred years. It fails to mention Immanuel Kant's work on the mind's shaping and structuring of human experience, Hegel's work on the dialectical nature of human thought, Marx's work on the economic and ideological foundations of human thought, Nietzsche's illumination of self-delusion in human thought, or Wittgenstein's work on the socio-linguistic foundations of human thought.

Another perspective conspicuously absent from *Dimensions of Thinking* is that of affective and social psychology, especially those studies that shed light on the major obstacles or blocks to rational thinking: prejudice, bias, self-deception, desire, fear, vested interest, delusion, illusion, egocentrism, sociocentrism, and ethnocentrism. The significance of this omission should be clear. The point behind the thinking skills movements (in both cognitive psychology and philosophy) is not simply to get students to think; all humans think spontaneously and continuously. The problem is to get them to think *critically* and *rationally* and this requires insight by students into the nature of uncritical and irrational thought. The massive literature in affective and social psychology bears on this problem; its seminal insights and concepts should be a significant part of any adequate framework for understanding how to reform education to cultivate rational, reflective, autonomous, empathic thought. (Philosophers, I might add, are often as guilty as cognitive psychologists of ignoring the work of affective and social psychologists.) Recently, when I did an ERIC search under the descriptors "prejudice or bias or self-deception or defense mechanism", the search turned up 8,673 articles! This then is a significant omission.

More important than the sheer numerical imbalance in scholarship cited is the imbalance in perspective. There are important differences between those features of thinking highlighted by philosophers in the critical thinking movement and the general approach to thinking fostered by cognitive psychologists and the educators influenced by them. And though there is much that each field is beginning to learn from the other, that learning can fruitfully take place only if some of their differences are clearly set out and due emphasis given to each. After I have spelled out these differences roughly, I will detail what I see as emerging common ground, what I see that gives me hope that these fields may yet work together. But first the down side.

In thinking of the relationship between the traditions of cognitive psychology and philosophy, I am reminded of a couple of remarks by the great 19th Century educator-philosopher John Henry Newman (1912) in his classic *Idea of a University*:

> I am not denying, I am granting, I am assuming, that there is reason and truth in the "leading ideas", as they are called and "large views" of scientific men; I only say that, though they speak truth, they do not speak the whole truth; that they speak a narrow truth, and think it a broad truth; that their deductions must be compared

with other truths, which are acknowledged to be truths, in order to verify, complete, and correct them. (p. 178)

  If different studies are useful for aiding, they are still more useful for correcting each other; for as they have their particular merits severally, so they have their defects. (p. 176)

In this case, the "scientific" views of cognitive psychologists need to be corrected by the insights of philosophers, for the whole truth to be apprehended.

Only when we see the differing emphases, assumptions, and concepts, even the differing value priorities of the two disciplines and how the work of those interested in critical thinking reflects them can we begin to appreciate the distinctive contributions of both cognitive psychology and philosophy to instruction for thinking. Few K–12 educators and their education department counterparts recognize the possible contribution of philosophy to instruction for thinking because their own educational background was heavily biased in favor of psychologically and scientistically-oriented courses. Rarely were they expected to articulate a philosophical perspective, to reason and synthesize across disciplinary lines, to formulate their philosophy. Moreover, few feel comfortable with philosophical argumentation and counter-argumentation as a means of establishing probable truth. Well-reasoned philosophical essays do not seem to them to be *research*, properly so called, because they rarely cite empirical studies.

With these thoughts in mind, let us examine 24 contrasting emphases between these two disciplines. I do not assume, of course, that all 24 are always present, but that, on the whole, there is a pattern of differences between the writings of *most* cognitive psychologists and *most* philosophers. In the case of *Dimensions of Thinking,* for example, I am confident that had the co-authors been Lipman, Ennis, Scriven, Scheffler, and Paul, a very different account of thinking would have emerged, one reflective of the contrasts which I now list.

Tendencies of		
Cognitive Psychologists		*Philosophers*
With Respect to:		
1. Approach to thinking		
Approach thinking descriptively.		Approach thinking normatively.
2. Methodology		
Focus on empirical fact-gathering. (This is not to imply that cognitive psychologists do not formulate theories or engage in conceptual analysis.)		Focus on the analysis of cases of "well-justified" thinking in contrast to cases of "poorly justified" thinking.

Tendencies of	
Cognitive Psychologists	*Philosophers*
With Respect to:	

3. Modes of thinking studied

Focus on expert versus novice thinking, intradisciplinary thinking, and monological thinking.	Focus on rational, reflective thinking, on interdisciplinary thinking, and on multilogical thinking.

4. Value emphasis

Emphasize the value of expertise.	Emphasize the values of rationality, autonomy, self-criticism, openmindedness, truth, and empathy.

5. Authority

Make the authority of the expert central.	Play down the authority of the expert and play up the authority of independent reason.

6. Language used

Generate more technical terminology and make their points in a technical fashion.	Take their terminology and concepts more from the critical, analytic vocabulary of a natural language (e. g., assumes, claims, implies, is consistent with, contradicts, is relevant to).

7. Role of values in thinking

Separate the cognitive from the domain of *a)* value-choices of the thinker and *b)* the overall world view of the thinker (at least when discussing basic mental skills and processes).	Emphasize the role in thinking of values and the overall conceptual framework of the thinker; hence, the significance of identifying and assessing points of view and frames of reference.

8. Place of dialogue

Play down the significance of dialogical and dialectical thinking.	Play up the significance of dialogical and dialectical thinking; view debate and argumentation as central to rational thinking.

Tendencies of	
Cognitive Psychologists	*Philosophers*
With Respect to:	

9. View of affect

Underemphasize the affective obstacles to rational thinking; fear, desire, prejudice, bias, vested interest, conformity, self-deception, egocentrism, and ethnocentrism.	Emphasize the affective obstacles to rational thinking (this emphasis is correlated with the emphasis on the philosophical ideal of becoming a rational person).

10. Role of teacher

Play down the role of the teacher as autonomous critical thinker (this is perhaps an emerging issue in cognitive psychology).	Make central the role of the teacher as autonomous critical thinker, the need to question her own biases, prejudices, point of view, and so forth.

11. Classroom climate

Play down the need to develop classrooms as communities of inquiry wherein dialogical and dialectical exchange is a matter of course.	Play up the need to develop classrooms as communities of inquiry where students learn the arts of analyzing, synthesizing, advocating, reconstructing, and challenging each other's ideas.

12. Place of intelligent skepticism

Ignore or play down the significance of the student as Socratic questioner, as intelligent skeptic (this too may be an emerging issue).	Make central the significance of questioning; view intellectual advancement more in terms of skill in the art of questioning than in the amassing of an unquestioned knowledge base (the thinker as questioner is connected by philosophers with the disposition to suspend judgment in cases in which the thinker is called upon to accept beliefs not justified by his or her own thinking.)

Tendencies of	
Cognitive Psychologists	**Philosophers**
With Respect to:	

13. Place of empirical research

Play up the significance of empirical research in settling educational issues.	Skeptical of empirical research as capable of settling significant educational issues without argumentation between conflicting educational viewpoints or philosophies on those issues.

14. View of the teaching process

Give more weight to the significance of teaching as embodying step-by-step procedures (although there is increasing dissent within cognitive psychology on this point).	Play up the significance of dialogical approaches that involve much criss-crossing and unpredictable back-tracking in teaching and thinking; skeptical of step-by-step procedures in teaching and thinking.

15. Identified micro-elements in thinking

Emphasize such categories as recalling, encoding and storing, and identifying relationships and patterns — all of which admit to empirical study.	Emphasize identification of issues, assumptions, relevant and irrelevant considerations, unclear concepts and terms, supported and unsupported claims, contradictions, inferences and implications — all of which shed light on thought conceived as the intellectual moves of a reasoning person.

16. Place of micro-skills

Separate the analysis of micro-skills from normative considerations.	Link the analysis of micro-skills with normative considerations since, for philosophers, micro-skills are intellectual moves which can be used to clarify, analyze, synthesize, support, elaborate, question, deduce, or induce.

Tendencies of	
Cognitive Psychologists	*Philosophers*
With Respect to:	

17. View of macro-processes

View macro-processes from the perspective of categories of research in cognitive psychology: problem solving, decision making, concept formation, and so forth.

View macro-processes from the perspective of the overall reasoning needs of a rational person: ability to analyze issues and distinguish questions of different logical types, ability to Socratically question, ability to engage in conceptual analysis, ability to accurately reconstruct the strongest case for opposing points of view, ability to reason dialogically and dialectically (each use of a macro-process is a unique orchestration of some sequence of micro-skills in the context of some issue, problem, or objective).

18. Teaching as a science or art

Present teaching for thinking as a quasi-science, with the assumption that there is a discrete body of information that can be "added up" or "united" and passed on "as is" to the teacher.

Present teaching for thinking as an intellectual art; play down the significance of technical, empirical information as necessary to skill in that art.

19. Place of philosophy of education

Ignore or play down the significance of teachers developing a philosophy of education into which rationality, autonomy, and self-criticism become central values.

Emphasize the importance of each teacher developing an explicit philosophy of education which is openly stated in the classroom; tend to encourage students to do the same, especially in relation to their philosophy of life.

20. Obstacles to rational thinking

Ignore the problem of prejudice and bias in parents and the community as possible obstacles to teaching for rational thinking.

Sensitive to the dangers of community and national bias as possible obstacles to teaching for rational thinking.

Tendencies of	
Cognitive Psychologists	**Philosophers**
With Respect to:	

21. Place of virtues and passions

Underemphasize the significance of rational passions and intellectual virtues.	Emphasize rational passions (a passion for clarity, accuracy, fairmindedness, a fervor for getting to the bottom of things or deepest root issues, for listening sympathetically to opposing perspectives, a compelling drive to seek out evidence, an intense aversion to contradiction and sloppy thinking, a devotion to truth over self-interest) and intellectual virtues (intellectual humility, intellectual courage, intellectual integrity, intellectual empathy, intellectual perseverance, faith in reason, and intellectual sense of justice).

22. Specialized versus mundane thinking

Orient themselves toward domain-specific thinking, with the "good" thinker often associated with the successful business or professional person, or with a specialist working within a discipline.	Emphasize the link between an emphasis on rational thought and the goals of a traditional liberal education, of the ideal of the liberally educated person and on mundane generalizable skills such as the art of reading the newspaper critically, detecting propaganda and bias in public discourse, advertising, and textbooks, and in rational reorientation of personal values and beliefs.

23. Place of ethics of teaching and the rights of students

Lay insufficient stress upon the relation of teaching for thinking to the ethics of teaching and the rights of students.	Emphasize the link between teaching for critical thinking and developing moral insight, with the rights of students; with the student's "right to exercise his independent judgment and powers of evaluation"; as Siegel (1980) puts it: "To deny the student this right is to deny the student the status of person of equal worth."

Tendencies of	
Cognitive Psychologists	*Philosophers*
With Respect to:	
24. Thinking and one's way of life	
Lay insufficient stress upon the relation of modes of thinking to fundamental ethical and philosophical choices concerning a way of life.	Link emphasis on critical thinking with an attempt to initiate students, as Israel Scheffler (1965) puts it, "into the rational life, a life in which the critical quest for reasons is a dominant and integrating motive."

Those whose thinking about thinking is basically shaped by scholars in one tradition differ from those shaped by the other. They differ in style, direction, and methods for improving thinking. Inevitably problems of misunderstanding and mutual prejudice remain as residues of the historical separation of psychology from philosophy. That psychologists are sometimes skeptical of philosophical approaches to teaching for thinking is poignantly demonstrated by Al Benderson (1984) of the Educational Testing Service. In characterizing "The View From Psychology" (on philosophy's contribution to teaching for thinking) Benderson says:

> Psychologists, who have their roots in research into mental processes, tend to view thinking from a different perspective than do philosophers. ETS Distinguished Research Scientist Irving Seigel, a psychologist, views philosophers who claim to teach thinking skills as encroaching upon a field in which they have little real expertise. "These philosophers are imperialists", he charges. "They don't know the first thing about how kids think." (p. 10)

R. S. Peters and C. A. Mace (1967), two philosophers in turn commenting on the separation of psychology from philosophy for the *Encyclopedia of Philosophy*, say:

> The trouble began when psychologists claimed the status of empirical scientists. At first the philosophers were the more aggressive, deriding the young science as a bogus discipline. The psychologists hit back and made contemptuous remarks about philosophical logic-chopping and armchair psychology. The arguments were charged with emotion and neither side emerged with great credit .... Not all issues between philosophers and psychologists have been resolved, but there has been notable progress toward a policy of coexistence, and here and there some progress toward cooperation has been made. (p. 26)

In the field of teaching for thinking there has been, in my view, much more coexistence than cooperation. The largest and oldest conference tradition in the field (the Sonoma Conferences: two national and six international conferences, the last with a registration of over 1,000 with over 100 presenters and 230 sessions) has had only token participation by cognitive psychologists. The conference on *Thinking* at Harvard, in turn, had only token participation by philosophers. It appears to me that few psychologists or philosophers read widely in the other tradition. The field of education has been dominated by various psychologically-based rather than philosophically-based models of instruction. It is understandable therefore why *Dimensions of Thinking*, written by a team that included no philosophers, fails to successfully represent or integrate the distinctive approach of philosophy toward the thinking skills movement.

Having said this much about the typical failure of cognitive psychologists and philosophers to appropriate the strengths and correct for the weaknesses of their two traditions, I nevertheless want to mention the signs of common themes emerging in the two traditions which may become the basis for integration. Representatives of both traditions are developing a profound critique of what I would call a "didactic" theory of knowledge, learning, and literacy and framing a "critical" alternative. Behind this critique and reconstruction is a growing common sense of how the didactic paradigm impedes the scholastic development of critical thinkers.

✦ Conclusion

Perhaps a growing joint recognition of the need for both cognitive psychologists and philosophers to make common cause against the didactic theory of education will be the impetus for an on-going fruitful exchange of ideas across these rich traditions. It is certainly in the interest of all who consider the ability to think critically to be at the heart of education rightly conceived, for this rapprochement to take place.

✦ References

Newman, John Henry. *The Idea of a University.* London: Langman's, Green, and Co. 1912.

Benderson, Al. "The View from Psychology." *Critical Thinking: Focus 15.* 1984.

Peters, R. S. & Mace, C. A. "Psychology" *Encyclopedia of Philosophy, Vol. 7.* New York: Macmillan Publishing Co., Inc. & The Free Press. 1967.

Paul, Richard W. "Critical Thinking in North America: A New Theory of Knowledge, Learning, and Literacy." *Argumentation: North American Perspectives on Teaching Critical Thinking.* (in press).

Siegel, Harvey. "Critical Thinking as an Educational Ideal" *National Forum.* November, 1980.

Scheffler, Israel. *The Conditions of Knowledge.* Chicago: Scott Foresman. 1965.

Section IV

The Affective and Ethical Dimension

Ethics Without Indoctrination

Critical Thinking, Moral Integrity, and Citizenship: Teaching for the Intellectual Virtues

Chapter 12

Ethics Without Indoctrination

Abstract

In this revised paper, originally published in Educational Leadership *(1988), Richard Paul argues that ethics ought to be taught in school, but only in conjunction with critical thinking. Without critical thinking at the heart of ethical instruction,* indoctrination *rather than ethical insight results. Moral principles do not apply themselves, they require a thinking mind to assess facts and interpret situations. Moral agents inevitably bring their perspectives into play in making moral judgments and this, together with the natural tendency of the human mind to self-deception when its interests are involved, is the fundamental impediment to the right use of ethical principles.*

Paul spells out the implications of this view for the teaching of ethics in literature, science, history, and civics. He provides a taxonomy of moral reasoning skills and describes an appropriate long term staff development strategy to foster ethics across the curriculum.

✦ The Problem of Indoctrination

*N*early everyone recognizes that even young children have moral feelings and ideas, make moral inferences and judgments, and develop an outlook on life which has moral significance for good or ill. Nearly everyone also gives at least lip service to a universal common core of general ethical principles — for example, that it is morally wrong to cheat, deceive, exploit, abuse, harm, or steal from others, that everyone has a moral responsibility to respect the rights of others, including their freedom and well-being, to help those most in need of help, to seek the common good and not merely their own self-interest and egocentric pleasures, to strive in some way to make this world more just and humane. Unfortunately, mere verbal agreement on general moral principles alone will not accomplish important moral ends nor change the world for the better. Moral principles mean something only when manifested in behavior. They have force only when embodied in action. Yet to put them into action requires some analysis and insight into the real character of everyday situations.

The world does not present itself to us in morally transparent terms. The moral thing to do is often a matter of disagreement even among people of good will. One and the same act is often morally praised by some, condemned by others. Furthermore, even when we do not face the morally conflicting claims of others, we often have our own inner conflicts as to what, morally speaking, we should do in some particular situation. Considered another way, ethical persons, however strongly motivated to do what is morally right, can do so only if they know what that is. And this they cannot do if they systematically confuse their sense of what is morally right with their self-interest, personal desires, or what is commonly believed in their peer group or community. Because of complexities such as these, ethically motivated persons must learn the art of self-critique, of moral self-examination, to become attuned to the pervasive everyday pitfalls of moral judgment: moral intolerance, self-deception, and uncritical conformity. These human foibles cause pseudo-morality, the systematic misuse of moral terms and principles in the guise of moral action and righteousness.

Unfortunately few have thought much about the complexity of everyday moral issues, can identify their own moral contradictions, or clearly distinguish their self-interest and egocentric desires from what is genuinely moral. Few have thought deeply about their own moral feelings and judgments, have tied these judgments together into a coherent moral perspective, or have mastered the complexities of moral reasoning. As a result, everyday moral judgments are often a subtle mixture of pseudo and genuine morality, moral insight and moral prejudice, moral truth and moral hypocrisy. Herein lies the danger of setting up ill-thought-out public school programs in moral education. Without scrupulous care, we merely pass on to students our own moral blindness, moral distortions, and closedmindedness. Certainly many who trumpet most loudly for ethics and morality in the schools merely want students to adopt *their* ethical beliefs and *their* ethical perspectives, regardless of the fusion of insight and prejudice those beliefs and perspectives doubtless represent. They take themselves to have *the Truth* in their pockets. They take their perspective to be exemplary of all morality rightly conceived. On the other hand, what these same people fear most is someone else's moral perspective taught as the truth: conservatives afraid of liberals being in charge, liberals of conservatives, theists of non-theists, non-theists of theists.

Now, if truth be told, all of these fears are justified. People, except in the most rare and exceptional cases, do have a strong tendency to confuse what they believe with the truth. It is always the others who do evil, who are deceived, self-interested, closedminded — never us. Given this universal blind spot in human nature, the only safe and justified basis for ethical education in the pubic schools is one precisely designed to rule out bias in favor of the substantive beliefs and conclusions of any particular group, whether religious, political, communal, or national. Indeed since one of our most fundamental responsibilities as educators is to *educate* rather than indoctrinate our students — to help them cultivate skills, insights, knowledge, and traits of mind and character that transcend narrow party and religious affiliations and help them to think beyond biased representations of the world — we must put special safeguards into moral education that prevent indoctrination. The world needs not more closed-minded zealots, eager to remake the world in their image, but more morally committed rational persons with respect for and insight into the moral judgments and perspectives of others, those least likely to confuse pseudo with genuine morality.

But how is this to be done? How can we cultivate morality and character in our students without indoctrinating them, without systematically rewarding them merely because they express our moral beliefs and espouse our moral perspective?

The answer is in putting *critical thinking* into the heart of the ethical curriculum, critical thinking for both teachers and students. To bring ethics and morality into the schools in an educationally legitimate way, administrators and teachers must think critically about what to emphasize and what to avoid. Intellectually discriminating minds and morally refined sensibilities must be in charge of both initial curriculum design and its subsequent classroom implementation. This is not an unreasonable demand, for, ethics aside, skill in the art of drawing important intellectual discriminations is crucial to education in any subject or domain, and proficiency in the art of teaching critically — encouraging students to question, think for themselves, develop rational standards of judgment — is the responsibility of all classroom teachers. Any subject, after all, can be taught merely to indoctrinate students and so to inadvertently stultify rather than develop their ability to think within it. Unfortunately, we have all been subjected to a good deal of indoctrination in the name of education and retain to this day some of the intellectual disabilities that such scholastic straight-jacketing produces. To allow ethics to be taught in the public schools this narrowly is unconscionable. It is to betray our ethical responsibility as educators in the name of ethics.

✦ *Integrating Critical Thinking and Ethics*

If we bring ethics into the curriculum — and we should — we must ensure that we do so morally. This requires us to clearly distinguish between espousing the universal, general principles of morality shared by people of good will everywhere, and the very different matter of defending some particular application of these principles to actual life situations as conceived from a particular moral standpoint (liberal, conservative, radical, theistic, non-theistic, U.S., Soviet, etc.). Any particular moral judgment arises from someone conceptualizing the facts of a situation from some moral perspective or standpoint. Every moral perspective in some way embodies the same general moral principles. The integration of *principles* with purported *facts* within a particular *perspective* produces the judgment that this or that act is morally right or wrong. Precisely because we often differ about the facts or about the proper perspective on the facts, we come to differing moral judgments.

The problem is not at the level of general moral principles. No people in the world, as far as I know, take themselves to oppose human rights or stand for injustice, slavery, exploitation, deception, dishonesty, theft, greed, starvation, ignorance, falsehood, and human suffering. In turn, no nation or group has special ownership over any general moral principle. Students, then, need skill and practice in moral reasoning, not indoctrination into the view that one nation rather than another is special in enunciating these moral principles. Students certainly need opportunities to explicitly learn basic moral principles, but more importantly they need opportunities to apply them to real and imagined cases, and to develop insight into both genuine and pseudo morality. They especially need to come to terms with the pitfalls of human moralizing, to recognize the ease with which we mask self-interest or egocentric desires with high-sounding moral language.

In any case, for any particular instance of moral judgment or reasoning, students should learn the art of distinguishing *principles* (which tell us in a general way what we ought or ought not to do) from *perspectives* (which characterize the world in ways which lead to an organized way of interpreting it) and *facts* (which provide the specific information for a particular moral judgment). In learning to discriminate these dimensions of moral reasoning, we learn how to focus on the appropriate questions at issue. Sometimes the dispute will depend on the facts: (Did John actually take the watch?) But, more often, they will be a matter of perspective (If you look at it this way, Jack did not take advantage of her, but if you look at it that way, he did. Which is more plausible given the facts?) Sometimes they will be a matter of both the facts and how to interpret them. (Do most people on welfare deserve the money they get? Should white collar crime be punished more severely?).

As people, students have an undeniable right to develop their own moral perspective — whether conservative, liberal, theistic, or non-theistic — but they should be able to analyze the perspective they do use, compare it accurately with other perspectives, and scrutinize the facts they conceptualize and judge as carefully as in any other domain of knowledge. They should, in other words, become as adept in using critical thinking principles in the moral domain as we expect them to be in scientific and social domains of learning.

To help students gain these skills, teachers need to see how one adapts the principles of critical thinking to the domain of ethical judgment and reasoning (see figure #1). Teachers also need insight into the intimate interconnection of intellectual and moral virtues. They need to see that being moral is something more than abstract good-heartedness, that our basic ways of knowing are inseparable from our basic ways of being, that how we think and judge in our daily life reflects who we are, morally and intellectually. To cultivate the kind of moral independence implied in being an educated moral person, we must foster in students moral humility, moral courage, moral integrity, moral perseverance, moral empathy, and moral fairmindedness (see figure #2). These moral traits are compatible with all moral perspectives (whether conservative, liberal, theistic, non-theistic, etc.).

Students who learn to think critically about moral issues and so develop moral virtues, can then develop their moral thinking within any tradition they choose. Critical thinking does not compel or coerce students to come to any particular substantive moral conclusions or to adopt any particular substantive moral point of view. Neither does it imply moral relativism, for it emphasizes the need for the same high intellectual standards in moral reasoning and judgment at the foundation of any bona fide domain of knowledge. Since moral judgment and reasoning presupposes and is subject to the same intellectual principles and standards that educated people use in all domains of learning, one can integrate consideration of moral issues into diverse subject areas, certainly into literature, science, history, civics, and society. Let us consider each of these areas very briefly.

✦ Ethics and Literature

Good literature represents and reveals, to the reflective critical reader, the deeper meanings and universal problems of real everyday life. Most of these problems have an important moral dimension or character. They are the kinds of problems all of us must think about and solve for ourselves; no one can simply tell us the "right" answers:

> Who am I? What kind of person am I? What is the world really like? What are my parents, my friends, and other people really like? How have I become the way I am? What should I believe in? Why should I believe in it? What real options do I have? Who are my real friends? Who should I trust? Who are my enemies? Need they be my enemies? How did the world become the way it is? How do people become the way they are? Are there any really bad people in the world? Are there any really good people in the world? What is good and bad? What is right and wrong? How should I decide? How can I decide what is fair and what is unfair? How can I be fair to others? Do I have to be fair to my enemies? How should I live my life? What rights do I have? What responsibilities?

Stimulating students to reflect upon questions like these in relationship to story episodes and their own experience enables them to draw upon their own developing moral feelings and ideas, to reason about them systematically, to tie them together and see where they lead. Careful reflection on episodes in literature — characters making sound or unsound moral judgments, sometimes ignoring basic moral principles or twisting them to serve their vested interests, sometimes displaying moral courage or cowardice, often caught in the throws of a moral dilemma — helps students develop a basic moral outlook on life. Furthermore, since moral issues are deeply embedded in everyday life, they often appear in literature. One need not unnaturally force discussion of literature into a moral framework. Moral issues are inevitably implicit there for the raising. However, it is important to realize that moral issues in literature, like the moral issues of everyday life, are rarely simplistic, and involved students will typically generate opposing viewpoints about how to respond to them. This, too, reflects the nature of the real world with its variety of moral outlooks vying for our allegiance.

As teachers of literature we should not impose authoritative interpretations upon the student; we should help them develop a reasoned, reflective, and coherent approach of their own. Each perspective, of course, should be respected; however, to be considered, each perspective must be *reasoned out*, not simply dogmatically asserted. In discussion, each student must learn the art of appealing to experience and reason, not merely to authority. Each student must therefore learn to reflect upon the grounds of his or her beliefs, to clarify ideas, support them with reasons and evidence, explore their implications, and so forth. Each student must also learn how to sympathetically enter into the moral perspectives of the others, not with the view that all moral perspectives are equally sound, but rather with the sense that we cannot judge another person's perspective until we genuinely understand it. Everyone is due the respect of at least being *understood*. And just as students will feel that they have something worth saying about the moral issues facing characters in stories and want their views to be understood, so they must learn to give that same respect to the others. Students then learn the art of reasoned dialogue, how to use moral reasoning skills to articulate their concerns about rights, justice, and the common good, from whatever moral viewpoint their experience and background predisposes them.

Essay writing is an excellent means of helping students organize their thinking on moral issues in literature. It provides the impetus to formulate moral principles explicitly, to carefully conceptualize and interpret facts, and to give and consider reasons in support of their own and contending moral conclusions. Needless to say we must grade students' moral writing, not on the basis of their substantive perspectives or conclusions, but rather on grounds of clarity, coherence, and sound reasoning. A clearly thought out, well-reasoned, well-illustrated piece of "moral" writing is what we are after. Such writing need not be long and complicated. Indeed it can begin in the early years with one-sentence "essays" such as "I think Jack (in "Jack and the Bean Stalk") was greedy because he didn't need to take all the golden eggs and the golden harp, too."

✦ Ethics and Science

Students should study science to **understand**, evaluate, and utilize scientific information. Most students will not, of course, become scientists but nevertheless need scientific knowledge to understand and solve problems within everyday personal and vocational life, problems having to do with such diverse areas as medicine, biology, chemistry, engineering, technology, the environment, and business. Science and technology play a greater and greater role in our lives, often generating major moral issues in the process. Scientific information is not simply *used*, it is used, and sometimes misused, for a variety of purposes, to advance the interests of a variety of groups, as those interests are conceived from a variety of perspectives. Its use must always be *assessed*.

In their daily lives students, like the rest of us, are bombarded with scientific information of every kind, typically in relation to some kind of advocacy. And they, like the rest of us, need to make decisions about the implications of that information. What are the real dangers of air pollution? Do people have a right to clean air and water? If so, how clean? What are the consequences of developing nuclear rather than solar power? To what extent should scientists be able to use animals in their experiments? Do animals have moral rights? To what extent should scientists be allowed to experiment with new viruses that might generate new diseases? Under what conditions should people be artificially kept alive? What life and death decisions should be left to doctors? What special moral responsibilities, if any, do scientists have to the broader society? These are but a few of the many weighty moral and scientific issues with which all of us as educated people are faced. Whether we develop an informed viewpoint or not, practical decisions are made everyday in each of these areas, and the public good is served or abused as a result of the rationality or irrationality of those decisions. Although many of these issues are ignored in traditional science instruction, there are good reasons not only to include but to emphasize them. First, they are more interesting and useful to most students than the more traditional "pure-science" emphasis. Second, they help students develop a more unified perspective on their values and personal beliefs and on the moral issues that science inevitably generates when applied to the real world.

✦ Ethics and History

There is no more important subject, rightly conceived, than history. Human life in all of its dimensions is deeply historical. Whatever experiences we have, the accounts that we give of things, our memories, our records, our sense of ourselves, the "news" we construct, the plans we form, even the daily gossip we hear — are historical. Furthermore, since we all have a deep-seated drive to think well of ourselves, and virtually unlimited powers to twist reality to justify ourselves, how we construct history has far-reaching ethical consequences. Not only do virtually all ethical issues have a historical component (moral judgment presupposes an account of what actually happened) but also virtually all historical issues have important ethical implications.

Issues arise among historians when they have conflicting accounts of events. Each major moral standpoint tends to *read* history differently and comes to importantly different moral conclusions as a result. The moral and the historical come together again and again in questions such as these: Morally speaking, what does the past *teach* us? What were the long-term effects of this kind of action as opposed to that? What kind of a world are we living in? What moral ideals can we actually live by and in what way? Is pacifism, for example, realistic? Are we justified in engaging in "unethical" practices in our own defense because our enemies use them to attack or harm us? What does it mean for countries to be "friendly" toward each other? How are friendships between countries like and unlike those between individuals? To what extent have we as a nation (and I as an individual) lived in accordance with the moral ideals we have set for ourselves? For example, was the historical treatment accorded Native Americans and other ethnic groups, has our foreign policy in general, been in keeping with our traditional espoused moral values? Morally speaking, how could our founding fathers justify slavery? Should they be morally criticized for accepting this violation of human rights or are there historical reasons why our criticism should be tempered with "understanding"? If our founding fathers, who eloquently formulated universal moral principles, were capable of violating them, are we now different from them, are we morally *better*, or are we also, without recognizing it, violating basic moral values we verbally espouse?

Once we grasp the moral significance of history, as well as the historical significance of morality, and recognize that historical judgment, like ethical judgement, is necessarily selective, that facts are conceptualized from some point of view, then we are well on our way toward constructing an unlimited variety of assignments in which history is no longer an abstraction from present and immediate concerns but rather an exciting, living, thought-provoking subject. Once students truly see themselves constructing history on a daily basis and, in doing so, coming to conclusions that directly affect the well-being of themselves and others, they will have taken a giant step toward becoming historically sensitive, ethical persons. As Carl Becker said in his presidential address to the American Historical Association over 50 years ago, every person, like it or not, "is his own historian". We must make sure that our students grasp the *moral* significance of that fact.

✦ Ethics, Civics, and the Study of Society

Just as all of us, to be ethical, must be our own historian, so too, to ethically fulfill our civic responsibilities, we must be our own sociologists. That is to say, each of us must study the underlying realities of social events, the unwritten rules and values that unreflectively guide our behavior; otherwise how can we justify using ethical principles to judge people and situations in the real world around us? We should be more than uncritical social observers and superficial moral judges. We have to recognize, as every sociologist since William Graham Sumner has pointed out, that most human behavior is a result of unanalyzed habit and routine based on unconsciously held standards and values. These embedded standards and values often differ from, even oppose, the ideals we express, and yet the conformist thinking which socialization tends to produce resists critical analysis. This resistance was recognized even from the early days of sociology as a discipline:

> Every group of any kind demands that each of its members shall help defend group interests ... group force is also employed to enforce the obligations of devotion to group interests. It follows that judgments are precluded and criticism is silenced. (Sumner, 1906)

Even patriotism, Sumner points out, "may degenerate into a vice ... chauvinism":

> It is a name for boastful and truculent group self-assertion. It overrules personal judgment and character, and puts the whole group at the mercy of the clique which is ruling at the moment. It produces the dominance of watchwords and phrases which take the place of reason and conscience in determining conduct. The patriotic bias is a recognized perversion of thought and judgment against which our education should guard us. (Sumner, 1906)

Ironically, true patriots in a democratic society serve their country by using their critical powers to ensure governmental honesty. Intelligent distrust rather than uncritical trust is the foundation necessary to keep officials acting ethically and in the public good. It was Jefferson who said:

> It would be a dangerous delusion were a confidence in the men of our choice to silence our fears for the safety of our rights. Confidence is everywhere the parent of despotism — free government is founded in jealousy, and not in confidence.

And Madison enthusiastically agreed: "The truth is, all men having power ought to be mistrusted."

What students need in civic education, then, is precisely what they need in moral education: not indoctrination into abstracted ideals, with the tacit implication that the ideals are generally practiced, not slogans and empty moralizing, but assignments that challenge their ability to use civic ideals to assess actual political behavior. Such assignments will, of course, produce divergent conclusions by students depending on their present political leanings. But, again, their thinking, speaking, and writing should be graded on the clarity, cogency, and intellectual rigor of their work, not on the substance of their answers. All students should learn the art of political analysis, the art of subjecting political behavior to critical assessment based on civic and moral ideals, on an analysis of important relevant facts, and on consideration of alternative political viewpoints. Virtually no students graduate today with this art in hand.

This means that words like "conservatism" and "liberalism", the "right" and "left", must become more than vague jargon; they must be recognized as names of different ways of thinking about human behavior. Students need experience actually thinking within diverse political perspectives. No perspective, not even one called "moderate", should be presented as *the* correct one. By the same token, we should be careful not to lead the students to believe that all perspectives are equally justified or that important insights are equally found in all points of view. We should continually encourage and stimulate our students to think and never do their thinking for them. We should, above all, be teachers and not preachers.

✦ Implementation Philosophy

Bringing ethics into the curriculum is essential but difficult. Many teachers are deeply committed to didactic lectorial modes of teaching. If ethics is taught in this way, indoctrination results, and we have lost rather than gained ground. Better no ethics than dogmatic moralizing.

To successfully establish a solid framework of ethical reasoning throughout the curriculum, we need excellent supplemental resources and well-designed in-service. Whenever possible, teachers should have access to books and materials that demonstrate how ethical and critical thinking principles can be integrated into subject matter instruction. They also need opportunities to air whatever misgivings they have about the paradigm shift this model represents for many of them. Above all, one should conceive of a move such as this as part of a long-term strategy in which implementation is achieved progressively over an extended time.

Just as educators should respect the autonomy of students, so in-service design should respect the autonomy of teachers. Teachers can and should be helped to integrate a critical approach to ethics into their everyday teaching. But they must actively think their way to this integration. It should not be imposed on them.

The model I suggest is one I have used successfully in in-service for both elementary and secondary teachers on numerous occasions. I call it the "Lesson Plan Remodeling Strategy" and have written three handbooks and an article explaining it in depth.

The basic idea is simple. Every practicing teacher works daily with lesson plans of one kind or another. To remodel lesson plans is to critique one or more lesson plans and formulate one or more new lesson plans based on that critical process. Thus, a group of teachers or staff development leaders with a reasonable number of exemplary remodels with accompanying explanatory principles can design practice sessions that enable teachers to develop new teaching skills as a result of experience in lesson remodeling.

Lesson plan remodeling can become a powerful tool in staff development for several reasons. It is action oriented and puts an immediate emphasis on close examination and critical assessment of what is taught on a day-to-day basis. It makes the problem of infusion more manageable by paring it down to the critique of particular lesson plans and the progressive infusion of particular principles. It is developmental in that, over time, more and more lesson plans are remodeled, and what has been remodeled can be remodeled again.

✦ Inservice Design

The idea behind inservice on this model is to take teachers step-by-step through specific stages of implementation. First of all, teachers must have an opportunity to become familiar with the basic concepts of critical thinking and ethical reasoning. They should first have an opportunity to formulate and discuss various general principles of morality and then to discuss how people with differing moral perspectives sometimes come to different moral conclusions when they apply these principles to actual events. Questions like "Is abortion morally justified?" or "Under what conditions do people have a right to welfare support?" or "Is capital punishment ever morally justified?" etc., can be used as examples to demonstrate this point.

Working together, the teachers should then construct examples of how they might encourage their students to apply one or more of the moral reasoning skills listed in figure #1. One table might focus on devising ways to help students clarify moral issues and claims *(S-8)*. Another table may discuss assignments that would help students develop their moral perspective *(S-7)*. A third might focus on ways to encourage one of the essential moral *virtues*, say, *moral integrity*. Of course teachers should have examples for each of the moral reasoning skills, as well as model classroom activities that foster them. Teachers should not be expected to work with nothing more than a list of abstract labels. The subsequent examples developed by the teachers working together should be written up and shared with all participants. There should be ample opportunity for constructive feedback.

Once teachers get some confidence in devising examples of activities they can use to help students develop various individual moral reasoning skills, they should try their hands at developing a full remodel. For this, each table has an actual lesson plan and they collectively develop a critique and remodel that embodies moral reasoning skills explicitly set out as objectives of the lesson. As before, exemplary remodels should be available for teachers to compare with their remodels. The following components should be spelled out explicitly:

1. *the original lesson plan* (or an abstract of it)

2. *a statement of the objectives of the plan*

3. *a critique of the original* (Why does it need to be revised? What does it fail to do that it might do? Does it indoctrinate students?)

4. *a listing of the moral reasoning skills to be infused*

5. *the remodeled lesson plan* (containing references to where in the remodel the various moral reasoning skills are infused)

Eventually school-wide or district-wide handbooks of lesson remodels can be put together and disseminated. These can be updated yearly. At least one consultant with unquestionable credentials in critical thinking should be hired to provide outside feedback on the process and its products.

For a fuller explanation of this inservice process and a wide selection of examples, I refer the reader to either *Critical Thinking Handbook: 4th-6th Grades*, or *Critical Thinking Handbook: K-3*, both are subtitled *A Guide for Remodeling Lesson Plans in Language Arts, Social Studies & Science*. Both integrate an emphasis on ethical reasoning into critical thinking infusion, though they do not explicitly express the component critical thinking skills with a moral reasoning emphasis (as I have in figure #1). The handbook examples are easily adaptable as illustrations for the upper grade levels. In any case, handbooks or not, what we should aim at is teacher practice in critiquing and revising standard lesson plans, based on a knowledgeable commitment to critical thinking and moral reasoning. We should not expect that teachers will begin with the knowledge base or even the commitment but only that with exposure, practice, and encouragement within a well planned long-term inservice implementation, proficiency and commitment will eventually emerge.

In my own experience in conducting inservices, I have found it easy to *begin* this process working with teachers. Though the early products of the teachers are of mixed quality, all of what is produced is workable as a basis for the development of further insights and teaching skills. The difficulty is not in getting the process started; it is in keeping it going. One

Moral Reasoning Skills

A Moral Affective Strategies
S-1 exercising independent moral thought and judgment
S-2 developing insight into moral egocentrism and sociocentrism
S-3 exercising moral reciprocity
S-4 exploring thought underlying moral reactions
S-5 suspending moral judgment

B Cognitive Strategies: Moral Macro-Abilities
S-6 avoiding oversimplification of moral issues
S-7 developing one's moral perspective
S-8 clarifying moral issues and claims
S-9 clarifying moral ideas
S-10 developing criteria for moral evaluation
S-11 evaluating moral authorities
S-12 raising and pursuing root moral questions
S-13 evaluating moral arguments
S-14 generating and assessing solutions to moral problems
S-15 identifying and clarifying moral points of view
S-16 engaging in Socratic discussion on moral issues
S-17 practicing dialogical thinking on moral issues
S-18 practicing dialectical thinking on moral issues

C Cognitive Strategies: Moral Micro-Skills
S-19 distinguishing facts from moral principles, values, and ideals
S-20 using critical vocabulary in discussing moral issues
S-21 distinguishing moral principles or ideas
S-22 examining moral assumptions
S-23 distinguishing morally relevant from morally irrelevant facts
S-24 making plausible moral inferences
S-25 supplying evidence for a moral conclusion
S-26 recognizing moral contradictions
S-27 exploring moral implication and consequences
S-28 refining moral generalizations

figure 1

Essential Moral Virtues

Moral Humility: Awareness of the limits of one's moral knowledge, including sensitivity to circumstances in which one's native egocentrism is likely to function self-deceptively; sensitivity to bias and prejudice in, and limitations of, one's viewpoint. Moral humility is based on the recognition that no one should claim to know more than one actually knows. It does not imply spinelessness or submissiveness. It implies the lack of moral pretentiousness, boastfulness, or conceit, combined with insight into the strengths and weaknesses of the logical foundations of one's beliefs.

Moral Courage: The willingness to face and assess fairly moral ideas, beliefs, or viewpoints to which we have not given serious hearing, regardless of our strong negative reaction to them. This courage arises from the recognition that ideas considered dangerous or absurd are sometimes rationally justified (in whole or in part), and that moral conclusions or beliefs espoused by those around us or inculcated in us are sometimes false or misleading.

Moral Empathy: Having a consciousness of the need to imaginatively put oneself in the place of others in order to genuinely understand them. We must recognize our egocentric tendency to identify truth with our immediate perceptions or longstanding beliefs. This trait correlates with the ability to reconstruct accurately the moral viewpoints and reasoning of others and to reason from moral premises, assumptions, and ideas other than our own. This trait also requires that we remember occasions when we were morally wrong, despite an intense conviction that we were right, as well as consider that we might be similarly deceived in a case at hand.

Moral Integrity: Recognition of the need to be true to one's own moral thinking, to be consistent in the moral standards one applies, to hold one's self to the same rigorous standards of evidence and proof to which one holds one's antagonists, to practice what one morally advocates for others, and to honestly admit discrepancies and moral inconsistencies in one's own thought and action.

Moral Perseverance: Willingness and consciousness of the need to pursue moral insights and truths despite difficulties, obstacles, and frustrations; firm adherence to moral principles despite irrational opposition of others; a sense of the need to struggle with confusion and unsettled questions over an extended period of time, to achieve deeper moral understanding or insight.

Moral Fairmindedness: Willingness and consciousness of the need to entertain all moral viewpoints sympathetically and to assess them with the same intellectual standards without reference to one's own feelings or vested interests, or the feelings or vested interests of one's friends, community, or nation; implies adherence to moral standards without reference to one's own advantage or the advantage of one's group.

figure 2

new lesson plan does not by itself change an established style of teaching. Like all creatures of habit, teachers tend to revert on Monday to their established teaching practices. A real on-going effort is essential for lesson plan remodeling to become a way of life and not just an interesting inservice activity.

✦ The Need for Leadership

I cannot overemphasize the need for leadership in this area. Teachers need to know that the administration is solidly behind them in this process, that the time and effort they put in will not only be appreciated but also visibly built upon. The school-wide or district-wide handbooks mentioned above are one kind of visible by-product that teachers should see. An excellent start is to have key administrators actively participate in the inservice along with the teachers. But the support should not end there. Administrators should facilitate on-going structures and activities to support this process: making and sharing video tapes, sending key personnel to conferences, establishing working committees, informal discussion groups, and opportunities for peer review. These are some among the many possibilities. Administrators should also be articulate defenders of an educational rather than a doctrinaire approach to morality. They should be ready, willing, and able to explain why and how critical thinking and ethics are integrated throughout the curriculum. They should make the approach intelligible to the school board and community. They should engender enthusiasm for it. They should fight to preserve it if attacked by those good hearted but closedminded people who see morality personified in their particular moral perspectives and beliefs. Above all, they should make a critical and moral commitment to a moral and critical education for all students and do this in a way that demonstrates to teachers and parents alike moral courage, perseverance, and integrity.

✦ References

Ralph W. Clark, *Introduction to Moral Reasoning*, West Publishing Company, St. Paul: 1986.

Ronald N. Giere, *Understanding Scientific Reasoning*, Holt, Rinehart, and Winston; New York: 1979.

Kuzirian and Madaras, *Taking Sides: Clashing Views on Controversial Issues in American History*, Dushkin Publishing Group; Guilford, Conn.: 1985.

Richard Paul, "Critical Thinking: Fundamental to Education for a Free Society," *Educational Leadership* 42, September, 1984.

Richard Paul, "Critical Thinking and the Critical Person," Forthcoming in *Thinking: Progress in Research and Teaching*, by Lawrence Erlbaum Associates, Inc. Publishers; Perkins, et al. editors.

Richard Paul, "Dialogical Thinking: Critical Thought Essential to the Acquisition of Rational Knowledge and Passions," *Teaching Thinking Skills; Theory and Practice*, by W.H. Freeman & Company, Publishers, Joan Baron and Robert Steinberg, editors, 1987.

Richard Paul, "Critical Thinking Staff Development: Lesson Plan Remodeling as the Strategy," *The Journal of Staff Development*, Fall 1987, Paul Burden, editor.

Paul, Binker, Jensen, and Kreklau, *Critical Thinking Handbook: 4th–6th Grades, A Guide for Remodeling Lesson Plans in Language Arts, Social Studies and Science*, Published by the Center for Critical Thinking and Moral Critique, (Sonoma State University, Rohnert Park, CA 94928) 1987.

Paul, Binker, Charbonneau *Critical Thinking Handbook: K–3, A Guide for Remodeling Lesson Plans in Language Arts, Social Studies and Science*, Published by the Center for Critical Thinking and Moral Critique, 1987.

Harvey Siegel, "Critical Thinking as an Education Ideal," *The Educational Forum*, Nov. 1980.

William Graham Sumner, *Folkways: A Study of the Sociological Importance of Usages, Manners, Customs, Mores, and Morals*, Dover Publications, Inc., New York: 1906.

Chapter 13

Critical Thinking, Moral Integrity, and Citizenship:
Teaching for the Intellectual Virtues

Abstract

Many are tempted to separate affective and moral dimensions of learning from cognitive dimensions. They argue that the cognitive and affective are obviously separate since many intelligent, well-educated people lack moral insight or sensitivity and many less intelligent, poorly-educated, or uneducated people are morally good. By distinguishing "strong" and "weak" senses of the terms 'critical thinking', 'moral integrity', and 'citizenship' Richard Paul suggests a novel answer to this objection.

Critical thinking, understood as skills alone separate from values, is often used to rationalize prejudice and vested interest. Moral integrity and responsible citizenship, understood merely as "good heartedness", are themselves susceptible to manipulation by propaganda. The human mind, whatever its conscious good will, is subject to powerful, self-deceptive, unconscious egocentricity of mind. The full development of each characteristic — critical thought, moral integrity, and responsible citizenship — in its strong sense requires and develops the others, in a parallel strong sense. The three are developed together only in an atmosphere which encourages the intellectual virtues: intellectual courage, intellectual empathy, intellectual good faith or integrity, intellectual perseverance, intellectual fairmindedness, and faith in reason. The intellectual virtues themselves are interdependent.

$\mathcal{E}$ducators and theorists tend to approach the affective and moral dimensions of education as they approach all other dimensions of learning, as compartmentalized domains, and as a collection of learnings more or less separate from other learnings. As a result, they view moral development as more or less independent of cognitive development. "And why not!" one might imagine the reply. "Clearly there are highly educated, very intelligent people who habitually do evil and very simple, poorly-educated people who consistently do good. If moral development were so intimately connected to cognitive development, how could this be so?"

In this paper, I provide the outlines of an answer to that objection by suggesting an intimate connection between critical thinking, moral integrity, and citizenship. Specifically, I distinguish a weak and a strong sense of each and hold that the strong sense ought to guide, not only our understanding of the nature of the educated person, but also our redesigning the curriculum.

There is little to recommend schooling that does not foster what I call intellectual virtues. These virtues include intellectual empathy, intellectual perseverance, intellectual confidence in reason, and an intellectual sense of justice (fairmindedness). Without these characteristics, intellectual development is circumscribed and distorted, a caricature of what it could and should be. These same characteristics are essential to moral judgment. The "good-hearted" person who lacks intellectual virtues will act morally only when morally grasping a situation or problem does not presuppose intellectual insight. Many, if not most, moral problems and situations in the modern world are open to multiple interpretations and, hence, do presuppose these intellectual virtues.

We are now coming to see how far we are from curricula and teaching strategies that genuinely foster basic intellectual and moral development. Curricula is so highly compartmentalized and teaching so committed to "speed learning" (covering large chunks of content quickly) that it has little room for fostering what I call the intellectual virtues. Indeed, the present structure of curricula and teaching not only strongly discourages their development but also strongly encourages their opposites. Consequently, even the "best" students enter and leave college as largely miseducated persons, with no real sense of what they do and do not understand, with little sense of the state of their prejudices or insights, with little command of their intellectual faculties — in short, with no intellectual virtues, properly so-called.

Superficially absorbed content, the inevitable by-product of extensive but shallow coverage, inevitably leads to intellectual arrogance. Such learning discourages intellectual perseverance and confidence in reason. It prevents the recognition of intellectual bad faith. It provides no foundation for intellectual empathy, nor for an intellectual sense of fair play. By taking in and giving back masses of detail, students come to believe that they *know* a lot about each subject — whether they understand or not. By practicing applying rules and formulas to familiar tasks, they come to feel that getting the answer should always be easy — if you don't know how to do something, don't try to figure it out, ask. By hearing and reading only one perspective, they come to think that perspective has a monopoly on truth — any other view must be completely wrong. By accepting (without understanding) that their government's past actions were all justified, they assume their government never would or could do wrong — if it doesn't seem right, I must not understand.

The pedagogical implications of my position include these: cutting back on coverage to focus on depth of understanding, on foundational ideas, on intellectual synthesis, and on intellectual experiences that develop and deepen the most basic intellectual skills, abilities, concepts, and virtues. A similar viewpoint was expressed by Whitehead:

> The result of teaching small parts of a large number of subjects is the passive reception of disconnected ideas, not illuminated with any spark of vitality. Let the main ideas which are introduced into a child's education be few and important, and let them be thrown into every combination possible. The child should make them his own, and should understand their application here and now in the circumstances of his actual life. From the very beginning of his education, the child should experience the joy of discovery. The discovery which he has to make is that general ideas give an understanding of that stream of events which pours through his life. (*The Aims of Education*, p. 14)

To accomplish this re-orientation of curriculum and teaching, we need new criteria of what constitutes success and failure in school. We need to begin this re-orientation as early as possible. Integrating teaching for critical thinking, moral integrity, and citizenship is an essential part of this re-orientation.

✦ Teaching for "Strong Sense" Skills

The term "critical thinking" can be used in either a weak or a strong sense, depending upon whether we think of critical thinking narrowly, as a list or collection of discrete intellectual skills, or, more broadly, as a mode of mental integration, as a synthesized complex of dispositions, values, and skills necessary to becoming a fairminded, rational person. Teaching critical thinking in a strong sense is a powerful, and I believe necessary means to moral integrity and responsible citizenship.

Intellectual skills in and of themselves can be used either for good or ill, to enlighten or to propagandize, to gain narrow, self-serving ends, or to further the general and public good. The micro-skills themselves, for example, do not define fairmindedness and could be used as easily by those who are highly prejudiced as those who are not. Those students not exposed to the challenge of strong sense critical thinking assignments (for example, assignments in which they must empathically reconstruct viewpoints that differ strikingly from their own) will not, as a matter of abstract morality or general good-heartedness, be fair to points of view they oppose, nor will they automatically develop a rationally defensible notion of what the public good is on the many issues they must decide as citizens.

Critical thinking, in its most defensible sense, is not simply a matter of cognitive skills. Moral integrity and responsible citizenship are, in turn, not simply a matter of good-heartedness or good intentions. Many good-hearted people cannot see through and critique propaganda and mass manipulation, and most good-hearted people fall prey at times to the powerful tendency to engage in self deception, especially when their own egocentric interests and desires are at stake. One can be good-hearted and intellectually egocentric at the same time.

The problems of education for fairminded independence of thought, for genuine moral integrity, and for responsible citizenship are not three separate issues but one complex task. If we succeed with one dimension of the problem, we succeed with all. If we fail with one, we fail with all. Now we are failing with all because we do not clearly understand the interrelated nature of the problem nor how to address it.

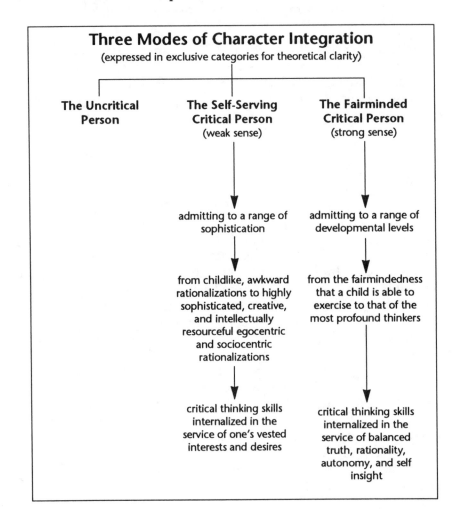

Three Modes of Character Integration
(expressed in exclusive categories for theoretical clarity)

The Uncritical Person	The Self-Serving Critical Person (weak sense)	The Fairminded Critical Person (strong sense)
	admitting to a range of sophistication	admitting to a range of developmental levels
	from childlike, awkward rationalizations to highly sophisticated, creative, and intellectually resourceful egocentric and sociocentric rationalizations	from the fairmindedness that a child is able to exercise to that of the most profound thinkers
	critical thinking skills internalized in the service of one's vested interests and desires	critical thinking skills internalized in the service of balanced truth, rationality, autonomy, and self insight

✦ The Intellectual and Moral Virtues of the Critical Person

Our basic ways of knowing are inseparable from our basic ways of being. How we think reflects who we are. Intellectual and moral virtues or disabilities are intimately interconnected. To cultivate the kind of intellectual independence implied in the concept of strong sense critical thinking, we must recognize the need to foster intellectual (epistemological) humility, courage, integrity, perseverance, empathy, and fairmindedness. A brief gloss on each will suggest how to translate these concepts into concrete examples. Intellectual humility will be my only extended illustration. I will leave to the reader's imagination what sorts of concrete examples could be marshalled in amplifying the other intellectual virtues.

Intellectual Humility: Having a consciousness of the limits of one's knowledge, including a sensitivity to circumstances in which one's native egocentrism is likely to function self-deceptively; sensitivity to bias, prejudice, and limitations of one's viewpoint. Intellectual humility depends on recognizing that one should not claim more than one actually knows. It does not imply spinelessness or submissiveness. It implies the lack of intellectual pretentiousness, boastfulness, or conceit, combined with insight into the logical foundations, or lack of such foundations, of one's beliefs.

To illustrate, consider this letter from a teacher with a Master's degree in Physics and Mathematics, with 20 years of high school teaching experience in physics:

> After I started teaching, I realized that I had learned physics by rote and that I really did not understand all I knew about physics. My thinking students asked me questions for which I always had the standard textbook answers, but for the first time it made me start thinking for myself, and I realized that these canned answers were not justified by my own thinking and only confused my students who were showing some ability to think for themselves. To achieve my academic goals I had to memorize the thoughts of others, but I had never learned or been encouraged to learn to think for myself.

This is a good example of what I call intellectual humility and, like all intellectual humility, it arises from insight into the nature of knowing. It is reminiscent of the ancient Greek insight that Socrates was the wisest of the Greeks because only he knew how little he really understood. Socrates developed this insight as a result of extensive, in-depth questioning of the knowledge claims of others. He had to think his way to this insight.

If this insight and this humility is part of our goal, then most textbooks and curricula require extensive modification, for typically they discourage rather than encourage it. The extent and nature of "coverage" for most grade levels and subjects implies that bits and pieces of knowledge are easily attained, without any significant consideration of the basis for the knowledge claimed in the text or by the teacher. The speed with which content is covered contradicts the notion that students must think in an extended way about content before giving assent to what is claimed. Most teaching and most texts are, in this sense, epistemologically unrealistic and hence foster intellectual arrogance in students, particularly in those with retentive memories who can repeat back what they have heard or read. *Pretending* to know is encouraged. Much standardized testing validates this pretense.

This led Alan Schoenfeld, for example, to conclude that "most instruction in mathematics is, in a very real sense, deceptive and possibly fraudulent". He cites numerous examples including the following. He points out that much instruction on how to solve word problems in elementary math

> ... is based on the "key word" algorithm, where the student makes his choice of the appropriate arithmetic operation by looking for syntactic cues in the problem statement. For example, the word 'left' in the problem "John had eight apples. He gave three to Mary. How many does John have left?" ... serves to tell the students that subtraction is the appropriate operation to perform. (p. 27)

He further reports the following:

> In a widely used elementary text book series, 97 percent of the problems "solved" by the key-word method would yield (serendipitously?) the correct answer.
>
> Students are drilled in the key-word algorithm so well that they will use subtraction, for example, in almost any problem containing the word 'left'. In the study from which this conclusion was drawn, problems were constructed in which appropriate operations were addition, multiplication, and division. Each used the word 'left' conspicuously in its statement and a large percentage of the students subtracted. In fact, the situation was so extreme that many students chose to subtract in a problem that began "Mr. Left ...".

Schoenfeld then provides a couple of other examples, including the following:

> I taught a problem-solving course for junior and senior mathematics majors at Berkeley in 1976. These students had already seen some remarkably sophisticated mathematics. Linear algebra and differential equations were old hat. Topology, Fourier transforms, and measure theory were familiar to some. I gave them a straightforward theorem from plane geometry (required when I was in the tenth grade). Only two of eight students made any progress on it, some of them by using arc length integrals to measure the circumference of a circle. (Schoenfeld, 1979). Out of the context of normal course work these students could not do elementary mathematics.

He concludes:

> In sum: all too often we focus on a narrow collection of well-defined tasks and train students to execute those tasks in a routine, if not algorithmic fashion. Then we test the students on tasks that are very close to the ones they have been taught. If they succeed on those problems, we and they congratulate each other on the fact that they have learned some powerful mathematical techniques. In fact, they may be able to use such techniques mechanically while lacking some rudimentary thinking skills. To allow them, and ourselves, to believe that they "understand" the mathematics is deceptive and fraudulent.

This approach to learning in math is paralleled in all other subjects. Most teachers got through their college classes mainly by "learning the standard textbook answers" and were neither given an opportunity nor encouraged to determine whether what the text or the professor said was "justified by their own thinking". To move toward intellectual humility, most teachers need to question most of what they learned, as the teacher above did, but such questioning would require intellectual courage, perseverance, and confidence in their own capacity to reason and understand subject matter through their own thought. Most teachers have not done the kind of analytic thinking necessary for gaining such perspective.

I would generalize as follows: just as the development of intellectual humility is an essential goal of critical thinking instruction, so is the development of intellectual courage, integrity, empathy, perseverance, fairmindedness, and confidence in reason. Furthermore, each intellectual (and moral) virtue in turn is richly developed only in conjunction with the others. Before we approach this point directly, however, a brief characterization of what I have in mind by each of these traits is in order:

Intellectual Courage: Having a consciousness of the need to face and fairly address ideas, beliefs, or viewpoints toward which we have strong negative emotions and to which we have not given a serious hearing. This courage is connected with the recognition that ideas considered dangerous or absurd are sometimes rationally justified (in whole or in part) and that conclusions and beliefs inculcated in us are sometimes false or misleading. To determine for ourselves which is which, we must not passively and uncritically "accept" what we have "learned". Intellectual courage comes into play here, because inevitably we will come to see some truth in some ideas considered dangerous and absurd, and distortion or falsity in some ideas strongly held in our social group. We need courage to be true to our own thinking in such circumstances. The penalties for non-conformity can be severe.

Intellectual Empathy: Having a consciousness of the need to imaginatively put oneself in the place of others in order to genuinely understand them, which requires the consciousness of our egocentric tendency to identify truth with our immediate perceptions or long-standing thought or belief. This trait correlates with the ability to reconstruct accurately the viewpoints and reasoning of others and to reason from premises, assumptions, and ideas other than our own. This trait also correlates with the willingness to remember occasions when we were wrong in the past despite an intense conviction that we were right, and with the ability to imagine our being similarly deceived in a case-at-hand.

Intellectual Good Faith (Integrity): Recognition of the need to be true to one's own thinking; to be consistent in the intellectual standards one applies; to hold one's self to the same rigorous standards of evidence and proof to which one holds one's antagonists; to practice what one advocates for others; and to honestly admit discrepancies and inconsistencies in one's own thought and action.

Intellectual Perseverance: Willingness and consciousness of the need to pursue intellectual insights and truths in spite of difficulties, obstacles, and frustrations; firm adherence to rational principles despite the irrational opposition of others; a sense of the need to struggle with confusion and unsettled questions over an extended period of time to achieve deeper understanding or insight.

Faith in Reason: Confidence that, in the long run, one's own higher interests and those of humankind at large will be best served by giving the freest play to reason, by encouraging people to come to their own conclusions by developing their own rational faculties; faith that, with proper encouragement and cultivation, people can learn to think for themselves, to form rational viewpoints, draw reasonable conclusions, think coherently and logically, persuade each other by reason and become reasonable persons, despite the deep-seated obstacles in the native character of the human mind and in society as we know it.

Fairmindedness: Willingness and consciousness of the need to treat all viewpoints alike, without reference to one's own feelings or vested interests, or the feelings or vested interests of one's friends, community, or nation; implies adherence to intellectual standards without reference to one's own advantage or the advantage of one's group.

✦ *The Interdependence of the Intellectual Virtues*

Let us now consider the interdependence of these virtues, how hard it is to deeply develop any one of them without also developing the others. Consider intellectual humility. To become aware of the limits of our knowledge we need the *courage* to face our own prejudices and ignorance.

To discover our own prejudices in turn we must often *empathize* with and reason within points of view toward which we are hostile. To do this, we must typically *persevere* over a period of time, for learning to empathically enter a point of view against which we are biased takes time and significant effort. That effort will not seem justified unless we have the *faith in reason* to believe we will not be "tainted" or "taken in" by whatever is false or misleading in the opposing viewpoint. Furthermore, merely believing we can survive serious consideration of an "alien" point of view is not enough to motivate most of us to consider them seriously. We must also be motivated by an *intellectual sense of justice*. We must recognize an intellectual *responsibility* to be fair to views we oppose. We must feel *obliged* to hear them in their strongest form to ensure that we do not condemn them out of our own ignorance or bias. At this point, we come full circle back to where we began: the need for *intellectual humility*.

Or let us begin at another point. Consider intellectual good faith or integrity. Intellectual integrity is clearly difficult to develop. We are often motivated — generally without admitting to or being aware of this motivation — to set up inconsistent intellectual standards. Our egocentric or sociocentric side readily believes positive information about those we like and negative information about those we dislike. We tend to believe what justifies our vested interest or validates our strongest desires. Hence, we all have some innate tendencies to use double standards, which is of course paradigmatic of intellectual bad faith. Such thought often helps us get ahead in the world, maximize our power or advantage, and get more of what we want.

Nevertheless, we cannot easily operate *explicitly* or overtly with a double standard. We must, therefore, avoid looking at the evidence too closely. We cannot scrutinize our own inferences and interpretations too carefully. Hence, a certain amount of *intellectual arrogance* is quite useful. I may assume, for example that I know just what you're going to say (before you say it), precisely what you are really after (before the evidence demonstrates it), and what actually is going on (before I have studied the situation carefully). My intellectual arrogance makes it easier for me to avoid noticing the unjustifiable discrepancy in the standards I apply to you and those I apply to myself. Of course, if I don't have to empathize with you, that too makes it easier to avoid seeing my duplicity. I am also better off if I don't feel a keen need to be *fair* to your point of view. A little background *fear* of what I might discover if I seriously considered the consistency of my own judgments also helps. In this case, my lack of intellectual integrity is supported by my lack of intellectual humility, empathy, and fairmindedness.

Going in the other direction, it will be difficult to maintain a double standard between us if I feel a distinct responsibility to be fair to your point of view, understand this responsibility to entail that I must view things from your perspective in an empathic fashion, and conduct this inner inquiry with some humility regarding the possibility of my being wrong and your being right. The more I dislike you personally or feel wronged in the past by you or by others who share your way of thinking, the more pronounced in my character must be the trait of intellectual integrity in order to provide the countervailing impetus to think my way to a fair conclusion.

✦ Defense Mechanisms and the Intellectual Virtues

A major obstacle to developing intellectual virtues is the presence in the human egocentric mind of what Freud has called "defense mechanisms". Each represents a way to falsify, distort, misconceive, twist, or deny reality. Their presence represents, therefore, the relative weakness or absence of the intellectual virtues. Since they operate in everyone to some degree, no one embodies the intellectual virtues purely or perfectly. In other words, we each have a side of us unwilling to face unpleasant truth, willing to distort, falsify, twist, and misrepresent. We also know from a monumental mass of psychological research that this side can be *powerful*, can dominate our minds strikingly. We marvel at, and are often dumfounded by, others whom we consider clear-cut instances of these modes of thinking. What is truly "marvelous", it seems to me, is how little we take ourselves to be victims of these falsifying thoughts, and how little we try to break them down. The vicious circle seems to be this: because we, by and large, lack the intellectual virtues, we do not have insight into them, but because we lack insight into them, we do not see ourselves as lacking them. They weren't explicitly taught to us, so we don't have to explicitly teach them to our children.

✦ Insights, Analyzed Experiences, and Activated Ignorance

Schooling has generally ignored the need for insight or intellectual virtues. This deficiency is intimately connected with another one, the failure of the schools to show students they should not only test what they "learn" in school by their own experience, but also test what they experience by what they "learn" in school. This may seem a hopeless circle, but if we can see the distinction between a critically analyzed experience and an unanalyzed one, we can see the link between the former and *insight,* and the latter and *prejudice,* and will be well on our way to seeing how to fill these needs.

We subject little of our experience to critical analysis. We seldom take our experiences apart to judge their epistemological worth. We rarely sort the "lived" integrated experience into its component parts, *raw data, our interpretation* of the data, or ask ourselves how the interests, goals, and desires we brought to those data shaped and structured that interpretation. Similarly, we rarely seriously consider the possibility that our interpretation (and hence our experience) might be selective, biased, or misleading.

This is not to say that our unanalyzed experiences lack meaning or significance. Quite the contrary, in some sense we assess *all* experience. Our egocentric side never ceases to catalogue experiences in accord with its common and idiosyncratic fears, desires, prejudices, stereotypes, caricatures, hopes, dreams, and assorted irrational drives. We shouldn't assume *a priori* that our rational side dominates the shaping of our experience. Our unanalyzed experiences are some combination of these dual contributors to thought, action, and being. Only through critical analysis can we hope to isolate the irrational dimensions of our experience. The ability to do so grows as we analyze more and more of our experience.

Of course, more important than the sheer *number* of analyzed experiences is their *quality* and *significance*. This quality and significance depends on how much our analyses embody the intellectual virtues. At the same time, the degree of our virtue depends upon the number and quality of experiences we have successfully critically analyzed. What links the virtues, as perfections of the mind, and the experiences, as analyzed products of the mind, is *insight*. Every critically analyzed experience to some extent produces one or more intellectual virtues. To become more rational it is not enough to have experiences nor even for those experiences to have meanings. Many experiences are more or less charged with *irrational* meanings. These important meanings produce stereotypes, prejudices, narrowmindedness, delusions, and illusions of various kinds.

The process of developing intellectual virtues and insights is part and parcel of our developing an interest in taking apart our experiences to separate their rational from their irrational dimensions. These meta-experiences become important benchmarks and guides for future thought. They make possible modes of thinking and maneuvers in thinking closed to the irrational mind.

✦ Some Thoughts on How to Teach for the Intellectual Virtues

To teach for the intellectual virtues, one must recognize the significant differences between the higher order critical thinking of a fairminded critical thinker and that of a self-serving critical thinker. Though both share a certain command of the micro-skills of critical thinking and hence would, for example, score well on tests such as the Watson-Glaser Critical Thinking Appraisal or the Cornell Critical Thinking Tests, they are not equally good at tasks which presuppose the intellectual virtues. The self-serving (weak sense) critical thinker would lack the insights that underlie and support these virtues.

I can reason well in domains in which I am prejudiced — hence, eventually, reason my way out of prejudices — only if I develop mental benchmarks for such reasoning. Of course one insight I need is that when I am prejudiced it will seem to me that I am not, and similarly, that those who are not prejudiced as I am will seem to me to be prejudiced. (To a prejudiced person, an unprejudiced person seems prejudiced.) I will come to this insight only insofar as I have analyzed experiences in which I was intensely convinced I was correct on an issue, judgment, or point of view, only to find, after a series of challenges, reconsiderations, and new reasonings, that my previous conviction was in fact prejudiced. I must take this experience apart in my mind, clearly understand its elements and how they fit together (how I became prejudiced; how I inwardly experienced that prejudice; how intensely that prejudice seemed true and insightful; how I progressively broke that prejudice down through serious consideration of opposing lines of reasoning; how I slowly came to new assumptions, new information, and ultimately new conceptualizations).

Only when one gains analyzed experiences of working and reasoning one's way out of prejudice can one gain the higher order abilities of a fairminded critical thinker. What one gains is somewhat "procedural" or sequential in that there is a *process* one must go through; but one also sees that the process cannot be followed out formulaically or algorithmically, it depends on principles. The somewhat abstract articulation of the intellectual virtues above will take on concrete meaning in the light of these *analyzed experiences*. Their true meaning to us will be given in and by these experiences. We will often return to them to recapture and rekindle the insights upon which the intellectual virtues depend.

Generally, to develop intellectual virtues, we must create a collection of analyzed experiences that represent to us intuitive models, not only of the pitfalls of our own previous thinking and experiencing but also processes for reasoning our way out of or around them. These model experiences must be charged with meaning for us. We cannot be *indifferent* to them. We must sustain them in our minds by our sense of their importance as they sustain and guide us in our thinking.

What does this imply for teaching? It implies a somewhat different content or material focus. Our own minds and experiences must become the subject of our study and learning. Indeed, only to the extent that the content of our own experiences becomes an essential part of study will the usual subject matter truly be learned. By the same token, the experiences of others must become part of what we study. But experiences of any kind should always be critically analyzed, and students must do their own analyses and clearly recognize what they are doing.

This entails that students become explicitly aware of the logic of experience. All experiences have three elements, each of which may require some special scrutiny in the analytic process: *1)* something to be experienced (some actual situation or other); *2)* an experiencing subject (with a point of view, framework of beliefs, attitudes, desires, and values); and *3)* some interpretation or conceptualization of the situation. To take any experience apart, then, students must be sensitive to three distinctive sets of questions:

1) What are the raw facts, what is the most neutral description of the situation? If one describes the experience this way, and another disagrees, on what description *can* they agree?

2) What interests, attitudes, desires, or concerns do I bring to the situation? Am I always aware of them? Why or why not?

3) How am I conceptualizing or interpreting the situation in light of my point of view? How else might it be interpreted?

Students must also explore the interrelationships of these parts: How did my point of view, values, desires, etc., affect what I noticed about the situation? How did they prevent me from noticing other things? How would I have interpreted the situation had I noticed those other things? How did my point of view, desires, etc., affect my interpretation? How *should* I interpret the situation?

If students have many assignments that require them to analyze their experiences and the experiences of others along these lines, with ample opportunity to argue among themselves about which interpretations make the most sense and why, then they will begin to amass a catalogue of critically analyzed experiences. If the experiences illuminate the pitfalls of thought, the analysis and the models of thinking they suggest will be the foundation for their intellectual traits and character. They will develop intellectual virtues because they had thought their way to them and internalized them as concrete understandings and insights, not because they took them up as slogans. Their basic values and their thinking processes will be in a symbiotic relationship to each other. Their intellectual and affective lives will become more integrated. Their standards for thinking will be implicit in their own thinking, rather than in texts, teachers, or the authority of a peer group.

✦ Conclusion

We do not now teach for the intellectual virtues. If we did, not only would we have a basis for integrating the curriculum, we would also have a basis for integrating the cognitive and affective lives of students. Such integration is the basis for strong sense critical thinking, for moral development, and for citizenship. The moral, social, and political issues we face in everyday life are increasingly intellectually complex. Their settlement relies on circumstances and events that are interpreted in a variety of (often conflicting) ways. For example, should our government publish misinformation to mislead another government or group which it considers terrorist? Is it ethical to tolerate a "racist" regime such as South Africa, or are we morally obligated to attempt to overthrow it? Is it ethical to support anti-communist groups that use, or have used, torture, rape, or murder as tools in their struggle? When, if ever, should the CIA attempt to overthrow a government it perceives as undemocratic? How can one distinguish "terrorists" from "freedom fighters"?

Or, consider issues that are more "domestic" or "personal". Should deliberate pollutors be considered "criminals"? How should we balance off "dollar losses" against "safety gains"? That is, how much money should we be willing to spend to save human lives? What is deliberate deception in advertising and business practices? Should one protect incompetent individuals within one's profession from exposure? How should one reconcile or balance one's personal vested interest against the public good? What moral or civic responsibility exists to devote time and energy to the public good as against one's private interests and amusements?

These are just a few of the many complex moral, political, and social issues that virtually all citizens must face. The response of the citizenry to such issues defines the moral character of society. These issues challenge our intellectual honesty, courage, integrity, empathy, and fairmindedness. Given their complexity, they require perseverance and confidence in reason. People easily become cynical, intellectually lazy, or retreat into simplistic models of learning and the world they learned in school and see and hear on TV. On the other hand, it is doubtful that the fundamental conflicts and antagonisms in the world can be solved or resolved by sheer power or abstract good will. Good-heartedness and power are insufficient for creating a just world. Some modest development of the intellectual virtues seems essential for future human survival and well-being. Whether the energy, the resources, and the insights necessary for this development can be significantly mustered remains open. This is certain: we will never succeed in cultivating traits whose roots we do not understand and whose development we do not foster.

Part B

How to Teach for Critical Thinking

Section I

Instruction

The Critical Connection: Higher Order
Thinking that Unifies Curriculum,
Instruction, and Learning

Dialogical and Dialectical Thinking

The Art of Redesigning Instruction

Socratic Questioning

Using Critical Thinking to Identify National
Bias in the News

Teaching Critical Thinking in the Strong
Sense: A Focus on Self-Deception, World
Views, and a Dialectical Mode of Analysis

Chapter 14

The Critical Connection:
Higher Order Thinking That Unifies
Curriculum, Instruction, and Learning

Abstract

*"Though education by its very nature comprises a set of high order goals, actu-
al school learning, given established practice, culminates in a set of lower order
results." "The problem," in Paul's view, "is unambiguous. How can we reconceptualize and restructure what we presently do to narrow the gap between goals and
results, to make high order goals a practical reality? ... What sorts of changes do
we need so that in math classes students learn to think mathematically, in history
classes they learn to think historically, in science classes they learn to think scientifically, and so that in general, not only in school but in their everyday lives as
well, students begin to think critically in a disciplined, self-directed fashion?"
Paul traces the problem to a tacit but large-scale acceptance of a network of
uncritically held assumptions about instruction, knowledge, and learning. He
argues for an alternative set of assumptions and spells out the kinds of changes
needed in curricula and staff development for these more critically held assumptions about instruction, knowledge, and learning to become embedded in practice.
Paul argues for long-term commitment to this process because of the deep-seated
nature of the changes needed and the depth of resistance that can be expected.*

✦ Introduction

*T*he fundamental problems in schooling today at all levels are fragmentation and lower order learning. Both within and between subject areas there is a dearth of connection and depth. Atomized lists dominate curricula, atomized teaching dominates instruction, and atomized
recall dominates learning. What is learned are superficial fragments, typically soon forgotten. What is missing is coherence, connection, and
depth of understanding.

Recognition of the economic implications of the pervasiveness of lower
order learning is illustrated in an open letter drafted by the president of
Stanford University, Donald Kennedy, co-signed by 36 other college leaders from across the USA and sent to 3,000 college and university presidents (Sept. 18, 1987). It warned of,

a national emergency ... rooted ... in the revolution of expectations about what our schools must accomplish ....

It simply will not do for our schools to produce a small elite to
power our scientific establishment and a larger cadre of workers
with basic skills to do routine work. Millions of people around the
world now have these same basic skills and are willing to work
twice as long for as little as one-tenth our basic wages. To maintain
and enhance our quality of life, we must develop a leading-edge
economy based on workers who can think for a living. If skills are
equal, in the long run wages will be too. This means we have to
educate a vast mass of people capable of thinking critically, creatively, and imaginatively.

There are reasons why teaching and learning are lower order and reasons
why they could and should be higher order. In this paper I explore both.

The bottom line, as we all well know, is not what is taught but what is
learned. Students often learn something very different from what is
taught. This dichotomy leads Alan Schoenfeld, the distinguished math
educator, to conclude that math instruction is on the whole "deceptive
and fraudulent". He uses strong words to underscore a wide gulf between
what math teachers think their students are learning and what in fact
they are. (Schoenfeld, 1982) He elaborates as follows:

All too often we focus on a narrow collection of well-defined
tasks and train students to execute those tasks in a routine, if not
algorithmic fashion. Then we test the students on tasks that are
very close to the ones they have been taught. If they succeed on
those problems, we and they congratulate each other on the fact
that they have learned some powerful mathematical techniques. In
fact, they may be able to use such techniques mechanically while
lacking some rudimentary thinking skills. To allow them, and ourselves, to believe that they "understand" the mathematics is deceptive and fraudulent. (p. 29)

Schoenfeld cites a number of studies to justify this characterization of
math instruction and its lower order consequences. He also gives a number of striking examples, at the tertiary as well as at the primary and secondary levels:

At the University of Rochester 85 percent of the freshman class
takes calculus, and many go on. Roughly half of our students see
calculus as their last mathematics course. Most of these students
will never apply calculus in any meaningful way (if at all) in their
studies, or in their lives. They complete their studies with the
impression that they know some very sophisticated and high-pow-
ered mathematics. They can find the maxima of complicated functions, determine exponential decay, compute the volumes of surfaces of revolution, and so on. But the fact is that these students
know barely anything at all. The only reason they can perform

with any degree of competency on their final exams is that the problems on the exams are nearly carbon copies of problems they have seen before; the students are not being asked to think, but merely to apply well-rehearsed schemata for specific kinds of tasks. Tim Keifer and I studied students abilities to deal with pre-calculus versions of elementary word problems such as the following:

As 8-foot fence is located 3 feet from a building. Express the length L of the ladder which may be leaned against the building and just touch the top of the fence as a function of the distance X between the foot of the ladder and the base of the building.

We were not surprised to discover that only 19 of 120 attempts at such problems (four each for 30 students) yielded correct answers, or that only 65 attempts produced answers of any kind. (p. 28)

Schoenfeld documents similar problems at the level of elementary math instruction. He reports on an experiment in which elementary students were asked questions like, "There are 26 sheep and 10 goats on a ship. How old is the captain?" 76 of the 97 students "solved" the problem by adding, subtracting, multiplying, or dividing. (Schoenfeld, 1989)

Schoenfeld cites many similar cases, including a study that demonstrated that "word problems", which are supposed to require thought, tend to be approached by students mindlessly with the *key word algorithm,* that is, by reading problems like "John had eight apples. He gave three to Mary. How many does John have left?" and looking for words like 'left' to tell them what operation to perform. As Schoenfeld puts it, "… the situation was so extreme that many students chose to subtract in a problem that began 'Mr. Left'." (Schoenfeld, 1982) This tendency to approach math problems and assignments with robotic lower order responses becomes obsessive in most students.

Robotic lower order learning is not, of course, peculiar to math. It is the common mode of learning in every subject area. This results in a kind of global self-deception that surrounds teaching and learning, often with the students clearer about what is really being learned than the teachers. Many students, for example, realize that in their history courses they merely learn to mouth names, dates, events, and outcomes whose significance they do not really understand and whose content they forget shortly after the test. Our stated goal may be to prepare students to think historically when dealing with public and private issues and problems, but that is not what happens. That is not the bottom line.

In other words, though education by its very nature comprises a set of higher order goals, actual school learning, given established practice, culminates in a set of lower order results. The problem is unambiguous. How can we reconceptualize and restructure what we presently do to narrow the gap between goals and results, to make higher order goals a practical reality, to reduce lower order goals to what they should be: mere means for higher order ends. What sorts of changes do we need to make so that in math classes students learn to think mathematically, in history classes they learn to think historically, in science classes they learn to think scientifically, and so that in general, not only in school but in their everyday lives as well, they begin to think critically in a disciplined, self-directed fashion?

✦ The Root of the Problem Is
Our Confidence in Didactic Teaching

Fundamental changes are needed, ones that require insight into a host of interrelated conditions. Consider some of the connections we need to grasp. We can improve student performance only by improving their thinking. We can improve their thinking only by creating opportunities and incentives for them to think. We can provide them with opportunities and incentives to think only if their teachers have time to thoughtfully redesign their instruction. We can give teachers time to thoughtfully redesign their instruction only if they do not feel compelled to cover huge amounts of subject matter. We can reduce the obsession to cover huge amounts of subject matter only if the curriculum is restructured to focus on basic concepts, understandings, and abilities. We can restructure the curriculum to focus on basic concepts, understandings, and abilities only if we understand why such a focus is essential to higher order learning. We will understand why such a focus is essential to higher order learning only if we clearly understand the profound differences between the present didactic model of education, which confuses acquiring knowledge with memorization, and the critical model of education which recognizes that acquiring knowledge intrinsically and necessarily depends on higher order critical thought.

In education the whole is greater than the sum of the parts. We need to forge connections that shape the parts to form a coherent educational whole. To achieve this, nothing is more important than a clear conception of education explicitly embedded in curriculum, inservice, and instruction. No significant reform of education can occur unless we face the didactic lower order conception of education that informs daily practice. Present instruction implies that parroting information is equivalent to the acquisition of knowledge. Hence, teachers often feel compelled to cover information, even though they realize their students do not really understand and will soon forget it. Behind this practice is a network of uncritically held assumptions that need to be made explicit and unequivocally refuted, namely:

1) that students learn *how* to think when they know *what* to think,

2) that knowledge can be given directly to students without their having to think it through for themselves,

3) that the process of education is, in essence, the process of storing content in the head like data in a computer,

4) that quiet classes with little student talk are evidence of student learning,

5) that students gain significant knowledge without seeking or valuing it,

6) that material should be presented from the point of view of the one who knows,

7) that superficial learning can later be deepened,

8) that coverage is more important than depth,

9) that students who correctly answer questions, provide definitions, and apply formulae demonstrate substantial understanding, and

10) that students learn best by working alone.

One who understands and values education as higher order learning holds a very different set of assumptions, namely:

1) that students learn *what* to think only as they learn *how* to think,

2) that one gains knowledge *only* through thinking,

3) that the process of education is the process of each student gathering, analyzing, synthesizing, applying, and assessing information for him or herself,

4) that classes with much student talk, focused on live issues, is a better sign of learning than quiet classes focused on a passive acceptance of what the teacher says,

5) that students gain significant knowledge only when they value it,

6) that information should be presented so as to be understandable from the point of view of the learner, hence continually related to the learner's experiences and point of view,

7) that superficial learning is often mis-learning and stands as an obstacle to deeper understanding,

8) that depth is more important than coverage,

9) that students can often provide correct answers, repeat definitions, and apply formulas while not understanding those answers, definitions, or formulas, and

10) that students learn best by working together with other students, actively debating and exchanging ideas.

These contrasting assumptions about education, knowledge, teaching, and learning have contrasting implications for how textbooks should be written, how teachers should teach, and how students should go about learning. Indeed they have very different implications for every dimension of school life. The first set of statements collectively define a *didactic* conception of education, the second a *critical* one. The first set encourages lower order learning, the second higher order. We must make a paradigm shift from a didactic to a critical model of education to make higher order thinking a classroom reality. This shift is like a global shift in our eating habits and lifestyle. It cannot be achieved in a one-day inservice or by any other short-term strategy. It must come over an extended period of time and be experienced as something of a conversion, as a new way of thinking about every dimension of schooling. Let us now consider some of the basic changes that must be made to effect this shift.

✦ Step One: Reconceive and Redesign the Curriculum

Curricula play a significant role in school life. Instruction arises from goals and objectives stated in them. When they are heavily loaded with lower order objectives and content, when higher order objectives are vaguely defined, when assessment is tied to content recall and lower order skills, a didactic conception of education, complete with extensive lower order teaching and learning, results.

As things now stand many teachers are — usually without knowing it — obsessed with the notion that they must cover so much content that they have no time to focus on depth of understanding at any point along the way, let alone at every point along the way. This compulsion blocks redesign of instruction. Teachers feel they have no time to focus on higher order learning and therefore on what has recently been called "high" content — the most basic ideas and issues within a content area approached in such a way that students think them through for themselves.

Only through an explicit shift to a critical conception of education, with an explicit critique and rejection of the assumptions of didactic education, can we achieve significant reform. Consider one of the conclusions of the studies conducted at the National Center on Effective Secondary Schools concerning teaching effectiveness in higher order thinking. These studies focus on high school social studies departments which have made an explicit commitment to teaching higher order critical thinking. They found, among other things, that even in departments with a special interest in higher order thinking numerous teachers lapse into didactic teaching and end up focusing more on coverage than depth. What is more, not only do didactic teachers score poorly on the teaching of higher order thinking, this failure correlates with their obsession with coverage:

> A careful interpretation of the above findings suggests that lower scorers, unlike high scorers, are caught in a contradiction. That is, lower scorers make the general statement that breadth of coverage is detrimental to thinking, yet at the same time: a) claim that specific breadth-oriented lessons enhance students' thinking, and b) impose coverage pressure on themselves equal to or greater than the coverage demands articulated by the department or district. (Newmann, 1988)

Similar conclusions are emerging in the field studies headed by Rexford Brown for the Policy and the Higher Literacies Project of the Education Commission of the States. Results of this sort underscore the need to attack the didactic model directly and explicitly. Subconscious habits of thought and instruction, internalized over many years of schooling, are not easily changed. Even with careful critique, ingrained habits of thought and behavior can only be abandoned by degrees as new ones take their place. The shift from a lecture-drill-recall paradigm to one focused upon engaged-deep-processing can only be achieved through long-term evolution. If we want a focus on *high content* we must make the implications of that commitment explicit and detailed. With this in mind, let us consider the connection to curricula.

Since most complete curricula contain a complex of elements — philosophy, goals, standards, objectives, assessment, and instructional examples — their formulation provides an important opportunity to confront the didactic model head on, and make the shift from low to high content inescapable. Unfortunately the philosophy expressed in most district curricula is typically little more than a set of empty platitudes, not an articulate analysis of the general conditions necessary for knowledge acquisition and learning. Given vagueness at the outset, a crucial opportunity is missed to nail down and avoid the misconceptions about knowledge and learning embedded in most didactic teaching. Nothing is done to forestall common misconceptions because there is no significant awareness that such misconceptions need to be forestalled. Nothing is done to make high content a priority.

As a result, teachers typically interpret the various goals and objectives as so many bits and pieces of information to be implanted in the students' minds by didactic instruction. Furthermore, systematic assessment often concentrates on recall and lower order skills. The result: higher order critical thinking lost in the rush to cover extended lists of content in preparation for testing. For this reason a major emphasis needs to be put on a detailed formulation of philosophy, one which highlights the essential role of thinking in the acquisition of knowledge, and contrasts lower order with higher order learning. Let us see how this might be stated as philosophy in the curriculum.

DEMONSTRATE HOW KNOWLEDGE IS EMBEDDED IN THOUGHT: A SAMPLE CURRICULAR STATEMENT

Imagine the following included under "philosophy" in a curriculum:

Higher order learning can be cultivated in almost any academic setting. By focusing on the rational capacities of students' minds, by designing instruction so that students explicitly grasp the sense, the logicalness, of what they learn, we can make all additional learning easier for them. Higher order learning multiplies comprehension and insight; lower order rote memorization and performance multiply misunderstanding and prejudice. Higher order learning stimulates and empowers, lower order discourages and limits the learner. Good teaching focuses on high content, basic ideas and issues taught in ways which actively engage student reflection and thought. Though very little present instruction deliberately aims at lower order learning, most results in it. "Good" students have developed techniques for short term rote memorization; "poor" students have none. But few know what it is to think analytically through the content of a subject, few use critical thinking as a tool for acquiring knowledge.

We often talk of knowledge as though it could be divorced from thinking, as though it could be gathered up by one person and given to another in the form of a collection of sentences to remember. When we talk in this way we forget that knowledge, by its very nature, depends on thought. Knowledge is produced by thought, analyzed by thought, comprehended by thought, organized, evaluated, maintained, and transformed by thought. Knowledge exists, properly speaking, only in minds that have comprehended and justified it through thought. And when we say *thought* we mean *critical thought*. Knowledge must be distinguished from the memorization of true statements. People can easily blindly memorize what they do not understand. A book contains knowledge only in a derivative sense, only because minds can thoughtfully read it and, through this analytic process, gain knowledge. We systematically forget this and design instruction as though recall were equivalent to knowledge.

We need to remember that all knowledge exists in and through critical thought. All the disciplines — mathematics, physics, chemistry, biology, geography, sociology, anthropology, history, philosophy, and so on — are modes of thinking. We know mathematics, not to the extent that we can recite mathematical formulas, but only to the extent that we can think mathematically. We know science, not to the extent that we can recall sentences from our science textbooks, but only to the extent that we can think scientifically. We understand sociology only to the extent that we can think sociologically, history only to the extent that we can think historically, and philosophy only to the extent that we can think philosophically.

When we teach each subject in such a way that students pass courses without thinking their way into the knowledge that these subjects make possible, students leave those courses with no more knowledge than they had when they entered them. *When we sacrifice thought to gain coverage, we sacrifice knowledge at the same time.*

There are numerous forms of lower order learning we must avoid. We can understand them by understanding the relative lack of student comprehension characteristic of them. Paradigmatically, lower order learning is learning by sheer association or rote. Hence students come to think of history class, for example, as a place where you hear names and dates and places; where you try to remember them and state them on tests, where you read that this event had this cause and that result. Math comes to be thought of as numbers, symbols, and formulas, mysterious things you mechanically manipulate as the teacher told you to get the right answer. Literature is often thought of as uninteresting stories to remember along with what the teacher said is important about them. Science means measuring, counting, and filling out graphs.

Consider history taught as a mode of thought. Viewed from the paradigm of a critical education, blindly memorized content ceases to be the focal point. Learning to think historically becomes the order of the day. Students learn historical content by thinking historically about historical questions and problems. They learn through their own thinking and classroom discussion that history is not a simple recounting of past events, but also an interpretation of events selected by and written from someone's point of view. In recognizing that each historian writes from a point of view, students begin to identify and assess points of view leading to various historical interpretations. They recognize, for example, what it is to interpret the American Revolution from a British as well as a colonial perspective. They role-play different historical perspectives and master content through in-depth historical thought. They relate the present to the past by discussing how their own stored-up interpretations of the events of their own lives shape their responses to the present and their plans for the future. They come to understand the daily news as a form of historical thought shaped by the profit-making agendas of news collecting outlets. They come to recognize that gossip is a kind of historical thought often shaped by bias.

Learning to think historically is, in short, a very different and much deeper approach to history than that adopted traditionally. The one-dimensional didactic approach, wherein students quickly forget what the teacher or text said, is abandoned as a misconceived anachronism. When students learn to think historically, they not only acquire information and higher order knowledge, but also insights, skills, abilities, and values — learnings that serve them well in grappling with real problems in a historically complex world. They learn that history is not principally what is found in dusty books, but what is actively embedded in people's minds as they interpret and shape events in the world about them.

Including language such as this in curriculum philosophy would go far toward flagging the problem of didactic lower order teaching, sensitizing teachers to the crucial shift needed. Of course we must follow up this curriculum philosophy with a redesigned articulation of curriculum goals, standards, objectives, assessment, and instructional examples.

✦ Step Two: Give Teachers Time to Thoughtfully Redesign Their Instruction

As teachers become increasingly aware of the difference between a didactic and a critical conception of education, and have a curriculum which articulates a coherent understanding of and commitment to higher order learning and high content for all students, they need the time and the incentive to thoughtfully redesign or remodel their own instruction. This is no simple, one-shot task. It must address deep-seated teaching habits and ways of thinking. It requires incremental change. It requires on-going critical thinking on the part of teachers and administrators. It requires long term planning. It requires a set of strategies for transforming instruction as well as an understanding of the nature of higher order thinking and of the conditions under which it can occur.

Consider this statement of what characterizes higher order thinking which Lauren Resnick made in a recent report on the research on the subject for the National Research Council (Resnick, 1987):

1) Higher order thinking is *nonalgorithmic*. That is, the path of action is not fully specified in advance.

2) Higher order thinking tends to be *complex*. The total path is not "visible" (mentally speaking) from any single vantage point.

3) Higher order thinking often yields *multiple solutions,* each with costs and benefits, rather than unique solutions.

4) Higher order thinking involves *nuanced judgment* and interpretation.

5) Higher order thinking involves the application of *multiple criteria,* which sometimes conflict with one another.

6) Higher order thinking often involves *uncertainty.* Not everything that bears on the task is known.

7) Higher order thinking involves *self-regulation* of the thinking process. We do not recognize higher order thinking in an individual when someone else "calls the plays" at every step.

8) Higher order thinking involves *imposing meaning,* finding structure in apparent disorder.

9) Higher order thinking is *effortful.* There is considerable mental work involved in the kinds of elaborations and judgments required.

This characterization warns us against conceptions of critical thinking that imply it can be proceduralized for students, reduced to predictable steps in a predictable order. Critical thinking needs to be understood globally not mechanistically. For example, we need to recognize that assignments that compel students to think their own way through the logic of the content, using their own experience, their own assumptions, their own ideas, call upon them to think in a higher order fashion virtually every step along the way. We also need to see that in doing such assignments no two students think it through in exactly the same way.

We cannot escape the brute fact that there are no algorithms for doing one's own thinking. Critical thinking is by its very nature *principled* not procedural thinking. Critical thinking requires thinkers to continually *monitor* their thinking by means of questions that test for clarity, accuracy, specificity, relevance, consistency, logic, depth, and significance. Since critical thinking often involves thinking within *multiple points of view and frames of reference,* it often yields multiple possible solutions. Since critical thinking enables a person to achieve *genuine knowledge* rather than mere recall, and since what one learns is always integrated into one's personal experience and previous knowledge, it always involves the *imposition of meaning.*

Critical thinking, in the deepest and fullest meaning of that phrase, is equivalent to higher order thinking. It engages us in an evolving process in which we progressively take control of our own thinking, disciplining it by degrees, making it more and more responsive to evidence and reason, and extending it to ever more domains and situations. We naturally use it to create, build upon, reform, modify, and redesign our beliefs and behavior. Teachers need time to assimilate this conception, to tie it into their experience, to try it out in their everyday life, to integrate it into their own thinking, to translate it into strategies for instructional reform.

Let us now look briefly at both the cognitive and affective dimensions, and the insights that underlie them. This will clarify the sort of reflective process teachers must go through.

PROVIDE OPPORTUNITIES FOR TEACHERS TO LEARN HOW TO TEACH FOR THE AFFECTIVE DIMENSIONS OF HIGHER ORDER THINKING

No one learns what they do not in some sense value. Knowledge has value because of its use. Consider, for example, things that students value, how quickly they learn them, how much they know about them, and how well they retain and use what they know. A list would include sports, music, television, movies, fashions, styles, video games, and so on. Taking any one of these, say skateboarding, we can easily see the connection between the cognitive and the affective. Students who value skateboarding spend much time and energy learning the differences between available wheels, trucks, and boards, the advantages and disadvantages of each, the kind of riding best suited to each, and how these components work together. They then use this knowledge to assemble a board appropriate to the kind of riding they prefer. Difficulties do not dampen their enthusiasm.

If we want students to learn to think in higher order ways we need to cultivate the traits essential to such thinking. Consider, for example, the most fundamental disposition necessary for all higher order thinking: the drive, disposition, or will to think independently. It is always easier in the short run to try to get someone else to do our thinking for us, for someone else to tell us what to do, for someone else to solve our problems for us, for someone else to figure out life for us. Students habitually expect the teacher or text to solve their scholastic problems for them — though they rarely expect teachers or texts to solve their real-world problems. In school, they look for algorithms, formulas, and fail-safe recipes or procedures. They expect to act robotically. Faced with problems at home or on the street they often, in contrast, show real independence of thought. Yet teachers rarely tap this independence. They rarely harness or discipline it. They cave in to the students' demand for mindless short-cuts, re-enforcing the students' expectations that they ought to have them. Indeed, teachers continually look for algorithms, formulas, and fail-safe recipes or procedures. They wrongly feel that this helps their students. Ironically and painfully, many teachers today are now looking for robotic procedures to teach higher order thinking.

Of course there are many ways teachers *can* cultivate independence of thought in their students, though none of these strategies involve formulas or mindless rules. Consider the following examples:

1) Rather than simply having students discuss ideas found in their texts, have them brainstorm their own ideas and argue among themselves about problems and the solutions to problems.

2) Routinely ask students for their point of view on issues, concepts, and ideas.

3) Before reading a section of text that explains a map, chart, time-line, or graph, have the students read and discuss what the map, etc., shows.

4) Whenever possible give students tasks that call upon them to develop their own categories and modes of classification instead of being provided with them in advance. For example, rather than providing them with ways of classifying literature, lead a discussion on how students *do* classify what they read, calling upon them to justify whatever labels they already use.

5) When giving written assignments, give the students a larger role in gathering and assembling information, in analyzing and synthesizing it, and in formulating and evaluating the conclusions or interpretations of others.

6) In science classes, have students devise their own hypotheses and experiments or seek out what they take to be examples of pseudo science, explaining how they came to this conclusion.

7) In math classes, devise activities that lead students to argue and debate various possible ways to solve standard math problems before you give them access to algorithms and formulas.

Teachers can devise innumerable such scenarios for the cultivation of every essential trait or disposition available. When teachers understand the importance of the affective dimension of thought and have some start-up examples, they are very creative in devising such strategies. Every teacher can devise ways of cultivating fairmindedness, intellectual humility, intellectual courage, intellectual perseverance, intellectual integrity, and confidence in reason, but only if they understand them, see them as important, and feel free to take the time to do so.

Of course, lest we be taken to be fostering an atomization of higher order thinking, it should be emphasized that the affective traits and dispositions we advocate are interdependent. Consider intellectual humility. To become aware of the limits of our knowledge, we need courage to face our prejudices and ignorance. To discover our prejudices, in turn, we often must empathize with and reason within points of view toward which we are hostile. To achieve this end, we must typically persevere over a period of time, for learning to empathically enter a point of view against which we are biased takes time and significant effort. That effort will not seem justified unless we have the confidence in reason to believe we will not be "tainted" or "taken in" by whatever is false or misleading in the opposing viewpoint. Furthermore, merely believing we can survive serious consideration of an "alien" point of view is not enough to motivate most of us to consider it seriously. We must also be motivated by an intellectual sense of justice. We must recognize an intellectual responsibility to be fair to views we oppose. We must feel obliged to hear them in their strongest form to ensure that we do not condemn them out of our own ignorance or bias. At this point, we come full circle back to where we began: the need for intellectual humility.

For a large catalog of examples K–12 the reader may want to consult the *Critical Thinking Handbook* series published by the Center for Critical Thinking and Moral Critique. They provide a "principled" rather than a "procedural" approach throughout.

The crucial point is this. Teachers need time to become aware of the variety of strategies available for cultivating the affective traits of mind essential to higher order thinking. They also need incentives for cultivating these traits. Ultimately, of course, teachers must come up with their own particular redesigned lessons. They must develop confidence in their own thinking, their own capacity to take a new idea and make it a reality in practice. Teachers who do not think independently and critically about their own instruction will never be able to teach independent critical thought to their students. No formulas, procedures, or recipes can substitute for independent critical thinking on the part of each and every teacher and, of course, each and every student.

PROVIDE OPPORTUNITIES FOR TEACHERS TO LEARN HOW TO TEACH FOR HIGHER ORDER COGNITIVE ABILITIES

There are a variety of critical thinking principles which can be transformed into teaching strategies for fostering higher order cognitive abilities and skills. These principles apply on the micro as well as the macro level. That is, in addition to developing the skills of identifying assumptions, evidence, conclusions, implications and consequences, and so forth, students have to learn to orchestrate those skills into more extended thought processes. They need to be able to read and write critically, to engage in Socratic discussions, to reason dialectically, to pursue root questions, and so forth. The upshot is that teachers have to learn how to teach for higher order cognitive abilities and skills. To do this they need to have the principles that underlie them spelled out with examples of the sorts of classroom activities and assignments that foster them.

Consider, for example, the concept of critical reading. Some people think of it as reading in an argumentative mind frame. This misses the essence of the process. Though critical readers do read with a healthy skepticism, their fundamental purpose is to understand the text, to grasp what is being said from the point of view of the person writing. They appreciate how, when humans think, they think within a point of view. Unless we sympathetically enter into the perspective of a writer we cannot make the best and most accurate sense of what is being said. Furthermore, a critical reader recognizes that whenever important ideas are dealt with they have important connections that a critical reader needs to determine. For example, all writers have a basic goal or purpose, make fundamental assumptions, reason from the assumptions they make, come to conclusions, and generate implications and consequences. Hence, a critical reader reads with a view to identifying these important elements, reads so as to better understand what precisely is being said, what portion should be accepted and what should be questioned and followed up with further reading.

When teachers have this principle of critical reading in mind, there are a number of things they can do to foster critical reading on the part of their students:

1) Call attention to the difference between uncritical impressionistic reading, on the one hand, and critical reading on the other, pointing out the differences between the two so that students begin to think about their own reading habits with a greater sense of what specific things they might try to do.

2) Have student's identify the author's point of view, purpose, conclusions, reasons given, assumptions made, issues raised, basic ideas used, and so forth.

3) Teach students to question as they read: "Can I summarize the last paragraph in my own words? Can I relate it to my experience? Can I see what the author is implying? Can I see reasons for what is said? Are there objections I might raise? Is this consistent with other things I know or believe?"

4) Lead a discussion on the relation of reading and listening. Compare asking questions of a speaker to asking questions while one reads.

5) Show by demonstration examples of poor and good reading.

6) Read aloud expressing your own questions as you proceed, using provisional answers expressed aloud to guide you in interpreting the text. Make your own critical reading explicit by thinking aloud. Have students take turns doing the same.

Teachers can take strategies such as these and work out the details with their own students, recognizing thereby that there are no formulas or pat procedures for producing critical readers. Each teacher committed to critical reading develops somewhat different ways of encouraging it. When teachers have time to exchange ideas on how to cultivate critical reading, they learn from each other and achieve higher levels of success.

✦ Step Three: Take the Long View

Short-term reform can do no more than foster surface reform. Deep change takes time, patience, perseverance, understanding, and commitment. This is not easy in an educational world saturated with glossy, superficial, quick-fixes and plagued historically by a very short attention span. Nevertheless, a well-devised long-term educational reform program, focused on the progressive ameliorization of instruction through the development of the critical thought of teachers, promises the kind of multiple long term payoffs that make in-depth reform cost-effective. Furthermore, the amount of money invested is in fact secondary, if the motivation and leadership are present.

A case in point is the Greensboro Plan, a reasoning and writing project which began in the city of Greensboro in the spring of 1986 and has been gathering momentum ever since. It was initially proposed by Associate Superintendent Sammie Parrish and approved by the Greensboro board of education as the spearhead of a commitment to infuse critical thinking and writing into K–12 curriculum. To ensure that the reform project had a life of its own, two full-time facilitators were hired: Kim DeVaney, an experienced elementary school teacher, and Janet Williamson, a high school teacher who had just completed a doctorate with a special emphasis on critical thinking. Williamson and DeVaney nurtured the project as a creature of the teaching staff. From the start they knew that the project needed a solid foundation. Accordingly, they began with a small group of 14 volunteers. These 14 read widely and diversely about critical thinking, developing their own thinking as they critically analyzed a variety of proposals for infusion. (For details about the Greensboro plan, see Chapter 21.)

I have included the Greensboro Plan in this anthology for a reason. It illustrates well the style, flavor, and thrust of a well-devised, well-run reform effort, tuned into the multiple connections that must be made to carry it through. Furthermore, Greensboro is not a wealthy suburban district. It is a medium sized urban district with 21,000 students and 1,389 classroom teachers. The students come from diverse economic and racial backgrounds. 46% of the student population is White; 52% Black; and 2% Asian, Hispanic, or Native American. Almost 28% of the student population has a family income low enough for them to receive either free or discounted lunches.

The Greensboro teachers and administrators know that even though they have been working hard for some three years, they are still, comparatively speaking, at the beginning of fundamental change. This is not a source of discouragement but of strength, of knowing what real change requires and how it comes to pass.

✦ Conclusion

There are a number of connections we must make conceptually and pragmatically to successfully reform education. All fundamental school practices presently cluster around or emerge from a didactic conception of education. The dominance of lower order learning is inevitable given this fact. Unless teachers and administrators come to terms with this dominance and its foundation in a mistaken conception of education, they will never be able to make the shift to higher order teaching and learning. Curricula will remain cluttered with details, superficial content, and low level skills. Schooling will remain a hurried race through undigested content. Students will remain largely passive and indifferent.

Substantial change can occur only by restructuring math classes so that students learn to think mathematically, history classes so that students learn to think historically, science classes so that students learn to think scientifically, and so that in general, not only in school but in everyday life as well, students — and teachers — begin to think critically in a deeply internalized, self-directed fashion. This requires that curricula be reconceptualized and recast by a critical model of higher order teaching and learning. It also requires long-term, in-depth staff development programs that remain focused on higher order learning for the foreseeable future. Teachers need years of practice critiquing and remodeling their instruction, to grow out of deeply ingrained compulsive didacticism. The obsession with didactic instruction is such that many will periodically relapse and begin again to treat the basic acquisition of knowledge as a mode of lower order memorization.

In this process it is important to involve the widest possible spectrum of people in discussing, articulating, and implementing the effort to infuse critical thinking. This includes teachers, administrators, board members, and parents. Incentives must be provided to those who move forward in the implementation process. Many small changes will be necessary before larger changes take place. Do not rush implementation. A slow but steady progress with continual monitoring and adjusting of efforts is best. Provide for refocusing on the long-term goal and ways of making the progress visible and explicit. Work continually to institutionalize the changes made as the understanding of higher order thinking grows, making sure that the goals and strategies being used are deeply embedded in school-wide and district-wide statements and articulations. Honor individual differences among teachers. Maximize the opportunities for teachers to pursue critical thinking strategies in keeping with their individual differences.

As you pursue these evolutionary changes, you will recognize additional implications and connections attendant on the process: a natural link with cooperative learning, with professionalizing teaching, with responsible assessment, with teacher involvement in school and district management decisions, and, not least, with preparing students to participate in a world — vocationally, personally, politically, and socially — in which fundamental change, adaptability, and higher order thinking are pressing needs in every dimension, in every conceivable domain of thought and action.

Chapter 15

Dialogical and Dialectical Thinking

Abstract

This paper is divided into two sections. Part I is theoretical. In it, Richard Paul discusses the importance of dialogical and dialectical thinking. He argues that students learn best in dialogical and dialectical situations, when their thinking involves dialogue or extended exchange between different points of view or frames of reference. Part II is pedagogical. In it, Paul discusses what can be done in a classroom to engage student thought dialogically and dialectically. He discusses how to distinguish multilogical issues (those having many logics) from monological issues (those having one logic). He then discusses Socratic questioning as a way to effectively involve students in a discussion and engage their thinking about an issue or topic. The value of cooperative learning is then discussed. Paul stresses that dialectical discussions are disciplined, that students must "learn how to bring intellectual standards into their work, how to hold themselves and their classmates to standards of good reasoning and analysis."

✦ Part I: Theory

INTRODUCTION

*W*hen as the result of a trial, the jury comes to a verdict of guilty or innocent; when as a result of political debate, a citizen decides to vote for one of the candidates; when as a result of reading the case that can be made for alternative political systems, one concludes that one is superior to the others; when as a result of hearing various sides of a family argument, one becomes persuaded that one side is more justified and accurate; when as a result of reading many reports on the need for educational reform, one is prepared to argue for one of them; when as a result of entertaining various representations of national security, one reasons to a position of one's own; when after reading and thinking about various approaches to the raising of children, one concludes that one is better than the others; when after interacting with a person for a number of years and entertaining various conflicting interpretations of her character, one decides that she would make a good marriage partner — *one is reasoning dialectically.*

Whenever students discuss their ideas, beliefs, or points of view with other students or the teacher; whenever students have to role play the thinking of others; whenever students have to use their thinking to figure out the thinking of another (say, that of the author of a textbook or of a story); whenever students have to listen carefully to the thoughts of another and try to make sense of them; whenever students, whether orally or in writing, have to arrange their thoughts in such a fashion as to be understood by another; whenever students have to enter sympathetically into the thinking of others or reason hypothetically from the assumptions of others, *they are reasoning dialogically.*

An open society requires open minds. One-sided egocentric and sociocentric thought, joined with massive technical knowledge and power, are not the foundations of a genuine democracy. The basic insight, formulated over a hundred years ago by John Stuart Mill, is as true today, and as ignored, as it was when he first wrote it:

> In the case of any person whose judgment is really deserving of confidence, how has it become so? Because he has kept his mind open to criticism of his opinions and conduct. Because it has been his practice to listen to all that could be said against him; to profit by as much of it as was just, and expound to himself, and upon occasion to others, the fallacy of what was fallacious. Because he has felt that the only way in which a human being can make some approach to knowing the whole of a subject, is by hearing what can be said about it by persons of every variety of opinion, and study.

This is the dialogical ideal. Dialogical and dialectical thinking involve dialogue or extended exchange between different points of view or frames of reference. Both are multilogical (involving *many* logics) rather than monological (involving *one* logic) because in both cases there is more than one line of reasoning to consider, more than one "logic" being formulated. Dialogue becomes dialectical when ideas or reasonings come into conflict with each other and we need to assess their various strengths and weaknesses.

In general, students learn best in dialogical situations, in circumstances in which they must continually express their views to others and try to fit others' views into their own. Even when dealing with monological problems (like many found in math and science) students need to move dialogically between their own thinking and "correct" thinking on the subject before they come to appreciate the one "right" (monological) way to proceed. They cannot simply leap directly to "correct" thought; they need to think dialogically first.

Unfortunately, the dominant mode of teaching at all levels is still didactic: teaching by telling, learning by memorizing. The problem it creates is evident in this excerpt from a letter by a teacher with a Master's degree in physics and mathematics:

> After I started teaching, I realized that I had learned physics by rote and that I really did not understand all I knew about physics. My thinking students asked me questions for which I always had the standard textbook answers, but for the first time made me start thinking for myself, and I realized that these canned answers were not justified by my own thinking and only confused my students who were showing some ability to think for themselves. To achieve my academic goals I had memorized the thoughts of others, but I had never learned or been encouraged to learn to think for myself.

Didactic teaching encourages monological thinking from beginning to end. There is little room for dialogical or dialectical thinking in the mind of the didactic teacher. Rather the teacher, usually focused on content coverage, tells students directly what to believe and think about subject matter, while students, in turn, focus on remembering what the teacher said in order to reproduce it on demand. In its most common form, this mode of teaching falsely assumes that one can directly give a person knowledge without that person having to think his or her way to it, that knowledge can directly be implanted in students' minds through memorization. It confuses *information* with *knowledge*. It falsely assumes that knowledge can be separated from understanding and justification. It confuses the ability to *state* a principle with *understanding* that principle, the ability to *supply a definition* with *comprehending* a concept. Didactic instruction flourishes when it appears that life's problems can be solved by one-dimensional answers and that knowledge is ready-made for passive absorption. Most teachers teach as if this were so without recognizing it.

Students today have very little experience in school of reasoning within opposing points of view. Indeed students today have little experience with reasoning at all. Most students do not know what inferences are, what it is to make assumptions, what it is to reason from an assumption to one or more conclusions. In the didactic classroom of today, the teacher is engaged in inculcating information. Classroom monologue (students passively listening) rather than active dialogue (students thoughtfully engaged) is the paradigm. Unfortunately, students then come away with the impression that knowledge can be obtained without struggle, without having to hear from more than one point of view, without having to identify or assess evidence, without having to question assumptions, without having to trace implications, without having to analyze concepts, without having to consider objections.

The result: students with no real sense of what the process of acquiring knowledge involves, students with nothing more than a jumble of information and beliefs, students with little sense of what it is to reason one's way to knowledge. The result: teachers oblivious of the fact that knowledge must be earned through thought, who teach as if knowledge were available to anyone willing to commit information to short-term memory. The result: school as a place where knowledge is didactically dispensed and passively acquired, something found principally in books, something that comes from authorities.

But if gaining knowledge really is a fundamental goal of education — and all curricula say it is — then most students should be spending most of their time actively reasoning. That is, most of the students most of the time should be gathering, analyzing, and assessing information. They should be considering alternative competing interpretations and theories. They should be identifying and questioning assumptions, advancing reasons, devising hypotheses, thinking up ways to experiment and test their beliefs. They should be following out implications, analyzing concepts, considering objections. They should be testing their ideas against the ideas of others. They should be sympathetically entering opposing points of view. They should be role playing reasoning different from their own. In short, they should be *reasoning dialogically and dialectically.*

Only when students have a rich diet of dialogical and dialectical thought, do they become prepared for the messy, multi-dimensional real world, where opposition, conflict, critique, and contradiction are everywhere. Only through a rigorous exposure to dialogical and dialectical thinking, do students develop intellectually fit minds.

ABSOLUTISTIC THINKING IN EARLY SCHOOL YEARS

Young children do not recognize that they have a point of view. Rather, they tend to make absolute judgments about themselves and others. They are not usually given an opportunity to rationally develop their own thoughts. Their capacity to judge reasons and evidence is usually not cultivated. Their intellectual growth is stunted.

As a result, young children uncritically internalize images and concepts of what they and others are like, of what, for example, Americans are like, of what atheists, Christians, communists, parents, children, business-people, farmers, liberals, conservatives, left-wingers, right-wingers, salespeople, foreigners, patriots, Palestinians, Kiwanis Club members, cheerleaders, politicians, Nazis, ballet dancers, terrorists, union leaders, guerrillas, freedom fighters, doctors, Marines, scientists, mathematicians, contractors, waitresses, are like. They then ego-identify with their conceptions, which they assume to be accurate, spontaneously using them as guides in their day-to-day decision making.

Children need assignments in multilogical issues to break out of their uncritical absolutism. They need to discover opposing points of view in nonthreatening situations. They need to put their ideas into words, advance conclusions, and justify them. They need to discover their own assumptions as well as the assumptions of others. They need to discover their own inconsistencies as well as the inconsistencies of others. They do this best when they learn how to role-play the thinking of others, advance conclusions other than their own, and construct reasons to support them. Children need to do this for the multilogical issues — issues involving conflicting points of view, interpretations, and conclusions — that they inevitably face in their everyday lives. But they also need to do so for the disciplined monological questions that they must of necessity approach from within the context of their own undisciplined minds.

Because children are not exposed to dialogical and dialectical activities, children do not learn how to read, write, think, listen, or speak in such a way as to rationally organize and express what they believe. They do not learn how uncritically they are responding to the mass media nor to what extent it is reinforcing their subconscious egocentric or sociocentric views. They feel deeply primarily about egocentric concerns, justifying getting what they want, and avoiding what they do not want. If school is to prepare students for life as it is, if it is to empower children to become rational persons, it must cultivate dialogical engagement and reasoned judgment from the outset.

FACT, OPINION, AND REASONED JUDGMENT

When critical thinking is introduced into the classroom — and very often it is not — it is often approached monologically, for example, by having students divide a set of statements into "facts" and "opinions".

Unfortunately, a taxonomy that divides all beliefs into either facts or opinions leaves out the most important category: reasoned judgment. Most important issues are not simply matters of fact, nor are they essentially matters of faith, taste, or preference. They are matters that call for reasoned reflection. They are matters that can be understood from different points of view through different frames of reference. We can, and many different people do, approach them with different assumptions, ideas and concepts, priorities, and ends in view. The tools of critical thinking enable us to grasp genuine strengths and weaknesses in thought only when they are analytically applied to divergent perspectives in dialectical contexts. Dialogical and dialectical experience enables us to develop a sense of what is most reasonable. Monological rules do not.

For example, it is exceedingly difficult to judge the case made by a prosecutor in a trial until we have heard the arguments for the defense. Only by stepping out of the perspective of the prosecutor and actually organizing the evidence in language designed to make the strongest case for the defense can we begin to grasp the true strength and weakness of the prosecutor's case.

This approach is the only proper way to deal with the important issues we face in our lives, and I am amazed that we and our textbooks refuse to recognize it. The most basic issues simply do not reduce to unadulterated fact or arbitrary opinion. True, they often have a factual dimension. But characteristically, some of what is apparently empirically true is also arguable. And we are often faced with the problem of deciding which facts are most important, which should be made central, and which should be deemed peripheral or even irrelevant. Finally, despite the common view, facts do not speak for themselves. They must be rendered meaningful by interpretation, by explanation, by construal. Make your own list of the ten most important issues and see if this is not true (but beware, of course, the tendency to see your own answers to these issues as self-evident facts!).

✦ Part II: Pedagogy

Everyday life, in contrast to school, is filled with multilogical problems for which there are competing answers and so require dialogical thinking. Furthermore, even when subject matter can be algorithmically and monologically expressed, students need to approach that subject matter through dialogical thought which brings their own thinking into play. Teachers do not, by and large, recognize these facts, nor when it is pointed out to them, do they know how to take them into account in the classroom. Being habituated to didactic instruction, dialogical instruction that does not result in predictable "correct" answers is a puzzle to them. They do not know how to foster it. They do not know how to assess it. They do not know how to use it to aid students in mastering content.

There are four interrelated things teachers need to learn: *1)* how to identify and distinguish multilogical from monological problems and issues, *2)* how to teach Socratically, *3)* how to use dialogical and dialectical thought to master content, and *4)* how to assess dialogical and dialectical thought. I should add that one does not master these understandings overnight, but only by degrees over an extended period of time. They cannot be taught, for example, in a one-day workshop. Let us consider each of these four learnings in order.

LEARNING TO IDENTIFY AND DISTINGUISH MULTILOGICAL FROM MONOLOGICAL PROBLEMS AND ISSUES

This involves distinguishing problems for which there is an established step-by-step procedure for solving them — What is the square root of 653? What is the boiling point of water? In what year did the American revolution begin? — from problems and issues that can be analyzed from different points of view leading to multiple competing answers, resolutions, or solutions — Was the American revolution justified? Should the colonists have used violence to achieve their ends? When should you conform to group pressure and when should you resist that pressure? What is the meaning of this story? What would a true friend do in this situation? What caused WWII? Could it have been avoided? How important is it to get a good education? How important is it to make a lot of money? Is money the root of all evil? What kind of a person are you? What are America's real values? How can you tell what to believe and what not to believe? These kinds of questions, we should note, can be raised from the earliest school years: Who was right in your argument with your sister, she or you? When should you share your toys? Was it right for Jack (in "Jack and the Bean Stalk") to take the golden eggs and the harp as well? Should the big Billy Goat have killed the Troll (in "Billy Goat Gruff")? Is this the best rule to have to avoid accidents in the playground or can you think of a better one? Do the advertisements on TV for toys give you good information about toys, or do they mislead you about them?

Of course, though there are multiple conflicting answers possible to multilogical questions, it does not follow that each is *equally* defensible or *equally* rational. The whole point of considering the reasoning behind conflicting positions is to assess their relative merits and debits in a rational way. After analysis and dialogue, we may be able to rule out some as simplistic, recognize the partiality of others, and gain some sense of what a deeper response to the issue would include. We will come out with better answers, if not *the* answer.

SOCRATIC QUESTIONING AND DIALOGICAL DISCUSSION

Dialogical discussion will naturally occur if teachers learn to stimulate student thinking through Socratic questioning. This consists in teachers wondering aloud about the meaning and truth of students' responses to questions. The Socratic teacher models a reflective, analytic listener. One that actively pursues clarity of expression. One that actively looks for evidence and reasons. One that actively considers alternative points of view. One that actively tries to reconcile differences of viewpoint. One that actively tries to find out not just what people think but whether what they think is actually so.

Socratic discussion allows students to develop and evaluate their thinking in comparison to that of other students. Since inevitably students respond to Socratic questions within their own points of view, the discussion inevitably becomes multi-dimensional.

By routinely raising root questions and root ideas in a classroom setting, multiple points of view get expressed, but in a context in which the seminal ideas, which must be mastered to master the content, are deeply considered and their interrelationships established.

Over time, students learn from Socratic discussions a sense of intellectual discipline and thoroughness. They learn to appreciate the power of logic and logical thinking. They learn that all thoughts can be pursued in at least four directions:

> 1) *Their origin:* How did you come to think this? Can you remember the circumstances in which you formed this belief?

2) *Their support:* Why do you believe this? Do you have any evidence for this? What are some of the reasons why people believe this? In believing this aren't you assuming that such and so is true? Is that a sound assumption do you think?

3) *Their conflicts with other thoughts:* Some people might object to your position by saying .... How would you answer them? What do you think of this contrasting view? How would you answer the objection that ...? and,

4) *Their implications and consequences:* What are the practical consequences of believing this? What would we have to do to put it into action? What follows from the view that ...? Wouldn't we also have to believe that ... in order to be consistent? Are you implying that ...?

Before a Socratic discussion, teachers should pre-think the issues and connections that underlie the area or subject to be discussed. Whenever possible they should figure out in advance what the fundamental ideas are and how they relate to fundamental problems. For example, before leading a Socratic discussion on the question "What is history?", teachers should pre-think the issue so that they are clear about the essential insights that the Socratic discussion is to foster, for example, that history is selective (it is not possible to include all of the past in a book), that historians make value judgments about what to include and exclude, that history is written from a point of view, and that historians with different view points often come to different historical judgments. Teachers should also recognize various related insights, for example, that all human thinking has a historical dimension (in that all our thinking is shaped by our life and times), that memory is a kind of internal historian, that the news is like the history of yesterday, that gossip is a form of historical thought, etc. This pre-thinking enables teachers to look for opportunities in discussion to help students to make connections and see the implications of their own thinking about history and things historical. Through Socratic discussion we do not teach students *our* view of history, but the ingredients in all historical views, however they may be particularized.

Of course, teachers must also follow up on the insights that are fostered through Socratic discussion. Hence, once a Socratic discussion has been held on the nature of history, students should be encouraged to raise questions about their history text. (What sorts of things would you guess were left out of this account of the battle? What point of view does the writer seem to have? Which of the sentences in this paragraph state facts? Which of the sentences interpret the facts or draw a conclusion from them? If you were a Native American do you think you would agree with this conclusion in your history text?...) Students should also have follow-up assignments which require them to further develop the insights being fostered. (For example, "I'd like each of you to imagine that you are one of the colonists loyal to the king and to write one paragraph in which you list your reasons why you think that armed revolution is not justified.")

No matter how much pre-thinking has been done, however, actual Socratic discussion will proceed, not in a predictable or straightforward direction, but in a criss-crossing, back-and-forth movement. Because Socratic instructors continually encourage the students to explore how what they think about x relates to what they think about y and z, students' thinking moves back and forth between their own basic ideas and those being presented by the other students, between their own ideas and those expressed in a book or story, between their own thinking and their own experience, between ideas within one domain and those in another, in short, between any of a variety of perspectives. This dialogical process will sometimes become dialectical when ideas clash or are inconsistent.

USING COOPERATIVE LEARNING TO FOSTER DIALOGICAL AND DIALECTICAL THINKING

Cooperative Learning fosters dialogical and dialectical thinking since individual students will inevitably have different points of view and will need to argue out those differences. The key is students learning to assess their own thinking so that they can make logical choices among the various proposals and suggestions they meet in cooperative learning. For example, we want students in cooperative groups to Socratically question each other in a supportive way. We want them to develop confidence in their capacity to reason together to find insightful answers to important questions. To do this they must probe each other's thinking for its support and implications. Along the way they must develop a sensitivity to what they and others are assuming. Most importantly if cooperative learning is not to be *cooperative mis-learning*, it is essential that students learn how to bring intellectual standards into their work, how to hold themselves and their classmates to standards of good reasoning and analysis.

ASSESSING DIALOGICAL AND DIALECTICAL THINKING

Since dialogical and dialectical activities focus on the process rather than the product of thinking, it is essential that both students and teachers learn how to assess thought processes. To do this it is essential that definite standards for thinking be established. Unfortunately, few teachers have had an education that emphasized the universal standards for thought. This deficiency is linked with the fact that the logic of thinking is not presently emphasized in schooling. Teachers must learn — while already in the classroom — how to distinguish and explain the difference between clear and unclear, precise and imprecise, specific and vague, relevant and irrelevant, consistent and inconsistent, logical and illogical, deep and superficial, complete and incomplete, significant and trivial, openminded and biased, adequate and inadequate ... reasoning and expression. Students, in turn, need to recognize their responsibility to express themselves in reasoning that is as clear, precise, specific, accurate, relevant, consistent, logical, deep, complete, and openminded as possible, irrespective of the subject matter. These are deep and substantial, even revolutionary, understandings. They provide an entirely new perspective on what knowledge and learning are all about.

How to Use Dialogical and Dialectical Thinking to Master Content

Because students do not come to the classroom with blank slates for minds, because their thinking is already developing in a direction, because they have already formed ideas, assumptions, beliefs, and patterns of inference, because they can learn new ideas, assumptions, and beliefs only through the scaffolding of their previously formed thinking, it is essential that dialogical and dialectical thinking form the core of their learning. There is no way around the need of minds to think their way to knowledge. Knowledge is discovered by thinking, analyzed by thinking, interpreted by thinking, organized by thinking, extended by thinking, and assessed by thinking. There is no way to take the thinking out of knowledge, neither is there a way to create a direct step-by-step path to knowledge that all minds can follow. In science classes students should be learning how to think scientifically, in math classes how to think mathematically, in history classes how to think historically, and so forth. It is scientific thinking that produces scientific knowledge, mathematical thinking that produces mathematical knowledge, historical thinking that produces historical knowledge. Dialogical exchange and dialectical clash are integral to the acquisition of all these forms of knowledge. To this day we have refused to face this reality.

Conclusion

Dialogical thinking refers to thinking that involves a dialogue or extended exchange between different points of view, cognitive domains, or frames of reference. Whenever we consider concepts or issues deeply, we naturally explore their connections to other ideas and issues within different domains or points of view. Critical thinkers need to be able to engage in fruitful, exploratory dialogue, proposing ideas, probing their roots, considering subject matter insights and evidence, testing ideas, and moving between various points of view. Socratic questioning is one form of dialogical thinking.

Dialectical thinking refers to dialogical thinking conducted in order to test the strengths and weaknesses of opposing points of view. Court trials and debates are dialectical in form and intention. They pit idea against idea, reasoning against counter-reasoning in order to get at the truth of a matter. As soon as we begin to explore ideas, we find that some clash or are inconsistent with others. If we are to integrate our thinking, we need to assess which of the conflicting ideas we will accept and which reject, or which parts of the views are strong and which weak, or, if neither, how the views can be reconciled. Students need to develop dialectical reasoning skills, so that their thinking moves comfortably between divergent points of view or lines of thought, assessing the relative strengths and weaknesses of the evidence or reasoning presented. Dialectical thinking can be practiced whenever two conflicting points of view, arguments, or conclusions are under discussion.

Because at present both teachers and students are largely unpracticed in either dialogical or dialectical thinking, it is important to move instruction in this direction slowly and carefully as part of a reflectively designed, long-term staff development plan, one with a sufficiently rich theoretical base and pedagogical translation to allow for individual teachers to proceed at their own rates. I recommend an approach that focuses on lesson remodeling and redesign, and have written four books to aid teachers in this redesign of instruction. Nevertheless, most teachers need to work with other teachers to carry through needed reforms. They need to work together with much encouragement and many incentives. Very few districts have taken up the challenge. Most have created the mere appearance of change. In most, didacticism remains — unchallenged in its arrogance, in its self-deception, and in its fruitlessness.

Chapter 16

The Art of Redesigning Instruction

Abstract

This paper is divided into two parts. The first part is entitled, "Why Should We Redesign Instruction?" Paul begins with an argument as to why reasoning should be recognized to be the essential mode of learning, for, only if we are reasoning while we are learning, do we truly figure out what we are striving to learn, and, thereby, truly make it our own. Paul extends the argument by suggesting that in a literal sense no one can teach us anything of importance, again, because reasoning is essential to quality learning and no one can reason for us. The best they can do is reason in front of us. Paul then discusses addictive and pseudo-learning and links them to the theme of the paper.

With this background established, Paul argues for three dimensions essential to education for reasoning: learning the principles that underlie reasoning, learning the moves that those principles define, and learning the standards that one must use to assess reasoning. He then extends this analysis to include the basic elements of reasoning (the source of critical thinking moves), the abilities intrinsic to reasoning (which are the basic moves), the modes of reasoning (patterned sequences of moves), the abilities as regulated by traits of mind (the attributes that motivate making the moves), and intellectual standards (the standards used to assess the moves). He provides an extended analysis of reading as a mode of reasoning.

The second part of the paper is entitled, "How Do We Redesign Instruction?" As you might expect, the idea of redesign follows from the argument developed in the first half of the paper. The crucial question for redesign is "How can I get my students to reason more and reason better?" As a teacher, you should be interested in the basic elements of reasoning "because they represent both a basic orientation and a resource for fundamental moves in reasoning". You will be interested in the component critical thinking abilities "because they represent the kinds of moves you want students to master". You will be interested in the modes of reasoning (reading, writing, speaking, and listening, for example) "because one cannot learn to reason without them."

Paul then provides a model for "Six Forms of Decision-Making in Designing Instruction", a sample redesigned lesson, a section on patterns in teaching, and a section on general recommendations for instruction. Paul's approach to the redesign of instruction "presupposes intellectual development on three fronts, a growing recognition of: 1) what is wrong with didactic instruction, 2) the nature and dimensions of critical thinking, and 3) pedagogical strategies that can be used to effectively integrate critical thinking into instruction (based on 1 and 2)."

✦✦ Why Should We Redesign Instruction?

THE PROBLEM OF "MOTHER ROBIN TEACHING"

*B*oth teaching and learning today are desperately in need of restructuring. However, grasping the how and why of it requires rare
insight into what is wrong with instruction: what is wrong with the way
teachers typically go about teaching, and what is wrong with the way students typically go about learning. The essential insight requires understanding of the dual roles that teaching and learning can play in the lives
of our students and how those roles correlate with very different, sometimes opposing, realities.

The most important starting point for that understanding is given in
the following truth: teaching, learning, and knowledge can be either
lower order or higher order, fragmented or organized, surface or deep.
Though all teachers, in theory, aspire to teaching so that students gain
higher order, organized, deep knowledge, the effect of most teaching is
otherwise: lower order, fragmented, superficial, and often transitory. A
significant part of this problem is due to what might be called "mother
robin teaching".

When we teach in "mother robin" fashion — trying to mentally chew
up everything for our students so we can put it into their intellectual
beaks to swallow — students tend to become, if I can slightly mix my
metaphor, "polly parrot" learners:

"I can't understand anything unless you tell me exactly how and what
to say and think. I need you to figure out everything for me. I shouldn't
have to do more than repeat what you and the textbook say."

Unfortunately, the more students grow in this direction, the more
teachers try to amplify their mother robin teaching to accommodate it.
Growth on either side produces a compensating growth on the other. By
the middle school level, most students are deeply entrenched in learning,
and teachers in teaching, nothing but lower order, fragmented, surface
knowledge. Teachers feel by this level that they have no choice but to
think for their students, or worse, that they should not require any thinking at all, that students are not really capable of it.

Rarely do students learn to reason well once such mutually-reinforcing,
lower order habits develop. Rarely do they integrate what they are learning into what they already know or believe. Rarely do they learn to grapple with, or grasp the logic of, what they are learning. Content comes and
goes as something independent of thought, dissociated from active
engagement, from give-and-take, from disciplined reading, writing,
speaking, or listening. Intellectual paralysis sets in. The trance-like state
that students bring typically to class becomes permanent.

THE SOLUTION: REASONING AS A MODE OF LEARNING

To learn how to teach critically, teachers must abandon mother robin teaching and make every effort to discourage polly parrot learning. To learn to think critically, students must learn to use reasoning as a pervasive tool of learning.

What is reasoning? Expressed most simply, it is the art of "figuring things out for yourself". It begins when we, in effect, say to ourselves something like this:

"Let's see, how can I understand this? Is it to be understood on the model of this experience or that? Shall I think of it in this way or that? Let me see. Ah, I think I see. It is just so... but, no, not exactly. Let me try again. Perhaps I can understand it from this point of view, by interpreting it thus. OK, now I think I am getting it...."

When we reason we puzzle something out, work out our understanding of it in relationship to what we already know. Reasoning contrasts, therefore, with thoughtlessly accepting what others say. It intrinsically involves *testing as we learn* to see if this or that is so. There are two ways we go about testing as we learn, and the two often work together: physical testing and mental testing. We physically test things by trying them out in the physical world. We mentally test things by trying them out in our minds. Hence we test ideas and beliefs by ideas, beliefs, and experiences we already have. For example, you tell me that you've just met a really *perfect* person and I, by thinking of my experience of people and my conception of human nature, inwardly decide that what you are saying *cannot be true*. I have tested out what you said in my mind and what you said "failed" the test.

In everyday life, of course, we continually have to figure things out for ourselves — for example, what our mothers, fathers, brothers and sisters, friends and acquaintances are *really* like, how to deal with personal and social problems, how to get what we want and avoid what we don't want. We are forced to develop theories about the world we live in and, of course, to test them in the crucible of day by day experience. Admittedly, our tests are often ill-conceived, our criteria often irrational. Nevertheless, there is a difference between what we personally reason through and what we mindlessly take in.

There are things, of course, we don't have to figure out for ourselves, that we can pick up merely by dint of lower order absorption and blind imitation. Much of this may, of course, be dysfunctional in some respects even as it is functional in others: for example, learning to be aggressive or passive, to attack or flee, to express ourselves outwardly or to "keep it all in".

There are still other learnings between the two extremes of the thoughtful and thoughtless: things which we figure out partially by ourselves through reasoning — physical or mental testing — and partially through others by mindless imitation. The reasoned and the unreasoned are thus sometimes combined.

✦ Learning from Others vs. Learning for Yourself

Very significant consequences follow from how students learn. The depth with which they understand anything is in direct proportion to the degree to which they have engaged in intellectual labor to figure it out *for* themselves. Whatever is to have meaning *to them* must be given meaning *by them*. They must work new meanings into the network of meanings they already have. They must relate new experiences to experiences they have already had. They must relate new problems to problems they have already solved. To create new meanings, to understand new experiences, to solve new problems, they must actively and intellectually participate in the "figuring out" process, going up and back between what they have already figured out and what they have not. They must do intellectual work. They must *reason to learn* — and to learn *well* they must *reason well*.

THE ADDICTIVE ILLUSION OF LEARNING FROM OTHERS

Of course, there are limited ways in which it is possible to learn things from others. Others can often help us get started. They can frequently point to or model the way. They can create environments which help shorten the "figuring out" process. The anchor point is this: There is no way to teach *that which requires understanding* so as to eliminate the "figuring out" process for the learner. When a teaching mode attempts to by-pass the processes by which each person individually figures things out, a mere illusion of learning takes place. When students do not engage in intellectual labor, they do not meaningfully learn, their learning is falsified.

Pseudo-learning mimics genuine learning. For example, students have not really learned why the earth spins on its axis if, in the last analysis, they believe that it does because their sixth grade teacher said it does. Neither do they understand because they memorized, but can't explain in their own words, the explanation in their sixth grade science text. They understand if and only if they can think it through for themselves in terms, and in the light of experiences, meaningful to each of them individually. Good teachers arrange circumstances and design activities to facilitate this process of "thinking something through". Nevertheless, there is no way on this earth or in the heavens above to eliminate the need for the process to be significantly structured by the active intellectual labor of the learner.

Pseudo-learning is addictive precisely because it appears to provide substantial learning with little effort. It seems genuine — when only parroted responses are called for. It seems substantial — as long as no one asks the students to explain what they have learned in their own words. It seems easy — as long as no one figures out how much time is wasted teaching the same content over and over and how little students retain after their schooling is completed.

This is the most fundamental problem in education today, that most teaching fosters various forms of pseudo-learning. It is because of pseudo-learning that most elementary students add, subtract, multiply, or divide when given the following "problem": "There are 75 sheep in the field and 5 sheep dogs. How old is the shepherd?" It is because of pseudo-learning that this tendency increases the more math instruction the students asked this question have had. It is because of pseudo-learning that most students are unable to explain in their own words what makes a scientific experiment scientific. It is because of pseudo-learning that most students are unable to solve problems that require more than one inference. It is because of pseudo-learning that students soon lose interest in the subjects they are "studying." (Who wants to study what one is not understanding?)

Most teaching attempts to achieve success without realistically taking into account the only conditions under which students can *genuinely* learn — and that is when they think things through for themselves. What most teachers fail to recognize, then, is that *students* (in the last analysis) *must teach themselves.*

Good teachers are not persons who know how to get students to learn without having to think. They are persons who know how to create conditions and activities, incentives and opportunities, in which those willing to think things through for themselves can achieve what they will. The statement "If you really knew how to teach, all your students would learn well and deeply" is as false as the statement: "If you really want to, you can by-pass the need for students to think for themselves. There are ways to teach which automatically inject knowledge, understanding, and skill into people without their active involvement or interested consent. Knowledge can be force-fed if you really know how to teach effectively."

Make no mistake; mother robins can be very useful to baby robins. But let us also not forget that baby robins are hungry when fed and instinctively swallow what is put into their beaks. And more. If mother robins never pushed their babies out of the nest, or expected them to do their own digging for worms, or their own chewing once found, neither they nor their species could or would survive.

Figuring things out has a crucial role in learning the simple and the complicated, the surface and the deep, the theoretical and the applied. Only a few things can be learned with a minimum of reasoning (e.g., copying the shapes of letters and numbers for the first time, practicing how to tie our shoes, learning to throw and catch a fluff ball, putting different colored objects into different colored boxes). And even though quite a few things, once learned, can be done more or less automatically and robotically — walking up and down stairs, riding a bicycle, eating with knife and fork, driving along a largely empty freeway, carrying the trash out to the trash bin — very often thoughtful interventions are essential to avoid unpredicted negatives: drunk drivers, slippery steps, holes in the road, and defective trash bags.

Furthermore, most of the curriculum of schools as well as most of the philosophy that accompanies that curriculum, if taken seriously, cannot legitimately be reduced to what can be learned automatically and robotically. Most of it, to be genuinely — i.e., meaningfully — learned, requires a lot of "figuring out" of things, a lot of good reasoning, a great deal of testing, much intellectual work. Unfortunately, research and experience tell us that good reasoning is about the last thing to expect in the typical classroom on a typical day.

There are a number of reasons for this. Most teachers are not aware of the nature and importance of reasoning — most teaching being a variation on a "mother robin" theme. And even when teachers do assign reasoning they frequently do not understand how to assess it appropriately. The result is that students rely on variations of "polly parrot" learning and save their reasoning for situations in which they must figure out how to subjectively please their teachers. ("I try to agree with my teachers, to say what pleases them.")

What Do Students Need to Learn, to Learn How to Reason Well?

We can best understand what is involved in teaching students to reason well by clarifying first what learning to reason is like. We can gain some leverage on this understanding by considering how reasoning well is analogous to doing a wide variety of things well.

Whenever one develops interrelated skills and abilities, there are three dimensions involved:

1) *broad principles* that articulate what is desirable, in general, in the light of the goals,

2) *skilled "moves"* based on "principles" that learners must practice in settings that enable them to assess the effectiveness of their performance by...

3) *appropriate "standards"*.

Unfortunately, we are more familiar with the mastery of skilled moves and strategies in the physical than in the intellectual domain. We are much better at disciplining our bodies than our minds. Let us therefore build an initial concept on this familiarity with the physical. If we keep in mind at least one clear example of the interrelation of *principles, moves,* and *standards* as formulated below, we will then have a benchmark in mind to guide us in thinking about the principles, moves, and standards to be learned in the art of reasoning well.

If students seek to join basketball, soccer, football, or tennis teams, they are well aware of the need to understand thoroughly the object of the game, the principles of sound play, the strategies and moves based on those principles, and the appropriate way to self-assess their moves in play. For example, for students to develop basketball skills and abilities, they must be willing to learn such principles as "square yourself to the basket whenever making a shot".

To learn this principle they practice by the hour doing what it calls for — squaring themselves to the basket — whenever they shoot. They also learn to integrate the skilled use of this move into a variety of strategic situations on the court. They do this with a combination of theoretical discussions and practical applications. They talk a lot about how to play the game — how to make this or that move, how to work with this or that strategy, how to counter this or that opposing strategy. And they spend a lot of time actually playing the game, trying in the process to put good theory into practice. They also spend considerable time critiquing their performance, making reference to the standards of excellent performance, as well as to the moves, principles, and strategies intrinsic to that excellence.

In tennis, students learn such principles as "always return to the ready position at the center of the court", "keep your weight distributed", "bend your knees when stroking the ball", "follow through whenever possible", "watch the ball closely when you hit it", and so forth. These principles are translated into moves on the court which are subject to assessment using the standards and strategies of good tennis play.

In learning ballet, one learns ballet principles, ballet moves, and ballet standards. In learning chess, one learns chess principles, chess moves and strategies, and chess standards. In learning architecture, one learns the principles of architecture, strategies and moves in design, and design assessment. In domain after domain, this same general pattern prevails. It holds as well for the art of sound reasoning, the art of disciplining the mind.

CRITICAL THINKING: THE ART OF TAKING CHARGE OF YOUR MIND

Learning to think critically, and to reason well as a result, is the intellectual analog of learning to play basketball, tennis, or chess well. It is analogous to learning how to dance ballet or do architecture well. As in the other domains, there are general principles and strategies intrinsic to the doing of it. There are skilled "moves" — critical thinking moves — to be learned. One must find the time to practice the moves, to talk about the principles that underlie them, to critique and assess one's own, and others', use of them. One must commit oneself to standards — intellectual standards. One must not only practice, but strive continually for excellence in practice. One must be willing to make mistakes and to learn from one's mistakes, to grow progressively in ability over an extended period of time. Insightfully conceived instruction is designed to create all of the above conditions: to facilitate students' learning the general principles and strategies intrinsic to the disciplined mastery of a body of content; to facilitate students' actively making critical thinking moves in reading, writing, speaking, and listening; to facilitate students' talking about intellectual standards, assessing their own and other students' reasoning; and to facilitate students' intellectual development over an extended period of time.

✦ What Does a Mind Need to Know About Itself to Reason Well?

It is important, then, to understand our minds as a potential repository of intellectual skills and abilities, of capacities that can be disciplined by critical thinking principles, strategies, and moves, and to begin to see why the mastery of reasoning is intrinsic to the task of taking charge of our mind and thus taking personal responsibility for the quality of our own thinking. To do this we must develop an interest in all of the components of reasoned thought:

1) basic *elements* (the source of critical thinking moves),

2) the elements combined into *abilities* (which are the basic moves),

3) the abilities in *modes of reasoning* (a patterned sequence of moves as in reading critically or writing critically or questioning Socratically, etc.)

4) the abilities as regulated by *traits* of mind (the attributes that motivate making the moves), and

5) intellectual *standards* (the standards used to assess the moves).

Each of these dimensions of reasoning is explained briefly in what follows. Each is discussed in the light of the role it plays in the intelligent redesign of instruction. Once we whet your appetite and provide some initial basis for seeing why it is that teachers tend to find it difficult both to develop assignments that require student reasoning and to assess the students' "reasoning" once completed, the stage will then be set for understanding how to go about redesigning instruction.

THE BASIC BUILDING BLOCKS OF REASONING: MASTERING THE ART OF BREAKING REASONING DOWN INTO ITS COMPONENT PARTS

As students of the art of reasoning, we must learn to take our thinking apart at the seams, to see the nuts and bolts of it, the very stuff, the elementary stuff, out of which critical thinking moves are inevitably structured. This includes nine elements:

a) the purpose that guides it

b) the questions or problems on which it is focused

c) the information it gathers and uses

d) the ideas and concepts by which it shapes the information it uses

e) the conclusions and interpretations to which it comes

f) the reasons it gives in justification

g) whatever it takes for granted

h) whatever it implies (or leads to in the way of consequences)

i) the point of view in which it is embedded as a whole

If we want to develop as critical thinkers, we need to develop an interest in making moves that probe these basic structures implicit in all our reasoning. Let me illustrate. As good reasoners we should be ever ready and disposed to probe our thinking with questions like the following, each of which constitutes a critical thinking move:

a) What am I trying to accomplish?

b) What problem or problems am I solving?

c) What information do I need and where can I get it?

d) What basic concepts do I need to clarify and carefully use?

e) What conclusion or conclusions shall I come to?

f) What do I base those conclusions on?

g) What am I taking for granted? Should I?

h) What is implied in my reasoning? To what consequences does it lead?

i) From what point of view am I reasoning? Do I need to consider others?

These are some of the most basic and fundamental considerations continually used by good reasoners to keep their reasoning functioning well.

Each of the elements of thought defines a domain of "moves" that good critical thinkers effectively make. There are a variety of moves one can make concerning one's purpose, a variety concerning the question at issue, a variety concerning information, etc.

SYNTHESIS: MASTERING THE MOVES THAT PUT THE PARTS OF REASONING TOGETHER

Each of these elements becomes a focus of skill and ability. Each becomes a shaping force in the nature of reasoning. By taking these elements into account in a variety of orchestrated ways, we are able to articulate a variety of important critical thinking moves in the process of figuring things out. We learn how to:

• uncover significant similarities and differences

• recognize contradictions, inconsistencies, and double standards

• refine generalizations and avoid oversimplifications

• create concepts, arguments, or theories

• clarify issues, conclusions, or beliefs

• clarify and analyze the meanings of words or phrases

• develop criteria for evaluation: clarify values and standards

• evaluate the credibility of sources of information

• compare analogous situations: transfer insights to new contexts

• compare and contrast ideals with actual practice

- analyze or evaluate arguments, interpretations, beliefs, or theories
- generate or assess solutions
- analyze or evaluate actions or policies
- rethink our thinking: metacognition
- question deeply: raise and pursue root or significant questions
- make interdisciplinary connections
- explore thoughts underlying feelings and feelings underlying thoughts
- design and carry out tests of concepts, theories, and hypotheses
- reason dialogically: compare perspectives, interpretations, or theories
- reason dialectically: evaluate perspectives, interpretations, or theories

Each of these abilities, depending upon the context and mode in which it is carried out, becomes a constituent in even larger structures of reasoning. We will touch upon these next.

MODES OF REASONING: LARGER STRUCTURES OF REASONING

All of the many component abilities of critical thinking, and the variety of critical thinking moves they presuppose, can be orchestrated in a number of basic ways. For example, reading, writing, speaking, and listening are four modes of reasoning. We reason while we do them and we use any of the full variety of critical thinking abilities and moves in the process. For example, if we were reading a book we might begin, for example, by trying to figure out the author's purpose in writing the book. In doing this we might make the following moves: What does the title of the book tell me about the purpose? What can I learn from the preface and introduction? Once we began to figure out the purpose, we might try to figure out the main question at issue and the main conclusion developed in relation to that question. Following any of a number of possible strategies, we would continue to reason through the text.

Consider the following example of two students engaged in reading a text. This example is taken from an important article by Stephen Norris and Linda Phillips ("Explanations of Reading Comprehension: Schema Theory and Critical Thinking Theory" in *Teachers' College Record*, Volume 89, Number 2, Winter 1987). Clearly the student who is reading the text well is reasoning his way through the text, carefully using the words of the text as "evidence" that must be taken into account in interpreting what the text means. We can see in these two readers a striking difference between good and bad reasoning embedded in the act of reading (the questions and commentaries within the text below are those of Norris and Phillips).

In what follows we will present, episode-by-episode, Steven's and Colleen's thinking aloud as they work through the passage. The experimenter's questions are given in brackets. We have chosen to make our example detailed, because we see this as the best route for providing specificity to otherwise vague generalizations about the relationship between reading and thinking. To simulate the task for you we present the passage without a title and one episode at a time, as was done with the children.

Episode 1

The stillness of the morning air was broken. The men headed down the bay.

Steven

The men were heading down the bay, I'm not sure why yet. It was a very peaceful morning. [Any questions?] No, not really. [Where do you think they're going?] I think they might be going sailing, water skiing, or something like that.

Colleen

The men are going shopping. [Why do you say that?] They're going to buy clothes at The Bay. [What is The Bay?] It's a shopping center. [Any questions?] No. [Where do you think they're going?] They're going shopping because it seems like they broke something.

Steven recognizes that there is insufficient information for explaining what the men are doing. On questioning, he tentatively suggests a couple of alternatives consistent with the information given, but indicates there are other possibilities. Colleen presents one explanation of the story, and seems fairly definite that the men are going to buy clothes at The Bay, a chain of department stores in Canada. On being queried she maintains her idea that the men are going shopping, but offers an explanation inconsistent with her first one that they are going to buy clothes. To do this she assumes that something concrete was broken, which could be replaced at The Bay.

Episode 2

The net was hard to pull. The heavy sea and strong tide made it even difficult for the girdie. The meshed catch encouraged us to try harder.

Steven

It was not a very good day as there were waves which made it difficult for the girdie. That must be some kind of machine for doing something. The net could be for pulling something out of the water like an old wreck. No, wait! It said "meshed catch." I don't know why but that makes me think of fish and, sure, if you caught fish you'd really want to get them. [Any questions?] No questions, just that I think maybe the girdie is a machine for helping the men pull in the fish or whatever it was. Maybe a type of pulley.

Colleen

I guess The Bay must have a big water fountain. [Why was the net hard to pull?] There's a lot of force on the water. [Why was it important for them to pull the net?] It was something they had to do. [What do you mean?] They had to pull the net and it was hard to do. [Any questions?] No. [Where do you think they're going?] Shopping.

For both children the interpretations of Episode 2 built on those of Episode 1. Steven continues to question what the men were doing. He raises a number of alternative interpretations dealing with the context of the sea. He refines his interpretations through testing hypothetical interpretations against specific details, and hypotheses of specific word meanings against his emerging interpretation of the story. At the outset he makes an inference that a girdie is a machine, but leaves details about its nature and function unspecified. He tentatively offers one specific use for the net, but immediately questions this use when he realizes that it will not account for the meshed catch, and substitutes an alternative function. He then confirms this interpretation with the fact from the story that the men were encouraged to try harder and his belief that if you catch fish you would really want to bring them aboard. Finally, he sees that he is in a position to offer a more definitive but tentative interpretation of the word girdie.

Colleen maintains her interpretation of going shopping at The Bay. When questioned about her interpretation, Colleen responds in vague or tautological terms. She seems not to integrate information relating to the terms net, catch, and sea, and she seemed satisfied to remain uninformed about the nature of the girdie and the reason for pulling the net. In the end, she concludes definitively that the men are going shopping.

Episode 3

With four quintels aboard, we were now ready to leave. The skipper saw mares' tails in the north.

Steven

I wonder what quintels are? I think maybe it's a sea term, a word that means perhaps the weight aboard. Yes maybe it's how much fish they had aboard. [So you think it was fish?] I think fish or maybe something they had found in the water but I think fish more because of the word "catch." [Why were they worried about the mares' tails?] I'm not sure. Mares' tails, let me see, mares are horses but horses are not going to be in the water. The mares' tails are in the north. Here farmers watch the north for bad weather, so maybe the fishermen do the same thing. Yeah, I think that's it, it's a cloud formation which could mean strong winds and hail or something which I think could be dangerous if you were in a boat and had a lot of weight aboard. [Any questions?] No.

Colleen
They were finished with their shopping and were ready to go home. [What did they have aboard?] Quintels. [What are quintels?] I don't know. [Why were they worried about the mares' tails?] There were a group of horses on the street and they were afraid they would attack the car. [Any questions?] No.

Steven is successful in his efforts to incorporate the new information into an evolving interpretation. From the outset Steven acknowledges that he does not know the meaning of quintel and seeks a resolution of this unknown. He derives a meaning consistent with his evolving interpretation and with the textual evidence. In his attempt to understand the expression *mares' tails* he first acknowledges that he does not know the meaning of the expression. Thence, he establishes what he does know from the background knowledge (mares are horses, horses are not going to be in the water, there is nothing around except sky and water, farmers watch the north for bad weather) and textual information (the men are on the bay, they have things aboard, the mares' tails are in the north) and inferences he has previously made (the men are in a boat, they are fishing). He integrates this knowledge into a comparison between the concerns of Alberta farmers with which he is familiar, and what he takes to be analogous concerns of fishermen. On seeing the pertinence of this analogy he draws the conclusion that the mares' tails must be a cloud formation foreboding inclement weather. He claims support for his conclusion in the fact that it would explain the skipper's concern for the mares' tails, indicating that he did not lose sight of the overall task of understanding the story.

Colleen maintains her original interpretation but does not incorporate all the new textual information into it. She works with the information on the men's leaving and the mares' tails, but appears to ignore or remain vague about other information. For example, she says the cargo was comprised of quintels but indicates no effort to determine what these things are. She cites the fact that the men were ready to leave and suggests that they have finished their shopping, but does not attempt to explain the use of such words as skipper, cargo, and aboard in the context of shopping for clothes. She interprets mares' tails as a group of horses that possibly would attack the men, but gives no account of what the horses might be doing on the street. Basically, she appears to grow tolerant of ambiguity and incompleteness in her interpretation.

Socratic questioning and role-playing are also modes of reasoning. The Socratic questioner orchestrates questioning in a variety of ways, using any of the full variety of critical thinking moves in the process. This is more obvious, of course, if we remember that typically Socratic questioning occurs during a discussion and therefore while both speaking and listening are going on. A similar point can be made for role-playing.

CRITICALITY, CREATIVITY, AND THE STANDARDS OF GOOD THINKING

Good thinking is thinking that does the job we set for it. It is thinking that figures things out, that poses problems to be solved and intricacies to reason through and then meets the challenge it has set itself with appropriate intellectual work. "Criticality" and "creativity" have an intimate relationship to this process. There is a natural marriage between them. Indeed, all thinking that is properly called "excellent" combines these two dimensions in an intimate way. Whenever our thinking excels, it excels because we succeed in designing or engendering, fashioning or originating, creating or producing results appropriate to our ends in thinking. It has, in a word, a creative dimension.

Like the body, the mind has its own form of fitness or excellence. Like the body, that fitness is caused by and reflected in activities done in accordance with standards (criticality). A fit mind can successfully engage in the designing, fashioning, formulating, originating, or producing of intellectual products worthy of its challenging ends. To achieve this fitness the mind must learn to take charge of itself, to energize itself, press forward when difficulties emerge, proceed slowly and methodically when meticulousness is necessary, immerse itself in a task, become attentive, reflective, and engrossed, circle back on a train of thought, re-check to ensure that it has been thorough, accurate, exact, and deep enough.

In a sense, of course, all minds create and produce in a manner reflective of their fitness or lack thereof. Minds indifferent to standards and judgment tend to judge inexactly, inaccurately, inappropriately, prejudicially. Prejudices, hate, irrational jealousies and fears, stereotypes and misconceptions — these too are "created", "produced", "originated" by minds. But they are not the products of "creative" minds. They reflect an undisciplined, an uncritical mode of thinking, and therefore are not properly thought of as products of "creativity". In short, except in rare circumstances, creativity presupposes criticality and criticality creativity.

INTELLECTUAL CHARACTER TRAITS

We can now begin to see why the mastery of reasoning is intrinsic to becoming a certain kind of person. At the highest level of development, the mastery of reasoning entails the development of a variety of interrelated character traits: intellectual humility, intellectual courage, intellectual perseverance, intellectual civility, intellectual integrity, intellectual curiosity, intellectual responsibility, intellectual autonomy, fairmindedness, and faith in reason.

Once we state the principles that underlie one of these traits, it becomes apparent what sort of critical thinking moves and strategies are intrinsic to them. Consider, for example, the principle behind intellectual humility:

> *Principle:* Awareness of the limits of one's knowledge, including sensitivity to circumstances in which one's native egocentrism is likely to function self-deceptively; sensitivity to bias and prejudice in, and limitations of one's viewpoint. Intellectual humility is based on the recognition that *no one should claim more than he or she actually knows.* It does not imply spinelessness or submissiveness. It implies the lack of intellectual pretentiousness, boastfulness, or conceit, combined with insight into the strengths or weaknesses of the logical foundations of one's beliefs: knowing what evidence one has, how one has come to believe, what further evidence one might look for or examine.

Given an understanding of and commitment to this principle, critical thinkers make moves such as the following. They question what they think they know. They admit the limitations of their knowledge. They readily admit to appropriate qualifications to their knowledge. They admit to mistakes when they make them. They modify their beliefs when the evidence requires such a modification. They listen with an open mind to people who have different experiences and perspectives. The acts of an intellectually humble mind readily lead to the expansion of knowledge and the development of insight. Needless to say, intellectual moves based on understanding the elements of thought, abilities, and modes are intrinsic to the development of these intellectual character traits.

✦✦ How Do We Redesign Instruction?

THE BASIC IDEA

The redesign of instruction is based upon a judgment as to what students are presently not learning that they should be learning. We have argued at length that the most fundamental failure in education is the failure to teach students to reason well. Reasoning, we have contended, is the only means by which people acquire knowledge, master content, and solve problems. If students become proficient in figuring things out — while reading, writing, speaking, and listening, while studying the subjects they should master, while tackling the problems of everyday life — then they get precisely what it is that schooling at its best should be "giving" them but is not.

As teachers, therefore, we should continually be asking:
How can I get my students to reason more and reason better?
How can I get my students when "studying" science to reason scientifically? How can I get them enthusiastic about and skilled in scientific reasoning? To pose scientific questions? To seek scientific data and information? To acquire scientific concepts? To question their non-scientific assumptions? To grasp scientific truths?

How can I get my students when "studying" math to reason mathematically? How can I get them enthusiastic about and skilled in mathematical reasoning? To pose mathematical questions? To seek mathematical data and information? To acquire mathematical concepts? To question their false mathematical assumptions? To grasp mathematical truths?

How can I get my students when "studying" history to reason historically? How can I get them enthusiastic about and skilled in historical reasoning? To pose historical questions? To seek historical data and information? To acquire historical concepts? To question their false historical assumptions? To grasp historical truths?

How can I get my students when "studying" geography to reason geographically? How can I get them enthusiastic about and skilled in geographical reasoning? To pose geographical questions? To seek geographical data and information? To acquire geographical concepts? To question their false geographical assumptions? To grasp geographical truths?

It is questions and concerns such as these that are essential to the successful redesign of instruction. If we put these questions continually at the center of our thinking as teachers, we will progressively move toward a model for instructional design and redesign which helps transform students into better thinkers and learners.

WHAT DOES THIS BASIC IDEA OF DESIGN ENTAIL?

If as a teacher you are continually concerned to get your students to reason while learning, in order to learn well and deeply, then you will be keenly interested in a variety of other concerns as a matter of course. You will be interested in *the basic elements of reasoning*, because they represent both a basic orientation and a resource for fundamental moves in reasoning. You will be interested in understanding the various *component critical thinking abilities*, because they represent the kinds of moves you want students to master. You will be interested in the *modes of reasoning* — reading, writing, speaking and listening — because one cannot learn without reasoning well within them. You will be interested in intellectual *traits of mind*, because without them students will be unmotivated to practice the abilities they initially learn. You will be interested in *intellectual criteria and standards*, because without them reasoning cannot be assessed. (See the figures on the following two pages: "Dimensions of Critical Thinking" and "A Selection of Critical Thinking Abilities".)

Dimensions of Critical Thinking

Elements of Reasoning

purpose or goalDimensions of Critical Thinking;intellectual abilities

problem or question at issue

empirical dimension

conceptual dimension

assumptions

conclusion, inference, or interpretation

implications and consequences

point of view or frame of reference

reasons

Intellectual Abilities

Identification & Recognition Abilities

Comprehension Abilities: Comparing & Clarifying

Application Abilities

Abilities of Analysis

Synthesis Abilities

Evaluation Abilities

Abilities to Create or Generate

(See next page for a list of some specific abilities)

Modes of Reasoning

reading critically

writing critically

speaking critically

listening critically

questioning Socratically: probing elements of thought

collaborative learning

role playing

Traits of Mind

intellectual independence

insight into egocentricity or sociocentricity

fairmindedness

intellectual humility and willingness to suspend judgment

intellectual courage

intellectual good faith or integrity

intellectual perseverance

confidence in reason

intellectual curiosity

intellectual civility

intellectual responsibility

intellectual discipline

intellectual empathy

Intellectual Standards

accurate

relevant

specific

clear

precise

plausible

consistent

logical

deep

broad

complete

significant

adequate

fair

A Selection of Critical Thinking Abilities

Identification & Recognition Abilities

identifying and recognizing elements of reasoning

uncovering significant similarities and differences

recognizing contradictions, inconsistencies, and double standards

Comprehension Abilities: Comparing & Clarifying

uncovering significant similarities and differences

refining generalizations and avoiding oversimplifications

clarifying and analyzing issues, conclusions, or beliefs

clarifying and analyzing the meanings of words or phrases

developing criteria for evaluation: clarifying values and standards

comparing and contrasting ideals with actual practice

reasoning dialogically: comparing perspectives, interpretations, or theories

Application Abilities

comparing analogous situations: transferring insights to new contexts

designing and carrying out tests of concepts, theories, and hypotheses

making interdisciplinary connections

Abilities of Analysis

clarifying and analyzing issues, conclusions, or beliefs

clarifying and analyzing the meanings of words or phrases

analyzing and evaluating arguments, interpretations, beliefs, or theories

analyzing and evaluating actions or policies

rethinking your thinking: metacognition

exploring thoughts underlying feelings and feelings underlying thoughts

Synthesis Abilities

reasoning dialogically: comparing perspectives, interpretations, or theories

comparing analogous situations: transferring insights to new contexts

making interdisciplinary connections

reasoning dialectically: evaluating perspectives, interpretations, or theories

Evaluation Abilities

refining generalizations and avoiding oversimplifications

comparing and contrasting ideals with actual practice

designing and carrying out tests of concepts, theories, and hypotheses

analyzing and evaluating arguments, interpretations, beliefs, or theories

analyzing and evaluating actions or policies

rethinking your thinking: metacognition

exploring thoughts underlying feelings and feelings underlying thoughts

reasoning dialectically: evaluating perspectives, interpretations, or theories

evaluating the credibility of sources of information

generating and assessing solutions

questioning deeply: raising and pursuing root or significant questions

Abilities to Create or Generate

designing and carrying out tests of concepts, theories, and hypotheses

generating and assessing solutions

creating concepts, arguments, or theories

Our idea for instructional design is built on a systematic approach that includes all of the dimensions above. The logic of the teaching process should reflect the logic by means of which students ought to learn.

✦ Six Forms of Decision-Making in Designing or Redesigning Instruction

There are six forms of decision-making in designing instruction:

I) Get Clear About What the Students Have to Reason About (the domain, the topic and the issue).

1) What is the domain about which the students will have to reason (e.g., within what subject or field: historical reasoning, economic reasoning, biological, anthropological, reasoning about a poem, about a short story, about...)?

2) Express, as specifically and as clearly as you can, the precise question at issue.

3) Ask yourself what sorts of things a person must do to reason well about this question (include here what sorts of facts persons must have, the understandings they must possess, the motivations or values they must have, the skills, etc.).

II) Find Something That Students Are Already Familiar With to Use as a Bridge or Crutch to Help Them Learn What They Are Not Familiar With

Decide where in their lives the students already deal with this question.

1) Once you have the problem or question-at-issue clearly in mind, scan the life-world of your students looking for questions in their lives that logically mirror or are analogous to the question at hand.

2) Two Back-Up Strategies: If for some reason you can't find a problem in the life-world of your students that mirrors the question at hand, consider two back-up strategies: *a)* Could you help them to reason to the answer on the basis of what they have already learned about the subject or *b)* Could you give them a group of examples from everyday life that they could examine and come to a conclusion about, pro or con?

III) Make Decisions About How You Are Going to Use Large and Small Groups

1) Typically you should begin with a large group Socratic discussion that helps the students to locate themselves with respect to the subject. Describe how you will do this.

2) As soon as the basic framework for the question is set in large group discussion, switch to small group discussion (groups of 3 or 4). The groups should have a specific amount of time and a specific task. They should have a clear sense of what is expected of them and of how they will have to report back.

3) You might from time to time have the groups report to another group, having the groups give feedback to each other. Describe.

IV) Get Clear About Assessment Issues

You should always think about how you are going to get the students to reason with discipline, how they are expected to get into the elements of what they are thinking about, how they are expected to use critical thinking abilities, what critical thinking standards are most important, and what traits can be cultivated. Decide on your overall plan for getting the students to reason with discipline in the lesson or unit, keeping in mind the major obstacles to disciplined reasoning about the topic.

V) Include Critical Writing as Well as Critical Speaking and Listening

The working groups should often culminate in an individual or group writing assignment. You should spell out what you want carefully and clearly, taking the time to make sure that the students understand what you are asking for and how they should assess themselves along the way.

VI) Gathering and Interpreting Information

At some point along the way, it will often be necessary to have the students gather and interpret information. When you do so, the students need to gain an appreciation of precisely what the task entails and what is expected of them. How will you do this?

WHY EACH OF THESE DIMENSIONS IS IMPORTANT:

1) Getting clear about what the students have to reason about forces us to become clear about the logic within which we want students to reason. The requirements for the reasoning will be importantly determined, first, by the general logic of the domain, and second, by the specific logic of the particular question at issue.

2) Finding something that students are already familiar with to use as a bridge to help them learn forces us to consider how to make the learning real and meaningful.

3) Making decisions about how we are going to use small and large groups forces us to consciously consider how to maximize the active involvement of the students in the learning process and maximize the knowledge base and idea pool available to all students.

4) Getting clear about assessment issues forces us to decide on how we are going to help the students to assess their own reasoning.

5) Getting clear about how and when students will read and write, as well as engage in Socratic questioning or role playing, forces us to decide on which of these important modes of reasoning the students will engage in.

6) Trying to find opportunities for students to gather information on their own maximizes the extent to which our students will free themselves from dependence on others for information.

✦ *A Sample Redesigned Lesson*

Let us now look at a sample redesigned lesson to see what the end product of this process might look like.

Geographical Thinking and Human Welfare

Deep Point: Getting insight into how "geographical thinking" is essential to human welfare.

Central Concept: geographical features

Central Issue: What is the relation between geographical features and the conditions of human life?

Present Practice

> Geography is often taught, like many other subjects, as a conglomeration of factoids that students are given to memorize and be tested upon. Rarely do students have to reason geographically in such instruction.

Critique

Geographical facts and concepts play an increasingly important role in schooling, and rightly so, but when they are taught didactically, students rarely learn how to *reason geographically*. Consequently, students rarely acquire geographical insights or an enthusiastic sense of how and why geographical thinking is essential to human welfare. Etymologically, the word 'geography' means "a description of the Earth". In fact geographers are most principally concerned — in contrast to, say, geologists — with the implications for human life of facts about the Earth. In studying the Earth from the geographical standpoint, one can concern oneself with mathematical questions (about the size, shape, and movements of the Earth), about "physical" questions (about the layers of the Earth's surface and about the forces historically shaping those surfaces), or about "biological" and "human" questions (about the life conditions of plants, animals, and humans). The result is that good geographical reasoning presupposes some ability to reason geologically, astronomically, zoologically, botanically, meteorologically, and historically. The central concept is "the Earth in evolution" and the central impact of informed reasoning with respect to that concept is insight into the way in which the evolution of the Earth has shaped and transformed, and continues to shape and transform, conditions for life on Earth.

Proposed Design for Instruction

I will bring some globes into class, divide my class into groups of four or five, and ask that each group figure out what they can tell about the planet from what they see on the globe itself (*collaborative learning, dialogical thinking, critical listening, independence of thought, intellectual perseverance*). I will ask, "Based on what you know right now about interpreting what you see represented on the globe, figure out what conclusions you can justifiably come to concerning the Earth and the conditions for life on it." I would stimulate thinking with more specific questions like this: "For example, are there areas of the world that you can see that you believe would have very few plants and animals? Are there areas of the Earth where people could not live except under very special circumstances?" (*thinking aloud*), etc.

I would give the groups a set amount of time to prepare a short report on the conclusions they came to and when the groups reported I would encourage the class to question how the individual groups came to the conclusions they came to and whether or not those conclusions were, in their view, justified (*formulating questions at issue, distinguishing evidence from conclusions, assessing inferences, noticing and questioning assumptions, analyzing concepts, critical listening, critical speaking, and dialogical, perhaps even dialectical, thinking*). As the reports and probings into the reports were taking place, I would be writing on the board the geographical *concepts* that were occurring, and *questions and problems* that were arising, in the *geographical reasoning* being presented.

Subsequent to this activity, I would lead a general discussion on the *assumptions*, including the assumed geographical *ideas*, implicit in their group's *reasoning* as well as in the subsequent *questioning* of that reasoning (*Socratic questioning*). I would outline the *issues* that arose (*identifying and clarifying issues*). I would ask the class to help me divide the issues into those that have to do with the nature of the Earth as a whole and those that have to do with specific areas of the Earth (*analyzing and classifying questions*). On the basis of the division I got, I would ask the group to choose which cluster of *questions* they wished to explore in working groups (which would be assigned as library research as the basis of a further report to the class as a whole) (*critical reading, collaborative learning, dialogical thinking*). I would underscore the importance of discussing in the group what to include and why (*seeking and giving good reasons*). I would ask the students to pay attention to what questions or issues they feel they have answered or resolved and which questions or issues they have not (*intellectual humility*).

The report would be a written report and I would spell out to the class how the report should be structured and why (*critical writing, asking root questions, clarifying purpose*). In doing this last, I would periodically stop and ask the question, "Why do you think it is important to do this in writing up your report?" For example, "Why do you think it is important to identify your sources?", "Why do you think it is important to put into quotes what you take literally from outside sources?", "Why do you think it is important to separate the conclusions you come to from what you are basing your conclusions on?", "Why do you think it is important to make us a short glossary of the important technical terms that you are using in your report?" (leading to *assessing the credibility of sources, clarifying evidence, making well-reasoned inferences*).

Four copies of each report would be made and each group would now become an assessment group for the report submitted by another group (*assessing reasoning, utilizing elements of thought and intellectual standards*). Before each group proceeded with the assessment, I would hold a discussion with the class as to how to go about assessing the reports (*designing and analyzing standards for evaluation*). This would involve, ultimately, detailed suggestions as to what to look for and why. The emphasis, of course, would be on constructive suggestions as to how the report could have been made more useful to the class, including comments on what further research would be required in the light of what the report did and did not accomplish (*intellectual civility, intellectual responsibility, intellectual humility*). I would emphasize the importance of trying to figure out what further questions or issues are raised in the light of the findings of the groups (*intellectual curiosity, intellectual perseverance*).

The next activity would be the reading, by a representative of the research group, of their report to the class as a whole (*critical speaking, critical listening*). The floor would then be opened for questions (because everyone has already served as part of an assessment team on some groups' report I would expect every group report to generate some good probing questions) (*dialogical thinking, asking root questions, analyzing and assessing reasoning, clarifying concepts, identifying assumptions, tracing implications, developing one's perspective*). After each report and question and answer period, a representative of the assessment team for that report would summarize the assessment teams' findings (*critical speaking*). The class would be given an opportunity to comment on the assessment (*critical listening, analyzing and assessing reasoning*, etc.). In this period any member of the group whose report was assessed could respond as well, agreeing or disagreeing with elements of the assessment (*critical speaking, dialogical and dialectical thinking, assessing reasoning, developing one's perspective*).

In the light of the issues and questions that arose from the reports, assessments, and discussions, new clusters of problems would be generated, new groups formed, and new research projects begun, leading to new assessments, new discussions, and yet further questions and issues. From this design for teaching "land forms" it is apparent that a conception is being formed that could be generalized to a whole semester. It illustrates therefore how, given skill in the art of instructional design based on critical thinking, one can avoid detailed lesson plan design for each class, and of how well-conceived overall design strategies can simplify, when they don't obviate entirely, the tasks of day-to-day design.

Now since all reasoning involves basic fundamental structures or elements (*elements of thought*), and since these elements are essential to reasoning well, it is important that, as we cultivate geographical thinking, we cultivate students' awareness, not only of their use, but of the need for *standards* in their use of these decisive structures. So, because all reasoning serves a *purpose* which directs it, we want our students to have a *clear* purpose in mind as they go about *reasoning geographically*. Because all reasoning generates *questions* that need to be expressed *clearly* and *precisely* in order to be answered, we want to teach in such a way that students get experience in putting their *geographical questions* into clear and precise form. Because all reasoning depends upon *accurate* and *sufficient information* about the "things" we are reasoning about, it is important that we design instruction so that students have opportunities to *gather, interpret,* and *assess geographical information*.

It is important that the specific content that we are focusing on — land forms in this case — not become an end in itself, that is, not be reduced to a series of surface facts about the shape and character of land. Finally, it is important that we not overwhelm our students with either questions or facts, nor proceed so quickly that they are not able to *reason* their way into the content on the basis of their previous *knowledge, beliefs,* and *experiences*.

✦ Patterns in Teaching

Every teacher teaches in a patterned way, though few teachers are explicitly aware of the patterns implicit in their teaching. For many teachers the pattern consists in nothing more than this: lecture, lecture, lecture, quiz; lecture, lecture, lecture, quiz; lecture, lecture, lecture, midterm exam, with occasional question and answer periods focused on recall with respect to lectures and the textbook. It is important for teachers who aspire to take command of their teaching to foster higher order learning to begin to develop a sense of the patterns implicit in their own instruction, to critique those patterns, and to begin to experiment with patterns that enable them more readily to cultivate the critical thinking of their students. For one thing, once one discovers one or two powerful patterns of teaching with which one can successfully work, it is possible to structure a whole semester of teaching around it.

Assuming that one has accepted the view that students must reason through what they are learning, there is a basic logic to deciding on the pattern of instruction to use. The basic logic comes in four variations (or schemas):

Schema One: Thinking to Conceptual Understandings and Insights

First, decide upon some kind of start-up activity which will help the students to begin thinking about the subject (typically this involves linking the subject with their experience). Next, decide how students can generate diversity: develop different approaches or points of view, explore different conceptualizations, gather different information. Then decide upon some way for the students to synthesize the insights, collect information together, or analyze what they have come up with, including identifying any conflicts or contradictions that have emerged. This design should require students to assess what they have successfully figured out and what still remains to be figured out.

On this model, our patterns of instruction should reveal many episodes of individuation, reconciliation, and assessment. The students begin their thinking on a topic, develop it, and then test it (figuring out at the end what they have learned and what is still to be learned). This pattern would hold whether or not the topic was a technical one — just so long as it required that students develop their concepts and understandings of something.

Schema Two: Reflective Modeled Practice of Skills

The skill-development schema has four parts: introduction (what are we going to try to learn), modeling (I model the skill slowly and carefully in front of the students, or Socratically lead students through the skill), and practice (the students try to emulate the example). The second two phases of this schema may well be repeated multiple times: "I do it —

they do it — I do it — they do it — I do it — they do it." Students and teacher will analyze and assess modeling and practice, though often this will be delayed until students have had sufficient practice.

Schema Three: A Reflective Performance

The performance schema also has three parts: *1)* start-up thinking, *2)* performance, *3)* analysis and assessment of their progress. Here, students are called on to *do* the sorts of things that practitioners in the field (for example, historians or biologists) do — students *use* the skills and insights of the field.

Schema Four: Thoughtful, Explicit Development of Traits

Finally, the traits schema, another three-part schema, begins with a start-up activity to help students begin to think about the trait and its importance. The next activity calls on students to develop their conceptualizations of the trait by comparing behavior that reflects the trait with behavior that reflects its lack. This will create some diversity. Finally, students can begin to develop the trait through experiences which duplicate circumstances requiring that trait. Clearly, the best method of developing any affective trait includes consistent modeling; this, however, cannot be done on command, written into a unit, but must be part of the teacher's character.

EXAMPLES OF EACH SCHEMA

Now consider the following variations on the four schemas above, each with different "modules" of instruction.

Schema One: For a lesson on discrimination: The main objective is to have students engage in moral reasoning; we might use the following pattern:

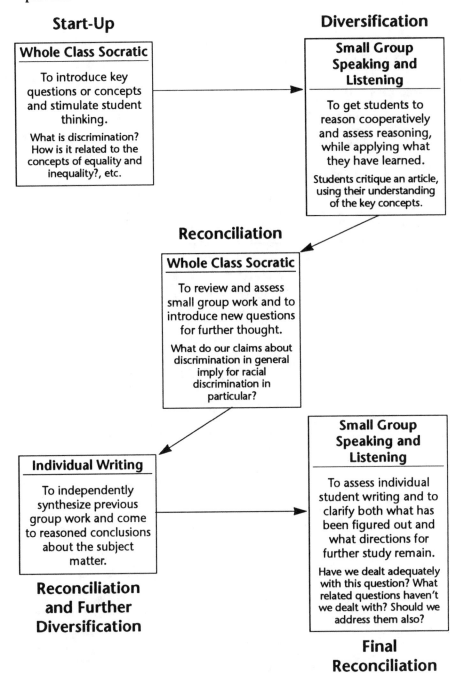

Start-Up

Whole Class Socratic

To introduce key questions or concepts and stimulate student thinking.

What is discrimination? How is it related to the concepts of equality and inequality?, etc.

Diversification

Small Group Speaking and Listening

To get students to reason cooperatively and assess reasoning, while applying what they have learned.

Students critique an article, using their understanding of the key concepts.

Reconciliation

Whole Class Socratic

To review and assess small group work and to introduce new questions for further thought.

What do our claims about discrimination in general imply for racial discrimination in particular?

Individual Writing

To independently synthesize previous group work and come to reasoned conclusions about the subject matter.

Reconciliation and Further Diversification

Small Group Speaking and Listening

To assess individual student writing and to clarify both what has been figured out and what directions for further study remain.

Have we dealt adequately with this question? What related questions haven't we dealt with? Should we address them also?

Final Reconciliation

Schema Two: For a lesson on critical reading: The main objective of the lesson is to get students to gain skill in critical reading through practice.

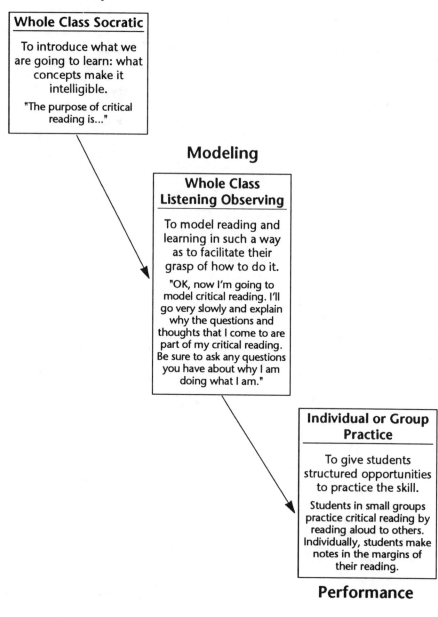

Start-Up

Whole Class Socratic

To introduce what we are going to learn: what concepts make it intelligible.

"The purpose of critical reading is..."

Modeling

Whole Class Listening Observing

To model reading and learning in such a way as to facilitate their grasp of how to do it.

"OK, now I'm going to model critical reading. I'll go very slowly and explain why the questions and thoughts that I come to are part of my critical reading. Be sure to ask any questions you have about why I am doing what I am."

Individual or Group Practice

To give students structured opportunities to practice the skill.

Students in small groups practice critical reading by reading aloud to others. Individually, students make notes in the margins of their reading.

Performance

Schema Three: For a lesson on the civil war: The main objective of this lesson is to have students engage in historical reasoning. We might use the following pattern:

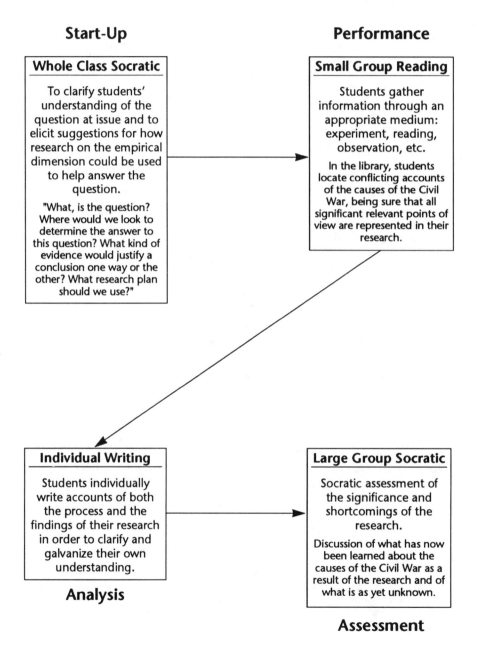

Start-Up

Whole Class Socratic

To clarify students' understanding of the question at issue and to elicit suggestions for how research on the empirical dimension could be used to help answer the question.

"What, is the question? Where would we look to determine the answer to this question? What kind of evidence would justify a conclusion one way or the other? What research plan should we use?"

Performance

Small Group Reading

Students gather information through an appropriate medium: experiment, reading, observation, etc.

In the library, students locate conflicting accounts of the causes of the Civil War, being sure that all significant relevant points of view are represented in their research.

Individual Writing

Students individually write accounts of both the process and the findings of their research in order to clarify and galvanize their own understanding.

Analysis

Large Group Socratic

Socratic assessment of the significance and shortcomings of the research.

Discussion of what has now been learned about the causes of the Civil War as a result of the research and of what is as yet unknown.

Assessment

Schema Four: Teaching for intellectual humility:

Start-Up

Whole Class Socratic

To stimulate student thinking about the concept of the trait (or value or standard) and its relation to other traits

What is intellectual humility? How does it relate to intellectual courage and confidence in reason? How is it related to the standard of having sufficient information for making a reasonable judgment?

Diversification

Large Group Work

To identify the earmarks of the trait in question and to identify earmarks of the opposite, negative trait also

What kinds of behavior do intellectually humble people show? What kinds of things do intellectually arrogant people typically do?

Diversification

Individual Writing

To get students clear on how developing the trait can have an impact on their own lives

How would I be better off if I could develop greater intellectual humility? What are the chief impediments to doing so?

Small Group

To develop the trait by acting within situations that call for its use

Students are assigned a number of topics. They discuss each one and students say when they don't have enough information to make a reasonable decision and when they do.

Development

Individual Writing

To help students gain some perspective on their own development of intellectual humility

Students assess their own progress in developing intellectual humility, paying particular attention to the process.

Assessment and Further Development

✦ *Tactical and Structural Recommendations*

1) *Design coverage so that students grasp more!* Plan instruction so students attain organizing concepts that enable them to retain more of what you teach. Cover *less* when *more* entails that they learn *less*.

2) *Speak less* so that they *think more!* (Try not to lecture more than 20% of total class time.)

3) *Don't be a mother robin* — chewing up the text for the students and putting it into their beaks through lecture! Teach them instead how to read the text for themselves, actively and analytically. Focus, in other words, on how to read the text, not on "reading the text for them".

4) *Focus on fundamental and powerful concepts with high generalizability.* Don't cover more than 50 basic concepts in any one course. Spend the time usually spent introducing more concepts applying and analyzing the basic ones while engaged in problem-solving and reasoned application.

5) *Present concepts,* as far as possible, *in the context of their use* as functional tools for the solution of real problems and the analysis of significant issues.

6) *Develop specific strategies for cultivating critical reading, writing, speaking, and listening.* Assume that your students enter your class — as indeed they do — with limited skills in these essential learning modes.

7) *Think aloud in front of your students.* Let them hear you thinking, better, *puzzling* your way slowly through problems in the subject. (Try to think aloud at the level of a good student, not as a speedy professional. If your thinking is too advanced or proceeds too quickly, they will not be able to internalize it.)

8) *Regularly question your students Socratically* — probing various dimensions of their thinking: their purpose; their evidence, reasons, data; their claims, beliefs, interpretations, deductions, conclusions; the implications and consequences of their thought; their response to alternative thinking from contrasting points of view, and so on.

9) *Call frequently on students who don't have their hands up.* Then, when one student says something, call on other students to summarize in their own words what the first student said (so that they actively listen to each other).

10) *Use concrete examples whenever you can* to illustrate abstract concepts and thinking. Cite experiences that you believe are more or less common in the lives of your students (relevant to what you are teaching).

11) *Require regular writing for class,* but grade using random sampling to make it possible for you to grade their writing without having to read it all (which you probably won't have time for). Or have the students themselves select their best work for you to assess.

12) *Spell out explicitly the intellectual standards you will be using in your grading*, and why. Teach the students, as well as you can, how to assess their own work using those standards.

13) *Break the class down frequently into small groups* (of two's, three's, four's, etc.), give the groups specific tasks and specific time limits, and call on particular groups afterward to report back on what part of their task they completed, what problems occurred, how they tackled those problems, etc.

14) *In general, design all activities and assignments, including readings, so that students must think their way through them.* Lead discussions on the kind of thinking that is required.

15) *Keep the logic of the most basic concepts in the foreground,* continually re-weaving new concepts into the basic ones. Talk about the whole in relation to the parts and the parts in relation to the whole.

16) *Let them know what they're in for.* On the first day of class, spell out as completely as possible what your philosophy of education is, how you are going to structure the class and why: why the students will be required to think their way through it, why standard methods of rote memorization will not work, what strategies you have in store for them to combat the strategies they use for passing classes without much thinking, etc.

✦✦ Conclusion

The redesign of instruction presupposes intellectual development on three fronts, a growing recognition of *1)* what is wrong with didactic instruction, *2)* the nature and dimensions of critical thinking, and *3)* pedagogical strategies that can be used to effectively integrate critical thinking into instruction (based on 1 and 2). Problems of understanding on any of these fronts can produce problems in implementation. It is not enough for our hearts to be in the right place. Nevertheless, it is possible to begin the process of moving forward on each of these fronts *simultaneously*. Indeed, that is the only way that significant progress can be made. We must continually teach with three considerations in mind: Am I falling into the traps of didactic instruction? Are the students reasoning their way through the class, or are they falling back into roles of passivity? What strategies and what patterns of instruction am I using to keep students involved in disciplined critical thinking?

Chapter 17

Socratic Questioning

with A. J. A. Binker

Abstract

Socratic questioning is at the heart of critical teaching. In this paper, published as a chapter in the Critical Thinking Handbook *series, Paul and Binker explain its nature and significance. Three types of Socratic questioning are described, uses of Socratic discussions are suggested, a taxonomy of Socratic questions is provided, and three extended examples of Socratic discussions are given.*

✦ Introduction

Socratic discussion, wherein students' thought is elicited and probed, allows students to develop and evaluate their thinking by making it explicit. By encouraging students to slow their thinking down and elaborate on it, Socratic discussion gives students the opportunity to develop and test their ideas — the beliefs they have spontaneously formed and those they learn in school. Thus, students can synthesize their beliefs into a more coherent and better-developed perspective.

Socratic questioning requires teachers to take seriously and wonder about what students say and think: what they mean, its significance to them, its relationship to other beliefs, how it can be tested, to what extent and in what way it is true or makes sense. Teachers who wonder about the meaning and truth of students' statements can translate that curiosity into probing questions. By wondering aloud, teachers simultaneously convey interest in and respect for student thought, and model analytical moves for students. Fruitful Socratic discussion infects students with the same curiosity about the meaning and truth of what they think, hear, and read and gives students the clear message that they are expected to think and to take everyone else's beliefs seriously.

Socratic questioning is based on the idea that all thinking has a logic or structure, that any one statement only partially reveals the thinking underlying it, expressing no more than a tiny piece of the system of interconnected beliefs of which it is a part. Its purpose is to expose the logic of someone's thought. Use of Socratic questioning presupposes the following points: All thinking has assumptions; makes claims or creates meaning; has implications and consequences; focuses on some things and throws others into the background; uses some concepts or ideas and not others; is defined by purposes, issues, or problems; uses or explains some facts and not others; is relatively clear or unclear; is relatively deep or superficial; is relatively critical or uncritical; is relatively elaborated or undeveloped; is relatively monological or multi-logical. Critical thinking is thinking done with an effective, self-monitoring awareness of these points.

Socratic instruction can take many forms. Socratic questions can come from the teacher or from students. They can be used in a large group discussion, in small groups, one-to-one, or even with oneself. They can have different purposes. What each form has in common is that someone's thought is developed as a result of the probing, stimulating questions asked. It requires questioners to try on others' beliefs, to imagine what it would be like to accept them and wonder what it would be like to believe otherwise. If a student says that people are selfish, the teacher may wonder aloud as to what it means to say that, how the student explains acts others call altruistic, what sort of example that student would accept as an unselfish act, or what the student thinks it means to say that an act or person was unselfish. The discussion which follows could help clarify the concepts of selfish and unselfish behavior, the kind of evidence required to determine whether or not someone is acting selfishly, and the consequences of accepting or rejecting the original generalization. Such a discussion enables students to examine their own views on such concepts as generosity, motivation, obligation, human nature, and right and wrong.

Some erroneously believe that a Socratic discussion is a chaotic free-for-all. In fact, Socratic discussion has distinctive goals and distinctive ways to achieve them. Indeed, any discussion — any thinking — guided by Socratic questioning is structured. The discussion, the thinking, is structured to take student thought from the unclear to the clear, from the unreasoned to the reasoned, from the implicit to the explicit, from the

---

Socratic Questioning

- raises basic issues
- probes beneath the surface of things
- pursues problematic areas of thought
- helps students to discover the structure of their own thought
- helps students develop sensitivity to clarity, accuracy, and relevance
- helps students arrive at judgment through their own reasoning
- helps students note claims, evidence, conclusions, questions-at-issue, assumptions, implications, consequences, concepts, interpretations, points of view — the elements of thought

unexamined to the examined, from the inconsistent to the consistent, from the unarticulated to the articulated. To learn how to participate in it, one has to learn how to listen carefully to what others say, look for reasons and evidence, recognize and reflect upon assumptions, discover implications and consequences, seek examples, analogies, and objections, discover, in short, what is really known and distinguish it from what is merely believed.

✦ Three Kinds of Socratic Discussion

We can loosely categorize three general forms of Socratic questioning and distinguish three basic kinds of preparation for each: the spontaneous, the exploratory, and the issue-specific.

SPONTANEOUS OR UNPLANNED

Every teacher's teaching should be imbued with the Socratic spirit. We should always keep our curiosity and wondering alive. If we do, we will often spontaneously ask students what they mean and explore with them how we might find out if something is true. If one student says that a given angle will be the same as another angle in a geometrical figure, we may spontaneously wonder how we might go about proving or disproving that. If one student says people in the U.S. love freedom, we may spontaneously wonder exactly what that means. (Does that mean, for example, that we love freedom more than other people do? How could we find out?) If in a science class a student says that most space is empty, we may be spontaneously moved to ask what that might mean and how we might find out.

Such spontaneous discussions provide models of listening critically as well as exploring the beliefs expressed. If something said seems questionable, misleading, or false, Socratic questioning provides a way of helping students to become self-correcting, rather than relying on correction by the teacher. Spontaneous Socratic discussion can prove especially useful when students become interested in a topic, when they raise an important issue, when they are on the brink of grasping or integrating something, when discussion becomes bogged down or confused or hostile. Socratic questioning provides specific moves which can fruitfully take advantage of the interest, effectively approach the issue, aid integration and expansion of the insight, move a troubled discussion forward, clarify or sort through what appears confusing, and diffuse frustration or anger.

Although by definition one cannot pre-plan for a particular spontaneous discussion, teachers can prepare themselves by becoming familiar and comfortable with generic Socratic questions, and developing the art of raising probing follow-up questions and giving encouraging and helpful responses. Ask for examples, evidence, or reasons, propose counter-examples, ask the other students if they agree with a point made, suggest parallel or analogous cases, ask for a paraphrase of opposing views, rephrase student responses clearly and succinctly. These are among the most common moves.

• If you see little or no relevance in a student comment, you may think, "I wonder why this student mentioned that now?" and ask, "What connection do you see between our discussion and your point that ...?" or "I'm not sure why you mentioned that now. Could you explain how it's related to this discussion?" or "What made you think of that?" Either the point is germane, and you can clarify the connection, or only marginally related, and you can rephrase it and say "A new issue has been raised." That new issue can be pursued then, or tactfully postponed, or can generate an assignment.

• If a student says something vague or general, you may think, "I wonder about the role of that belief in this student's life, the consequences of that belief, or how the student perceives the consequences, or whether it has any practical consequences at all" and so may ask, "How does that belief affect how you act? What, for example, do you do or refrain from doing because you believe that?" You might have several students respond and compare their understandings, or suggest an alternative view and have students compare its consequences.

Because we begin to wonder more and more about meaning and truth, and so think aloud in front of our students by means of questions, Socratic exchanges will occur at many unplanned moments in our instruction. However, in addition to these unplanned wonderings we can also design or plan at least two distinct kinds of Socratic discussion: one that explores a wide range of issues and one that focuses on one particular issue.

EXPLORATORY

Exploratory Socratic questioning enables teachers to find out what students know or think and to probe into student thinking on a variety of issues. Hence you may use it to learn students' impressions of a subject to assess their thought and ability to articulate it, you may use it to see what students value, or to uncover problematic areas or potential biases, or find out where students' thought is clearest and fuzziest. You may use it to discover areas or issues of interest or controversy, or to find out where and how students have integrated school material into their belief systems. Such discussions can serve as a general preparation for later study or analysis of a topic, as an introduction, as review, to see what students understood from their study of a unit or topic before a test, to suggest where they should focus study for a test, as a basis for or guide to future assignments, or to prepare for an assignment. You might have students take (or pick) an issue raised in discussion and give their own views, or have students form groups to discuss the issue or topic.

This type of Socratic questioning raises and explores a broad range of interrelated issues and concepts. It requires minimal pre-planning or pre-thinking. It has a relatively loose order or structure. You can prepare by having some general questions ready to raise when appropriate by considering the topic or issue, related issues, and key concepts. You can also prepare by predicting students' likeliest responses and preparing some follow-up questions. Remember, however, that once students' thought is stimulated no one can predict exactly where discussion will go.

Here are some suggestions and possible topics for Socratic discussions:

- "What is social studies?" If students have difficulty, ask, "When you've studied social studies, what have you talked about?" If students list topics, put them on the board. Then have students discuss the items and try to group them. "Do these topics have something in common? Are there differences between these topics?" Encourage students to discuss details they know about the topics. If, instead of listing topics, they give a general answer or definition, or if they can give a statement about what the topics listed have in common, suggest examples that fit the definition but are not social studies. For example, if a student says, "It's about people", mention medicine. Have them modify or improve their definition. "How is social studies like and unlike other subjects? What basic questions does the subject address? How does it address them? Why study social studies? Is it important? Why or why not? How can we use what we learn in social studies? What are the most important ideas you've learned from this subject?"
- When, if ever, is violence justified? Why are people as violent as they are? What effects does violence have? Can violence be lessened or stopped?
- What is a friend?
- What is education? Why learn?
- What is most important?
- What is right and wrong? Why be good? What is a good person?
- What is the difference between living and non-living things?
- Of what sorts of things is the universe made?
- What is language?
- What are the similarities and differences between humans and animals?

Sometimes you may not know whether to call a discussion exploratory or issue-specific. Which you call it is unimportant. What is important is what happens in the discussion. For example, consider this group of questions:

- What does 'vote' mean?

- How do people decide whom to elect? How should they decide? How could people predict how a potential leader is likely to act? If you don't know about an issue or the candidates for an office, should you vote?
- Is voting important? Why or why not? What are elections supposed to produce? How? What does that require? What does that tell us about voting?
- Why have elections? Why is democracy considered good? What does belief in democracy assume about human nature?
- How do people become candidates?
- Why does the press emphasize how much money candidates have? How does having lots of money help candidates win?
- Why do people give money to candidates? Why do companies?
- Is voting the same thing as marking a ballot?

These questions could be the list generated as possible questions for an exploratory discussion. Which of them are actually used would depend on how students respond. For an issue-specific discussion, these questions and more could be used in an order which takes students from ideas with which they are most familiar to those with which they are least familiar.

ISSUE-SPECIFIC

You will often approach your instruction with specific areas and issues to cover. This is the time for issue-specific Socratic questioning. To really probe an issue or concept in depth, to have students clarify, sort, analyze and evaluate thoughts and perspectives, distinguish the known from the unknown, synthesize relevant factors and knowledge, students can engage in an extended and focused discussion. This type of discussion offers students the chance to pursue perspectives to their most basic assumptions and through their furthest implications and consequences. These discussions give students experience in engaging in an extended, ordered, and integrated discussion in which they discover, develop, and share ideas and insights. It requires pre-planning or thinking through possible perspectives on the issue, grounds for conclusions, problematic concepts, implications, and consequences. You can further prepare by reflecting on those subjects relevant to the issue: their methods, standards, basic distinctions and concepts, and interrelationships — points of overlap or possible conflict. You may also prepare by considering likeliest student answers.

All three types of Socratic discussion require developing the art of questioning. They require the teacher to develop familiarity with a wide variety of intellectual moves and sensitivity to when to ask which kinds of questions, though there is rarely one best question at any particular time.

Some Suggestions for Using Socratic Discussion

• Have an initial exploratory discussion about a complex issue in which students break it down into simpler parts. Students can then choose the aspects they want to explore or research. Then have an issue-specific discussion where students share, analyze, evaluate, and synthesize their work.

• The class could have a "fishbowl" discussion. One third of the class, sitting in a circle, discusses a topic. The rest of the class, in a circle around the others, listens, takes notes, then discusses the discussion.

• Assign an essay asking students to respond to a point of interest made in a discussion.

• Have students write summaries of their discussions immediately afterwards. They could also add new thoughts or examples, provide further clarification, etc. They could later share these notes.

✦ A Taxonomy of Socratic Question

It is helpful to recognize, in light of the universal features in the logic of human thought, that there are identifiable categories of questions for the adept Socratic questioner to dip into: questions of clarification, questions that probe assumptions, questions that probe reasons and evidence, questions about viewpoints or perspectives, questions that probe implications and consequences, and questions about the question. Here are some examples of generic questions in each of these categories:

QUESTIONS OF CLARIFICATION

• What do you mean by _____?
• Could you give me an example?
• What is your main point?
• Would this be an example: ___?
• How does _____ relate to ___?
• Could you explain that further?
• Could you put that another way?
• Would you say more about that?
• Is your basic point _____ or _____?
• Why do you say that?
• What do you think is the main issue here?
• Let me see if I understand you; do you mean _____ or _____?
• How does this relate to our discussion (problem, issue)?
• What do you think John meant by his remark? What did you take John to mean?
• Jane, would you summarize in your own words what Richard has said? ... Richard, is that what you meant?

Socratic Discussion
Anyone's thinking can be pursued in four directions

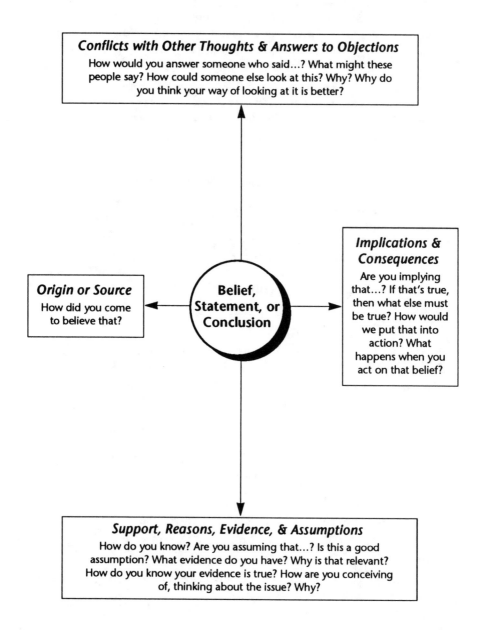

Conflicts with Other Thoughts & Answers to Objections
How would you answer someone who said...? What might these people say? How could someone else look at this? Why? Why do you think your way of looking at it is better?

Origin or Source
How did you come to believe that?

Belief, Statement, or Conclusion

Implications & Consequences
Are you implying that...? If that's true, then what else must be true? How would we put that into action? What happens when you act on that belief?

Support, Reasons, Evidence, & Assumptions
How do you know? Are you assuming that...? Is this a good assumption? What evidence do you have? Why is that relevant? How do you know your evidence is true? How are you conceiving of, thinking about the issue? Why?

QUESTIONS THAT PROBE ASSUMPTIONS

- What are you assuming?
- What is Karen assuming?
- What could we assume instead?
- You seem to be assuming _____. Do I understand you correctly?
- All of your reasoning depends on the idea that ____. Why have you based your reasoning on _____ rather than _____?
- You seem to be assuming ____. How would you justify taking this for granted?
- Is it always the case? Why do you think the assumption holds here?
- Why would someone make this assumption?

QUESTIONS THAT PROBE REASONS AND EVIDENCE

- What would be an example?
- How do you know?
- Why do you think that is true?
- Do you have any evidence for that?
- What difference does that make?
- Are these reasons adequate?
- Why did you say that?
- What led you to that belief?
- How does that apply to this case?
- What would change your mind?
- What are your reasons for saying that?
- What other information do we need?
- Could you explain your reasons to us?
- But is that good evidence to believe that?
- Is there reason to doubt that evidence?
- Who is in a position to know if that is so?
- What would you say to someone who said ____?
- Can someone else give evidence to support that response?
- By what reasoning did you come to that conclusion?
- How could we find out whether that is true?

QUESTIONS ABOUT VIEWPOINTS OR PERSPECTIVES

- You seem to be approaching this issue from _____ perspective. Why have you chosen this rather than that perspective?
- How would other groups/types of people respond? Why? What would influence them?
- How could you answer the objection that _____ would make?
- What might someone who believed ___ think?
- Can/did anyone see this another way?
- What would someone who disagrees say?
- What is an alternative?
- How are Ken's and Roxanne's ideas alike? Different?

QUESTIONS THAT PROBE IMPLICATIONS AND CONSEQUENCES

- What are you implying by that?
- When you say _____, are you implying _____?
- But if that happened, what else would happen as a result? Why?
- What effect would that have?
- Would that necessarily happen or only probably happen?
- What is an alternative?
- If this and this are the case, then what else must also be true?
- If we say that this is unethical, how about that?

QUESTIONS ABOUT THE QUESTION

- How can we find out?
- What does this question assume?
- Would __ put the question differently?
- Why is this question important?
- How could someone settle this question?
- Can we break this question down at all?
- Is the question clear? Do we understand it?
- Is this question easy or hard to answer? Why?
- Does this question ask us to evaluate something?
- Do we all agree that this is the question?
- To answer this question, what questions would we have to answer first?
- I'm not sure I understand how you are interpreting the main question at issue.
- Is this the same issue as ____?
- How would ____ put the issue?

To participate effectively in Socratic questioning, one must:

- listen carefully to what others say
- take what they say seriously
- look for reasons and evidence
- recognize and reflect upon assumptions
- discover implications and consequences
- seek examples, analogies, and objections
- seek to distinguish what one *knows* from what one merely *believes*
- seek to enter empathetically into the perspectives or points of view of others
- be on the alert for inconsistencies, vagueness, and other possible problems in thought
- look beneath the surface of things
- maintain a healthy sense of skepticism
- be willing to helpfully play the role of devil's advocate

✦ *Wondering (and Wondering About Your Wonderings)*

As a blossoming critical thinker, you will find yourself wondering in many directions. You will often, however, be unsure about how to share many of these wonderings with your students. You certainly don't want to overwhelm them. Neither do you want to confuse them or lead them in too many directions at once. So when do you make the wonderings explicit in the form of a question and when do you keep them in the privacy of your mind?

There is no pat formula or procedure for answering these questions, though there are some principles:

- "Test and find out." There is nothing wrong with some of your questions misfiring. You won't always be able to predict what questions will stimulate students' thought. So you must engage in some trial-and-error questioning.

- "Tie into student experience and perceived needs." You may think of numerous examples of ways students can apply what they learn, and formulate questions relating academic material to students' lives.

- "Don't give up too soon." If students don't respond to a question, wait. If they still don't respond, you could rephrase the question or break it down into simpler questions.

You should use care and caution in introducing students to Socratic questioning. The level of the questions should match the level of the students' thought. Furthermore, it should not be assumed that students will be fully successful with it, except over a considerable length of time. Nevertheless, properly used, it can be introduced in some form or other at virtually any grade level.

✦ *Socratic Interludes in Class*

#1 HELPING STUDENTS ORGANIZE THEIR THOUGHTS FOR WRITING

The following Socratic interlude represents an initial attempt to get students to think about what a persuasive essay is and how to prepare to write one. Of course, like all Socratic questioning it goes beyond one objective, for it also stimulates students to think critically in general about what they are doing and why. It helps them to see that their own ideas, if developed, are important and can lead to insights.

Transcript (A Reconstruction)

> T: *You are all going to be writing a persuasive essay, so let's talk about what you have to do to get your ideas organized. There are two ways to persuade people of something, by appealing to their reason, a rational*

appeal, and by appealing to their emotions, an emotional appeal. What is the difference between these? Let's take the rational appeal first, what do you do when you appeal to someone's reason?

John: You give them good reasons for accepting something. You tell them why they should do something or what they can get out of it or why it's good for them.

T: But don't they already have reasons why they believe as they do? So why should they accept your reasons rather than theirs?

Bob: Well, maybe mine are better than theirs.

T: Have you ever given someone, say your mother or father, good reasons for what you wanted to do, but they just did not accept your reasons even though they seemed compelling to you?

Susan: Yeah, that happens a lot to me. They just say that I have to do what they say whether I like it or not because they're my parents.

T: So is it hopeless to give people good reasons for changing their minds because people will never change their minds?

Grace: No, people sometimes do change their minds. Sometimes they haven't thought about things a lot or they haven't noticed something about what they're doing. So you tell them something they hadn't considered and then they change their minds ... sometimes.

T: That's right, sometimes people do change their minds after you give them a new way of looking at things or reasons they hadn't considered. What does that tell you about one thing you want to be sure to do in deciding how to defend your ideas and get people to consider them? What do you think, Tom?

Tom: I guess you want to consider different ways to look at things, to find new reasons and things.

T: Where can you find different ways to look at things? What do you think, Janet?

Janet: I would look in the library.

T: How? What would you look for, could you be more specific?

Janet: Sure. I'm going to write about why women should have the same rights as men, so I'll look for books on feminism and women.

T: How will that help you to find different ways to look at things, could you spell that out further?

Janet: I think that there will probably be different ideas in different books. Not all women think alike. Black women and white women and religious women and Hispanic women all have their own point of view. I will look for the best reasons that each gives and try to put them into my paper.

T: OK, but so far we have just talked about giving reasons to support your ideas, what I called in the beginning a 'rational appeal'. What about the emotional side of things, of appealing to people's emotions? John, what are some emotions and why appeal to them?

John: Emotions are things like fear and anger and jealousy, what happens when we feel strongly, or are excited.

T: Right, so do you know anyone who appeals to our emotions? Are your emotions ever appealed to?

Judy: Sure, we all try to get people involved in feeling as we do. When we talk to friends about kids we don't like we describe them so that our friends will get mad at them and feel like we do.

T: How do we do this, could you give me an example, Judy?

Judy: OK, like I know this girl who's always trying to get her hands on boys, even if they already have girl friends. So I tell my friends how she acts. I give them all the details, how she touches them when she talks to them and acts like a dip. We really get mad at her.

T: So what do you think, should you try to get your reader to share your feeling? Should you try to get their emotions involved?

Judy: Sure, if you can.

T: But isn't this the way propaganda works? How we get people emotional so that they go along with things they shouldn't? Didn't Hitler get people all emotional and stir up their hate?

Judy: Yeah, but we do that too when we play the national anthem or when we get excited about Americans winning medals at the Olympics.

T: So what do you think of this Frank, should we or shouldn't we try to get people's emotions stirred up?

Frank: If what we are trying to get people to do is good we should do it, but if what we are trying to get them to do is bad we shouldn't.

T: Well, what do you think about Judy's getting her friends mad at a girl by telling them how she flirts with boys?

Frank: Are you asking me? ... I think she ought to clean up her own act first. (laughter)

Judy: What do you mean by that?!

Frank: Well, you're one of the biggest flirts around!

Judy: I never flirt with boys who have girl friends and anyway I'm just a friendly person.

Frank: Yes you are, *very* friendly!

T: OK, calm down you guys. I think you better settle this one in private. But look, there's an important point here. Sometimes we do act inconsistently, sometimes there are contradictions in our behavior, and we criticize people for doing what we do. And that's one thing we should think about when writing our papers, are we willing to live by what we are preaching to others? Or another way to put this is by asking whether our point of view is realistic. If our point of view seems too idealistic then our reader may not be persuaded.

We don't have much time left today, so let me try to summarize what I see as implied in what we have talked about. So far, we have agreed about a number of things important to persuasive writing: 1) you need to give good reasons to support your point of view, 2) you should be clear about what your reasons are, 3) you should consider the issue from more than one point of view, including considering how your reader might look at it, 4) you should check out books or articles on the subject to get different points of view, 5) you should consider how you might reach your reader's feelings, how what you say ties into what they care about, 6) following Judy's example you should present specific examples and include the details that make your example realistic and moving, 7) in line with Frank's point, you should watch out for contradictions and inconsistencies, and 8) you should make sure that what you are arguing for is realistic. For next time I would like you all to write out the introductory paragraph to your paper in which you basically tell the reader what you are going to try to persuade him or her of and how you are going to do it, that is, how the paper will be structured. Don't worry that your first draft is rough; you will be working in groups of threes to sharpen up what you have written.

#2 HELPING STUDENTS TO THINK MORE DEEPLY ABOUT BASIC IDEAS

Introduction

We tend to pass by basic ideas quickly to get into more derivative ideas. This is part of the didactic mind set of giving-students-content-to-remember. What we need to do, in contrast, is to stimulate student's thinking right from the start, especially about the most basic ideas in a subject so that they are moti348vated from the beginning to use their thinking in trying to understand things, and so that they base their thinking on foundational ideas that make sense to them.

Transcript (A Reconstruction)

T: This is a course in Biology. What kind of a subject is that? What do you know about Biology already? Kathleen, what do you know about it?

Kathleen: It's a science.

T: And what's a science?

Kathleen: Me? A science is very exact. They do experiments and measure things and test things.

T: What other sciences are there besides biology? Marisa, could you name some?

Marisa: Sure, there's chemistry and physics.

T: What else?

Blake:There's botany and math?

T: Math ... math is a little different from the others, isn't it? How is math different from biology, chemistry, physics, and botany? Blake, what would you say?

Blake: You don't do experiments in math.

T: And why not?

Blake: I guess 'cause numbers are different.

T: Yes, studying numbers and other mathematical things is different from studying chemicals or laws in the physical world or living things and so forth. You might ask your math teacher about why numbers are different or do some reading about that, but let's focus our attention here on what are called the life sciences. Why are biology and botany called life sciences?

Peter: Because they both study living things.

T: How are they different? How is biology different from botany? Jennifer, what do you think?

Jennifer: I don't know.

T: Well, let's all of us look up the words in our dictionaries and see what it says about them.

(Students look up the words)

T: Jennifer, what did you find for biology?

Jennifer: It says: "The science that deals with the origin, history, physical characteristics, life processes, habits, etc., of plants and animals: It includes botany and zoology."

T: So what do we know about the relationship of botany to biology? Rick?

Rick: Botany is just a part of biology.

T: Right, and what can we tell about biology from just looking at its etymology. What does it literally mean? If you break the word into two parts "bio" and "logy". Blake, what does it tell us?

Blake: The science of life or the study of life.

T: So, do you see how etymology can help us get an insight into the meaning of a word? Do you see how the longer definition spells out the etymological meaning in greater detail? Well, why do you think experiments are so important to biologists and other scientists? Have humans always done experiments do you think? Marisa.

Marisa: I guess not, not before there was any science.

T: Right, that's an excellent point, science didn't always exist. What did people do before science existed? How did they get their information? How did they form their beliefs? Peter.

Peter: From religion.

T: Yes, religion often shaped a lot of what people thought. Why don't we use religion today to decide, for example, what is true of the origin, history, and physical characteristics of life?

Peter: Some people still do. Some people believe that the Bible explains the origin of life and that the theory of evolution is wrong.

T: What is the theory of evolution, Jose?

Jose: I don't know.

T: Well, why don't we all look up the name Darwin in our dictionaries and see if there is anything there about Darwinian theory.

(Students look up the words)

T: Jose, read aloud what you have found.

Jose: It says, "Darwin's theory of evolution holds that all species of plants and animals developed from earlier forms by hereditary transmission of slight variations in successive generations and that the forms which survive are those that are best adapted to the environment."

T: What does that mean to you ... in ordinary language? How would you explain that? Jose.

Jose: It means the stronger survive and the weaker die?

T: Well, if that's true why do you think the dinosaurs died out? I thought dinosaurs were very strong?

Shannon: They died because of the ice age, I think.

T: So I guess it's not enough to be strong, you must also fit in with the changes in the environment. Perhaps fitness or adaptability is more important than strength. Well, in any case why do you think that most people today look to science to provide answers to questions about the origin and nature of life rather than to the Bible or other religious teachings?

Shannon: Nowadays most people believe that science and religion deal with different things and that scientific questions cannot be answered by religion.

T: And by the same token, I suppose, we recognize that religious questions cannot be answered by science. In any case, how were scientists able to convince people to consider their way of finding answers to questions about the nature of life and life processes. Kathleen, you've been quiet for a while, what do you think?

Kathleen: To me science can be proved. When scientists say something we can ask for proof and they can show us, and if we want we can try it out for ourselves.

T: Could you explain that further?

Kathleen: Sure, in my chemistry class we did experiments in which we tested out some of the things that were said in our chemistry books. We could see for ourselves.

T: That's right, science is based on the notion that when we claim things to be true about the world we should be able to test them to see if, objectively, they are true. Marisa, you have a question?

Marisa: Yes, but don't we all test things. We test our parents and our friends. We try out ideas to see if they work.

T: That's true. But is there any difference between the way you and I test our friends and the way a chemist might test a solution to see if it is acidic?

Marisa: Sure, ... but I'm not sure how to explain it.

T: Blake, what do you think?

Blake: Scientists have laboratories; we don't.

T: They also do precise measurements and use precise instruments, don't they? Why don't we do that with our friends, parents, and children? Adrian, do you have an idea why not?

Adrian: We don't need to measure our friends. We need to find out whether they really care about us.

T: Yes, finding out about caring is a different matter than finding out about acids and bases, or even than finding out about animal behavior. You might say that there are two different kinds of realities in the world, the qualitative and the quantitative, and that science is mostly concerned with the quantitative, while we are often concerned with the qualitative. Could you name some qualitative ideas that all of us are concerned with? Rick, what do you think?

Rick: I don't know what you mean.

T: *Well, the word qualitative is connected to the word quality. If I were to ask you to describe your own qualities in comparison to your brother or sister, would you know the sort of thing I was asking you?*

Rick: I guess so.

T: *Could you, for example, take your father and describe to us some of his best and some of his worst qualities as you see them?*

Rick: I guess so.

T: *OK, why don't you do it. What do you think some of your father's best qualities are?*

Rick: To me he is generous. He likes to help people out when they are in trouble.

T: *And what science studies generosity?*

Rick: I don't know. None, I guess.

T: *That's right, generosity is a human quality, it can't be measured scientifically. There is no such thing as generosity units. So science is not the only way we can find things out. We can also experience qualities in the world. We can experience kindness, generosity, fear, love, hate, jealousy, self-satisfaction, friendship, and many, many other things as well. In this class we are concerned mainly with what we can find out about life quantitatively or scientifically. For next time, I want you to read the first chapter in your text book and I want you to be prepared to explain what the first chapter says. I will be dividing you up into groups of four and each group of four will develop a short summary of the first chapter (without looking at it, of course) and then we will have a spokesperson from each group explain your summary to the class. After that, we will have a discussion of the ideas mentioned. Don't forget today's discussion, because I'll be asking you some questions that will see if you can relate what we talked about today with what was said in your first chapter. Any questions? ... OK, ... See you next time.*

#3 HELPING STUDENTS TO THINK SERIOUSLY ABOUT COMPLEX SOCIAL ISSUES

Introduction

In the following extended discussion, Rodger Halstead, Homestead High School Social Studies teacher, Socratically questions students about their views about the Middle East. He links up the issue with the death-camps of WWII and, ultimately, with the problem of how to correct one injustice without committing another.

Part One

I thought what we'd do now is to talk a little about the Middle East. And remember we saw a film, and title of the film was, "Let My People Go". And in the process of seeing that film, we took a look at some of the things that happened in the concentration camps; in the death-camps of Nazi Germany during World War II. Remember that? It's pretty hard to forget, so I'm sure that you do remember that. Who do you hold responsible for what happened to the Jewish people during the holocaust, the Nazi holocaust of the 1940's and the late 1930's? Who do you hold responsible for that? Laura?

Laura: Everyone. Um ...

What do you mean, everyone?

Student: It started in Germany. I would ... My first thought goes to Hitler; then it goes to the German people that allowed him to take control without ... without seeing what he was doing before it was too late.

Let's see if we understand. Are you talking now about what I call moral responsibility, that they hold some moral responsibility for what happened, or are you talking about legal responsibility? What I'd like to really have us talk about is legal responsibility. Who would you punish for the responsibility for what happened to the Jewish people? Would you punish all Germans? No. OK, then who would you punish?

Student: Hitler.

Hitler. OK, if he had been alive and we'd been able to capture him, you would have punished him.

Student: Absolutely.

OK. I think probably we'd all agree to that, alright? Anybody else?

Student: Probably his five top men. I ... I'm not sure ....

Well, whatever. Whether it's five or six or ten or whatever. The top guys, the SS ....

Student: (several talking) Well, that's a good question ... and, there are a lot of Nazis out there.

Well, are you sure everyone was a member of the Nazi party? Not all Germans were.

Student: Well, not all Germans were ... um ...

Want to think about it?

Student: Yeah.

How about somebody else? First of all, we all agree that somebody should have been punished, right? Alright, these are not acts that should have gone unpunished. OK, Steve?

Steve: Well, it'd be kind of hard, but, like, I think that every soldier or whatever, whoever took a life, theirs should be taken. (Several speaking)

Every person who ... every ... every Nazi soldier who was in the camps ....

Steve: Who had something to do with ...

Who had something to do with the killing of the people in the camps. The Jews, the gypsies, the opponents of Hitler, all those people. All the 12 million killed. Anybody that had a direct ... played a direct role. You would punish them. What if we had a corporal here, Steve, and the corporal said, "The reason I did this is because I was ordered to do it. And if I didn't do it, my family was going to be injured, or something was going to happen to my family." Are you going to punish that corporal?

Steve: Well, I guess ... well, I mean ... ah, they ... They still took a life, you know, but they're ... what they're ... You know, they were just following the rules. What ... (Laughter) Yes, but I mean ... I, I, I believe that, you know, if you take a life ...

What if they didn't take a life? What if they just tortured somebody?

Steve: Then they ... then ... then they should be tortured in the same way.

So you say anybody who was directly responsible for any injury, torture, murder, whatever in the camps, they themselves should get a similar kind of punishment. What about the people who were in the bureaucracy of the German government who, uh, set up the trains and the time schedule of the trains? What about the engineer on the train? You're looking at me, Amy. I'm not sure if ...

Amy: Well, yeah, I guess ....

All those people?

Amy: Yeah, because if you think about it, if they hadn't of done that, they couldn't have gotten the people there.

OK, and what about the people standing on the streets while the Jews had to get in the trucks ...?

Amy: No, I think that's going a little too ...

OK, so anybody who participates in any way in the arrest, the carrying out of all these activities, including even people who, uh ... what about people who typed up the memos?

Amy: Yeah, I guess.

(Several Speaking)

No, says Manuel. Why not no? Why no?

Manuel: Like, for example, if they're put under a lot of duress. Like, uh, "We're going to kill your family, we're going to hurt your family, put them in a concentration camp, too ...."

Yes. Yes?

Manuel: It, it's just total ... you just can't hold them responsible because their family ... it's just like, uh ... the next, the closest thing to them, and you can't just say you have to punish them because I don't think they did it on purpose. They didn't do it because we hate the Jews, we don't like you ... we're not doing it because we want to see you suffer. They're doing it because they don't want to see their family suffer.

Anybody who enjoyed what they were doing, Manny, clearly needs to be punished, in your ... right? What if I do it, but I don't enjoy it? "Oh, God! I don't want to do this! Ohhh! But you made me do it."

Manuel: I don't think they should be punished.

OK, the war's over, Manny. Let's get the man in here for a second. The war's over, Manny, and we now have the rest of these people. Leslie, did you do that because you wanted to do that? (jumps to Rodger)

(Laughter)

Student: No.

No. Gail, did you do it because you wanted to do it?

Gail: No.

Did you do it because you wanted to do it, Ariel? Did you do it, Laurel? 'Cause you wanted, Brad?

Student: No.

Manny, what we got? None of them did it because they wanted to. They all did it because it was orders.

Manuel: Well, uh ...

How do we know?

Manuel: That's a good question.

You want to get off the hot seat for a second, Manny?

Manuel: Yeah.

OK, I don't know ... eeny, meeny, Stacy?

Stacy: Well, ah ... that's why I think that it should maybe just be the leadership because they're the ones ...

Just Hitler, and the ...

Stacy: Yeah, 'cause they're the ones who made up the concentration camps, and they're the ones who tell the people to do it. And some people will want to do these things, and some people won't, and you can't determine who wants to do it and who doesn't.

Student: Yeah, but how far do you go down?

Stacy: See ... Well, that's why you just do ... it'd just be those top ...

Student: What's the top ...?

Stacy: Hitler and his five or six men.

Stacy, would I gather that you agree with Manny that if somebody really enjoyed doing it and wanted to do it, 'doing it' meaning hurting, killing, torture; if they really wanted to do it and enjoyed it, those people should be punished.

Stacy: Yeah, they should, but you can't decide, you can't tell who really wanted to be ...

OK, someone who did it reluctantly, you shouldn't punish them, is that right?

Stacy: Right.

Suppose you and I are in the mafia. And suppose you and I are in the mafia, and I order you to kill ... uh, Katherine. OK?

Stacy: OK.

You happen to be ... uh, acquaintances with Kathy, and you don't want to do it, but I order you to do it. And, in fact you do, you carry it out because I tell ya, if you don't do it, I'm going to pull your fingernails out, and your toenails, and I'm going to shoot off your kneecap. And so you kill Katherine. Now, along comes Brad. He's a policeman. And he arrests you for killing Katherine, OK? And you say, "I didn't want to do it. My toenails were going to go out, my fingernails were going to go out, my kneecaps were going to go." Should we say, "You're home free, Stacy."?

Stacy: No, I'd lead them to you, is what I'd do.

So, they're going to arrest me?

Stacy: Yeah.

Alright. Now should you be arrested? Should we just say, "I'm sorry, Stacy." Should you be arrested? Should you be punished?

Stacy: Yeah, I should be arrested but maybe not .... You should be *really* punished, yeah.

Really punished?

Stacy: Yeah.

Should you be punished too?

Stacy: I'm in the Mafia, I shouldn't be in the Mafia.

So anybody who is in the camp who does these deeds because even though they did it because they did not want to do them they should also be held responsible and punished.

Stacy: You can't. There are too many of them. It's stooping to the Nazi's level by killing, by punishing all these people.

So will you let some of them go free because you can't punish all?

Stacy: Right, you can't, you can't punish a whole entire group of people that's like millions of people.

Why can't you do that?

Stacy: Because it's doing what they were doing to the Jewish people.

We'll get some disagreement here. Jeannette?

Jeannette: If you can't call a person responsible for making a decision, where does that leave society?

What kind of decision?

Jeannette: They made a decision to follow the order.

And you are saying we can't be responsible for a major ...

(voices)

Oh, I'm sorry. Oh you have to ... the front row is answering ... why must you hold them responsible?

(Laughter.)

Jeannette: Because they made the decision, they did it.

But what if they did it under duress?

Jeannette: They could've ... faced the responsibilities, you have to face responsibilities either way, you can't just do something.

Suppose, suppose I say to you, "Jeannette you, I want you to uh pull Bill's eyeballs out of his head. (Laughter) And if you don't do that, I am going to kill you, Jeannette."

Jeannette: I am responsible.

Are you responsible?

Jeannette: I'm responsible.

You're going to die!

Jeannette: I'm responsible!

So we should punish you because you do this deed even though you would have died if you hadn't done it?

Jeannette: No! it's still my decision.

Student: Yeah.

Stacy: But they, what if they were drafted into being in the Nazi camps and they were forced to do that — and they did not want to do that?

Student: How did they force ...

Stacy: Just like we had American troops in Vietnam, they were killing people.

Student: And they were drafted. A lot of people ran, though ....

Student: A lot of people didn't.

Time out! Time out, we have a real important discussion and that is the issue of the people who — what about the people who did not willingly do it, who did it because of orders, are they or are they not responsible?

Student: No.

Jody: I agree with Jeannette. They are responsible, they made the decision to do it, — they have a choice but some people, I'm sure, made the choice to die rather than to do this. I'm sure there were people that did that. And that was their decision because they could not go through with the order. You can't live with that. They went through it and made that decision. They have to live with what they did and they have to be punished for it because they took the lives of other people.

Wait a minute, no, no, no, no, no. Do you know the story of Patty Hearst at all? I know its ancient history to you. She was kidnapped by a group call the SLA. She was brainwashed and she was beaten. She was abused and eventually she joins the group and they rob a bank and she had a part in the bank robbery up in Carmichael, California, it's up near Sacramento. And in the process of doing that — after she is freed, she argued that during the bank robbery they had a gun on her and she didn't have any choice.

Now, she's arrested for the bank robbery and she's going to be put on trial. Is she responsible for her acts in that bank robbery Jody? Does she go free or do you punish her for the bank robbery?

Jody: That's a hard question. (yeah, no fair) Was it proven that there was a gun on her?

Yes, they had tape. It was not clear whether there were bullets in the gun or so forth. There is tape of a gun.

Jody: Well, if there's really proof, that's different.

What do you mean that's different?

Jody: Well, than someone who was a Nazi.

No, no, no, let's not get to Nazis yet. You're on a jury, Jody, are you going to vote guilty or innocent?

Jody: Innocent.

Why?

Jody: Because there was proof that she was forced; it wasn't a threat that something was going to happen. She was forced.

Did she do it under threat of her own life?

Student: Yes.

All right. Leslie here is a Nazi. OK, Gayle is just a neutral. Leslie tells Gayle if you don't kill Ariel the Jew, you will be punished. Gayle kills Ariel the Jew. The reason she does, is, because Leslie told her to do it.

Jody: No, I guess.

Leslie held the gun on her. Are we not going to punish Gayle — Gayle "Patty Hearst"?

Jody: No. I would probably have to say that she would have to be responsible.

Patty Hearst? Patty Hearst?

Jody: Yeah.

Because you see the inconsistency with the previous position and you want to hold the position that in fact everyone who does things even under orders and compulsion are responsible for what they do. Is that right? Would I be clear that in any future argument with your parents, you will not argue a line that might say, "The reason I did that is because somebody else told me I had to do that." You'll never argue that?

Jody: Your parents always say, "But it was your decision."

And you agree to that.

Jody: And you don't have to listen to what everyone else says.

And you believe that.

Jody: Yeah.

And you will follow it?

Jennifer.

Jennifer: Um, I agree with Janet, but I think its conditional because ...

What is conditional?

Jennifer: Well, that, that the people are ultimately responsible for their actions because in the Patty Hearst case, she umm, it was a bank robbery, and that wasn't directly, I mean that was, — you're not supposed to steal people's money and that would affect people but it's not physically, its not physical pain and it's not, you know, killing them, and so I think they should of, um, punish all the people who are in the Nazi camp because they were responsible for — physical pain and uh their deaths.

Now let's see. Let's change it just slightly to make sure we understand. So far, we have pretty wide — all the leaders get punished, right? We had some disagreement on who in the camps will be punished and some of you think all the people involved in the camps and others think not quite all the people. Anybody beyond that? What about Germans who knew what was going on and did nothing to stop it?

Student: (many voices)

Student: It's too broad.

It's too broad?

Student: Yeah.

Is there anybody in the room right now who thinks that we should punish all the Germans who knew what was going on and did nothing to stop it. OK, so obviously you would not agree to punish Americans who knew about it, right? Or the British, right? So you're keeping your level of punishment to the leaders and those who are directly involved, and you have some disagreement on who is directly involved and should be punished. Have I got it right?

Part Two

You're in the U.N. It's 1947. You have now been given the legal right, whether you believe it is the moral right or not, you have been given the legal right to decide what to do with Palestine. OK, we are not talking about moral. No, we are talking about legal. You are a country, you are going to have to vote on what to do with the state of Palestine. What are you going to do?

Student: Vote for the Arabs.

For the Arabs. You are going to vote that the Arabs have — why?

Student: Additionally, I would give the Jews a piece of Germany.

OK, OK, Would you today be somewhat sympathetic to a Palestinian who comes to you and says, "My land has been taken wrongly from me and I have been driven off my land by a people and by an organization for an act that I had no responsibility for." Would you be sympathetic to a Palestinian who said that?

Jeannette: Yes.

What would you say to the Palestinian, other than to say that I am sympathetic?

Jeannette: I would say what my Daddy always says to me, that life is not fair.

So the world is not fair and life is not fair. We do the best we can. Do the Palestinians have, in your mind, some right to oppose what was done to them?

Jeannette: Yes.

Do they have the right to use force to try to, uh, change what was done to them?

Jeannette: They have a right.

In your mind?

Jeannette: Yes, they do.

How do we get out of this dilemma?

Jeannette: I don't know.

It is a real dilemma isn't it?

Jeannette: Yeah.

Anybody else? John.

John: No wait, I want to clarify a couple of things first.

OK.

John: OK, the land that is, uh, that is in question, Palestine, was once the Jews'. If we go back far enough ... it was their holy land, right?

Yes. Correct.

John: And the Arabs drove them off a long time ago.

Well, actually the Romans drove them off.

John: The Romans drove them off, OK, but they've had a history of persecution, so isn't that ...

Student: The Jews?

John: Isn't that — yeah the Jews — isn't that the significance of giving them that piece of land instead of a piece of Germany is because that's originally theirs and they have pride and heritage there and they were driven off ...?

John, would you then argue the proposition that anybody who, any group of people, who have been persecuted and driven off their land, at some time in the future should be given that land back?

John: No.

That's not your proposition?

John: That's a Halstead generalization.

Well, I thought that's what you said; did I not get what you said correct?

John: I'm talking about the Jews specifically.

All right, explain it to me again, let's see if I hear it right.

John: OK, the Jews have been burned all through history.

All right.

John: You agree with that?

Yes, I do.

John: OK, and you agree that that was once their holy land.

I agree to that.

John: So, if in fact, the UN decides to give them a piece of land, which they did, the significance of giving them that land in contrast to giving them a piece of Germany is because it was once theirs and it was, it had some significance to them, in fact we're trying to compensate for 'em, not just push them into the corner, OK.

I agree to all that, now are you saying to me that you personally, if you had been a delegate in the UN would have voted to give a portion of Palestine to the Jewish people because of that argument?

John: Correct.

Is that an argument that is valid for any other group of people or is that argument only valid to the Jewish people?

John: It's, yeah, it depends.

Well, I ... suppose ... suppose I can find, John, suppose I can find another group of people who have been persecuted for a good portion of their life and had their land taken away by another group and now these people are trying to find someplace to live where they in fact can live a fruitful life, would you in fact agree to those people getting their land back?

John: Yeah.

All right, let's talk about the American Indian. Were the American Indians persecuted?

Class: Yes.

Were they driven off their land?

Class: Yes.

Were they put in reservations?

Class: Yes.

Have we taken their land away from them?

Class: Yes.

John: And I'm not saying that's right.

Are the, are the American Indians today that are alive basically on land areas where they are not able to survive fruitfully as a people? Should they be given their land back?

Student: Some.

John: Seems logical, I mean ...

Am I correct then that, John, that you're arguing, that you would agree that we in the United States should give this land back to the American Indian because of all those circumstances?

John: They should get something, in proportion to the size of their people.

They should get something, something of the United States ... and they should get something that is worthwhile and fruitful and that they can live and survive not some junk land down in the desert ... is that correct?

Class: Yes.

Would you agree perhaps maybe Santa Clara Valley? Would you personally, John, be willing to move out of your house and turn it over to the Indians?

Class laughs.

Student: Give Ohio.

Well, that's too easy for John to give away Ohio. Would you give away your home?

John: I wouldn't be happy about it.

No you wouldn't, you would feel wronged if it happened, right?

John: Right.

Would you, would you, if the government came down and said "John Rimenshutter and family, your house has just been given away to an Indian couple". Would you feel right in taking some force against that Indian couple at a later time to get your house back?

John: Yeah.

Laurel: I wouldn't, I would ...

Laurel, you wouldn't what?

Laurel: I wouldn't.

You wouldn't what?

Laurel: I wouldn't feel comfortable using force to get my house back from the Indian couple. I would go to the government.

John: Well, yeah.

Laurel: And, and .... Well, but the question was, would you feel force ...

Laurel, you're in the UN. Would you vote to give a piece of that land to the Jewish people, or would you vote to give it to the Arabs in its entirety?

Laurel: I really ... I want to be able to feel good about giving that homeland to the Jews.

All right.

Laurel: I think they deserve it ... and I think I would vote no because the Arabs are there and it is Arab land.

So then what do we do with the Jews? It's 1946, 1947.

Laurel: And you know a lot of the time ... Jody was telling me a lot of Jews didn't want to go back to their homes that they've been ... they didn't want to go back to their German homes.

Is that rightfully so? Would you, would you agree that there is logical reason why they would not want to go back?

Laurel: Absolutely, oh absolutely ....

So what do we do with them maybe we've got thousands maybe hundreds of thousands of Jews who were in the camps they don't want to go back to Germany, they don't want to go back to Poland?

Laurel: Maybe ...

John has raised what is actually true, they want to go back to where is their historical place.

Laurel: Right, right.

You do not believe that's right, because the majority of the people who live there are Arabs now. So what are we going to do with the Jews?

Laurel: Somehow, uh ...

It's a heck of a dilemma, isn't it?

Laurel: Somehow, split up Israel so that, um, the Arabs, but yeah, but, but they didn't do that totally, I mean a lot of, there's like what, in Lebanon there's a lot of — there's many camps up there for, for ...

Palestinians.

Laurel: Palestinians and I don't think that that's fair.

OK.

Laurel: And, um, I think somehow both sides ...

In trying to correct one injustice have we created another injustice?

Laurel: Yes!

And do we, do we have in the Middle East, two groups of people who believe rightfully so, that they have been injured, and that there is a solution to their problem and that is that the solution to their problem, for both of them, is to have the land of Palestine? Now the Palestinians feel injured because their land was given away and their solution is to give them back Palestine, and the Jews feel that they have been injured historically and specifically the Holocaust and the solution to them is to give them Palestine. Haven't we got a heck of a dilemma on our hands? Yeah, Katherine.

Katherine: Well, not all of the Jews that live in Israel are survivors of the Holocaust.

I agree.

Laurel: I mean they're from, it's their homeland for people from all around the world so now they can practice freely and have a place, a place to be without being persecuted. And, when I was there, the feeling is that they are more than willing to live with the Arabs only as long as they can just be there, but, the Arabs, it seems that the Arabs only they want to be in there and they don't want — they don't — they aren't willing to live with the Jews.

Chapter 18

Using Critical Thinking to Identify National Bias in the News

with Kenneth R. Adamson

Abstract

In this previously unpublished paper, Paul and Adamson present a model for teaching students how to identify national bias in the news. This model, they argue, can be extended to any form of bias in the news. They fit the task of detecting bias into a coherent theory which illuminates the logic or pattern of sociocentric thought. Possible student instructions and samples of strong and weak student work are included.

✦ Introduction

One of the most destructive forms of bias in the world today is national bias, the tendency to analyze and assess world events through a nationalistic mind set. Though many teachers recognize that much news coverage is biased in one way or another, few see clearly how to teach students to identify bias. The purpose of this article is to explain how students can become critical consumers of the news.

The ability to identify bias is an important dimension of critical thinking and, as other dimensions, requires practice. We need: *1)* a reasonably clear theory why bias exists, how it affects our thinking, and the forms it takes; and *2)* practice identifying it. We need, then, good theory and good practice. There are many forms and dimensions of bias, so it is useful to begin with one basic form. Other forms can be added as time goes on.

Teaching students to identify bias will be no easy task, for when we are biased it appears to us that we are not. We resist the notion that we might have a bias. Many students also feel reluctant to accept this. Teachers need to be aware of this tendency in themselves and their students, and their pedagogy must reflect this awareness.

✦ The Importance of Recognizing Bias

Bias exerts a subtle, but powerful, influence on our thinking. None of us is free of it. Some biases are personal, while others are socially shared. National bias is a socially shared bias in which most citizens of a country hold a common view of themselves, their country, and the world. For example, most people in Iran believe in tenets of the Shiite Moslem religion, most people in the U.S.S.R. believe in communism, and most people in the U.S. believe in capitalism. These views are transmitted as biases to children by members of each society, most notably parents, peers, and the media. Piaget (1976) noticed this tendency and commented, "... everything suggests that, on discovering the values accepted in his immediate circle, the child felt bound to accept the circle's opinions of all other national groups". These acquired images of other countries are less favorable than one's image of one's own country, and sometimes are extremely negative. This tendency has very deep historical and psychological roots. To quote Sam Keene (1986):

> Sadly, the majority of tribes and nations create a sense of social solidarity and membership in part by systematically creating enemies. The corporate identity of most peoples depends upon dividing the world into a basic antagonism:
>
> | Us | versus | Them |
> | Insider | versus | Outsiders |
> | The tribe | versus | The enemy |

Those who teach social studies struggle against this acquired bias, for they want their students not only to understand their own culture and society, but also to develop an understanding of cultures and societies different from their own. To simply impart facts about these cultures to students and hope that understanding will follow, is too optimistic. If Piaget and Keene are right, we have strong reason to suspect the adequacy of the simple transmission of facts and pleas for fairness as sufficient to foster in students a genuine understanding of, not to mention an appreciation for, other countries and cultures. The us/them dichotomy pervades our cultural, political, and social thought, is passed on and reinforced overtly and covertly, becomes deeply entrenched in our and the students' minds, and cannot be dislodged by simply learning facts. These views have become part of the students' individual and social identity. This struggle for fairness, then, is a battle to be waged against egocentricity and sociocentricity. Students have to fight against their own deep-seated views, by itself a very powerful influence, and against uncritically held mainstream cultural conceptions of the world. Facts, by themselves, cannot win this battle. Neither is general encouragement to be fair sufficient for the student to actually be fair. Students need to gain insight into the nature of bias, the ways it influences their thought, and the methods by which it is passed on and reinforced. Only then can the student critically and fairly appraise the facts about "them". When we have biases, especially deep-seated ones, we need to *think* our way out of them. Someone else's thinking will not do.

✦ The Roots of National Bias

All of our thinking depends on our beliefs about the world. Our beliefs form the basis of how we classify, interpret, and experience things. In this sense, to have a "bias" is inevitable, for we approach all situations with some expectations and a point of view. This "inevitable bias" is compatible with objectivity *if we recognize it* and acknowledge other possible ways to classify and interpret. Indeed we become objective only to the degree that we develop this openmindedness: "I see it this way for this reason, in the light of this evidence. How do you see it? What is your point of view?"

Conversely, the illegitimately biased person regularly equates his or her point of view with *the Truth*, and so is unlikely to grant any significant truth to other systems of belief, to other perspectives. Such a person is not openminded. To move students toward objectivity we need to help them become explicitly conscious of the beliefs they implicitly hold, so that they can become skilled in recognizing when and how those beliefs shape their experience. They need to recognize, for example, that when the members of a nation are raised to implicitly believe that the motives of their leaders are "pure" while the motives of the leaders of "enemy" countries are "evil", then, though both countries might do the same thing, say, intervene in the affairs of another country, the events will be experienced differently. Objective persons see that the events can be distinguished only to the degree that these assumptions they are making about themselves and others are truly justifiable. They can see, in other words, how news items about the intervention in *our* newspapers present interpretations of events based upon *our* assumptions and beliefs, while *their* newspapers present interpretations of events based upon *their* assumptions and beliefs. We (and they) do not recognize, and even resist recognizing, that we (and they) have a picture of the world, a picture quite different from other possible pictures. Each picture may have merit but all highlight some facts at the expense of others and no picture includes, or could include, *all* of reality.

If to "have a bias" (a partial view) is inevitable, to recognize it is essential. Consider this analogy. In bowling, the word 'bias' refers to a weight that is sometimes built into the bowling ball causing it to curve toward the weighted direction. If one uses a weighted ball, and is aware that the ball is weighted, one will bowl differently. When beginning bowlers use weighted balls they usually attribute the curve to themselves. Similarly, to fail to recognize that we have a bias increases the likelihood of our seeing other beliefs and points of view as "defective", rather than seeing the partiality in our own perspective. To be aware of our bias allows us to "bowl with a biased ball", as it were, to appreciate other points of view and learn how they structure the world.

Few of us continually recognize that we see the world from some point of view. We often see our own picture of the world as the simple truth; not merely as the *best* of possible views, but as the *only* view. Those who agree with us and hold to their views strongly and unfalteringly we see as committed and dedicated, not as opinionated and dogmatic. As a case in point, consider Oliver North and the Iran-Contra scandal. Many U.S. citizens did not review the issue in any depth, but saw North's patriotic confidence in his actions as sufficient justification of them. What North said agreed perfectly with their bias, namely, that what the United States does, and what is done in the name of patriotism, is the right thing to do, even if "questionable".

Often we do not even know exactly what we believe or why we believe it. Many things just seem true to us even if we can think of no reasons to support them. We often do not consider that there may be elements of truth in other beliefs. We need to learn, then, how to fairly and accurately assess beliefs, both our own and others'. To quote Israel Scheffler (1973), the knower "must typically earn the right to confidence in his belief by acquiring the capacity to make a reasonable case for the belief in question". This task of making a reasonable case is fatally hampered if we do not recognize how our point of view and beliefs influence our thinking.

✦ Egocentricity: The Theory

'Egocentricity' is the tendency to view everything in relation to one's self, viewing the world only from one's own perspective. Since we want to bolster our self-respect and protect our self-image, we often make ourselves the standard by which we judge others. Here is a familiar example. If a driver carelessly pulls in front of me, cutting me off, I see this person as a reckless driver, and I will probably be irritated or even angry. However, if I do the same, I tend to think of myself not as "cutting another person off" but only as "pulling in close". I generally have an excuse for myself. I will not see myself, as I would see another, as careless or stupid.

This egocentric tendency manifests itself in a variety of ways. We tend to think that the beliefs and values we hold are better than the beliefs and values of others. ("*My* beliefs are accurate and true; *you* are deceived.") We also tend to believe that our attitudes are more appropriate than another's ("*I* have good reason to be angry; *you* just have a bad temper."), and that our actions are more reasonable and moral than the actions of another ("I plan; you plot."). And it is psychologically understandable that we would think this way, for if we thought that another's beliefs, attitudes, or actions were in some way better than our own, we would be faced with a problem: Why do I believe or act as I do?

This tendency toward egocentric thinking provides the basis for the creation of a dichotomous view of the world and the people in it: "We are number one!" To be unaware of this tendency allows us to propagate and preserve this illusion. We then dichotomize: We are good, they are bad or evil. Our friends are seen by us as good, but not as good as we are. Our view of our enemies, however, is typically antagonistic and hostile. Of course, we are not denying that sometimes we have solid evidence and good reasons to believe that one country is better than another in some specific way. For example, we may have statistics to demonstrate that infant mortality is lower in one country than another, or that one commits fewer human rights violations. The point is that given our eagerness to believe we are best, our minds often use evidence only after the fact, to justify what we are committed to believing in advance.

✦ Sociocentricity and National Bias: The Theory

A perfect parallel exists between egocentricity and sociocentricity: the "I" of the individual becomes the "We" of the group, since judgments are made from the perspective of the group rather than the individual. Since sociocentricity is a direct extension of egocentricity, the reader will notice here a repetition of those tendencies of egocentricity. The same basic principles apply to the one as to the other, and very little needs to be changed. We see the beliefs, values, attitudes, and actions of our group as better than those of other groups. The groups or countries that we consider friends we view positively, while groups and countries we think of as unfriendly, as rivals, or as enemies, we view negatively. Consider this thought from Jerome Frank (1982):

> Behind the arms race and wars lies a trait humans share with all social animals: fear and distrust of members of groups other than their own. When two human groups compete for the same goal, this distrust rapidly escalates into the mutual "image of the enemy".

Taking the notion of group or sociocentric bias we can apply these tendencies to a much larger group, our nation. There is, again, a perfect parallel between egocentricity and national bias (sociocentrism). We easily extend our "group think" from that of local groups to the nation as a whole. Consider the point as made by Jerome Frank (1982), focusing on how national bias influences our choice of words:

> Enemy-images mirror each other — that is, each side attributes the same virtues to itself and the same vices to the enemy. "We" are trustworthy, peace-loving, honorable, and humanitarian, "they"

are treacherous, warlike, and cruel. In surveys of Americans conducted in 1942, the first five adjectives chosen to characterize both Germans and Japanese (enemies) included warlike, treacherous, and cruel, none of which appeared among the first five describing the Russians (allies); in 1966 all three had disappeared from American characterizations of the Germans and Japanese (allies), but now the Russians (no longer allies, but more rivals than enemies) were warlike and treacherous. In 1966 the Mainland Chinese, predictably, were seen as warlike, treacherous, and sly. After President Nixon's visit to China, these adjectives disappeared from our characterizations of the Chinese, whom we now see as hardworking, intelligent, artistic, progressive, and practical.

The tendency to think egocentrically and sociocentrically, then, influences the judgments we form regarding "us" and "them", as we tend to assess the people and groups we like by different standards than those we dislike. Some predictable results follow:

A. Since we are more eager to praise those people and groups we like, we tend to notice the good things about ourselves more than we do the good things about them. We often fail to see in those people and groups we dislike the positive qualities we clearly see and readily praise in ourselves. In short, we tend to play down or ignore the good things about those we dislike, as we play up or emphasize the good things about us and those we like.

B. Since we are more eager to criticize those people and groups we dislike, we often fail to see in ourselves the negative qualities we see and readily criticize in those we dislike. In short, we tend to play up or emphasize negative qualities of those we dislike, while we tend to play down or ignore the negative qualities in ourselves.

C. Since we tend to have more positive images of ourselves and the people and groups we like, we often project into people and groups we like more noble intentions and purer motives.

It may be helpful to illustrate how these tendencies actually become articulated in the media. If we or those we like engage in some activity of a questionable or negative nature, we try to justify the activity by an appeal to motive or intent. ("We meant well.") A clear example from the *San Francisco Chronicle* (1988) illustrates this:

> For the United States the war in Vietnam was humbling, draining public hubris and setting the precedent for a deficit economy. Vietnam, with Soviet support, taught America that purity of motive does not always prevail.

While most people now consider Vietnam a tragic mistake, many believe that our motives were "pure". On the other hand, if those we dislike engage in some apparently commendable action, we tend to question their motives, often dismissing the activity as scheming or treacherous. Consider, for example, how we view the Soviet involvement in Afghanistan. For another example, consider a recent edition of "Global Affairs" (1988); in it an almost direct analogy is drawn between the Hitler of 1938 Germany and the Gorbachev of 1988 USSR:

> Despite the half century anniversary of the fatal consequences deriving from the acceptance by the Western Allies of Adolph Hitler's promises ... that he had no further political ambitions in Europe, the vision of the West is once again obscured by a smiling, apparently reasonable, and seemingly sincere authoritarian leader.

To be cautious in accepting Gorbachev's proposals is one thing, to dismiss it at the outset as Hitlerian scheming is quite another. It is easy to see the importance of an awareness of these tendencies. If unrecognized and unchecked, bias easily and quickly becomes prejudice. Only when we become sensitized to how we habitually sanitize our own behavior and negatively portray that of our "enemies", can we begin to evaluate beliefs and actions more fairly and reasonably. Only then can we see the truth in the views of others and the falsehood in our own. Only then can we see the parallels in all human behavior, the general consistency in most group rationalizations and judgments. Only then can we say that we have "earned the right to confidence in our beliefs".

✦ Language: The Importance of Precision

Many words have evaluative connotations, and when used voice our approval or censure of the subject under discussion. Rarely, however, are related words perfectly synonymous, for all words have nuances not duplicated by other words. Consider the following list of related words:

Column A:	Column B:
self-assured	arrogant
dedicated	obstinate
quiet	dull
sympathetic	indulgent
educated	indoctrinated
informed	propagandized
defenders	attackers
clever	sneaky
planners	plotters

The words in column A are related to the corresponding words in column B, but have different meanings and implications, and hence require different evidence to justify them. We use the words in column A when we approve of the subject under discussion; we use the words in column B when we disapprove. In describing ourselves or our friends we tend to use the words in column A, but in describing those we dislike, we tend to use the words in column B. "We are dedicated, they are fanatic." "We intervene to aid other countries, but they invade." "We protect our interests, but they commit acts of aggression." "We support freedom fighters, they support terrorists."

Notice that each of the examples above could have been described as an example of "sloppy" language or of misuse of terms. This is an important recognition: all biased uses of language are to that extent *incorrect* uses of language. We often use language imprecisely, allowing for the strengthening of our images of ourselves and them. To help students detect bias in language use, we must teach them how to identify misuses of words. To notice their biased language, students must learn that each word has a specific range of meaning somewhat different from every other word choice. Students must become sensitized into their use of language, they must control it as reflective, rational agents.

✦ United States' National Bias

One must first become aware of our biases before one can look for and recognize instances of it. We must, therefore, have a clear idea what mainstream United States viewpoints are, for they form the basis for our biases.

How do citizens of the U.S. see themselves and the world? Citizens of the U.S. see themselves as citizens of the greatest country in the world. They see themselves as supporting neither the extreme right or left, but as being in the well-balanced middle. They see their country as peace-loving, just, democratic and free, honest in international dealings, and abhorring terrorism. They see the United States as fundamentally right, at least on all important issues, even if the world disagrees.

It is easy to see how these attitudes influence the way we view our country and our country's actions. If we are peace-loving, it is inconceivable that we would be the aggressor in any conflict. If we intervene in the affairs of another country, it is therefore only to help them toward a more democratic government. We are there to help, even if they do not appreciate our help at the time. We are criticized only because we are misunderstood, or lied about. Even if the world is against our actions or decisions (for example, in denying Arafat a visa or invading Panama) it is because they do not understand or are unfairly set against us. With these as examples, we can move onto some classroom assignments and actual student work.

✦ Classroom Assignments

The long assignment given below is probably too much to give students without some prior in-class activities designed to foster their practical insight into national bias. You may decide to present these points to students in smaller chunks, passing them out only after group discussion. Here are some examples of what could be done initially:

1. Bring samples of articles displaying national bias into class. Read each aloud and ask the class to comment on how, if at all, the article reflects national bias.

2. Ask students to imagine how an article might have been written in a Soviet newspaper. Have students work in groups to rewrite it accordingly. How would the wording be different? What about the size of the article or its placement in the paper? Articles could even be selected from a Soviet paper, such as *Pravda*, without telling students its source. Most would probably immediately recognize its bias. They could then be asked *why and how* it is biased. After being told the article's source, students could be asked to suggest how it would have been written differently had it appeared in our press. Students will thus have a clear example of how much easier it is to spot another's bias than one's own.

3. Break the class into small groups of two or three students. Students could be asked to explain to the rest of the group what it means to talk about a national bias. As one student is explaining, the others could ask questions. Those asking the questions could be encouraged to argue the case for the objectivity of national news reporting. Roles could then be reversed.

4. Have students to bring newspapers to class and seek out examples of bias. They could work on this in groups. As articles are suggested by members of the group, the others could question why it was selected.

POSSIBLE STUDENT INSTRUCTIONS

1. Be cautious as you attempt to identify instances of national bias. Ask yourself: "To what extent is the article written with a sociocentric bias, slanting the news to reinforce a U.S. point of view?" Ignore other biases. Remember, you are not identifying regional, professional, religious, or any other bias but national.

2. Keep in mind that before you can identify our national bias in news stories, you must have a clear picture of how "Americans", as against, say, Soviets, see ourselves and the world. It is helpful to have a clear picture of how the Soviets see the world (as a point of contrast). A good way to test yourself is to take a story and imagine how that story might be written for *Isvestia* or *Pravda*.

2a. Be certain you are looking for the mainstream American point of view. Do not confuse this with your own point of view, or with that of some other group within the U.S. In any country there will always be some who dissent from the mainstream view, but this is not what we want.

3. Be sure you know what is meant by 'national bias'. Keep in mind that some of our biases may be shared by other countries. For example, the idea that our country is peaceful is part of our national bias, but many other countries may also see themselves as peaceful. Some biases are unique to the U.S., for example, belief in the superiority of the two-party system. Both the unique biases and the shared biases are part of our country's mainstream bias. Do not look only for biases peculiar to the U.S.

4. Make specific predictions about how some given story about "us" or "them" will be written before you actually read the story. Do this in order to look for specific bias. See the examples below, and try to think of others yourself.

    4a. Remember, most countries like to see themselves as peaceful and unaggressive. We are no exception. If this is so, how might our newspapers describe the deployment and use of U.S. troops in another country? As an invasion? As an act of aggression? How would you predict our newspapers would describe the deployment and use of Soviet troops in another country? Are they there by the invitation of that country's legitimate government? Then reverse the positions. How are Soviet newspapers likely to describe the deployment and use of our troops in another country?

    4b. Try to predict how the Soviets might write about, say, Israel. What words do you think they might choose to describe some of Israel's recent activities? The following article appeared on the front page of Pravda, April 2, 1988:

> Occupied Territories: Despite the *draconian repressive* measures of the occupational authorities, Palestinians took to the streets in the past 24 hours to express protest against the *terror unleashed on them by the aggressors.* A UN spokesman stated that on Wednesday, Land Day, the Israeli *aggressors* killed eight people and wounded 250 in carrying out *punitive actions* against the Palestinians.

    Notice the italicized words. What do they tell you about a mainstream Soviet viewpoint? How would you predict the Soviets might write about the Palestinians? How might *we* describe some of their actions?

5. Remember to pay attention to story placement. Is it on the front page, inside the paper? If a story does not support the mainstream U.S. point of view, where would we expect to find it? Will it be given much space or little space? Other than trivial "fillers" used by the press to fill space, what sorts of articles can we predict will be buried within the paper?

6. Look for key information within the article. What occurs at the beginning of the article? What at the end? For example, the *San Francisco Chronicle* once ran a front page story reporting on some Palestinian "terrorist" attacks on Israeli villages. At the end of the last paragraph, which was continued on the back page, it briefly mentioned that the Palestinians said they had done this in response to Israeli "terrorist" attacks made against them. Its placement toward the end suggests to those few who had read this far that the Palestinian allegations of Israeli terrorist attacks on Palestinians were insignificant, or even wrong.

7. What is the headline of the story? Imagine other possible headlines.

8. Pay attention to word choice, especially note charged words. Who gets the positive words? Who gets the negative words?

9. Remember the general logic of nationally biased communications:

9a. They play up what is positive about us and our allies or friends.

9b. They play down what is negative about us and our allies or friends.

9c. They play up what is negative about our enemies, their allies and friends.

9d. They play down what is positive about our enemies, their allies and friends.

10. Finally, note exceptions to this rule: When might you expect to see our news play up some positive news about "them"? If the Soviet Union is making some changes that we consider positive, for example, toward free enterprise, this may become front page news. ("They finally have to admit that free enterprise is the best economic system.") Conversely, when might you expect to see our news play up some negative news about this country? What negative news about this country can be criticized by the media, and what cannot?

11. Here is a way to try out your skills. Go through the newspaper page by page, identifying stories, editorials, advertisements, etc., that may be biased. Examine them one by one to determine whether they are biased, and if they are, whether you need to make a number of points about them, or just one. If you are making just one point, you may be able to group it with others. For example, you might group together a set of articles which are "buried" (that is, where negative information about "us" or positive information about "them" is being played down by placement).

12. When you do have a number of points to make, underline passages in the article and number them. Write your points clearly and give your reasons for them. Do this on a separate attached page, or at least make sure the reader can understand what you are saying.

13. When you have all your evidence assembled, write an introduction that explains to the reader what you have done and why. Write it so as to help the reader figure out exactly what you are presenting. Assume that the reader has never heard of national bias in the news.

✦ Examples of Student Work

As would be expected, student work will demonstrate a wide range of understanding, from superficial and impressionistic, to deep and insightful. What follows are examples of actual student work on the identification of national bias. Some of the examples betray a superficial understanding, others deep and insightful understanding. In reading both good and bad examples of work, the teacher will see the kinds of misunderstanding to anticipate, as well as the kind of work to have as a goal.

EXAMPLES OF WEAK WORK

Some students have trouble going beyond an impressionistic understanding of national bias. In the examples that follow, the students' commentaries reflect basic misunderstandings. One tendency is to go to extremes, as in the following: "If bias tends to influence us to look at the bad things about them and the good things about us, then *any* bad news about them is biased and *any* good news about us is biased."

This first example illustrates how some students see any bad news as biased. Of course, the fact that it contains negative news is not enough to suggest bias. The article quite fairly points out that the United States also has a serious drug and AIDS problem which the student, eager to see bias, failed to acknowledge.

> Quote From Article (Source not cited) The headline reads: "Heroin problem in Italy growing at alarming rate" Quotes from the article: "Overdose deaths skyrocket ... spread of AIDS among addicts ... two-thirds of those with AIDS are intravenous drug users .... Italians have cause for worry."

> *Student Commentary* "This article is plainly biased. The huge heading of Italy's drug problem says it all. Throughout the article the press is stating fact for fact how terrible Italy's drug and AIDS problem is."

This second article shows how positive news about the U.S. is seen by the student as being biased. The article, however, was not obviously biased.

> Quote From Article (Source not cited) Headline: "Even War-Torn Nations Aid Armenia, Rare Soviet Acceptance of Help." First paragraph: "From Los Angeles and New York, from Argentina and Cuba,

from Britain, Scandinavia, Israel and Japan, people around the world sent food, medical supplies, and rescue equipment to victims of the earthquake in Soviet Armenia."

Student Commentary "This front page article, with a huge heading, flashes "good deed" in front of the American readers eyes. Of course, it is a good thing for war-torn nations to aid Armenia, but as you read on in the article you notice that it is making the U.S. first on the list of contributors."

This next example shows a student making unsupported allegations. The student was probably having difficulty in finding articles with bias, and so had to "make" one with a bias. This commentary probably gives us more insight into the student's own bias than into any actual bias the article may contain.

Quote From Article (Source not cited.) The headline reads: "Abortion most cited issue". The article reads: "Despite all the T.V. ads and speeches on prison furloughs and the Pledge of Allegiance, few voters cited these as key issues. The No. 1 issue: abortion, cited by nearly a third of voters interviewed by ABC News. And those who cited abortion went for Bush. The issues that dominated the campaigns were cited less frequently, about 10 percent each on furloughs and the Pledge. One in four voters mentioned the drug problem and split nearly evenly between the candidates."

Student Commentary "The paper did not want the public to know that the issues the two candidates used against each other so viciously were not the issues that the people wanted to hear the answers to. The issue of abortion was not a commercial for Bush or Dukakis, but why is it the No. 1 danced around issue? Because the conservatives avoid the issue until the election is over in order to steal some of the votes of the liberals, then put their beliefs and views into action once elected."

EXAMPLES OF STRONG WORK

The following excerpts illustrate work in which students demonstrate a basic understanding of bias in general, and national bias in particular. The student commentary is not perfect, and should not be taken by the reader as exemplary work. It serves only to illustrate a student's first steps toward understanding and identifying national bias.

The following article is a fairly good example of a buried story, one placed in the background either because it puts us in a negative light or one of our enemies in a somewhat positive light.

Quote From Article *(Los Angeles Times,* 11–14–88 p. 12) Headline: "Grim Picture of Reagan's Legacy to U.S. Defenses" First paragraph: "Today's high technology weapons are so expensive that President

Bush will not have enough money to operate them and still pay for all the new ones that President Reagan has ordered but not paid for, according to military budget analysts."

Student Commentary "This story is buried because it contradicts the popular assumption that the U.S. defense industry has been strengthened through heavy financial support by the Reagan administration .... Because it identifies fallacies in administration and defense department assumptions, and verifies the assessment of failure from normally supportive sources, this information has been buried. Though it has national significance, it runs counter to the belief of many Americans that national defense has been strengthened by the Reagan administration."

This next article illustrates how word choice influences our perception of the situation. In this example, our position is made to look better, and the "enemy" made to look worse.

Quote From Article *(San Francisco Chronicle,* 12–01–88 p. A25) Headline: "Envoy to U.N. Downplays Flap Over Arafat." The first paragraph reads: "U.N. Ambassador Vernon Walters told a San Francisco audience yesterday that the Reagan administration is right in denying an entry visa to PLO chairman Yasser Arafat, and that the whole controversy will blow over in a couple of weeks."

Student Commentary "This headline's use of the word 'flap' implies that the controversy surrounding the U.S. denial of Arafat's visa to speak before the U.N. is trivial. Other word choices could have been 'outrage' or 'protest'.... Asserting that the U.S. 'never signed an agreement allowing criminals into the country' sidesteps the fact that the U.S. signed an agreement not to impede access to the U.N. forum for any representative of an issue before that body .... Shunting attention to other issues, also biased, he attacked the Vietnamese government with emotive words, characterizing it as an 'abominable, tyrannical regime'. He follows with the assertion that the U.S. 'forced' the Soviets to realize their 'failure' as an imperialistic nation. Neither of these two last issues have any bearing on the story, but rather try to shore up a very weak position by diverting attention."

✦ From National Bias to Bias Detection in General

Once we and our students understand how to identify national bias, we should be well on the way to recognizing how to identify other forms of bias: personal, professional, religious, regional, etc. In each case we need to recognize that we do have a point of view we favor and that this commitment to one way of seeing things affects the way we represent and experience particular events.

For example, consider a professional bias — that of the American Medical Association. To recognize that doctors who belong to the AMA have a bias is to realize that they have a particular way of viewing issues which affect the medical profession, a view which supports their interests regardless of the evidence. Identifying these biases will help us predict the stance taken by the AMA on major issues. For example, the approach of the AMA to health care is generally pharmacological and surgical. We would expect, then, that they would be opposed to such things as home birth, holistic medicine and chiropractics. Furthermore, given their financial interests, we can be confident that the official position of the AMA on socialized medicine will be negative, unless at some later date it becomes possible to make more money under a national health act than under a private system.

To sum up, people typically presuppose their points of view to be the truth. This uncritical closedmindedness perpetuates prejudice. Individuals are not inclined to examine and question their own biases, unless they develop critical insight into them. Neither are they inclined to consider whether another's point of view is more accurate or insightful than their own. We must help students discover that no single point of view contains all the truth, that no single perspective is without limitations and weaknesses, that confusing one's own point of view with reality inevitably produces biases and prejudices. These recognitions require extensive practice. Only when students grasp this explicitly, and systematically begin to critically assess their own biases can they begin to correct and improve how they look at the world. It is our responsibility as teachers to design activities and assignments that directly facilitate this end.

✦ References

Frank, Jerome. "Psychological Causes of the Nuclear Arms Race." *CHEMTECH* August, 1982, p. 467.

Friedlander, Robert A. "The Munich Affliction: Will It Happen Again?" *Global Affairs,* Fall, 1988, p. 18.

Keene, Sam. *Faces of the Enemy.* Harper and Row, San Francisco. 1986 p. 18.

Piaget, Jean. "The Transition From Egocentricity to Reciprocity" *Piaget Sampler, An Introduction to Jean Piaget Through His Own Words.* Campbell, Sarah F. (ed.) John Wiley and Sons, New York. 1976 p. 48.

"Dawning of a New World Order." Briefing section, *San Francisco Chronicle,* December 8, 1988 p. 1.

Scheffler, Israel "Philosophical Models of Teaching." *Reason And Teaching,* Bobbs-Merrill and Co., Inc. New York. 1973 p. 7.

Chapter 19

Teaching Critical Thinking in the Strong Sense:
A Focus on Self-Deception, World Views, and a Dialectical Mode of Analysis

Abstract

This revised paper, originally published in Informal Logic *in (1982), is one of the most influential of Richard Paul's writings among philosophers interested in critical thinking. In it, Paul questions some of the major assumptions that underlie much instruction in critical thinking at the college level. In so doing, Paul implicitly broadens the concept of critical thinking and links it with the problem of rationality. He links the assessment of "arguments" ultimately to the assessment of "forms of life". He argues that a world view is implicit in our behavior as well as in our public pronouncements, and further, that there are inevitable contradictions and conflicts between what we do and how we describe what we do. In this view reasoning is implicit in and intrinsic to human life and behavior. Because much of our reasoning is buried in our lives, and because there are multiple points of view possible in which to reason, the ability to enter sympathetically into divergent perspectives and to explicate the deepest substructure in reasoning are crucial to Paul's view of critical thinking. Finally, in this paper Paul emphasizes the significance of human interests, often vested interests, lurking behind, shaping, and distorting reasoning. Understanding this, it is easy to see why Paul argues against an atomistic approach to assessment of the strengths and weaknesses of reasoning, why he believes that to appreciate a line of reasoning we must appreciate how it stands up under criticism from opposing lines of reasoning, and why he so often sees strengths as implicit insights and weaknesses as distortions, as obfuscation of counter insights. For Paul there is often unexpressed motivation behind "mistakes" in reasoning. Humans often make the "mistakes" that serve their interests. We develop our ethical sensitivity only by recognizing the subtlety and pervasiveness of the dark side of human thought and reason. Given the decisions that all adults, like it or not, must make for human good or ill, it is not possible to be both intellectually naive and an ethical adult.*

... no abstract or analytic point exists out of all connection with historical, personal thought: ... every thought belongs, not just somewhere, but to someone, and is at home in a context of other thoughts, a context which is not purely formally prescribed. Thoughts ... are something to be known and understood in these concrete terms.

Isaiah Berlin, *Concepts and Categories*, xii

✦ *The Weak Sense: Dangers and Pitfalls*

*T*o teach a critical thinking course is to make important and often frustrating decisions about what to include and exclude, what to conceive as one's primary goals and what secondary, and how to tie all of what one includes into a coherent relationship to one's goals. There have been considerable and important debates on the value of a "symbolic" versus a "non-symbolic" approach, the appropriate definition and classification of fallacies, appropriate analysis of extended and non-extended arguments, and so forth. There has been little discussion, and as far as I know, virtually no debate, on how to avoid the fundamental dangers in teaching such a course: that of "sophistry" on the one hand (inadvertently teaching students to use critical concepts and techniques to maintain their most deep-seated prejudices and irrational habits of thought by making them appear more rational and putting their opponents on the defensive), and that of "dismissal" (the student rejects the subject either as sophistry or in favor of some supposed alternative — feeling, intuition, faith, higher consciousness, ...).

Students, much as we might sometimes wish it, do not come to us as "blank slates" upon which we can inscribe the inference-drawing patterns, analytic skills, and truth-facing motivations we value. Students studying critical thinking at the university level have highly developed belief systems buttressed by deep-seated uncritical, egocentric, and sociocentric habits of thought by which they interpret and process their experiences, whether academic or not, and place them into some larger perspective. Consequently, most students find it easy to question *only* those beliefs, assumptions, and inferences they have already "rejected", and very difficult, often traumatic, to question those in which they have a personal, egocentric investment.

I know of no way of teaching critical thinking so that the student who learns to recognize questionable assumptions and inferences only in "egocentrically neutral" cases, *automatically* transfers those skills to the egocentric and sociocentric ones. Indeed, I think the opposite more commonly occurs. Those students who already have sets of biased assumptions, stereotypes, egocentric and sociocentric beliefs, taught to recognize "bad" reasoning in "neutral" cases (or in the case of the "opposition") become *more* sophistic rather than less so, more skilled in rationalizing and intellectualizing their biases. They are then *less* rather than *more* likely to abandon them if they later meet someone who questions them. Like the religious believer who studies apologetics, they now have a variety of critical moves to use in defense of their *a priori* egocentric belief systems.

This is not the effect, of course, we wish our teaching to have. Virtually all teachers of critical thinking want their teaching to have a global "Socratic" effect, making major inroads into the everyday reasoning of the student, enhancing to some degree that healthy, practical, and skilled skepticism one naturally and rightly associates with the *rational* person. Therefore, students need experience in seriously questioning previously held beliefs and assumptions and in identifying contradictions and inconsistencies in personal and social life. When we think along these lines and get glimpses into the everyday lives and habits of our students, most of us probably experience moments of frustration and cynicism.

I don't think the situation is hopeless, but I do believe the time has come to raise serious questions about how we now teach critical thinking. Current methods, as I conceive them, often inadvertently encourage critical thinking in the "weak" sense. The most fundamental and questionable assumption of these approaches (whether formal or informal) is that critical thinking can be successfully taught as a battery of technical skills which can be mastered more or less one-by-one without giving serious attention to self-deception, background logic, and multi-categorical ethical issues.

The usual scenario runs something like this. One begins with some general pep-talk on the importance of critical thinking in personal and social life. In this pep-talk one reminds students of the large scale social problems created by prejudice, irrationality, and sophistic manipulation. Then one launches into a discussion of the difference between arguments and non-arguments and students are led to believe that, without any further knowledge of contextual or background considerations, they can learn to analyze and evaluate arguments by parsing them into, and examining the relation between, "premises" and "conclusions". (The "non-arguments" presumably do not need critical appraisal.) To examine that relationship, students look for formal or informal fallacies, conceived as atomically determinable and correctable "mistakes". Irrationality is implied thereby to be reducible to complex combinations of atomic mistakes. One roots it out, presumably, by rooting out the atomic mistakes, one-by-one.

Models of this kind do not effectively teach critical thinking. This atomistic "weak sense" approach and the questionable assumptions underlying it should be contrasted with an alternative approach specifically designed to avoid its pitfalls.

This alternative view rejects the idea that critical thinking can be taught as a battery of atomic technical skills independent of egocentric beliefs and commitments. Instead of "atomic arguments" (a set of premises and a conclusion) it emphasizes argument *networks* (world views); instead of evaluating atomic arguments it emphasizes a more dialectical and dialogical approach. Arguments need to be appraised in relation to counter-arguments. One can make moves that are very difficult to defend or ones that strengthen one's position. An atomic argument is merely a limited set of moves within a more complex set of moves reflecting a variety of logically significant engagements in the world. Argument exchanges are means by which contesting points of view are brought into rational conflict. A line of reasoning can rarely be refuted by an individual charge of fallacy, however well supported. The charge of fallacy is a move, however it is rarely logically compelling, it virtually never refutes a point of view. This approach more accurately reflects our own and the student's experience of argument exchanges.

By immediately introducing students to these more "global" problems in the analysis and evaluation of reasoning, we help them more clearly see the relationship between world views, forms of life, human engagements and interests, what is at stake (versus what is at issue), how what is at issue is often itself at issue, how the unexpressed as well as the expressed may be significant, the difficulties of judging credibility, and the ethical dimension in most important and complex human problems.

✦ Some Basic Theory: World Views, Forms of Life

Here are some basic theoretical underpinnings for a "strong sense" approach:

1) As humans we are — first, last, and always — engaged in inter-related life projects which, taken as a whole, define our personal "form of life" in relation to broader social forms. Because we are engaged in some projects rather than others, we organize or conceptualize the world and our place in it in somewhat different terms than others do. We have somewhat different *interests,* somewhat different *stakes,* and somewhat different *perceptions* of what is so. We make somewhat different assumptions and reason somewhat differently from them.

2) We also express to ourselves and others a more articulated view of how we see things, a view only partially consistent at best with the view presupposed by and reflected in our behavior. We have, then, *two* world views overlapping each other, one implicit in our activity and engagements, another implicit in how we describe our behavior. One must recognize contradictions between these conflicting views to develop as a critical thinker and as a person in good faith with one's self. Both traits are measured by the degree to which we can articulate what we live and live what we articulate.

3) Reasoning is an essential and defining operation presupposed by all human acts. To reason is to use elements in a logical system to generate conclusions. Conclusions may be explicit in words or implicit in behavior. Sometimes reasoning is explicitly cast into the form of an argument, sometimes not. However, since reasoning presupposes a system or systems of which it is a manifestation, the full implications of reasoning are rarely (if ever) exhausted or displayed in arguments in which they are cast. Arguments presuppose questions at issue. Questions at issue presuppose a point of view and interests at stake. Different points of view frequently differ, not simply in answers to questions, but in the appropriate formulations of questions themselves.

4) When we, including those of us who are logicians, analyze and evaluate arguments important to us (this includes all arguments which, if accepted, would strengthen or weaken beliefs to which we have committed ourselves in word or deed), we do so in relationship to prior belief-commitments. The best we can do to move toward increased objectivity is to bring to the surface the set of beliefs, assumptions, and inferences from the perspective of which our analysis proceeds, and to see explicitly the dialectical nature of our task, the critical moves we might make at various points, and the various possible counter-moves to them.

5) Skill in analyzing and evaluating reasoning is skill in reciprocity, the ability to reason within more than one point of view, understanding strengths and weaknesses through comprehending the objections that could be raised at various points in the arguments by alternative points of view.

6) Laying out elements of reasoning in deductive form is useful, not principally to see whether a "mistake" had been made, but to see critical moves one might make to determine the strengths and weaknesses of the reasoning in relation to alternatives.

7) Since vested interest typically influences perception, assumptions, reasoning in general, and specific conclusions, we must become aware of the nature of our own and others' engagements to recognize strengths and weaknesses in reasoning.

   a) Only when we recognize that a given argument reflects or, if justified, would serve a given interest can we, by imaginatively entertaining a competing interest, construct an opposing point of view and so an opposing argument or set of arguments. By developing both arguments dialectically, we can see their strengths and weaknesses.

   b) Arguments are not things-in-themselves but constructions of specific people who must further interpret and develop them, for example, to answer objections. By recognizing the interests typically correlated with given arguments, we can often challenge the credibility of others' premises by alluding to discrepancies between what they say and what they do. In doing so we force them to critique their own behavior in line with the implications of their arguments, or to abandon the line of argument. There are a variety of critical moves they may make upon being so challenged.

 c) By reflecting on interests as implicit in behavior, one can often much more effectively construct the assumptions most favorable to those interests. Once formulated, one can begin to formulate alternative competing assumptions. Both can then be more effectively questioned and arguments for and against them can be entertained.

8) The total set of factual claims that buttress a world view, hence the various arguments generated by it, is usually indefinitely large and often involves shifting conceptual problems and implicit judgments of value (especially shifts in how to formulate the "facts"). The credibility of an individual claim often depends on the credibility of many other claims; very often the claims themselves are very difficult to verify "directly" and atomically. Very often then, to analyze an argument, we must judge relative credibility. These judgments are more plausible if they take into account the vested interests and the track records of the sources.

9) The terms in which an argument is cast often reflects the biased interest of the person who formulated it. Calling into question the very concepts used or the use to which they are put is an important critical move. To become adept at this, we must practice recognizing how social groups systematically and selectively move back and forth between usage in keeping with the logic of ordinary language and that which accords with the ideological commitments of the group (and so conflicts with ordinary use). Consider the ways many people use key terms in current international debate — say, 'freedom fighter', 'liberator', 'revolutionary', 'guerrilla', 'terrorist' — and reflect on:

 a) what is implied by the *logic* of the terms apart from the usage of any particular social group (say U.S. citizens, Germans, Israelis, Soviets);

 b) what is implied by the usage of a particular group with vested interests (say, U.S. citizens, Germans, Israelis, Soviets);

 and

 c) the various historical examples that suggest inconsistency in the use of these by that group, and how this inconsistency depends on fundamental, typically unexpressed, assumptions. Through such disciplined reflection, one can identify predictable, self-serving inconsistencies.

✦ Multi-Dimensional Ethical Issues

Teaching critical thinking in the strong sense helps students develop reasoning skills precisely in those areas where they are most likely to have egocentric and sociocentric biases. Such biases exist most profoundly in areas of their identities and vested interests. Their identities and interests are linked in turn to their unarticulated world views. One's unarticulated world view represents the person that one *is* (the view implicit in the principles which guide one's actions). One's articulated view represents the person that one *thinks* one is (the view implicit in the principles used to *justify* one's actions). Excepting honest mistakes, the contradictions or inconsistencies between these two represent the degree to which one reasons and acts in bad faith or self-deceptively.

Multi-dimensional issues involving proposed ethical justifications for behavior are ideal for teaching critical thinking. Most political, social, and personal issues which most concern us and students are of this type — abortion, nuclear energy, nuclear arms, the nature of national security, poverty, social injustices of various kinds, revolution and intervention, socialized medicine, government regulation, sexism, racism, problems of love and friendship, jealousy, rights to private property, rights to world resources, faith and intuition versus reason, and so forth.

Obviously one can cover only a few such issues, and I believe that the advantages lie in covering fewer of them deeply and intensively. I am certainly unsympathetic to inundating the student with an array of truncated arguments set up to "illustrate" atomic fallacies.

Since I teach in the United States, and since the media here as everywhere else in the world reflects, and most students have internalized, a profoundly nationalistic bias, I focus one segment of my course on identifying national bias in the news. In doing this, students must face issues that, to be approached dialectically, require them to discover that mainstream "American" reasoning and the mainstream "American" point of view on world issues is not the only dialectical possibility. I identify as mainstream American views any which have significant support with the Democratic and Republican parties. This segment of the course serves a number of purposes:

1) Though most students have internalized much media "propaganda", so that their egos are partly identified with it, they are neither totally taken in by that propaganda nor incapable of beginning to systematically question it.

2) The students become more adept at constructing and more empathetic toward alternative lines of reasoning as the *sociocentric assumptions* of mainstream media coverage come more and more to the surface — for example, the assumptions that:

a) the U.S. government, compared to other governments, is more committed to ideals;

b) U.S. citizens have more energy, more practical know-how, and more common sense than others;

c) the world as a whole would be better off (freer, safer, more just) if the U.S. had *more* power;

d) U.S. citizens are less greedy and self-deceived than others;

e) U.S. lives are more important than the lives of other peoples.

3) Explicitly addressing and constructing dialectical alternatives to political and national as well as professional and religious "party lines" and exploring their contradictions enables students to draw parallels to their personal and their peer groups' "party lines" and the myriad contradictions in their talk and behavior. Such "discoveries" explicitly and dramatically forge the beginnings of a commitment to developing the "critical spirit", the foundation for "strong sense" skills and insights.

✦ *A Sample Assignment and Results*

It is useful to provide one sample assignment to indicate how my concerns and objectives can be translated into assignments. The following was assigned last semester (1984) as a take-home mid-term examination, approximately six weeks into the semester. The students were allowed three weeks to complete it.

> The objective of this mid-term is to determine the extent to which you understand and can effectively use the basic concepts of the course: world view, assumptions, concepts (personal, social, implicit in language, technical), evidence (empirical claims), implications, consistency, conclusions, premises, questions-at-issue.
>
> You are to view and critically and sympathetically analyze two films: *Attack on the Americas* (a right-wing think-tank film alleging Communist control of Central American revolutionaries) and *Revolution or Death* (a *World Council of Church's* film defending the rebels in El Salvador). Two incompatible world views are presented in those films. After analyzing the films and consulting whatever background material you deem necessary to understand the two world views, construct a dialogue between two of the most intelligent defenders of each perspective. They should each demonstrate skills in explicating the basic assumptions, the questionable claims, ideas, inferences, values, and conclusions of the other side. Both should be able to make some concessions to the other point of view without conceding their basic positions. Each should be able to summarize some of the inferences of the other side and raise questions

about those inferences (e.g., "You appear to me to be arguing in the following way. You assume that .... You ignore that .... And then you conclude that ....").

In the second part of your paper, write a third-person commentary on the debate, indicating which point of view is in the strongest position logically in your view. Argue for your position; do not simply assert it. Give good reasons for rejecting or accepting whatever aspects of the two world views you reject or accept. Make clear to the reader how your position reflects your world view. The dialogue should have at least 14 exchanges (28 entries) and the commentary should be at least 4 typewritten pages.

A variety of background materials were made available, including the U.S. State Department "White Paper", an open letter from the late Archbishop of San Salvador, a copy of the Platform of the El Salvador rebels, and numerous current newspaper and magazine articles and editorials on the issue. The students were encouraged to discuss and debate the issue outside of class (which they did). The students were expected to document how the major newspapers were covering the story (e.g., that accounts favorable to the State Department position tended to be given front page coverage while accounts critical of the State Department position, say from *Amnesty International,* were de-emphasized on pages 9 through 17). There was also discussion of internal inconsistencies within the accounts. Many of the students came to see one or more of the following points:

1) That in a conflict such as this the two sides disagree not only on conclusions but even about how the issue ought to be put. One side will put the issue, for example, in terms of the dangers of a communist takeover, the other in terms of the need for people to over-throw a repressive regime. One will see the fundamental problem as caused by Cuban and Soviet intervention, the other side by U.S. intervention. Each side will see the other as begging the essential question.

2) That a debate on how to word the issue will often become a debate on a series of factual questions. This debate will be extended into a series of historical questions. Each side will typically see the other as suppressing evidence. Those favorable to the Duarte regime, for example, will see the other side as suppressing evidence of the extent of communist involvement in El Salvador. Those favorable to the rebels will see the other side as suppressing evidence of government complicity in terrorist acts of the right. There will be disagreement about which side is committing most of the violent acts.

3) That these factual disagreements will at some point or another lead to a shifting of ground to *conceptual disagreements:* which acts should be called 'terrorist' which 'revolutionary', and which 'acts of liberation'. This debate will at some point become a debate about *values,* about which acts are reprehensible or justified. Very often the acts which from one perspective seem required by circumstances will be morally condemned by the other.

4) That at various points in the discussion the debate will become "philosophical" or "anthropological", involving broad issues concerning "the nature of man" and "the nature of human society". The side supporting the government tends to take a philosophical position that plays down the capacity of "mass man" to make rational and appropriate judgments in its own behalf, at least when under the influence of outside agitators and subversives. The other side tends to be more favorable to "mass man" and suspicious of our government's capacity or right to make what appear to them to be decisions that should be left to the people. Each side thinks the other begs important questions, suppresses evidence, stereotypes, uses unjustified analogies, uses faulty causal reasoning, misuses concepts, and so forth.

Such assignments help students appreciate the kinds of moves that typically occur in everyday argument, put them into perspective, and construct alternative arguments, precisely because they more clearly see how arguments develop in relation to each other and so in relation to a broader perspective. They give students more practical insight into the motivated nature of argument "flaws" than the traditional approach. They are therefore better able to anticipate them and more sensitive to the special probing moves that need to be made. Finally, they are much more sensitive (than I believe they would be under most "weak sense" approaches) to the profound ethical consequences of ego-serving reasoning, and to the ease with which we can fall prey to it. If we can indeed accomplish something like these results, then there is much to be said for further work and development of "strong sense" approaches. What I have described here is, I hope, the beginning of such work.

Postscript

In the five years since I wrote this paper, I have become increasingly convinced that if students are to learn to think critically in a strong sense, they must be exposed to critical thinking over an extended period of time, over years not months. To think critically in a strong sense is to become a critical person. It is to develop particular values and traits of mind in addition to particular skills and abilities. If we are committed to critical thinking, we must then be committed to major reform of education, for most schooling is didactic in nature and discourages rather than encourages critical thinking and the values and dispositions essential to it.

As time passes it becomes increasingly apparent that the field of critical thinking is only now beginning to develop. If critical thinking is to be encouraged in every discipline, every discipline must reconceptualize the manner in which students acquire its knowledge. Knowledge and thought are in a reciprocal relation. The traits of mind essential to critical thinking should be fostered in every subject area or domain, not just in selected assignments.

Section II

Staff Development

Critical Thinking Staff Development: The Lesson Plan Remodeling Approach

The Greensboro Plan: A Sample Staff Development Plan

Critical Thinking and Learning Centers

Chapter 20

Critical Thinking Staff Development:
The Lesson Plan Remodeling Approach

with A. J. A. Binker

Abstract

No one can teach critical thinking who does not think critically. Unfortunately, most teachers did not have their own critical thinking developed when they were students. Furthermore, few have time to take courses in critical thinking to develop their own thinking. The result is that staff development in critical thinking must be designed to accomplish two ends: 1) to stimulate and develop the critical thinking of teachers and 2) to help them transform their teaching from a didactic to a critical, dialogical model of education. In this paper from the Critical Thinking Handbook *series, Binker and Paul summarize "the basic idea behind lesson plan remodeling as a strategy for staff development in critical thinking."*

$\mathcal{T}$he basic idea behind lesson plan remodeling as a strategy for staff development in critical thinking is simple. Every practicing teacher works daily with lesson plans of one kind or another. To remodel lesson plans is to critique one or more lesson plans and to formulate one or more new lesson plans based on that critical process. It is well done when the remodeler understands the strategies and principles used in producing the critique and remodel, when the strategies are well-thought-out, and when the remodel clearly follows from the critique. The idea behind our particular approach to staff development in lesson plan remodeling is also simple. A group of teachers or a staff development leader with a reasonable number of exemplary remodels and explanatory principles can design practice sessions that enable teachers to begin to develop new teaching skills as a result of experience in lesson remodeling.

When teachers have clearly contrasting "befores" and "afters", lucid and specific critiques, a set of principles clearly explained and illustrated, and a coherent unifying concept, they can increase their own skills in this process. One learns how to remodel lesson plans to incorporate critical thinking only through practice. The more one does it the better one gets, especially when one has examples of the process to serve as models.

Of course, a lesson remodeling strategy for critical thinking in-service is not tied to any particular handbook of examples, but it is easy to see the advantages of having such a handbook, assuming it is well-executed. Some teachers lack a clear concept of critical thinking. Some stereotype it as negative, judgmental thinking. Some have only vague notions, such as "good thinking", or "logical thinking", with little sense of how such ideals are achieved. Others think of it simply in terms of a laundry list of atomistic skills and so cannot see how these skills need to be orchestrated or integrated, or how they can be misused. Teachers rarely have a clear sense of the relationship between the component micro-skills, the basic, general concept of critical thinking, and the obstacles to using it fully.

It is theoretically possible but, practically speaking, unlikely that most teachers will sort this out for themselves as a task in abstract theorizing. In the first place, few teachers have much patience with abstract theory or little experience in developing it. In the second place, few school districts could give them the time to do so, even if they were qualified and motivated enough themselves. But sorting out the basic concept is not the only problem. Someone must also translate that concept into "principles", link the "principles" to applications, and implement them in specific lessons.

On the other hand, if we simply give teachers prepackaged finished lesson plans designed by someone else, using a process unclear to them, then we have lost a major opportunity for the teachers to develop their own critical thinking skills, insights, and motivations. Furthermore, teachers who cannot use basic critical thinking principles to critique and remodel their own lesson plans probably won't be able to implement someone else's effectively. Providing teachers with the scaffolding for carrying out the process for themselves and examples of its use opens the door for continuing development of critical skills and insights. It begins a process which gives the teacher more and more expertise and success in critiquing and remodeling the day-to-day practice of teaching.

Lesson plan remodeling can become a powerful tool in critical thinking staff development for other reasons as well. It is action-oriented and puts an immediate emphasis on close examination and critical assessment of what is taught on a day-to-day basis. It makes the problem of critical thinking infusion more manageable by paring it down to the critique of particular lesson plans and the progressive infusion of particular principles. It is developmental in that, over time, more and more lesson plans are remodeled, and what has been remodeled can be remodeled again; more strategies can be systematically infused as they become clear to the teacher. It provides a means of cooperative learning for teachers. Its results can be collected and shared, at both the site and district levels, so teachers can learn from and be encouraged by what other teachers do. The dissemination of plausible remodels provides recognition for motivated teachers. Lesson plan remodeling forges a unity between staff development, curriculum development, and student development. It avoids recipe solutions to critical thinking instruction. And, finally, properly conceptualized and implemented, it unites cognitive and affective goals and integrates the curriculum.

Of course, the remodeling approach is no panacea. It will not work for the deeply complacent or cynical, or for those who do not put a high value on students' learning to think for themselves. It will not work for those who lack a strong command of critical thinking skills and self-esteem. It will not work for those who are "burned out" or have given up on change. Finally, it will not work for those who want a quick and easy solution based on recipes and formulas. It is a long-term solution that transforms teaching by degrees as teachers' critical insights and skills develop and mature. Teachers who can develop the art of critiquing their lesson plans and using their critiques to remodel them more and more effectively, will progressively 1) refine and develop their own critical thinking skills and insights; 2) re-shape the actual or "living" curriculum (what is in fact taught); and 3) develop their teaching skills.

The approach to lesson remodeling developed by the Center for Critical Thinking and Moral Critique depends on the publication of handbooks which illustrate the remodeling process, unifying well-thought-out critical thinking theory with practical application. They explain critical thinking by translating general theory into specific teaching strategies. The strategies are multiple, allowing teachers to infuse more strategies as they clarify more dimensions of critical thought. This is especially important since the skill at, and insight into, critical thought varies.

This approach, it should be noted, respects the autonomy and professionalism of teachers. *They* choose which strategies to use in a particular situation and control the rate and style of integration. It is a flexible approach, maximizing the teacher's creativity and insight. The teacher can apply the strategies to any kind of material: textbook lessons, the teacher's own lessons or units, discussion outside of formal lessons, discussion of movies, etc.

In teaching for critical thinking in the strong sense, we are committed to teaching in such a way that children, as soon and as completely as possible, learn to become responsible for their own thinking. This requires them to learn how to take command of their thinking, which requires them to learn how to notice and think about their own thinking, and the thinking of others. Consequently, we help children talk about their thinking in order to be mindful and directive in it. We want them to study their own minds and how they operate. We want them to gain tools by which they can probe deeply into and take command of their own mental processes. Finally, we want them to gain this mentally skilled self-control to become more honest with themselves and more fair to others, not only to "do better" in school. We want them to develop mental skills and processes in an ethically responsible way. This is not a "good-boy/bad-boy" approach to thinking, for people must think their own way to the ethical insights that underlie fairmindedness. We are careful not to judge the content of the student's thinking. Rather, we facilitate a process whereby the student's own insights can be developed.

The global objectives of critical thinking-based instruction are intimately linked to specific objectives. Precisely because we want students to learn how to think for themselves in an ethically responsible way we use the strategies we do – help them gain insight into their tendency to think in narrowly self-serving ways (egocentricity); encourage them to empathize with the perspectives of others; to suspend or withhold judgment when they lack sufficient evidence to justify making a judgment; to clarify issues and concepts; to evaluate sources, solutions, and actions; to notice when they make assumptions, how they make inferences and where they use, or ought to use, evidence; to consider the implications of their ideas; to identify contradictions or inconsistencies in their thinking; to consider the qualifications or lack of qualifications in their generalizations; and do all of these things in encouraging, supportive, non-judgmental ways. The same principles of education hold for staff development.

✦ Beginning to Infuse Critical Thinking

Let us now consider how to incorporate these general understandings into in-service design. Learning the art of lesson plan remodeling can be separated into five tasks. Each can be the focus of some stage of in-service activity:

1) *Clarifying the global concept* — How is the fairminded critical thinker unlike the self-serving critical thinker and the uncritical thinker? What is it to think critically? Why think critically?

2) *Understanding component principles* underlying the component critical thinking values, processes, and skills — What are the basic values that (strong sense) critical thinking presupposes? What are the micro-skills of critical thinking? What are its macro-processes? What do critical thinkers do? Why? What do they avoid doing? Why?

3) *Seeing ways to use the various component strategies in the classroom* — When can each aspect of critical thought be fostered? When is each most needed? What contexts most require each dimension? What questions or activities foster it?

4) *Getting experience in lesson plan critique* — What are the strengths and weaknesses of this lesson? What critical principles, concepts, or strategies apply to it? What important concepts, insights, and issues underlie this lesson? Are they adequately emphasized and explained? What use would the well-educated person make of this material? Will that usefulness be clear to the students?

5) *Getting experience in lesson plan remodeling* — How can I take full advantage of the strengths of this lesson? How can this material best be used to foster critical insights? Which questions or activities should I drop, use, alter, or expand upon? What should I add to it? How can I best promote genuine and deep understanding of this material?

Let us emphasize at the outset that these goals or understandings are interrelated and that achieving any or all of them is a matter of degree. We therefore warn against trying to achieve "complete" understanding of any one of them before proceeding to the others. Furthermore, we emphasize that understanding should be viewed practically or pragmatically. One does not learn about critical thinking by memorizing a definition or a set of distinctions. The teacher's mind must be actively engaged at each point in the process — concepts, principles, applications, critiques, and remodels. At each level, "hands-on" activities should immediately follow any introduction of explanatory or illustrative material. When, for example, teachers read a handbook formulation of one of the principles, they should then have a chance to brainstorm applications of it, or an opportunity to formulate another principle. When they read the critique of one lesson plan, they should have an opportunity to remodel it or to critique another. When they read a complete remodel set — original lesson plan, critique, and remodel — they should have a chance to critique their own, individually or in groups. This back-and-forth movement between example and practice should characterize the staff development process overall. These practice sessions should not be rushed, and the products of that practice should be collected and shared with the group as a whole. Teachers need to see that they are fruitfully engaged in this process; dissemination of its products demonstrates this fruitfulness. Staff development participants should understand that initial practice is not the same as final product, that what is remodeled today by critical thought can be re-remodeled tomorrow and improved progressively thereafter as experience, skills, and insights grow.

Teachers should be asked early on to formulate what critical thinking means to them. You can examine some teacher formulations in the chapter, "What Critical Thinking Means to Me" (Appendix A). However, do not spend too much time on the general formulations of what critical thinking is before moving to particular principles and strategies. The reason for this is simple. People tend to have trouble assimilating general concepts unless they are clarified through concrete examples. Furthermore, we want teachers to develop an *operational* view of critical thinking, to understand it as particular intellectual behaviors derivative of basic insights, commitments, and principles. Critical thinking is not a set of high-sounding platitudes, but a very real and practical way to think things out and to act upon that thought. Therefore, we want teachers to make realistic translations from the general to the specific as soon as possible and to periodically revise their formulations of the global concept in light of their work on the details. Teachers should move back and forth between general formulations of critical thinking and specific strategies in specific lessons. We want teachers to see how acceptance of the general concept of critical thinking translates into clear and practical critical thinking teaching and learning strategies, and to use those strategies to help students develop as rational and fair thinkers.

For this reason, all the various strategies explained in the handbook are couched in terms of behaviors. The principles express and describe a variety of behaviors of the "ideal" critical thinker; they become applications to lessons when teachers canvass their lesson plans for places where each can be fostered. The practice we recommend helps guard against teachers using these strategies as recipes or formulas, since good judgment is always required to apply them.

✦ Some Staff Development Design Possibilities

1) Clarifying the global concept

After a brief exposition or explanation of the global concept of critical thinking, teachers might be asked to reflect individually (for, say, 10 minutes) on people they have known who are basically uncritical thinkers, those who are basically selfish critical thinkers, and those who are basically fairminded critical thinkers. After they have had time to think of meaningful personal examples, divide them into groups of two to share and discuss their reflections.

Or one could have them think of dimensions of their own lives in which they are most uncritical, selfishly critical, and fairminded.

2) Understanding component teaching strategies that parallel the component critical thinking values, processes, and skills

Each teacher could choose one strategy to read and think about for approximately 10 minutes and then explain it to another teacher, without reading from the handbook. The other teacher can ask questions about the strategy. Once one has finished explaining his or her strategy, roles are reversed. Following this, pairs could link up with other pairs and explain their strategies to each other. At the end, each teacher should have a basic understanding of four strategies.

3) Seeing how the various component strategies can be used in classroom settings

Teachers could reflect for about 10 minutes on how the strategies that they chose might be used in a number of classroom activities or assignments. They could then share their examples with other teachers.

4) Getting experience in lesson plan critique

Teachers can bring one lesson, activity, or assignment to the inservice session. This lesson, or one provided by the inservice leader, can be used to practice critique. Critiques can then be shared, evaluated, and improved.

5) Getting experience in lesson plan remodeling

Teachers can then remodel the lessons which they have critiqued and share, evaluate, and revise the results.

Other activities and ideas include the following:

- Copy a remodel, eliminating strategy references. Groups of teachers could mark strategies on it; share, discuss, and defend their versions. Remember, ours is not "the right answer". In cases where participants disagree with, or do not understand why we cited the strategies we did, they could try to figure out why.

- Over the course of a year, the whole group can work on at least one remodel for each participant.

- Participants could each choose several strategies and explain their inter-relationships, mention cases in which they are equivalent, or how they could be used together. (For example, refining generalizations could be seen as evaluating the assumption that all x's are y's.)

- To become more reflective about their teaching, teachers could keep a teaching log or journal, making entries as often as possible, using prompts such as these: What was the best question I asked today? Why? What was the most effective strategy I used today? Was it appropriate? Why or why not? What could I do to improve that strategy? What did I actively do today to help create the atmosphere that will help students to become critical thinkers? How and why was it effective? What is the best evidence of clear, precise, accurate reasoning I saw in a student today? What factors contributed to that reasoning? Did the other students realize the clarity of the idea? Why or why not? What was the most glaring evidence of irrationality or poor thinking I saw today in a student? What factors contributed to that reasoning? How could I (and did I) help the student to clarify his or her own thoughts? (From *The Greensboro Plan*)

The processes we have described thus far presuppose motivation on the part of the teacher to implement changes. Unfortunately, many teachers lack this motivation. We must address this directly. This can be done by focusing attention on the insights that underlie each strategy. We need to foster discussion of them so that it becomes clear to teachers not only *that* critical thinking requires this or that kind of activity but *why*, that is, what desirable consequences it brings about. If, for example, teachers do not see why thinking for themselves is important for the well-being and success of their students, they will not take the trouble to implement activities that foster it, even if they know what these activities are.

To meet this motivational need, we have formulated "principles" to suggest important insights. For example, consider this brief introduction to the strategy "exercising fairmindedness:"

Principle

To think critically about issues, we must be able to consider the strengths and weaknesses of opposing points of view; to imaginatively put ourselves in the place of others in order to genuinely understand them; to overcome our egocentric tendency to identify truth with our immediate perceptions or long-standing thought or belief. This trait correlates with the ability to reconstruct accurately the viewpoints and reasoning of others and to reason from premises, assumptions, and ideas other than our own. This trait also correlates with the willingness to remember occasions when we were wrong in the past, despite an intense conviction that we were right, and the ability to imagine our being similarly deceived in a case at hand. Critical thinkers realize the unfairness of judging unfamiliar ideas until they fully understand them.

The world consists of many societies and peoples with many different points of view and ways of thinking. To develop as reasonable persons, we need to enter into and think within the frameworks and ideas of different peoples and societies. We cannot truly understand the world if we think about it only from *one* viewpoint, as North Americans, as Italians, or as Soviets.

Furthermore, critical thinkers recognize that their behavior affects others, and so consider their behavior from the perspective of those others.

Teachers reflecting on this principle in the light of their own experience should be able to give their own reasons why fairmindedness is important. They might reflect upon the personal problems and frustrations they faced when others — spouses or friends, for example — did not or would not empathically enter their point of view. Or they might reflect on their frustration as children when their parents, siblings, or schoolmates did not take their point of view seriously. Through examples of this sort, constructed by the teachers themselves, insight into the need for an intellectual sense of justice can be developed.

Once teachers have the insight, they are ready to discuss the variety of ways that students can practice thinking fairmindedly. As always, we want to be quite specific here, so that teachers understand the kinds of behaviors they are fostering. The handbooks provide a start in the *application* section following the *principle*. For more of our examples, one can look up one or more remodeled lesson plans in which the strategy was used, referenced under each. Remember, it is more important for teachers to think up their own examples and applications than to rely on the handbook examples, which are intended as illustrative only.

Lesson plan remodeling as a strategy for staff and curriculum development is not a simple, one-shot approach. It requires patience and commitment. But it genuinely develops the critical thinking of teachers and puts them in a position to understand and help structure the inner workings of the curriculum. While doing so, it builds confidence, self-respect, and professionalism. With such an approach, enthusiasm for critical thinking strategies will grow over time. It deserves serious consideration as the main thrust of a staff development program. If a staff becomes proficient at critiquing and remodeling lesson plans, it can, by redirecting the focus of its energy, critique and "remodel" any other aspect of school life and activity. In this way, the staff can become increasingly less dependent on direction or supervision from above and increasingly more activated by self-direction from within. Responsible, constructive critical thinking, developed through lesson plan remodeling, promotes this transformation.

Besides devising in-service days that help teachers develop skills in remodeling their lessons, it is important to orchestrate a process that facilitates critical thinking infusion on a long-term, evolutionary basis. As you consider the "big picture", remember the following principles:

✔ *Involve the widest possible spectrum of people* in discussing, articulating, and implementing the effort to infuse critical thinking. This includes teachers, administrators, board members, and parents.

✔ *Provide incentives to those who move forward in the implementation process.* Focus attention on those who make special efforts. Do not embarrass or draw attention to those who do not.

✔ *Recognize that many small changes are often necessary before larger changes can take place.*

✔ *Do not rush implementation.* A slow but steady progress with continual monitoring and adjusting of efforts is best. Provide for refocusing on the long-term goal and ways of making the progress visible and explicit.

✔ *Work continually to institutionalize the changes made* as the understanding of critical thinking grows, making sure that the goals and strategies being used are deeply embedded in school-wide and district-wide statements and articulations. Foster discussion on how progress in critical thinking instruction can be made permanent and continuous.

✔ *Honor individual differences among teachers.* Maximize the opportunities for teachers to pursue critical thinking strategies in keeping with their own educational philosophy. Enforcing conformity is incompatible with the spirit of critical thinking.

It's especially important to have a sound long-term plan for staff development in critical thinking. The plan of the Greensboro City Schools is especially noteworthy for many reasons. *1)* It does not compromise depth and quality for short-term attractiveness. *2)* It allows for individual variations between teachers at different stages of their development as critical thinkers. *3)* It provides a range of incentives to teachers. *4)* It can be used with a variety of staff development strategies. *5)* It is based on a broad philosophical grasp of the nature of education, integrated into realistic pedagogy. *6)* It is long-term, providing for evolution over an extended period of time. Infusing critical thinking into the curriculum cannot be done overnight. It takes a commitment that evolves over years. The Greensboro plan is in tune with this inescapable truth.

Consider these features of the Greensboro plan:

> A good staff development program should be realistic in its assessment of time. Teachers need time to reflect upon and discuss ideas, they need opportunities to try out and practice new strategies, to begin to change their own attitudes and behaviors in order to change those of their students, to observe themselves and their colleagues — and then they need more time to reflect upon and internalize concepts.
>
> Furthermore, we think that teachers need to see *modeled* the teacher attitudes and behaviors that we want them to take back to the classroom. We ask teachers to participate in Socratic discussion, we ask teachers to write, and we employ the discovery method in our workshops. We do *not* imply that we have "the answer" to the problem of how to get students to think and we seldom lecture.
>
> In planning and giving workshops, we follow these basic guidelines. Workshop leaders:
>
> 1. model for teachers the behaviors they wish them to learn and internalize. These teaching behaviors include getting the participants actively involved, calling upon and using prior experiences and knowledge of the participants, and letting the participants process and deal with ideas rather than just lecturing to them.
>
> 2. use the discovery method, allowing teachers to explore and to internalize ideas and giving time for discussion, dissension, and elaboration.
>
> 3. include writing in their plans — we internalize what we can process in our own words.

Here is what Greensboro said about the remodeling approach:

> After studying and analyzing a number of approaches and materials, this nucleus recommends Richard Paul's approach to infusing critical thinking into the school curriculum (which has a number of advantages).

1. It avoids the pitfalls of pre-packaged materials, which often give directions which the teacher follows without understanding why or even what the process is that she/he is following. Pre-packaged materials thus do not provide an opportunity for the teacher to gain knowledge in how to teach for and about thinking, nor do they provide opportunity for the teacher to gain insight and reflection into his/her own teaching.

2. It does not ask teachers to develop a new curriculum or a continuum of skills, both of which are time-consuming and of questionable productivity. The major factor in the productivity of a curriculum guide is how it is used, and too many guides traditionally remain on the shelf, unused by the teacher.

3. It is practical and manageable. Teachers do not need to feel overwhelmed in their attempts to change an entire curriculum, nor does it need impractical expenditures on materials or adoption of new textbooks. Rather, the teacher is able to exercise his/her professional judgment in deciding where, when, at what rate, and how his or her lesson plans can be infused with more critical thinking.

4. It infuses critical thinking into the curriculum rather than treating is as a separate subject, an "add on" to an already crowded curriculum.

5. It recognizes the complexity of the thinking process, and rather than merely listing discreet skills, it focuses on both affective strategies and cognitive strategies.

This focus on affective and cognitive strategies may seem confusing at first, but the distinction is quite valid. Paul's approach recognizes that a major part of good thinking is a person's affective (or emotional) approach, in other words, attitudes or dispositions. Although a student may become very skilled in specific skills, such as making an inference or examining assumptions, he or she will not be a good thinker without displaying affective strategies such as exercising independent judgment and fairmindedness or suspending judgment until sufficient evidence has been collected. Likewise, Paul also emphasizes such behavior and attitudes as intellectual humility, perseverance, and faith in reason, all of which are necessary for good thinking.

Paul's approach also gives specific ways to remodel lesson plans so that the teacher can stress these affective and cognitive skills. Thirty-one specific strategies are examined and numerous examples of how to remodel lesson plans using these strategies are presented. These concrete suggestions range from ways to engage students in Socratic dialogue to how to restructure questions asked to students.

A critical factor in this approach is the way that a teacher presents material, asks questions, and provides opportunities for students to take more and more responsibility on themselves for thinking and learning. The teacher's aim is to create an environment that fosters and nurtures student thinking.

This nucleus recommends that this approach be disseminated through the faculty in two ways. First, a series of workshops will familiarize teachers with the handbooks. Secondly, nucleus teachers will work with small numbers of teachers (two or three) using peer collaboration, coaching, and cooperation to remodel and infuse critical thinking into lesson plans.

Since no two districts are alike, just as no two teachers are alike, any plan must be adjusted to the particular needs of a particular district. Nevertheless, all teachers assess their lessons in some fashion or other, and getting into the habit of using critical thought to assess their instruction cannot but improve it. The key is to find an on-going process to encourage and reward such instructional critique.

Chapter 21

The Greensboro Plan:
A Sample Staff Development Plan

by Janet L. Williamson

Abstract

This chapter from the second edition of The Greensboro Plan, *written by Janet Williamson, describes the Greensboro School District's Reasoning and Writing Project, which is using the lesson plan remodeling method of bringing critical thinking into instruction. It is included in this volume as a model of staff development in critical thinking.*

$\mathcal{G}$ reensboro, North Carolina is a medium-sized city nestled in the rolling hills of the Piedmont, near the Appalachian Mountains. The school system enrolls approximately 21,000 students and employs 1,400 classroom teachers. Although our school system is a relatively small one, Greensboro has recently implemented a program that is beginning successfully to infuse critical thinking and writing skills into the K–12 curriculum.

The Reasoning and Writing Project began in the spring of 1986 when the school board approved the project and affirmed as a priority the infusion of thinking and writing into the K–12 curriculum. The school system hired two educators to coordinate the program. The two current facilitators are Carolyn Eller, who is a former coordinator for the Academically Gifted program, and myself, Janet L. Williamson, a former English teacher who had recently returned from a leave of absence during which I completed my doctorate with a special emphasis on critical thinking.

Carolyn and I are teachers on special assignment, relieved of our regular classroom duties in order to facilitate the project. We stress this fact; we are facilitators, not directors; we are teachers, not administrators; the project is primarily teacher directed and implemented. In fact, this tenet of teacher empowerment is one of the major principles of the project, as is the strong emphasis on and commitment to a philosophical and theoretical basis of the program.

We began the program with some basic beliefs and ideas. We combined reasoning and writing because we think that there is an interdependence between the two processes and that writing is an excellent tool for making ideas clear and explicit. We also believe that no simple or quick solution would bring about a meaningful change in the complex set of human attitudes and behaviors that comprise thinking. Accordingly, we began the project at two demonstration sites where we could slowly develop a strategic plan for the program. A small group of fourteen volunteers formed the nucleus with whom we primarily worked during the first semester of the project.

Even though I had studied under Dr. Robert H. Ennis, worked as a research assistant with the Illinois Critical Thinking Project, and written my dissertation on infusing critical thinking skills into an English curriculum, we did not develop our theoretical approach to the program quickly or easily. I was aware that if this project were going to be truly teacher-directed, my role would be to guide the nucleus teachers in reading widely and diversely about critical thinking, in considering how to infuse thinking instruction into the curriculum, and in becoming familiar with and comparing different approaches to critical thinking. My role would not be, however, to dictate the philosophy or strategies of the program.

This first stage in implementing a critical thinking program, where teachers read, study, and gather information, is absolutely vital. It is not necessary, of course, for a facilitator to have a graduate degree specializing in critical thinking in order to institute a sound program, but it is necessary for at least a small group of people to become educated, in the strongest sense of the word, about critical thinking and to develop a consistent and sound theory or philosophy based on that knowledge. There are a number of ways to develop this knowledge — read (and reread), question, develop a common vocabulary of critical thinking terms and the knowledge of how to use them, take university or college courses in thinking, seek out local consultants such as professors, and attend seminars and conferences.

In the beginning stages of our program, we found out that the importance of a consistent and sound theoretical basis is not empty educational jargon. We found inconsistencies in our stated beliefs and our interactions with our students and in our administrators' stated beliefs and their interactions with teachers. For example, as teachers we sometimes proclaim that we want independent thinkers and then give students only activity sheets to practice their "thinking skills"; we declare that we want good problem solving and decision making to transfer into all aspects of life and then tend to avoid controversial or "sensitive" topics; we bemoan the lack of student thinking and then structure our classrooms so that "guessing what is in the teacher's mind" is the prevailing rule. We also noted a tendency of some principals to espouse the idea that teachers are professionals and then declare that their faculty prefer structured activities rather than dealing with theory or complex ideas. Although most administrators state that learning to process information is more important than memorizing it, a few have acted as if the emphasis on critical thinking is "just a fad." One of the biggest contradictions we have encountered has been the opinion of both teachers and administrators that "we're already doing a good job of this (teaching for thinking)" while they admit that students are not good thinkers.

While recognizing these contradictions is important, that does not in and of itself solve the problem. In the spirit of peer coaching and collegiality, we are trying to establish an atmosphere that will allow us to point out such contradictions to each other. As our theories and concepts become more internalized and completely understood, such contradictions in thought and action become less frequent. In all truthfulness, however, such contradictions still plague us and probably will for quite a while.

We encountered, however, other problems that proved easier to solve. I vastly underestimated the amount of time that we would need for an introductory workshop, and our first workshops failed to give teachers the background they needed; we now structure our workshops for days, not hours. There was an initial suggestion from the central office that we use a "packaged program" as the basis of our program, or at least as a starting point. To the credit of central office administration, although they may have questioned whether we should use an already existing program, they certainly did not mandate that we use any particular approach. As we collected evaluations of our program, from our teachers, neighboring school systems, and outside consultants, however, there seemed to be a general consensus that developing our own program, rather than adopting a pre-existing one, has been the correct choice.

Finally, teachers became confused with the array of materials, activities, and approaches. They questioned the value of developing and internalizing a concept of critical thinking and asked for specifics, activities they could use immediately in the classroom. This problem, however, worked itself out as teachers reflected on the complexity of critical thinking and how it can be fostered. We began to note and collect instances such as the following: a high school instructor, after participating in a workshop that stressed how a teacher can use Socratic questioning in the classroom, commented that students who had previously been giving unsatisfactory answers were now beginning to give insightful and creative ones. Not only had she discovered that the quality of the student's response is in part determined by the quality of the teacher's questions, she was finding new and innovative ways to question her students. Another teacher, after having seen how the slowest reading group in her fourth grade class responded to questions that asked them to think and reflect, commented that she couldn't believe how responsive and expressive the children were. I can think of no nucleus teacher who would now advocate focusing on classroom activities rather than a consistent and reflective approach to critical thinking.

As the nucleus teachers read and studied the field, they outlined and wrote the tenets that underscore the program. These tenets include the belief that real and lasting change takes place not by writing a new curriculum guide, by having teachers attend a one day inspirational workshop at the beginning of each new year, by adopting new textbooks that emphasize more skills, or by purchasing pre-packaged programs and activity books for thinking. Rather, change takes place when attitudes and priorities are carefully and reflectively reconsidered, when an atmosphere is established that encourages independent thinking for both teachers and students, and when we recognize the complex interdependence between thinking and writing.

The nucleus teachers at the demonstration schools decided that change in the teaching of thinking skills can best take place by remodeling lesson plans not by creating new ones, and a committee dealing with thinking skills wrote a position paper adopting Richard Paul's Critical Thinking Handbook. This approach, they wrote, is practical and manageable. It allows the teacher to exercise professional judgment and provides opportunity for the teacher to gain insight into his or her own teaching. In addition, it recognizes the complexity of the thinking process and does not merely list discrete skills.

The primary-level nucleus teachers decided to focus upon language development as the basis for critical thinking; their rationale was that language is the basis for both thinking and writing, that students must master language sufficiently to be able to use it as a tool in thinking and writing, and that this emphasis is underdeveloped in many early classrooms. This group of teachers worked on increasing teacher knowledge and awareness of language development as well as developing and collecting materials, techniques, and ideas for bulletin boards for classroom use.

By the second semester, the project had expanded to two high schools. By the second year of the program, we had expanded to sixteen new schools, including all six middle schools. Now in our fourth year, we have held workshops in over thirty schools and we have conducted workshops for interested central office and school based administrators. Also, workshops have been conducted or planned that are led by the original nucleus teachers for their colleagues at a number of schools.

It is certainly to the credit of the school board and the central administration that we have had an adequate budget on which to operate. As I have mentioned, Carolyn and I are full-time facilitators of the program. Substitutes have been hired to cover classes when teachers worked on the project during school hours. We were able to send teachers to conferences led by Richard Paul and we were able to bring in Professor Paul for a very successful two day workshop. One of the Seventeen Underpinnings of Quality Critical Thinking Staff Development is:

Allocate special resources on a permanent basis.

Without at least one full-time facilitator and resources for substitutes, conferences, a newsletter, books, and materials, the program would have had little impact.

Our teachers work individually and in pairs, and in small and large groups at various times during the day. A number of teachers have video-taped themselves and their classes in action, providing an opportunity to view and reflect on ways that they and their colleagues could infuse more thinking opportunities into the curriculum. Essentially, we have worked on three facets in the program:

1) workshops that provide baseline information,

2) follow-up that includes demonstration teaching by facilitators, individual study, collegial sharing of ideas, peer coaching, individual and group remodeling of lesson plans, teachers writing about their experiences both for their personal learning and for publication, team planning of lessons, peer observation, and

3) dissemination of materials, including our popular newsletter and the materials in our growing professional library.

As the program expands, we have found that critical thinking is not an isolated instructional methodology. Rather, as one elementary teacher recently expressed, "Critical thinking is the framework on which we build, the basis of all teaching and learning." Sound instructional techniques such as cooperative learning and integrated education naturally dovetail with our endeavors in the Reasoning and Writing Program, and we constantly talk about them and infuse them into workshops and follow-up. It is our contention that educationally sound instructional methods, such as cooperative learning, must have as their basis these assumptions: *1)* knowledge can only be achieved through thinking, *2)* students are active learners only when they are involved in processing information and not just memorizing factual material, and *3)* students must learn how to make meaning for themselves, not passively accept the ideas which are given to them. Thus, critical thinking instruction can be an underlying assumption upon which other methods of instruction are based. Without a solid understanding of and commitment to critical thinking instruction, cooperative learning can degenerate into cooperative worksheets. With critical thinking instruction as an underlying assumption, cooperative learning can help students to think dialogically, consider other perspectives, and develop more complexity in their thinking.

Therefore, the Reasoning and Writing Program is committed to these Underpinnings of Quality Critical Thinking Staff Development:

Formulate a comprehensive philosophy of education focused on critical thinking, one that makes clear that knowledge can be achieved only through thinking.

> *Make critical thinking the essential mode of*
> *instruction for all subjects, all students,*
> *all grade levels.*

We are expanding slowing and only on a volunteer basis. Another assumption, one of the Seventeen Underpinnings of the program, is:

> *Rely on voluntary participation. There is*
> *no gain in "forcing" teachers to teach in a way*
> *they do not favor.*

Currently, we have approximately over two hundred nucleus teachers working in over thirty schools in the system. Plans for the future should include two factors: ways for the nucleus groups to continue to expand their professional growth and knowledge of critical thinking and an expansion of the program to include more teachers. We plan to continue to build on the essential strengths of the program — the empowerment of teachers to make decisions, the thorough theoretical underpinnings of the program, the slow and deliberate design and implementation plan, and our adherence to another of the Seventeen Underpinnings of Quality Critical Thinking Staff Development:

> *Don't use a canned program*
> *or an algorithmic approach.*

Our teachers generally seem enthusiastic and committed. In anonymous, written evaluations of the program, they have given the program overwhelming support. One teacher stated:

It is the most worthwhile project the central office has ever offered.... Because

- It wasn't forced on me.
- It wasn't touted as the greatest thing since sliced bread.
- It was not a one-shot deal that was supposed to make everything all better.
- It was not already conceived and planned down to the last minute by someone who had never been in a classroom or who hadn't been in one for x years.

It was, instead,

- led by professionals who were still very close to the classroom.
- designed by us,
- a volunteer group of classroom teachers,
- who had time to reflect and read and talk after each session
- who had continuing support and information from the leaders, not just orders and instructions.

✦ 17 Underpinnings of Quality Critical Thinking Staff Development

1) Formulate a *comprehensive philosophy of education* focused on critical thinking, one that makes clear that knowledge can be achieved only through thinking.

2) Make *critical teaching the essential mode of instruction* for all subjects, all students, all grade levels.

3) Rely on *voluntary participation*. There is no gain in "forcing" teachers to teach in a way they do not favor.

4) Systematically *cultivate the critical thinking of teachers*. Do not assume that all teachers are automatically good critical thinkers.

5) *Don't use a canned program.* or an algorithmic approach.

6) Make *a long-term, system-wide, open-ended commitment to critical thinking* that provides for the different rates of growth of different teachers.

7) Create *multiple incentives* for teachers. Teachers like everyone else are busy and not likely to do what they are not rewarded for doing.

8) Allocate *special resources* on a permanent basis.

9) Find at least *one committed driving force*, one passionate critical thinking enthusiast, to head the effort.

10) Adopt *a broad and rich concept of critical thinking* that is consistent not only with the variety of subject matter areas and disciplines but with the individuality of teachers as well.

11) Provide for *diverse critical thinking staff development activities*.

12) Give each teacher a *critical thinking handbook* that contains lessons shown before and after critical thinking has been infused.

13) Set up a *library* of critical thinking books and video tapes.

14) Create a *critical thinking newsletter*.

15) Set *modest short-term goals*.

16) Provide for *on-going, site-based follow up*.

17) *Involve parents* as completely as you can.

These are the keys to quality critical thinking staff development and they are the keys to quality education as well. If critical teaching and learning are not nurtured — and today very largely they are not — then there is little chance that our young people will become critical thinkers on their own.

Chapter 22

Critical Thinking and
Learning Centers

Abstract

*In this paper, originally presented as a keynote address at the annual meeting
of the Western Reading and Learning Association, Richard Paul explains the
relationship of critical thinking to learning. He distinguishes between student survival skills (those tactics and strategies which enable students to "beat the system", as it were) and student critical thinking skills (which enable students to
master content and learn deeply). This distinction becomes the basis for a further
distinction between a "minimalist" and a "maximalist" approach to structuring
a learning center. In a minimalist approach, students learn the study skills that
students use to get good grades, particularly short term recall strategies. In a
maximalist approach, students learn to critically process and master content
through critical reading, writing, and listening skills.*

✦ What Is Critical Thinking?

*I*t is always frustrating, and a challenge, to talk about notions as complex and rich as critical thinking. To illuminate, at the same time,
particular practical concerns, in this case those of directors of learning
centers, adds a further dimension of difficulty. So let me say now that I
will not canvass every dimension of critical thinking. I will telescope my
remarks on many fronts, for there is much more to critical thinking and
evaluation than I can possibly span in one talk.

A definition of critical thinking is in order, of course, but before I give
you one, let me caution against overemphasizing any particular definition, including the one I shall give. Definitions of complex realities are at
best aids to the beginnings of understanding. They necessarily emphasize
some features of the defined reality more than others. They are possible
traps by which we sometimes convince ourselves that our depth of understanding is greater than it is. You can perhaps see my point best by
remembering how misleading a three or four sentence definition of *you*
would be, how little the intricate workings of your mind and character
and experience could be captured in a short sequence of words. Your

417

mother, your father, your sisters, your brothers, and your peers might all give different characterizations that would illuminate different parts, elements, or aspects of you. But no one person could give a definition which could capture you totally, as Browning once said, "root and all, and all in all". I hope you remember this essential qualification when you think later about what critical thinking is. In the last analysis, your knowledge of it, your insight into it, will grow over time as you interest yourself more and more, if you do, in helping students become critical thinkers.

In the future, when schools commit themselves more than they yet have to helping students think for themselves actively and independently, the nature and richness of critical thinking will become more commonly understood. Today the term does no more for most people than conjure up vague notions, or worse, misleading stereotypes. Hence, some people think of critical thinking as negative thinking, as fault-finding, even nit-picking or judgmentalism. Some people think of it merely as a summary term that stands for a heterogeneous list of atomistic intellectual skills. Others think of it as one of many forms of thinking, to be used on occasion. These latter sometimes contrast critical thinking with creative thinking, sometimes with problem-solving or decision-making.

From my vantage point, however, critical thinking is best understood as a global way of disciplining and taking control of one's own thinking so as to accomplish more effectively the purposes of thinking through disciplined self-command. Of course, there are multiple possible purposes for thinking, and multiple possible domains or fields into which thinking may venture. Therefore, how we discipline our thinking, how we self-direct our thinking, varies according to purpose and domain. To become a proficient critical thinker is not simply to become well trained in a variety of loosely connected disciplines, but more precisely to develop an over-arching commitment to think beyond specialized techniques and technical concepts to take command of one's cognitions overall, to grasp global or universal obstacles to independence of thought, and to develop generalizable insights and skills across multiple domains of human thought and action.

With these thoughts in mind, I offer the following definition:

> Critical thinking is disciplined, rational, self-directed thinking that skillfully pursues the purpose for thinking within some domain of knowledge or human concern.

Now let me take this definition apart and indicate my understanding of its various elements. First, critical thinking is *disciplined* and *self-directed*. Everyone thinks. It is of the very nature of the mind to think. Whether we like it or not, will it or not, our minds are continually engaged in acts of cognition: conceptualizing, interpreting, and evaluating aspects of our lives, our values, and our experiences. Indeed, experiences and meaning are constructed by the mind, continuously and automatically. Nonetheless, despite the pervasiveness of thinking in human life, much of it is undisciplined and therefore not under the direction of ourselves — the thinker.

Thus, we interpret the world in ways that we do not consciously realize. We make assumptions of which we are unaware. We judge without knowing how we are judging, without conscious reflection on our criteria for judgment. We make inferences without any sense of the movement of the mind from premise to conclusion, without any sense of the need to validate evidence or justify our line of reasoning. We choose and use concepts to shape our experiences and organize them within our point of view. We often don't realize we have created the very points of view that dominate our thinking. We sometimes assume that what we have created through our thinking — our interpretations, beliefs, points of view — are not simply various ways of getting at reality, but are reality itself. We uncritically assume we are in touch with things as they are in themselves, with no sense of our involvement in mental selectiveness or distortion. We think, in other words, largely in an undisciplined and unself-directed fashion. In a word, we typically think uncritically.

We do this because we never learned how to do otherwise. We do this because those who raised and shaped us did not realize that conscious and deliberate *thinking about thinking* is essential to the fullest development of thinking. We do this because most people around us think uncritically. Most of our teachers were given subject content to learn, but little insight into how content must be organized and shaped to be genuinely, deeply, or rationally learned. Our teachers learned content just as we did from them, without deeply understanding, without grasping it in relation to other things learned inside and outside of school, without testing what they were learning within the crucible of their own experiences, without discipline or self-directedness of thought.

Of course, the best students and learners stumble upon some standards for thinking simply by being exposed to organized content. Because academic content itself has been thought-out and organized by disciplined minds, the best students pick up something of that discipline merely because they try to take that content into their minds and keep it there for testing purposes. Furthermore, some students are exposed to other people (parents, teachers, peers) who do have some command of critical thought, and so pick up some intellectual skills from the give-and-take of discussion and debate with them.

But most students go through school largely on the outside looking in, largely alienated from intellectual discipline and skills of self-directed thinking; they do not know how to make learning exciting, powerful, and educational. Most students never know the power of bringing their thinking under their control. They are like people trying to learn to dance by looking at hundreds of still pictures of people dancing, with no more than a faint sense of music in the background, with little vision of how picture and music come together, and with little grasp of how to move their own bodies to the beat of the music. Somehow knowledge is discovered. Somehow it gets put into categories and subject fields. Somehow it gets into books and teachers' heads. And then somehow it is there before them waiting to be "learned". It's all discontinuous still pictures. There is no beat or rhythm to it. There is no power or beauty in it. There is no theme or harmony within it.

Classrooms are, on the whole, fairly dull and boring places to most students precisely because most students do not know how to make them otherwise. Yet all teachers should be skilled in helping students discover the nature and power of learning, for that is precisely what all classrooms and schools ought to be — centers of skilled and significant learning. Indeed, it is paradoxical that we should need learning centers at institutionally established centers of learning. We do need them precisely because students have not learned how to make their own minds, and teachers have not learned how to make their classrooms, *true* centers of learning.

It all comes down to the virtual impossibility for the mind to become disciplined and self-directed, unless it is systematically stimulated to turn inward upon itself and so become consciously aware of its own operations, its own powers and disabilities. In its natural state, the mind unconsciously absorbs beliefs and sets up pathways of thought through mere association and what Freud called pleasure-principle thinking. We believe what we want to believe, what people around us believe, what we are rewarded for believing, what *seems* or appears to be true. Raised in the U.S., we believe what U.S. citizens believe. Raised in Iran, we would believe what Iranians believe. Raised in the Soviet Union, we would believe what Soviets believe. We do not individually reason our way to our basic beliefs. They are, in essence, given to us, insinuated, repeated, and approved of so often by those with influence over us that we find them in possession of our minds. Rather than running our minds, our minds typically run us. This uncritical process of belief-absorption is the natural state of affairs in societies as we know them. Rational belief formation is not automatic or natural — the propensity to question what those around you believe, to do your own thinking, to form your own beliefs, to withhold assent to beliefs until you have adequate reason or evidence to support them.

So we should not be surprised that most students lack discipline and self-direction in their thinking, that they are not in command of the shaping forces in their own minds, and that they do not know how to achieve self-command. At the same time, it is possible to describe what students need to learn to become more rational, to transform their thinking from passive, undisciplined, other-directedness to disciplined self-command. They need three things: 1) explicit standards or criteria for assessing their thought, 2) insight into the elements of thought, and 3) practice orchestrating those elements to improve their thinking, to take charge of it.

Let us look first at the standards for, or perfections of, thinking, implicit in what may properly be called universal ideals of thought:

1)	clarity	*6)*	breadth
2)	accuracy	*7)*	fairness
3)	relevance	*8)*	logicalness
4)	consistency	*9)*	significance
5)	depth	*10)*	adequacy

We don't often think of perfections of thought, even though we consciously recognize perfection or its lack in most other human activities. We recognize perfection in dance, in playing musical instruments, in sports, in the manual arts, in the fitness of the body. We recognize in a skilled dancer command of physical movements. We recognize that skilled dancers can do with their bodies what others cannot. We also recognize that to develop that command one has to self-monitor one's body movements and practice extensively. We line dance studios with mirrors so students can watch their own dancing in process, and notice their relative perfection or lack of perfection of line and form.

We don't generally recognize the parallel facts for the mind. We don't know, as it were, how to bring mirrors for the mind into classes. We don't know how to help students monitor their own thinking. We don't know how to demonstrate mental moves so that students can usefully practice them. We are quite unclear about the kind of time and energy necessary for disciplined thinking to be fostered, practiced, and refined.

We need to bring the perfections of thought into central focus in education. Classrooms should become places where teachers and students routinely talk about clarity of thought, precision of thought, exactness, specificity, logicalness, reflectiveness, fairness, depth, consistency of thought — these universal standards for thought. Teachers and students need to recognize that in any context we may be more or less clear or unclear, more or less precise or imprecise, exact or inexact, relevant or irrelevant, logical or illogical in our thinking. As we recognize the possibility of achieving or failing to achieve these ideals or perfections, we grasp the basis for the critique and improvement of thinking. I can fault your thinking if, and to the degree that, I can show that it is unclear, vague, inexact, irrelevant, illogical, inconsistent, superficial, narrow, or inadequate to the purpose at hand.

Needless to say, most students do not scan their thinking, speech, writing, or reading to see whether it is clear, precise, accurate, relevant, consistent, logical, or fair. They do not, in other words, have these standards intelligibly available to them. They do not aspire to these ideals. And unfortunately most teachers and professors are not clear enough in their own thinking about thinking to help students grasp these standards. Most assume they are learned more or less automatically simply by exposing students to, and questioning them on, content in their field.

Before I continue, I should draw attention to two importantly different forms of critical thinking: what I call "weak sense" and "strong sense" critical thinking. This distinction is based on two fundamentally different ends that can underlie the critical thinking of any individual: selfish interests or fairmindedness. In all critical thinking we discipline our thinking, gain command over it, direct it toward serving our purposes. But purposes may be narrow and selfish or broad and fairminded. And there is a significant difference in the educational strategies one must use to achieve these qualitatively different ends.

As things now stand in the world at large, it is *selfish* critical thinking that is most valued and practiced, skilled thinking that serves some special interest, whether commercial, political, religious, or personal. So if one works for the Democratic or Republican parties, one is expected to develop skilled defenses of party policy and practice. In neither case is a party member to publically acknowledge significant insights on the other side. Similarly, if you are a "patriotic American", in the vulgar sense of the term, you are to defend official governmental practices, not concede insight or justification in the thinking of countries that might oppose them. Finally, if you work for one company you are not expected to admit equal quality in the products of competing companies.

In each case, weak sense critical thinking is fostered, thinking that is at once skilled, narrowminded, and one-sided, thinking that lends itself to propaganda, public relations, advertisements, rationalizations, and other forms of selfish, manipulative thought. Skill in it is highly prized and paid for. A world of special interests struggling for power and advantage needs an army of skilled thinkers to defend and advance those interests.

Strong sense critical thinking is harder to develop, for it requires that one apply the same standards, the same rules of assessment, to one's own thinking as one applies to one's enemies or opposition. It requires that one think *broadly* as well as *skillfully*. To this end, students need to learn to think sympathetically and accurately within a wide variety of divergent points of view, especially within points of view to which they are most unsympathetic. To accurately represent, to appreciate, the insights of one's opponents is a necessary challenge to face in developing one's fairmindedness. Only by extensive practice in empathic reconstruction of opposing points of view does it become possible. There is virtually no emphasis on it in schooling today. This is the single most significant flaw in schooling today.

Having considered the perfections of critical thought, as well as its possible dual functions, I shall briefly review the elements of thought, the various basic structures that a disciplined thinker orchestrates and uses when achieving self-command and self-directedness in thought.

They are:

1) beliefs	7) ideas/concepts
2) inferences	8) purposes/goal
3) reasons	9) issues
4) evidence	10) implications
5) experiences	11) consequences
6) assumptions	12) points of view

None of these terms, as you can see, are specialized, technical terms. They are all available in what might be called the critical, analytic vocabulary of the English language. Integrated into one's thinking about thinking, they enable a thinker to focus attention now on one, now on another, aspect or dimension of thought. They are essential terms of reference to translate the general perfections of thought into workable standards for the analysis and assessment of thought.

I can't get very far in understanding your thinking if I don't understand your basic *beliefs*. But, to understand whether to accept your beliefs, I have to understand what supports them, what *reasons*, what *evidence*, what *experiences* you would cite to support them. Thinking about these reasons, evidence, and experiences I should look for *assumptions* you may have made as you thought out your reasons, gathered your evidence, and interpreted your experience. You may have taken something for granted which should have been questioned. You may have assumed when you should have verified or tested. Furthermore, I cannot understand your thought unless I know your *purposes* or *goals*. What are you trying to accomplish and under what conditions and constraints? How are you conceiving the *issues(s)* or *problem(s)?* Are there other ways to conceive them? What *ideas* or *concepts* are you using? What are the relationships between them? How do you apply them? Are you applying them appropriately?

Then, where is your thinking taking us, what are its *implications* and *consequences?* If we accept this or that of what you claim, what else are we committed to accepting? What are some of the practical consequences that follow from this acceptance?

Finally, within what *point of view* or *frame of reference* are you thinking? Are you looking at the problem from the perspective of a particular discipline (biology, psychology, anthropology), or with a special focus (moral, economic, political)? Are you thinking within the perspective of some ideology or overarching system of beliefs (as a Christian, Muslim, Capitalist, Marxist)? Your point of view serves as a screen and selective organizer of thought and information. I should notice how your point of view is structuring your thought. Finally, I should notice how mine is doing the same.

My ability to refocus my analysis on different dimensions of thinking, my ability to analyze the elements in some process of thought, puts me in the best position to understand its strengths and weaknesses. Of course, the spirit in which I do all of the above is crucial, whether I proceed empathically and fairmindedly, or narrowly and selfishly. If I analyze your thinking only to destroy or defeat it, I will doubtless distort it, exaggerating its weaknesses while underestimating its strengths. Much of our personal experience of people critically analyzing others' thought is, as I have said, of this narrowminded sort. Most of us have had more than our fair share of egocentric argument, emotional charge and counter-charge, skilled stereotyping and intellectual sleight-of-hand. One of the difficulties we face, therefore, is giving students a different paradigm for intellectual give-and-take, helping them to grasp the nature and importance of fairminded critical thought.

✦ Deciding Between a Maximalist and a Minimalist Approach

Having roughly laid out my conception of critical thinking, I will now turn my attention to your circumstances and problems. Of what relevance is critical thinking to those who run learning centers? This question cannot be answered except in the light of some further ones. Under what conditions or circumstances do you operate? What level of support do you have? What are you expected to accomplish, and under the circumstances, what is it reasonable to try to accomplish? What are your personal goals for your learning center? What would you like it to be and how much time and energy are you willing to expend to make it that? Does the faculty support you strongly or weakly? Has your school, college, or university made a real commitment to critical thinking? Different centers exist under different circumstances, and it is therefore unreasonable for all to be structured the same way, or to have the same goals and obligations.

From this point on, I shall draw a distinction between a *minimalist* and a *maximalist* approach to education, to critical thinking, and to conceiving of and structuring a learning center. If your college's commitment to critical thinking is minimal, if your are minimally funded, if your students are minimally motivated, if you have the minimum amount of time to spend with each student, then you have little choice but to work from a minimalist conception of your center and education. Working from such a minimalist conception, there will be a minimal role for critical thinking to play. Perhaps I can make this clearer by putting a couple of these conceptions into formal definitions:

1. *A minimalist conception of education:* education is passing courses, and passing courses is memorizing enough of what the teachers and professors want to satisfy them on tests and assignments.

2. *A minimalist conception of critical thinking:* strategies for studying to survive classes, regardless of whether or not one becomes educated in the process.

3. A minimalist learning center: a center which helps disadvantaged or slower students to learn minimalist study skills to survive their classes.

Most students today are much more minimalist than maximalist in their orientation toward education, much more concerned with surviving than with learning deeply. There are different skills appropriate to being a minimalist and maximalist student. A minimalist student needs survival skills, and academic survival skills differ from in-depth learning skills. You can get through college and learn very little in-depth; such deep learning is unnecessary, unfortunately, to get through most courses in college. In fact, a lot of research by cognitive psychologists demonstrates the superficiality of learning, even that of some of our best students. This has led some distinguished educators, like Alan Schoenfeld, to say that most instruction (he refers to mathematics instruction) is deceptive and fraudulent in that it leads us and the students to believe that they understand subjects in more than a superficial way.

Let me give you an example. Alan Schoenfeld gave his senior math majors at the University of California, Berkeley, — a most prestigious university, — a tenth grade geometry problem on a test. Only 20% got it right. First, they didn't recognize it as a tenth grade geometry problem, then they used the wrong math trying to solve it. Schoenfeld believes that most students would get the wrong answers if we put problems on their tests from previous math courses they had taken, problem types they did not expect. This is because most mathematics instruction is structured in a patterned, predictable way: from algorithm to practice to test. Students perform reasonably well because they are programmed to use particular algorithms and formulas. They know basically what to expect on each test.

Other studies have been done in other subject areas. For example, in one study, physics students were asked questions like, "If you were driving down the freeway and threw a piece of paper out the window, what would happen to that piece of paper and why. Explain using physics." Analysis of the responses by graduate students tells us that most of them use Aristotelian physics to answer the question, a physics they'd never studied in school because it was obsolete after Newton. The thinking they used spontaneously was inconsistent with the thinking they presumably learned in class. This leads people in this area of research to distinguish "gut knowledge", beliefs learned outside of school, from school knowledge. The mind is schizophrenic, as it were — inert, academic knowledge over here and activated ignorance over there. We rarely *use* our academic knowledge because deep down, experientially, we don't *believe* it. We believe what we personally experienced, even if what we experienced was biased and distorted. When inert academic knowledge is in a contest with activated ignorance, activated ignorance wins. What cognitive psychologists are telling us is that what we think the students are learning and what they really are learning are radically different.

If this problem concerns you, you are a maximalist at heart, for you are concerned with the problem of transfer, of making academic learning effective in the real world, not just in the contrived world of academic assignments and tests. But if you feel that your first responsibility is to help students do their assignments and pass their tests, irrespective of whether those assignments and tests generate *real* knowledge, you are a minimalist.

Once again, there are often political and/or budgetary reasons for being a minimalist. There are reasons why a person might say, "I am a minimalist, but a good minimalist, and my program does help students survive, and that is all that I can realistically hope to achieve. I don't have the budget, I don't have the staff, I don't have the credibility, I don't have the respect, I don't have the conditions to be a maximalist." That makes sense to me, and so I say be a good minimalist if you are going to be a minimalist; but call a spade a spade, don't say that you are teaching higher order critical thinking skills when you aren't, when you are focused only on low level academic survival skills.

Academic survival skills are a grab bag of strategies tailor-made for specific purposes. I learned many of them when I was going through college, yet most students struggle along oblivious of them. For example, the student survivalist pays considerable attention to the prejudices of the instructors; this is an important survival skill. As an undergraduate, I took a course in Shakespeare and wrote an essay on *Romeo and Juliet*. My thesis was that the play was flawed as a tragedy because it depended too much on chance. I went through it and found all the events that turned on chance happenings — a person arrives a minute too late or too early. I systematically laid out the flaws. I turned my paper in, very happy with it, got my paper back and read words to the effect, "You reason very well for your conclusions, but I disagree: C–". I got an "A" on every subsequent paper; I learned not to disagree with my instructor. I learned a student survival skill.

I was in another course, a sociology course, and on all of my exams I put "according to the lectures," and then wrote what I was going to say. The instructor was a wonderful fellow, very bright and insightful in many respects, but he seemed to me to overestimate the scientificness of sociology. Sociology was everything, all human behavior could be explained by it. It seemed to me then, and it seems to me now, that though sociology sheds important light on human behavior, it is far from explaining it totally. In any case, my professor took me aside one day and asked me why I kept writing "according to the lectures" before I wrote out my answers to the test questions. In this case, he was quite understanding. He was willing to accept some level of dissent as long as I gave the "correct" answers on the tests. I got my "A" though I had taken a bit of a chance by revealing to the professor that I did not fully believe what was taught in class.

One can learn a variety of basic study skills that help one survive in courses, skills which do not involve anything but the lowest level of critical thinking. To give you another example, I routinely put my notes on a tape recorder, emphasizing the fundamental points made in the lectures. Then I played them back while washing the dishes or otherwise passing the time in my apartment. By maximizing my exposure to what the professor said, I did better. This, again, is not in-depth learning. This is not critical thinking, in the fullest sense of the words; it is academic survival. Techniques like these made me a better, but not a less prejudiced, student. If what I was taught was prejudiced or distorted, then what I internalized was prejudiced or distorted. It didn't teach me to go into depth in what I was learning, it didn't lead to my taking seriously what I was learning, nor relate it to my experience, but it certainly made it a lot easier to get an "A" and so was functional. This is what I have in mind by the distinction between academic survival skills and in-depth learning skills. I think students have the right to learn academic survival skills. But if this is all that school is about, then we are in a sorry mess because education, rightly conceived, is a much higher conception than that embodied in surviving a scholastic rat race. After all, at the end of a rat race everyone is still a rat. And we would like education to do more than teach people to survive mazes that others devise for them.

✦ Critical Thinking as In-Depth Learning Skills

As we begin to take command of our own thinking, as we learn to recognize and to focus upon the basic structures present in our thinking, we begin to study and learn in a new way. We become aware of how the majority of ideas and beliefs we have imbibed we have not formed through an independent, rational process. We become attuned to the need to critique our own ideas as well as those of others. In learning anything, we seek to find, to analyze, to relate basic ideas to our own experience. For example, in a history course, we seek to come to terms with the very concept of history. We break this idea down to its simplest terms, for example, into that of a process whereby people select an infinitesimal number of facts or events from the past, and organize them by a perspective or point of view into a narrative for others to accept as "true". We key in on each essential feature. First, that it is highly selective. Out of the countless actual events, only some few hundreds will be cited in books. Secondly, that this selectivity presupposes value judgments as to which facts are most important. Thirdly, that value judgments presuppose a point of view which generates standards of value.

Recognizing this much about the basic logic of history, we are in a position to recognize that there will be many possible histories of any given era, just as there are many possible points of view from which we could

approach each. Seeing this, we are in a position to appreciate the nature
of historical thinking and so can see where we need to focus our attention, both in understanding and assessing historical writing. Armed with
critical insights, we then look for what was *left out*. We look specifically
for the interpretations in the text that reveal the point of view and the
value judgments of the historian. We read other historians, especially
those who approach the same period from alternative points of view.

Finally, we begin to notice the presence of historical thinking in everyday life. We recognize in our memories of things past something analogous to the construction of history: the selectivity, the point of view, the
value judgments. We recognize the analogy between history and everyday
activities such as gossip. We recognize the analogy between history and
"the news". The daily news becomes for us the history of yesterday: highly
selective, structured within a point of view, embodying value judgments.
Our mode of reading the news is transformed as is our mode of listening to
gossip — by our transformed reading and understanding of history.

We critically analyze the basic concept of history and that analysis has
a profound influence on how we relate to history and to its everyday ana-
logues. Critical analysis in this sense takes us far beyond academic survival skills.

We gain similar insights into the nature of reading, writing, speaking,
and listening. To speak or to write, if we think critically, is not simply to
follow a stream of conscious associations. It is not simply to say or write
everything that pops into our heads. It is a selective process that organizes
thought within a disciplined point of view in order to accomplish a particular purpose with a particular audience. As we better understand our
purpose, what exactly we want to accomplish, we see more clearly what
we need to include and exclude. We also recognize that we must organize,
shape, and order what we have to say. We recognize that our listeners or
readers will not have precisely the same experiences, the same ideas, the
same points of view that we do. We will therefore need to find ways to
elaborate our ideas to maximize connections between what we want to
say and what our audience has experienced. We seek out, therefore, common experiences; we look for everyday examples. We do this to build
bridges for our readers or listeners to make contact with our thoughts, to
enter our point of view, to think our thoughts.

When we read or listen as critical thinkers, we recognize special problems. We recognize the difficulty of entering into and appreciating the
thoughts, the experiences, the point of view of others. We recognize the
need to engage in a dialogue with the text we are reading or the person to
whom we are listening. We recognize at the outset that there are many different points of view from which different people experience and inwardly
organize the world. We recognize the need to read and listen actively to
enter into the mind of another, especially if that person thinks differently
from us. We immediately recognize the difficulty of re-creating in our own

mind the thoughts of others based simply on hearing their words. Knowing the elements universally present in all thinking, we know, however, how to begin; we know what to look for, and how to look for it. We know how to question the structure of other people's thought, how to probe for their points of view, how to look into their reasons, their experiences, the evidence that underlies their ideas, beliefs, and conclusions. We know how to clarify and draw out their thought, how to generate examples which may make their thinking more concrete, how to dig for their assumptions and underlying ideas and values. We know how to identify possible problems or objections that might be raised to their thinking, and how to contrast their thinking with other thinking. We know, in short, how to actively engage in the give-and-take of intellectual exchange.

Reading, writing, speaking, and listening are all recognized by us to be forms of *thought*, and we appreciate the arts necessary to coming to terms with thought. Through these arts, we recognize ourselves to be getting an education, to be sharpening, deepening, and refining our own skills and insights while we progressively lessen our prejudices and biases. In the process we acquire a vast deal of information, not inert or scattered about in our minds, but organized within a framework that integrates academic learning with everyday experiences, information we can screen, structure, and restructure from multiple points of view. We can use the information we gather to reason within diverse frames of reference. We can take information apart to consider the same situations from different points of view: psychologically, sociologically, historically, philosophically, and personally. We are not dominated by information, rather we are in command of it.

✦ Learning Centers and In-Depth Learning

Learning centers can lead in heightening faculty and student awareness of the need for higher order thinking and in-depth learning. They can play a significant role, not simply in helping students get by in the standard routines of lower order learning, but also in generating campus-wide awareness of the nature of and need for in-depth higher order learning. Unfortunately, most academic departments are too myopic to interest themselves in the question of generalized in-depth learning. Most academic departments see the whole of education merely from the perspective of their own part in it, and they see their part mainly in narrow academic terms. Few faculty concern themselves with developing students' general critical thinking, with helping students go beyond technical vocabularies, academic jargon, standard formulas, routine procedures, isolated facts, and narrow professionalism. They do not think in these terms. No one has clear or significant academic responsibility for the education of the whole person and for the conditions under which that education takes place. Academicians continually assume that students will put the parts together automatically, and that specialized training in intradisciplinary skills and perspectives provides everything students need for generalized integration. Nothing could be further from the truth.

Specialized training, wherein terminology and technical procedures emphasize distinctiveness within a traditional discipline, impedes rather than encourages generalization and synthesis. We live in fragmented societies, and colleges and universities unambiguously reflect and serve that fragmentation, that atomism of daily life. We need structures in higher education that function college-wide to provide an impetus for synthesis, built upon in-depth learning and generalized critical thinking skills. Very specific skills and insights are needed to accomplish this foundational educational end. Unfortunately, critical thinking is now nothing more than a vague idea in the minds of most faculty, one they cannot translate into concrete teaching and testing practices.

✦ Evaluating a Learning Center

I would evaluate a minimalist center differently from a maximalist center; I would not expect the same things. It's not fair to expect a center to accomplish maximalist ends with a minimalist budget. One can only do what one is budgeted to do, unless, of course, one chooses to donate extensive time and energy to what one is not paid for. So one should begin with a clear conception of what a particular center can and cannot do, whether it can merely provide for minimalist survival skills of a few students or provide for maximalist in-depth learning skills for most. Is it possible for the center staff to work directly with faculty, or are faculty largely uninterested in the center and in the generalized critical thinking skills of the students?

Of course, all campuses have some faculty members concerned with in-depth critical thinking, who recognize the failure of college instruction to produce liberally educated persons. They will also have a few administrators willing to move in this direction if supported by the faculty. Herein lies the opportunity to move in a maximalist direction. In principle, any director of a learning center could take an interest in galvanizing interested faculty and administrators and hence provide some impetus for a concerted "maximalist" effort on campus. A clear definition of objectives for a learning center should in any case be coordinated with clearly defined goals of the college, and, in my view, every institution of higher education should take the time to clarify and specify goals and objectives. Consider the following hypothetical statement:

> All students are expected to take responsibility for their own learning. This means that students are expected to learn the art of independent study and develop sound intellectual and occupational skills and habits. All work turned in should reflect care, thor-

oughness, and precision, should reveal command of the processes of critical reading, writing, speaking, and listening, and should demonstrate independent critical thought. Students should not approach their classes as so many unconnected fields, each with a mass of information to be blindly memorized, but rather as organized systems for thinking clearly, accurately, and precisely about interconnected domains of human life and experience. In science classes, students should learn to think scientifically, in math classes to think mathematically, in history classes to think historically, and so on, in such a way that if later called upon to respond to an issue in one of these domains, students will know how to begin to interpret and analyze it, to find and organize information appropriate to it, to reason well concerning it, and to devise a clear and reasonable way to answer or solve it.

To develop into disciplined and independent critical thinkers and learners, all students should be actively involved in their own learning, looking to find in each of their classes the most basic ideas, principles, and meanings that underlie the field and to use these as a basis for analyzing, synthesizing, and assessing all of the remaining information or content covered. Students should recognize that fundamental concepts and processes must be mastered before one can successfully understand a given domain of knowledge and that it is better to learn what is basic to a field deeply and well than to rush on to half-learn, and so mis-learn, what is less basic. Classes will be designed to emphasize in-depth learning of fundamentals as a foundation for more advanced learning. Fundamental concepts and principles will continually be used as organizers for more advanced understandings.

Some such statement could be made the basis for a campus-wide commitment to critical thinking. It could then be followed up with more specific statements from each department. For example, a history department might begin to formulate its goals, vis-a-vis critical thinking, in something like the following way:

All of the history courses have the goal of helping students learn how to think historically in a critical and insightful manner. This includes learning how to identify historical viewpoints, gather and organize historical information, distinguish basic historical facts from historical interpretations, to recognize historical relationships and patterns, and to see the relevance of historical insight to the understanding of current events and problems ....

Once there was not only a campus-wide statement but also a network of departmental statements such as that above, individual instructors could follow up with even more specific statements for their particular courses. For example, a professor teaching a course in U.S. history might follow up the departmental statement above with something like the following:

The fundamental aim of the study of U.S. history will be to aid students in thinking critically, insightfully, and knowledgeably about the U.S. historical past, focusing on the basic issues upon which historians organize and base their research and the development of their divergent viewpoints. Students will learn how to write a historical essay in which they will defend a historical interpretation based on organized, analytic, historical reasoning, reflecting their careful reading of professional historians ....

These statements could be correlated with a campus-wide effort to make students aware of the universal elements of and standards for thinking, so the learning center staff could help each student see the common goals, skills, and standards at the basis of all of their classes. A core critical thinking class could also be established to provide special emphasis on critical thinking. Additionally, the learning center could begin to disseminate the research results daily accumulating which emphasize the need for a shift in instruction from didactic, memory-oriented modes of instruction to those which more actively engage students in their own learning and challenge them to think their way critically through class material and content.

Well, I have gone on at great length and it is now time for me to close. I should like to end with a word of philosophical advice, and that is this: Take the long view of things and keep yourself continually aware of what Matthew Arnold once called "the extreme slowness of things". Classroom instruction will not be changed significantly in a short time. What happens in colleges and schools is a product of many potent forces, each with deep social and psychological roots. The deeper the reform that is needed — and in my view, as you have seen, deep reform is indeed needed — the longer the time that must be allowed for it.

On the other hand, nothing is accomplished by cynicism or defeatism. Creative critical discontent is our only dependable agent for change. So if you are moved by a maximalist conception of education yet forced to live within a minimalist budget, steel yourself for the long term by integrating intense and enthusiastic commitment into long term patience. Remember, the possibility of change is before us daily. Each new day offers to each of us another chance to begin again. But substantial change is not something that happens and is done; it is something that begins, grows, and evolves by degrees in keeping with the ever present, ever powerful, "extreme slowness of things".

Section III

Critical Thinking and Academic Subjects

The Contribution of Philosophy to Thinking

Critical Thinking and Social Studies

Critical Thinking and Language Arts

Critical Thinking and Science

Chapter 23

The Contribution of Philosophy to Thinking

Abstract

In this paper, originally part of "Philosophy and Cognitive Psychology", Paul argues for the power of philosophy and philosophical thinking for intellectual autonomy. He claims that even children have a need and right to think philosophically and are very much inclined to do so, but are typically discouraged by the didactic absolutistic answers and attitudes of adults. Consequently, the inquiring minds of children soon become jaded by the self-assured absolutistic environment which surrounds them.

The potential of children to philosophize is suggested in a transcript of a 4ᵗʰ grade classroom discussion of a series of abstract questions. Following the transcript, Paul illustrates a variety of ways in which traditional school subjects can be approached philosophically. He closes with a discussion of the values and intellectual traits fostered by philosophical thought, the skills and processes of thought, and the relation of philosophical to critical thought.

In this paper I lay the foundation for a philosophy-based, in contrast to a psychology-based, approach to teaching critical thinking across the curriculum. I lay out the general theory and provide some examples of how it could be used to transform classroom instruction and activities. Nevertheless, I want to underscore the point that I lack the space to cover my subject comprehensively. Interested readers must independently pursue the leads I provide, to see the power and flexibility of philosophy-based approaches to critical thinking instruction. I must content myself with modest goals, with a few basic insights into philosophical thinking, with a few of its advantages for instruction.

There are three overlapping senses of *philosophy* that can play a role in explicating the nature of philosophical thinking: philosophy as a field of study, philosophy as a mode of thinking, and philosophy as a framework for thinking. In what follows, I focus on philosophy as a mode of and framework for thinking and will say least about it as a field of study. Nevertheless, some characterization of the field of philosophy is useful.

Philosophy is steeped in dialogical and dialectical thought. Philosophy is an art rather than a science, a discipline that formulates issues that can be approached from multiple points of view and invites critical dialogue and reasoned discourse between conflicting viewpoints. Critical thought and discussion are its main instruments of learning. More so than any other field, philosophy requires all participants to think their own way to whatever system of beliefs ultimately constitute their thought within the field. This entails that all philosophers develop their own unique philosophies.

In contrast, science students are not expected to construct their own science. Sciences have emerged because of the possibility of specialization and joint work within a highly defined shared frame of reference. Its ground rules exclude what is not subject to quantification and measurement. Sciences are cooperative, collaborative ventures whose practitioners agree to limit strictly the range of issues they consider and how they consider them.

Philosophy, on the other hand, is largely an individualistic venture wherein participants agree, only in the broadest sense on the range and nature of the issues they will consider. Philosophers have traditionally been concerned with big questions, root issues that organize the overall framework of thinking itself, in all domains, not just one. Philosophers do not typically conduct *experiments*. They rarely form *hypotheses* or make *predictions* as scientists do. Philosophical tradition gives us a tapestry rich in the development of individual syntheses of ideas across multiple subject domains: syntheses carefully and precisely articulated and elaborately argued. There is reason for this basic difference between the history of science and that of philosophy.

Some questions, by their nature, admit of collaborative treatment and solution; others do not. For example, we do not need to individually test for the chemical structure of lead or determine the appropriate theory of that structure; we can rely on the conclusions of those who have done so. But we cannot learn the structure of our own lives or the best way to plan for the future by looking up the answer in a technical manual or having an answer determined for us by a collaborative scientific effort. We must each individually analyze these questions to obtain rationally defensible answers. There is a wide range of ways human lives can be understood and a variety of strategies for living them. Rarely, if ever, can answers to philosophical questions be validated by one person for another.

The method of philosophy, or the *mode* of thinking characteristic of philosophy, is that of critical discussion, rational cross examination, and dialectical exchange. Every person who would participate in that discussion must create and elaborate a framework for thinking comprehensively. This discipline in the mode of thinking characteristic of philosophy has roots in the ideal of learning to think with a clear sense of the ultimate foundations of one's thinking, of the essential logic of one's thought, and of significant alternative, competing ways of thinking.

Consider philosophical thinking as a framework for thought. When one engages in philosophical thinking, one thinks within a self-constructed network of assumptions, concepts, defined issues, key inferences, and insights. To think philosophically as a liberal, for example, is to think within a different framework of ideas than conservatives do. What is more, to think philosophically, in this sense, is to *know* that one is thinking within a different framework of ideas than other thinkers. It is to know the foundations of liberalism compared to those of conservativism.

✦ Philosophical and Un-Philosophical Minds: Philosophy as a Mode of Thinking and a Framework for Thinking

Perhaps the best way to show what lies at the heart of the uniqueness and power of philosophy is to consider the contrast in general between un-philosophical and philosophical minds. In doing so, I present the two as idealized abstractions for the purpose of clarifying a paradigm; I realize that no one perfectly illustrates these idealizations.

The un-philosophical mind thinks without a clear sense of the foundations of its own thought, without conscious knowledge of the most basic concepts, aims, assumptions, and values that define and direct it. The un-philosophical mind is unaware that it thinks within a system, within a framework, within, if you will, a *philosophy*. Consequently, the un-philosophical mind is trapped within the system it uses, unable to deeply understand alternative or competing systems. The un-philosophical mind tends toward an intra-system closedmindedness. The un-philosophical mind may learn to think within different systems of thought, if the systems are compartmentalized and apply in different contexts, but it cannot compare and contrast whole systems, because, at any given time, it thinks within a system without a clear sense of what it means to do so. This kind of intra-system thinking can be skilled, but it lacks foundational self-command. It functions well when confronted with questions and issues that fall clearly within its system, but is at its worse when facing issues that cross systems, require revising a system, or presuppose explicit critique of the system used.

Un-philosophical liberals, for example, would be hard pressed to think clearly and accurately within a conservative point of view, and hence would not do well with issues such as "What are some of the most important insights of conservatism?" Un-philosophical psychologists, to take another example, would find it difficult to integrate sociological or economic insights into their thinking. Indeed, thinking un-philosophically in any discipline means thinking reductionistically with respect to insights from other disciplines: one either reduces them to whatever can be absorbed into concepts in one's field or ignores them entirely.

An un-philosophical mind is at its best when routine methods, rules, or procedures function well and there is no need to critically reconceptualize them in the light of a broad understanding of one's framework for thinking. If one lacks philosophical insight into the underlying logic of those routines, rules, or procedures, one lacks the ability to mentally step outside of them and conceive of alternatives. As a result, the un-philosophical mind tends toward conformity to a system without grasping clearly what the system is, how it came to be thus, or how it might have been otherwise.

The philosophical mind, in contrast, routinely probes the foundations of its own thought, realizes its thinking is defined by basic concepts, aims, assumptions, and values. The philosophical mind gives serious consideration to alternative and competing concepts, aims, assumptions, and values, enters empathically into thinking fundamentally different from its own, and does not confuse its thinking with reality. By habitually thinking globally, the philosophical mind gains foundational self-command, and is comfortable when problems cross disciplines, domains, and frameworks. A philosophical mind habitually probes the basic principles and concepts that lie behind standard methods, rules, and procedures. The philosophical mind recognizes the need to refine and improve the systems, concepts, and methods it uses and does not simply conform to them. The philosophical mind deeply values gaining command over its own fundamental modes of thinking.

The discipline of philosophy is the only one at present that routinely fosters the philosophical mind, though there are philosophical minds at work in every discipline. The philosophical mind is most evident in other disciplines in those working on foundational concepts and problems. In everyday life, the philosophical mind is most evident in those who deeply value doing their own thinking about the basic issues and problems they face and giving serious reasoned consideration to the ideas and thinking of others. In everyday life, the philosophical mind is most evident in those not afraid to probe conventional thought, rules, mores, and values, those skeptical of standard answers and standard definitions of questions and problems.

In teaching, the philosophical mind is most evident in those who routinely probe the concepts, aims, assumptions, and values that underlie their teaching;who routinely raise fundamental issues through Socratic questions;who routinely encourage students to probe the foundation and source of their own ideas and those of others; and who routinely encourage students to develop their own philosophy or approach to life or learning based on their own disciplined, rational thought. Need I add that philosophical thinking is not habit for most?

✦ Why Children Need to Think Philosophically

There is a sense in which everyone has a philosophy, since human thought and actions are always embedded in a framework of foundational concepts, values, and assumptions which define a "system" of some sort. Humans are by nature inferential, meaning-creating animals. In this sense, all humans use "philosophies" and even in some sense create them. Even the thinking of very young children presupposes philosophical foundations, as Piaget so ably demonstrated. Of course, if by 'philosophy' we mean explicit and systematic reflection on the concepts, values, aims, and assumptions that structure thinking and underlie behavior, then in that sense most children do *not* philosophize. It all depends on whether one believes that one can have a philosophy without *thinking* one's way to it.

Most children have at least the impulse to philosophize and for a time seem driven by a strong desire to know the most basic *what* and *why* of things. Of course parents or teachers rarely cultivate this tendency. Usually children are given didactic answers in ways that discourage, rather than stimulate, further inquiry. Many parents and teachers seem to think that they or textbooks have appropriate and satisfactory answers to the foundational questions that children raise, and the sooner children accept these answers the better. Such authorities unwittingly encourage children to assent to, without truly understanding, basic beliefs. In effect, we teach answers to philosophical questions as though they were like answers to chemical questions. As a result, children lose the impulse to question, as they learn to mouth the standard answers of parents, peers, and other socializing groups. How many of these mouthed answers become a part of children's lived beliefs is another matter.

Children learn behaviors as well as explanations. They learn to act as well as to speak. Thus they learn to behave in ways inconsistent with much of their conscious talk and thought. Children learn to live, as it were, in different and only partially integrated worlds. They develop unconscious worlds of meaning that do not completely square with what they are told or think they believe. Some of these meanings become a source of pain, frustration, repression, fear, and anxiety. Some become a source of harmless fantasizing and day-dreaming. Some are embedded in action, albeit in camouflaged, or in tacit, unarticulated ways.

In any case, the process of unconsciously taking in or unknowingly constructing a variety of meanings outstrips the child's initial impulse to reflect on or question those meanings. In one sense, then, children become captives of the ideas and meanings whose impact on their own thought and action they do not themselves determine. They have in this sense two philosophies (only partially compatible with each other): one verbal but largely unlived; the other lived but mainly unverbalized. This split continues into adulthood. On the emotional level, it leads to anxiety and stress. On the moral level, it leads to hypocrisy and self-deception. On the intellectual level, it results in a condition in which lived beliefs and spontaneous thought are unintegrated with school learning which in turn is ignored in "real life" situations.

As teachers and parents we seldom consider the plight of children from this perspective. We tend to act as though there were no real need for children to reflect deeply about the meanings they absorb. We fail to see the conflicting meanings they absorb, the double messages that capture their minds. Typically our principal concern is that they absorb the meanings that we think are correct and act in ways that we find acceptable. Reflecting upon their thoughts and actions seems important to us only to get them to think or act correctly, that is, as we want them to think and act. We seldom question whether they deeply agree or even understand. We pay little attention as parents to whether or not conflicting meanings and double messages become an on-going problem for them.

In some sense we act as though we believe, and doubtless many do believe, that children have no significant capacity, need, or right to think for themselves. Many adults do not think that children can participate mindfully in the process which shapes their own minds and behavior. Of course, at the same time we often talk to our children as though they were somehow responsible for, or in control of, the ideas they express or act upon. This contradictory attitude toward children is rarely openly admitted. We need to deal explicitly with it.

I believe that children have the need, the capacity, and the *right* to freedom of thought, and that the proper cultivation of that capacity requires an emphasis on the philosophical dimension of thought and action. Again, by 'the philosophical dimension', I mean precisely the kind of deliberative thought that gives to thinkers the on-going disposition to mindfully create, analyze, and assess their own most basic assumptions, concepts, values, aims, and meanings, in effect to choose the very framework in which they think and on the basis of which they act. I would not go so far as to say, as Socrates was reputed to have said, that the unreflective life is not worth living, but I would say that an unreflective life is not a truly *free* life and is often a basic cause of personal and social problems. I claim at least this much, that philosophical thinking is necessary to freedom of thought and action and that freedom of thought and action are good in themselves and should be given a high priority in schooling. They are certainly essential for a democracy. How can the people rule, as the word *democracy* implies, if they do not think for themselves on issues of civic importance? And if they are not encouraged to think for themselves *in* school, why should they do so once they leave it?

Let me now discuss whether children are in fact capable of this sort of freedom of thought, reflection upon ultimate meanings, values, assumptions, and concepts. The question is both conceptual and empirical. On the conceptual side, the issue is one of *degree*. Only to the degree that children are encouraged in supportive circumstances to reflect philosophically, will they develop proficiency in it. Since few parents and teachers value this sort of reflection or are adept at cultivating it, it is understandable that children soon give up their instinctive philosophical impulses (the basic *why* and *what* questions). It would be foolish to assume that it is the *nature* of children to think and act unreflectively when indeed our experience indicates that they are socialized into unreflectiveness. Since we do not encourage children to philosophize why should they do so?

Furthermore, in many ways we penalize children for philosophizing. Children will sometimes innocently entertain an idea in conflict with the ideas of their parents, teachers, or peers. Such ideas are often ridiculed and the children made to feel ashamed of their thoughts. It is quite common, in other words, for people to penalize unconventional thought and reward conventional thought. When we think only as we are rewarded to think, however, we cease to think freely or deeply. Why should we think for ourselves if doing so may get us into trouble and if teachers, parents, and powerful peers provide authoritative didactic answers for us? Before we decide that children cannot think for themselves about basic ideas and meanings, we ought to give them a real and extended opportunity to do so. No society has yet done this. Unless we are willing to exercise some faith in freedom of thought, we will never be in a position to reap the benefits of it or to discover its true limits, if any.

Let me now explore the conceptual side of the question further by suggesting some kinds of philosophical issues embedded, not only in the lives of children, but also in the lives of adults:

> Who am I? What am I like? What are the people around me like? What are people of different backgrounds, religions, and nations like? How much am I like others? How much am I unlike them? What kind of a world do I live in? When should I trust? When should I distrust? What should I accept? What should I question? How should I understand my past, the pasts of my parents, my ethnic group, my religion, my nation? Who are my friends? Who are my enemies? What is a friend? How am I like and unlike my enemy? What is most important to me? How should I live my life? What responsibilities do I have to others? What responsibilities do they have to me? What responsibilities do I have to my friends? Do I have any responsibilities to people I don't like? To people who don't like me? To my enemies? Do my parents love me? Do I love them? What is love? What is hate? What is indifference? Does it matter if others do not approve of me? When does it matter? When should I ignore what others think? What rights do I have? What rights should I give to others? What should I do if others do not respect my rights? Should I get what I want? Should I question what I want? Should I take what I want if I am strong or smart enough to get away with it? Who comes out ahead in this world, the strong or the good person? Is it worthwhile to be good? Are authorities good or just strong?

I do not assume that children must reflect on all or even most of the questions that professional philosophers consider — although the preceding list contains many concepts that professional philosophers tackle. To cultivate philosophical thinking, one does not force students to think in a sophisticated way before they are ready. Each student can contribute to a philosophical discussion thoughts which help other students to orient themselves within a range of thoughts, some of which support or enrich and some of which conflict with other thoughts. Different students achieve different levels of understanding. There is no reason to try to force any given student to achieve a particular level of understanding. But the point is that we can lead young students into philosophical discussions which help them begin to:

1) see the significance and relevance of basic philosophical questions to understanding themselves and the world about them,

2) understand the problematic character of human thought and the need to probe deeply into it,

3) gain insights into what it takes to make thinking more rational, critical, and fairminded,

4) organize their thinking globally across subject matter divisions,

5) achieve initial command over their own thought processes, and

6) come to believe in the value and power of their own minds.

In the transcript that follows, a normal 4th grade class is led to discuss a variety of basic ideas: how the mind works, the nature of mind, why different people interpret the same events differently, the relationship between emotions and mental interpretations, the nature and origin of personality, nature versus nurture, peer group influence on the mind, cultural differences, free will versus determinism, the basis for ethical and unethical behavior, the basis for reputation, the relation of reputation to goodness, mental illness, social prejudice and sociocentrism, and the importance of thinking for oneself. This transcript represents the first philosophical discussion this particular class had and although it is clear from some of their answers that their present degree of insight into the ideas being discussed is limited, it is also clear that they are capable of pursuing those insights and of articulating important philosophical ideas that could be explored in greater and greater depth over time.

✦ Transcript

The following is a transcript of a 4th grade Socratic discussion. The discussion leader was with these particular students for the first time. The purpose was to determine the status of the children's thinking on some of the abstract questions whose answers tend to define our broadest thinking. The students were eager to respond and often seemed to articulate responses that reflected potential insights into the character of the human mind, its relation to the body, the forces that shape us, the influence of parents and peer groups, the nature of morality and of ethnocentric bias. The insights are disjointed, of course, but the questions that elicited them and the responses that articulated them could be used as the basis of future discussions or simple assignments with these students.

➤ *How does your mind work?*
Where's your mind?

Student: In your head. (Numerous students point to their heads.)

➤ *Does your mind do anything?*

Student: It helps you remember and think.

Student: It helps, like, if you want to move your legs. It sends a message down to them.

Student: This side of your mind controls this side of your body and that side controls this other side.

Student: When you touch a hot oven it tells you whether to cry or say ouch.

➤ *Does it tell you when to be sad and when to be happy?*
How does your mind know when to be happy and when to be sad?

Student: When you're hurt it tells you to be sad.

Student: If something is happening around you is sad.

Student: If there is lightning and you are scared.

Student: If you get something you want.

Student: It makes your body operate. It's like a machine that operates your body.

➤ *Does it ever happen that two people are in the same circumstance but one is happy and the other is sad? Even though they are in exactly the same circumstance?*

Student: You get the same toy. One person might like it. The other gets the same toy and he doesn't like the toy.

➤ *Why do you think that some people come to like some things and some people seem to like different things?*

Student: 'Cause everybody is not the same. Everybody has different minds and is built different, made different.

Student: They have different personalities?

➤ *Where does personality come from?*

Student: When you start doing stuff and you find that you like some stuff best.

➤ *Are you born with a personality or do you develop it as you grow up?*

Student: You develop it as you grow up.

➤ *What makes you develop one rather than another?*

Student: Like, your parents or something.

➤ *How can your parent's personality get into you?*

Student: Because you're always around them and then the way they act, if they think they are good and they want you to act the same way, then they'll sort of teach you and you'll do it.

Student: Like, if you are in a tradition. They want you to carry on something that their parents started.

➤ *Does your mind come to think at all the way the children around you think? Can you think of any examples where the way you think is like the way children around you think? Do you think you behave like other American kids?*

Student: Yes.

➤ *What would make you behave more like the kids around you than like Eskimo kids?*

Student: Because you're around them.

Student: Like, Eskimo kids probably don't even know what the word 'jump-rope' is. American kids know what it is.

➤ *And are there things that the Eskimo kids know that you don't know about?*

Student: Yes.

Student: And also we don't have to dress like them or act like them and they have to know when a storm is coming so they won't get trapped outside.

➤ *O.K., so if I understand you then, parents have some influence on how you behave and the kids around you have some influence on how you behave. ... Do you have some influence on how you behave? Do you choose the kind of person you're going to be at all?*

Student: Yes.

➤ *How do you do that do you think?*

Student: Well if someone says to jump off a five-story building, you won't say O.K. You wouldn't want to do that ....

➤ *Do you ever sit around and say, "Let's see shall I be a smart person or a dumb one?"*

Student: Yes.

➤ *But how do you decide?*

Student: Your grades.

➤ *But I thought your teacher decided your grades. How do you decide?*

Student: If you don't do your homework you get bad grades and become a dumb person but if you study real hard you'll get good grades.

➤ *So you decide that, right?*

Student: And if you like something at school like computers you work hard and you can get a good job when you grow up. But if you don't like anything at school you don't work hard.

Student: You can't just decide you want to be smart, you have to work for it.

Student: You got to work to be smart just like you got to work to get your allowance.

➤ *What about being good and being bad, do you decide whether you're good or you're bad? How many people have decided to be bad? (Three students raise their hands.) (To first student,) Why have you decided to be bad?*

Student: Well, I don't know. Sometimes I think I've been bad too long and I want to go to school and have a better reputation but sometimes I feel like just making trouble and who cares.

➤ *Let's see, is there a difference between who you are and your reputation? What's your reputation? That's a pretty big word. What's your reputation?*

Student: The way you act. If you had a bad reputation people wouldn't like to be around you and if you had a good reputation people would like to be around you and be your friend.

➤ *Well, but I'm not sure of the difference between who you are and who people think you are. Could you be a good person and people think you bad? Is that possible?*

Student: Yeah, because you could try to be good. I mean, a lot of people think this one person's really smart but this other person doesn't have nice clothes but she tries really hard and people don't want to be around her.

➤ *So sometimes people think somebody is real good and they're not and sometimes people think that somebody is real bad and they're not. Like if you were a crook, would you let everyone know you're a crook?*

Students: [Chorus of "NO!"]

➤ *So some people are really good at hiding what they are really like. Some people might have a good reputation and be bad; some people might have a bad reputation and be good.*

Student: Like, everyone might think you were good but you might be going on dope or something.

Student: Does reputation mean that if you have a good reputation you want to keep it just like that? Do you always want to be good for the rest of your life?

➤ *I'm not sure ....*

Student: So if you have a good reputation you try to be good all the time and don't mess up and don't do nothing?

➤ *Suppose somebody is trying to be good just to get a good reputation — why are they trying to be good?*

Student: So they can get something they want and they don't want other people to have?

Student: They might be shy and just want to be left alone.

Student: You can't tell a book by how it's covered.

➤ *Yes, some people are concerned more with their cover than their book. Now let me ask you another question. So if its true that we all have a mind and our mind helps us to figure out the world and we are influenced by our parents and the people around us, and sometimes we choose to do good things and sometimes we choose to do bad things, sometimes people say things about us and so forth and so on.... Let me ask you: Are there some bad people in this world?*

Student: Yeah.

Student: Terrorists and stuff.

Student: Nightstalker.

Student: The TWA hijackers.

Student: Robbers.

Student: Rapers.

Student: Bums.

➤ *Bums, are they bad?*

Student: Well, sometimes.

Student: The Klu Klux Klan.

Student: The Bums ... not really, cause they might not look good but you can't judge them by how they look. They might be really nice and everything.

➤ *O.K., so they might have a bad reputation but be good, after you care to know them. There might be good bums and bad bums.*

Student: Libyan guys and Machine Gun Kelly.

➤ *Let me ask you, do the bad people think they're bad?*

Student: A lot of them don't think they're bad but they are. They might be sick in the head.

→ *Yes, some people are sick in their heads.*

Student: A lot of them (bad guys) don't think they're bad.

→ *Why did you say Libyan people?*

Student: Cause they have a lot 'o terrorists and hate us and bomb us ....

→ *If they hate us do they think we are bad or good?*

Student: They think we are bad.

→ *And we think they are bad? And who is right?*

Student: Usually both of them.

Student: None of us are really bad!

Student: Really, I don't know why our people and their people are fighting. Two wrongs don't make a right.

Student: It's like if there was a line between two countries, and they were both against each other, if a person from the first country crosses over the line, they'd be considered the bad guy. And if a person from the second country crossed over the line he'd be considered the bad guy.

→ *So it can depend on which country you're from who you consider right or wrong, is that right?*

Student: Like a robber might steal things to support his family. He's doing good to his family but actually bad to another person.

→ *And in his mind do you think he is doing something good or bad?*

Student: It depends what his mind is like. He might think he is doing good for his family or he might think he is doing bad for the other person.

Student: It's like the underground railroad a long time ago. Some people thought it was bad and some people thought it was good.

→ *But if lots of people think something is right and lots of people think something is wrong, how are you supposed to figure out the difference between right and wrong?*

Student: Go by what you think!

→ *But how do you figure out what to think?*

Student: Lots of people go by other people.

→ *But somebody has to decide for themselves, don't they?*

Student: Use your mind?

➤ *Yes, let's see, suppose I told you: "You are going to have a new classmate. Her name is Sally and she's bad." Now, you could either believe me or what could you do?*

Student: You could try to meet her and decide whether she was bad or good.

➤ *Suppose she came and said to you: "I'm going to give you a toy so you'll like me." And she gave you things so you would like her, but she also beat up on some other people, would you like her because she gave you things?*

Student: No, because she said I'll give you this so you'll like me. She wouldn't be very nice.

➤ *So why should you like people?*

Student: Because they act nice to you.

➤ *Only to you?*

Student: To everybody!

Student: I wouldn't care what they gave me. I'd see what they're like inside.

➤ *But how do you find out what's on the inside of a person?*

Student: You could ask, but I would try to judge myself.

Socratic questioning is flexible. The questions asked at any given point will depend on what the students say, what ideas the teacher wants to pursue, and what questions occur to the teacher. Generally, Socratic questions raise basic issues, probe beneath the surface of things, and pursue problematic areas of thought.

The above discussion could have gone in a number of different directions. For instance, rather than focussing on the mind's relationship to emotions, the teacher could have pursued the concept 'mind' by asking for more examples of its functions, and having students group them. The teacher could have followed up the response of the student who asked, "Does reputation mean that if you have a good reputation you want to keep it just like that?" He might, for instance, have asked the student why he asked that, and asked the other students what they thought of the idea. Such a discussion may have developed into a dialogical exchange about reputation, different degrees of goodness, or reasons for being bad. Or the concept 'bad people' could have been pursued and clarified by asking students why the examples they gave were examples of bad people. Students may then have been able to suggest tentative generalizations which could have been tested and probed through further questioning. Instead of exploring the influence of perspective on evaluation, the teacher might have probed the idea, expressed by one student, that no one is "really bad". The student could have been asked to explain the remark, and other students could have been asked for their responses. In these cases and others, the teacher has a choice between any number of equally thought provoking questions. No one question is the 'right' question.

A general discussion such as this lays the foundation for subsequent discussions by raising and briefly covering a variety of interrelated issues. This can be followed up in small group discussions or made the basis of brief writing assignments or integrated into the discussion of literature, history, or other subject areas. Note the variety of questions that were raised in the preceding discussion:

1) Is the mind like a machine that operates your body?

2) How is it influenced by events?

If something happening around you is sad.

If you get something you want.

3) How is it influenced by its own interpretations and meanings?

You get the same toy. One person might like it. The other gets the same toy and he doesn't like the toy.

When you start doing stuff and you find that you like some stuff best.

4) How is it shaped by significant persons like parents?

Because you're always around them and then the way they act, if they think they are good and they want you to act the same way, then they'll sort of teach you and you'll do it.

5) How is it shaped by cultural forces like peer groups?

Because you're around them.

Like, Eskimo kids probably don't even know what the word 'jump-rope' is. American kids know what it is.

And also we don't have to dress like them or act like them and they have to know when a storm is coming so they won't get trapped outside.

6) Does free will involve more than just inwardly deciding?

You can't just decide you want to be smart, you have to work for it.

You got to work to be smart just like you got to work to get your allowance.

Sometimes I think I've been bad too long and I want to go to school and have a better reputation, but sometimes I feel like just making trouble and who cares.

7) Are minds sometimes deceived by others or self-deceived?

Like, everyone might think you were good but you might be going on dope or something.

You can't tell a book by how it's covered.

The bums, ... not really 'cause they might not look good but you can't judge them by how they look. They might be really nice and everything.

A lot of them don't think they're bad but they are. They might be sick in the head.

A lot of them (bad guys) don't think they're bad.

It depends what his mind is like. He might think he is doing good for his family or he might think he is doing bad for the other person.

Yeah, because you could try to be good. I mean, a lot of people think this one person's really smart but this other person doesn't have nice clothes but she tries really hard and people don't want to be around her.

8) What are people really like? Should you approach anyone as if they were evil?

None of us are really bad!

Really, I don't know why our people and their people are fighting. Two wrongs don't make a right.

They might be shy and just want to be left alone.

9) Should you think as others think or do your own thinking?

Lots of people go by other people.

You could ask, but I would try to judge myself.

You could try to meet her and decide whether she was bad or good.

When teachers approach their subjects philosophically, they make it much easier for students to begin to integrate their thinking across subject matter divisions. In the preceding discussion, for example, the issues considered involved personal experience, psychology, sociology, ethics, culture, and philosophy. The issues, philosophically put, made these diverse areas relevant to each other. And just as one might inquire into a variety of issues by first asking a basic philosophical question, so one might proceed in the other direction: first asking a question within a subject area and then, by approaching it philosophically, explore its relationships to other subjects. These kinds of transitions are quite natural and unforced in a philosophical discussion, because all dimensions of human study and experience are indeed related to each other. We would see this if we could set aside the blinders that usually come with conventional discipline-specific instruction. By routinely considering root questions and root ideas philosophically, we naturally pursue those connections freed of these blinders.

As teachers teaching philosophically, we are continually interested in what the students themselves think on basic matters and issues. We continually encourage students to explore how what they think about X relates to what they think about Y and Z. This necessarily requires that students' thought moves back and forth between their own basic ideas and those presented in class by other students, between their own ideas and those expressed in a book, between their thinking and their experiences, between ideas within one domain and those in another.

This *dialogical* process (moving back and forth between divergent domains and points of view) will sometimes become *dialectical* (some ideas will clash or be inconsistent with others). The act of *integrating* thinking is deeply tied to the act of *assessing* thinking, because, as we consider a diversity of ideas, we discover that many of them contradict each other. Teachers should introduce the critical, analytic vocabulary of English (to be discussed presently) into classroom talk, so that students increasingly learn standards and tools they can use to make their integrative assessments. Skilled use of such terms as 'assumes', 'implies', and 'contradicts' is essential to rational assessment of thinking.

It would be unrealistic to expect students to suddenly and deeply grasp the roots of their own thinking, or to immediately be able to honestly and fairmindedly assess it — to instantly weed out all beliefs to which they have not consciously assented. In teaching philosophically, one is continually priming the pump, as it were, continually encouraging responsible autonomy of thought, and making progress in degrees across a wide arena of concerns. The key is to continually avoid forcing the student to acquiesce to authoritative answers without understanding them. To the extent that students become submissive in their thinking, they stop thinking for themselves. When they comply tacitly or passively without genuine understanding, they are set back intellectually.

To cultivate students' impulses to think philosophically, we must continually encourage them to believe that they can figure out where they stand on root issues, that they themselves have something worthwhile to say, and that what they have to say should be given serious consideration by the other students and the teacher.

All subjects, in sum, can be taught philosophically or un-philosophically. Let me illustrate by using the subject of history. Since philosophical thinking tends to make our most basic ideas and assumptions explicit, by using it we can better orient ourselves toward the subject as a whole and mindfully integrate the parts into the whole.

Students are introduced to history early in their education, and that subject area is usually required through high school and into college, and with good reason. But the un-philosophical way history is often taught fails to develop students' ability to think historically for themselves. Indeed, history books basically tell students what to believe and what to think about history. Students have little reason in most history classes to relate the material to the framework of their own ideas, assumptions, or values. Students do not know that they have a philosophy and even if they did it is doubtful that without the stimulation of a teacher who approached the subject philosophically they would see the relevance of history to it.

But consider the probable outcome of teachers raising and facilitating discussion questions such as the following:

What is history? Is everything that happened part of history? Can everything that happened be put into a history book? Why not? If historians have to select some events to include and leave out others, how do they do this? If this requires that historians make value judgments about what is important, is it likely that they will all agree? Is it possible for people observing and recording events to be biased or prejudiced? Could a historian be biased or prejudiced? How would you find out? How do people know what caused an event? How do people know what outcomes an event had? Would everyone agree about causes and outcomes? If events, to be given meaning, have to be interpreted from some point of view, what is the point of view of the person who wrote our text?

Do you have a history? Is there a way in which everyone develops an interpretation of the significant events in his or her own life? If there is more than one point of view that events can be considered from, could you think of someone in your life who interprets your past in a way different from you? Does it make any difference how your past is interpreted? How are people sometimes harmed by the way in which they interpret their past?

These questions would not, of course, be asked at once. But they should be the *kind* of question routinely raised as part of stimulating students to take history seriously, to connect it to their lives, minds, values, and actions. After all, many of the most important questions we face in everyday life do have a significant historical dimension, but that dimension is not given by a bare set of isolated facts. For example, arguments between spouses often involve disagreements on how to interpret events or patterns of past events or behaviors. How we interpret events in our lives depends on our point of view, basic values and interests, prejudices, and so forth.

Few of us are good historians or philosophers in the matter of our own lives. But then, no one has encouraged us to be. No one has helped us grasp these kinds of connections nor relate to our own thought or experience in these ways. We don't see ourselves as shaping our experience within a framework of meanings, because we have not learned how to isolate and identify central issues in our lives. Rather we tend to believe, quite egocentrically, that we directly and immediately grasp life as it is. The world must be the way we see it, because we see nothing standing between us and the world. We seem to see it directly and objectively. We don't really see the need therefore to consider seriously other ways of seeing or interpreting it.

As we identify our point of view (philosophy) explicitly, and deliberately put its ideas to work in interpreting our world, including seriously considering competing ideas, we are freed from the illusion of absolute objectivity. We begin to recognize egocentric subjectivity as a serious problem in human affairs. Our thought begins to grapple with this problem in a variety of ways. We begin to discover how our fears, insecurities, vested interests, frustrations, egocentricity, ethnocentricity, prejudices, and so forth, blind us. We begin to develop intellectual humility. We begin, in short, to think philosophically. Children have this need as much as adults, for children often take in and construct meanings that constrain and frustrate their development and alienate them from themselves and from healthy relationships to others.

✦ Values and Intellectual Traits

Philosophical thinking, like all human thinking, is infused with values. But those who think philosophically make it a point to understand and assent to the values that underlie their thought. One thinks philosophically because one *values* coming to terms with the meaning and significance of one's life. If we do so sincerely and well, we recognize problems that challenge us to decide the kind of person we want to make ourselves, including deciding the kind of mind we want to have. We have to make a variety of value judgments about ourselves regarding, among other things, fears, conflicts, and prejudices. This requires us to come to terms with the traits of mind we are developing. For example, to be truly open to knowledge, one must become intellectually humble. But intellectual humility is connected with other traits, such as intellectual courage, intellectual integrity, intellectual perseverance, intellectual empathy, and fairmindedness. The intellectual traits characteristic of our thinking become for the philosophical thinker a matter of personal concern. Philosophical reflection heightens this concern.

Consider this excerpt from a letter from a teacher with a Masters degree in physics and mathematics:

> After I started teaching, I realized that I had learned physics by rote and that I really did not understand all I knew about physics. My thinking students asked me questions for which I always had the standard textbook answers, but for the first time made me start thinking for myself, and I realized that these canned answers were not justified by my own thinking and only confused my students who were showing some ability to think for themselves. To achieve my academic goals I had memorized the thoughts of others, but I had never learned or been encouraged to learn to think for myself.

This is a good example of intellectual humility and, like all intellectual humility, is based on a philosophical insight into the nature of knowing. It is reminiscent of the ancient Greek insight that Socrates himself was the wisest of the Greeks because only he realized how little he really knew. Socrates developed this insight as a result of extensive, deep questioning of the knowledge claims of others. He, like all of us, had to think his way to this insight and did so by raising the same basic *what* and *why* questions that children often ask. We as teachers cannot hand this insight to children on a silver platter. All persons must do for themselves the thinking that leads to it.

Unfortunately, though intellectual virtues cannot be conditioned into people, intellectual failings can. Because of the typically un-philosophical way most instruction is structured, intellectual arrogance rather than humility is typically fostered, especially in those who have retentive minds and can repeat like parrots what they have heard or read. Students are routinely rewarded for giving standard textbook answers and encouraged to believe that they understand what has never been justified by their own thinking. To move toward intellectual humility most students (and teachers) need to think broadly, deeply, and foundationally about most of what they have "learned", as the teacher in the previous example did. Such questioning, in turn, requires intellectual courage, perseverance, and faith in one's ability to think one's way to understanding and insight.

Genuine intellectual development requires people to develop intellectual traits, traits acquired only by thinking one's way to basic philosophical insights. Philosophical thinking leads to insights which in turn shape basic skills of thought. Skills, values, insights, and intellectual traits are mutually and dynamically interrelated. It is the whole person who thinks, not some fragment of the person.

For example, intellectual empathy requires the ability to reconstruct accurately the viewpoints and reasoning of others and to reason from premises, assumptions, and ideas other than one's own. But if one has not developed the philosophical insight that different people often think from divergent premises, assumptions, and ideas, one will never appreciate the need to entertain them. Reasoning from assumptions and ideas other than our own will seem absurd to us precisely to the degree that we are unable to step back philosophically and recognize that differences exist between people in their very frameworks for thinking.

Philosophical differences are common, even in the lives of small children. Children often reason from the assumption that their needs and desires are more important than anyone else's to the conclusion that they ought to get what they want in this or that circumstance. It often seems absurd to children that they are not given what they want. They are trapped in their egocentric viewpoints, see the world from within them, and unconsciously take their viewpoints (their philosophies, if you will) to define reality. To work out of this intellectual entrapment requires time and much reflection.

To develop consciousness of the limits of our understanding we must attain the *courage* to face our prejudices and ignorance. To discover our prejudices and ignorance in turn we often have to *empathize* with and reason within points of view toward which we are hostile. To achieve this end, we must *persevere* over an extended period of time, for it takes time and significant effort to learn how to empathically enter a point of view against which we are biased. That effort will not seem justified unless we have the *faith in reason* to believe we will not be tainted or taken in by whatever is false or misleading in this opposing viewpoint. Furthermore, the belief alone that we can survive serious consideration of alien points of view is not enough to motivate most of us to consider them seriously. We must also be motivated by an *intellectual sense of justice*. We must recognize an intellectual *responsibility* to be fair to views we oppose. We must feel *obliged* to hear them in their strongest form to ensure that we do not condemn them out of ignorance or bias.

If we approach thinking or teaching for thinking atomistically, we are unlikely to help students gain the kind of global perspective and global insight into their minds, thought, and behavior which a philosophical approach to thinking can foster. Cognitive psychology tends to present the mind and dimensions of its thinking in just this atomistic way. Most importantly, it tends to leave out of the picture what should be at its very center: the active, willing, judging agent. The character of our mind is one with our moral character. How we think determines how we behave and how we behave determines who we are and who we become. We have a moral as well as an intellectual responsibility to become fairminded and rational, but we will not become so unless we cultivate these traits through specific modes of thinking. From a philosophical point of view, one does not develop students' thinking skills without in some sense simultaneously developing their autonomy, their rationality, and their character. This is not fundamentally a matter of drilling the student in a battery of skills. Rather it is essentially a matter of orchestrating activities to continually stimulate students to express and to take seriously their own thinking: what it assumes, what it implies, what it includes, excludes, highlights, and foreshadows; and to help the student do this with intellectual humility, intellectual courage, intellectual empathy, intellectual perseverance, and fairmindedness.

✦ The Skills and Processes of Thinking

Philosophers do not tend to approach the micro-skills and macro-processes of thinking from the same perspective as cognitive psychologists. Intellectual skills and processes are approached not from the perspective of the needs of empirical research but from the perspective of achieving personal, rational control. The philosophical is, as I have suggested, a *person-centered* approach to thinking. Thinking is always the thinking of some actual person, with some egocentric and sociocentric tendencies, with some particular traits of mind, engaged in the problems of a particular life. The need to understand one's own mind, thought, and action cannot be satisfied with information from empirical studies about aspects or dimensions of thought. The question foremost in the mind of the philosopher is not "How should I conceive of the various skills and processes of the human mind to be able to conduct empirical research on them?" but "How should I understand the elements of thinking to be able to analyze, assess, and rationally control my own thinking and accurately understand and assess the thinking of others?" Philosophers view thinking from the perspective of the needs of the thinker trying to achieve or move toward an intellectual and moral ideal of rationality and fairmindedness. The tools of intellectual analysis result from philosophy's 2,500 years of thinking and thinking about thinking.

Since thinking for one's self is a fundamental presupposed value for philosophy, the micro-skills philosophers use are intellectual moves that a reasoning person continually makes, independent of the subject matter of thought. Hence, *whenever one is reasoning,* one is reasoning about some issue or problem (hence needs skills for analyzing and clarifying issues and problems). Likewise, *whenever one is reasoning,* one is reasoning from some point of view or within some conceptual framework (hence needs skills for analyzing and clarifying interpretations or interpretive frameworks.) Finally, *whenever one is reasoning,* one is, in virtue of one's inferences, coming to some conclusions from some beliefs or premises which, in turn, are based on some assumptions (hence needs skills for analyzing, clarifying, and evaluating beliefs, judgments, inferences, implications, and assumptions.) For virtually any reasoning, one needs a variety of interrelated processes and skills.

Hence, from the philosophical point of view, the fundamental question is not whether one is solving problems or making decisions or engaging in scientific inquiry or forming concepts or comprehending or composing or arguing, precisely because one usually does most or all of them in *every* case. Problem solving, decision-making, concept formation, comprehending, composing, and arguing are in some sense common to all reasoning. What we as reasoners need to do, from the philosophical point of view, is not to decide which of these things we are doing, but rather to orchestrate any or all of the following macro-processes:

1) Socratic Questioning: questioning ourselves or others so as to make explicit the salient features of our thinking:

  a) What precisely is at issue? Is this the fairest way to put the issue?

  b) From what point of view are we reasoning? Are there alternative points of view from which the problem or issue might be approached?

  c) What assumptions are we making? Are they justified? What alternative assumptions could we make instead?

  d) What concepts are we using? Do we grasp them? Their appropriateness? Their implications?

e) What evidence have we found or do we need to find? How dependable is our source of information?

f) What inferences are we making? Are those inferences well supported?

g) What are the implications of our reasoning?

h) How does our reasoning stand up to competing or alternative reasoning?

i) Are there objections to our reasoning we should consider?

2) *Conceptual Analysis:* Any problematic concepts or uses of terms must be analyzed and their basic logic set out and assessed. Have we done so?

3) *Analysis of the Question-at-Issue:* Whenever one is reasoning, one is attempting to settle some question at issue. But to settle a question, one must understand the kind of question it is. Different questions require different modes of settlement. Do we grasp the precise demands of the question-at-issue?

4) *Reconstructing Alternative Viewpoints in their Strongest Forms:* Since whenever one is reasoning, one is reasoning from a point of view or within a conceptual framework, one must identify and reconstruct those views. Have we empathically reconstructed the relevant points of view?

5) *Reasoning Dialogically and Dialectically:* Since there are almost always alternative lines of reasoning about a given issue or problem, and since a reasonable person sympathetically considers them, one must engage in dialectical reasoning. Have we reasoned from a variety of points of view (when relevant) and rationally identified and considered the strengths and weaknesses of these points of view as a result of this process?

Implicit in the macro-processes, as suggested earlier, are identifiable micro-skills. These constitute moves of the mind while thinking in a philosophical, and hence in a rational, critically-creative way. The moves are marked in the critical-analytic vocabulary of everyday language. Hence in Socratically questioning someone we are engaging in a *process* of thought. Within that process we make a variety of moves. We can make those moves explicit by using analytic terms such as these:

> claims, assumes, implies, infers, concludes, is supported by, is consistent with, is relevant to, is irrelevant to, has the following implications, is credible, plausible, clear, in need of analysis, without evidence, in need of verification, is empirical, is conceptual, is a judgment of value, is settled, is at issue, is problematic, is analogous, is biased, is loaded, is well confirmed, is theoretical, hypothetical, a matter of opinion, a matter of fact, a point of view, a frame of reference, a conceptual framework, etc.

To put the point another way, to gain command of our thinking we must be able to take it apart and put it back together in light of its *logic*, the patterns of reasoning that support it, oppose it, and shed light on its rational acceptability. We don't need a formal or technical language to do this, but we do need a command of the critical-analytic terms available in ordinary English. Their careful use helps discipline, organize, and render self-conscious our ordinary inferences and the concepts, values, and assumptions that underlie them.

✦ Philosophical and Critical Thinking

Those familiar with some of my other writings will recognize that what I am here calling *philosophical* thinking is very close to what I have generally called *strong sense critical thinking*. The connection is not arbitrary. The ideal of strong sense critical thinking is implicit in the Socratic philosophical ideal of living a reflective life (and thus achieving command over one's mind and behavior). Instead of absorbing their philosophy from others, people can, with suitable encouragement and instruction, develop a critical and reflective attitude toward ideas and behavior. Their outlook and interpretations of themselves and others can be subjected to serious examination. Through this process, our beliefs become more our own than the product of our unconscious absorption of others' beliefs. Basic ideas such as 'history', 'science', 'drama', 'mind', 'imagination', and 'knowledge' become organized by the criss-crossing paths of one's reflection. They cease to be compartmentalized subjects. The philosophical questions one raises about history cut across those raised about the human mind, science, knowledge, and imagination. Only deep philosophical questioning and honest criticism can protect us from the pronounced human tendency to think in a self-serving way. It is common to question only within a fundamentally unquestioned point of view. We naturally use our intellectual skills to defend and buttress those concepts, aims, and assumptions already deeply rooted in our thought.

The roots of thinking determine the nature, direction, and quality of that thinking. If teaching for thinking does not help students understand the roots of their thinking, it will fail to give them real command over their minds. They will simply make the transition from uncritical thought to weak sense critical thought. They will make the transition from being unskilled in thinking to being narrowly, closedmindedly skilled.

David Perkins (1986) has highlighted this problem from a somewhat different point of view. In studying the relationship between people's scores on standard IQ tests and their openmindedness, as measured by their ability to construct arguments against their points of view on a public issue, Perkins found that:

intelligence scores correlated substantially with the degree to which subjects developed arguments thoroughly on their own sides of the case. However, there was no correlation between intelligence and elaborateness of arguments on the other side of the case. In other words, the more intelligent participants invested their greater intellectual endowment in bolstering their own positions all the more, not in exploring even-handedly the complexities of the issue.

Herein lies the danger of an approach to thinking that relies fundamentally, as cognitive psychology often does, on the goal of technical competence, without making central the deeper philosophical or normative dimensions of thinking. Student skill in thinking may increase, but whatever narrowness of mind or lack of insight, whatever intellectual closedmindedness, intellectual arrogance, or intellectual cowardice the students suffer, will be supported by that skill. It is crucial therefore that this deeper consideration of the problem of thinking be highlighted and addressed in a significant and global manner. Whether one labels it 'philosophical' thinking or 'strong sense critical thinking' or 'thinking that embodies empathy and openmindedness' is insignificant.

A similar point can be made about the thinking of teachers. If we merely provide teachers with exercises for their students that do no more than promote technical competence in thinking, if inservice is not long-term and designed to develop the critical thinking of teachers, they will probably be ineffective in fostering the thinking of their students.

Teachers need to move progressively from a didactic to a critical model of teaching. In this process, many old assumptions will have to be abandoned and new ones taken to heart as the basis for teaching and learning. This shift can be spelled out systematically as follows.

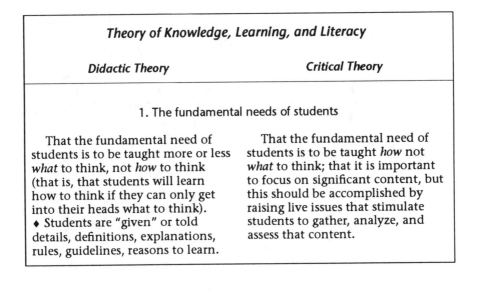

Theory of Knowledge, Learning, and Literacy

Didactic Theory	Critical Theory
1. The fundamental needs of students	
That the fundamental need of students is to be taught more or less *what* to think, not *how* to think (that is, that students will learn how to think if they can only get into their heads what to think). ♦ Students are "given" or told details, definitions, explanations, rules, guidelines, reasons to learn.	That the fundamental need of students is to be taught *how* not *what* to think; that it is important to focus on significant content, but this should be accomplished by raising live issues that stimulate students to gather, analyze, and assess that content.

Theory of Knowledge, Learning, and Literacy

Didactic Theory	Critical Theory

2. The nature of knowledge

That knowledge is independent of the thinking that generates, organizes, and applies it. ♦ Students are said to *know* when they can repeat what has been covered. Students are given the finished products of someone else's thought.

That all knowledge of "content" is generated, organized, applied, analyzed, synthesized, and assessed by thinking; that gaining knowledge is unintelligible without engagement in such thinking. (It is *not* assumed that one can think without some content to think about, nor that all content is equally significant and useful.) ♦ Students are given opportunities to puzzle their way through to knowledge and explore its justification, *as part of* the process of learning.

3. Model of the educated person

That educated, literate people are fundamentally repositories of content analogous to an encyclopedia or a data bank, directly comparing situations in the world with facts that they carry about fully formed as a result of an absorptive process. That an educated, literate person is fundamentally a true believer, that is, a possessor of truth, and therefore claims much knowledge. ♦ Texts, assignments, lectures, discussions, and tests are detail-oriented, and content dense.

That an educated, literate person is fundamentally a repository of strategies, principles, concepts, and insights embedded in processes of thought rather than in atomic facts. Experiences analyzed and organized by critical thought, rather than facts picked up one-by-one, characterize the educated person. Much of what is known is constructed by the thinker *as needed* from context to context, not *prefabricated* in sets of true statements about the world. That an educated, literate person is fundamentally a seeker and questioner rather than a true believer, therefore cautious in claiming knowledge. ♦ Classroom activities consist of questions and problems for students to discuss and discover how to solve. Teachers model insightful consideration of questions and problems, and facilitate fruitful discussions.

Theory of Knowledge, Learning, and Literacy

Didactic Theory   *Critical Theory*

4. The nature of knowledge

That knowledge, truth, and understanding can be transmitted from on person to another by verbal statements in the form of lectures or didactic teaching. ◆ For example, social studies texts present principles of geography and historical explanations. Questions at the end of the chapter are framed in identical language and can be answered by repeating the texts. "The correct answer" is in bold type or otherwise emphasized.

That knowledge and truth can rarely, and insight never, be transmitted from one person to another by the transmitter's verbal statements alone; that one cannot directly give another what one has learned — one can only facilitate the conditions under which people learn for themselves by figuring out or thinking things through. ◆ Students offer their own ideas and explore ideas given in the texts, providing their own examples and reasons. Students come to conclusions by practicing reasoning historically, geographically, scientifically, etc.

5. The nature of listening

That students do not need to be taught skills of listening to learn to pay attention and this is fundamentally a matter of self-discipline achieved through will power. Students should therefore be able to listen on command by the teacher. ◆ Students are told to listen carefully and are tested on their abilities to remember details and to follow directions.

That students need to be taught how to listen critically — an active and skilled process that can be learned by degrees with various levels of proficiency. Learning what others mean by what they say requires questioning, trying on, testing, and, hence, engaging in public or private dialogue with them, and this involves critical thinking. ◆ Teachers continually model active critical listening, asking probing and insightful questions of the speaker.

6. The relationship of basic skills to thinking skills

That the basic skills of reading and writing can be taught without emphasis on higher order critical thinking. ◆ Reading texts provide comprehension questions requiring recall of random details. Occasionally, "main point," "plot," and

That the basic skills of reading and writing are inferential skills that require critical thinking; that students who do not learn to read and write critically are ineffective readers and writers, and that critical reading and writing involve

Theory of Knowledge, Learning, and Literacy

Didactic Theory	Critical Theory
"theme" lessons cover these concepts. Literal comprehension is distinguished from "extras" such as inferring, evaluating, thinking beyond. Only after basic literal comprehension has been established is the deeper meaning probed.	dialogical processes in which probing critical questions are raised and answered. (For example, What is the fundamental issue? What reasons, what evidence, is relevant to this issue? Is this source or authority credible? Are these reasons adequate? Is this evidence accurate and sufficient? Does this contradict that? Does this conclusion follow? Is another point of view relevant to consider?) ◆ Teachers routinely require students to *explain* what they have read, to reconstruct the ideas, and to evaluate written material. Students construct and compare interpretations, reasoning their way to the most plausible interpretations. Discussion moves back and forth between what was said and what it means.

7. The status of questioning

That students who have no questions typically are learning well, while students with a lot of questions are experiencing difficulty in learning; that doubt and questioning weaken belief.	That students who have no questions typically are not learning, while having pointed and specific questions, on the other hand, is a significant sign of learning. Doubt and questioning, by deepening understanding, strengthen belief by putting it on more solid ground. ◆ Teachers evaluate their teaching by asking themselves: Are my students asking better questions — perceptive questions, questions which extend and apply what they have learned? ("Is that why ...?" Does this mean that ...?" "Then what if ...?")

Theory of Knowledge, Learning, and Literacy

Didactic Theory   *Critical Theory*

---

8. The desirable classroom environment

That quiet classes with little student talk are typically reflective of students learning while classes with a lot of student talk are typically disadvantaged in learning.

That quiet classes with little student talk are typically classes with little learning while classes with much student talk focused on live issues is a sign of learning (provided students learn dialogical and dialectical skills).

---

9. The view of knowledge (atomistic vs. holistic)

That knowledge and truth can typically be learned best by being broken down into elements, and the elements into sub-elements, each taught sequentially and atomically. Knowledge is additive. ♦ Texts provide basic definitions and masses of details, but have little back-and-forth movement between them. They break knowledge into pieces, each of which is to be mastered one by one: subjects are taught separately. Each aspect is further broken down: each part of speech is covered separately; social studies texts are organized chronologically, geographically, etc.

That knowledge and truth is heavily systemic and holistic and can be learned only by many on-going acts of synthesis, many cycles from wholes to parts, tentative graspings of a whole guiding us in understanding its parts, periodic focusing on the parts (in relation to each other) shedding light upon the whole, and that the wholes that we learn have important relations to other wholes as well as their own parts and hence need to be frequently canvassed in learning any given whole. (This assumption has the implication that we cannot achieve in-depth learning in any given domain of knowledge unless the process of grasping that domain involves active consideration of its relation to other domains of knowledge.) That each learner creates knowledge. ♦ Education is organized around issues, problems, and basic concepts which are pursued and explored through all relevant subjects. Teachers routinely require students to relate knowledge from various fields. Students compare analogous events or situations, propose examples, apply new concepts to other situations.

Theory of Knowledge, Learning, and Literacy

Didactic Theory	Critical Theory

10. The place of values

That people can gain significant knowledge without seeking or valuing it, and hence that education can take place without significant transformation of values for the learner. ♦ For example, texts tend to inform students of the importance of studying the subject or topic covered, rather than proving it by *showing* its immediate usefulness and having students use it.

That people gain only the knowledge they seek and value. All other learning is superficial and transitory. All genuine education transforms the basic values of the person educated, resulting in persons becoming life-long learners and rational persons. ♦ Instruction poses problems meaningful to students, requiring them to use the tools of each academic domain.

11. The importance of being aware of one's own learning process

That understanding the mind and how it functions, its epistemological health and pathology, are not important or necessary for learning. To learn the basic subject matter one need not focus on such matters, except perhaps with certain disadvantaged learners.

That understanding the mind and how it functions, its health and pathology, are important and necessary parts of learning. To learn subject matter in-depth, we must gain some insight into how we as thinkers and learners process that subject matter.

12. The place of misconceptions

That ignorance is a vacuum or simple lack, and that student prejudices, biases, misconceptions, and ignorance are automatically replaced by their being given knowledge. ♦ Little if any attention is given to students' beliefs. Material is presented from the point of view of the authority, the one who knows.

That prejudices, biases, and misconceptions are built up through actively constructed inferences embedded in experience and must be broken down through a similar process; hence, that students must reason their way out of their prejudices, biases, and misconceptions. ♦ Students have many opportunities to express their views in class, however biased or prejudiced, and a non-threatening environment to argue their way out of their internalized misconceptions. Teachers cultivate in themselves genuine curiosity about how students see things, why they think as they do, and the structure of students' thought. The educational process starts where students are, and walks them through to insight.

Theory of Knowledge, Learning, and Literacy

Didactic Theory	*Critical Theory*

13. The level of understanding desired

That students need not understand the rational ground or deeper logic of what they learn to absorb knowledge. Extensive but superficial learning can later be deepened. ◆ For example, historical and scientific explanations are presented to students as givens, not as having been reasoned to. In language arts, skills and distinctions are rarely explicitly linked to such basic ideas as 'good writing' or 'clear expression.'

That rational assent is an essential facet of all genuine learning and that an in-depth understanding of basic concepts and principles is an essential foundation for rational concepts and facts. That in-depth understanding of root concepts and principles should be used as organizers for learning within and across subject matter domains. ◆ Students are encouraged to discover how the details relate to basic concepts. Details are traced back to the foundational purposes, concepts, and insights.

14. Depth versus breadth

That it is more important to cover a great deal of knowledge or information superficially than a small amount in depth. That only after the facts are understood, can students discuss their meaning; that higher order thinking can and should only be practiced by students who have mastered the material. That thought-provoking discussions are for the gifted and advanced, only.

That it is more important to cover a small amount of knowledge or information in depth (deeply probing its foundation) than to cover a great deal of knowledge superficially. That all students can and must probe the significance of and justification for what they learn.

15. Role definition for teacher and student

That the roles of teacher and learner are distinct and should not be blurred.

That we learn best by teaching or explaining to others what we know. ◆ Students have many opportunities to teach what they know, to formulate their understanding in different ways, and to respond to questions from others.

Theory of Knowledge, Learning, and Literacy

Didactic Theory   **Critical Theory**

16. The correction of ignorance

That the teacher should correct the learners' ignorance by telling them what they do not know.

That students need to learn to distinguish for themselves what they know from what they do not know. Students should recognize that they do not genuinely know or comprehend what they have merely memorized. Self-directed recognition of ignorance is necessary to learning. ♦ Teachers respond to mistakes and confusion by probing with questions, allowing students to correct themselves and each other. Teachers routinely allow students the opportunity to supply their own ideas on a subject before reading their texts.

17. The responsibility for learning

That the teacher has the fundamental responsibility for student learning. Teachers and texts provide information, questions, and drill.

That progressively the student should be given increasing responsibility for his or her own learning. Students need to come to see that only they can learn for themselves and that they will not do so unless they actively and willingly engage themselves in the process. ♦ The teacher provides opportunities for students to decide what they need to know and helps them develop strategies for finding or figuring it out.

18. The transfer of learning to everyday situations

That students will automatically transfer the knowledge that they learn in didactically taught courses to relevant real-life situations. ♦ For example, students are told to perform a given skill on a given group of items. The text will *tell* students when, how, and why to use that skill.

That most knowledge that students memorize in didactically taught courses is either forgotten or rendered "inert" by their mode of learning it, and that the most significant transfer is achieved by in-depth learning which focuses on experiences meaningful to the student and aims directly at transfer.

Theory of Knowledge, Learning, and Literacy

Didactic Theory   *Critical Theory*

19. Status of personal experiences

That the personal experience of the student has no essential role to play in education.

That the personal experience of the student is essential to all schooling at all levels and in all subjects; that it is a crucial part of the content to be processed (applied, analyzed, synthesized, and assessed) by the student.

20. The assessment of knowledge acquisition

That a student who can correctly answer questions, provide definitions, and apply formulae while taking tests has proven his or her knowledge or understanding of those details. Since the didactic approach tends to assume, for example, that knowing a word is knowing its definition (and an example), didactic instruction tends to overemphasize definitions. Students practice skills by doing exercises, specifically designed as drill. Successfully finishing the exercise is taken to be equivalent to having learned the skill.

That students can often provide correct answers, repeat definitions, and apply formulae while yet not understanding those questions, definitions, or formulae. That proof of knowledge or understanding is found in the students' ability to explain in their own words, with examples, the meaning and significance of the knowledge, why it is so, and to *spontaneously* recall and use it when relevant.

21. The authority validating knowledge

That learning is essentially a private, monological process in which learners can proceed more or less directly to established truth, under the guidance of an expert in such truth. The authoritative answers that the teacher has are the fundamental standards for assessing students' learning.

That learning is essentially a public, communal, dialogical, and dialectical process in which learners can only proceed indirectly to truth, with much "zigging and zagging" along the way, much back-tracking, misconception, self-contradiction, and frustration in the process. In this process, authoritative answers are replaced by authoritative standards for engagement in the communal, dialogical process of enquiry.

✦ Bringing a Philosophical Approach Into the Classroom

Unfortunately a general case for the contribution of philosophy to thinking and to teaching for thinking, such as this one, must lack a good deal of the concrete detail regarding how one would, as a practical matter, translate the generalities discussed here into action in the classroom or in everyday thinking. There are two basic needs. The first is an ample supply of concrete models that bridge the gap between theory and practice. These models should come in a variety of forms: video tapes, curriculum materials, handbooks, etc. Second, most teachers need opportunities to work on their own philosophical thinking skills and insights. These two needs are best met in conjunction with each other. It is important for the reader to review particular philosophy-based strategies in detail.

The most extensive program available is *Philosophy for Children*, developed by Matthew Lipman in association with the *Institute for the Advancement of Philosophy for Children*. It is based on the notion that philosophy ought to be brought into schools as a separate subject, and philosophical reflection and ideas used directly as an occasion for teaching thinking skills. The program introduces philosophy in the form of children's novels. Extensive teachers' handbooks are provided and a thorough inservice required to ensure that teachers develop the necessary skills and insights to encourage classroom discussion of root ideas in such a way that students achieve philosophical insights and reasoning skills. In a year-long experiment conducted by the *Educational Testing Service* significant improvements were recorded in reading, mathematics, and reasoning. *Philosophy for Children* achieves transfer of reasoning skills into the standard curriculum but is not designed to directly infuse philosophical reflection into it.

In contrast, the *Center for Critical Thinking and Moral Critique* at Sonoma State University in California is developing a philosophy-based approach focused on directly infusing philosophical thinking across the curriculum. Handbooks of lesson plans K–12 have been remodeled by the Center staff to demonstrate that, with redesign, philosophically-based critical thinking skills and processes can be integrated into the lessons presently in use, if teachers learn to remodel the lessons they presently use with critical thinking in mind.

We provide a 'before' and 'after', (the lesson plan before remodeling and after remodeling); a critique of the un-remodeled lesson plan to clarify how the remodel was achieved; a list of specific objectives; and the particular strategies used in the remodel. Here is one such example.

Two Ways to Win

(Language Arts — 2nd Grade)
Objectives of the remodeled lesson
The student will:
- use analytic terms such as assume, infer, and imply to analyze and assess story characters' reasoning
- make inferences from story details
- clarify 'good sport' by contrasting it with its opposite, 'bad sport' and exploring its implications

Original Lesson Plan

Abstract
Students read a story about a brother and sister named Cleo and Toby. Cleo and Toby are new in town and worried about making new friends. They ice skate at the park every day after school, believing that winning an upcoming race can help them make new friends (and that they won't make friends if they don't win). Neither of them wins; Cleo, because she falls, Toby, because he forfeits his chance to win by stopping to help a boy who falls. Some children come over after the race to compliment Toby on his good sportsmanship and Cleo on her skating.

Most of the questions about the story probe the factual components. Some require students to infer. Questions ask what 'good sport' means and if Cleo's belief about meeting people is correct.

from *Mustard Seed Magic,*
Theodore L. Harris et al. Economy
Company. © 1972. pp. 42–46

Critique

The original lesson has several good questions which require students to make inferences, for example, "Have Toby and Cleo lived on the block all their lives?" The text also asks students if they know who won the race. Since they do not, this question encourages students to suspend judgment. Although 'good sportsmanship' is a good concept for students to discuss and clarify, the text fails to have students practice techniques for clarifying it in sufficient depth. Instead, students merely list the characteristics of a good sport (a central idea in the story) with no discussion of what it means to be a bad sport or sufficient assessment of specific examples. The use of opposite cases to clarify concepts helps students develop fuller and more accurate concepts. With such practice a student can begin to recognize borderline cases as well — where someone was a good sport in some respects, bad in others, or not clearly either. This puts students in a position to develop criteria for judging behavior.

STRATEGIES USED TO REMODEL

S-10 clarifying the meanings of words or phrases
S-28 supplying evidence for a conclusion
S-23 using critical vocabulary
S-25 examining assumptions

Remodeled Lesson Plan

Where the original lesson asks, "What does 'a good sport' mean?" we suggest an extension. *S-10* The teacher should make two lists on the board of the students' responses to the question "How do good sports and bad sports behave?" Students could go back over the story and apply the ideas on the list to the characters in the story, giving reasons to support any claims they make regarding the characters' sportsmanship. *S-28* In some cases there might not be enough information to determine whether a particular character is a good or bad sport. Or they might find a character who is borderline, having some characteristics of both good and bad sports. Again, students should cite evidence from the story to support their claims.

The students could also change details of the story to make further points about the nature of good and bad sportsmanship. (If the girl had pushed Cleo down to win the race, that would have been very bad sportsmanship.) To further probe the concept of good sportsmanship, ask questions like the following: How did Toby impress the other children? Why did they think he did a good thing? If you had seen the race, what would you have thought of Toby? Why do we value the kind of behavior we call 'good sportsmanship'? Why don't we like bad sportsmanship? Why are people ever bad sports? *S-10*

There are a number of places in the lesson where the teacher could introduce, or give students further practice using critical thinking vocabulary. Here are a few examples "What can you *infer* from the story title and picture? What parts of the story *imply* that Toby and Cleo will have some competition in the race? What do Toby and Cleo *assume* about meeting new people and making new friends? Is this a good or a bad *assumption?* Why? Why do you think they made this assumption? Have you ever made similar assumptions? Why? *S-25* What can you infer that Cleo felt at the end of the story? How can you tell?" *S-23*

Only after close examination of specific classroom materials and teaching strategies, can teachers begin to understand how to translate philosophically-based approaches into classroom practice. This requires long-term staff development with ample provision for peer collaboration and demonstration teaching. Only then can one reasonably assess the value and power of a philosophical approach.

✦ Summary and Conclusion

A strong case can be made for a philosophically-based approach to thinking and teaching for thinking. Such an approach differs fundamentally from most cognitive psychology-based approaches. Philosophy-based approaches reflect the historic emphases of philosophy as a field, as a mode of thinking, and as a framework for thinking. The field is historically committed to specific intellectual and moral ideals, and presupposes people's capacity to live reflective lives and achieve an understanding of and command over the most basic ideas that rule their lives. To achieve this command, people must critically examine the ideas on which they act and replace those ideas when, in their own best judgment, they can no longer rationally assent to them. Such an ideal of freedom of thought and action requires that individuals have a range of intellectual standards by which they can assess thought. These standards, implicit in the critical-analytic terms that exist in every natural language, must be applied in a certain spirit — a spirit of intellectual humility, empathy, and fairmindedness. To develop insight into proper intellectual judgment, one must engage in and become comfortable with dialogical and dialectical thinking. Such thinking is naturally stimulated when one asks basic questions, inquires into root ideas, and invites and honestly considers a variety of responses. It is further stimulated when one self-reflects. The reflective mind naturally moves back and forth between a variety of considerations and sources. The reflective mind eventually learns how to inwardly generate alternative points of view and lines of reasoning, even when others are not present to express them.

A teacher who teaches philosophically brings these ideals and practices into the classroom whatever the subject matter, for all subject matter is grounded in ideas which must be understood and related to ideas pre-existing in the students' minds. The philosophically-oriented teacher wants all content to be critically and analytically processed by all students in such a way that they can integrate it into their own thinking, rejecting, accepting, or qualifying it in keeping with their honest assessment. All content provides grist for the philosophical mill, an opportunity for students to think further, to build upon their previous thought. The philosophically oriented teacher is careful not to require the students to take in more than they can intellectually digest. The philosophically oriented teacher is keenly sensitive to the ease with which minds become passive and submissive. The philosophically oriented teacher is more concerned with the global state of students' minds (Are they developing their own thinking, points of view, intellectual standards and traits, etc.) than with the state of the students' minds within a narrowly defined subject competence. Hence it is much more important to such a teacher that students learn how to think historically (how to look at their own lives and experience and the lives and experiences of others from a historical vantage point) than that they learn how to recite information from a history text. History books are read as aids to historical thought, not as ends-in-themselves.

The philosophically oriented teacher continually looks for deeply rooted understanding and encourages the impulse to look more deeply into things. Hence, the philosophically oriented teacher is much more impressed with how little we as humans know than with how much information we have collected. They are much more apt to encourage students to believe that they, as a result of their own thinking, may design better answers to life's problems than have yet been devised, than they are to encourage students to submissively accept established answers.

What stands in the way of successful teaching for thinking in most classrooms is not as much the absence of technical, empirical information about mental skills and processes, as a lack of experience of and commitment to teaching philosophically. As students, most teachers, after all, were not themselves routinely encouraged to think for themselves. They were not exposed to teachers who stimulated them to inquire into the roots of their own ideas or to engage in extended dialogical and dialectical exchange. They have had little experience in Socratic questioning, in taking an idea to its roots, in pursuing its ramifications across domains and subject areas, in relating it critically to their own experience, or in honestly assessing it from other perspectives.

To appreciate the power and usefulness of a philosophy-based approach, one must understand not only the general case that can be made for it but also how it translates into specific classroom practices. One will achieve this understanding only if one learns how to step outside the framework of assumptions of cognitive psychology and consider thinking, thinking about thinking, and teaching for thinking from a different and fresh perspective. If we look at thinking only from the perspective of cognitive psychology, we will likely fall into the trap which Gerald W. Bracey (1987) recently characterized as,

> ... the long and unhappy tendency of American psychology to break learning into discrete pieces and then treat the pieces in isolation. From James Mill's "mental mechanics", through Edward Titchener's structuralism, to behavioral objectives and some "componential analysis" in current psychology, U.S. educators have acted as if the whole were never more than the sum of its parts, as if a house were no more than the nails and lumber and glass that

went into it, as if education were no more than the average number of discrete objectives mastered. We readily see that this is ridiculous in the case of a house, but we seem less able to recognize its absurdity in the case of education. (p. 684)

In thinking, if nowhere else, the whole is greater than the sum of its parts, and cannot be understood merely by examining its psychological leaves, branches, or trunk. We must also dig up its philosophical roots and study its seed ideas as ideas: the "stuff" that determines the very nature of thought itself.

✦ References

Bracey, Gerald W. "Measurement-Driven Instruction: Catchy Phrase, Dangerous Practice." *Phi Delta Kappan.* May, 1987. pp. 683–688.

Paul, Richard W., Binker, A. J. A., & Charbonneau, Marla. *Critical Thinking Handbook: K–3, A Guide for Remodeling Lesson Plans in Language Arts, Social Studies, and Science.* Rohnert Park, California: Center for Critical Thinking and Moral Critique. 1987.

Paul, Richard W., Binker, A. J. A., Jensen, Karen, & Kreklau, Heidi. *Critical Thinking Handbook: 4th–6th Grades, a Guide for Remodeling Lesson Plans in Language Arts, Social Studies, and Science.* Rohnert Park, California: Center for Critical Thinking and Moral Critique. 1987.

Perkins, David. "Reasoning as it Is and Could Be: An Empirical Perspective." Paper given at *American Educational Research Association* Conference, San Francisco. April, 1986.

Chapter 24

Critical Thinking and Social Studies

with A. J. A. Binker

Abstract

In this paper, originally published as a chapter in the Critical Thinking Handbooks 6*th*–9*th* Grades, and High School, *Paul and Binker outline a critical approach to teaching social studies emphasizing the need to focus instruction on the basic questions of social studies. They first argue that thinking about social studies is multi-dimensional or dialogical and that students must think their way to knowledge, then they list common flaws in social studies texts (both in general and within the fields of history, politics, economics, anthropology, and geography). They then provide recommendations for educational reform. Finally they list key questions, first in the various disciplines of social studies, and then basic questions which suggest their overlap and interrelationships, which can help teachers and students unify social studies.*

✦ Introduction

*T*he major problem to overcome in remodeling social studies units and lessons is that of transforming didactic instruction within one point of view into dialogical instruction within multiple points of view. As teachers, we should see ourselves not as dispensers of absolute truth nor as proponents of relativity, but as careful reflective seekers after truth, a search in which we invite our students to participate. We continually need to remind ourselves that each person responds to social issues from one of many mutually inconsistent points of view. Each point of view rests on assumptions about human nature. Thinking of one point of view as *the truth* limits our understanding of issues. Practice entering into and coming to understand divergent points of view, on the other hand, heightens our grasp of the real problems of our lives. Children, in their everyday lives, already face the kinds of issues studied in social studies and are engaged in developing assumptions on questions like the following:

> What does it mean to belong to a group? Does it matter if others do not approve of me? Is it worthwhile to be good? What is most important to me? How am I like and unlike others?

475

Whom should I trust? Who are my friends and enemies? What are people like? What am I like? How do I fit in with others? What are my rights and responsibilities? What are others' rights and responsibilities?

Humans live in a world of humanly constructed meanings. There is always more than one way to conceptualize human behavior. Humans create points of view, ideologies, and philosophies that often conflict with each other. Students need to understand the implications of these crucial insights: that all accounts of human behavior are expressed within a point of view; that no one account of what happened can possibly cover all the facts; that each account stresses some facts over others; that when an account is given (by a teacher, student, or textbook author), the point of view in which it is given should be identified and, where possible, alternative points of view considered; and finally, that points of view need to be critically analyzed and assessed.

Adults, as well as children, tend to assume the truth of their own unexamined points of view. People often unfairly discredit or misinterpret ideas based on assumptions differing from their own. To address social issues critically, students must continually evaluate their beliefs by contrasting them with opposing beliefs. From the beginning, social studies instruction should encourage dialogical thinking, that is, the fairminded discussion of a variety of points of view and their underlying beliefs. Of course, this emphasis on the diversity of human perspectives should not be covered in a way that implies that all points of view are equally valid. Rather, students should learn to value critical thinking skills as tools to help them distinguish truth from falsity, insight from prejudice, accurate conception from misconception.

Dialogical experience in which students begin to use critical vocabulary to sharpen their thinking and their sense of logic, is crucial. Words and phrases such as 'claims', 'assumes', 'implies', 'supports', 'is evidence for', 'is inconsistent with', 'is relevant to' should be integrated into such discussions. Formulating their own views of historical events and social issues enables students to synthesize data from divergent sources and to grasp important ideas. Too often, students are asked to recall details with no synthesis, no organizing ideas, and no distinction between details and basic ideas or between facts and common U.S. interpretations of them.

Students certainly need opportunities to explicitly learn basic principles of social analysis, but more importantly they need opportunities to *apply* them to real and imagined cases and to develop insight into social analysis. They especially need to come to terms with the pitfalls of human social analyses, to recognize the ease with which we mask self-interest or egocentric desires with "social scientists'" language. For any particular instance of social judgment or reasoning, students should learn the art of distinguishing *perspectives on the world* from *facts* (which provide the specific information or occasion for a particular social judgment).

As people, students have an undeniable right to develop their own social perspective — whether conservative or liberal, whether optimistic or pessimistic — but they should also be able to analyze their perspectives, compare them accurately with other perspectives, and scrutinize the facts they conceptualize and judge in the social domain with the same care required in any other domain of knowledge. They should, in other words, become as adept in using critical thinking principles in the social domain as we expect them to be in scientific domains of learning.

Traditional lessons cover several important subjects within social studies: politics, economics, history, anthropology, and geography. Critical education in social studies focuses on basic questions in each subject, and prepares students for their future economic, political, and social roles.

✦ Some Common Problems with Social Studies Texts

• End-of-chapter questions often ask for recall of a random selection of details and key facts or ideas. Minor details are often given the same emphasis as important events and principles. Students come away with collections of sentences but little sense of how to distinguish major from minor points. The time and space given to specifics should reflect their importance.

• Often the answers to review questions are found in the text in bold or otherwise emphasized type. Thus, students need not even understand the question, let alone the answer, to complete their assignments.

• Timelines, maps, charts and graphs are presented and read as mere drill rather than as aids to understanding deeper issues. Students do not learn to *read* them or *use* them. Students do not develop useful schemas of temporal or spatial relationships — timelines and globes in their heads.

• Texts rarely have students extend insights to analogous situations in other times and places. Students do not learn to *use* insights or principles to understand specifics. They do not learn to recognize recurring patterns.

• Although texts treat diversity of opinion as necessary, beliefs are not presented as subject to examination or critique. Students are encouraged to accept that others have different beliefs but are not encouraged to understand why. Yet only by understanding *why* others think as they do, can students profit from considering other points of view. The text writers' emphasis on simple tolerance serves to end discussion, whereas students should learn to consider judgments as subject to rational assessment.

• Students are not encouraged to recognize and combat their own natural ethnocentricity. Texts encourage ethnocentricity in many ways. They often present U.S. ideals as uniquely ours when, in fact, every nation shares at least some of them. Although beliefs about the state of the world and about how to achieve ideals vary greatly, the U.S. version of these is often treated as universal or self-evident. Students should learn not to confuse their limited perspective with universal belief.

• Ethnocentricity is reflected in word choices that assume a U.S. or Western European perspective. For example, cultures are described as "isolated" rather than as "isolated from Europe". Christian missionaries are described as spreading or teaching "religion" rather than "Christianity". Cultures are evaluated as "modern" according to their similarity to ours. In addition, texts often assume, imply, or clearly state that most of the world would prefer to be just like us. The "American Way of Life" and policies, according to the world view implied in standard texts, is the pinnacle of human achievement and presents the best human life has to offer. That others might believe the same of their own cultures is rarely mentioned or considered.

• Texts often wantonly omit crucial concepts, relationships, and details. For example, in discussing the opening of trade relations between Japan and the U.S., one text failed to mention why the Japanese had cut off relations with the West. Another text passed over fossil fuels and atomic energy in two sentences.

• Most texts treat important subjects superficially. There seems to be more concern for the outward appearance of things and trivial details than for their underlying dynamics. Texts often cover different political systems by merely listing the titles of political offices. Most discussions of religion reflect the same superficiality. Texts emphasize names of deities, rituals, and practices. But beliefs are not explored in depth; the inner life is ignored, the personal dimension omitted. Geography texts are filled with such trivia as names of currencies, colors of flags, vegetation, and so on. Students do not learn important information about other countries. Important information that is covered is usually lost amidst the trivia and so soon forgotten.

• Many texts also tend to approach the heart of the matter and then stop short. Important topics are introduced, treated briefly, and dropped. History, for instance, is presented as merely a series of events. Texts often describe events briefly but seldom mention how people perceived them, why they accepted or resisted them, or what ideas and assumptions influenced them. Problems are dismissed with, "This problem is very complicated. People will have to work together to solve it." In effect, this tells students that when something is complicated, they shouldn't think about it or try to understand it. Students do not learn how to sort out the contributing factors or develop and assess specific solutions.

• Texts often encourage student passivity by providing all the answers. They are not held accountable for providing significant answers on their own. Texts usually err by asking questions students should be able to answer on their own, and then immediately providing the answer.

Once students understand the system, they know that they don't have to stop and think for themselves because the text will do it for them in the next sentence.

- After lengthy map skills units, students are asked to apply those skills to answer simple questions. ("Find the following cities:") Students practice reading maps in their texts for reasons provided by the texts. They are not required to determine for themselves what questions a map can answer, what sort of map is required, or how to find it. Map reading practice could be used to develop students' confidence in their abilities to reason and learn for themselves, but rarely is. Graphs and charts are treated similarly.

- Although the rich selections of appendices are convenient for the students, they discourage students from discovering where to find information on their own. In real life, problems are not solved by referring to a handy chart neatly labeled and put into a book of information on the subject. In fact few, if any, complex issues are resolved by perusing one book. Instead we should teach students to decide what kind of information is necessary and how to get it. In addition, many of the appendices are neatly correlated, designed and labeled to answer precisely those questions asked in the text. Students therefore do not develop the strategies they need to transfer their knowledge to the issues, problems, and questions they will have as adults.

- Texts often emphasize the ideal or theoretical models of government, economic systems, and institutions without exploring real (hidden) sources of power and change. Texts rarely distinguish ideals from the way a system might really operate in a given situation. They often give people's *stated* reasons as the *real* reasons for their actions.

- Explanations are often abstract and lack detail or connection to that which they explain, leaving students with a vague understanding. Texts fail to address such questions as: *How* did this bring about that? What was going on in people's minds? Why? How did that relate to the rest of society? Why is this valued? Without context, the bits have little meaning and therefore, if remembered at all, serve no function and cannot be recalled for use.

✦ Subject-Specific Problems

There are somewhat different problems which emerge in each of the areas of social studies. It is important to identify them.

HISTORY

- Although texts *mention* that to understand the present one must understand the past, they fail to *show* students the necessity of knowing historical background. They fail to illustrate *how* current situations, events, problems, conflicts, and so on can be better understood and addressed by those who understand how they came to be. "It is important to understand the past" becomes a vague slogan rather than a crucial insight which guides thought.

• Although texts refer to past problems, give the solutions attempted, and mention results, students don't evaluate them *as solutions*. They don't look at what others did about the same problem, nor do they analyze causes or evaluate solutions for themselves. We recommend that teachers ask, "To what extent and in what ways did this solve the problem? Fail to solve it? Create new problems?" Students should assess solutions tried and argue for their own solutions.

• When discussing causes and results of historical events, texts present the U.S. interpretation as though it were fact. They often treat historical judgment and interpretation as though they were facts on the order of dates. Thus, students gain little or no insight into historical reasoning, into how one reasonably decides that this caused that.

• When texts present negative information about the U.S., they don't encourage students to explore its consequences or implications. Students are not encouraged to refine their judgment by judging past actions and policies.

• Primary sources, when used or referred to at all, are not examined as sources of information or as explications of important attitudes and beliefs which shaped events. Their assessment is not discussed, nor are influences which shape that assessment. Texts fail to mention, for example, that most history was written by victors of wars and by the educated few. Much information about other points of view has been lost. Most selections from primary sources are trivial narratives.

POLITICS

• Traditional lessons stress that we should all be good citizens, but fail to explore what that entails (for example, the importance of assessing candidates and propositions before voting).

• Texts tend to make unfair comparisons, such as comparing the *ideal* of governments of the U.S. and its allies to the *real* Soviet government.

• Important ideals, such as freedom of speech, are taught as mere slogans. Students read, recall, and repeat vague justifications for ideals rather than deepen their understanding of them and of the difficulty in achieving them. In effect, such ideas are taught as though they were facts on the order of the date a treaty was signed. Texts do not, for example, have students discuss the positive aspects of dissent such as the need to have a wide-ranging open market of ideas.

• Texts often confuse facts with ideals and genuine patriotism with show of patriotism or false patriotism. The first confusion discourages us from seeing ourselves, others, and the world accurately; we fail to see the gap between how we want to be and how we are. The second encourages us to reject constructive criticism. The concept of love of one's country is reduced to a pep rally.

ECONOMICS

- Texts assume a capitalist perspective on economics. They fail to explain how other systems work. Students are ill-prepared to understand how the economies of other countries work.

- Texts generally contrast *ideal* capitalism with *real* socialism. Students come away with the idea that what we have needs no improvement and with a set of overly negative stereotypes of others.

- Texts cover economic systems superficially, neglecting serious and in-depth coverage of *how* they are supposed to work (for example, in our system, people must make rational choices as consumers, employers, employees, and voters). Students are left with vague slogans rather than realistic understanding and the ability to *use* principles to understand issues, problems, and specific situations.

ANTHROPOLOGY

- Cultural differences are often reduced to holidays and foods rather than values, perspectives, habits, and more significant customs, giving students little more than a superficial impression of this field. Students fail to learn how much people (themselves included) are shaped by their cultures, that their culture is only one way of understanding or behaving, or how much hostility is generated by culture clashes. For example, what happens when someone from a culture wherein looking someone in the eye is rude meets someone from a culture wherein avoiding another's eye is rude? Each feels offended, becomes angry at the other who breaks the rules. Are "Germans cold", or do "Americans smile too much?" Texts overemphasize tolerance for food and clothing differences but often neglect developing insight into more important or problematic differences.

GEOGRAPHY

- Texts more often use maps to show such trivialities as travelers' and explorers' routes than to illuminate the history and culture of the place shown and the lives of the people who actually live there.

- Texts fail to explain *why* students should know specific details. For example, texts mention chief exports, but don't have students explore their implications or consequences: What does this tell us about this country? The people there? It's relationships with other countries? Environmental problems? Economic problems? International and domestic politics?

What ties many of these criticisms together and points to their correction is the understanding that study of each subject should teach students how to *reason* in that subject, and this requires that students learn how to synthesize their insights into each subject to better understand their world. The standard didactic approach, with its emphasis on giving students as much information as possible, neglects this crucial task. Even those texts which attempt to teach geographical or historical reasoning do so only occasionally, rather than systematically. By conceptualizing education primarily as passing data to students, texts present *products* of reasoning. A critical approach, emphasizing root questions and independent thought, on the other hand, helps students get a handle on the facts and ideas and offers students crucial tools for thinking through the problems they will face throughout their lives.

Students need assignments that challenge their ability to assess actual political behavior. Such assignments will, of course, produce divergent conclusions by students depending on their present leanings. And don't forget that student thinking, speaking, and writing should be graded not on some authoritative set of substantive answers, but rather on the clarity, cogency, and intellectual rigor of their work. All students should be expected to learn the art of social and political analysis — the art of subjecting political behavior and public policies to critical assessment — based on an analysis of relevant facts and on consideration of reasoning within alternative political viewpoints.

✦ Some Recommendations for Action

Students in social studies, regardless of level, should be expected to begin to take responsibility for their own learning. This means that they must develop the art of independent thinking and study and cultivate intellectual and study skills. This includes the ability to critique the text one is using, discovering how to learn from even a poor text. And since it is unreasonable to expect the classroom teacher to remodel the format of a textbook, the teacher must choose how to use the text as given.

Discussions and activities should be designed or remodeled by the teacher to develop the students' use of critical reading, writing, speaking, and listening. Furthermore, students should begin to get a sense of the interconnecting fields of knowledge within social studies, and the wealth of connections between these fields and others, such as math, science, and language arts. The students should not be expected to memorize a large quantity of unrelated facts, but rather to think in terms of interconnected domains of human life and experience. This includes identifying and evaluating various viewpoints; gathering and organizing information for interpretation; distinguishing facts from ideals, interpretations, and judgments; recognizing relationships and patterns; and applying insights to current events and problems.

Students should repeatedly be encouraged to identify the perspective of their texts, imagine or research other perspectives, and compare and evaluate them. This means, among other things, that words like 'conservatism' and 'liberalism', the 'right' and 'left', must become more than vague jargon; they must be recognized as names of different ways of thinking about human nature and society. Students need experience actually thinking within diverse political perspectives. No perspective, not even one called 'moderate', should be presented as *the* correct one. By the same token, we should be careful not to lead the students to believe that all perspectives are equally justified or that important insights are equally found in all points of view. Beware especially of the misleading idea that the truth always lies in the middle of two extremes. We should continually encourage and stimulate our students to think and never do their thinking for them. We should, above all, teach, not preach.

HISTORY

History lessons should show students how to reason historically and why historical reasoning is necessary to understanding the present and to making rational decisions regarding the future. To learn to reason historically, students must discuss issues dialogically, generating and assessing multiple interpretations of events they study. This requires students to distinguish facts from interpretations. It also requires that they develop a point of view of their own.

* Many crucial historical insights have analogies in students' lives which you can use to clarify historical events. For example, as with wars between nations, relatively few childhood conflicts are entirely caused by *one* participant. Most result from an escalation of hostilities in which both sides participate.

* Dates are useful not so much as things-in-themselves, but as markers placing events in relation to each other and within a context (historical, political, anthropological, technological, etc.). To reason with respect to history, we need to orient ourselves to events in relation to each other. So when you come across a particular date, you might ask the students to discuss in pairs what events came before and after it and to consider the significance of this sequence. They might consider the possible implications of different conceivable sequences. (Suppose dynamite had been invented 50 years earlier. What are some possible consequences of that?)

* What do we know about this time? What was happening in other parts of the world? What countries or empires were around? What technology existed? What didn't exist? What were things like then?

* Why is this date given in the text? What dates are the most significant according to the text? To us? To others? Notice that many dates significant to other groups, such as to Native Americans, are not mentioned. All dates that are mentioned result from a value judgment about the significance of that event.

All students should leave school with a timeline in their heads of basic eras and a few important dates with a deeply held and thoroughly understood conviction that all history is history from a point of view, and that one needs to understand how things came to be and why.

ECONOMICS

When reasoning economically, North Americans reason not only from a capitalist perspective, but also as liberals, conservatives, optimists, or pessimists. Lessons on economics should stress not only how our system is supposed to work but also how liberals, conservatives, etc. tend to interpret the same facts differently. Students should routinely consider questions like the following: "What can I learn from conservative and liberal readings of these events? What facts support each interpretation?" They should also have an opportunity to imagine alternative economic systems and alternative incentives, other than money, to motivate human work. Students should analyze and evaluate their own present and future participation in the economy by exploring reasoning and values underlying particular actions, and the consequences of those actions.

✦ Some Key Questions in Subject Areas

Instruction for each subject should be designed to highlight the basic or root questions of that subject and help students learn how to reason within each field. To help you move away from the didactic, memorization-oriented approach found in most texts, we have listed below some basic questions, to suggest what sort of background issues could be used to unify and organize instruction and relate it to students' lives. We have made no attempt to provide a comprehensive list. Consider the questions as suggestions only.

HISTORY

Why are things the way they are now? What happened in the past? Why? What was it like to live then? How has it influenced us now? What kinds of historical events are most significant? Why? How do I learn what happened in the past? How do I reconcile conflicting accounts? How can actions of the past best be understood? Evaluated? How does study of the past help me understand present situations and problems? To understand this present-day problem, what sort of historical background do I need, and how can I find and assess it? Is there progress? Is the world getting better? Worse? Always the same? Do people shape their times or do the times shape people?

ANTHROPOLOGY

Why do people have different cultures? What shapes culture? How do cultures change? How have you been influenced by our culture? By ideas in movies and TV? How does culture influence people? What assumptions underlie my culture? Others' cultures? To what extent are values universal? Which of our values are universal? To what extent do values vary between cultures? Within cultures? How can cultures be categorized? What are some key differences between cultures that have writing and those that don't? What are the implications and consequences of those differences? How might a liberal critique our culture? A socialist? Is each culture so unique and self-contained, and so thoroughly defining of reality that cultures cannot be compared or evaluated? How is your peer group like a culture? How are cultures like and unlike other kinds of groups — clubs, nations, groups of friends, families, generations?

GEOGRAPHY

How do people adapt to where they live? What kinds of geographical features influence people the most? How? How do people change their environment? What effects do different changes have? How can uses of land be evaluated? How can we distinguish geographical from cultural influences? (Are Swedes hardy as a result of their geography or as a result of their cultural values?) Which geographical features in our area are the most significant? Does our climate influence our motivation? How so? Would you be different if you had been raised in the desert? Explain how. Why is it important to know what products various countries export? What does that tell us about that country, its relationships to other countries, its problems, its strengths?

POLITICS

What kinds of governments are there? What is government for? What should governments do? What shouldn't they do? What is my government like? What are other governments like? How did they come to be that way? Who has power? Who should have power? What ways can power be used? How is our system designed to prevent abuse of power? To what extent is that design successful? What assumptions underlie various forms of government? What assumptions underlie ours? On what values are they theoretically based? What values are actually held? How is the design of this government supposed to achieve its ideals? To what extent should a country's political and economic interests determine its foreign relations? To what extent should such ideals as justice and self-determination influence foreign policy decisions? Take a particular policy and analyze the possible effects of vested interests. How can governments be evaluated? How much should governments do to solve political, social, or economic, problems?

ECONOMICS

What kinds of economic decisions do you make? What kinds will you make in the future? On what should you base those decisions? How should you decide where your money goes? When you spend money, what are you telling manufacturers? How is a family like an economic system? What kinds of economies are there? In this economy, who makes what kinds of decisions? What values underlie this economy? What does this economic system assume about people and their relationship to their work — why people work? According to proponents of this economic system, who should receive the greatest rewards? Why? Who should receive less reward? How can economic systems be evaluated? What problems are there in our economy according to liberals? Conservatives? Socialists? What features of our economy are capitalistic? Socialistic? How does ideal capitalism (socialism) work? In what ways do we depart from ideal capitalism? Are these departures justified? What kinds of things are most important to produce? Why? What kinds of things are less important? Why?

✦ Unifying Social Studies Instruction

Although it makes sense to say that someone is reasoning historically, anthropologically, geographically, etc., it does not make the same sense to say that someone is reasoning socio-scientifically. There is no one way to put all of these fields together. Yet, understanding the interrelationships between each field and being able to integrate insights gained from each field is crucial to social studies. We must recognize the need for students to develop their own unique perspectives on social events and arrangements. This requires that questions regarding the interrelationships between the fields covered in social studies be frequently raised and that lessons be designed to require students to apply ideas from various fields to one topic or problem. Keep in mind the following questions:

- What are people like? How do people come to be the way they are? How does society shape the individual? How does the individual shape society?

- Why do people disagree? Where do people get their points of view? Where do I get my point of view?

- Are some people more important than others?

- How do people and groups of people solve problems? How can we evaluate solutions?

- What are our biggest problems? What has caused them? How should we approach them?

- What are the relationships between politics, economics, culture, psychology, history, and geography? How do each of these influence the rest? How does the economy of country X influence its political decisions? How does the geography of this area affect its economy? How is spending money like voting?

- How can governments, cultures, and economic systems be evaluated?

- Could you have totalitarian capitalism? Democratic communism?
- Are humans subject to laws and, hence, ultimately predictable?

In raising these questions beware the tendency to assume a "correct" answer from our social conditioning as U.S. citizens, especially on issues dealing with socialism or communism. Remember, we, like all peoples, have biases and prejudices. Our own view of the world must be critically analyzed and questioned.

Try to keep in mind that it takes a long time to develop a person's thinking. Our thinking is connected with every other dimension of us. All of our students enter our classes with many "mindless" beliefs, ideas which they have unconsciously picked up from TV, movies, small talk, family background, and peer groups. Rarely have they been encouraged to think for themselves. Thinking their way through these beliefs takes time. We therefore need to proceed very patiently. We must accept small payoffs at first. We should expect many confusions to arise. We must not despair in our role as cultivators of independent critical thought. In time, students will develop new modes of thinking. In time they will become more clear, more accurate, more logical, more openminded — if only we stick to our commitment to nurture these abilities. The social studies provide us with an exciting opportunity, since they address issues central to our lives and well-being. It is not easy to shift the classroom from a didactic-memorization model, but, if we are willing to pay the price of definite commitment, it can be done.

Chapter 25

Critical Thinking and Language Arts

with A. J. A. Binker

Abstract

In this paper, originally published as a chapter in the Critical Thinking Hand-books *for 6ᵗʰ–9ᵗʰ Grades and High School, Paul and Binker outline a critical approach to teaching language arts, emphasizing the need to help students gain command over language. Binker and Paul outline the essential disciplined and questioning attitude of the ideal student of the language arts (as critical reader, writer, and listener), outline characteristics and goals of language arts instruction (emphasizing mastery of the logic of language), point out common flaws in standard texts, and list generic questions students could learn to raise about the aspects of language arts (reading, writing, listening, and grammar).*

✦ Introduction

*L*anguage arts, as a domain of learning, mainly covers the study of literature and the arts of reading and writing. All three areas — literature, reading and writing — deal with the art of conceptualizing and representing *in language* how people live and might live their lives. All three are primarily concerned with gaining command of language and expression. Of course, there is no command of language separate from command of thought and no command of thought without command of language.

Very few students will ever publish novels, poems, or short stories, but presumably all should develop insight into what can be learned from literature. Students should develop a sense of the art involved in writing a story and, hence, of putting experiences into words. At its root is the need everyone has to make sense of human life. This requires command of our own ideas, which requires command over the words in which we express them.

In words and ideas there is power — power to understand and describe, to take apart and put together, to create systems of beliefs and multiple conceptions of life. Literature displays this power, and reading apprehends it. Students lack insight into these processes. Few have command of the language they use or a sense of how to gain that command. Not having a command of their own language, they typically struggle when called upon to read literature. They often find reading and writing frustrating and unrewarding. And worse, they rarely see the value of achieving such command. Literature seems a frill, something artificial, irrelevant, and bookish, outside of the important matters of life. Reading, except in its most elementary form, seems expendable as a means of learning. Writing is often viewed as a painful bore and, when attempted, reduced to something approaching stream-of-consciousness verbalization.

The task of turning students around, stimulating them to cultivate a new and different conception of literature, of reading, and of writing, is a profound challenge. If we value students thinking for themselves, we cannot ignore this challenge. If a basic goal of English classes is to instill the love of lifelong reading, we must seriously confront why most students have little or no interest in literature. We need to think seriously about the life-world in which they live: the music they listen to, the TV programs and movies they watch, the desires they follow, the frustrations they experience, the values they live for.

Most teachers can probably enumerate the most common features and recurring themes of, say, students' favorite movies: danger, excitement, fun, sex, romance, rock music, car chases, exploding planets, hideous creatures, mayhem, stereotypes, cardboard characters, and so on. The lyrics and values of most popular music are equally accessible, expressing as they do an exciting, fast-moving, sentimentalized, superficial world. Much student talk consists in slang. Though sometimes vivid it is more often vague, imprecise, and superficial. (He, like totally freaked out! It was awesome. He got totally weird.) Most quality literature seems dull to students in comparison.

Good English instruction must respect and challenge students' attitudes. Ignoring student preferences doesn't alter them. Students must assess for themselves the relative worth of popular entertainment and quality works. Students need opportunities to scrutinize and evaluate the forms of entertainment they prefer. They need to assess the messages they receive from them, the conceptions of life they presuppose, and the values they manifest. As instruction is now designed, students typically ignore what they hear, read, and reiterate in school work and activities. They may follow the teacher's request to explain why a particular classic has lasted many generations, but this ritual performance has little influence on students' real attitudes. Critical thinking can help encourage students to refine their tastes, and we should encourage it with this end in mind. Nevertheless, under no conditions should we try to order or force students to say what they don't believe. A well-reasoned, if wrong-headed, rejection of Shakespeare is better than mindless praise of him.

✦ The Ideal English Student

In addition to the need to enter sympathetically into the life-world of our students, appreciating how and why they think, speak, and act as they do, we must also have a clear conception of what changes we want to cultivate in them. We must clearly see the ideals we are striving for as teachers. Consider language itself and the way in which an ideal student might approach it. We want students to be sensitive to their language, striving to understand it and use it thoughtfully, accurately, and clearly. We want them to become autonomous thinkers and so command, rather than be commanded by, language.

AS CRITICAL READER

Critical readers of literature approach literature as an opportunity to live within another's world or experience, to consider someone else's view of human nature, relationships, and problems. Critical readers familiarize themselves with different uses of language to enhance their understanding and appreciation of literature. They choose to read literature because they recognize its worth. They can intelligently discuss it with others, considering the interpretations of others as they support their own.

Critical readers approach a piece of nonfiction with a view to entering a silent dialogue with the author. They realize they must actively reconstruct the author's meaning. They read because there is much that they know they do not know, much to experience that they have not experienced. Thus, critical readers do not simply pass their eyes over the words with the intention of filling their memories. They question, organize, interpret, synthesize, and digest what they read. They question, not only what was said, but also what was implied and presupposed. They organize the details, not only around key ideas in the work, but also around their own key ideas. They not only interpret, they recognize their interpretations *as interpretations,* and consider alternative interpretations. Recognizing their interpretations as such, they revise and refine them. They do not simply accept or reject; they work to make ideas their own, accepting what makes most sense, rejecting what is ill-thought-out, distorted, and false, fitting their new understanding into their existing frameworks of thought.

AS CRITICAL WRITER

Command of reading and command of writing go hand-in-hand. All of the understanding, attitudes, and skills we have just explored have parallels in writing. When writing, critical writers recognize the challenge of putting their ideas and experiences into words. They recognize that inwardly many of our ideas are a jumble, some supporting and some contradicting other ideas, some vague, some clear, some true, some false, some expressing insights, some reflecting prejudices or mindless conformity. Since critical writers recognize that they only partially understand

and only partially command their own ideas and experiences, they recognize a double difficulty in making those ideas and experiences accessible to others.

As readers they recognize they must *actively* reconstruct an author's meaning; as writers they recognize the parallel need to *actively* construct their own meanings as well as the probable meanings of their readers. In short, critical writers engage in parallel tasks when writing to those of reading. Both are challenging. Both organize, engage, and develop the mind. Both require the full and heightened involvement of critical and creative thought.

AS CRITICAL LISTENER

The most difficult condition in which to learn is in that of a listener. People naturally become passive when listening, leave to the speaker the responsibility to express and clarify, to organize and exemplify, to develop and conclude. The art of becoming a critical listener is therefore the hardest and the last art that students develop. Of course, most students never develop this art. Most students remain passive and impressionistic in their listening throughout their lives.

Yet this need not be the case. If students can come to grasp the nature of critical reading and writing, they can also grasp the nature of critical listening. Once again, each of the understandings, attitudes, and skills of reading and writing have parallels in listening. There is the same challenge to sort out, to analyze, to consider possible interpretations, the same need to ask questions, to raise possible objections, to probe assumptions, to trace implications. As listeners we must follow the path of another person's thought. Listening is every bit as dialogical as reading and writing, though harder, since we cannot go back over the words of the speaker as we can when reading.

What is more, our students face a special problem in listening to a teacher, for if they listen so as to take seriously what is being said, they may appear to their peers to be playing up to the teacher, or may appear foolish if they seem to say a wrong or dumb thing. Student peer groups often expect students to listen with casual indifference, even with passive disdain. To expect students to become active classroom listeners is, therefore, to expect them to rise above the domination of the peer group. This is very difficult for most students.

The ideal English student, as you can see, is quite like the ideal learner in other areas of learning, in that critical reading, writing, and listening are required in virtually all subject areas. Yet the language arts are more central to education than perhaps any other area. Without command of one's native language, no significant learning can take place. Other domains of learning rely on this command. The ideal English student should therefore come close to being the ideal learner, and while helping our students to gain command of reading, writing, and listening we should see ourselves as laying the foundation for all thought and learning.

✦ Ideal Instruction

Considering the ideal reader, writer, and listener paves the way for a brief overview of ideal instruction. We should use our understanding of the ideal as a model to move toward, as an organizer for our behavior, not as an empty or unrealistic dream. Reading, writing, and listening, as critical thinking activities, help organize and develop learning. Each depends on recognizing that if we actively probe and analyze, dialogue and digest, question and synthesize, we will begin to understand alternative schemes of meaning and belief. The world of Charles Dickens is not the same as that of George Eliot, nor are either the same as those of Hemingway or Faulkner. Similarly, each of us lives in a somewhat different world. Each of us has somewhat different ideas, goals, values, and experiences. Each of us constructs somewhat different meanings to live by. In ideal instruction, we want students to discover and understand different worlds so that they can better understand and develop their own. We want them to struggle to understand the meanings of others so they can better understand their own.

Unfortunately, most texts do not have a unified approach toward this goal. They are often a patchwork, as if constructed by a checklist mentality, as if each act of learning were independent of the one that precedes or follows it. Texts typically lack a global concept of literature, language, reading, writing, and listening. Even grammar is treated as a separate, unconnected set of rules and regulations. This is not what we want, and this is not how we should design our instruction. Rather, we should look for opportunities to tie dimensions of language arts instruction together. There is no reason for treating any dimension of language arts instruction as unconnected to the rest.

Thus far, we have talked about reading, writing, listening, and literature as ways of coming to terms with constructing and organizing meanings. We can now use this central concept to show how one can tie grammar to the rest of language arts instruction, for clearly grammar itself can be understood as an organized system for expressing meanings. Each "subject" of each sentence, after all, represents a focus for the expression of meaning, something that we are thinking or talking about. Each "predicate" represents what is said about, the meaning we are attributing to, the subject. All adjectives and adverbs qualify or render more precise the meanings we express in subjects and predicates. By the same token, each sentence we write has some sort of meaningful relationship to the sentences that precede and follow it. The same principle holds for the paragraphs we write. In each paragraph, there must be some unifying thing that we are talking about and something that we are saying about it.

To put this another way, at each level of language arts instruction we should aim at helping the student gain insight into the idea that there is a "logic" to the language arts. This key insight builds upon the idea of constructing and organizing meanings; it makes even clearer how we can tie all of the language arts together. It reminds us of the established uses for all facets and dimensions of language, and that the reasons behind these uses can be made intelligible. Basic grammar has a logic to it, and that logic can be understood. Individual words and phrases also have a logic to them, and, therefore, they too can be understood. When we look into use of language realizing that there is intelligible structure to be understood, our efforts are rewarded. Unfortunately, we face a special obstacle in accomplishing this purpose.

Usually, students treat the meanings of words as "subjective" and "mysterious". I have my meanings of words, and you have your meanings of them. On this view, problems of meaning are settled by asking people for their personal definitions. What do *you* mean by 'love', 'hate', 'democracy', 'friendship', etc.? Each of us is then expected to come forward with a "personal definition". *My* definition of love is this .... *My* definition of friendship is that ....

To persuade students that it is possible to use words precisely, we must demonstrate to them every word in the language had an established use with established *implications* that they must learn to respect. For example, consider the words 'rise', 'arise', 'spring', 'originate', 'derive', 'flow', 'issue', 'emanate', and 'stem'. They cannot be used however one pleases, according to a merely personal definition in mind. Each has different implications:

> 'Rise' and 'arise' both imply a coming into being, action, notice, etc., but 'rise' carries an added implication of ascent (empires *rise* and fall) and 'arise' is often used to indicate causal relationship (accidents *arise* from carelessness); 'spring' implies sudden emergence (weeds *sprang* up in the garden); 'originate' is used in indicating a definite source, beginning, or prime cause (psychoanalysis *originated* with Freud); 'derive' implies a proceeding or developing from something else that is the source (this word *derives* from the Latin) 'flow' suggests a streaming from a source like water ("Praise God, from whom all blessings *flow*"); 'issue' suggests emergence through an outlet (not a word *issued* from his lips); 'emanate' implies the flowing forth from a source of something that is non-material or intangible (rays of light *emanating* from the sun); 'stem' implies outgrowth as from a root or a main stalk (modern detective fiction *stems* from Poe).

Or consider the words 'contract', 'shrink', 'condense', 'compress', and 'deflate'. Each of them, too, has definite implications in use:

> 'Contract' implies a drawing together of surface or parts and a resultant decrease in size, bulk, or extent; to 'shrink' is to contract so as to be short of the normal or required length, amount, extent, etc. (those shirts have *shrunk*); 'condense' suggests reduction of something into a more compact or more dense form without loss of essential content (*condensed* milk); to 'compress' is to press or squeeze into a more compact, orderly form (a lifetime's work *com-*

pressed into one volume); 'deflate' implies a reduction in size or bulk by the removal of air, gas, or in extended use, anything insubstantial (to *deflate* a balloon, one's ego, etc.)

There is a parallel insight necessary for understanding how to arrange sentences in logical relationships to each other. Our language provides a wide variety of adverbial phrases that can make connections between our sentences clearer. Here, as above, students need to learn and respect this established logic.

Connectives	How they are used
besides what's more furthermore moreover in addition	To add another thought
for example for instance in other words	To add an illustration or explanation.
therefore consequently accordingly	To connect an idea with another one that follows from it.
of course to be sure although though	To grant an exception or limitation.
still however on the other hand nevertheless rather	To connect two contrasting ideas.
first next finally meanwhile later afterwards nearby eventually above beyond in front	To arrange ideas in order, time, or space.
in short in brief to sum up in summary in conclusion	To sum up several ideas.

✦ Common Problems With Texts

A critical thinking approach to language arts instruction, with its emphasis on helping students understand the *logic* of what they study, can provide a strong unifying force in all of the basic dimensions of the language arts curriculum: reading, writing, language, grammar, and appreciation of literature. Unfortunately, this unifying stress is rare in language arts textbooks. Consequently, the emphases in reading, writing, language, grammar, and literature do not "add-up" for students. They don't recognize common denominators between reading and writing. They don't grasp how words in language have established uses and so can be used precisely or imprecisely, clearly or vaguely. Their lack of understanding of the logic of language in turn undermines their clarity of thought when reading and writing.

Similarly, grammar seems to students to be nothing more than a set of arbitrary rules. Most texts take a didactic approach. They introduce principles or concepts, then provide drills. Specific skills are often torn from their proper contexts and practiced merely for the sake of practice. Yet, without context, skills have little or no meaning. An occasional simple reiteration of basic purposes or ideas is insufficient. Students need to see for themselves when, how, and why each skill is used specifically as it is.

Texts rarely even mention that most crucial distinction: well written versus poorly written. Students rarely, if ever, evaluate what they read. Students do not explore their standards for evaluating written material, or distinguish for themselves when a written work is clear or unclear, engaging or dull, profound or superficial, realistic or unrealistic, well-organized or disjointed, and so on.

Texts occasionally have a short lesson or activity on "describing plot", "identifying theme", and "finding the main point". But students are rarely, if ever, called upon to describe the plots of selections they read. Yet these basic concepts are worthy of frequent discussion. Students should continually be required to describe the plot and state the theme of literature they read or state the main point of nonfiction passages.

Unfortunately, texts seldom have students examine work for themselves, discovering strengths and flaws, distinguishing main points from details, exploring the use of various techniques, formulating their conceptions of theses, plots, and themes.

SOME QUESTIONS TO RAISE ABOUT THE LOGIC OF LANGUAGE AND GRAMMAR

Keeping in mind the idea that language and grammar are, on the whole, logical, we should ask questions that help students discover this logic. Students should learn *how* to use grammatical distinctions, and *why*. For example, though students "cover" the distinction between transitive and intransitive verbs, they see no reason to make this distinction when they read or write. They should learn to supply implied objects of transitive verbs when they read or write. They should *use* grammatical analysis to help them read vague or difficult writing and to edit writing, not merely practice parsing sentences as drill.

"What is a sentence? How is it different from a group of words? What is a paragraph? How is it different from a group of sentences? What are words for? What do they do? How? How are words alike? Different? What kinds of words are there? How is each used? Why are some ways of using a word right and others wrong? What different kinds of sentences are there? When and how should each be used? Why follow the rules of grammar? How does punctuation help the reader? How does knowing about grammar help me write? Read? When do I need to know this distinction or concept? How should I use it? How does knowing this help me as a writer? A reader? Why and how do different types of writing differ? What do they have in common?"

SOME QUESTIONS TO RAISE ABOUT THE LOGIC OF LITERATURE

Stories have their own logic. Events don't just happen. They make sense within the meanings and thinking of their authors. When we ask a question, there should be method to it. The questions should lead students to discover how to come to terms with the logic of the story. We should always have students support their answers by reference to passages in the story. It is not their particular answers that are of greatest importance, but rather how they support their answers with reasons and references to the story.

"What happened? Why? What is the author trying to convey? Why is this important? What is the main character like? How do you know? What parts of the book gave you that idea? What has shaped the main character? How has this person shaped others? Why do the characters experience their worlds as they do? How do those experiences relate to my experience or to those of people around me? How realistic are the characters? How consistent? If they aren't (realistic, consistent) why not? Is it a flaw in the work, or does it serve some purpose? What conflicts occur in the story? What is the nature of this conflict? What is its deeper meaning? What relationship does it have to my life? What meaning does that conflict have for the character? For me? Though the world, society, lifestyle, or characters are obviously different than what I know, what does this work tell me about my world, society, life, character, and the characters of those around me? What needs, desires, and ideas govern these characters? Can I identify with them? Should I? How does the view presented in this work relate to my view? To what extent do I accept the conception of humanity and society expressed or implicit in this work? To what extent or in what way is it misleading? How does it relate to conceptions I've found in other works? How good is this work?"

SOME QUESTIONS TO RAISE ABOUT THE LOGIC OF PERSUASIVE WRITING

Persuasive writing has a straightforward logic. In it, an author attempts to describe some dimension of real life and hopes to persuade us to take it seriously. We, as readers, need to grasp what is being said and judge whether it does make sense or in what way or to what degree it makes sense.

"What parts of this work do I seem to understand? What parts don't I understand? What, exactly, is the author trying to say? Why? How does the author support what is said with reasons, evidence, or experiences? What examples can I give to further illuminate these ideas? What counter-examples can I cite? How could the author respond to my counter-examples? What are the basic parts of this work? How are the pieces organized? Which claims or ideas support which other claims or ideas? What beliefs does this claim presuppose? What does it imply? What are the consequences of believing or doing as the author says? What kind of writing is this? How has the writer attempted to achieve this purpose? Given that this is what I think is meant, how does this statement fit in? Could this be meant instead? Which of these interpretations makes more sense? How does the writer know what he or she claims to know? Have I good reason to accept these claims? Doubt them? How could I check, or better evaluate what it says? How are such questions settled, or such claims evaluated? What deeper meaning does this work have? What criticisms can I make? What is left out? Distorted? How are opponents addressed? Are these opponents represented fairly? Does the evidence support exactly the conclusions drawn? If not, am I sure I understand the conclusions and evidence? What is the source of the evidence? How should I evaluate it? What is left unexplained? What would the writer say about it? Of all the ideas or concepts, which is the most fundamental or basic? How are these concepts used? To what other concepts are they related? How does the writer's use of concepts relate to mine and to that of others? Should other concepts have been used instead? How can I reconcile what has been said with what others have said?"

SOME QUESTIONS TO ASK WHILE WRITING

Writing has a logic. Good substance poorly arranged loses most of its value. Whatever the principle of order chosen, thought must progress from somewhere to somewhere else. It must follow a definite direction, not ramble aimlessly. In the entire piece, as well as in section and paragraph, ideally, each sentence should have a place so plainly its own that it could not be shifted to another place without losing coherence. Remember, disorderly thinking produces disorderly writing, and, conversely, orderly thinking produces orderly writing.

"What do I want to communicate? Why? What am I talking about? What do I want to say about it? What else do I want to say about it and why? What else do I know or think about this? How is what I am saying like and unlike what others have said? What am I sure of? What questions do I have? What must I qualify? How can I divide my ideas into intelligible parts? What are the relationships between the parts? How can I show those relationships? How does this detail fit in? How does that claim illuminate my main point? What form of expression best gets this idea across? Would the reader accept this? What questions would the reader have? How can I answer those questions? If I word it this way, would the reader understand it the way I intended? How can I clarify my meaning? How could someone judge this idea or claim? How can it be supported? How would others refute it? Which of those criticisms should I take into account? How can I reconcile the criticisms with my ideas? How should I change what I've said? Will the support seem to the reader to justify the conclusion? Should I change the conclusion, or beef up the support? What counter-examples or problems would occur to the reader here? What do I want to say about them? How am I interpreting my sources? How would someone else interpret them? How can I adjust or support my interpretation? What implications do I want the reader to draw? How can I help the reader see that I mean this and not that? Which of all of the things I'm saying is the most important? How will the reader know which is most important? Why is this detail important? Have I assumed the reader knows something he or she may not know?"

✦ Conclusion

As a teacher of language arts, you should develop a clear sense of the logic of language and of the unity of the language arts. If you model the insight that every dimension of language and literature makes sense, can be figured out, can be brought under our command, can be made useful to us, your students will be much more apt to make this same discovery for themselves. Remember that students are not used to unifying what they study. They are more used to fragmented learning. They are used to forgetting, for everything to begin anew, for each part to be self-contained.

Furthermore, they are not used to clear and precise use of language. They are usually satisfied with any words that occur to them to say or write. They are unfamiliar with good writing. Disciplined thinking is something foreign to their lives and being. Therefore, don't expect the shift from a didactic approach ("The teacher tells us and we repeat it back" "We do the sentences in chapter one, then in chapter two.") to a critical one ("We figure it out for ourselves and integrate it into our own thought") to occur quickly and painlessly. Expect a slow transition. Expect the students to experience many frustrations along the way. Expect progress to come by degrees over time. Commit yourself to the long view, to what Matthew Arnold called "the extreme slowness of things", and you will have the attitude necessary for success. Teaching critically, with a critical spirit, is a global transformation. Global transformations take a long time to achieve, but their effect is then often permanent. And that is what we want — students who learn to use language clearly and precisely for the rest of their lives, students who listen and read critically for the rest of their lives, students who become critical and creative persons for the rest of their lives.

Chapter 26

Critical Thinking and Science

with A. J. A. Binker

Abstract

In this brief paper, originally published as a chapter in the Critical Thinking Handbook 4th–6th Grades, Paul and Binker discuss the key features of education in science. They argue for the need to teach students to think scientifically and to examine and critique their preconceptions of science and the physical world. They then point out common flaws in standard instructional practices, and provide generic questions students can consider when studying science.

A critical approach to teaching science is concerned less with students accumulating undigested facts and scientific definitions and procedures, than with students learning to *think scientifically*. As students learn to think scientifically they inevitably do organize and internalize facts, learn terminology, and use scientific procedures. But they learn them deeply, tied into ideas they have thought through, and hence do not have to "re-learn" them again and again.

The biggest obstacle to science education is students' previous misconceptions. Although there are well-developed, defensible methods for settling many scientific questions, educators should recognize that students have developed their own ideas about the physical world. Merely presenting established methods to the student does not usually affect those beliefs; they continue to exist in an unarticulated and therefore unchallenged form. Rather than transferring the knowledge they learn in school to new settings, students continue to use their pre-existing frameworks of knowledge. Students' own emerging egocentric conceptions about events in their immediate experience seem much more real and true to them than what they have superficially picked up in school.

For example, in one study, few college physics students could correctly answer the question, "What happens to a piece of paper thrown out of a moving car's window?" They reverted to a naive physics inconsistent with what they learned in school; they used Aristotelian rather than Newtonian physics. The *Proceedings of the International Seminar on Misconceptions in*

Science and Mathematics offers another example. A student was presented with evidence about current flow incompatible with his articulated beliefs. In response to the instructor's demonstration, the student replied, "Maybe that's the case here, but if you come home with me you'll see it's different there."[1] This student's response graphically illustrates one way students can retain their own beliefs while simply juxtaposing them with a new belief. Unless students practice expressing and defending their own beliefs, and listening critically to those of others, they will not critique their own beliefs and modify them in light of what they learn, a process essential for genuine understanding.

> As children discover they have different solutions, different methods, different frameworks, and they try to convince each other, or at least to understand each other, they revise their understanding in many small but important ways.[2]

Science texts suffer from serious flaws which give students false and misleading ideas about science. Scientists are not given experiments; they begin with a problem or question, and have to figure out, through trial and error, how to solve it. Typical science texts, however, present the student with the finished products of science. These texts present information, and tell students how to conduct experiments. They have students sort things into given categories, rather than stimulating students to discover and assess their own categories. Texts require students to practice the skills of measuring, graphing, and counting, often for no reason but practice or mindless drill. Such activities merely reinforce the stereotype that scientists are people who run around counting and measuring and mixing bizarre liquids together for no recognizable reason.

Texts also introduce scientific concepts. But students must understand scientific concepts through ordinary language and ordinary concepts. After a unit on photosynthesis, a student who was asked, "Where do plants get their food?" replied, "From water, soil, and all over." The student misunderstood what the concept 'food' means for plants and missed the crucial idea that *plants make their own food.* He was using his previous (ordinary, human) concept of 'food'. Confusion often arises when science concepts that have another meaning in ordinary language (e.g. 'work') are not distinguished in a way that highlights how purpose affects use of language. Students need to see that the each concept is correct for its purpose.

Students are rarely called upon to understand the reasons for doing their experiments or for doing them in a particular way. Students have little opportunity to come to grips with the concept of 'the controlled experiment' or understand the reasons for the particular controls used. Furthermore texts often fail to make the link between observation and conclusion explicit. "How do scientists get from *that* observation to *that* conclusion?" Sometimes the experiment or study is not obviously related to the question it's supposed to answer. Scientific reasoning remains a mystery to students, whereas education in science should combat the common assumption that, "Only scientists and geniuses can understand science."

To learn from a science activity, students should understand its purpose. A critical approach to science education would allow students to ponder questions, propose solutions, and develop and conduct their own experiments. Although many of their experiments would fail, the attempt and failure provide a valuable learning experience which more accurately parallels what scientists do. When an experiment designed by students fails, those students are stimulated to amend their beliefs.

Many texts also treat the concept of *"the* scientific method" in a misleading way. Scientific thinking is not a matter of running through a set of steps once. Rather it is a kind of thinking in which we continually move back and forth between questions we ask about the world and observations we make and experiments we devise to test out various hypotheses, guesses, hunches, and models. We continually think in a hypothetical fashion: "If this idea of mine is true, then what will happen under these or those conditions? Let me see, suppose we try this. What does this result tell me? Why did this happen? If *this* is why, then *that* should happen when I ...." We have to do a lot of critical thinking in the process, because we must ask clear and precise questions in order to devise experiments that can give us clear and precise answers. Typically the results of experiments — especially those devised by students — will be open to more than one interpretation. What one student thinks the experiment has shown often differs from what another student thinks. Here then is another opportunity to try to get students to be clear and precise in what they are saying. Exactly how are these two different interpretations different? Do they agree at all? If so, where do they agree?

Furthermore, not all scientists do the same kinds of things — some experiment, others don't, some do field observations, others develop theories. Compare what chemists, theoretical physicists, zoologists, and paleontologists do.

As part of learning to think scientifically, clearly, and precisely, students need opportunities to transfer ideas to new contexts. This can be linked with the scientific goal of bringing different kinds of phenomena under one scientific law, and the process of clarifying our thinking through analogies. Students should seek connections, and assess explanations and models. "How do the concepts of gravity, mass, and air resistance explain the behavior of pebbles and airplanes, boulders and feathers?"

Finally, although science is much more monological than social studies, students should learn to do their own thinking about scientific questions from the beginning. Once students give up on trying to do their own scientific thinking and start passively taking in what their textbooks tell them, the spirit of science, the scientific attitude and frame of mind, is lost. Never forget the importance of "I can figure this out for myself! I can find some way to *test* this!" as an essential scientific stance for students in relationship to how they think about themselves as *knowers*. If they reach the point of believing that knowledge is something in books that other people smarter than them figured out, then they have lost the fundamental drive that ultimately distinguishes the educated from the uneducated person. Unfortunately this shift commonly occurs in the thinking of most students some time during elementary school. We need to teach science, and indeed all subjects, in such a way that this shift never occurs, so that the drive to figure out things for oneself does not die, but is continually fed and supported.

Students often mindlessly do their science work. We should look for opportunities that call upon them to explain or make intelligible what they are doing and why it is necessary or significant.

When students perform experiments, we should ask questions such as these:

- What exactly are you doing? Why? What results do you expect? Why?

- Have you designed any controls for this experiments? (Why do you have to use the same amount of liquid for both tests? Why do these have to be the same temperature? Size? What would happen if they weren't?)

- What might happen if we ... instead?

When students make calculations or take measurements, we should ask questions like these:

- What are you measuring? Why? What will that tell you?

- What numbers do you need to record? In what units? Why?

- What equation are you using? Why? Which numbers go where in the equation? What does the answer tell you? What would a different answer mean?

When studying anatomy, students can apply what they learn by considering such questions as these:

- If this part of the body has this function, what would happen if it no longer functioned fully or at all? Why do you say so? What would that be like for the person?

- What if it functioned on "overdrive"? What other parts of the body would such breakdowns affect? Why?

When students use theoretical concepts in biology or zoology, for example, they could be asked to explain the purpose and significance of those concepts by answering questions like these:

- How important is this distinction? Let's look at our chart of categories of living things. Where on the chart is this distinction? Why?

- What distinction is more important? Why? Less important? Why? (Why is the distinction between vertebrates and invertebrates more important to zoologists than the distinction between warm-blooded and cold-blooded animals?)

- Did any categorizations surprise you or seem strange? Do zoologists group together animals that seem very different to you? Which?

- How can we find out why they are grouped this way?

In general, students should be asked to explain the justification for scientific claims.

- Why does your text say this? How did scientists find this out? How would that prove this conclusion?

- Could we explain these results another way? How? Then how could we tell which was right? What would we have to do? Why?

- What results would you expect if *this* were so, rather than *that?*

Whenever possible, students should be encouraged to express their ideas and try to convince each other to adopt them. Having to listen to their fellow students' ideas, to take those ideas seriously, and to try to find ways to test those ideas with observations and experiments are necessary experiences. Having to listen to their fellow students' objections will facilitate the process of self critique in a more fruitful way than if they are merely corrected by teachers who are typically taken as absolute authorities on "textbook" matters. Discussion with peers should be used to make reasoning from observation to conclusion explicit, help students learn how to state their own assumptions and to recognize the assumptions of others.

✦ Footnotes

[1] Hugh Helm & Joseph D. Novak, "A Framework for Conceptual Change with Special Reference to Misconceptions," *Proceedings of the International Seminar on Misconceptions in Science and Mathematics,* Cornell University, Ithaca, NY, June 20–22, 1983, p. 3.

[2] Jack Easley, "A Teacher Educator's Perspective on Students' and Teachers' Schemes: Or Teaching by Listening," *Proceedings of the Conference on Thinking, Harvard Graduate School of Education,* August, 1984, p. 8.

Appendices

*What Critical Thinking Means to Me:
The Views of Teachers*

*Glossary: A Guide to Critical Thinking
Terms and Concepts*

Recommended Readings

Index

Appendix A

What Critical Thinking Means to Me:
The Views of Teachers

Abstract

The following passages were written by teachers from Greensboro School District following a workshop on critical thinking.

Critical thinking is a process through which one solves problems and makes decisions. It is a process that can be improved through practice, though never perfected. It involves self-discipline and structure. Sometimes it can make your head hurt, but sometimes it comes naturally. I believe, for critical thinking to be its most successful, it must be intertwined with creative thinking.

Kathryn Haines
Grade 5

Thinking critically gives me an organized way of questioning what I hear and read in a manner that goes beyond the surface or literal thought. It assists me in structuring my own thoughts such that I gain greater insight into how I feel and appreciation for the thoughts of others, even those with which I disagree. It further enables me to be less judgmental in a negative way and to be more willing to take risks.

Patricia Wiseman
Grade 3

Critical thinking is being able and willing to examine all sides of an issue or topic, having first clarified it; supporting or refuting it with either facts or reasoned judgment; and in this light, exploring the consequences or effects of any decision or action it is possible to take.

Kim V. DeVaney
Facilitator, WATTS

All of us think, but critical thinking has to do with becoming more aware of how we think and finding ways to facilitate clear, reasoned, logical, and better-informed thinking. Only when our thoughts are backed

509

with reason and logic, and are based on a process of careful examination of ideas and evidence, do they become critical and lead us in the direction of finding what is true. In order to do this, it seems of major importance to maintain an openminded willingness to look at other points of view. In addition, we can utilize various skills which will enable us to become more proficient at thinking for ourselves.

Nancy Johnson
Kindergarten

Critical thinking is necessary to a happy and full life. It provides me the opportunity to analyze and evaluate my thoughts, beliefs, ideas, reasons, and feelings as well as those of other individuals. Utilizing this process, it helps me to understand and respect others as total persons. It helps me in instructing my students and in my personal life. Critical thinking extends beyond the classroom setting and has proven to be valid in life other than the school world.

Veronica Richmond
Grade 6

Critical thinking is the ability to analyze and evaluate feelings and ideas in an independent, fairminded, rational manner. If action is needed on these feelings or ideas, this evaluation motivates meaningfully positive and useful actions. Applying critical thinking to everyday situations and classroom situations is much like Christian growth. If we habitually evaluate our feelings and ideas based on reasonable criteria, we will become less likely to be easily offended and more likely to promote a positive approach as a solution to a problem. Critical thinking, like Christian growth, promotes confidence, creativity, and personal growth.

Carolyn Tarpley
Middle School
Reading

Critical thinking is a blend of many things, of which I shall discuss three: independent thinking; clear thinking; and organized Socratic questioning.

As for the first characteristic mentioned above, a critical thinker is an independent thinker. He doesn't just accept something as true or believe it because he was taught it as a child. He analyzes it, breaking it down into its elements; he checks on the author of the information and delves into his or her background; he questions the material and evaluates it; and then he makes up his own mind about its validity. In other words, he thinks independently.

A second criterion of critical thinking is clarity. If a person is not a clear thinker, he can't be a critical thinker. I can't say that I agree or disagree with you if I can't understand you. A critical thinker has to get very particular, because people are inclined to throw words around. For example, they misuse the word 'selfish'. A person might say: "You're selfish, but I'm motivated!" A selfish person is one who systematically ignores the rights of others and pursues his own desires. An unselfish one is a person who systematically considers the rights of others while he pursues his own desires. Thus, clarity is important. We have to be clear about the meanings of words.

The most important aspect of critical thinking is its spirit of Socratic questioning. However, it is important to have the questioning organized in one's mind and to know in general the underlying goals of the discussion. If you want students to retain the content of your lesson, you must organize it and help them to see that ideas are connected. Some ideas are derived from basic ideas. We need to help students to organize their thinking around basic ideas and to question. To be a good questioner, you must be a wonderer — wonder aloud about meaning and truth. For example, "I wonder what Jack means." "I wonder what this word means?" "I wonder if anyone can think of an example?" "Does this make sense?" "I wonder how true that is?" "Can anyone think of an experience when that was true?" The critical thinker must have the ability to probe deeply, to get down to basic ideas, to get beneath the mere appearance of things. We need to get into the very spirit, the "wonderment" of the situation being discussed. The students need to feel, "My teacher really wonders; and really wants to know what we think." We should wonder aloud. A good way to stimulate thinking is to use a variety of types of questions. We can ask questions to get the students to elaborate, to explain, to give reasons, to cite evidence, to identify their points of view, to focus on central ideas, and to raise problems. Socratic questioning is certainly vital to critical thinking.

Thus, critical thinking is a blend of many characteristics, especially independent thinking, clear thinking, and Socratic questioning. We all need to strive to be better critical thinkers.

Holly Touchstone
Middle School
Language Arts

Critical thinking is wondering about that which is not obvious, questioning in a precise manner to find the essence of truth, and evaluating with an open mind. As a middle school teacher, critical thinking is a way to find out where my students are coming from (a way of being with-it). Because of this "with-itness", produced by bringing critical thinking into the classroom, student motivation will be produced. This motivation fed by fostering critical thinking will produce a more productive thinker in society. Thus, for me, critical thinking is a spirit I can infuse into society by teaching my students to wonder, question, and evaluate in search of truth while keeping an open mind.

Malinda McCuiston
Middle School
Language Arts, Reading

Critical thinking means thinking clearly about issues, problems, or ideas, and questioning or emphasizing those that are important to the "thinker". As a teacher, I hope to develop Socratic questioning so that my students will feel comfortable discussing why they believe their thoughts to be valid. I hope that they will develop language skills to communicate with others and that they will be open to ideas and beliefs of others.

Jessie Smith
Grade 1

The spirit of critical thinking is a concept that truly excites me. I feel the strategies of critical thinking, implemented appropriately in my classroom, can enable me to become a more effective teacher. By combining this thinking process with my sometimes overused emotions and intuitive power, I can critically examine issues in my classroom as well as in my personal life. I feel it is of grave importance for us as educators to provide a variety of opportunities for our students to think critically by drawing conclusions, clarifying ideas, evaluating assumptions, drawing inferences, and giving reasons and examples to support ideas. Also, Socratic dialogue is an effective means of enabling the students to discover ideas, contradictions, implications, etc., instead of being told answers and ideas by the teacher. Critical thinking is an excellent tool for the teacher to help the students learn *how* to think rather than just *what* to think. Hopefully critical thinking will help me be a more effective teacher as well as excite my students.

Beth Sands
Middle School
Language Arts

Critical thinking is what education should be. It is the way I wish I had been taught. Although I left school with a wealth of facts, I had never learned how to connect them or to use them. I loved learning but thought that being learned meant amassing data. No one ever taught me how to contrast and compare, analyze, and dissect. I believed that all teachers knew everything, all printed material was true and authority was always right. It took me years to undo the habits of "good behavior" in school. I want to save my students the wasted time, the frustration, the doubts that I encountered during and after my school years. And teaching and using critical thinking is the way to do that.

Nancy Poueymirou
High School
Language Arts

For me, critical thinking is a combination of learning and applying a data-base of learning to evaluate and inter-relate concepts from diverse academic disciplines. Critical thinking is understanding that knowledge, wisdom, and education are not divided into math, science, English, etc. It is the fairness of tolerance combined with a strong sense of ethics and morals. It is the fun of feeling your mind expand as you accomplish intellectual challenges that attain your own standards. It is the zest of life.

Joan Simons
High School
Biology

Both as teacher and individual, I find critical thinking skills essential elements of a full and enjoyable life. With the ability to think critically, one can both appreciate and cope with all aspects of life and learning. When dealing with problems, from the most mundane to the most complex, the ability to think critically eliminates confusion, dispels irrational emotion, and enables one to arrive at an appropriate conclusion. At the same time, as we ponder the beauty and creativity of our environment, we are free to "wonder" and enjoy the complexity around us, rather than be perplexed or intimidated by it, because we have the mental capability to understand it. To live is to be ever curious, ever learning, ever investigating. Critical thinking enables us to do this more fully and pleasurably.

Mary Lou Holoman
High School
Language Arts

A critical thinker never loses the joy of learning, never experiences the sadness of not caring or not wondering about the world. The essence of the truly educated person is that of being able to question, inquire, doubt, conclude, innovate. And beyond that, to spread that enthusiasm to those around him, obscuring the lines that divide teacher and student, enabling them to travel together, each learning from the other.

Jane Davis-Seaver
Grade 3

Critical thinking is a means of focusing energy to learn. The learning may be academic (proscribed by an institutional curriculum or self-directed) or non-academic (determined by emotional need). It provides a systematic organization for gathering information, analyzing that information, and evaluating it to reach reasonable, acceptable conclusions for yourself.

Blair Stetson
Elementary
Academically Gifted

Critical thinking is the ability to reason in a clear and unbiased way. It is necessary to consider concepts or problems from another's point of view and under varying circumstances in order to make reasoned judgments. Awareness of one's own reasoning processes enables one to become a more fairminded and objective thinker.

Karen Marks
Elementary
Academically Gifted

Critical thinking is questioning, analyzing, and making thoughtful judgments about questions, ideas, issues, or concepts. It refines thoughts to more specific or definite meanings. The critical thinker must be an active listener who does not simply accept what he or she hears or reads at face value without questioning, but looks for deeper meaning. Critical thinking also involves evaluating the ideas explored or problems addressed and better prepares a student to be able to think about the world around him or her.

Becky Hampton
Grade 6

Critical thinking has given me a broader means of evaluating my daily lesson plans. It has helped me better understand the thinking principles of each student I teach. It has also enabled me to practice strategies in lesson planning and to become a more effective classroom teacher.

Pearl Norris Booker
Grade 2

Critical thinking provides me the opportunity to broaden the thinking process of my students. It can be used to have the students reason and think about different ideas of a problem or a given situation.

Portia Staton
Grade 3

Critical thinking is a process that takes all the ideas, questions, and problems that we are faced with each day and enables us to come up with solutions. It is the process by which we are able to search for evidence that supports already-existing answers, or better yet, to come up with new solutions to problems. Through critical thinking, one begins to realize that many times there is more than one solution whereupon decisions can be made. To me, critical thinking has helped and will continue to help me understand myself and the world around me.

Debbie Wall
Grade 4

Critical thinking is a skill that involves the expansion of thoughts and the art of questioning. This skill must be developed over a period of time. It is a way of organizing your thoughts in a logical sequence. Knowledge is gained through this process.

Carolyn Smith
Grade 5

Critical thinking is questioning, analyzing, and evaluating oral or written ideas. A critical thinker is disciplined, self-directed, and rational in problem solving. Reaching conclusions of your own rather than accepting everything as it is presented, is internalizing critical thinking.

Denise Clark
Grade 2

To think critically, one must analyze and probe concepts or ideas through reasoning. It makes one an active reasoner, not a passive accepter of ideas (or facts). It turns one into a doer, an evaluater, or re-evaluater. Critical thinking occurs everywhere, is applicable everywhere, and while it can be tedious, need not be, because as one thinks critically, new ideas are formed, conclusions are drawn, new knowledge is acquired.

Janell Prester
Grade 3

Critical thinking means to think through and analyze a concept or idea. You are able to back up your reasoning and think through an idea in a manner which allows an over-all focus. If a person is a critical thinker, a yes-no answer is too brief. An answer to a problem or idea must have an explanation and reasoning backing it.

Donna Phillips
Grade 4

Critical thinking is a tool that teachers can use to offer a new dimension of education to their students: that of thinking about, questioning, and exploring the concepts in the curriculum. When critical thinking is an integral part of the teaching-learning process, children learn to apply thinking skills throughout the curriculum as well as in their daily lives. Socratic dialogue fosters critical thinking and motivates the teacher and learner to share and analyze experiences and knowledge. Critical thinking involves the child in the learning process and makes education more meaningful to the individual, thus facilitating learning.

Andrea Allen
Grade 1

The most important part of critical thinking, to me, is discovery. We discover a deeper level of thinking. We discover the reasons for ideas instead of just accepting ideas. We are motivated by action, interaction, and involvement. We discover we have the ability to expand our thoughts to include all aspects and perspectives of our beliefs.

Mandy Ryan
Grade 5

Critical thinking, to me, is the process of analyzing new and old information to arrive at solutions. It's the process of learning to question information that you may have taken for granted. It's being independent. Critical thinking is letting people think for themselves and make judgments for themselves.

Leigh Ledet
Grade 4

Critical thinking is the process of taking the knowledge you have gained through past experience or education and re-evaluating conclusions on a certain situation or problem. Because students must evaluate the reasons for their beliefs, they become actively involved in learning through the teacher's use of Socratic questioning. Allowing students to clarify their reasons through the writing process further stimulates the students to become critical thinkers. The ultimate goal for students in using critical thinking is to become active thinkers for themselves.

Robin Thompson
Middle School
Language Arts

Critical thinking, to me, is to be open-ended in my thoughts. It is like opening a door which leads to many other doors through which ideas may evolve, move about, change, and come to rest. It is like a breath of freshness in which one can gain new insight over long-established opinions. It stimulates and generates endless new possibilities.

Eutha M. Godfrey
Grades 2–3

Critical thinking is thinking that demonstrates an extension of an idea or concern beyond the obvious. A critical thinker's values are significant to his learning.

Frances Jackson
Grade 2

To me, critical thinking means independence. It gives me a tool which lets me explore my own mind extending beyond basic recall to a higher level of reasoning. I then feel more in touch with myself and my own inner feelings. This results in my becoming a better decision-maker.

Jean Edwards
Grade 5

Critical thinking is the process of working your mind through different channels. It is the process of thinking logically. Critical thinking is analyzing your thoughts through questions. It is the process of seeing that your ideas and concepts may not be the same as another's. It is opening your mind to those who have different views and looking at their views.

Cathy L. Smith
Grade 3

Critical thinking is to question in-depth at every possible angle or point of view, to look at someone else's point of view without making hasty judgments. Critical thinking is to logically and fairly re-orient your own personal point of view, if necessary. To think critically, you are self-directed in your thinking process, as well as disciplined.

Mary Duke
Grade 1

Critical thinking is the vehicle by which I encourage students to become active participants in the learning process. I allow more time for and become more aware of the need for students to express ideas verbally and in written form to clarify ideas in their own minds. I recognize the importance of developing skills for analyzing and evaluating. Ultimately, once students become comfortable using critical thinking skills, they assume greater responsibility for their learning.

Dora McGill
Grade 6

Critical thinking is clear, precise thinking. I believe that all human actions and expressions involve in some way, thinking. For example, I believe that feelings, emotions, and intuitions are much the results of earlier thought (reactions to stimuli). I think that this, in one way, explains the variations of emotional responses in some people to similar stimuli. Thus, I believe that critical thinking not only has the potential to clarify new and former conscious thoughts but also to affect/change likely (future) emotive and intuitive reactions/responses.

More concrete and less theoretical outcomes of critical thinking may be more relevant to me as an educator. Better questioning skills on the part of the students and the teacher is an obvious outcome. There seem to be several positive outcomes of better questioning: more opportunity for in-depth understanding of content, a natural (built-in) process for assessing the effectiveness of lessons, and more opportunity for student participation, self-assessment, and direction are three apparent outcomes. There are, of course, many other outcomes of developing better questioning skills, and from the other skills of critical thinking.

I simply believe that critical thinking improves the overall integrity of the individual and the collective group, class, school, community, etc.

Richard Tuck
High School
Art

I perceive critical thinking in teaching as a tool for my learning. As I attempt to develop the critical thinker, I will become more aware of the students' thoughts, values, and needs. I must learn from what students offer, and develop acceptance and sensitivity to the individual. The knowledge I gain from the student will determine what I utilize as strategies or principles of critical thinking.

Loretta Jennings
Grade 1

Critical thinking is the ability to look at a problem or issue with a spirit of openmindedness and to take that problem and analyze or evaluate it based on the facts or good, "educated" hypotheses. Critical thinking is being flexible enough to suspend one's bias towards an issue in order to study all sides to formulate an opinion or evaluation.

Mark Moore
Grade 4

Critical thinking to me involves mental conversations and dialogues with myself. I try first to establish the facts. Then I try to search for criteria to examine my "facts". The next question is whether or not there are distortions and irrelevancies. I have to examine whether I have a personal bias which has led me to select only certain facts and leave others out.

I then try to mentally list facts and arguments on both sides of a question and, finally, draw logical questions and conclusions.

Barbara Neller
Middle School
Social Studies

Critical thinking is a systematic, logical approach to life in which an individual, using this method, truly learns and understands a concept rather than imitates or mimics. Knowledge and intellectual growth are achieved by a variety of strategies which include examining a variety of viewpoints, making assumptions based on viable evidence and forming well thought out conclusions.

Jane S. Thorne
High School
Math

Critical thinking allows students to become active participants in their learning. Socratic dialogue stimulates communication between teacher and students, thus creating an atmosphere where everyone is encouraged to become risk-takers. A teacher needs to become a model of critical thinking for the students. Through this interaction, content can be analyzed, synthesized, and evaluated with thinking.

Carol Thanos
Grade 6

Critical thinking is the complex process of exploring an issue, concept, term, or experience which requires verbal as well as non-verbal involvement from the participant. It involves listing ideas related to the subject, so that the person involved can objectively examine the relationship of the ideas thought of. It demands that the person involved in the process investigates the issue, concept, or process from varied vantage points, in order that intuitions, assumptions, and conclusions are presented with reasoned opinions or experienced evidences. Critical thinking is a task that involves the participant's in-depth assessment of his or her body of knowledge, experience, and emotions on the subject in question.

Ariel Collins
High School
Language Arts

Critical thinking is thinking that is clear, fairminded, and directed. It is not sloppy or self-serving thinking, but deep and probing thought aimed at finding the truth. It is skillful thinking aimed at genuine understanding, not superficial head-shaking. It is the tool used by and descriptive of an educated person whose mantra would be "veritas".

Helen Cook
Middle School
Science

Critical thinking is a process of questioning and seeking truth and clarity. It is a continual endeavor as one is constantly exposed to new knowledge which must be reconciled with prior conclusions. As one's body of knowledge grows, it is all the more important to be able to critically consider and determine what is truth.

Critical thinking demands certain prerequisites: openmindedness, willingness to withhold snap judgments, commitment to exploring new ideas. The development of such qualities empowers me to participate in the various facets of critical thinking, e.g., clarifying ideas, engaging in Socratic discussions. These skills are not nearly so difficult as achieving the mindset which must precede them. Only a commitment to question and persevere and honestly pursue truth will supply the impetus necessary to delve beneath the surface of issues and concepts. Yet this predisposition is difficult to achieve, because it necessitates taking risks, making mistakes, being wrong, and being corrected — activities very threatening to our safe ego-boundaries.

Only in transcending these ego-boundaries does growth occur and genuine learning transpire. Critical thinking is comprised of a sense of wonderment, daring, and determination. It is undergirded by a value for truth and personal growth. It is the continual learning process of the individual.

Deborah Norton
High School
Social Studies

The definition of critical thinking that I now hold is one that explains some things that I have felt for some time. I am convinced that everything that I know, that is a part of my education, I have figured or found out for myself. I have had close to twenty years of formal, didactic education, but I could tell you very little about anything that was presented to me in lecture through all those classes, except perhaps some trivia. In college, I did my real learning through the writing that I did, either from research or from contemplation. I have felt that this was true, but a lot of my own teaching has continued to be didactic and students have learned to be very accepting and non-questioning and to expect to be told what the right answer is, what someone else has decided the right answer is. I hope that I can change that now. I now feel that it is imperative that my students learn to be critical thinkers, and I hope that I can model that belief and, through all my activities in class, lead them in that direction. We all need to be openminded, to realize that there are often many sides to a problem, many points of view, and that there are strategies and techniques for analyzing, making decisions, and making learning our own. I want to be, and I want my students to be, questioning, openminded, fairminded, synthesizing individuals — in other words, critical thinkers.

Liza Burton
High School
Language Arts

Appendix B

Glossary:
A Guide to
Critical Thinking Terms and Concepts

with A. J. A. Binker

accurate: Free from errors, mistakes, or distortion. *Correct* connotes little more than absence of error; *accurate* implies a positive exercise of one to obtain conformity with fact or truth; *exact* stresses perfect conformity to fact, truth, or some standard; *precise* suggests minute accuracy of detail. Accuracy is an important goal in critical thinking, though it is almost always a matter of degree. It is also important to recognize that making mistakes is an essential part of learning and that it is far better that students make their own mistakes, than that they parrot the thinking of the text or teacher. It should also be recognized that some distortion usually results whenever we think within a point of view or frame of reference. Students should think with this awareness in mind, with some sense of the limitations of their own, the text's, the teacher's, the subject's perspective. See *perfections of thought.*

ambiguous: A sentence having two or more possible meanings. Sensitivity to ambiguity and vagueness in writing and speech is essential to good thinking. *A continual effort to be clear and precise in language usage is fundamental to education.* Ambiguity is a problem more of sentences than of individual words. Furthermore, not every sentence that can be construed in more than one way is problematic and deserving of analysis. Many sentences are clearly intended one way; any other construal is obviously absurd and not meant. For example, "Make me a sandwich." is never seriously intended to request metamorphic change. It is a poor example for teaching genuine insight into critical thinking. For an example of a problematic ambiguity, consider the statement, "Welfare is corrupt." Among the possible meanings of this sentence are the following: Those who administer welfare programs take bribes to administer welfare policy unfairly; Welfare policies are written in such a way that much of the money goes to people who don't deserve it rather than to those who do; A government that gives money to people who haven't earned it corrupts both the giver and the recipient. If two people are arguing about whether or not welfare is corrupt, but interpret the claim differently, they can make little or no progress; they aren't arguing about the same point. Evidence and considerations relevant to one interpretation may be irrelevant to others.

analyze: To break up a whole into its parts, to examine in detail so as to determine the nature of, to look more deeply into an issue or situation. *All learning presupposes some analysis of what we are learning,* if only by categorizing or labeling things in one way rather than another. Students should continually be asked to analyze their ideas, claims, experiences, interpretations, judgments, and theories and those they hear and read. See *elements of thought.*

argue: There are two meanings of this word that need to be distinguished: *1)* to argue in the sense of *to fight* or to emotionally disagree; and *2)* to give reasons for or against a proposal or proposition. In emphasizing critical thinking, we continually try to get our students to move from the first sense of the word to the second; that is, we try to get them to see the importance of *giving reasons* to support their views without getting their egos involved in what they are saying. This is a fundamental problem in human life. To argue in the critical thinking sense is to use logic and reason, and to bring forth facts to support or refute a point. It is done in a spirit of cooperation and good will.

argument: A reason or reasons offered for or against something, the offering of such reasons. This term refers to a discussion in which there is disagreement and suggests the use of logic and bringing forth of facts to support or refute a point. See *argue.*

to assume: To take for granted or to presuppose. Critical thinkers can and do make their assumptions explicit, assess them, and correct them. Assumptions can vary from the mundane to the problematic: I heard a scratch at the door. I got up to let the cat in. I *assumed* that only the cat makes that noise, and that he makes it only when he wants to be let in. Someone speaks gruffly to me. I feel guilty and hurt. I assume he is angry *at me,* that he is only angry at me when I do something bad, and that if he's angry at me, he dislikes me. *Notice that people often equate making assumptions with making false assumptions.* When people say, "Don't assume", this is what they mean. In fact, we cannot avoid making assumptions and some are justifiable. (For instance, we have assumed that people who buy this book can read English.) Rather than saying "Never assume", we say, "Be aware of and careful about the assumptions you make, and be ready to examine and critique them." See *assumption, elements of thought.*

assumption: A statement accepted or supposed as true without proof or demonstration; an unstated premise or belief. *All human thought and experience is based on assumptions.* Our thought must begin with something we take to be true in a particular context. We are typically unaware of what we assume and therefore rarely question our assumptions. Much of what is wrong with human thought can be found in the uncritical or unexamined assumptions that underlie it. For example, we often experience the world in such a way as to assume that we are observing things just as they are, as though we were seeing the world without the filter of a point of view. People we disagree with, of course, we recognize as *having a point of view.* One of the key dispositions of critical thinking is the on-going sense that as humans we always think within a perspective, that we virtually never experience things totally and absolutistically. There is a connection, therefore, between thinking so as to be *aware of our assumptions* and being *intellectually humble.*

authority: 1) The power or supposed right to give commands, enforce obedience, take action, or make final decisions. *2)* A person with much knowledge and expertise in a field, hence reliable. Critical thinkers recognize that ultimate authority rests with reason and evidence, since it is only on the assumption that purported experts have the backing of reason and evidence that they rightfully gain authority. Much instruction discourages critical thinking by encouraging students to believe that whatever the text or teacher says is true. As a result, students do not learn how to assess authority. See *knowledge.*

bias: A mental leaning or inclination. We must clearly distinguish two different senses of the word 'bias'. One is neutral, the other negative. In the neutral sense we are referring simply to the fact that, *because of one's point of view, one notices some things rather than others,* emphasizes some points rather than others, and thinks in one direction rather than others. This is not in itself a criticism because *thinking within a point of view is unavoidable.* In the negative sense, we are implying *blindness or irrational resistance to weaknesses within one's own point of view* or to the strength or insight within a point of view one opposes. Fairminded critical thinkers try to be aware of their bias (in sense one) and try hard to avoid bias (in sense two). Many people confuse these two senses. Many confuse bias with emotion or with evaluation, perceiving any expression of emotion or any use of evaluative words to be biased (sense two). Evaluative words that can be justified by reason and evidence are not biased in the negative sense. See *criteria, evaluation, judgment, opinion.*

clarify: To make easier to understand, to free from confusion or ambiguity, to remove obscurities. *Clarity* is a fundamental perfection of thought and *clarification* a fundamental aim in critical thinking. Students often do not see why it is important to write and speak clearly, why it is important to *say what you mean and mean what you say.* The key to clarification is *concrete, specific* examples. See *accurate, ambiguous, logic of language, vague.*

concept: An idea or thought, especially a generalized idea of a thing or of a class of things. Humans think within concepts or ideas. *We can never achieve command over our thoughts unless we learn how to achieve command over our concepts or ideas.* Thus we must learn how to identify the concepts or ideas we are using, contrast them with alternative concepts or ideas, and clarify what we include and exclude by means of them. For example, most people say they believe strongly in democracy, but few can clarify with examples what that word does and does not imply. *Most people confuse the meaning of words with cultural associations,* with the result that 'democracy' means to people whatever *we* do in running *our* government — any country that is different is undemocratic. We must distinguish the concepts implicit in the English language from the psychological associations surrounding that concept in a given social group or culture. The failure to develop this ability is a major cause of uncritical thought and selfish critical thought. See *logic of language.*

conclude/conclusion: To decide by reasoning, to infer, to deduce; the last step in a reasoning process; a judgment, decision, or belief formed after investigation or reasoning. All beliefs, decisions, or actions are based on human thought, but rarely as the result of conscious reasoning or deliberation. *All that we believe is,* one way or another, *based on conclusions* that we have come to during our lifetime. Yet, we rarely monitor our thought processes, we don't critically assess the conclusions we come to, to determine whether we have sufficient grounds or reasons for accepting them. People seldom recognize when they have come to a conclusion. They confuse their conclusions with evidence, and so cannot assess the reasoning that took them from evidence to conclusion. Recognizing that *human life is inferential,* that we continually come to conclusions about ourselves and the things and persons around us, is essential to thinking critically and reflectively.

consistency: To think, act, or speak in agreement with what has already been thought, done, or expressed; to have intellectual or moral integrity. Human life and thought is filled with inconsistency, hypocrisy, and contradiction. We often say one thing and do another, judge ourselves and our friends by one standard and our antagonists by another, lean over backwards to justify what we want or negate what does not serve our interests. Similarly, we often confuse desires with needs, treating our desires as equivalent to needs, putting what we want above the basic needs of others. *Logical and moral consistency are fundamental values of fairminded critical thinking.* Social conditioning and native egocentrism often obscure social contradictions, inconsistency, and hypocrisy. See *personal contradiction, social contradiction, intellectual integrity, human nature.*

contradict/contradiction: To assert the opposite of; to be contrary to, go against; a statement in opposition to another; a condition in which things tend to be contrary to each other; inconsistency; discrepancy; a person or thing containing or composed of contradictory elements. See *personal contradiction, social contradiction.*

criterion (criteria, pl): A standard, rule, or test by which something can be judged or measured. Human life, thought, and action are based on human values. The standards by which we determine whether those values are achieved in any situation represent criteria. Critical thinking depends upon making explicit the standards or criteria for rational or justifiable thinking and behavior. See *evaluation.*

critical listening: A mode of monitoring how we are listening so as to maximize our accurate understanding of what another person is saying. By understanding the logic of human communication — that *everything spoken expresses point of view,* uses some ideas and not others, has implications, etc. — critical thinkers can listen so as to enter sympathetically and analytically into the perspective of others. See *critical speaking, critical reading, critical writing, elements of thought, intellectual empathy.*

critical person: One who has mastered a range of intellectual skills and abilities. If that person generally uses those skills to advance his or her own selfish interests, that person is a critical thinker only in a weak or qualified sense. If that person generally uses those skills fairmindedly, entering empathically into the points of view of others, he or she is a critical thinker in the strong or fullest sense. See *critical thinking.*

critical reading: Critical reading is an active, intellectually engaged process in which the reader participates in an inner dialogue with the writer. Most people read uncritically and so miss some part of what is expressed while distorting other parts. A critical reader realizes the way in which *reading, by its very nature, means entering into a point of view other than our own,* the point of view of the writer. A critical reader actively looks for assumptions, key concepts and ideas, reasons and justifications, supporting examples, parallel experiences, implications and consequences, and any other structural features of the written text, to interpret and assess it accurately and fairly. See *elements of thought.*

critical society: A society which rewards adherence to the values of critical thinking and hence *does not use indoctrination and inculcation as basic modes of learning* (rewards reflective questioning, intellectual independence, and reasoned dissent). Socrates is not the only thinker to imagine a society in which independent critical thought became embodied in the concrete day-to-day lives of individuals; William Graham Sumner, North America's distinguished anthropologist, explicitly formulated the ideal:

The critical habit of thought, if usual in a society, will pervade all its mores, because it is a way of taking up the problems of life. Men educated in it cannot be stampeded by stump orators and are never deceived by dithyrambic oratory. They are slow to believe. They can hold things as possible or probable in all degrees, without certainty and without pain. They can wait for evidence and weigh evidence, uninfluenced by the emphasis or confidence with which assertions are made on one side or the other. They can resist appeals to their dearest prejudices and all kinds of cajolery. Education in the critical faculty is the only education of which it can be truly said that it makes good citizens. (*Folkways*, 1906)

Until critical habits of thought pervade our society, however, there will be a tendency for schools as social institutions to transmit the prevailing world view more or less uncritically, to transmit it as reality, not as a picture of reality. Education for critical thinking, then, requires that the school or classroom become a microcosm of a critical society. See *didactic instruction, dialogical instruction, intellectual virtues, knowledge.*

critical thinking: 1) Disciplined, self-directed thinking which exemplifies the perfections of thinking appropriate to a particular mode or domain of thinking. *2)* Thinking that displays mastery of intellectual skills and abilities. *3)* The art of thinking about your thinking while you are thinking in order to make your thinking better: more clear, more accurate, or more defensible. Critical thinking can be distinguished into two forms: "selfish" or "sophistic", on the one hand, and "fairminded", on the other. In thinking critically we use our command of the elements of thinking to adjust our thinking successfully to the logical demands of a type or mode of thinking. See *critical person, critical society, critical reading, critical listening, critical writing, perfections of thought, elements of thought, domains of thought, intellectual virtues.*

critical writing: To express ourselves in language requires that we arrange our ideas in some relationships to each other. When accuracy and truth are at issue, then we must understand what our thesis is, how we can support it, how we can elaborate it to make it intelligible to others, what objections can be raised to it from other points of view, what the limitations are to our point of view, and so forth. *Disciplined writing requires disciplined thinking; disciplined thinking is achieved through disciplined writing.* See *critical listening, critical reading, logic of language.*

critique: An objective judging, analysis, or evaluation of something. The purpose of critique is the same as the purpose of critical thinking: to appreciate strengths as well as weaknesses, virtues as well as failings. *Critical thinkers critique in order to redesign, remodel, and make better.*

cultural association: Undisciplined thinking often reflects associations, personal and cultural, absorbed or uncritically formed. If a person who was cruel to me as a child had a particular tone of voice, I may find myself disliking a person who has the same tone of voice. Media advertising juxtaposes and joins logically unrelated things to influence our buying habits. Raised in a particular country or within a particular group within it, we form any number of mental links which, if they remain unexamined, unduly influence our thinking. See *concept, critical society.*

cultural assumption: Un-assessed (often implicit) belief adopted by virtue of upbringing in a society. Raised in a society, we unconsciously take on its point of view, values, beliefs, and practices. At the root of each of these are many kinds of assumptions. Not knowing that we perceive, conceive, think, and experience within assumptions we have taken in, we take ourselves to be perceiving "things as they are", not "things as they appear from a cultural vantage point". Becoming aware of our cultural assumptions so that we might critically examine them is a crucial dimension of critical thinking. It is, however, a dimension almost totally absent from schooling. Lip service to this ideal is common enough; a realistic emphasis is virtually unheard of. See *ethnocentricity, prejudice, social contradiction.*

data: Facts, figures, or information from which conclusions can be inferred, or upon which interpretations or theories can be based. As critical thinkers we must make certain to distinguish hard data from the inferences or conclusions we draw from them.

dialectical thinking: Dialogical thinking (thinking within more than one perspective) conducted to test the strengths and weaknesses of opposing points of view. (Court trials and debates are, in a sense, dialectical.) When thinking dialectically, reasoners pit two or more opposing points of view in competition with each other, developing each by providing support, raising objections, countering those objections, raising further objections, and so on. Dialectical thinking or discussion can be conducted so as to "win" by defeating the positions one disagrees with — using critical insight to support one's own view and point out flaws in other views (associated with critical thinking in the restricted or weak sense), or fairmindedly, by conceding points that don't stand up to critique, trying to integrate or incorporate strong points found in other views, and using critical insight to develop a fuller and more accurate view (associated with critical thinking in the fuller or strong sense). See *monological problems.*

dialogical instruction: Instruction that fosters dialogical or dialectic thinking. Thus, when considering a question, the class brings all relevant subjects to bear and considers the perspectives of groups whose views are not canvassed in their texts — for example, "What did King George think of the *Declaration of Independence,* the Revolutionary War, the Continental Congress, Jefferson and Washington, etc.?" or, "How would an economist analyze this situation? A historian? A psychologist? A geographer?" See *critical society, didactic instruction, higher order learning, lower order learning, Socratic questioning, knowledge.*

dialogical thinking: Thinking that involves a dialogue or extended exchange between different points of view or frames of reference. Students learn best in dialogical situations, in circumstances in which they continually express their views to others and try to fit other's views into their own. See *Socratic questioning, monological thinking, multilogical thinking, dialectical thinking.*

didactic instruction: Teaching by telling. In didactic instruction, the teacher directly tells the student what to believe and think about a subject. The student's task is to remember what the teacher said and reproduce it on demand. In its most common form, this mode of teaching falsely assumes that one can directly give a person knowledge without that person having to think his or her way to it. It falsely assumes that knowledge can be separated from understanding and justification. It confuses the ability to *state* a principle with *understanding* it, the ability to *supply* a definition with *knowing* a new word, and the act of *saying* that something is important with *recognizing* its importance. See *critical society, knowledge.*

domains of thought: Thinking can be oriented or structured with different issues or purposes in view. *Thinking varies in accordance with purpose and issue.* Critical thinkers learn to discipline their thinking to take into account the nature of the issue or domain. We see this most clearly when we consider the difference between issues and thinking within different academic disciplines or subject areas. Hence, mathematical thinking is quite different from, say, historical thinking. Mathematics and history, we can say then, represent different domains of thought. See the *logic of questions.*

egocentricity: A tendency to view everything in relationship to oneself; to confuse immediate perception (how things *seem*) with reality. One's desires, values, and beliefs (seeming to be self-evidently correct or superior to those of others) are often uncritically used as the norm of all judgment and experience. Egocentricity is one of the fundamental impediments to critical thinking. As one learns to think critically in a strong sense, one learns to become more rational, and less egocentric. See *human nature, strong sense critical thinker, ethnocentrism, sociocentrism, personal contradiction.*

elements of thought: All thought has a universal set of elements, each of which can be monitored for possible problems: Are we clear about our *purpose or goal?* about the *problem or question at issue?* about our *point of view or frame of reference?* about our *assumptions?* about the *claims* we are making? about the *reasons or evidence* upon which we are basing our claims? about our *inferences and line of reasoning?* about the *implications and consequences* that follow from our reasoning? Critical thinkers develop skills of identifying and assessing these elements in their thinking and in the thinking of others.

emotion: A feeling aroused to the point of awareness, often a strong feeling or state of excitement. When our egocentric emotions or feelings get involved, when we are excited by infantile anger, fear, jealousy, etc., our objectivity often decreases. Critical thinkers need to be able to monitor their egocentric feelings and use their rational passions to reason themselves into feelings appropriate to the situation as it really is, rather than to how it seems to their infantile ego. Emotions and feelings themselves are not irrational; however, it is common for people to feel strongly when their ego is stimulated. One way to understand the goal of strong sense critical thinking is as the attempt to develop rational feelings and emotions at the expense of irrational, egocentric ones. See *rational passions, intellectual virtues.*

empirical: Relying or based on experiment, observation, or experience rather than on theory or meaning. *It is important to continually distinguish those considerations based on experiment, observation, or experience from those based on the meaning of a word or concept or the implications of a theory.* One common form of uncritical or selfish critical thinking involves distorting facts or experience in order to preserve a preconceived meaning or theory. For example, a conservative may distort the facts that support a liberal perspective to prevent empirical evidence from counting against a theory of the world that he or she holds rigidly. Indeed, within all perspectives and belief systems many will distort the facts before they will admit to a weakness in their favorite theory or belief. See *data, fact, evidence.*

empirical implication: That which follows from a situation or fact, not due to the logic of language, but from experience or scientific law. The redness of the coil on the stove empirically implies dangerous heat.

ethnocentricity: A tendency to view one's own race or culture as central, based on the deep-seated belief that one's own group is superior to all others. Ethnocentrism is a form of egocentrism extended from the self

to the group. Much uncritical or selfish critical thinking is either egocentric or ethnocentric in nature. ('Ethnocentrism' and 'sociocentrism'
are used synonymously, for the most part, though 'sociocentricity' is
broader, relating to *any* group, including, for example, sociocentricity
regarding one's profession.) The "cure" for ethnocentrism or sociocentrism is empathic thought within the perspective of opposing groups
and cultures. Such empathic thought is rarely cultivated in the societies
and schools of today. Instead, many people develop an empty rhetoric
of tolerance, saying that others have different beliefs and ways, but
without seriously considering those beliefs and ways, what they mean
to those others, and their reasons for maintaining them.

evaluation: To judge or determine the worth or quality of. *Evaluation has
a logic and should be carefully distinguished from mere subjective preference.* The elements of its logic may be put in the form of questions
which may be asked whenever an evaluation is to be carried out: *1)*
Are we clear about *what precisely we are evaluating?; 2)* Are we clear
about *our purpose?* Is our purpose legitimate?; *3)* Given our purpose,
what are the *relevant criteria or standards* for evaluation?; *4)* Do we have
sufficient information about that which we are evaluating? Is that *information relevant to the purpose?;* and *5)* Have we *applied our criteria accurately and fairly to the facts* as we know them? Uncritical thinkers often
treat evaluation as mere preference or treat their evaluative judgments
as direct observations not admitting of error.

evidence: The data on which a judgment or conclusion might be based or
by which proof or probability might be established. Critical thinkers
distinguish the evidence or raw data upon which they base their interpretations or conclusions from the inferences and assumptions that
connect data to conclusions. Uncritical thinkers treat their conclusions as something given to them in experience, as something they
directly observe in the world. As a result, they find it difficult to see
why anyone might disagree with their conclusions. After all, the truth
of their views is, they believe, right there for everyone to see! Such
people find it difficult or even impossible to describe the evidence or
experience without coloring that description with their interpretation.

explicit: Clearly stated and leaving nothing implied; *explicit* is applied to
that which is so clearly stated or distinctly set forth that there should
be no doubt as to the meaning; *exact and precise* in this connection
both suggest that which is strictly defined, accurately stated, or made
unmistakably clear; *definite* implies precise limitations as to the nature,
character, meaning, etc. of something; *specific* implies the pointing up
of details or the particularizing of references. Critical thinking often
requires the ability to be explicit, exact, definite, and specific. Most
students cannot make what is *implicit* in their thinking *explicit.* This
deficiency hampers their ability to monitor and assess their thinking.

fact: What actually happened, what is true; verifiable by empirical means; distinguished from interpretation, inference, judgment, or conclusion; the raw data. There are distinct senses of the word 'factual': "True" (as opposed to "claimed to be true"); and "empirical" (as opposed to conceptual or evaluative). You may make many "factual claims" in one sense, that is, claims which can be verified or disproven by observation or empirical study, but I must evaluate those claims to determine if they are true. People often confuse these two senses, even to the point of accepting as true, statements which merely "seem factual", for example, "29.23 % of Americans suffer from depression." Before I accept this as true, I should assess it. I should ask such questions as "How do you know? How *could* this be known? Did you merely ask people if they were depressed and extrapolate those results? How exactly did you arrive at this figure?" Purported facts should be assessed for their accuracy, completeness, and relevance to the issue. Sources of purported facts should be assessed for their qualifications, track records, and impartiality. Education which stresses retention and repetition of factual claims stunts students' desire and ability to assess alleged facts, leaving them open to manipulation. Activities in which students are asked to "distinguish fact from opinion" often confuse these two senses. They encourage students to *accept as true* statements which merely "look like" facts. See *intellectual humility, knowledge.*

fair: Treating both or all sides alike without reference to one's own feelings or interests; *just* implies adherence to a standard of rightness or lawfulness without reference to one's own inclinations; *impartial* and *unbiased* both imply freedom from prejudice for or against any side; *dispassionate* implies the absence of passion or strong emotion, hence, connotes cool, disinterested judgment; *objective* implies a viewing of persons or things without reference to oneself, one's interests, etc.

faith: 1) Unquestioning belief in anything. 2) Confidence, trust, or reliance. A critical thinker does not accept faith in the first sense, for every belief is reached on the basis of some thinking, which may or may not be justified. Even in religion one believes in one religion rather than another, and in doing so implies that there are good reasons for accepting one rather than another. A Christian, for example, believes that there are good reasons for not being an atheist, and Christians often attempt to persuade non-Christians to change their beliefs. In some sense, then, everyone has confidence in the capacity of his or her own mind to judge rightly on the basis of good reasons, and does not believe simply on the basis of blind faith.

fallacy/fallacious: An error in reasoning; flaw or defect in argument; an argument which doesn't conform to rules of good reasoning (especially one that appears to be sound). Containing or based on a fallacy; deceptive in appearance or meaning; misleading; delusive.

higher order learning: Learning through exploring the foundations, justification, implications, and value of a fact, principle, skill, or concept.
Learning so as to deeply understand. One can learn in keeping with the
rational capacities of the human mind or in keeping with its irrational
propensities, cultivating the capacity of the human mind to discipline
and direct its thought through commitment to intellectual standards,
or one can learn through mere association. Education for critical
thought produces higher order learning by helping students actively
think their way to conclusions; discuss their thinking with other students and the teacher; entertain a variety of points of view; analyze
concepts, theories, and explanations in their own terms; actively question the meaning and implications of what they learn; compare what
they learn to what they have experienced; take what they read and
write seriously; solve non-routine problems; examine assumptions;
and gather and assess evidence. Students should learn each subject by
engaging in thought within that subject. They should learn history by
thinking historically, mathematics by thinking mathematically, etc.
See *dialogical instruction, lower order learning, critical society, knowledge,
principle, domains of thought.*

human nature: The common qualities of all human beings. People have
both a primary and a secondary nature. Our primary nature is spontaneous, egocentric, and strongly prone to irrational belief formation. It
is the basis for our instinctual thought. People need no training to
believe what they want to believe: what serves their immediate interests, what preserves their sense of personal comfort and righteousness,
what minimizes their sense of inconsistency, and what presupposes
their own correctness. People need no special training to believe what
those around them believe: what their parents and friends believe,
what is taught to them by religious and school authorities, what is
repeated often by the media, and what is commonly believed in the
nation in which they are raised. People need no training to think that
those who disagree with them are wrong and probably prejudiced.
People need no training to assume that their own most fundamental
beliefs are self-evidently true or easily justified by evidence. People
naturally and spontaneously identify with their own beliefs. They
experience most disagreement as personal attack. The resulting defensiveness interferes with their capacity to empathize with or enter into
other points of view.

On the other hand, *people need extensive and systematic practice to develop their secondary nature, their implicit capacity to function as rational persons.* They need extensive and systematic practice to recognize the tendencies they have to form irrational beliefs. They need extensive
practice to develop a dislike of inconsistency, a love of clarity, a passion to seek reasons and evidence and to be fair to points of view other

than their own. People need extensive practice to recognize that they indeed have a point of view, that they live inferentially, that they do not have a direct pipeline to reality, that it is perfectly possible to have an overwhelming inner sense of the correctness of one's views and still be wrong. See *intellectual virtues.*

idea: Anything existing in the mind as an object of knowledge or thought; *concept* refers to generalized idea of a class of objects, based on knowledge of particular instances of the class; *conception,* often equivalent to concept, specifically refers to something conceived in the mind or imagined; *thought* refers to any idea, whether or not expressed, that occurs to the mind in reasoning or contemplation; *notion* implies vagueness or incomplete intention; *impression* also implies vagueness of an idea provoked by some external stimulus. Critical thinkers are aware of what ideas they are using in their thinking, where those ideas came from, and how to assess them. See *clarify, concept, logic, logic of language.*

imply/implication: A claim or truth which follows from other claims or truths. One of the most important skills of critical thinking is the ability to distinguish between what is actually implied by a statement or situation from what may be carelessly inferred by people. Critical thinkers try to *monitor their inferences to keep them in line with what is actually implied* by what they know. When speaking, critical thinkers *try to use words that imply only what they can legitimately justify.* They recognize that there are established word usages which generate established implications. To say of an act that it is murder, for example, is to imply that it is intentional and unjustified. See *clarify, precision, logic of language, critical listening, critical reading, elements of thought.*

infer/inference: An inference is a step of the mind, an intellectual act by which one concludes that something is so in light of something else's being so, or seeming to be so. If you come at me with a knife in your hand, I would probably infer that you mean to do me harm. Inferences can be strong or weak, justified or unjustified. Inferences are based upon assumptions. See *imply/implication.*

insight: The ability to see and clearly and deeply understand the inner nature of things. Instruction for critical thinking fosters insight rather than mere performance; it cultivates the achievement of deeper knowledge and understanding through insight. *Thinking one's way into and through a subject leads to insights* as one synthesizes what one is learning, relating one subject to other subjects and all subjects to personal experience. Rarely is insight formulated as a goal in present curricula and texts. See *dialogical instruction, higher order learning, lower order learning, didactic instruction, intellectual humility.*

intellectual autonomy: Having rational control of ones beliefs, values, and inferences. The ideal of critical thinking is to learn to think for oneself, to gain command over one's thought processes. Intellectual autonomy does not entail willfulness, stubbornness, or rebellion. It entails a commitment to analyzing and evaluating beliefs on the basis of reason and evidence, to question when it is rational to question, to believe when it is rational to believe, and to conform when it is rational to conform. See *know, knowledge.*

intellectual civility: A commitment to take others seriously as thinkers, to treat them as intellectual equals, to grant respect and full attention to their views — a commitment to persuade rather than browbeat. It is distinguished from intellectual rudeness: verbally attacking others, dismissing them, stereotyping their views. Intellectual civility is not a matter of mere curtesy, but arises from a sense that communication itself requires honoring others' views and their capacity to reason.

(intellectual) confidence or faith in reason: Confidence that in the long run *one's own higher interests and those of humankind at large will best be served by giving the freest play to reason* — by encouraging people to come to their own conclusions through a process of developing their own rational faculties; faith that (with proper encouragement and cultivation) people can learn to think for themselves, form rational viewpoints, draw reasonable conclusions, think coherently and logically, persuade each other by reason, and become reasonable, despite the deep-seated obstacles in the native character of the human mind and in society. Confidence in reason is developed through experiences in which one reasons one's way to insight, solves problems through reason, uses reason to persuade, is persuaded by reason. Confidence in reason is undermined when one is expected to perform tasks without understanding why, to repeat statements without having verified or justified them, to accept beliefs on the sole basis of authority or social pressure.

intellectual courage: The willingness to face and fairly assess ideas, beliefs, or viewpoints to which we have not given a serious hearing, regardless of our strong negative reactions to them. This courage arises from the recognition that *ideas considered dangerous or absurd are sometimes rationally justified* (in whole or in part), and that *conclusions or beliefs espoused by those around us or inculcated in us are sometimes false or misleading.* To determine for ourselves which is which, we must not passively and uncritically "accept" what we have "learned". Intellectual courage comes into play here, because inevitably we will come to see some truth in some ideas considered dangerous and absurd and some distortion or falsity in some ideas strongly held in our social group. It takes courage to be true to our own thinking in such circumstances. Examining cherished beliefs is difficult, and the penalties for non-conformity are often severe.

intellectual curiosity: A strong desire to deeply understand, to figure things out, to propose and assess useful and plausible hypotheses and explanations, to learn, to find out. People do not learn well, do not gain knowledge, unless they *want* knowledge — deep, accurate, complete understanding. When people lack passion for figuring things out (suffer from intellectual apathy), they tend to settle for an incomplete, incoherent, sketchy "sense" of things incompatible with a critically developed, richer, fuller conception. This trait can flourish only when it is allowed and encouraged, when people are allowed to pose and pursue questions of interest to them and when their intellectual curiosity pays off in increasing understanding.

intellectual discipline: The trait of thinking in accordance with intellectual standards, intellectual rigor, carefulness, order, conscious control. The undisciplined thinker neither knows nor cares when he or she comes to unwarranted conclusions, confuses distinct ideas, fails to consider pertinent evidence, and so on. Thus, intellectual discipline is at the very heart of becoming a critical person. It takes discipline of mind to keep oneself focused on the intellectual task at hand, to locate and carefully assess needed evidence, to systematically analyze and address questions and problems, to hold one's thinking to sufficiently high standards of clarity, precision, completeness, consistency, etc. Such discipline is achieved slowly, bit by bit, only in an atmosphere of intellectual rigor and is acquired only to the degree that one develops insight into elements and standards of reasoning.

intellectual empathy: Understanding the need to imaginatively put oneself in the place of others to genuinely understand them. We must recognize our egocentric tendency to identify truth with our immediate perceptions or longstanding beliefs. Intellectual empathy correlates with the ability to accurately reconstruct the viewpoints and reasoning of others and to *reason from premises, assumptions, and ideas other than our own.* This trait also requires that we remember occasions when we were wrong, despite an intense conviction that we were right, and consider that we might be similarly deceived in a case at hand.

intellectual humility: Awareness of the limits of one's knowledge, including sensitivity to circumstances in which one's native egocentrism is likely to function self-deceptively; sensitivity to bias and prejudice in, and limitations of one's viewpoint. Intellectual humility is based on the recognition that *no one should claim more than he or she actually knows.* It does not imply spinelessness or submissiveness. It implies the lack of intellectual pretentiousness, boastfulness, or conceit, combined with insight into the strengths or weaknesses of the logical foundations of one's beliefs.

intellectual integrity: Recognition of the need to be true to one's own thinking, to be consistent in the intellectual standards one applies, to hold oneself to the same rigorous standards of evidence and proof to which one holds one's antagonists, to practice what one advocates for others, and to honestly admit discrepancies and inconsistencies in one's own thought and action. This trait develops best in a supportive atmosphere in which people feel secure and free enough to honestly acknowledge their inconsistencies, and can develop and share realistic ways of ameliorating them. It requires honest acknowledgment of the difficulties of achieving greater consistency.

intellectual perseverance: Willingness and consciousness of the need to pursue intellectual insights and truths despite difficulties, obstacles, and frustrations; firm adherence to rational principles despite irrational opposition of others; a sense of the need to struggle with confusion and unsettled questions over an extended period of time in order to achieve deeper understanding or insight. This trait is undermined when teachers and others continually provide the answers, do students' thinking for them or substitute easy tricks, algorithms, and short cuts for careful, independent thought.

intellectual responsibility: The responsible person keenly feels the obligation to fulfill his or her duties; intellectual responsibility is the application of this trait to intellectual matters. Hence, the intellectually responsible person feels strongly obliged to achieve a high degree of precision and accuracy in his or her reasoning, is deeply committed to gathering complete, relevant, adequate evidence, etc. This sense of obligation arises when people recognize the need for meeting the intellectual standards required by rational, fairminded thought.

intellectual sense of justice: Willingness and consciousness of the need to entertain all viewpoints sympathetically and to assess them with the same intellectual standards, without reference to one's own feelings or vested interests, or the feelings or vested interests of one's friends, community, or nation; implies adherence to intellectual standards without reference to one's own advantage or the advantage of one's group.

intellectual standards: Principles by which reasoning can be judged; requirements of quality reasoning. Intellectual standards are a pervasive part of critical; thinking. Thinking that qualifies as critical thinking is thinking clear, accurate, relevant to the question at issue, fair, precise, specific, plausible, consistent, logical, deep, broad, complete, and significant. Such standards are implicit in all aspects of critical thinking: where standards are not explicitly stated, they are presupposed. (For example, the critical thinker does not merely identify assumptions, but *accurately* identifies *significant* assumptions.)

intellectual virtues: The traits of mind and character necessary for right action and thinking; the traits of mind and character essential for fairminded rationality; the traits that distinguish the narrowminded, self-serving critical thinker from the openminded, truth-seeking critical thinker. These *intellectual traits are interdependent.* Each is best developed while developing the others as well. They cannot be imposed from without; they must be cultivated by encouragement and example. People can come to deeply understand and accept these principles by analyzing their experiences of them: learning from an unfamiliar perspective, discovering you don't know as much as you thought, and so on. They include: intellectual sense of justice, intellectual perseverance, intellectual integrity, intellectual humility, intellectual empathy, intellectual courage, (intellectual) confidence in reason, and intellectual autonomy.

interpret/interpretation: To give one's own conception of, to place in the context of one's own experience, perspective, point of view, or philosophy. Interpretations should be distinguished from the facts, the evidence, the situation. (I may interpret someone's silence as an expression of hostility toward me. Such an interpretation may or may not be correct. I may have projected my patterns of motivation and behavior onto that person, or I may have accurately noticed this pattern in the other.) The best interpretations take the most evidence into account. Critical thinkers recognize their interpretations, distinguish them from evidence, consider alternative interpretations, and reconsider their interpretations in the light of new evidence. *All learning involves personal interpretation, since whatever we learn we must integrate into our own thinking and action.* What we learn must be given a meaning by us, must be meaningful to us, and hence involves interpretive acts on our part. Didactic instruction, in attempting to directly implant knowledge in students' minds, typically ignores the role of personal interpretation in learning.

intuition: The direct knowing or learning of something without the conscious use of reasoning. We sometimes seem to know or learn things without recognizing how we came to that knowledge. When this occurs, we experience an inner sense that what we believe is true. The problem is that sometimes we are correct (and have genuinely experienced an intuition) and sometimes we are incorrect (having fallen victim to one of our prejudices). A critical thinker does not blindly accept that what he or she thinks or believes but cannot account for is necessarily true. A critical thinker realizes how easily we confuse intuitions and prejudices. Critical thinkers may follow their inner sense that something is so, but only with a healthy sense of intellectual humility.

There is a second sense of 'intuition' that is important for critical thinking, and that is the meaning suggested in the following sentence: "To develop your critical thinking abilities, it is important to develop your critical thinking *intuitions*." This sense of the word is connected to the fact that we can learn concepts at various levels of depth. If we learn nothing more than an abstract definition for a word and do not learn how to apply it effectively in a wide variety of situations, one might say that we end up with no *intuitive* basis for applying it. We lack the insight into how, when, and why it applies. Helping students to develop critical thinking intuitions is helping them gain the practical insights necessary for a ready and swift application of concepts to cases in a large array of circumstances. We want critical thinking to be "intuitive" to our students, ready and available for immediate translation into their everyday thought and experience.

irrational/irrationality: 1) Lacking the power to reason. 2) Contrary to reason or logic. 3) Senseless, absurd. Uncritical thinkers have failed to develop the ability or power to reason well. Their beliefs and practices, then, are often contrary to reason and logic, and are sometimes senseless or absurd. It is important to recognize, however, that in societies with irrational beliefs and practices, it is not clear whether challenging those beliefs and practices — and therefore possibly endangering oneself — is rational or irrational. Furthermore, suppose one's vested interests are best advanced by adopting beliefs and practices that are contrary to reason. Is it then rational to follow reason and negate one's vested interests or follow one's interests and ignore reason? These very real dilemmas of everyday life represent on-going problems for critical thinkers. Selfish critical thinkers, of course, face no dilemma here because of their consistent commitment to advance their narrow vested interests. Fairminded critical thinkers make these decisions self-consciously and honestly assess the results.

irrational learning: All rational learning presupposes rational assent. And, though we sometimes forget it, not all learning is automatically or even commonly rational. *Much that we learn in everyday life is quite distinctively irrational.* It is quite possible — and indeed the bulk of human learning is unfortunately of this character — *to come to believe any number of things without knowing how or why.* It is quite possible, in other words, to believe for irrational reasons: because those around us believe, because we are rewarded for believing, because we are afraid to disbelieve, because our vested interest is served by belief, because we are more comfortable with belief, or because we have ego identified ourselves, our image, or our personal being with belief. In all of these cases, our beliefs are without rational grounding, without good reason and evidence, without the foundation a rational person demands. We become rational, on the other hand, to the extent that our beliefs and actions are grounded in good reasons and evidence; to the extent that we recognize and critique our own irrationality; to the extent that we are not moved by bad reasons and a multiplicity of irrational motives, fears, and desires; to the extent that we have cultivated a passion for clarity, accuracy, and fairmindedness. These global skills, passions, and dispositions, integrated into behavior and thought, characterize the rational, the educated, and the critical person. See *higher and lower order learning, knowledge, didactic instruction.*

judgment: 1) The act of judging or deciding. 2) Understanding and good sense. A person has good judgment when they typically judge and decide on the basis of understanding and good sense. Whenever we form a belief or opinion, make a decision, or act, we do so on the basis of implicit or explicit judgments. All thought presupposes making judgments concerning what is so and what is not so, what is true and what is not. To cultivate people's ability to think critically is to foster their judgment, to help them to develop the habit of judging on the basis of reason, evidence, logic, and good sense. Good judgment is developed, not by merely learning about principles of good judgment, but by frequent practice judging and assessing judgments.

justify/justification: The act of showing a belief, opinion, action, or policy to be in accord with reason and evidence, to be ethically acceptable, or both. Education should foster reasonability in students. This requires that both teachers and students develop the disposition to ask for and give justifications for beliefs, opinions, actions, and policies. Asking for a justification should not, then, be viewed as an insult or attack, but rather as a normal act of a rational person. Didactic modes of teaching that do not encourage students to question the justification for what is asserted fail to develop a thoughtful environment conducive to education.

know: To have a clear perception or understanding of, to be sure of, to have a firm mental grasp of; *information* applies to data that are gathered in any way, as by reading, observation, hearsay, etc. and does not necessarily connote validity; *knowledge* applies to any body of facts gathered by study, observation, etc. and to the ideas inferred from these facts, and connotes an *understanding* of what is known. Critical thinkers need to distinguish knowledge from opinion and belief. See *knowledge.*

knowledge: The act of having a clear and justifiable grasp of what is so or of how to do something. Knowledge is based on understanding or skill, which in turn are based on thought, study, and experience. 'Thoughtless knowledge' is a contradiction. 'Blind knowledge' is a contradiction. 'Unjustifiable knowledge' is a contradiction. Knowledge implies justifiable belief or skilled action. Hence, when students blindly memorize and are tested for recall, they are not being tested for knowledge. *Knowledge is continually confused with recall in present-day schooling.* This confusion is a deep-seated impediment to the integration of critical thinking into schooling. *Genuine knowledge is inseparable from thinking minds.* We often wrongly talk of knowledge as though it could be divorced from thinking, as though it could be gathered up by one person and given to another in the form of a collection of sentences to remember. When we talk in this way, we forget that *knowledge,* by its very nature, *depends on thought.* Knowledge is produced by thought, analyzed by thought, comprehended by thought, organized, evaluated, maintained, and transformed by thought. Knowledge can be *acquired only* through thought. Knowledge exists, properly speaking, only in minds that have comprehended and justified it through thought. Knowledge is not to be confused with belief nor with symbolic representation of belief. Humans easily and frequently believe things that are false or believe things to be true without knowing them to be so. A book contains knowledge only in a derivative sense, only because minds can thoughtfully read it and through that process gain knowledge.

logic: 1) Correct reasoning or the study of correct reasoning and its foundations. 2) The relationships between propositions (supports, assumes, implies, contradicts, counts against, is relevant to, ...). 3) The system of principles, concepts, and assumptions that underlie any discipline, activity, or practice. 4) The set of rational considerations that bear upon the truth or justification of any belief or set of beliefs. 5) The set of rational considerations that bear upon the settlement of any question or set of questions. The word 'logic' covers a range of related concerns all bearing upon the question of rational justification and explanation. *All human thought and behavior is to some extent based on logic* rather than instinct. Humans try to figure things out using ideas, meanings, and thought. Such intellectual behavior inevitably involves "logic" or considerations of a logical sort: some sense of what is relevant and irrelevant, of what supports and what counts against a belief, of what we should and should not assume, of what we should and should not claim, of what we do and do not know, of what is and is not implied, of what does and does not contradict, of what we should or should not do or believe. *Concepts have a logic* in that we can investigate the conditions under which they do and do not apply, of what is relevant or irrelevant to them, of what they do or don't imply, etc. *Questions have a logic* in that we can investigate the conditions under which they can be settled. *Disciplines have a logic* in that they have purposes and a set of logical structures that bear upon those purposes: assumptions, concepts, issues, data, theories, claims, implications, consequences, etc. The concept of logic is a seminal notion in critical thinking. Unfortunately, it takes a considerable length of time before most people become comfortable with its multiple uses. In part, this is due to people's failure to monitor their own thinking in keeping with the standards of reason and logic. This is not to deny, of course, that logic is involved in all human thinking. It is rather to say that the logic we use is often implicit, unexpressed, and sometimes contradictory. See *knowledge, higher and lower order learning, the logic of a discipline, the logic of language, the logic of questions.*

the logic of a discipline: The notion that every technical term has logical relationships with other technical terms, that some terms are logically more basic than others, and that every discipline relies on concepts, assumptions, and theories, makes claims, gives reasons and evidence, avoids contradictions and inconsistencies, has implications and consequences, etc. Though all students study disciplines, most are ignorant of the logic of the disciplines they study. This severely limits their ability to grasp the discipline as a whole, to think independently within it, to compare and contrast it with other disciplines, and to apply it outside the context of academic assignments. Typically now, students do not look for seminal terms as they study an area. They do not strive to translate technical terms into analogies and ordinary words they understand or distinguish technical from ordinary uses of terms. They do not look for the basic assumptions of the disciplines they study. Indeed, on the whole, they do not know what assumptions are nor why it is important to examine them. What they have in their heads exists like so many BB's in a bag. Whether one thought supports or follows from another, whether one thought elaborates another, exemplifies, presupposes, or contradicts another, are matters students have not learned to think about. They have not learned to use thought to understand thought, which is another way of saying that they have not learned how to use thought to gain knowledge. *Instruction for critical thinking cultivates the students' ability to make explicit the logic of what they study.* This emphasis gives depth and breath to study and learning. It lies at the heart of the differences between lower order and higher order learning. See *knowledge.*

the logic of language: For a language to exist and be learnable by persons from a variety of cultures, it is necessary that *words have definite uses and defined concepts that transcend particular cultures.* The English language, for example, is learned by many peoples of the world unfamiliar with English or North American cultures. Critical thinkers must learn to use their native language with precision, in keeping with educated usage. Unfortunately, many students do not understand the significant relationship between precision in language usage and precision in thought. Consider, for example, how most students relate to their native language. If one questions them about the meanings of words, their account is typically incoherent. They often say that people have their own meanings for all the words they use, not noticing that, were this true, we could not understand each other. Students speak and write in vague sentences because they have no rational criteria for choosing words — they simply write whatever words pop into their heads. They do not realize that every language has a highly refined logic one must learn in order to express oneself precisely. They do not realize that even words similar in meaning typically have different implications. Consider, for example, the words explain, expound, explicate, elucidate, interpret, and construe. *Explain* implies the process of making clear and intelligible something not understood or known. *Expound* implies a systematic and thorough explanation, often by an expert. *Explicate* implies a scholarly analysis developed in detail. *Elucidate* implies a shedding of light upon by clear and specific illustration or explanation. *Interpret* implies the bringing out of meanings not immediately apparent. *Construe* implies a particular interpretation of something whose meaning is ambiguous. See *clarify, concept.*

the logic of questions: The range of rational considerations that bear upon the settlement of a given question or group of questions. A critical thinker is adept at analyzing questions to determine what, precisely, a question asks and how to go about rationally settling it. A critical thinker recognizes that different kinds of questions often call for different modes of thinking, different kinds of considerations, and different procedures and techniques. Uncritical thinkers often confuse distinct questions and use considerations irrelevant to an issue while ignoring relevant ones.

lower order learning: Learning by rote memorization, association, and drill. There are a variety of forms of lower order learning in the schools which we can identify by understanding the relative *lack of logic informing them.* Paradigmatically, lower order learning is learning by sheer association or rote. Hence students come to think of history class, for example, as a place where you hear names, dates, places, events, and outcomes; where you try to remember them and state them on tests. Math comes to be thought of as numbers, symbols, and formulas — mysterious things you mechanically manipulate as the teacher told you in order to get the right answer. Literature is often thought of as uninteresting stories to remember along with what the teacher said is important about them. Consequently, students leave with a jumble of undigested fragments, scraps left over after they have forgotten most of what they stored in their short-term memories for tests. Virtually never do they grasp the logic of what they learn. Rarely do they relate what they learn to their own experience or critique each by means of the other. Rarely do they try to test what they learn in everyday life. Rarely do they ask "Why is this so? How does this relate to what I already know? How does this relate to what I am learning in other classes?" To put the point in a nutshell, very few students think of what they are learning as worthy of being arranged logically in their minds or have the slightest idea of how to do so. See *didactic instruction, monological and multilogical problems and thinking.*

monological (one-dimensional) problems: Problems that can be solved by reasoning exclusively within one point of view or frame of reference. For example, consider the following problems: *1)* Ten full crates of walnuts weigh 410 pounds, whereas an empty crate weighs 10 pounds. How much do the walnuts alone weigh?; and *2)* In how many days of the week does the third letter of the day's name immediately follow the first letter of the day's name in the alphabet? I call these problems and the means by which they are solved "monological". They are settled within one frame of reference with a definite set of logical moves. When the right set of moves is performed, the problem is settled. The answer or solution proposed can be shown by standards implicit in the frame of reference to be the "right" answer or solution. *Most important human problems are multilogical rather than monological,* non-atomic problems inextricably joined to other problems, with some conceptual messiness to them and very often with important values lurking in the background. When the problems have an empirical dimension, that dimension tends to have a controversial scope. In multilogical problems, it is often arguable how some facts should be considered and interpreted, and how their significance should be determined. When they have a conceptual dimension, there tend to be arguably different ways to pin the concepts down. Though life presents us with predominantly multilogical problems, schooling today over-emphasizes monological problems. Worse, and more frequently, present instructional practices treat multilogical problems as though they were monological. The posing of multilogical problems, and their consideration from multiple points of view, play an important role in the cultivation of critical thinking and higher order learning.

monological (one-dimensional) thinking: Thinking that is conducted exclusively within one point of view or frame of reference: figuring our how much this $67.49 pair of shoes with a 25% discount will cost me; learning what signing this contract obliges me to do; finding out when Kennedy was elected President. A person can think monologically whether or not the question is genuinely monological. (For example, if one considers the question, "Who caused the Civil War?" only from a Northerner's perspective, one is thinking monologically about a multilogical question.) The strong sense critical thinker avoids monological thinking when the question is multi-logical. Moreover, higher order learning requires multi-logical thought, even when the problem is monological (for example, learning a concept in chemistry), since students must explore and assess their original beliefs to develop insight into new ideas.

multilogical (multi-dimensional) problems: Problems that can be analyzed and approached from more than one, often from conflicting,
points of view or frames of reference. For example, many ecological
problems have a variety of dimensions to them: historical, social, economic, biological, chemical, moral, political, etc. A person comfortable thinking about multilogical problems is comfortable thinking
within multiple perspectives, in engaging in dialogical and dialectical
thinking, in practicing intellectual empathy, in thinking across disciplines and domains. See *monological problems, the logic of questions, the
logic of disciplines, intellectual empathy, dialogical instruction.*

multilogical thinking: Thinking that sympathetically enters, considers,
and reasons within multiple points of view. See *multilogical problems,
dialectical thinking, dialogical instruction.*

national bias: Prejudice in favor of one's country, it's beliefs, traditions,
practices, image, and world view; a form of sociocentrism or ethnocentrism. It is natural, if not inevitable, for people to be favorably disposed toward the beliefs, traditions, practices, and world view within
which they were raised. Unfortunately, this favorable inclination commonly becomes a form of prejudice: a more or less rigid, irrational
ego-identification which significantly distorts one's view of one's own
nation and the world at large. It is manifested in a tendency to mindlessly take the side of one's own government, to uncritically accept
governmental accounts of the nature of disputes with other nations,
to uncritically exaggerate the virtues of one's own nation while playing down the virtues of "enemy" nations. National bias is reflected in
the press and media coverage of every nation of the world. Events are
included or excluded according to what appears significant within the
dominant world view of the nation, and are shaped into stories to validate that view. Though constructed to fit into a particular view of the
world, the stories in the news are presented as neutral, objective
accounts, and uncritically accepted as such because people tend to
uncritically assume that their own view of things is the way things
really are. To become responsible critically thinking citizens and
fairminded people, students must practice identifying national bias in
the news and in their texts, and to broaden their perspective beyond
that of uncritical nationalism. See *ethnocentrism, sociocentrism, bias,
prejudice, world view, intellectual empathy, critical society, dialogical
instruction, knowledge.*

opinion: A belief, typically one open to dispute. Sheer unreasoned opinion should be distinguished from reasoned judgment — beliefs formed
on the basis of careful reasoning. See *evaluation, judgment, justify,
know, knowledge, reasoned judgment.*

the perfections of thought: Thinking, as an attempt to understand the world as it is, has a natural excellence or fitness to it. This excellence is manifest in its *clarity, precision, specificity, accuracy, relevance, consistency, logicalness, depth, completeness, significance, fairness, and adequacy.* These perfections are general canons for thought; they represent legitimate concerns irrespective of the discipline or domain of thought. To develop one's mind and discipline one's thinking with respect to these standards *requires extensive practice and long-term cultivation.* Of course, achieving these standards is a relative matter and varies somewhat among domains of thought. Being *precise* while doing mathematics is not the same as being precise while writing a poem, describing an experience, or explaining a historical event. Furthermore, one perfection of thought may be periodically incompatible with the others: adequacy to purpose. Time and resources sufficient to thoroughly analyze a question or problem is all too often an unaffordable luxury. Also, since the social world is often irrational and unjust, because people are often manipulated to act against their interests, and because skilled thought often serves vested interest, thought adequate to these manipulative purposes may require *skilled violation of the common standards for good thinking.* Skilled propaganda, skilled political debate, skilled defense of a group's interests, skilled deception of one's enemy may require the violation or selective application of any of the above standards. Perfecting one's thought as an instrument for success in a world based on power and advantage differs from perfecting one's thought for the apprehension and defense of fairminded truth. *To develop one's critical thinking skills merely to the level of adequacy for social success is to develop those skills in a lower or weaker sense.*

personal contradiction: An inconsistency in one's personal life, wherein one says one thing and does another, or uses a double standard, judging oneself and one's friends by an easier standard than that used for people one doesn't like; typically a form of hypocrisy accompanied by self-deception. Most personal contradictions remain unconscious. People too often ignore the difficulty of becoming intellectually and morally consistent, preferring instead to merely admonish others. Personal contradictions are more likely to be discovered, analyzed, and reduced in an atmosphere in which they can be openly admitted and realistically considered without excessive penalty. See *egocentricity, intellectual integrity.*

perspective (point of view): Human thought is relational and selective. It is impossible to understand any person, event, or phenomenon from every vantage point simultaneously. Our purposes often control how we see things. Critical thinking requires that this fact be taken into account when analyzing and assessing thinking. This is not to say that human thought is incapable of truth and objectivity, but only that human truth, objectivity, and insight is virtually always limited and partial, virtually never total and absolute. The hard sciences are themselves a good example of this point, since qualitative realities are systematically ignored in favor of quantifiable realities.

precision: The quality of being accurate, definite, and exact. The standards and modes of precision vary according to subject and context. See *the logic of language, elements of thought.*

prejudice: A judgment, belief, opinion, point of view — favorable or unfavorable — formed before the facts are known, resistant to evidence and reason, or in disregard of facts which contradict it. Self-announced prejudice is rare. Prejudice almost always exists in obscured, rationalized, socially validated, functional forms. It enables people to sleep peacefully at night even while flagrantly abusing the rights of others. It enables people to get more of what they want, or to get it more easily. It is often sanctioned with a superabundance of pomp and self-righteousness. Unless we recognize these powerful tendencies toward selfish thought in our social institutions, even in what appear to be lofty actions and moralistic rhetoric, we will not face squarely the problem of prejudice in human thought and action. Uncritical and selfishly critical thought are often prejudiced. Most instruction in schools today, because students do not think their way to what they accept as true, tends to give students prejudices rather than knowledge. For example, partly as a result of schooling, people often accept as authorities those who liberally sprinkle their statements with numbers and intellectual-sounding language, however irrational or unjust their positions. This prejudice toward pseudo-authority impedes rational assessment. See *insight, knowledge.*

premise: A proposition upon which an argument is based or from which a conclusion is drawn. A starting point of reasoning. For example, one might say, in commenting on someone's reasoning, "You seem to be reasoning from the premise that everyone is selfish in everything they do. *Do* you hold this belief?"

principle: A fundamental truth, law, doctrine, value, or commitment, upon which others are based. Rules, which are more specific, and often superficial and arbitrary, are based on principles. Rules are more algorithmic; they needn't be understood to be followed. Principles must be understood to be appropriately applied or followed. Principles go to the heart of the matter. Critical thinking is dependent on principles, not rules and procedures. Critical thinking is principled, not procedural, thinking. Principles cannot be truly grasped through didactic instruction; they must be practiced and applied to be internalized. See *higher order learning, lower order learning, judgment.*

problem: A question, matter, situation, or person that is perplexing or difficult to figure out, handle, or resolve. Problems, like questions, can be divided into many types. Each has a (particular) logic. See *logic of questions, monological problems, multilogical problems.*

problem-solving: Whenever a problem cannot be solved formulaically or robotically, critical thinking is required: first, to determine the nature and dimensions of the problem, and then, in the light of the first, to determine the considerations, points of view, concepts, theories, data, and reasoning relevant to its solution. Extensive practice in independent problem-solving is essential to developing critical thought. Problem-solving is rarely best approached procedurally or as a series of rigidly followed steps. For example, problem-solving schemas typically begin, "State the problem." Rarely can problems be precisely and fairly stated prior to analysis, gathering of evidence, and dialogical or dialectical thought wherein several provisional descriptions of the problem are proposed, assessed, and revised.

proof (prove): Evidence or reasoning so strong or certain as to demonstrate the truth or acceptability of a conclusion beyond a reasonable doubt. How strong evidence or reasoning have to be to demonstrate what they purport to prove varies from context to context, depending on the significance of the conclusion or the seriousness of the implications following from it. See *domain of thought.*

rational/rationality: That which conforms to principles of good reasoning, is sensible, shows good judgment, is consistent, logical, complete, and relevant. Rationality is a summary term like 'virtue' or 'goodness'. It is manifested in an unlimited number of ways and depends on a host of principles. There is some ambiguity in it, depending on whether one considers only the logicalness and effectiveness by which one pursues one's ends, or whether it includes the assessment of ends themselves. There is also ambiguity in whether one considers selfish ends to be rational, even when they conflict with what is just. Does a rational person have to be just or only skilled in pursuing his or her interests? Is it rational to be rational in an irrational world? See *perfections of thought, irrational/irrationality, logic, intellectual virtues, weak sense critical thinking, strong sense critical thinking.*

rational emotions/passions: R. S. Peters has explained the significance of the affective side of reason and critical thought in his defense of the necessity of "rational passions":

> There is, for instance, the hatred of contradictions and inconsistencies, together with the love of clarity and hatred of confusion without which words could not be held to relatively

constant meanings and testable rules and generalizations stated. A reasonable man cannot, without some special explanation, slap his sides with delight or express indifference if he is told that what he says is confused, incoherent, and perhaps riddled with contradictions.

Reason is the antithesis of arbitrariness. In its operation it is supported by the appropriate passions which are mainly negative in character — the hatred of irrelevance, special pleading, and arbitrary fiat. The more developed emotion of indignation is aroused when some excess of arbitrariness is perpetuated in a situation where people's interests and claims are at stake. The positive side of this is the passion for fairness and impartial consideration of claims ....

A man who is prepared to reason must feel strongly that he must follow the arguments and decide things in terms of where they lead. He must have a sense of the giveness of the impersonality of such considerations. In so far as thoughts about persons enter his head they should be tinged with the respect which is due to another who, like himself, may have a point of view which is worth considering, who may have a glimmering of the truth which has so far eluded himself. A person who proceeds in this way, who is influenced by such passions, is what we call a reasonable man.

rational self: Our character and nature to the extent that we seek to base our beliefs and actions on good reasoning and evidence. Who we are, what our true character is, or our predominant qualities are, is always somewhat or even greatly different from who we *think* we are. Human egocentrism and accompanying self-deception often stand in the way of our gaining more insight into ourselves. We can develop a rational self, become a person who gains significant insight into what our true character is, only by reducing our egocentrism and self-deception. Critical thinking is essential to this process.

rational society: See *critical society.*

reasoned judgment: Any belief or conclusion reached on the basis of careful thought and reflection, distinguished from mere or unreasoned opinion on the one hand, and from sheer fact on the other. Few people have a clear sense of which of their beliefs are based on reasoned judgment and which on mere opinion. Moral or ethical questions, for example, are questions requiring reasoned judgment. One way of conceiving of subject-matter education is as developing students' ability to engage in reasoned judgment in accordance with the standards of each subject.

reasoning: The mental processes of those who reason; especially the drawing of conclusions or inferences from observations, facts, or hypotheses; the evidence or arguments used in this procedure. A critical thinker tries to develop the capacity to transform thought into reasoning at will, or rather, the ability to make his or her inferences explicit, along with the assumptions or premises upon which those inferences are based. Reasoning is a form of explicit inferring, usually involving multiple steps. When students write a persuasive paper, for example, we want them to be clear about their reasoning.

reciprocity: The act of entering empathically into the point of view or line of reasoning of others; learning to think as others do and by that means sympathetically assessing that thinking. (Reciprocity requires creative imagination as well as intellectual skill and a commitment to fairmindedness.)

relevant: Bearing upon or relating to the matter at hand; *relevant* implies close logical relationship with, and importance to, the matter under consideration; *germane* implies such close natural connection as to be highly appropriate or fit; *pertinent* implies an immediate and direct bearing on the matter at hand (a pertinent suggestion); *apposite* applies to that which is both relevant and happily suitable or appropriate; *applicable* refers to that which can be brought to bear upon a particular matter or problem. Students often have problems sticking to an issue and distinguishing information that bears upon a problem from information that does not. Merely reminding students to limit themselves to relevant considerations fails to solve this problem. The usual way of teaching students the term 'relevant' is to mention only clear-cut cases of relevance and irrelevance. Consequently, students do not learn that not everything that *seems* relevant is, or that some things which *do not seem* relevant are. Sensitivity to (ability to judge) relevance can only be developed with continual practice — practice distinguishing relevant from irrelevant data, evaluating or judging relevance, arguing for and against the relevance of facts and considerations.

self-deception: Deceiving one's self about one's true motivations, character, identity, etc. One possible definition of the human species is "The Self-Deceiving Animal". Self-deception is a fundamental problem in human life and the cause of much human suffering. Overcoming self-deception through self-critical thinking is a fundamental goal of strong sense critical thinking. See *egocentric, rational self, personal contradiction, social contradiction, intellectual virtues.*

social contradiction: An inconsistency between what a society preaches and what it practices. In every society there is some degree of inconsistency between its image of itself and its actual character. Social contradiction typically correlates with human self-deception on the social or cultural level. Critical thinking is essential for the recognition of inconsistencies, and recognition is essential for reform and eventual integrity.

sociocentricity: The assumption that one's own social group is inherently and self-evidently superior to all others. When a group or society sees itself as superior, and so considers its views as correct or as the only reasonable or justifiable views, and all its actions as justified, there is a tendency to presuppose this superiority in all of its thinking and thus, to think closedmindedly. All dissent and doubt are considered disloyal and rejected without consideration. Few people recognize the sociocentric nature of much of their thought.

Socratic questioning: A mode of questioning that deeply probes the meaning, justification, or logical strength of a claim, position, or line of reasoning. Socratic questioning can be carried out in a variety of ways and adapted to many levels of ability and understanding. See *elements of thought, dialogical instruction, knowledge.*

specify/specific: To mention, describe, or define in detail; limiting or limited; specifying or specified; precise; definite. Student thinking, speech, and writing tend to be vague, abstract, and ambiguous rather than specific, concrete, and clear. Learning how to state one's views specifically is essential to learning how to think clearly, precisely, and accurately. See *perfections of thought.*

strong sense critical thinker: One who is predominantly characterized by the following traits: *1)* an ability to question deeply one's own framework of thought; *2)* an ability to reconstruct sympathetically and imaginatively the strongest versions of points of view and frameworks of thought opposed to one's own; and *3)* an ability to reason dialectically (multilogically) in such a way as to determine when one's own point of view is at its weakest and when an opposing point of view is at its strongest. Strong sense critical thinkers are not routinely blinded by their own points of view. They know they have points of view and therefore recognize on what framework of assumptions and ideas their own thinking is based. They realize the necessity of putting their own assumptions and ideas to the test of the strongest objections that can be leveled against them. Teaching for critical thinking in the strong sense is teaching so that students explicate, understand, and critique their own deepest prejudices, biases, and misconceptions, thereby discovering and contesting their own egocentric and sociocentric tendencies. Only if we contest our inevitable egocentric and sociocentric habits of thought, can we hope to think in a genuinely rational fashion. Only dialogical thinking about basic issues that genuinely matter to the individual provides the kind of practice and skill essential to strong sense critical thinking.

Students need to develop all critical thinking skills in dialogical settings to achieve ethically rational development, that is, genuine fairmindedness. If critical thinking is taught simply as atomic skills separate from the empathic practice of entering into points of view that students are fearful of or hostile toward, they will simply find additional means of rationalizing prejudices and preconceptions, or convincing people that their point of view is the correct one. They will be transformed from vulgar to sophisticated (but not to strong sense) critical thinkers.

teach: The basic inclusive word for the imparting of knowledge or skills. It usually connotes some individual attention to the learner; *instruct* implies systematized teaching, usually in some particular subject; *educate* stresses the development of latent faculties and powers by formal, systematic teaching, especially in institutions of higher learning; *train* implies the development of a particular faculty or skill or instruction toward a particular occupation, as by methodical discipline, exercise, etc. See *knowledge.*

theory: A systematic statement of principles involved in a subject; a formulation of apparent relationships or underlying principles of certain observed phenomena which has been verified to some degree. Often without realizing it, we form theories that help us make sense of the people, events, and problems in our lives. Critical thinkers put their theories to the test of experience and give due consideration to the theories of others. Critical thinkers do not take their theories to be facts.

think: The general word meaning to exercise the mental faculties so as to form ideas, arrive at conclusions, etc.; *reason* implies a logical sequence of thought, starting with what is known or assumed and advancing to a definite conclusion through the inferences drawn; *reflect* implies a turning of one's thoughts back on a subject and connotes deep or quiet continued thought; *speculate* implies a reasoning on the basis of incomplete or uncertain evidence and therefore stresses the conjectural character of the opinions formed; *deliberate* implies careful and thorough consideration of a matter in order to arrive at a conclusion. Though everyone thinks, few people think critically. We don't need instruction to think; we think spontaneously. We need instruction to learn how to discipline and direct our thinking on the basis of sound intellectual standards. See *elements of thought, perfections of thought.*

truth: Conformity to knowledge, fact, actuality, or logic: a statement proven to be or accepted as true, not false or erroneous. Most people uncritically assume their views to be correct and true. Most people, in other words, assume themselves to possess the truth. Critical thinking is essential to avoid this, if for no other reason.

uncritical person: One who has not developed intellectual skills (naive, conformist, easily manipulated, dogmatic, easily confused, unclear, closedminded, narrowminded, careless in word choice, inconsistent, unable to distinguish evidence from interpretation). Un-criticalness is a fundamental problem in human life, for when we are uncritical we nevertheless think of ourselves as critical. The first step in becoming a critical thinker consists in recognizing that we are uncritical. Teaching for insight into un-criticalness is an important part of teaching for criticalness.

vague: Not clearly, precisely, or definitely expressed or stated; not sharp, certain, or precise in thought, feeling, or expression. Vagueness of thought and expression is a major obstacle to the development of critical thinking. We cannot begin to test our beliefs until we recognize clearly what they are. We cannot disagree with what someone says until we are clear about what they mean. Students need much practice in transforming vague thoughts into clear ones. See *ambiguous, clarify, concept, logic, logic of questions, logic of language.*

verbal implication: That which follows, according to the logic of the language. If I say, for example, that someone used flattery on me, I *imply* that the compliments were insincere and given only to make me feel positively toward that person, to manipulate me against my reason or interest for some end. *See imply, infer, empirical implication, elements of thought.*

weak sense critical thinkers: 1) Those who do not hold themselves or those with whom they ego-identify to the same intellectual standards to which they hold "opponents". 2) Those who have not learned how to reason empathically within points of view or frames of reference with which they disagree. 3) Those who tend to think monologically. 4) Those who do not genuinely accept, though they may verbally espouse, the values of critical thinking. 5) Those who use the intellectual skills of critical thinking selectively and self-deceptively to foster and serve their vested interests (at the expense of truth); able to identify flaws in the reasoning of others and refute them; able to shore up their own beliefs with reasons.

world view: All human action takes place within a way of looking at and interpreting the world. As schooling now stands, very little is done to help students to grasp how they are viewing the world and how those views determine the character of their experience, their interpretations, their conclusions about events and persons, etc. In teaching for critical thinking in a strong sense, we make the discovery of one's own world view and the experience of other people's world views a fundamental priority. See *bias, interpret.*

Appendix C

Recommended Readings

The General Case for Critical Thinking

Bailin, Sharon. *Achieving Extraordinary Ends: An Essay of Creativity.* Kluwer-Academic Publishers, Norwell, MA, 1988.

Baron, Joan and Robert Sternberg. *Teaching Thinking Skills: Theory and Practice.* W. H. Freeman Co., New York, NY, 1987.

Blair, J. Anthony and Ralph H. Johnson, eds. *Informal Logic (First International Symposium).* Edgepress, Point Reyes, CA, 1980.

Glaser, Edward M. *An Experiment in the Development of Critical Thinking.* AMS Press, New York, NY, reprint of 1941 edition.

Kennedy, Mary. "Policy Issues in Teacher Education." *Phi Delta Kappan.* May, 1991

Mill, John Stuart. *On Liberty.* AHM Publishing Corp., Arlington Heights, IL, 1947.

Resnick, Lauren. *Education and Learning to Think.* National Academy Press, Washington, D.C., 1987.

Scriven, Michael. *Evaluation Thesaurus.* Point Reyes, CA, Edge Press, 1991

Scheffler, Israel. *Reason and Teaching.* Hackett Publishing, Indianapolis, IN, 1973.

Siegel, Harvey. *Educating Reason: Rationality, Critical Thinking, & Education.* Routledge Chapman & Hall, Inc., New York, NY, 1988.

Sumner, William G. *Folkways.* Ayer Co., Publishing, Salem, NH, 1979.

Toulmin, Stephen E. *The Uses of Argument.* Cambridge University Press, New York, NY, 1958.

Critical Thinking Pedagogy

Brookfield, Stephen D. *Developing Critical Thinkers.* Jossey-Bass, San Francisco, CA, 1987.

Costa, Arthur L. *Developing Minds: A Resource Book for Teaching Thinking.* Revised Edition, Volume 1. Alexandria, VA: ASCD, 1991.

D'Angelo, Edward. *The Teaching of Critical Thinking.* B. R. Grüner, N. V., Amsterdam, 1971.

Lipman, Matthew. *Ethical Inquiry.* Institute for the Advancement of Philosophy for Children, Upper Montclair, N.J., 1977.

Lipman, Matthew. *Harry Stottlemeier's Discovery.* Institute for the Advancement of Philosophy for Children, Upper Montclair, N.J., 1982.

Lipman, Matthew. *Lisa.* Institute for the Advancement of Philosophy for Children, Upper Montclair, N.J., 1976.

Lipman, Matthew. *Mark.* Institute for the Advancement of Philosophy for Children, Upper Monclair, N.J., 1980.

Lipman, Matthew, Ann M. Sharp, and Frederick S. Oscanyan. *Philosophical Inquiry.* University Press of America, Lanham, MD, 1979.

Lipman, Matthew, and Ann M. Sharp. *Philosophy in the Classroom.* 2nd edition, Temple University Press, Philadelphia, PA, 1980.

Lipman, Matthew. *Social Inquiry.* Institute for the Advancement of Philosophy for Children, Upper Montclair, N.J., 1980.

Meyers, Chet. *Teaching Students to Think Critically: A Guide for Faculty in all Disciplines.* Jossey-Bass, San Francisco, CA, 1986.

Norris, Stephen P, and Ennis, Robert H. *Evaluating Critical Thinking.* Pacific Grove, CA: Midwest Publications, 1989.

Paul, Richard and Binker, A. J. A., et al. *Critical Thinking Handbook: K–3rd Grades. A Guide for Remodelling Lesson Plans in Language Arts, Social Studies, & Science.* 2nd edition, Santa Rosa, CA: Foundation for Critical Thinking 1990.

Paul, Richard and Binker, A. J. A., et al. *Critical Thinking Handbook: 4th–6th Grades. A Guide for Remodelling Lesson Plans in Language Arts, Social Studies, & Science.* 2nd edition, Santa Rosa, CA: Foundation for Critical Thinking, 1990.

Paul, Richard and Binker, A. J. A., et al. *Critical Thinking Handbook: 6th–9th Grades. A Guide for Remodelling Lesson Plans in Language Arts, Social Studies, & Science.* Rohnert Park, CA: Center for Critical Thinking and Moral Critique 1989.

Paul, Richard and Binker, A. J. A., et al. *Critical Thinking Handbook: High School A Guide for Redesigning Instruction,* Rohnert Park, CA: Center for Critical Thinking and Moral Critique 1989.

Raths, Louis. *Teaching for Thinking: Theories, Strategies, and Activities for the Classroom.* 2nd edition, Teachers College Press, New York, NY, 1986.

Ruggiero, Vincent. *Thinking Across the Curriculum.* Harper & Row, New York, NY, 1988.

Ruggiero, Vincent. *Art of Thinking.* 2nd edition, Harper & Row, New York, NY, 1988.

Williamson, Janet L. *The Greensboro Plan: Infusing Reasoning and Writing into the K–12 Curriculum.* Santa Rosa, CA, Foundation for Critical Thinking 1990.

College Textbooks (Not Focused on a Specific Discipline)

Barker, Evelyn M. *Everyday Reasoning.* Prentice-Hall, Englewood Cliffs, NJ, 1981.

Barry, Vincent E., and Joel Rudinow. *Invitation to Critical Thinking.* 2nd edition, Holt, Rinehart & Winston, New York, NY, 1990.

Brown, Neil and Stuart Keely. *Asking the Right Questions: A Guide to Critical Thinking.* 2nd edition, Prentice-Hall, Englewood Cliffs, NJ, 1986.

Capaldi, Nicholas. *The Art of Deception.* 2nd edition, Prometheus Books, Buffalo, New York, 1979.

Cederblom, Jerry. *Critical Reasoning.* 2nd edition, Wadsworth Publishing Co., Belmont, CA, 1986.

Chaffee, John. *Thinking Critically.* 2nd edition, Houghton Mifflin, Boston, MA, 1988.

Damer, T. Edward. *Attacking Faulty Reasoning.* 2nd edition, Wadsworth Publishing Co., Belmont, CA, 1987.

Engel, Morris. *Analyzing Informal Fallacies.* Prentice-Hall, Englewood Cliffs, NJ, 1980.

Engel, Morris. *With Good Reason: An Introduction to Informal Fallacies.* 3rd edition, St. Martin's Press, New York, NY, 1986.

Fahnestock, Jeanne and Marie Secor. *Rhetoric of Argument.* McGraw-Hill Book Co., New York, NY, 1982.

Fisher, Alec. *The Logic of Real Arguments.* Cambridge University Press, New York, NY, 1988.

Govier, Trudy. *A Practical Study of Argument.* 2nd edition, Wadsworth Publishing Co., Belmont, CA, 1988.

Hitchcock, David. *Critical Thinking: A Guide to Evaluating Information.* Methuan Publications, Toronto, Canada, 1983.

Hoagland, John. *Critical Thinking.* Vale Press, Newport News, VA, 1984.

Johnson, Ralph H. and J. A. Blair. *Logical Self-Defense.* 2nd edition, McGraw-Hill, New York, NY, 1983.

Kahane, Howard. *Logic and Contemporary Rhetoric.* 5th edition, Wadsworth Publishing Co., Belmont, CA, 1988.

Meiland, Jack W. *College Thinking: How to Get the Best Out of College.* New American Library, New York, NY, 1981.

Michalos, Alex C. *Improving Your Reasoning.* Prentice-Hall, Englewood Cliffs, NJ, 1986.

Miller, Robert K. *Informed Argument.* 2nd edition, Harcourt, Brace, Jovanovich, San Diego, CA, 1989.

Missimer, Connie. *Good Arguments: An Introduction to Critical Thinking.* 2nd edition, Prentice-Hall, Englewood Cliffs, NJ, 1986.

Moore, Brooke N. *Critical Thinking: Evaluating Claims and Arguments in Everyday Life.* 2nd edition, Mayfield Publishing Co., Palo Alto, CA, 1989.

Moore, Edgar. *Creative and Critical Reasoning.* 2nd edition, Houghton Mifflin, Boston, MA, 1984.

Nickerson, Raymond S. *Reflections on Reasoning.* L. Erlbaum, Assoc., Hillsdale, NJ, 1986.

Nosich, Gerald. *Reasons and Arguments.* Belmont, CA Wadsworth 1981.

Ruggiero, Vincent. *Moral Imperative.* Mayfield Publishing, Palo Alto, CA, 1984.

Scriven, Michael. *Reasoning.* McGraw-Hill Book Co., New York, NY, 1976.

Seech, Zachary. *Logic in Everyday Life: Practical Reasoning Skills.* Wadsworth Publishing Co., Belmont, CA, 1988.

Shor, Ira. *Critical Teaching & Everyday Life.* University of Chicago Press, Chicago, IL, 1987.

Toulmin, Stephen E., Richard Rieke, and Alan Janik. *An Introduction to Reasoning.* Macmillan Publishing Co., New York, NY, 1979.

Weddle, Perry. *Argument: A Guide to Critical Thinking.* McGraw-Hill, New York, NY, 1978.

Wilson, John. *Thinking with Concepts.* 4th edition, Cambridge University Press, New York, NY, 1987.

Mathematics and Critical Thinking

Schoenfeld, Alan. *Mathematical Problem Solving: Issues in Research.* Lester, F.K. and Garofalo, J., ed's. Philadelphia, PA: The Franklin Institute Press 1982.

Curriculum and Evaluation Standards for School Mathematics, by the Working Groups of the Commission on Standards for School Mathematics of the National Council of Teachers of Mathematics, Reston, VA 1989.

Professional Standards for Teaching Mathematics, by the Working Groups of the Commission on Standards for School Mathematics of the National Council of Teachers of Mathematics, Reston, VA 1991.

Social Studies and Critical Thinking

Holt, Tom. *Thinking Historically: Narrative, Imagination, and Understanding,* College Entrance Examination Board. New York, 1990

Science and Critical Thinking

Giere, Ronald N. *Understanding Scientific Reasoning.* Holt, Rinehart, and Winston, New York, NY, 1979. (Out of print.)

Radner, Daisie and Radner, Michael. *Science and Unreason.* Wadsworth Publishing Co., Belmont, CA, 1982.

Language Arts and Critical Thinking

Adler, Mortimer. *How to Read a Book.* Simon and Schuster, New York, NY, 1972.

Horton, Susan. *Thinking Through Writing.* Johns Hopkins, Baltimore, MD, 1982.

Kytle, Ray. *Clear Thinking for Composition.* 5th edition, McGraw-Hill Book Co., New York, NY, 1987.

Mayfield, Marlys. *Thinking for Yourself: Developing Critical Thinking Skills Through Writing.* Wadsworth Publishing Co., Belmont, CA, 1987.

Rosenberg, Vivian. *Reading, Writing, and Thinking: Critical Connections.* McGraw-Hill Book Co., New York, NY, 1989.

Scull, Sharon. *Critical Reading and Writing for Advanced ESL Students.* Prentice-Hall, Englewood Cliffs, NJ, 1987.

Zinser, William. *Writing to Learn: How to Write — and Think — Clearly About Any Subject at All,* Harper & Row, Publishers, New York, 1988.

Critical Thinking and the Media

Lazere, Donald. *American Media & Mass Culture.* University of California Press, Berkeley, CA, 1987.

Also of Interest

Baker, Paul J., and Louis Anderson. *Social Problems: A Critical Thinking Approach.* Wadsworth Publishing Co., Belmont, CA, 1987.

Bloom, Benjamin. *Taxonomy of Educational Objectives.* David McKay Co., Inc., New York, 1956.

Dorman, William and Farhang, Mansour. *The U.S. Press and Iran: Foriegn Policy and the Journalism of Deference.* UC Berkeley Press, Berkeley, CA. 1987.

Goffman, Erving. *Presentation of Self in Everyday Life*. Doubleday & Co., New York, NY, 1959.

Lappé, Francis Moore. *Rediscovering America's Values*. Ballantine Books, New York, NY, 1989.

Siegel, Harvey. *Relativism Refuted*. Kluwer-Academic Publishers, Norwell, MA, 1987.

Tavris, Carol. *Anger: The Misunderstood Emotion*. Simon & Schuster, New York, NY, 1987.

Webster, Yehudi. *The Racialization of America*, St. Martin's Press, New York, NY. 1992.

Wilson, Barrie. *The Anatomy of Argument*. University Press of America, Lanham, Maryland, 1980.

Index

ethics, cont'd
  basic issues of 245
  clarity of 245
  closemindedness and 240
  cognitive strategies and 251
  coherence and 245
  complexity of 240
  critical thinking and 241
  critical thinking principles and 248
  curriculum design and 241
  daily life and 245
  didactic teaching and 248
  disputes and 242
  dogmatism and 244
  education and 241
  egocentric desires and 240
  empathy and 244
  ethical judgment and 242
  ethical reasoning and 248
  everyday life and 243
  general moral principles and 242
  good-heartedness and 243
  history and 246
  human suffering and 242
  ideas and 244
  ignorance and 242
  inservice design and 249
  insight and 243
  lesson plans and 249
  literature and 243
  misuse of moral terms and 240
  moral affective strategies and 251
  moral conclusions and 244
  moral courage and 243, 252
  moral dilemma and 244
  moral empathy and 243, 252
  moral fairmindedness and 252
  moral feelings and 244
  moral humility and 243, 252
  moral independence and 243
  moral integrity and 243, 252
  moral issues and 244
  moral judgment and 243
  moral micro-skills and 251
  moral perseverance and 243, 252
  moral reasoning skills and 251
  moral relativism and 243
  moral virtues and 252
  perspectives in 242
  pitfalls of, the 240, 242
  point of view and 242
  pseudo morality and 240
  rational standards and 241
  religious belief and 240
  science and 245
  scientific information and 245
  self-deception and 240
  self-interest and 240
  skills and 241
  sound reasoning and 245
  technology and 245
  truth and 240
  universal principles and 241
  writing and 244
  zealotry and 241
Ethnocentricity
  defined 529
  explained 529
Evaluation
  defined 530
  explained 530
  objective vs. subjective, ff 173
  reasoning 182
Evidence
  defined 530
  explained 530
Experience
  three elements of 267
Explicit
  defined 530
  explained 530

Fact
  defined 531
  explained 531
Fair
  defined 531
  explained 531
Fairmindedness 422-423, 456
  defined 262
Faith in Reason
  defined 262, 534
  explained 534
Faith
  defined 531
  explained 531
Fallacy
  defined 531
  explained 531
Fragmentation 273
Frame of Reference
  see point of view 155
Frank 371
Freud 264, 420

Geography
  key questions in 485
Gimmicks 93
Global Affairs 373
Global Realities, ff 1

Grammar
  as a system 5
  precise word usage and 5
  problems with textbooks and 8
  teaching, and 5
  the logic of, ff 5

Greensboro Plan 409
  history and design 409
  noteworthy aspects of 406
  philosophy of 413
  seventeen underpinnings 415

Harvard 99

Hegel 228

Heilbroner 3, 11

Higher Literacies Project 279

Higher Order Learning
  defined 532
  explained 532

Higher Order Thinking 98, 273
  algorithms and 284
  assignments and 284
  complex 282
  critical reading and 286
  defined 282
  educational reform and 287
  formulas and 284
  involves imposing meaning 282
  involves nuanced judgment 282
  multiple criteria 282
  nonalgorithmic 282
  recipes and 284
  self-regulation 282
  teaching for cognitive abilities 286
  teaching for independence of
    thought 284
  teaching of 305
  yields multiple solutions 282

Historical Roots of Anti-Intellectualism
  Berkeley and 40
  Beveridge and 41
  Mann and 41

History
  conflicting accounts of 246
  didactic instruction and 281
  everyday life, and 246
  historical content and 281
  interpretations and 281
  judgment, and 246
  key questions in 484
  mode of thought, as a 281
  moral significance of 246
  moral standpoint and 246
  news and 281
  points of view and 281
  profit and 281
  well-being and 246

Hitler 74, 79

Holt 16

Human Nature
  defined 532
  explained 532

Idea
  defined 533
  explained 533

Implication 156, 163
  defined 209, 533
  explained 533

Indoctrination
  general moral principles and 239
  nature of 239
  outlook on life and 239
  verbal agreement and 239

Inference 164
  conceptualization and 201
  defined 533
  explained 533

Inferences 156, 167
  defined 208

Infusing Critical Thinking
  lesson plan remodeling and 398

Inservice
  handbooks and 249
  lesson plans and 249
  moral reasoning and 249

Insight
  defined 533
  explained 533

Institute for the Advancement of
  Philosophy for Children 468

Instruction 273
  deceptive 274
  fraudulent 274
  habits of thought 282
  incremental change and 282
  math instruction 274
  redesigning of 282, 303
  Socratic 336

Instructional Reform
  emphasis on critical thinking 105

Intellect
  misuse of, ff 57

Intellectual Autonomy
  defined 534
  explained 534

Intellectual Civility
  defined 534
  explained 534

Intellectual Courage
 defined 261, 534
 explained 534
Intellectual Curiosity
 defined 535
 explained 535
Intellectual Development 454
Intellectual Discipline
 defined 535
 explained 535
Intellectual Empathy
 defined 261, 535
 explained 535
 requirements of 454
Intellectual Good Faith (Integrity)
 defined 262
Intellectual Humility
 defined 259, 535
 example of 453
 explained 535
Intellectual Integrity
 defined 536
 explained 536
Intellectual Perseverance
 defined 262, 536
 explained 536
Intellectual Responsibility
 defined 536
 explained 536
Intellectual Sense of Justice
 defined 536
 explained 536
Intellectual Skills 257
Intellectual Skills and Abilities
 basic elements of, ff 310
 intellectual standards, ff 310
 modes of reasoning, ff 310
 traits of mind, ff 310
Intellectual Standards 20
 academic disciplines, in 53
 defined 131, 536
 derivation of 214
 explained 536
 lack or misuse of, ff 54
 reading and writing assessment
  and 63
Intellectual Traits 22, 57, 454
Intellectual Virtues 256
 defined 537
 explained 537
 how to teach for 265
 interdependence of 262
Intellectual Work 98
 challenges of, ff 13

Interpretation
 defined 537
 explained 537
Intuition
 defined 537
 explained 537
Irrational Learning
 defined 538
 explained 538
Irrationality
 defined 538
 explained 538

Jefferson 247
Judgment 8
 defined 539
 explained 539
Justification
 defined 539
 explained 539

Kant 227
Keene 368
Kennedy 104, 170
Knowledge 61
 achievement, as 222
 defined 539
 explained 539
 lower order learning and 281
 pursuit of 53
 recall vs., ff 56

Language Arts 1
 grammar and 5
 logic of, the 5
 precise use of words and 5
Language
 concepts and 202
 connection to bias 374
 importance of precision and,
  the 373
 logic and, ff 204
Leadership
 administrators and 253
 ethics across the curriculum and
  253
 ethics and 253
 moral commitment and 253
Learning Centers 417, 424, 429
Learning 273
 collaborative 8

Science Instruction
cooperative learning and 505
flaws of experimentation 502
independent thinking and 503
obstacles to 501
scientific method, the 503
Socratic questioning and 504
students' egocentric
misconceptions 501
textbook flaws and 502
thinking scientifically 501
transferring ideas to new
contexts 503

Sculley 15

Self-Critique 240

Self-Deception
defined 549
explained 549

Self-Esteem
competence and 95
pseudo self-esteem and 95
self-worth and 95

Self-Examination 240

Shideler 225

Social Contradiction
defined 549
explained 549

Social Studies
anthropology and 481
common problems with 477
critical vocabulary 476
economics and 481
geography and 481
history and 479
integrating curriculum and 486
need for reasoning and 482
perspectives vs. facts 476
point of view and 476
politics and 480
recommendations for teaching
and 482-483

Society
human behavior and 247

Socio-Logic
defined 202

Sociocentricity
assumptions and, ff 389
defined 550
explained 550
results of 372
theory 371

Sociology 247
civic education, in 248
not indoctrination, and 248

Socrates 440, 453

Socratic Discussion 335
common moves 338
example of 348, 352, 442
exploratory 338
possible topics for 339
issue-specific 340
role of wondering 345
spontaneous or unplanned 337

Suggestions 341
three kinds of 337

Socratic Questioning 335-336, 456
characteristics of 448
defined 550
dialogical discussion and 297
effective participation in 344
explained 550
follow up questions and 298
four types of questions and 297
preparation for 298
probing assumptions 343
probing implications and
consequences 344
probing reasons and evidence 343
probing the question 344
probing viewpoints or
perspectives 343
questions of clarification 341
taxonomy 341

Socratic Spirit 337

Speaking
logic of, the 95

Staff development 397
design possibilities 402
Greensboro Plan 409
inservice and 405
principles of 405
recommendations for 401
teacher motivation and 403

Standards 197
minds indifferent to 197

Standards and Assessment
higher order thinking, for 99

Strong Sense Critical Thinker
defined 550
explained 550

Strong Sense Critical Thinking 383
conceptual analysis and 388
elements of reasoning and 386
evaluating elements and 386
philosophical thinking and 458
reasoning and 386
reciprocity and 386
theoretical underpinnings 386
vested interest 386

Writing
  assessment of   80
  criteria in assessing   71
  logic of, the   95
  misassessment of, ff   76
  problem of subjectivity vs.
    reasonability, ff 73
  response to, in workplace   63